Understanding Physical Anthropology and Archeology

◇ THIRD EDITION

Understanding Physical Anthropology and Archeology

ROBERT JURMAIN
Department of Anthropology
San Jose State University

HARRY NELSON
Department of Anthropology
Foothill College, Los Altos, California

WILLIAM A. TURNBAUGH
Department of Sociology and Anthropology
University of Rhode Island

WEST PUBLISHING COMPANY
St. Paul   New York   Los Angeles   San Francisco

Library of Congress Cataloging in Publication Data

Jurmain, Robert.
  Understanding physical anthropology and archeology.

  Bibliography: p.
  Includes index.
  1. Physical anthropology.   2. Archaeology.   I. Nelson,
Harry.   II. Turnbaugh, William A.   III. Title.
GN60.J84   1987   573   86–26789
ISBN: 0–314–30395–2

Design: Janet Bollow
Copy editor: Stuart Kenter
Illustrations: Brenda Booth, Sue Sellars, Evanell Towne
Composition: Janet Hansen & Associates
Cover: Photo by A. J. Jelinik. Used with permission of *Science*
magazine. Copyright 1982 by the AAAS.

Credits

Chapter 1: 5 (top) Public Relations, San Francisco State University; (bottom) H. Nelson. 6 H. Nelson. 8 (a) Baron Hugo van Lawick; (b) Leakey Foundation; (c) Rod Brindamour; (d) National Geographic Society. 9 R. Jurmain. 10 Georg Gerster; Photo Researchers, Inc. 11 (top) R. Jurmain; (bottom) John E. Hall, University of Miami. 15 Diana L. Davis, University of Oklahoma.

Chapter 2: 21, 23, 25, 28, 29, 30, 31 Courtesy of the American Museum of Natural History. 33 Courtesy Library of the New York Academy of Medicine. 37 M.W.F. Tweedie, Photo Researchers, Inc.

Chapter 3: 42 Dr. Linus Pauling, Institute of Orthomolecular Medicine. 43 From J. D. Watson, *The Double Helix*, Atheneum, New York, 1968, p. 215. © 1968 by J. D. Watson. 46 Prenatal Diagnosis and Cytogenetics Laboratory, University of California, San Francisco.

Chapter 4: 69 Courtesy of the American Museum of Natural History. 71, 72 Malcolm Gutter. 85 Courtesy of *Annual Reviews of Genetics*.

Chapter 5: 111 Courtesy of R. Heglar; photo by H. Nelson. 112 Courtesy of New York Academy of Medicine. 113 H. Nelson.

Chapter 6: 134 Courtesy of Biological Sciences Curriculum Study. Permission to use this figure does not constitute an endorsement. 135 Courtesy of the American Museum of Natural History. 140 Reprinted by permission of *American Scientist*. 143 Courtesy of Biological Sciences Curriculum Study. Permission to use this figure does not constitute an endorsement. 144 (top) San Diego Zoo photo; (bottom) New York Zoological Society photo. 144 From *Life: An Introduction to Biology* by Simpson, Pittendrigh, and Tiffany. Copyright © 1957 by Harcourt Brace Jovanovich, Inc. Redrawn by permission of the publishers. Redrawn from Romer, *The Vertebrate Body*, W. B. Saunders.

Chapter 7: 151 © National Geographic Society. Courtesy Dr. Dian Fossey. 155 Redrawn with permission of Quadrangle/The New York Times Book Co. from *The Antecedents of Man* by W. E. Le Gros Clark. Also

redrawn by permission Edinburgh University Press, Edinburgh, Scotland. 158, 160 San Diego Zoo photo. 161 (a) Ron Garrison, San Diego Zoo; (b) R. D. Schmidt, San Diego Zoo photo. 162, 163 San Diego Zoo photo. 164 H. Nelson. 168 (upper) Ron Garrison, San Diego Zoo photo; (lower) San Diego Zoo photo. 169 (left) Ron Garrison, San Diego Zoo photo; (right) Courtesy of Dr. Faren R. Akins, National Aeronautics and Space Administration, Ames Research Center. 170 San Diego Zoo photo. 171 (top) H. Nelson; (bottom) Ron Garrison, San Diego Zoo photo. 172 H. Nelson.

Chapter 8: 178 David Bygott, © National Geographic Society. 186 (upper) T. W. Ranson; (lower) San Diego Zoo photo. 187 (upper) H. Nelson; (left) courtesy of Masao Kawai; (right) Gladys Porter Zoo, Brownsville, Texas. 188 (top) Ron Garrison, San Diego Zoo photo; 188 (a) San Diego Zoo photo; (b) H. Nelson. 189 H. Nelson. 190 H. F. Harlow, University of Wisconsin Primate Laboratory. 192 Courtesy of Hans Kummer. 194 Photograph courtesy of T. W. Ransom. 198, 200 Baron Hugo van Lawick © National Geographic Society. 205 Geza Teleki. 208 Courtesy of Masao Kawai. 209 Courtesy of Beatrice Gardner. 216 Courtesy of Beatrice Gardner. 219 Phyllis Dolinhow. 221, 222 From George Schaller, *The Serengeti Lion*, University of Chicago Press, © 1972 by the University of Chicago. 226, 227, 228, 229 Courtesy of Jon Yellen.

Chapter 9: 244 Courtesy of Dr. E. L. Simons (lateral view). 249 (top) Courtesy the British Museum; (bottom) R. Jurmain. 253, 256 Courtesy of Dr. David Pilbeam. 257 The Bettmann Archive. 258 R. Jurmain. 264 From *Populations, Species and Evolution* by Ernest Mayr, Harvard University Press. Copyright © 1963, 1970 by the President and Fellows of Harvard College.

Chapter 10: 272 R. Jurmain. 277 M. D. Leakey, *Olduvai Gorge*, Vol. III. Cambridge University Press, 1971. 278 David Siddon, L. S. B. Leakey Foundation. 281, 282 R. Jurmain. 283 H. Nelson. 290, 291 R. Jurmain. 298 Photo by L. H. Keeley. 300 Tools manufactured by A. Leventhal; photographed by H. Nelson and R. Jurmain. Used by permission of A. Leventhal.

Chapter 11: 306 R. Jurmain. 307 Courtesy of the Geological Society of London, British Museum. 308 Courtesy of Dr. Raymond Dart, photo by Alun R. Hughes. 309 Photo by Alun R. Hughes; reproduced by permission of Professor P. V. Tobias. 311 San Diego Zoo photo. 312 Courtesy of the American Museum of Natural History. 314 Photo provided courtesy of Transvaal Museum, South Africa (also source of specimen). 315 The Bettmann Archive. 317 R. Jurmain. 318 (top) H. Nelson; (bottom) Photo provided courtesy of the Transvaal Museum, South Africa (also source of the specimen). 322 Ron Garrison, San Diego Zoo.

Chapter 12: 328 From C. K. Brain, "New Finds at the Swartkrans Australopithecine Site," *Nature*, Vol. 225:1112–1119. Redrawn with permission of the publisher and author. 333 Photograph by Peter R. Jones, Laetoli Research Project, 1978. 335 Courtesy of Dr. D. C. Johanson. 337 Courtesy the Cleveland Museum of Natural History. 338 Reproduced with permission of the National Museums of Kenya. Copyright reserved. 340 D. C. Johanson. 341 Courtesy the Cleveland Museum of Natural History. 345 Photo by T. White. Reconstruction by W. H. Kimbel and T. White. Courtesy of the Cleveland Museum of Natural History. 346 (top) H. Nelson; (middle and bottom) Reproduced with permission of the National Museums of Kenya. Copyright reserved. 347 H. Nelson. 348 Photo by Tim White. 349 (top) Courtesy of Richard Leakey; Dr. I. C. Findlater, photographer. (bottom) Reproduced with permission of the National Museums of Kenya. Copyright reserved. 350 H. Nelson.

Chapter 13: 358 (top) Reproduced with permission of the National Museums of Kenya. Copyright reserved. (bottom) Photo by R. J. Clarke (SK 847 is housed at the Transvaal Museum, Pretoria, South Africa). 360 Photo by A. R. Hughes; reproduced by permission of Professor P. V.

(continued following Index)

◇ CONTENTS

Human Diversity

Evolutionary Record

Living Primates

◇ CHAPTER EIGHT
  ISSUE: Killer Apes   178

Models for Human Behavior   **177**

Primate Evolution

Paleoanthropology

Homo Erectus

◇ CHAPTER FOURTEEN
ISSUE: Seeking the Peking
Bones 370

Homo Sapiens

◇ CHAPTER FIFTEEN
ISSUE: The Frozen Neandertal 412

◇ CHAPTER SIXTEEN
Issue: Why Was Stonehenge
Built?   452

Post-Pleistocene Adaptations in the Old World   451

Prehistory of the Americas

Conclusion
Evolution: The Human Adventure

◇ PREFACE

Because physical anthropology and archeology are so closely interrelated, many instructors—rather than teach these subjects in two separate courses—prefer to teach a single course in human physical and behavioral evolution from this combined point of view. This textbook is intended to serve that purpose.

The text begins with physical anthropology, covering the topics of evolution, genetics, and primates. Since human evolution is best understood within the context of both organic and cultural evolution, archeology and paleoanthropology are integrated with materials on fossil hominids.

The study of human origins is a rapidly unfolding and often exciting pursuit. Since the second edition of this book was published (1984), new discoveries have come to light, especially in Africa. These new finds, and their resulting interpretations and controversies, are thus discussed at some length in this edition. Further discoveries will, no doubt, be made in the next few years. We hope the background students gain from this text, and the course of which it is a part, will enable them to better understand these finds.

In the first six chapters students are introduced to the discipline of anthropology, the biological basis of evolution, and a chronological overview of the evolutionary record. This material is followed by three chapters on primates, including living primates, primates as possible models of human behavior, and primate evolution.

Chapters 10 through 17 deal with the events of hominid evolution and the development and growth of culture. Paleoanthropological and archeological methods are discussed in Chapter 10. Chapters 11, 12, and 13 are devoted to early fossil and archeological finds and their interpretations (that is, Plio-Pleistocene material from Africa).

H. erectus and *H. sapiens* are discussed in similar fashion—both biologically and culturally. Archeological sites as well as fossil hominid sites are included in Chapters 14 and 15.

With the appearance of anatomically modern human beings, the growth of culture becomes the major topic of the next two chapters. In Chapter 16 the origins of domestication and urbanism in the Old World are discussed and, likewise, New World prehistory is presented in Chapter 17. The last chapter—the conclusion—briefly presents an interpretation and summary of human physical and cultural evolution.

We have aimed our textbook mainly at those students with little background in the biological or physical sciences. We have, therefore, restricted use of technical and professional jargon. When such terms become necessary, a running glossary in the margin of the text (in addition to the alphabetical glossary at the back of the book) defines unfamiliar terms. Also, we have made a definite effort to maintain a writing style that is completely comprehensible and not at all condescending to beginning students.

To help understand the more complex concepts and events, an abundance of diagrams, line drawings, charts, maps, and photographs have been added. Today's students are accustomed to visual presentations, and this kind of material is indeed helpful in grasping new facts and concepts.

As a further study aid incorporated into this edition, we have divided those materials enclosed in boxes: In boxes that are tinted blue are topical subjects placed there for general interest; in untinted boxes are included materials we consider more central to physical anthropology and archeology.

The authors wish to express their appreciation to Clyde Perlee, our editor at West Publishing Company; Janet Bollow, the text designer; Stuart Kenter for copy editing; Wayne Fogle, John Yellen, Milford Wolpoff and Loring Brace for assistance with photographs; and to Lynn Kilgore and Sandy Nelson for help with proofing and indexing. And, finally, to all our students who have helped us see physical anthropology and archeology through their eyes.

Robert Jurmain
Harry Nelson
William Turnbaugh

◇ THIRD EDITION

Understanding Physical Anthropology and Archeology

Introduction

CONTENTS

◇ ISSUE   Fact, Fantasy, and Anthropology

At the beginning of each chapter throughout this book you will find brief discussions of an assortment of contemporary issues. Some of these—for example, the existence and implications of such phenomena as Bigfoot, extraterrestrials, and frozen Neandertals—may seem too bizarre to be discussed in a scholarly textbook. However, scientists and scholars cannot make these issues disappear by ignoring them. Someone in the scientific community must deal with them, hopefully in a rational way. This task often falls to the physical anthropologist.

Since the public is concerned about these topics, we shall address them. You may not always agree with our conclusions (you may notice, by the way, that our own personal biases occasionally emerge), but to induce you to agree or disagree with us is not the point. What you should do, is think seriously and rationally about these issues. In light of all the bizarre and ridiculous claims floating around today in pseudoscientific guise, you will do best by adopting the cautious "show me" approach attributed to inhabitants of Missouri. Without hard evidence no distinction may be made among fiction, fantasy, and fact. Judge for yourself!

◇ What Is Anthropology?

Anthropology is the study of human beings. As a scientific discipline, anthropology is concerned with all aspects of humankind: social behavior, language, attitudes, values, personality, government, kinship, history, prehistory, art, illness, healing, religion, economics, technology, and clothing, to name just a few. Furthermore, anthropology is concerned with such biological aspects of humans as body build, pigmentation, blood types and other biochemical traits, our ancestry and ancestors, and the evolutionary processes involved in our physical development.

Anthropology, therefore, is a **holistic** science, with the entire gamut of humankind as the focus of study. Other disciplines that deal with people—sociology, psychology, economics, political science, history, and others—tend to specialize in single aspects of human activity. Economists, for example, study the production, distribution, and consumption of goods; the market system; and systems of exchange; but they would rarely consider the effect of religion or kinship on the economic system. Anthropology, however, takes a broader, holistic approach and considers the findings of all academic fields pertaining to humans; in fact, anything associated with humankind is considered within the scope of our discipline.

The division of anthropology into two* broad categories—cultural and physical—illustrates its breadth. Cultural anthropology, often divided into *sociocultural anthropology*, **archeology**, and *linguistics*, is involved with the **culture** of peoples, both past and present. The sociocultural anthropologist concentrates on the culture of existing peoples, traditionally focusing on the less technologically complex societies of the world. Studying, say, the Yurok, a California Indian society, the sociocultural anthropologist would not restrict investigation to clothing, food, and religious practices, but would include the entire range of Yurok behavior.

An archeologist would be concerned with the same society through attempting to reconstruct its ancient culture. By studying the **artifacts** obtained by excavation, the archeologist could learn the kinds of food the Yurok once gathered, hunted, and ate; what kinds of tools and weapons they made and used; what sort of housing they had erected and clothing they had worn; how they disposed of the dead and, perhaps, their attitudes toward death; what goods they traded with neighbors, etc. The archeologist would, in a sense, do what the sociocultural anthropologist does, but data would come mainly from artifacts rather than from informants and actual observation of the people.

As a focus of culture, the linguist would take the description and history of language. Anthropological linguistics is considered a part of cultural anthropology because language is such an integral part of culture. Language is

Anthropology
anthropos: man
logos: science or study of

Holism
Viewing the whole in terms of an integrated system; cultural and ecological systems as wholes.

Archeology
(ar-kee-ol'-o-jee)
arche: beginning, ancient
logos: discourse, science or study of
The study of material things (artifacts) of past human life and activities; reconstruction of culture of peoples no longer in existence.

Culture
The set of rules, standards, and norms shared by members of a human society; transmitted by learning, and responsible for the behavior of those members. The human adaptive strategy for survival.

Artifact
artis: art
fact: make
Any object made or modified by humans.

---

*Anthropology is sometimes divided into four branches: physical anthropology, cultural anthropology, archeology, and linguistics.

Biocultural
A combination of the biological, cultural, and ecological. An approach to the study of human evolution and behavior that stresses the influence of each of these three clusters and their reciprocating effects on one another.

Primates
(pry'-mates; also, pry-may'-tees) The order of mammals to which humans, apes, monkeys, and prosimians belong.

the basic means by which humans communicate, organize themselves, and transmit their culture from one generation to the next. In investigating the Yurok, the linguist would probably look at the entire culture, but would concentrate, perhaps, on the relationship of the Yurok language to the languages of neighboring societies, would analyze the structure of the language, or would trace the history of the language or the relationship of the language to the culture.

Unlike anthropologists whose main concern is culture, the physical anthropologist, in a comprehensive study of the Yurok, would collect data on all aspects of inherited physical characteristics, such as body build, blood types, pigmentation, ability to tolerate cold, and susceptibility to various diseases. The physical anthropologist would also include notes on such cultural behavior as marriage and kinship, population patterns, migrations, dietary practices, and other cultural behavior that may affect Yurok biology.

In order to understand the human condition, anthropologists believe it necessary to investigate human biological *and* cultural behavior. Since we are both animal and human, such a broad perspective—what is known as a **biocultural approach**—makes sense. Examining only cultural behavior fails to consider our animal capabilities and limitations, and concentrating on our biology omits the single most important attribute of humans: *culture*.

This biocultural approach to the study of human beings makes anthropology a unique discipline. As a social science, cultural anthropology is the study of culture—that broad area of learned behavior that humans have developed as their basic strategy for survival. As a biological science, physical anthropology is the study of the biological aspects of humans. Combining the biological and social aspects, we have a comprehensive view of the animal *Homo sapiens*, which we call human.

◇ What Is Physical Anthropology?

As already indicated, anthropology may be divided into cultural and physical approaches to the study of human beings. Whereas it is possible to emphasize one or the other, it is impossible to separate completely the subject matter of these two branches.

In order to understand the physical human being, we must of necessity consider the special way of life of this organism. Unlike all other creatures in the Animal Kingdom, we human beings have developed a strategy of adaptation (obtaining food, producing the next generation, protecting the group against enemies and the elements, developing concepts of life's meaning) that is learned, not biologically inherited. Although other animals, especially mammals, may learn some things, most of their behavior is built into their nervous system from birth. **Primates** are capable of much more learning, and the learning ability of the great apes is now well recognized; nevertheless, no other mammal is as dependent on learning as are humans. While possessing a biologically based capacity for culture, we humans must learn behavior anew every generation. We must learn what, when, where, and with whom to obtain food, eat, marry, associate, etc. We must learn what is right and

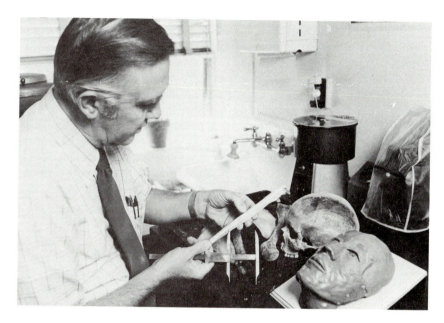

Figure 1-1   Physical anthropologist in his lab.

wrong, what to wear and not wear, what weapons and utensils to use and when, and how to relate to parents, cousins, and friends. All of this learning process comes under the heading of culture.

Culture, then, is the way humans discover, invent, and develop in order to survive; that is to say, culture is an adaptive strategy enabling humans to adapt to the environments in which they live. One cannot imagine humans today surviving without culture. Indeed, such a case is very likely impossible. Obtaining and preparing food, coping with severe climatic conditions, trying to understand the world around us, cooperating with others—all of these normal and daily activities require cultural solutions. Our bodies alone are not adequate for the task of living. We must have material items to help us acquire what we need and ideas to help us communicate with one another.

Figure 1-2   Humans are biocultural animals who developed culture as an adaptive strategy for survival and thus became human. Note the many items of material culture and social behavior that make the human way possible.

Cultural anthropology is the comprehensive study of what humans have learned to do, and are doing, in order to survive and adapt. What is the connection between these learned processes and our biological constitution? Was our evolutionary development dependent on culture? Was the development of culture dependent on our biological constitution?

In the biocultural view, culture and our biological structure are critically related. Had we not come from primate beginnings, culture as we know it would never have developed, and had our ancestors not developed culture, we would not have evolved our present physical form. The two are inextricably associated, and if we wish to learn something of physical anthropology, we *must* understand the role culture has played in the process of human evolution. As one anthropologist has stated it:

> Our present biological makeup is a consequence among other things of cultural selection pressures. We are, therefore, biologically constituted to produce culture, not simply because by some accident we got a brain that could do cultural things, but because the cultural things themselves propelled us into getting a larger brain. We are not simply the *producers* of institutions like the family, science, language, religion, . . . we are the product of them (Fox, 1971, p. 59).

With this introduction, let us examine more closely the field of physical anthropology and archeology, the concerns of this book. Although physical anthropologists are not in complete agreement on precisely what is to be included within their field, they do generally agree that two areas are basic: **human variation** and **human evolution**.

Human variation (the subject of Chapter 5) examines the differences within and between human populations. Within a population such as the Eskimos or San, variation occurs in body shapes and sizes; in anatomical structures, organs, and tissues; and in physiological responses to heat, cold, humidity, and exercise. Physical anthropologists are interested in the environmental and hereditary bases of this diversity and attempt to make evolutionary explanations of it.

Figure 1-3 Early humans possessed a small and simple tool kit. At a modern hardware store, an overwhelming variety of tools, utensils, and weapons is available.

As human biologists, physical anthropologists in the field or laboratory collect such data as susceptibility and immunity to disease, the effects of malnutrition, and patterns of human growth. These data may be used by medical scientists, physicians, and government agencies in their efforts to combat disease and improve the health of peoples around the world.

While all human beings belong to the same genus and species (*Homo sapiens*) and can interbreed and produce fertile offspring, there is a wide variation within the species. As comparative human geneticists, physical anthropologists study these variations and in the past have classified the world's population into physical types called **races**. Many anthropologists today are dissatisfied with the concept of race and do not believe it to be a useful or valid tool for the investigation of human diversity.

The second focus of physical anthropology, human evolution, may itself be subdivided into two areas: paleoanthropology and primatology.

Paleoanthropology is the study of the fossil remains of our ancestors. Physical anthropologists, together with archeologists, geologists, and other scientists, have unearthed fossil remains in many parts of the world. With their knowledge of **osteology**, paleoanthropologists examine, measure, and reconstruct these remains, often from mere fragments. This has enabled physical anthropologists to propose possible lines of descent from our ancient ancestors to our present form, *Homo sapiens*.

Primatology, as the word suggests, is the study of nonhuman primates, the group (*order* is the technical term) of the Animal Kingdom to which humans, apes, monkeys, and **prosimians** belong. Because of the remarkable similarities among monkeys, apes, and humans, researchers have been able, through laboratory experiments with monkeys and apes, to learn what effects certain diseases, stresses, and other conditions might have on humans.

A fascinating area of primate investigation concerns observing primates in their natural habitat. Such studies have uncovered important patterns of social interactions, such as the relationships between dominant and subordinate males, mothers and offspring, and the young and old. In addition, toolmaking and the ability to learn complex tasks have also been discovered with surprising frequency among certain species of primates.

Physical anthropologists hope these current, rapidly accumulating data will help in tracing human evolution from our primate ancestors, as well as aid in understanding the behavior of humans today.

We have been discussing what might be termed *academic anthropology*. A more utilitarian branch, called *applied anthropology*, relates the principles and data of anthropology to practical situations. Many years ago, for example, physical anthropologists were already applying their knowledge by developing standard sizes for the clothing industry and the military, and more comfortable seats for automobiles and airplanes. Space requirements for industrial workers were also analyzed, and mechanical problems associated with the body, such as the placement of foot pedals and hand controls for machine operators, were studied.

Physical anthropologists sometimes also assist judicial and law enforcement agencies. Practitioners of **forensic** anthropology, as the field is called, may be asked to ascertain the age and sex of a corpse, and how long it has been buried and, in some cases, even the cause of death (to determine if homicide has occurred).

Human variation
Physical differences among humans.

Human evolution
Physical changes over time leading to anatomically modern human beings.

Races
Breed or variety; subdivisions of a species. Large divisions of humans, based on physical traits. As it applies to humans, the term is not favored by many anthropologists.

Osteology
(os-tee-ol'-o-jee)
osteon: bone
The study of bones.

Prosimians
(pro-sim'-ee-ens)
pro: before
simian: ape or monkey
Common form of Prosimii, a suborder of primates, composed of small primates such as lemurs and tarsiers.

Forensic
(from forum)
Pertaining to courts of law. In anthropology, the use of anthropology in questions of law.

Figure 1-4 Primatologists. (*a*) Jane Goodall; (*b*) Shirley Strum; (*c*) Biruté Galdikas; (*d*) Dian Fossey;* (*e*) Phyllis Dolhinow. [(*a*), (*b*), (*c*), (*d*), © National Geographic Society; (*e*) photograph by Phyllis Dolhinow.]

*We regret to report the death of Dian Fossey, who was murdered December 26, 1985, in her cabin in Rwanda's National Volcanic Park.

For many years physical anthropology has had application in the field of medicine. The relationship between body build and disease, and the question of whether a particular disease is hereditary or social, have been among those investigated by physical anthropologists. Data on diseases have been collected from many countries in an effort to determine what special social conditions might be involved in the causes and cures.

Physical anthropologists are also interested in the history of disease in human populations, and this area of research, known as human *paleoepidemiology* or **paleopathology**, may shed light on the causes and possible cures of such conditions as arthritis, malnutrition, and numerous hereditary syndromes.

Paleopathology
(pay'-lee-o-path-ol'-o-jee)
pathos: suffering
The study of ancient diseases.

◇ What Is Archeology?

Archeology is the study of ancient human cultures (especially those that existed before the invention of writing), as well as the methods used in this study. Grahame Clark, a noted British prehistorian, has said that archeology is the study of the past distribution of culture traits in time and space, and of the factors governing their distribution (Clark, 1967). Culture is uniquely human; it is learned behavior, patterned, and highly perishable. No one has ever excavated a language, a set of religious beliefs, or a political system. However, the archeologist assumes that the patterning observed in surviving material remains reflects the patterning of the culture that produced those remains.

Material remains of human activity are the focus of archeologists. Objects made of stone, wood, horn, metal, and so forth compose the body of evidence archeologists use, but study of such objects is not an end in itself. It is, rather, a means of arriving at an understanding of particular cultures (as much as the evidence permits) and it ultimately contributes to an understanding of human behavior in general. There are, of course, other sciences and humanistic disciplines with similar goals, but archeologists, because of the specialized techniques and concepts they have developed in the analysis of material objects, contribute a knowledge of human behavior that would otherwise be unobtainable.

In pursuit of their data, archeologists have developed a number of approaches that we may categorize into two groups: (a) those who use written records to supplement their material data, and (b) those who work with the material remains of prehistoric societies. These divisions will be discussed in the following sections.

HISTORIC ARCHAEOLOGY

Classical archaeologists,* academically trained in departments of fine arts or classics, rather than anthropology departments, are primarily interested in

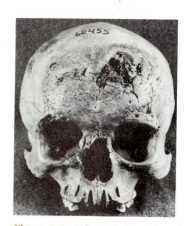

Figure 1-5 Paleopathology. The infectious reaction on the frontal part of this twelfth-century Pueblo Indian skull suggests syphilis. Other diseases are also a possibility.

The word "archeology" is often spelled "archaeology." It is always spelled with the additional *a* when used in association with classical archaeology.

Figure 1-6 Classical archaeologists often
excavate great architectural complexes,
such as this temple at Aswan, Egypt.

ancient history and fine arts. Thus they usually work in the Old World,
especially around the Mediterranean, although areas in Southeast Asia, China,
and other historic regions have also been excavated. While classical archaeologists use methods similar to those of other archeologists, they supplement
their findings and interpretations from the historical records. (The excavation
of King Tut's tomb is an example.) Also, they tend to place more emphasis
on artifacts as art objects.

Some classical archaeologists specialize in the study of Near East sites
associated with events mentioned in the Old and New Testaments. This area
of investigation may be called *Biblical Archaeology*.

Other historical archeologists work at sites dating from fairly recent times.
These may be located in our own or other still-functioning cultures. Written
documents associated with such sites are almost always incomplete. They
often lack such basic information as descriptions of ordinary artifacts or other
details of interest in analyzing the culture involved. For example, in the
reconstruction of colonial Williamsburg in Virginia, historical archeologists
were able to provide many details lacking in the written historical record of
that period.

In recent years, a number of archeologists have investigated contemporary
activities of Americans, such as swap meets, drive-in movies, and one of the
most interesting, the Garbage Project conducted by Professor William Rathje
of the University of Arizona. Rathje's team collected garbage from over 7,000
households in Tucson, Arizona, in Milwaukee, Wisconsin, and in Marin County
(California). It was found that the average household "discarded between
7 and 14 percent . . . of its purchased food, estimated . . . to come to about
$11 billion a year nationally. This represents enough food to feed the entire
population of Canada for one year" (Rathje and Schiffer, 1982, p. 35).

Another kind of historic archeology is *Underwater (Marine) Archeology*.
Using diving equipment, underwater archeologists explore ancient ship-
wrecks and other submerged sites. They are able to recover numerous details
of the structure of the ships and their respective cargoes. Some marine

Figure 1-7 The colonial town of Williamsburg, now a tourist attraction, was reconstructed with archeological assistance. (An example of historic archeology.)

archeologists have attempted to excavate sites on the continental shelf, where ancient people might have camped during glacial times, when the oceans were much lower than they are today.

Prehistoric Archeology

Most archeologists fall into this category. Since 99% of human history extends back beyond the invention of writing, prehistoric archeologists work with this vast period of over 2 million years. Without the assistance of historical records, prehistoric archeologists pursue several goals (Binford, 1968):

1. Reconstruction of culture history
2. Reconstruction of extinct lifeways
3. Delineation of culture process

Culture history is an account of the growth and development of culture in space and time, and considers such questions as: When and where were the first tools made? Were our early ancestors hunters or scavengers? Who were the first farmers? When was metal first used? Prehistoric archeologists, using material data from their excavations, seek answers to these questions, and arrange their data into a spatial and temporal sequence of events.

Until recently, prehistoric archeologists spent much of their time trying to reconstruct the way of life of earlier people from the material remains they excavated: What animals were hunted? What techniques may have been used for hunting and for making tools and weapons? What foods were eaten? What was the architecture of their structures? In short, what lifeways did earlier people follow?

More recently, archeologists have come to feel that such description comprises only part of their work. Also important is to understand the processes of culture; that is, to *explain* what happened in the past. It is not enough to simply describe the lifeways of ancient peoples and compile a history of culture, it is also absolutely necessary to understand the how and the why

Figure 1-8 An archeologist, using diving equipment, examines underwater artifacts.

Ethnography
(eth-nog'-ra-fee)
ethnos: nation
graphy: a writing or description
The study and description of a culture through fieldwork done by a sociocultural anthropologist.

Phylogeny
(fy-loj'-en-ee)
phylon: tribe or race
The evolutionary history of a species; evolutionary relationships of organisms; a "family tree."

Geochemistry
(jee-o)
ge: earth
The study of the chemical composition of the earth's crust.

Chronometric dating
Dating by methods that give time in years, also known as absolute dating (compared with relative dating). It includes radiometric techniques (carbon 14 and potassium-argon) and dendrochronology (tree-ring dating).

of past cultural events. *How* did the domestication of plants and animals originate? *How* can the origin of the state be explained? *Why* did the Indians of North America fail to develop the sophisticated political, religious, and economic institutions of Mesoamerica? And that fundamental question always confronting prehistoric archeologists: Did definable patterns of culture growth and change even exist—or was it all accidental?

In addition to these goals, a movement toward developing a more rigorous methodology (led by Professor Binford of the University of New Mexico) began in the 1960s. "The archeologist," Binford stated (1968, p. 14)

> must make use of his data as documents of past conditions, proceed to formulate propositions about the past and devise means for testing them against archeological remains.

Thus, a problem such as the origins of agriculture should be stated in hypothetical terms. The fieldwork would then be planned to evaluate the hypothesis, and the data collected would be used to accept, reject, or modify the hypothesis. The conclusions could then be applied to theories concerning general cultural processes.

Ethnoarcheology   In order to understand the behavior of the people whose remains they excavated, prehistoric archeologists referred to data collected by ethnographers for descriptions of analagous behavior that might be useful in interpreting the artifacts they had uncovered. Because the **ethnographic** material was not always helpful, archeologists began making their own studies of living societies. They are interested in such data as settlement patterns, population size, the relationship of population to subsistence systems, social organization, migrations, and environment. Many such studies have been made. Much of the description of the !Kung San in Chapter 8, for example, is taken from an ethnological study made by John Yellen.

◇ Paleoanthropology and Other Disciplines

Searching for ancient human remains—organic and cultural—is the work of *paleoanthropologists* (see Chapter 10). Organic material, such as bones and teeth, is examined and analyzed by physical anthropologists; cultural material, such as tools, weapons, shelters, and so forth, by archeologists.

However, as our discussion suggests, paleoanthropology is quite closely associated with other disciplines. In fact, a paleoanthropologist could not operate without cooperation from a host of other scientists. For example, in working out the **phylogeny** of our species, one must have the vital knowledge (as accurately as possible) concerning the dates of fossil remains. To obtain this crucial information, the paleoanthropologist consults the **geochemist** for a **chronometric dating** of the fossils themselves, or of the matrix containing the fossil material.

If these facts are unobtainable, then a **geologist** may be able to give some idea of the dating from an analysis of the rock strata holding the material, and may also be able to reconstruct the physical landscape of the period in which these ancient creatures were living. Thus, armed with such information, the physical anthropologist may justifiably speculate about the environment of the now-fossilized creatures—how they lived, how they obtained their food, how they used their bodies, and, to some extent, what kind of stone was available for tools.

In reconstructing the way of life of our ancient ancestors, one must have certain important facts concerning what other animals and plants were living at the same time. Such information would suggest clues to the kinds of food eaten, the hunting and gathering techniques, the possible materials for clothing and shelter and, in general, considerable other anthropological data about how these ancient peoples adapted to their environment. For this knowledge, the paleoanthropologist looks to the **paleontologist** and **palynologist**.

Much of paleoanthropology deals with evolution, including physical changes within a species and the transmission of physical characteristics from one generation to the next. Scientists from all the biological sciences have contributed insights to evolutionary theory, and geneticists in recent years have greatly expanded their understanding of the processes of biological heredity. This knowledge has been of considerable theoretical assistance to physical anthropologists as they speculate about how the transition from prehuman to human may have occurred.

Since cultural information would shed light on the evolution of the human form, paleoanthropologists have currently become increasingly interested in how our early ancestors lived. Necessarily, then, we have come to rely on the findings of cultural anthropologists who work with less technologically complex societies. As discussed in the previous section, living patterns seen today, such as family structure, division of labor, and hunting techniques, suggest ideas and concepts to paleoanthropologists in their reconstructions of the life of early humans and the evolution of physical form.

Similarly, primate anatomy and behavior studies done by zoologists, psychologists, psychiatrists, medical scientists, linguists, and others have contributed to the paleoanthropologist's exploration of human evolution.

Geology
The study of the history and structure of the earth, as recorded in rocks.

Paleontology
(pay'-lee-on-tol'-o-jee)
onta: existing things
The study of ancient forms of life based on fossil bones.

Palynology
Identifying ancient plants by examining pollen from archeological sites.

Hominid
The common term for Hominidae.

Hominidae
The family, of the order Primates, to which humans belong.

Australopithecines
(os-tray-lo-pith'-e-seens)
australo: southern
pithecus: ape
The earliest hominids known; located in South and East Africa.

Orthograde
ortho: straight, upright
grade: walking
Upright walking.

Prehensile
Capable of seizing; ability to grasp.

◇ What Is Human?

The word **hominid**, from the Latin *homo*, meaning man, is an abbreviated or anglicized form of **Hominidae**, the family to which we belong as opposed to, say, Pongidae, the ape family. Because hominid is a neutral term (that is, it does not indicate sex, intelligence, or stage of evolution), we shall make extensive use of this happy term, which has the further advantage of including those early ancestors we would prefer to keep out of our exclusive human category. These ancestors, we know them as **australopithecines**, may not have possessed all the criteria we assign to humans, especially the complex brain.

A hominid may be defined as a bipedal and **orthograde** creature with a wide pelvis, **prehensile** hands but not prehensile feet, and a brain larger in proportion to body size than in nonhominid primates. Footprints, found in Africa and dated to almost 4 mya,* reflect a creature with bipedality, wide pelvis, and a nonprehensile foot. Although we would not include these early ancestors within our own exclusive human group, we are willing and even eager to embrace them as fellow hominids.

*mya = million years ago. The footprints are discussed in Chapter 12.

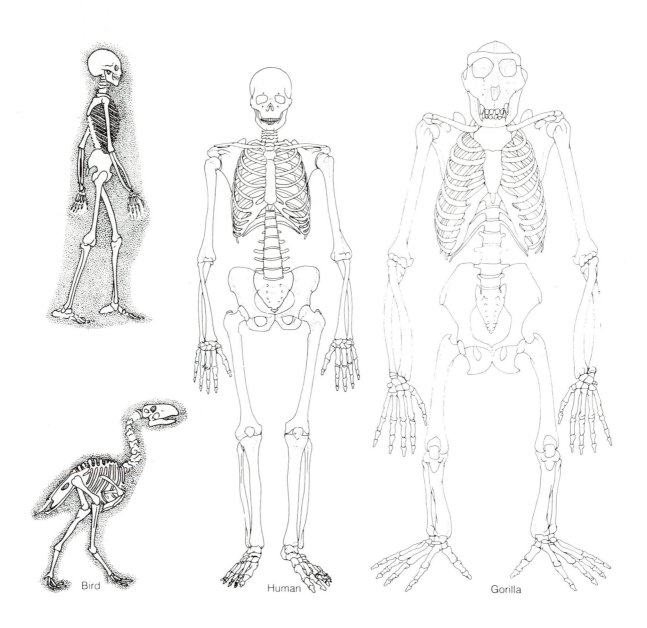

Figure 1-9 Bipedal animals. An upright (orthograde) posture evolving from an apelike structure explains the short, wide human pelvis.

The concept "human" is more difficult to clarify. What makes human beings unique and thereby different from all other animals is a perplexing and age-old question that has been the subject of religious, philosophical, and sociological inquiry. Human uniqueness is based on two general classes of criteria: the biological and the behavioral.

From the biological view, the differences between humans and other animals are quantitative. The difficulty is not that we possess physical characteristics lacking in, or radically different from, other animals, but that we possess the same attributes to a greater or lesser degree. We are larger than most animals, but have less hair; our brain is not the largest in relative or absolute size, but it is very large according to the standards of both these categories. We are not the only animal that is bipedal (birds are, too), but we have a skeleton adapted for standing upright and walking, which leaves the hands free for purposes other than mobility. All these traits, elaborated and coordinated under the control of a brain capable of abstract thought, give us our remarkable physical uniqueness.

In the behavioral area, human uniqueness is even more noteworthy. Every species, in adapting to its **ecological niche** (econiche), has developed its own distinct behavior, but human uniqueness is revealed in behaviors absent in other animals. For example, our sexual behavior does not include a mating season or **estrus** for females. Or, as another example, most animals build shelters for themselves and eat in ways particular to their species; but among humans, activities like the building of shelters and preparing of food are learned, vary in each society, and can be successfully accomplished only with the assistance of tools. Without tools, it is unlikely that any human society could survive.

Our social relationships are not only learned but also vary from society to society. Cultural anthropologists have routinely observed societal differences in marriage, residence, and kinship patterns, in attitudes toward the elderly and the young, and in behavior between the sexes. This diversity is unlike other animal species, where flexibility occurs to a much lesser degree than among humans. Mammals exhibit more flexibility than other vertebrates, with primates displaying the most of all. Recent observations of the variety of behavior among chimpanzees in the wild, along with the ability of captive chimpanzees to learn sign language in a number of experiments, have astonished scientists. Nevertheless, no community of chimpanzees displays the degree of variety in behavior found in *any* human society.

One of the most important factors that differentiates humans from other species is our ability to communicate symbolically through language, an activity that, as far as we know, is specific to humans. Chimpanzee, gorilla, and orangutan achievements in learning sign language (discussed in Chapter 8) *taught them by humans* are truly remarkable. Even when these intelligent apes sign to other apes, such a display in no way compares to the crucial reliance humans place on symbolic communication.

What then is "human"? There may well be as many definitions as there are human beings! We suggest, however, that a sound explanation of the term be based on the two criteria previously mentioned: first, a body structured for standing upright and walking on two legs (**bipedalism**), thus leaving the arms and hands free for functions other than locomotion; second, a complex brain that provides the abilities for abstract thought, symbolic communication, and the development of culture as an adaptive strategy for the human way of life. With this dual emphasis on biology and culture, our definition once again underlines the biocultural view of human evolution.

◇ Summary

Anthropology is the study of human beings and their primate ancestors. It is a holistic science divided into two main branches: cultural and physical. Cultural anthropology is the study of what humans have learned to do in

Ecological niche
(econiche)
The life style of an organism or species in relation to its habitat; the habitat of an organism or species that makes life possible; the feeding habits of an organism or species.

Estrus
(also oestrus)
oistros: sting, frenzy
Period of sexual heat of female mammals; receptive period.

Bipedalism
(by-pee'-dal-ism)
bi: two
ped: feet
Habitually walking on two feet as among hominids and some other animals.

Figure 1-10 Jesabel, a six-year-old chimp signing "drink."

order to adapt to their environment; physical anthropology, the study of humans as animals, is mainly concerned with human variation and human evolution.

Specialized fields within physical anthropology include comparative human genetics, growth and development, human paleontology, human osteology, and primatology. Some physical anthropologists have specialized in applied anthropology, forensic anthropology, and human paleoepidemiology. For assistance in their research, physical anthropologists work closely with a variety of biological, social, and physical scientists.

Seeking cultural remains of ancient humans by digging for them is the task of archeologists. Archeologists may be divided into two groups: historical and prehistorical. Historical archaeologists include the classical scholars who work especially in the Near East and emphasize an interest in the fine arts. Other historical archeologists work in a more recent time period (the past several hundred years), at contemporary sites and underwater sites.

Prehistoric archeologists, on the other hand, work with sites ranging over a vast time period—from those of nonliterate societies of recent date to those of ancient hominids dating back several million years. A recent trend among prehistoric archeologists is the emphasis on a more rigid scientific methodology, as well as investigating contemporary societies in order to help interpret past events.

Two terms of similar meaning—hominid and human—are discussed. "Human" is defined similarly to hominid, but its definition includes the phenomenon of a complex brain capable of abstract thought, symbolic communication, and culture.

◇ Questions for Review

1. What is meant by "holistic," and why is anthropology a holistic science?
2. Explain the biocultural approach in anthropology.
3. What are the two main branches of anthropology?
4. What are the two main areas of physical anthropology?
5. Define archeology and explain how it differs from physical anthropology.
6. List the various kinds of archeology and the approach of each.
7. How does the recent field of contemporary archeology seek a more rigorous scientific method?
8. How do other disciplines assist paleoanthropological research?
9. What are the fields of specialization within physical anthropology?
10. How does the concept "hominid" differ from the concept "human"?
11. In what ways are humans unique from other animals?
12. What role does culture play in human uniqueness?

Principles of Evolution

CONTENTS

That it shall be unlawful for any teacher in any of the universities, normals and all other public schools of the State . . . to teach any theory that denies the story of the Divine Creation of man as taught in the Bible, and to teach instead that man has descended from a lower order of animals (Section 1 of the Butler Act, March 21, 1925, State of Tennessee).

In May, 1925, several leading citizens of Dayton, Tennessee (population 1,800) were sitting around Doc Robinson's drug store, the town's social center, discussing various and sundry topics of great import. To settle an argument, they sent for John T. Scopes, a local high school coach and teacher of algebra, physics, and chemistry. Scopes came over from his tennis game not realizing that he was about to enter the most dramatic period of his life, one he would never forget.

One of the men, a local businessman, said, "John, we've been arguing, and I said that nobody could teach biology without teaching evolution."

"That's right," said Scopes, and showed them the biology textbook that had been adopted by the state of Tennessee.

"Then," said Doc Robinson, "you've been violating the law."

Although he did not teach biology, Scopes had, one day in April, substituted for the principal, who did. Technically, therefore, it could be said that he had taught biology and had thus violated the newly passed law.

As the discussion continued, and it became clear that Scopes felt strongly on the matter of academic freedom, Robinson asked him whether he would stand for a test case. Scopes said he would, whereupon Robinson called the *Chattanooga News* and reported, "This is

F. E. Robinson in Dayton. I'm chairman of the school board here. We've just arrested a man for teaching evolution." The man who had been "arrested" finished his soft drink and returned to his tennis game. (Writing forty years later in 1967, Scopes suggested that the trial was deliberately planned by Dayton businessmen to put that town on the map and bring in business, which is precisely what happened.)

The "arrest" made front page news across the country. William Jennings Bryan—three times Democratic nominee for President, Secretary of State under Woodrow Wilson, famous for his Cross of Gold speech at the Democratic convention of 1896, and acknowledged leader of the crusade against Darwinism—offered his services to the prosecution as the representative of the World's Christian Fundamentals Association.

With Bryan's entry into the fray, Clarence Darrow, nationally known labor and criminal lawyer, offered his services to the defense without fee or expense. The American Civil Liberties Union was in charge of the case for the defense and provided other well-known lawyers: John Randolph Neal, Arthur Garfield Hayes, and Dudley Field Malone.

In the weeks before the trial, the town of Dayton took on the atmosphere of a circus. The trial was referred to as "the monkey business." Merchants used monkey motifs in their advertising: little cotton apes were featured in store windows; pins that read "Your Old Man's a Monkey" could be purchased; and at Doc Robinson's drug store, a monkey fizz was available for refreshment from the summer heat. Hot dog stands, lemonade peddlers, booths selling books on biology or religion, and Bryan's truck, equipped with loud-

speaker touting Florida real estate, all added spice and noise to the carnival.

The trial began on Friday, July 10, 1925, with Judge John T. Raulston on the bench, and ended on Tuesday, July 21. It was clear from the start that Scopes would be convicted. The court, strongly religious, consistently favored the prosecution and forbade the testimony of expert defense witnesses—scientists—who were prepared to prove that evolution was a valid scientific concept. The prosecution insisted that the trial was not about the validity of evolution but that the real issue was simply whether or not Scopes had violated the law.

There were magnificent speeches. On Monday, July 13, in his support of the motion to squash the indictment against Scopes, Darrow displayed his famous forensic ability, and the crowded courthouse hung on every word. If the teaching of evolution is outlawed, he argued, then:

After a while, Your Honor, it is the setting of man against man and creed against creed until with flying banners and beating drums we are marching backward to the glorious age of the sixteenth century when bigots lighted faggots to burn the men who dared to bring any intelligence and enlightenment and culture to the human mind.

On Thursday, Bryan stood up to speak against the admissibility of scientific testimony. The crowd had been waiting for this moment, but they were to be disappointed. Bryan was an old man, not the man he once was; the fire was missing. H. L. Mencken, the acidulous reporter from the *Baltimore Sun*, attended the trial and wrote:

His . . . speech was a grotesque performance and downright touching in its imbecility. Its climax came when he launched into a furious denunciation of the doctrine that man is a mammal. It seemed a sheer impossibility that any literate man should stand up in public and discharge any such nonsense. Yet the poor old fellow did it. . . . To call man mammal, it appeared, was to flout the revelation of God (Tompkins, 1965, p. 48).

Malone replied to Bryan, his former superior officer at the State Department, and his eloquence carried the day even among the spectators who fully supported Bryan. Bryan himself recognized this when he told Malone afterwards, "Dudley, that was the greatest speech I have ever heard."

The climax of the trial came on Monday afternoon, July 20, when the defense called Bryan as an expert witness on the Bible. The prosecutors immediately jumped to their feet protesting, aware of the danger inherent in the questions that might be asked and the answers that might be given. However, Bryan himself insisted on testifying, perhaps because he felt compelled to defend the Bible and "show up" the evolutionists. It was an opportunity not to be missed.

Darrow's strategy was to question Bryan about his literal interpretation of the Bible. The Bible, Bryan held, was true, every word of it, every comma. Every miracle recorded in the Bible actually happened. And it was on these points that Darrow broke Bryan, made him appear foolish, unthinking, and even a "traitor" to the cause of fundamentalism. At one point Darrow asked, "Do you think the earth was made in six days?"

"Not in six days of twenty-four hours," Bryan replied.

The crowd gasped at this heresy.

The Bible read six days, and a day was obviously twenty-four hours. What was Bryan thinking of? Toward the end of the afternoon Darrow brought up the Bible story of Adam and Eve and the serpent. Had God punished the serpent by making him crawl on his belly? Bryan said he believed that. Then, Darrow asked, "Have you any idea how the snake went before that time?"

"No, sir."

"Do you know whether he walked on his tail or not?"

"No, sir, I have no way to know."

The crowd laughed and Bryan's hands nervously trembled and his lips quivered.*

The trial ended the next day. The jury (excused for most of the trial) was called back and charged to decide whether Scopes had violated the law; no other question was to be considered. The jury took but a short time and returned with their verdict—guilty! Judge Raulston fined Scopes $100 and the trial closed.

The case was appealed to the Tennessee Supreme Court, which handed down its decision on January 15, 1927. The Court upheld the Butler Act and also recommended that the State drop the indictment against Scopes on the technicality that the judge had imposed the fine, instead of the jury, as Tennessee law required. The Court thus made it impossible to appeal the case before the United States Supreme Court.

Update

In the sixty years since the Scopes trial, religious fundamentalists have not ceased their attempts to remove the teaching of evolution from the public schools of the nation. Known as "creationists" because they explain the existence of the universe, energy, and life as a result of sudden creation, they are determined either to eliminate the teaching of evolution or to introduce antievolutionary subject matter. In a ploy developed in recent years, creationists have insisted that "creation-science" is just as much science as what they term "evolution science." Therefore, they claim, in the interest of fair play, a balanced view should be offered to students—if evolution is taught as science, then creationism should also be taught as science.

So-called "creation-science" is not science as we know it.† Far from the spirit of science, creationists, for instance, assert that their position is absolute and not subject to error. Therefore, it is impossible for any sort of evidence to alter their position, for anything that might modify creationism is automatically rejected.

Creationists have been active in state legislatures, promoting the passage of laws mandating the inclusion of creationism in school curricula wherever evolution is taught. To this effect, creationists successfully lobbied the legislature of the State of Arkansas, which passed Act 590 in March of 1981.

As used in the Act, "creation-science" means the scientific "evidence" for creation, as well as inferences based on such evidence, including:

1. sudden creation of the universe, energy, and life, from nothing
2. inadequacy of mutation and natural selection to explain how all liv-

---

*A diabetic and in ill health, Bryan died on Sunday, July 26, five days after the trial ended.

†See Eldridge, Niles, "Creationism Isn't Science," *The New Republic*, Apr. 14, 1981, pp. 15–20.

ing kinds developed from a single organism

3. changes of forms of life only within fixed limits of originally created kinds of plants and animals
4. idea of a separate ancestry for man and apes
5. explanation of the earth's geology by catastrophism
6. concept of a relatively recent inception of the earth and living kinds

The American Civil Liberties Union (ACLU) challenged Act 590 (also known as the "Balanced Treatment for Creation-Science and Evolution-Science Act") in the case of McLean vs. Arkansas State Board of Education. The case came to trial in federal district court in December, 1981. ACLU contended that Act 590 infringed on three separate rights guaranteed under the United States Constitution:

1. separation of church and state, guaranteed by the First Amendment
2. academic freedom, guaranteed by the First Amendment
3. the right to due process under the Fourteenth Amendment: the act was vague, and teachers could be placed in jeopardy since it would be easy to misinterpret such phrases as "fixed limits" and "kinds of plants and animals," these being too unclear for identification

On January 5, 1982, Judge William Ray Overton ruled against the State of Arkansas. He found that "creation science has no scientific merit or education value," that "a theory that is by its own terms dogmatic, absolutist and never subject to revision is not a scientific theory," and that "since creation is not science, the conclusion is inescapable that the only real effect of Act 590 is the advancement of religion."

Judge Overton declared that the Act violated the Constitution's guarantees of separation of church and state, and he accompanied his decision with an injunction against the enforcement of the Act.

This was not, by the way, the first Arkansas attempt to introduce anti-evolution legislation. In 1928, just three years after the Scopes trial ended, the Arkansas legislature passed a law that forbade

any teacher or other instructor in any university, college, normal, public or any other institution of the state . . . to teach the theory or doctrine that mankind ascended or descended from a lower order of animals.

The law was finally challenged in 1965 by Susan Epperson, a high-school biology teacher. Trial was held on April 1, 1966, and the court found the 1928 statute unconstitutional because it violated the First and Fourteenth Amendments. On appeal, the Arkansas Supreme Court overturned the lower court decision, but, on fur-

ther appeal, the U.S. Supreme Court decided that the 1928 law violated the First Amendment, and was an intrusion of religion into the state schools.

A similar Louisiana law was declared unconstitutional by a federal appeals court on June 8, 1985.

Although Act 590 was declared unconstitutional, creationists continue their efforts. In Texas, California, Kentucky, and other states, creationist legislation and biology textbook censorship remain as goals of the religious fundamentalists.

SOURCES FOR ISSUE:

Ginger, Ray. *Six Days or Forever?*, Boston: Beacon Press, 1958.

Scopes, John T. and James Presley. *Center of the Storm*, New York: Holt, Rinehart and Winston, 1967.

Tompkins, Jerry R. (ed.). *D-Days at Dayton*, Baton Rouge: Louisiana State University Press, 1965.

SOURCES FOR UPDATE:

New York Times, Jan. 6, 1982.

New York Times, Jan. 12, 1982.

Science. 215 (4531) pp. 381–384, Jan. 22, 1982.

Science 229 (4711) pp. 368–369, July 26, 1985.

◇ CHAPTER TWO

◇ Introduction

As a concept, evolution, during the Middle Ages, was not a view seriously considered by medieval philosophers. Scholarly interpretations of the Bible, especially Genesis, had given European philosophers a *Weltanschauung* (world view) in which change had no place. Evolution, therefore, is an idea that would not only have been considered heretical, but "common sense" of the era would have labeled it ridiculous.

Nevertheless, scholars of the fifteenth, sixteenth, and seventeenth centuries demonstrated that the universe—planets (including the earth) and stars (including the sun)—was not rigidly fixed, and the belief that organic beings were similarly not fixed was being entertained. Attempts to explain how the process of evolution worked failed until Charles Darwin, in the nineteenth century, succeeded with his theory of natural selection.

How we understand evolution today is drawn directly from Darwin's work, as well as from contributions, mainly from the field of genetics, made during the twentieth century. Our focus throughout this text is *human evolution*, but, in this chapter, we discuss the general evolutionary principles applicable to all organisms. The evolutionary process is a unified one, and the principles are the same for all life forms, including humans. We will examine the changes in intellectual thought that led to the theory of natural selection, acclaimed as the most important scientific contribution of the nineteenth century. First, though, let's take a brief look at the man responsible for this theory: Charles Darwin.

◇ Darwin's Life

Charles Darwin (1809–1882) was the son of Dr. Robert and Susannah Darwin and grandson of the eminent Dr. Erasmus Darwin. Charles, one of six children, was thought by his family and by himself to be a "very ordinary boy." As an ordinary boy, he did the usual things (collecting shells, stamps, coins) and, at school, he displayed no special inclination for scholarship.

Because he showed little interest in, or aptitude for, anything particular (with the possible exception of science), Dr. Darwin decided that Charles should study medicine at Edinburgh. After two years, Charles conceded medicine was not for him, and instead turned to hunting and fishing, which he thoroughly enjoyed. His father complained that Charles was only interested in "shooting, dogs and rat-catching."

For sons who had no discernible academic leanings, parents could, as a last refuge, turn them to the church. Although indifferent to religion, Charles dutifully took up residence at Christ's College, Cambridge, in 1828, at the age of 19. While ostensibly enrolled in theology, Charles became interested in what we today call natural science. He became a constant companion of the

Figure 2-1   Charles Darwin (at age 32).

21

Figure 2-2 Examples of some of Darwin's finches. Note the similarities and differences in beak structure.

Reverend John Stevens Henslow, professor of botany, and often joined his classes in their botanical excursions.

Darwin was graduated in 1831, at the age of 22, not with a distinguished record, but one good enough to satisfy his family, and he could look forward to a serene future as a country cleric. However, that was not to be, for something happened that summer that Darwin referred to as "the most important event of my life."

He received a letter from his friend, Professor Henslow, informing him that he had recommended Darwin as the best-qualified person he knew for the position as naturalist on a scientific expedition that would circle the globe. (See Box 2-1.) Darwin was willing, even eager, for this opportunity to combine travel with the pursuit of botany, zoology, and geology, but his father objected and Charles regretfully declined. However, Charles found a champion in his uncle, Josiah Wedgewood, who persuaded Dr. Darwin that the voyage would be desirable. Dr. Darwin reluctantly gave his consent. With mixed feelings of elation and dismay, Charles set sail on board the H.M.S. *Beagle*, December 27, 1831, on a voyage where attacks of seasickness would place him in his hammock for days on end. Having begun the voyage as a clergyman (at least such had been his intent) with hobbies of zoology, botany, and geology, Darwin found, within a short time, that his true calling was natural science. Through his industrious and diligent work of collecting, arranging, and dissecting specimens, Darwin matured from an amateur observer into a professional naturalist.

Darwin went aboard the *Beagle* not as an evolutionist but as a believer in the fixity of species. His observations, however, quickly raised evolutionary suspicions in his mind. As early as 1832, for example, he noted in his diary that a snake with rudimentary hind limbs marked "the passage by which Nature joins the lizards to the snakes." He came across fossils of ancient giant animals that looked, except for size, very much like forms living in the same vicinity, and wondered whether the fossils were the ancestors of those forms. He observed that the Andean Mountain Range constituted a natural barrier to life and, as might be expected according to geologists, flora and fauna on opposite sides of the range differed.

The stopover at the Galapagos Islands profoundly impressed Darwin. He noted that the flora and fauna of South America were very similar—yet dissimilar—to those of the Galapagos. Even more surprising, the inhabitants of the various islands differed slightly. The thirteen kinds of finches resembled one another in the structure of their beaks, body forms, and plumage, and yet each constituted a separate species despite the fact that few geographic differences existed among the islands. What, he asked himself, could cause this modification if the physical geography and climate were not responsible? These observations, and the questions they raised, caused Darwin to wonder whether the theory of fixity of species was a valid one after all.

This abbreviated account of Darwin and his research on the *Beagle* does not do justice to the significant role the voyage played in Darwin's intellectual growth. He returned to England on board the *Beagle* on October 2, 1836, just short of five years from the date he sailed.

In 1842, Darwin wrote a short summary of his views on natural selection and revised it in 1844. The 1844 sketch was surprisingly similar to the

◇ Box 2-1   Darwin: Naturalist or Companion?

Robert Fitzroy, Captain of the *Beagle*.

Was Darwin invited to sail aboard the H.M.S. *Beagle* as a naturalist or as a companion to **Captain Fitzroy**?* Since Darwin had been recommended as a naturalist, and had acted in that capacity throughout the *Beagle's* five-year voyage (during which he developed ideas that ultimately led to his concept of natural selection), the answer has always seemed obvious.

However, Dr. Stephen Jay Gould (1976) has suggested that Darwin was invited to be Fitzroy's companion, and that the position of naturalist was an enticement to that end. The reasons, says Gould, were that a captain in the British navy was not permitted to speak to members of his crew except on ship's business; that Fitzroy was aware of the awful loneliness of a captain who had to dine by himself in his own cabin; and that he, Fitzroy, was not too stable. Therefore, someone to share his cabin, meals, and conversation was absolutely mandatory. For this, Fitzroy required someone of the proper social rank—a gentleman—and in order to persuade such a person, the captain offered the position of naturalist.

The interesting and important aspect of this, according to Gould, is that Darwin's view of evolution may have grown out of the strained relationship that developed between the two men. They argued on several subjects: slavery, for one; God and nature, for another. Fitzroy's dogmatic assertions about the universe, suggests Gould, acted as the catalyst that drove Darwin to an opposite view, leading to "an evolutionary theory based on chance variation and natural selection by a largely external environment: a rigidly materialistic (and basically atheistic) version of evolution."

Today it is difficult to know why Fitzroy wanted a naturalist on board. He has been described as "a public spirited and zealous officer." Since the purpose of the *Beagle's* voyage was entirely scientific, it is certainly possible that Fitzroy may have been serious in his search for a naturalist who might also — as a subordinate function — serve as companion.

Darwin's correspondence to his friend and professor Dr. Henslow (who first recommended him for the position), and to his father, seems to leave no doubt about why he thought he was sailing: to work as a naturalist. Darwin was aware that he was expected to be a companion to Captain Fitzroy (Henslow mentioned it in his letter to Darwin), but this function must have impressed him very little. He never referred to it in his correspondence.

*The captain's name is spelled variously as Fitz-Roy, FitzRoy, and Fitzroy.

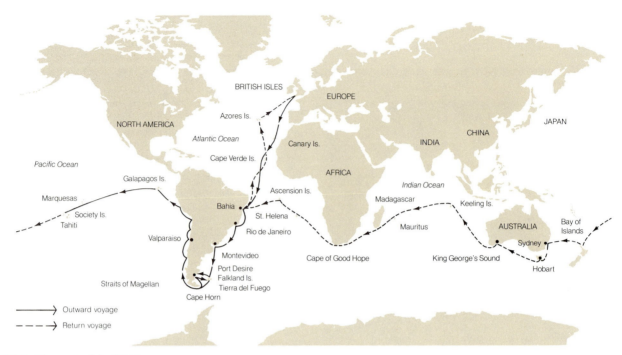

Figure 2-3a   The route of the H.M.S. *Beagle*.

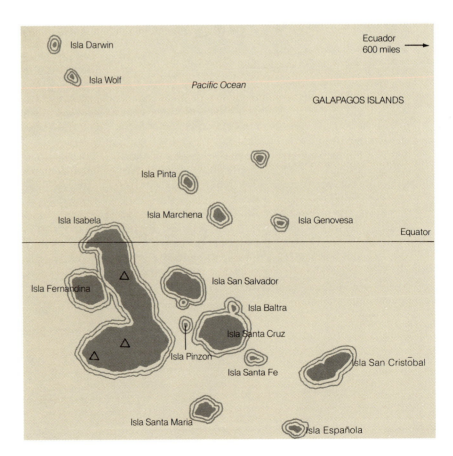

Figure 2-3b   The Galapagos Islands. Finches (because of their variety) and tortoises (because each island was inhabited by its own variety) influenced Darwin's thinking about evolution.

argument he presented fifteen years later in *Origin of Species*, but Darwin did not feel he had sufficient data to support his views, and he continued to accumulate facts.

Time passed. In 1855, an article by Alfred Russel Wallace on the succession of species impressed Darwin because it supported his views on species' mutability. Darwin was not disturbed at this time by the possibility that the publication of his own theory might be anticipated. Darwin had been encouraged by his close friends, especially Lyell (see p. 36) and Hooker (a well-known botanist) to publish his "theory," but he declined because he felt there was much more evidence to collect. His friends cautioned him that someone else might publish before he did, and, indeed, his friends' warning was realized in June, 1858, when Wallace sent him his paper on natural selection.

Alfred Russel Wallace (1823–1913) was born in a small English village into a family of modest means. He went to work at 14 and, without any special talent, moved from one job to the next. He became interested in collecting, and joined an expedition to the Amazon Valley in 1848, at the age of 25. After four happy years of collecting specimens in South America, Wallace returned to England and two years later, in 1854, he sailed to the Malayan Archipelago to continue his study and collection of bird and insect specimens. He remained there eight years, collected 125,660 specimens, and often thought about the problem of the succession of species.

Figure 2-4   Alfred Russel Wallace.

In 1858, on the island of Ternate, just off the coast of the Celebes Islands, Wallace was in bed suffering from one of his periodic attacks of fever. Suddenly, the solution to the problem he had so long thought about flashed through his mind. Recalling the phrase, "the positive checks to increase," from Malthus' *Essay* (p. 33), he immediately realized that this phenomenon could apply to animals as well as to human beings. If there were no checks, the earth would quickly be overrun by the most prolific breeders. Why, then, did some species of plants or animals perish while others survived? The answer came at once: the best adapted survived; the less well adapted perished. Wallace at once set his thoughts down on paper and sent Darwin his essay, "On the Tendency of Varieties to Depart Indefinitely from the Original Type" (Löwenberg, 1959).

When Darwin read Wallace's paper he was thoroughly depressed. He wrote Lyell, "Your words have come true with a vengeance—that I should be forestalled" (F. Darwin, 1950, p. 199). With the publication of Wallace's paper, Wallace would be given credit for a theory that Darwin felt belonged to him, since he had thought of it at least twenty years before. What to do? Darwin considered publishing a resumé of his own work but wondered whether it would be honorable to do so. He told Lyell, "I would far rather burn my whole book, than that he [Wallace] or any other man should think I have behaved in a paltry spirit" (F. Darwin, 1950, p. 201). After much indecision, Darwin finally decided to let his close friends, Lyell and Joseph Hooker, devise a formula that would be fair to both Wallace and himself.

This difficult task was achieved by his friends, who decided that joint papers by Wallace and Darwin would be read before a meeting of the Linnaean Society. The Society agreed, and the papers were read on the evening of July 1, 1858, with Darwin ill in bed and Wallace in the Far East. What is remarkable is that the papers did not create a furor at the meeting, since most members of the Society disagreed with the concepts of natural selection.

The solution to the problem of Wallace's paper pleased Darwin, and Wallace was delighted that he had been so fairly treated. After the presentation of the two papers, the trustees of the Linnaean Society brought urgent pressure on Darwin to publish as speedily as possible a full account of his "theory." Darwin returned to his work with exemplary energy and, within a year, in 1859, had completed and published his great work, *On the Origin of Species*.*

With publication, the storm broke, and has not abated even to this day. While there was much praise for the book from many quarters, the gist of opinion was negative. Scientific opinion gradually came to Darwin's support, assisted especially by Darwin's able friend, Thomas Huxley (known as "Darwin's bulldog"), who for years wrote and spoke in favor of natural selection. The riddle of species was now explained: species were not fixed, but mutable; they evolved from other species through the mechanism of natural selection. Science was never to be the same again.

◇ Darwin's Theory of Evolution

Darwin did not originate the idea of evolution, which had been suggested (or at least hinted at) 200 years previously—and much longer, if we include Greek thought of 2000 years ago. Darwin's grandfather, Erasmus Darwin, had written in defense of evolution before Charles was born, and Lamarck, a French scientist, had drawn up a schema trying to explain how new species were formed. However, his explanation met with unfavorable criticism and, in fact, did not accurately explain how the evolutionary process functioned.

Nor were the basic ideas used by Darwin completely of his own invention. Struggle for existence, extinction of species, variation, adaptation—these were all known and discussed for years by many European scientists. Darwin's great contribution was to bring these divergent ideas together and add the key: natural selection.

In his book, *On the Origin of Species*, published in 1859, Darwin explained his concept of evolution:

1. All species are capable of producing offspring faster than the food supply increases (see Malthus, p. 33)
2. All living things show variations; no two individuals of a species are exactly alike
3. Because there are more individuals than can possibly survive, there is a fierce struggle for existence and those with a favorable variation in size, strength, running ability, or whatever characteristics are necessary for survival, will possess an advantage over others (see Malthus, p. 33)
4. These favorable variations are inherited and passed on to the next generation
5. Over long periods of geologic time, these successful variations produce great differences that result in new species

*The complete title of Darwin's book is *On the Origin of Species by Means of Natural Selection, or the Preservation of Favoured Races in the Struggle for Life.*

Darwin called this process "natural selection." He did not believe in creation by design; that is, that life forms were placed on earth by creation, that variation in plants and animals was part of a grand divine design, or that the inorganic and the organic could be viewed as a progression from inferior to superior types, with humans at the top.

Darwin did not arrive at natural selection—his solution to the process of evolution—without assistance. When we look at the intellectual climate of Europe of the Middle Ages, we find that Christianity was associated with certain views of the universe. Since the time of Ptolemy, a Greco-Egyptian mathematician, geographer, and astronomer of the second century A.D., the earth was considered to be fixed at the center of a universe of spheres that revolved with perfect regularity around it. Not only was the inorganic world fixed and unchanging, but the organic world was believed to be equally static. It was believed that all species of the earth had been created (according to Genesis of the Old Testament) on a progression from the simplest forms to the most complex—humans. This progression was not evolutionary; that is, one species did not lead to or evolve into the next. The forms and sequence were fixed, no new ones had appeared since creation, and none had disappeared.

This progression was known as the Great Scale of Being, and the plan of the entire universe was seen as the Grand Design, that is, God's Design. The limbs of men and animals seemed designed to meet the purpose for which they are required. The wings of birds, eyes, etc., all of these structures were interpreted as neatly fitting the functions they performed. It was considered to be a deliberate plan, a design of the Grand Designer. Furthermore, it had all occurred in quite a short time, since creation was dated at 4004 B.C. by Archbishop James Ussher (1581–1656), an Irish prelate and scholar, who worked out the date by analyzing the "begat" chapter of Genesis.

Until these concepts of fixity and time were changed, it would be very unlikely that the idea of natural selection could even be conceived. What, then, upset the medieval belief in a rigid universe of planets, stars, plants, and animals? What scientific philosophy would, within the following 150 years, strike a death blow to the whole medieval system of thought? How would the scientific method as we know it today develop and, especially with Newton and Galileo in the seventeenth century, demonstrate a moving, not unchanging, universe?

The man who began this revolution was Copernicus (1473–1543), a Polish mathematician and astrologer, who simplified the Ptolemaic system by placing the sun at the center of the universe and the earth as one of the planets revolving around it. "The Copernican Revolution," as it is sometimes called, "is the supreme symbol of the passage from the medieval to the modern world, from an outlook which now seems like that of fairyland to the matter-of-fact outlook of the present day" (Dingle, 1959, p. 18).

Copernicus may not have realized the far-reaching effects of his new celestial system, but scientists of the seventeenth century—Bacon (inductive method), Harvey (circulation of the blood), Galileo (experimental science, central position of the sun, gravity, etc.), Newton (laws of motion and gravity)— gave the intellectual thought of their era a definite naturalistic basis. Although scientists remained religiously oriented, their observations and experiments

Figure 2-5 Linnaeus.

provoked notions of the universe that were new, exciting, and challenging, although sometimes condemned as heretical, Darwin, in the nineteenth century, was heir to the thinking and ideas of these seventeenth-century giants. At Cambridge, Darwin associated with professors (all churchmen) who were anti-evolutionists, but the radical change in intellectual thought of the seventeenth century enabled scientists of the eighteenth to think about the universe in a manner that made the idea of evolution possible, and paved the way for Darwin.

By the early decades of the 1700s, motion, not fixity, had become accepted for the physical universe, but most biological scientists held that change was unacceptable for living forms. Species had been fixed at creation, they still insisted, and since then there had been no new species formed or old species driven to extinction—there had simply been no change. Without change there cannot, of course, be evolution, and until it was recognized that species could alter, evolution and Darwin's natural selection could not be considered. This view of fixity of species was solidly held by one of the leading naturalists of his day, **Carolus Linnaeus**, who believed that "There are just as many species as there were created in the beginning," and again, "There is no such thing as a new species" (quoted in Singer, 1959, 379–380).

The son of a Lutheran pastor, Linnaeus (1707–1778) was born at Roeshult, Sweden. He is best known for developing a classification system for plants and animals, first published in 1835, which he called *Systema Naturae*. Linnaeus isolated those particular physical traits that best characterized a particular group of organisms. In plants, for instance, he used blossoms; in insects, wings; and in fish, scales. He even included humans in his classification of animals, thus defying the then-contemporary thought that humans, made in God's image, should be considered separately and outside the Animal Kingdom.

Linnaeus' scheme was well received throughout Europe, and, when applied to collections in museums and botanical gardens, it worked. He then proceeded to assign names to the animals and plants. Linnaeus hit upon the simple but effective idea of assigning two Latin names to each organism. The first word would be the generic term—the genus—for the organism and the second word, the specific term—the species. Thus, the two words together would become a unit internationally recognized as the name for that particular form. This system of binomial (or binominal) nomenclature was widely accepted, and is still used today.

We are concerned not so much with the problems and solutions that resulted in Linnaeus' *Systema Naturae* as we are in his ideas about evolution, which reflected the scientific thought of his time. Linnaeus saw nature as a "rationally ordained system of means and ends"; that is, every living thing is created perfectly adapted to the environment in which it lives, making further change unnecessary. According to Linnaeus (and many other scientists as well as laymen), this natural relationship did not exist for its own sake, but for the glory of God. It is, they believed, the duty of humans to study nature diligently, so that God might be glorified. Although some scientists had abandoned the age-old notion that nature was fixed, Linnaeus still adhered to the idea that species, once divinely created, had never changed, and "to study nature diligently" meant assigning to every living thing its proper name.

This Linnaean emphasis on classification, and his concept of the perfection of nature once fixed by creation and never altered, neatly delineated the views of the opponents of evolutionary thought. However, there were other voices, especially in France, raised loudly and clearly in favor of a universe based on change, and much more to the point, of the relationship between similar forms based on descent from a common ancestor.

The leading advocate of this point of view was Georges Louis Leclerc, who came from an old noble family in Burgundy and was later raised to the rank of Count, under the name of Buffon by Louis XV. **Buffon** (1707–1788), as he is known, was born the same year as Linnaeus. He knew of his contemporary and disagreed with him on most points. Buffon's writings made natural science popular drawing-room conversation, in which he himself excelled with sly wit. Talking one day with his female visitors, he said, "Nothing stands still. Everything moves. Even the seed of man does so, otherwise it would never reach its goal. May I show it to you under the microscope?" (Wendt, 1963, p. 83).

Buffon believed neither in the perfection of nature nor in the idea that nature had purpose. He stressed again and again the importance of change in the universe, and he underlined the changing nature, or mutability, of species.

In contrast to Linnaeus' static "rationally ordained system of means and ends," Buffon emphasized the variety and minute gradations of nature, which he explained in terms of "a system of laws, elements and forces." Thus, nature could be seen as functioning by natural means rather than through a divine mind. Buffon considered it important to see life as a dynamic system of processes instead of a static pattern of structure. He felt that the true aim of natural history was to discover and understand these processes, not simply to classify their result. Buffon

Figure 2-6   Buffon.

> put the hypothesis of organic evolution . . . in clear and definite form. He called . . . attention to the facts of comparative anatomy which constitute one of the principal evidences for that hypothesis. . . . He, finally, did more than any one else to habituate the mind of his time to a vastly (though not yet sufficiently) enlarged time-scale in connection with the history of organic nature, a necessary prerequisite to the establishment of transformation (Lovejoy, 1959, pp. 111–112).

The contrast between the thinking of Linnaeus and that of Buffon reflects not merely the old and the new, but also the response of many scientists and clergymen to the publication of Darwin's *Origin*. Although Linnaeus appeared to have changed his mind about fixity late in life, the concept of immutability of species continued to be the dominant theme among most scientists. Darwin was familiar with the writings of Buffon, which helped to make a belief in evolution acceptable. With the voluminous publications of Buffon and others, it is not at all surprising that when we arrive at the latter portion of the eighteenth century, the ideas of mutability of species and the possibility of unlimited organic change were well known throughout Europe. This doctrine of organic change was not widely accepted, but at least it was being discussed at length in intellectual circles.

In this enlightened era of the popularization of science (which saw the beginnings of archeology and the recognition that fossil bones belonged to

Figure 2-7   Erasmus Darwin.

Figure 2-8   Lamarck.

species of animals since perished), we must take notice of a most interesting figure who saw clearly the force of evolutionary ideas. Charles Darwin was well aware of the writings of this man, his grandfather, **Erasmus Darwin** (1731–1802), who was a country physician, poet, and versatile and eccentric scientist. More than fifty years before his grandson was to startle the world with his views on natural selection, Erasmus had expressed such ideas as "evolution by natural and sexual selection, protective adaptation, inheritance of acquired characteristics, and even the evolution of mankind" (Francoeur, 1965, p. 68). In fact, one biographer wrote of Erasmus Darwin, "the theory of natural selection was the only cardinal one in the evolution system on which Erasmus Darwin did not actually forestall his more famous and greater namesake" (Clodd, 1897, p. 114).

Although Charles Darwin had read his grandfather's writings, it is not possible to say what influence these had on his views. Erasmus had not solved the problem of the evolutionary process, but it is likely that his discussion of evolution made it easier for Charles to approach it. Erasmus Darwin had little influence on the scientific thought of his day, which is not difficult to understand, since he described his scientific ideas in ambiguous verse. For example, he expressed his thoughts on the struggle for existence thus:

Where milder skies protect the nascent brood
And earth's warm bosom yields salubrious food,
Each new descendant with superior powers
Of sense and motion speeds the transient hours;
Braves every season, tenants every clime,
And nature rises on the wings of Time.
(Wendt, 1955, p. 138)

During the eighteenth century, Erasmus Darwin wrote about and believed in evolution, but was never able to explain the process. He came close but, as Buffon before him and Lamarck afterwards, he relied on the concept of acquired characteristics to indicate how species were transformed: " 'All animals undergo perpetual transformations; which are in part produced by their own exertions . . . and many of these acquired forms or propensities are transmitted to their posterity' " (E. Darwin, quoted in Singer, 1959, p. 505). However, neither Buffon nor E. Darwin codified their beliefs into a comprehensive system. The first European scientist to do this was Jean Baptiste Pierre Antoine de Monet de **Lamarck** (1744–1829).

Like Erasmus Darwin and Buffon, Lamarck also developed most of the ingredients of the concept of evolution, but he went beyond these men by organizing his ideas. Ernst Heinrich Haeckel, the well-known scientist of the late nineteenth century, said that to Lamarck "will always belong the immortal glory of having for the first time worked out the Theory of Descent as an independent scientific theory of the first order, and as the philosophical foundation of the whole science of Biology" (Clodd, 1897, p. 115).

One of the points stressed by Lamarck was the interaction of organic forms with their environment. He believed the stability of organic forms was directly proportionate to the stability of the conditions of life, and, as the conditions of life changed, organic forms were altered.

The alterations were caused by the *effort* the form makes in using those parts of its body that are most adaptive under given environmental conditions. Little by little, as time goes on, these changes result in new organs that are passed on through heredity. What is the mechanism that induces change?

If a particular part of the body feels a certain need, "fluids and forces" would be directed toward that point and a new organ would be slowly produced to satisfy that need. That the environment affects and can eventually induce change in organic forms is commonplace knowledge today, but that felt needs are the mechanism, while an intriguing idea, is not true.

Lamarck also believed that a characteristic acquired in the manner described above for a new organ could be passed on through heredity to the next generation. This theory of acquired characteristics, or Lamarckism, had already been suggested by Erasmus Darwin, but was not really questioned until it was carefully scrutinized by one of the leading scientists of France, Georges Cuvier, whose ideas we shall discuss shortly.

It should be stressed, on the other hand, that many of Lamarck's views of nature and evolution are as valid today as they were 150 years ago. His emphasis on the dynamic interaction of organic forms with the environment and the consequent adaptation is well placed. He brought together vast quantities of materials to support his evolutionary ideas, carrying them beyond those of Buffon. The world of science, especially biology, owes him a great debt.

Figure 2-9   Cuvier.

However, like E. Darwin, he failed to solve the riddle of "how it works." It is true enough that all living forms may acquire characteristics during their lifetime. We know, for example, that a man may develop large muscles simply through exercise, but we also know that the physical characteristics we acquire in our lifetime (with the possible exception of mutations) are not transmitted to our offspring. Our highly muscled man does not pass on his overdeveloped muscles to his children. It is interesting to note that Charles Darwin, while he used natural selection as the mechanism for evolution, also used, at times, the belief that acquired characteristics could be inherited.

Lamarck, we might say, popularized the idea of evolution, but there remained vehement opposition to the notion that species may change and develop into new species. The outstanding opponent of evolution at this time was one of the great scientists of his day. He was not only a contemporary of Lamarck, but a man to whom Lamarck had given a position at the Jardin des Plantes, the institution where Buffon had worked for so many years. This was **Georges Cuvier** (1769–1832), who was to become famous as the "Pope of Bones," the father of zoology, paleontology, and comparative anatomy.

Our interest in Cuvier resides mainly in his unwavering, obstinate, and at times nasty criticism of Lamarck's views on evolution. Although not an especially religious person, Cuvier insisted upon the fixity of species with almost religious fervor, refusing to believe that a new species could evolve from an old one. By this time, most scientists thought it quite obvious that new species of animals and plants had come into existence, and, if Cuvier was to successfully counteract the growing interest in evolution, he had to offer an alternative explanation about how new species could appear. He did so by proposing a theory of catastrophism.

This theory was based on the assumption of a series of violent and sudden catastrophes.* These catastrophes were produced by natural, not divine,† means, such as the formation of the Alps, and were responsible for ending each major stratigraphical sequence (see geologic table, p. 132). All creatures living in those parts of the world where "revolutions" or catastrophes took place were destroyed. Then, after things settled down, these areas were restocked with new forms, different from those previously living there. These new forms came from neighboring areas unaffected by the catastrophes. Cuvier's representation thus avoided the idea of evolution to explain the appearance of new forms.

Cuvier was an antievolutionist and one of the most brilliant scientists of his time. Did his antievolutionary views retard the development of evolutionary ideas? As we have seen, they did not affect Lamarck, who developed his evolutionary scheme despite Cuvier. Oldroyd (1980) suggests that, on the contrary, Cuvier's work led to Darwin!

Cuvier divided the Animal Kingdom into four divisions or embranchements: vertebrates, molluscs, jointed or segmented animals, and zoophytes (no special nervous system or sense organs). Each of these major groupings was seen as a separate organizational type, and each one had its particular anatomical and physiological characteristics functionally adaptive for the conditions of its environment. Thus, each of these divisions, one separate from the other, was not rigidly set in an inseparable Chain of Being, as was the Linnaean arrangement. Although separate, Cuvier believed these divisions fixed and not subject to change. However, since Cuvier separated these four divisions, thus eliminating the Chain of Being concept, he also opened the way for someone else to explain the appearance and disappearance of forms by an evolutionary theory.

Changes necessary from Cuvier's representation had to suggest mutability instead of fixity and to link species with their environments. Darwin did this, and added natural selection to complete the scheme. Thus, as Oldroyd suggests (1980, p. 43), "the route from Linnaeus to Darwin lay through the antievolutionist Cuvier, as much as the evolutionist Lamarck."

Cuvier's influence on Darwin was indirect, since his ideas did not act specifically on matters discussed by Darwin. Still, it may have made it easier for Darwin to argue (and others to accept) the notion that the Chain of Being concept was inadequate. On the other hand, Cuvier's catastrophism was of no help to Darwin; it is quite likely that, early in his thinking, Darwin rejected catastrophism because of the influence of Lyell, the period's most influential opponent of Cuvier's view.

Charles Lyell (1797–1875) was a lawyer by training and geologist by choice. When Darwin returned to England in 1836, he became Lyell's close friend and confidant, a relationship that was to last a lifetime despite differences on a number of intellectual points.

*A recent school of thought suggests that evolution can occur with sudden and rapid change. This idea (quite different from catastrophism) is known as "punctuated equilibrium" and is discussed on p. 9.

†Cuvier's catastrophism had no religious basis, and he was careful to separate his religious beliefs from his scientific work. Creationists mistakenly use Cuvier's views to support their position.

Lyell's important contribution to science was his popular three-volume work, *Principles of Geology* (1830–1833), in which he rejected the catastrophism of Cuvier. Lyell reaffirmed the principle of **uniformitarianism**; that is, no forces had been active in the past history of the earth that are not also working today—an idea introduced into European thought in 1785 by James Hutton. Lyell showed, through the process of uniformitarianism, that the earth's crust was formed via a series of slow and gradual changes. Mountains, rivers, valleys, lakes, deserts, and coastlines were not the sudden result of cataclysms, but rather the result of purely natural forces, such as erosion by land, water, frost, ice, and rain. These forces, which could be seen operating in the present, could (assuming sufficient time) have caused all geological events of the past.

When he embarked on the *Beagle*, Darwin was more interested in geology than in any other science. In 1832, while in South America, Darwin received the second volume of Lyell's *Principles* (Professor Henslow had presented Darwin with the first volume just before the *Beagle* sailed, but cautioned Darwin not to believe everything Lyell had written). Lyell's work immediately struck a responsive chord as Darwin observed the mountains, rocks, and coastline of South America. From Lyell, Darwin learned first of all about the development of the earth's crust, the environmental conditions that, through the struggle for existence, could modify living forms, and, secondly, about the immense age of the earth, far beyond Archbishop Ussher's 4004 B.C.

Two important points in Darwin's explanation of evolution are the struggle for existence and descent with modification. The principle of struggle for existence was basic to Darwin's evolutionary theory, and this he credits to Lyell, though the idea was not original with him. Descent with modification Darwin saw as a slow and gradual process and, for this to work, time would be necessary. Lyell believed the earth was extremely old, on the order of hundreds or thousands of million years (much older than Buffon had suggested in the previous century), thus giving to Darwin a notion of time that would have made the gradual process of evolution possible.

Shortly after his return to England, Darwin opened his first notebook in July, 1837. He planned to collect evidence on the subject of the gradual modification of species since, as he said "... the subject haunted me" (F. Darwin, 1950, p. 15). As he worked, he came to realize that "selection was the keystone of man's success in making useful races of animals and plants. But how selection could be applied to organisms living in a state of nature remained for some time a mystery to me" (F. Darwin, 1950, p. 53). The mystery was solved for Darwin in October, 1838, fifteen months after he had begun his systematic enquiry, when he happened "to read for amusement" Malthus' essay on the principle of population.

Thomas Robert Malthus (1766–1834) was an English clergyman, political economist, and devotee of the natural sciences. His work was to become a standard consulted by politicians dealing with population problems and a source of inspiration to both Charles Darwin and Alfred Wallace in their separate discoveries of the principle of natural selection.

In his *Essay*, Malthus pointed out that if human population growth is unrestrained by natural causes, it will double every twenty-five years, but that the capacity for food production increases only in a straight arithmetic

Uniformitarianism
The thesis that geological processes have always been the same as they are today.

Figure 2-10   Lyell.

progression. In nature, Malthus noted, this impulse to multiply was *checked by the struggle for existence*, but humans had to apply artificial restraints. Malthus emphasized two facts: the infinite fertility of humankind, and the limited size and resources of the earth.

Upon reading this, Darwin wrote:

> . . . it at once struck me that under these circumstances favourable variations would tend to be preserved, and unfavourable ones to be destroyed. The result of this would be the formation of a new species. *Here then I had at last got a theory by which to work* (F. Darwin, 1950, pp. 53–54). (Emphasis added.)

While Darwin had already realized that selection was the key to evolution, it was due to Malthus that he saw how selection in nature could be explained. In the struggle for existence, those *individuals* with favorable variations would survive; those with unfavorable variations would not. The significance here is that Darwin was thinking in terms of individuals (not species) that interact with one another. This was quite different from the nineteenth-century philosophy prevalent in Europe since the time of Plato. It was the significance of individuals in the struggle for existence that led Darwin to his concept of natural selection.

Before Darwin, scientists (Linnaeus and Lyell, for example) thought of species as an entity that could not change, and, if species changed, they were not species. It was species that were at the basis of the discussions of plants and animals. Individuals within the species did not appear to be significant and, therefore, it was difficult for many scientists to imagine how change could occur. Darwin, as we have pointed out, saw that variation of individuals could explain how selection occurred. Favorable variations were selected by nature for survival; unfavorable ones eliminated (Malthus, of course, believed God did the selecting, not nature). Thus, "Population thinkers stress the uniqueness of everything in the organic world. What is important for them is the individual, not the type. They emphasize that every individual in sexually reproducing species is uniquely different from all others. . . . There is no 'typical' individual, . . ." (Mayr, 1982, p. 46).

This emphasis on the uniqueness of the individual (the variation that occurs in all populations—that a population is a group of interacting individuals and not a type) led Darwin to natural selection as the mechanism that made evolution work. Natural selection operates on individuals, favorably or unfavorably, but it is the population that evolves. As pointed out on p. 89, the unit of natural selection is the individual; the unit of evolution is the population.

Darwin's Evidence

By 1859, Darwin had accumulated a tremendous amount of data. In addition to the thousands of observations made during his five-year voyage on the *Beagle*, Darwin read voluminously in geology, paleontology, and related disciplines, and meticulously collected observations on domesticated plants and animals. Darwin had originally planned to detail all this information in a huge multivolume treatise. But when Wallace forced his hand, Darwin—in *Origin*—summarized his conclusions in what he modestly called an "abstract."

Domesticated Plants and Animals   Through what Darwin called "unconscious selection," animal and plant breeders had greatly modified varieties of domestic species during historic times. Darwin believed such observations provided strong support for the process of natural selection, and was particularly impressed with pigeons (which he had studied and bred for years):

> Altogether at least a score of pigeons might be chosen, which if shown to an ornithologist, and he were told that they were wild birds, would certainly, I think, be ranked by him as well-defined species. Moreover, I do not believe that any ornithologist would place the English carrier, the short-faced tumbler, the runt, the barb, pouter, and fantail in the same genus; more especially as in each of these breeds several truly-inherited sub-breeds, or species as he might have called them, could be shown him.
>
> Great as the differences are between the breeds of pigeons, I am fully convinced that the common opinion of naturalists is correct, namely, that all have descended from the rock-pigeon (*Columba livia*) including under this term several geographical races or sub-species, which differ from each other in the most trifling respects (Darwin, 1859, pp. 22–23).

Geographic Distribution of Life Forms   Darwin drew widely upon his experience from the *Beagle* voyage, as well as an intimate knowledge of the flora and fauna of his native England, to argue further for the role of natural selection:

> Isolation, also, is an important element in the process of natural selection. In a continued or isolated area, if not very large, the organic and inorganic conditions of life will generally be in a great degree uniform; so that natural selection will tend to modify all the individuals of a varying species throughout the area in the same manner in relation to the same conditions. Intercrosses, also, with the individuals of the same species, which otherwise would have inhabited the surrounding and differently circumstanced districts, will be prevented (Darwin, 1859, p. 104).

The Geological and Paleontological Record   Darwin clearly understood that the major verification for his theory of slow and gradual evolutionary modification must come from fossil evidence embedded within the earth's strata. He also recognized that the paleontological record could never be complete (much less, of course, was known about this record at that time). Even given these limitations, Darwin's perceptive use of paleontological examples strengthened his argument and provided a great stimulus for future research:

> We can understand how it is that all the forms of life, ancient and recent, make together one grand system; for all are connected by generation. We can understand, from the continued tendency to divergence of character, why the more ancient a form is, the more it generally differs from those now living. Why ancient and extinct forms often tend to fill up gaps between existing forms, sometimes blending two groups previously classed as distinct into one; but more commonly only bringing them a little closer together. The more ancient a form is, the more often, apparently, it displays characters in some degree intermediate between groups now distinct; for the more ancient a form is, the more nearly it will be related to, and consequently resemble, the common progenitor of groups since become widely divergent (Darwin, 1859, pp. 344–345).

Comparative Anatomy   A basic element of biological interpretation in Darwin's time (as well as our own) involves anatomical comparison. How do we know whether two living forms are really related to each other, or to whom a fossil form is related?

> We have seen that the members of the same class, independently of their habits of life, resemble each other in the general plan of their organisation. This resemblance is often expressed by the term "unity of type," or by saying that the several parts and organs in the different species of the class are homologous. The whole subject is included under the general name of Morphology. This is the most interesting department of natural history, and may be said to be its very soul. What can be more curious than that the hand of a man, formed for grasping, that of a mole for digging, the leg of the horse, the paddle of the porpoise, and the wing of the bat, should all be constructed on the same pattern, and should include the same bones, in the same relative positions? (Darwin, 1859, p. 434).

Embryology   It has long been known that the immature stages organisms pass through during development can give important clues concerning evolutionary relationships—a fact that did not escape Darwin's attention.

> The embryos, also, of distinct animals within the same class are often strikingly similar; a better proof of this cannot be given, than a circumstance mentioned by Agassiz, namely, that having forgotten to ticket the embryo of some vertebrate animal he cannot now tell whether it be that of a mammal, bird, or reptile. The vermiform larvae of moths, flies, beetles, &c., resemble each other much more closely than do the mature insects (Darwin, 1859, p. 439).

Vestigial Organs   A final line of evidence presented by Darwin concerned those "rudimentary, atrophied, or aborted" organs that appeared to no longer perform any apparent function. If life had not evolved, what possible "Design" could explain their presence?

> Rudimentary organs may be compared with the letters in a word, still retained in the spelling, but become useless in the pronunciation, but which serve as a clue in seeking for its derivation. On the view of descent with modification, we may conclude that the existence of organs in a rudimentary, imperfect, and useless condition, or quite aborted, far from presenting a strange difficulty, as they assuredly do on the ordinary doctrine of creation, might even have been anticipated, and can be accounted for by the laws of inheritance (Darwin, 1859, pp. 455–456).

NATURAL SELECTION IN ACTION

A modern example of natural selection can be shown through research on the process in operation. The best historically documented case of natural selection acting in modern populations deals with changes in pigmentation among peppered moths near Manchester, England. Before the nineteenth century, the common variety of moth was a mottled gray color that provided extremely effective camouflage against lichen-covered tree trunks. Also present, though in much lower frequency, was a dark variety of moth. While resting on such trees, the dark, uncamouflaged moths against the light tree trunks were more visible to birds, and were therefore eaten more often. Thus, in the end, they produced fewer offspring than the light, camouflaged moths. Yet, in fifty years, by the end of the nineteenth century, the common gray, camouflaged form had been almost completely replaced by the black variety.

What had brought about this rapid change? The answer lies in the rapidly changing environment of industrialized nineteenth-century England. Pollutants released in the area settled on trees, killing the lichen and turning the bark a dark color. Moths living in the area continued to rest on trees, but the gray (or light) variety was increasingly conspicuous as the trees became darker. Consequently, they began to be preyed upon more frequently by birds and contributed fewer genes to the next generation. This process caused the gene for gray-colored moths to decrease in frequency. On the other hand, the black variety had greater reproductive success, and the gene for black increased from one generation to the next.

In the twentieth century, increasing control of pollutants has allowed some forested areas to return to their lighter, preindustrial conditions with lichen growing again on the trees. As would be expected, in these areas the black variety is now being supplanted by the gray.

The substance that produces pigmentation is called *melanin* and the evolutionary shift in the peppered moth, as well as many other moth species, is termed *industrial melanism*. Such an evolutionary shift in response to environmental change is called **adaptation**.

This example provides numerous insights into the mechanism of evolutionary change by natural selection:

1. A trait must be inherited to have importance in natural selection. A characteristic that is not hereditary (such as a change in hair pigmentation brought about by dye) will not be passed on to succeeding generations. Therefore, gene frequencies will not change and evolution will not occur. In moths, pigmentation is a demonstrated hereditary trait.

2. Natural selection cannot occur without variation in inherited characteristics. If all the moths had initially been gray (you will recall some dark forms were present) and the trees became darker, the survival and reproduction of all moths may have been so low that the population would have become extinct. Such an event is not unusual in evolution and, without variation, would nearly always occur. *Selection can only work with variation already present.*

3. "Fitness" is a relative measure that will change as the environment changes. Fitness is simply reproductive success. In the initial stage, the gray moth was the most-fit variety, but as the environment changed, the black moth became more fit, and a further change reversed the adaptive pattern. It should be obvious that statements regarding the "most-fit" life form mean nothing without reference to specific environments.

The example of peppered moths shows how different death rates influence natural selection, for moths that die early tend to leave fewer offspring. But mortality is not the entire picture. Another important aspect of natural selection is fertility, for an animal that gives birth to more young would pass its genes on at a faster rate than those who bear fewer offspring. However, fertility is not the whole picture either, for the crucial element is the number of young raised successfully to the point where they reproduce themselves. We may

Adaptation
An evolutionary shift in a population in response to environmental change; the result of natural selection.

(a)

(b)

Figure 2-11 Variation in the peppered moth. In (*a*), the dark form is more visible to bird predators on the light (unpolluted) trees. In (*b*), the light form is more visible: trees are darker due to pollution.

state this simply as *differential net reproductive success*. The way this mechanism works can be demonstrated through another example.

In a common variety of small birds called swifts, data show that giving birth to more offspring does not necessarily guarantee that more young will be successfully raised. The number of eggs hatched in a breeding season is a measure of fertility. The number of birds that mature and are eventually able to leave the nest is a measure of net reproductive success, or offspring successfully raised. The following tabulation shows the correlation between the number of eggs hatched (fertility) and the number of young that leave the nest (reproductive success) averaged over four breeding seasons (Lack, 1966).

Number of eggs hatched (fertility)	2 eggs	3 eggs	4 eggs
Average number of young raised (reproductive success)	1.92	2.54	1.76
Sample size	72	20	16

As the tabulation shows, the most efficient fertility number is three eggs, for that yields the highest reproductive success. Raising two is less beneficial to the parents since the *end result* is not as successful as with three eggs. Trying to raise more than three young is actually detrimental, since the parents may not be able to provide adequate nourishment for any of the offspring. An offspring that dies before reaching reproductive age is, in evolutionary terms, an equivalent of never having been born in the first place. Actually, such a result may be an evolutionary minus to the parents, for this offspring will drain their resources and may inhibit their ability to raise other offspring, thereby lowering their reproductive success even further. Selection will favor those genetic traits that yield the maximum net reproductive success. If the number of eggs laid* is a genetic trait in birds (and it seems to be), natural selection in swifts should act to favor the laying of three eggs as opposed to two or four.

DARWIN'S FAILURES

Darwin argued eloquently for the notion of evolution in general and the role of natural selection in particular, but he did not entirely comprehend the exact mechanisms of evolutionary change.

As we have seen, natural selection acts on *variation* within species. Neither Darwin, nor anyone else in the nineteenth century, understood the source of all this variation. Consequently, Darwin speculated about variation arising from "use"—an idea similar to Lamarck's. Darwin, however, was not as dogmatic in his views as Lamarck, and most emphatically argued against inner "needs" or "effort." Darwin had to confess that when it came to explaining variation, he simply did not know.

> Our ignorance of the laws of variation is profound. Not in one case out of a hundred can we pretend to assign any reason why this or that part differs, more or less, from the same part in the parents. But whenever we have the means of instituting a comparison, the same laws appear to have acted in producing the lesser differ-

*The number of eggs hatched is directly related to the number of eggs laid.

ences between varieties of the same species, and the greater differences between species of the same genus. The external conditions of life, as climate and food, &c., seem to have induced some slight modifications. Habit in producing constitutional differences, and use in strengthening, and disuse in weakening and diminishing organs, seem to have been more potent in their effects (Darwin, 1859, pp. 167–168).

In addition to his inability to explain the origins of variation, Darwin also did not completely understand the mechanism by which parents transmitted traits to offspring. Almost without exception, nineteenth-century scholars were confused about the laws of heredity, and the popular consensus was that inheritance was *blending* by nature. In other words, offspring were always expected to express intermediate traits as a result of a blending of their parents' contributions. Given this view, we can see why the actual nature of genes was thus unimaginable. Without any viable alternatives, Darwin accepted this popular misconception. As it turned out, a contemporary of Darwin had systematically worked out the rules of heredity. However, the work of this obscure Augustinian monk, Gregor Mendel (whom you shall meet in Chapter 4), was not recognized until the beginning of the twentieth century.

◇ Summary

The concept of evolution as we know it today is directly traceable to developments in intellectual thought in Western Europe over the last 300 years. In particular, the contributions of Linnaeus, Lamarck, Buffon, Lyell, and Malthus all had significant impact upon Darwin. The year 1859 marks a watershed in evolutionary theory for, in that year, the publication of Darwin's *On the Origin of Species* crystallized the evolutionary process (particularly the crucial role of natural selection) and, for the first time, thrust evolutionary theory into the consciousness of the common person. Debates both inside and outside the sciences continued for several decades (and in some corners persist today), but the theory of evolution irrevocably changed the tide of intellectual thought. Gradually Darwin's formulation of the evolutionary process became accepted almost universally by scientists as the very foundation of all the biological sciences, physical anthropology included. In this, the twentieth century, contributions from genetics allow us to demonstrate the mechanics of evolution in a way unknown to Darwin and his contemporaries.

Natural selection is the central determining factor influencing the long-term direction of evolutionary change. How natural selection works can best be explained as differential reproductive success, meaning, in other words, how successful individuals are in leaving offspring to succeeding generations.

◇ Questions for Review

1. Trace the history of evolutionary ideas from Copernicus to the time of Darwin.
2. In what ways do Linnaeus and Buffon differ in their approach to the concept of evolution?

3. What are the bases of Lamarck's theory of acquired characteristics? Why is this theory unacceptable?
4. What was Lamarck's contribution to nineteenth-century evolutionary ideas?
5. Explain Cuvier's catastrophism.
6. What did Malthus and Lyell contribute to Darwin's thinking on evolution?
7. What major areas of evidence did Darwin use to strengthen his argument concerning evolution?
8. How did Darwin's explanation of the source of variation compare with that of Lamarck?
9. What hereditary mechanism did Darwin utilize to explain transmission of traits from parents to offspring?
10. What is meant by adaptation? Illustrate through the example of industrial melanism.

Biological Basis of Life

CONTENTS

Linus Pauling.

At Cambridge University's Cavendish Laboratory, from 1951 to 1953, a brash young American scientist from Chicago, **James D. Watson** and a garrulous Englishman from Northampton, **Francis H. C. Crick**, worked more or less together (with the assistance of English physicist Maurice Wilkins and others) to solve the puzzle of DNA structure.

Watson should have been hard at work in Copenhagen learning chemistry to help him in his postdoctoral biological research, and Crick, already at Cambridge, should have been busily engaged researching hemoglobin crystals for his Ph.D. Neither should have been involved in DNA research, but, as a matter of fact, both men were very much involved, and they hoped not only to discover the structure of DNA and win a Nobel Prize, but to beat **Linus Pauling** who, they were quite sure, was close to success on the same project at California Institute of Technology.

But Pauling was not as close to success as Crick and Watson believed. In November, 1951, Pauling started working on a triple helix and thought he succeeded, "although the structure was described as 'an extraordinarily tight one, with little opportunity for change in positions of the atoms'" (Pauling, 1974). A copy of the paper on his experiment was sent to Crick and Watson, who had themselves built an unsuccessful triple helix model a year earlier. They had considered their model a failure, and, after reading Pauling's paper (and catching an error in basic chemistry), knew his to be a failure also.

As Watson tells the story, he knew that Pauling was wrong, and that the earlier model he and Crick had constructed was also wrong, and now he was stumped. It was not until Wilkins showed him an X-ray diffraction photograph of DNA (taken by Cavendish scientist Rosalind Franklin) early in 1953, that Watson thought he saw a bit of light. The X-ray indicated that a helix was the correct structure, which he had been sure of anyway, and, further, that a 2-chain model—a double helix rather than a triple helix—might possibly be the answer. Watson and Crick deliberately kept the X-ray photograph from Pauling, since they feared that if he saw the X-ray, he would solve the problem before they did.

Watson designed a 2-chain metal helical model of DNA for experimental purposes to be built by the Cavendish Laboratory. The key to the mystery occurred abruptly to Watson while he was impatiently waiting for the Lab machine shop to complete the model. He had cut accurate representations of the four bases from stiff cardboard and was shifting them around trying out various pairing possibilities when:

Suddenly I became aware that an adenine-thymine pair held together by two hydrogen bonds was identical in shape to a guanine-cytosine pair held together by at least two hydrogen bonds. All the hydrogen bonds seemed to form naturally; no fudging was required to make the two types of base pairs identical in shape (Watson, 1968, p. 194).

The enigma of the basic DNA structure was solved and the race won. In 1962, the Nobel Prize for Medicine and Physiology was awarded to Crick, Watson, and Wilkins.

Actually, Watson and Crick need not have worried about Pauling's beating them to the DNA solution since Pauling did not consider this research a race (Pauling, personal communication); however, Pauling does believe there was a chance, had he seen the X-ray photograph,

. . . that I would have thought of the Watson-Crick structure during the next few weeks. . . . Nevertheless, I myself think that the chance is rather small that I would have thought of the double helix in 1952, before Watson and Crick made their great discovery (Pauling, 1974, p. 771).

SOURCES:

Pauling, Linus. "Molecular Basis of Biological Specificity," *Nature*, **248** (no. 5451):769, 771, April 26, 1974.

Olby, Robert. *The Path to the Double Helix*, Seattle: University of Washington Press, 1974.

Watson, James D. *The Double Helix*, New York: Atheneum, 1968.

James Watson and Francis Crick, 1953.

◇ CHAPTER THREE

◇ Introduction

In the preceding chapter, evolution was discussed from a conceptual point of view, but the mechanics of evolution—how hereditary characteristics are actually passed on from one generation to the next—were not included in that generalized presentation. In the body, what physiological processes operate to produce and distribute variation and enable natural selection to function? In this chapter, we shall examine the specifics, beginning with the nature of the cell, since that is where, in a sense, the evolutionary process begins. The basic evolutionary process applies to all forms of life—to plants as well as to animals; however, our interest is mainly humankind, and cells and genetics will be discussed for the most part from the point of view of human beings. Nevertheless, we should keep in mind that the cell is basic to all forms of life, and that cellular characteristics (such as genes, chromosomes, and DNA) are found in the cells of all animals and plants. Finally, we should remember that the process of heredity is essentially similar in all species. Heredity, as we deal with it here, refers simply to the passage of genetic information from the cells of one generation to those of the next.

◇ The Cell

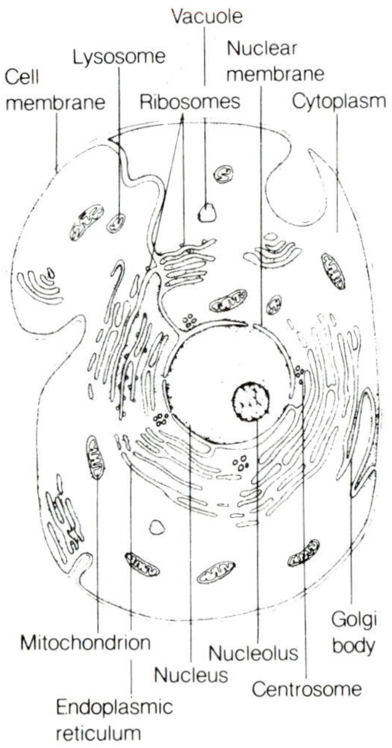

SOMATIC AND SEX CELLS

Basically, two kinds of cells are directly involved with heredity: **somatic cells** and **sex cells**. The body is composed of various kinds of specialized tissues (blood, liver, muscle, skin, nerve) consisting of billions of somatic cells continually being manufactured to replace those that have died. Indeed, one estimate has it that the cells of the human body are replaced every seven years.

Sex cells are similar to somatic cells but play no part in the structural composition of the body. They originate in the testes of males and ovaries of females, and their only function is to transmit life and hereditary information from parents to offspring.

The focal point of heredity is the **nucleus**, usually located in the center of the cell and separated from the cytoplasm by a thin nuclear membrane. Within the nucleus are two nucleic acids central to understanding the hereditary process: ribonucleic acid (RNA) and deoxyribonucleic acid (DNA). Just outside the nucleus and associated with its function, are two small cylindrical bodies called *centrioles*.

Chromosomes   During division of the cell, **chromosomes** become readily visible within the nucleus. The structure of a chromosome may be portrayed as two arms held together by a circle (**centromere**). (See Fig. 3-2.) The number of chromosomes in different plant and animal species varies, but normally

---

Somatic cells
soma: body
Cells that do not divide by meiosis and do not become gametes.

Sex cells
Cells that divide by meiosis and become gametes.

Nucleus
A body, present in most types of cells, containing chromosomes.

Chromosome
chrome: color
soma: body
Threadlike, gene-containing body found in the nucleus.

Centromere
centro: central
mere: part
That part of the chromosome to which spindle fibers are attached during mitosis and meiosis.

Figure 3-1   Generalized diagram of a cell.

◇ Box 3-1   Terms Used in Discussion of Chromosomes

Autosomes   In humans, the first 22 pairs of chromosomes; not sex chromosomes.

Diploid   (*dipl*: double; *oid*: resembling, similar to). The full set of chromosomes, 46 in humans. Since there are 23 different chromosomes, doubling that makes 46, the diploid number. There are two (a pair) of each kind of chromosome.

Haploid   (*hapl*: single, simple; *oid*: resembling, similar to). Simple here means uncomplicated, the basic number, referring to the 23 different chromosomes found in the gamete after the second division. There is a single representative, not a pair, of each kind of chromosome.

Homologous chromosomes   A matched pair of chromosomes.

Locus   (pl. *loci*, pronounced lo'-sigh, lo'-see, lo'-kee). The place of a gene on a chromosome.

Oocyte   (oh-oh-site). Female sex cell; a cell that undergoes meiosis and produces an egg, or ovum.

Ootid   A haploid cell produced by meiosis and differentiating into an ovum.

Oogenesis   Division process of the female sex cell that produces ova.

Spermatocyte   A cell that undergoes meiosis and produces a spermatid. A male sex cell.

Spermatogenesis   Division process of the male sex cell that produces sperm.

Spermatid   A haploid cell produced by meiosis and differentiating into a sperm cell.

---

all the members of a single species possess the same number of chromosomes (46 for humans).

The 46 chromosomes found in the somatic cells of all human beings are more accurately considered as 23 pairs, since there are two sets of 23 different chromosomes (Fig. 3-4). The first 22 pairs of chromosomes are known as *autosomes*; the 23rd pair (or *sex chromosomes*) is known alphabetically as XX or XY. (A female carries two X chromosomes and a male one X and one Y.)

Chromosomes play their role during division of the somatic and sex cells. We can better understand these functions as we follow chromosome behavior during somatic cell division (*mitosis*) and sex cell division (*meiosis*) in the following sections.

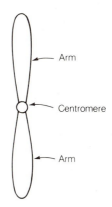

Figure 3-2   A normal chromosome.

◇ Cell Division: Mitosis

The nature of cells is to divide. Since division of the two kinds of cells differs, let us first take the less complex somatic cell division, called **mitosis**.

Somatic cell division serves several functions. As cells divide, they multiply, thus aiding in the growth of the organism. Cell division is also a means by which old cells are replaced by new ones. What is of interest to us is the part of this process of cell division resulting in the development of two daughter cells identical to the mother cell. In this way, as new body cells are produced they are exactly the same as those they replace, and the body, except for maturation and degeneration, remains essentially the same throughout life.

"Twin" chromosomes or chromatids

Figure 3-3   When a chromosome replicates itself, each unit is known as a *chromatid*.

Figure 3-4 Human chromosomes; a male karyotype. *Upper portion*: Chromosomes as they appear under a microscope. *Lower portion*: Each pair of chromosomes is identified by the size of the arms on each side of the centromere and arranged, by number, from large to small.

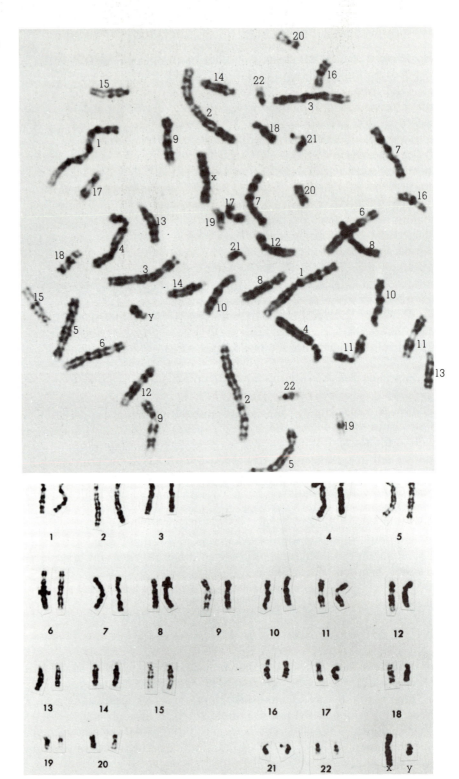

Mitosis operates in ingenious fashion in order to produce these two identical daughter cells (Fig. 3-5). A cell with 46 chromosomes divides into two daughter cells, each containing the exact number of chromosomes as the mother cell. This is accomplished in the following manner:

1. At the beginning of the division process, each chromosome duplicates itself and actually consists of two longitudinal components called *chromatids*. There are now 46 doubled chromosomes, or 92 chromatids. (See Fig. 3-3.)
2. The doubled chromosomes position themselves along the equator of the nucleus and, as the cell divides, the chromatids separate.
3. As the cell continues to divide, the chromatids move away from each other in opposite directions. When the cell completes its division, there are two daughter cells, each with a complete set of 46 chromosomes.

The result of this division is the production of two daughter cells, each identical to the other and to the mother cell. Each daughter cell contains the same 46 chromosomes; that is, the same genetic material as the mother cell.

Cell Division: Meiosis

We have seen how mitosis produces two daughter cells with the same number of chromosomes and genetic material as the mother cell. Reproduction, however, is quite another matter, requiring a specialized division process called **meiosis**.

The function of meiosis also appears simple—the production of cells with 23 chromosomes by dividing a cell of 46 chromosomes. However, it is not merely a matter of dividing 46 by 2, since that could result in cells with a random collection of any 23 chromosomes. The problem is to produce cells (called **gametes**) containing one of each of the 23 different kinds of chromosomes, no more and no less. A normal gamete, following the meiotic process, will have a complete set of 23 chromosomes, one of each homologous pair (Fig. 3-6).

The process of reducing the number of chromosomes from 46, the *diploid* number, to 23, the *haploid* number, takes two divisions, referred to as Meiosis I and Meiosis II.

Meiosis I Since the production process of sperm (*spermatogenesis*) and ova (*oogenesis*) differs, it will be simpler to take up one process at a time. We will begin with the production of sperm and follow with the production of ova. In meiosis I, the chromosomes appear as two chromatids, or twin chromosomes. The same-numbered chromosomes, 1A and 1B, for example, come into physical contact, a pairing known as *synapsis*. During synapsis, the chromatids of a chromosome pair often exchange segments, a process called **crossing-over**, one of the mechanisms that creates new genetic combinations.

Following synapsis, the chromosomes align themselves along the cell's equatorial plane, and, as the cell divides, the chromosome pair separates. When the division of the *primary* spermatocyte is completed, each of the two

Karyotype
(care'-ee-o-type)
karyo: nut, kernel
In biology, refers to the nucleus—a description or illustration of the number, size, and shapes of the chromosomes in the cells of an organism.

Mitosis
(my-toe'-sis)
mit: thread
osis: process or state
Somatic cell division producing two daughter cells identical to the parental cell.

Meiosis
(my-oh'-sis)
meioun: to make smaller
osis: process or state
Reduction division; sex cell division; reduction of a diploid cell, through two divisions, to a haploid (gamete) cell.

Gamete
A haploid cell (sperm or ovum) that may combine with a haploid cell of the other sex to form a fertilized cell.

Somatic cell with 46 chromosomes in nucleus

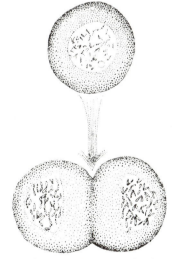

Cell divides; the nucleus of each daughter cell contains 46 chromosomes

Figure 3-5 An "ingenious" method of dividing a cell with 46 chromosomes and producing two daughter cells with 46 chromosomes identical to each other and to the mother cell.

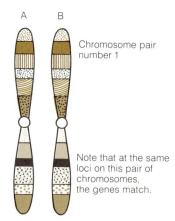

A   B

Chromosome pair
number 1

Note that at the same
loci on this pair of
chromosomes,
the genes match.

Figure 3-6 Idealized chromosome form. Each space represents a locus; 12 are shown here. Actually, there are thousands, perhaps several million, loci on a chromosome. The figure is a diagrammatic representation of a pair of chromosomes with matching genes: a homologous pair.

Figure 3-7 Spermatogenesis and oogenenis.

new cells, the *secondary* spermatocytes, contains a chromosome consisting of two joined chromatids. However, the number of chromosomes is reduced to half of those in the primary spermatocyte. For this reason, meiosis I is known as *reduction division*.

Meiosis II   The secondary spermatocytes divide, producing four cells called *spermatids*. During the second division, the joined chromatids separate, resulting in 23 single-stranded chromosomes in each of the four spermatids. With some further changes, the spermatids become sperm, or male gametes.

Ova, female gametes, are developed in essentially the same process as the sperm, except for one major difference: Instead of the primary *oocyte* producing two secondary oocytes during meiosis I, as in spermatogenesis, it creates one large cell—the secondary oocyte—and one tiny one—the polar body.* The process is repeated in meiosis II, the secondary oocyte producing one large cell and one small one; the polar body producing two more polar bodies.

If the paternal and maternal **gametes** combine in the female, the result is a fertilized cell, called a **zygote**, which carries the full complement of 23 pairs of homologous chromosomes, one member of each pair coming from the father and one from the mother. The zygote divides by mitosis and develops into an embryo and then a fetus.

To understand the process of heredity, it is necessary to examine chromosomes more carefully. The 23 pairs of chromosomes we have been discussing are actually 23 pairs of *homologous* chromosomes. To be homologous, the **genes** on two chromosomes must occupy the same place, called a **locus**. On a chromosome there are thousands of loci, each one occupied by a gene.

*Polar bodies are rarely viable.

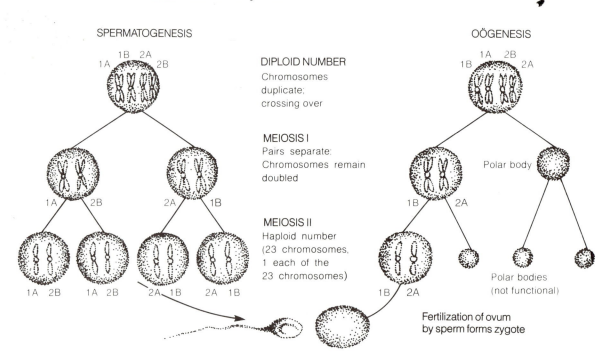

SPERMATOGENESIS

1B 2A
1A   2B

DIPLOID NUMBER
Chromosomes
duplicate;
crossing over

MEIOSIS I
Pairs separate:
Chromosomes remain
doubled

MEIOSIS II
Haploid number
(23 chromosomes,
1 each of the
23 chromosomes)

1A   2B   2A   1B

1A 2B   1A 2B   2A 1B   2A 1B

OÖGENESIS

1A 2B
1B   2A

Polar body

1B   2A

1B   2A

Polar bodies
(not functional)

Fertilization of ovum
by sperm forms zygote

When the genes at the same locus on two chromosomes affect the same trait, the two chromosomes are considered an homologous pair. The chromosome of one pair will not share the same corresponding genes at the same loci with any other chromosome except its homologous partner.

A further point of interest concerning chromosomes involves the 23rd pair, known as the *sex chromosomes*. Earlier, we noted that, in females, the 23rd pair consists of two X chromosomes, whereas in males there is one X and one Y. These are called the sex chromosomes because they are the determiners of sex of the offspring.

As we have seen, each parent contributes 23 chromosomes. The mother contributes only an X; however, since the father has both an X and a Y, there is a 50% chance that he will contribute one or the other. If he transmits an X, the offspring will be female; if a Y, it will be male.

Two functions of meiosis have now been discussed: (1) the reduction of the number of chromosomes in a sex cell from 46 to 23, and (2) separation of X and Y chromosomes in the male sex cells so that sex determination of the offspring becomes possible.

There is another significant function, especially in terms of natural selection and evolution: the production of *variation* (discussed in Chapter 4). Without variation, natural selection would be impossible; without natural selection, evolution would be impossible; and without evolution, life as we know it on earth would be impossible.

In addition to mutation (also discussed in Chapter 4), variation is produced in at least two other ways. First, a child is the result of a recombination of genes derived from the father *and* mother; therefore, an individual is always different, to a greater or lesser degree, from either parent. Furthermore, each time a sex cell divides, the 23 chromosome pairs position themselves differently so that when first division occurs, a new alignment of chromosomes takes place (Fig. 3-8). Since there are 23 pairs of chromosomes, the number

Zygote
(yoked)
A fertilized cell formed by the union of a male gamete and a female gamete.

Gene
A segment of a DNA molecule with a detectable function; sometimes used synonymously with locus and allele.

Locus
(pl. loci)
The place a gene occupies on a chromosome.

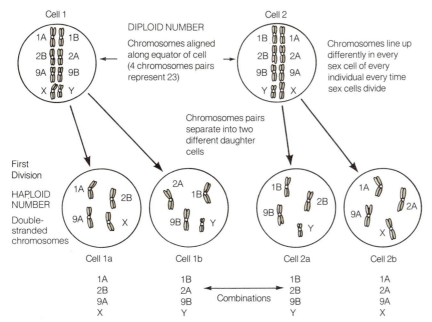

Figure 3-8 At alignment before division, chromosomes assort themselves randomly (but always in homologous pairs). Each different alignment produces a different random assortment of chromosomes in the daughter cells after first division. In the two daughter cells of cell 1, for example, cell 1a carries an X, and cell 1b a Y. Since chromosomes carry genes, the varying combinations of chromosomes result in the recombination of genes. In cell 1a, genes on X chromosomes are combined with those on 1A, 2B, and 9A. In cell 2b, Y is combined with the opposite members of those chromosomes. This particular combination of chromosomes and genes (if all 23 were considered) is unique. It probably never occurred before and will probably never occur again.

of different possible combinations is over 8 million. This number represents the possibility of only one gamete: the sperm, for example. An equal number of possibilities exists for the gamete of the other parent, so the possible different kinds of individuals that could result from one human mating is about *70 trillion*. This mind-boggling number represents more than all the human beings who have ever lived or are ever likely to live.

Another way of looking at this process is to consider that *a human male can produce several hundred million sperm every day, from puberty until death, and the chances are that no two of these sperm will be identical.*

These endless recombinations of genes provide variation which, in terms of natural selection, is extremely significant. They assure, to a population, the availability of genes that may be adaptive in a changing environment. With less variation, natural selection would have less to choose from, a circumstance that would perhaps even lead to extinction of the group.

Figure 3-9 (a) Recombination of genes at cross-over. (b) Four examples of crossing-over. An infinite number of gene combinations may easily be imagined. The single chromosomes show how the genes contributed by parents may be recombined.

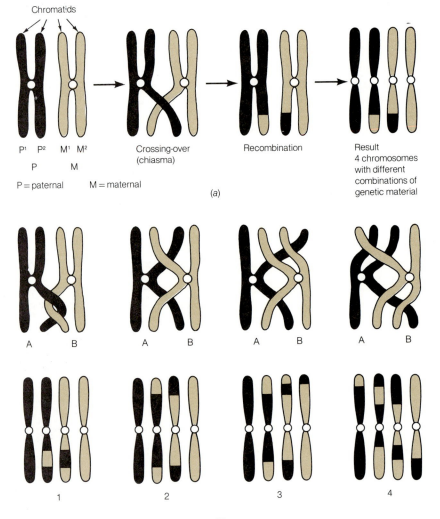

Variation occurs in yet another way. Known as **crossing-over**, this process occurs during the tetrad stage of the chromosomes. The chromosomes are arranged in pairs that have duplicated themselves, resulting in 4 chromatids. Before division, sections of each of the chromatids may exchange segments with other chromatids. The right-hand side of Figure 3-9(a) shows the result of the exchange. At crossing-over, a section of an M^2 chromatid has crossed-over with a section of P^1. (M stands for the maternal chromosome; P for the paternal chromosome.) When the chromatids "straighten out," a segment of M^2 has become part of the P^1 chromatid.

◇ DNA: Structure

We have now seen how heredity is influenced through what might be called mechanical processes. Sex cells divide, chromosomes cross-over, and genes recombine. These mechanical processes do not, however, transmit actual characteristics; in fact, parents do not pass on physical traits, they pass on information. Cell division, crossing-over, and gene recombination do not explain how the information passes from parents to offspring. For that, we must turn to the chemical nature of the phenomena involved.

Heredity is transmitted through information chemically coded in deoxyribonucleic acid (DNA), which is usually referred to as the carrier of the genetic code. An examination of the structure and process of DNA will help us understand how the information carried in chemically coded form is transformed from a code to actual physical characteristics of the body.

DNA is a large molecule consisting of four (among other) chemical substances that are its building blocks, or *bases*: *adenine*, *guanine*, *cytosine*, and *thymine*. Adenine (A) and guanine (G) belong to the class of substances known as **purines**; cytosine (C) and thymine (T) are **pyrimidines**. Each base is combined with a sugar (deoxyribose) and a phosphate residue which, all together, are called a *nucleotide*. The DNA molecule is formed by linking many nucleotides into a long chain (Fig. 3-10). The sugar and phosphate alternate to form a backbone of the molecule, and the base may be any one of the four (A, G, C, T) mentioned above.

Each base of this long chain is attached to another base (shown in Fig. 3-10), so that the DNA molecule is actually composed of two long chains, or strands, of nucleotides. The bonding of the pairs follows a pattern called the *base pairing rule*, which states that one of the purines—adenine (A) and guanine (G)—must pair with one of the pyrimidines—cytosine (C) and thymine (T). In other words, A, a purine, must pair with T, a pyrimidine; and C must pair with G. The purine A does not pair with C or G, and C and G do not pair with T. Figure 3-10 illustrates the base pair rule.

In Figure 3-11(a), the DNA molecule is represented as a flat structure, which might be compared to a ladder. The alternating sugar and phosphates represent the sidepieces of the ladder and the bases represent the rungs. Actually, the two chains twist around each other to form a loose spiral called a **helix**. Since there are two strands, and each one forms a helix, DNA is referred to as a **double helix**. If the ladder in Figure 3-11(a) were twisted to

Crossing-over
Exchange of genetic maaterial between chromatids of homologous chromosomes.

Purines
A class of organic compounds to which adenine and guanine bases belong.

Pyrimidines
A class of organic compounds to which cytosine, thymine, and uracil belong.

Helix
A spiral or anything having a spiral form.

Double helix
The structure of DNA, composed of a pair of matching helices.

Figure 3-10 Part of a DNA molecule.

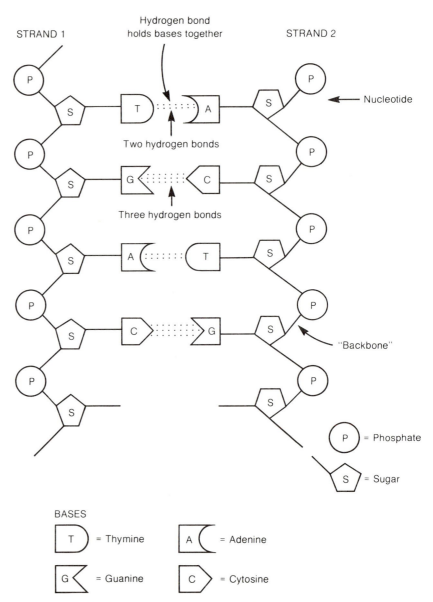

form a double helix, the representation would be more accurate, as in Figure 3-11(*b*). The discovery of the DNA molecule structure as a double helix was made by James Watson and Francis Crick, an American and English team. Their work, which earned them a Nobel Prize, sparked a phenomenal period of research in molecular biology. (See Issue, this chapter.)

Figure 3-10 illustrates the double helix nature of the DNA molecule. Alternating sugar and phosphates represent the backbone of the DNA chain, and the bases are paired according to rule. For our purposes, the significance of the DNA structure lies in the bases, especially in the sequence of the bases, because this location is where the hereditary information is stored. In the following sections on DNA *process*, note carefully the role of the bases in transmitting the genetic message.

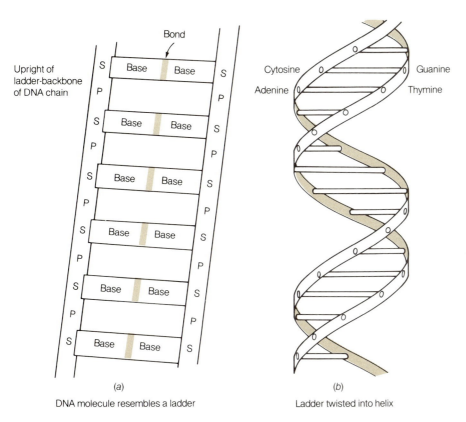

Figure 3-11 (*a*) DNA molecule resembles a ladder. (*b*) Ladder twisted into a helix.

(*a*)

DNA molecule resembles a ladder

(*b*)

Ladder twisted into helix

◇ DNA: The Genetic Code

We have mentioned that the genetic information is contained within the DNA molecule, and it is this information that is passed on from parent to offspring. The first requirement of the genetic material (DNA) is, then, that it have some efficient means of *self-replication*, so that hereditary information can be accurately reproduced and passed on to succeeding generations of individuals (or, even more basically, to succeeding generations of cells). Replication is essential because it enables parents to retain the master copy, so to speak, of the genetic information and send the duplicate copy to offspring. Without replication, the only set parents possessed would be transmitted to offspring, and parents would then be left without genetic material for future transmissions.

The way replication is accomplished is revealed directly in the beautifully simple structure of the DNA molecule itself. Figure 3-11(*a*) shows the DNA molecule simplified as a ladderlike structure. As we can easily see, the molecule has two sides, with each base on one side paired with a specific base on the other side. In other words, T only pairs with A; G with C; A with T; and C with G. In this way, one entire side of one strand of the molecule is *complementary* to the other side. To put it even more simply, one side of the molecule forms a complementary pairing of the opposite side.

◇ Box 3-2   Terms Used in Discussion of DNA

Base   One of the four chemicals attached to a sugar molecule and a phosphate to make up a nucleotide; in DNA and RNA, a base is always paired with another base.

Adenine ⎫
Guanine ⎬   The four chemical bases.
Cytosine ⎬   Adenine and thymine are
Thymine ⎭   paired; cytosine and guanine are paired.

Uracil   A chemical base found in RNA in the same position as thymine in DNA.

Amino acids   Small molecules that are the building blocks of protein.

Codon   A triplet sequence of bases on DNA and mRNA.

Anticodon   A triplet sequence of bases on tRNA.

DNA   Deoxyribonucleic acid; a large molecule composed of adenine, guanine, cytosine, and thymine plus phosphate and sugar; carries the genetic code.

RNA   Ribonucleic acid; slightly different chemically from DNA; found in the nucleus and the cytoplasm.

mRNA   Messenger RNA; carries genetic information from DNA in the nucleus to the ribosomes in the cytoplasm.

tRNA   Transfer RNA; brings an amino acid to match the mRNA bases.

rRNA   Ribosomal RNA; a major constituent of ribosomes.

Molecule   Smallest portion of a substance (element or compound) that acts like that substance and is capable of existing independently. Several to many atoms constitute a molecule.

Nucleotide   A base attached to a sugar and a phosphate group; a subunit of DNA and RNA.

Peptide   A compound of two or more amino acids joined by peptide bonds. Linked peptides form polypeptides which, in turn, join to form proteins.

Polypeptide   A group of peptides linked together.

Protein   A macromolecule, composed of one or more polypeptide chains of amino acids, responsible for carrying out most of the cell's metabolic activities; also contributes to cell structure.

Ribosomes   Small, minute bodies found in the cytoplasm of the cell; composed of rRNA and proteins; site of protein synthesis.

Protein synthesis   The manufacture of a protein. The process by which amino acids are linked (by a peptide bond) to form a polypeptide chain. The completed chain or chains form a protein.

In order for the DNA to replicate, the two strands must first unwind—much in the manner of a zipper unzipping—and separate, as indicated in Figure 3-12. The two single strands then attract free DNA nucleotides (bases, phosphates, and sugars), thus forming a complementary strand. The result is that where we started with one double-stranded molecule, we now have two identical double-stranded molecules. The genetic information has been completely replicated.

We have already discussed, earlier in this chapter, the mechanics of cell division (mitosis, meiosis), working through the duplication and distribution of chromosomes. These processes take place at a fairly gross level, and are clearly visible through a light microscope. What goes on in the DNA operates at the *molecular* level. While not visible by current methods, the process can be detected by biochemical methods and radioactive labeling. However, we can observe a direct association between the replication of DNA at the molecular level and the duplication of chromosomes. In fact, current thinking considers a chromosome as one giant DNA molecule. When a single-stranded chromosome duplicates to become a double-stranded (two chromatids) chromosome in the late interphase of both mitosis and meiosis, what we are actually seeing is the result of the DNA molecules unwinding and replicating their complementary strands. And, for example, when the chromosomes during mitosis are later distributed to respective daughter cells, they carry the same genetic information. Each has equal and identical amounts of DNA produced by simple replication.

◇ DNA: Process

Hereditary information, we know, is transmitted from parents to children through the process of meiosis. Once the father and mother contribute a sex cell each with 23 chromosomes, the result (if fertilization occurs) is a cell with 46 chromosomes called a zygote. The zygote acts as a body cell and passes through the stages of embryo, fetus, and birth. During this period of growth, and for the rest of the individual's life, the hereditary information (coded in the DNA of the nucleus) is taken from the DNA by RNA out into the cytoplasm, where the protein-synthesizing machinery is located. Here, it is converted into proteins, which build and maintain the body according to

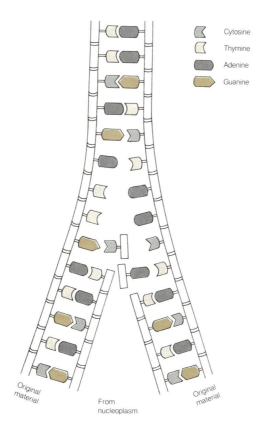

Cytosine
Thymine
Adenine
Guanine

Original material

From nucleoplasm

Original material

Figure 3-12 The replication of a DNA molecule. The double helix uncoils and then unzips, separating base pairs. Complementary base pairs are attracted and attach to the exposed nucleotides. When replication is completed, each daughter strand is composed of one strand of the parent DNA and one new strand.

Figure 3-13 Formation of mRNA strand. (a) DNA has separated. One DNA strand attracts complementary RNA nucleotide (uracil in RNA replaces thymine), a basic step in the transmission of genetic information. (b) RNA strand completed. Note that RNA bases are exact complements of DNA bases. The sequence of the bases is important.

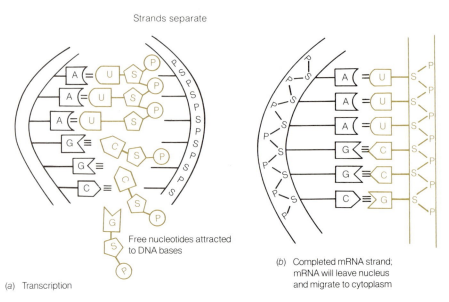

Strands separate

Free nucleotides attracted to DNA bases

(a) Transcription

(b) Completed mRNA strand; mRNA will leave nucleus and migrate to cytoplasm

that hereditary information. The information is coded in the *sequence of bases*, and the student is again asked to bear in mind the significant role of the sequence.

How is the information taken out of the nucleus? How is it decoded? And how is it converted into protein? The process begins when a gene receives the stimulus to send out information.

Transcription   The two strands of DNA separate (unzip), and one of the strands, acting as a template, assembles a strand of messenger RNA (mRNA) by attracting mRNA nucleotides that match the DNA bases (Fig. 3-13a). A DNA nucleotide sequence of CGG, for example, will be complemented on the mRNA strand by a GCC codon. DNA AAA will transcribe as UUU, instead of TTT, because mRNA does not contain thymine but substitutes uracil instead.

When transcription is completed (Fig. 3-13b), the mRNA strand will be an exact copy of the DNA sequence but with corresponding bases. At this point mRNA, acting as a messenger, carries its coded message out of the nucleus into the cytoplasm of the cell.

Translation   Once in the cytoplasm, mRNA is chemically bonded to a ribosome. The ribosome then moves along, reading the mRNA codons and attracting transfer RNA (tRNA) molecules that match the sequences of mRNA codons. In Figure 3-14, the ribosome has moved to, and is bonded with, codons 6 and 7. Anticodons 6 and 7, on two different mRNAs, are attracted and bond with corresponding mRNA codons.

Each tRNA is attached to a specific amino acid (Fig. 3-15). Since there are 20 different amino acids, there are 20 different tRNAs. As the tRNA moves away from codon 6 (Fig. 3-14), the amino acid is detached from its tRNA and is bonded to the existing chain 1-2-3-4-5. This process continues until the ribosome reaches a stop codon, and the synthesis of the polypeptide chain is complete. The completed polypeptide chain of amino acids is a protein, or part of one, and the process of converting the DNA genetic code for this particular protein has ended.

Proteins are the basic structural and functional compounds of the cell; they are responsible for carrying out most of the metabolic functions of the cell, as well as making up most of the cell structure. The structural components of tissue, hormones, enzymes, hemoglobins, etc., are proteins. In turn, the kind of protein that is synthesized depends upon the information that comes from the DNA. Consequently, the body the proteins build (pigmenta-

Codon
A triplet sequence of bases on DNA and mRNA.

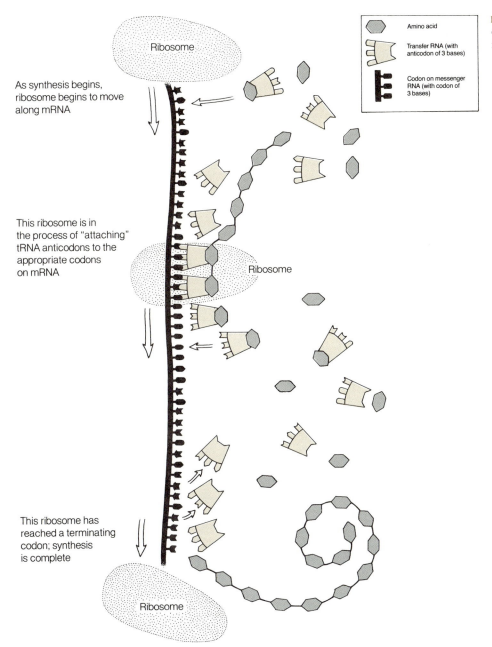

As synthesis begins, ribosome begins to move along mRNA

This ribosome is in the process of "attaching" tRNA anticodons to the appropriate codons on mRNA

This ribosome has reached a terminating codon; synthesis is complete

Ribosome

Ribosome

Ribosome

Amino acid

Transfer RNA (with anticodon of 3 bases)

Codon on messenger RNA (with codon of 3 bases)

Figure 3-14 Translation of the genetic code into strings of amino acids and finally into polypeptides and proteins.

Figure 3-15 tRNA. The cloverleaf molecular configuration of tRNA. (*a*) The open end is the end that attaches to free amino acids. (*b*) The anticodon loop attaches to a codon on mRNA.

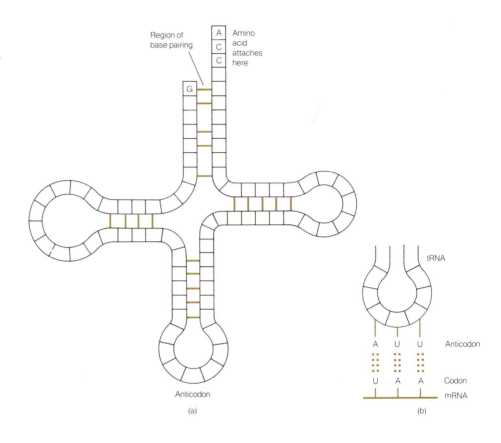

(a)

(b)

tion, body build, blood type, etc.) is largely determined by the sequence of bases found in DNA.

◇ Theory of the Gene

DNA structure and function are directly related to what we have called genes. An understanding of a gene may be gained through a demonstration of the way it changes, or mutates. The best-known example of a mutation in humans concerns the gene that produces adult hemoglobin, a globular molecule found in red blood cells.

POINT MUTATION

Normal adult hemoglobin is made up of protein chains that are direct products of gene action. One of these chains, called the *beta chain*, is in turn made up of 146 amino acids. Individuals with **sickle-cell anemia** inherit from *both* their parents mutant genes that produce a different type of hemoglobin. As a result, these individuals usually have major circulatory disturbances, destruction of red blood cells, and severe anemia often resulting in early death. Individuals who inherit this gene from only one of their parents are much less severely affected and usually have a normal life span.

The cause of all these dramatic changes in the individual's health is a seemingly minute change in the gene that produces hemoglobin. Both normal adult hemoglobin and the sickle-cell variety have 146 amino acids and, of these, 145 are identical. A substitution of only one amino acid (at position #6—see Fig. 3-16) causes all the problems.

We know, of course, that it is the sequence of bases in the DNA that codes for the sequence of amino acids in the final protein product. We also know that 3 bases (1 codon) code for one amino acid. Therefore, it takes 438 bases (146 × 3) to produce the chain of 146 amino acids seen in the adult hemoglobin beta chain.

Recent research has shown that, within the DNA, there are considerably more nucleotides than just those that are eventually translated into amino acid sequences. In fact, in human DNA (and other organisms with nucleated cells, but *not* bacteria) most genes are fragmented. Between those sections that are eventually coded there are often long intervening sequences called **introns**, which do not contribute information for protein synthesis. For example, for the hemoglobin beta locus we have seen there is a total of 438 nucleotides, which code for the eventual polypeptide chain. However, when

Sickle-cell anemia
A disease caused by a mutant form of hemoglobin (when inherited in double dose).

Intron
Within a genetic locus, a section of DNA that is not coded.

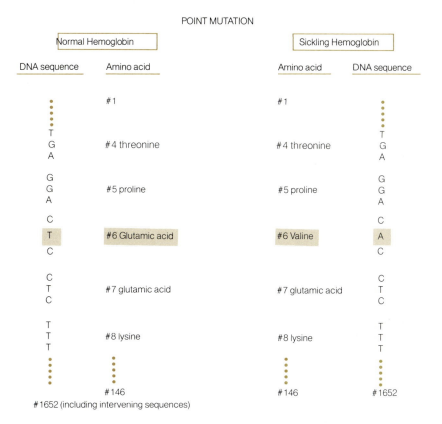

POINT MUTATION

Normal Hemoglobin

DNA sequence	Amino acid
⋮	#1
T	
G	#4 threonine
A	
G	
G	#5 proline
A	
C	
T	#6 Glutamic acid
C	
C	
T	#7 glutamic acid
C	
T	
T	#8 lysine
T	
⋮	#146

#1652 (including intervening sequences)

Sickling Hemoglobin

Amino acid	DNA sequence
#1	⋮
	T
#4 threonine	G
	A
	G
#5 proline	G
	A
	C
#6 Valine	A
	C
	C
#7 glutamic acid	T
	C
	T
#8 lysine	T
	T
#146	⋮
	#1652

Figure 3-16 Substitution of one base at position #6 produces a sickling hemoglobin.

Point mutation
The change in a single base in the DNA molecule.

one also counts those sections at the beginning and end of the locus (promoter and termination regions), as well as two long introns, the entire locus is 1,652 nucleotides long.

While all this genetic information is not utilized directly in protein synthesis, it may serve some function. The entire locus is transcribed onto mRNA. However, before the molecule leaves the nucleus, the intervening sequences are excised and the coded regions are spliced precisely back together. Such apparent DNA superfluity may provide an evolutionary basis for flexible recombination of genetic components. Another possible role in *direct* cell metabolism might operate through the excised sequences being used as "messages" sent to other genes—informing them that the synthesis of a particular polypeptide chain is taking place (Lewin, 1981).

Bear in mind that whereas DNA replication is highly efficient and accurate, it is not perfect—mistakes can and *do* occur. The difference between normal and sickling hemoglobin, however, concerns a change at only one point in the hemoglobin gene. The first 5 and the last 140 amino acids in the protein chains of both varieties of hemoglobin are identical. Only at position #6 (Fig. 3-16) is there an alteration.

Figure 3-16 shows a possible DNA base sequence and the resulting amino acid products for both normal and sickling hemoglobin. As can be seen, a single base substitution (from CTC to CAC) could result in an altered amino acid sequence (... proline–*glutamic acid*–glutamic acid ... to ... proline–*valine*–glutamic acid ...). This, in turn, would alter the properties of the whole protein (hemoglobin), resulting in differently shaped red blood cells, oxygen-bonding properties, etc. In other words, the only difference between normal hemoglobin and sickling hemoglobin is a change in *one base* out of the 438 bases that make up the coded portion of this gene. Such an alteration is called a **point mutation** and, in evolution, is probably the most common and most important source of new variation.

Point mutations probably occur relatively frequently during cell division, but a new mutation will have evolutionary significance only if it is passed on to offspring through the gametes. Once such a new mutation has occurred, its fate in the population will depend on the other evolutionary forces, especially natural selection. Sickle-cell, in fact, is the best-demonstrated example of natural selection acting in human beings, and we will take this point up in considerably more detail in Chapter 5.

DEFINITION OF THE GENE

Although not all biologists agree on the definition, we have defined the gene as that section of DNA—a sequence of codons on the DNA template—responsible for the ultimate synthesis of a specific polypeptide chain of amino acids. To put it another way, a gene is that portion of a DNA molecule that specifies the manufacture (synthesis) of a protein (hemoglobin, say) that will produce, or assist in the production of, one or more physical traits. A gene, then, is not a discrete unit operating in the nucleus or the cell; it is part of a large DNA molecule.

HEREDITY AND ENVIRONMENT

For years scientists, debating societies, philosophers, writers, preachers and others have debated, often acrimoniously, the question of what is more important: heredity or environment, nature or nurture. The question is whether human beings—physically, behaviorally, and psychically—are the result of their heredity or are fashioned and molded by their environment. Or, if both, which is more influential? Differences of opinion on this subject have been bitter.

The English philosopher John Locke (1632–1704) believed that, at birth, the mind of the human being is a blank slate (*tabula rasa*), and all differences are environmentally produced. On the other hand, the French writer Count Joseph Arthur de Gobineau (1816–1882), notorious for his belief in the inequality of races, held that differences in ability are inherited. The behavioral psychologist, J. B. Watson, left no doubt of his position:

> Give me a dozen healthy infants, well-formed, and my own specified world to bring them up, and I'll guarantee to take any one at random and train him to become any type of specialist I might select—doctor, lawyer, artist, merchant and yes, even beggar and thief, regardless of the talents, penchants, tendencies, abilities, vocations, and race . . . (Watson, 1924, p. 42).

To demonstrate whether heredity or environment is the primary factor responsible for human development is very difficult. Genetics teaches that it is not an either-or proposition, since both factors contribute to what we are physically and behaviorally. From our discussion of genes, we might infer that heredity determines exactly what the nature of a physical trait will be. This circumstance may be so with some genes, but probably not so with most. In the case of the ABO blood system mentioned above, the genes do determine blood type, and, as far as we know, the environment has no effect on the expression of the blood-group genes. If both parents are O, then all their children will be O, regardless of environmental conditions.

Genotypes and Phenotypes   The underlying basis of what we have called heredity in the preceding discussion is known as the *genotype*—"the sum total of the hereditary materials received by an individual from its parents and other ancestors" (Dobzhansky, 1979, p. 32).

An individual's genotype does not change during his or her lifetime—with the exception of some cells in aberrant tissue lines that arise from what are called *somatic mutations*. The consequences may be quite significant for the individual, since experimental work with animals suggests some cancers may well arise from somatic mutations. However, in no case are these somatic mutations passed to offspring. Moreover, for the vast majority of genes in the vast majority of one's cells, we could say the genotype is "fixed" at birth and does not change.

When we observe, probe, or measure people, what we see is their *phenotypes*; for example, a person's skin color, stature, blood type, etc. The phenotype is the *ascertainable* aspect of an organism (see p. 73 for a more complete definition). Phenotypes, as such, are partly products of the genotype, but, because of their plasticity, they *also* can be modified by the environment.

However, other more complex traits, such as stature, weight, personality, or intelligence, are often modified dramatically by the environment (see pp. 000–000). In these cases, a person's phenotype could be said to result from an interaction of the genotype with the environment.

Diet, good or poor, may affect stature and weight; sun exposure may affect skin pigmentation; phenotypes of monozygotic twins, genetically identical individuals, may vary if the twins are raised in different environments. Thus, it is obvious that an individual's phenotype changes continuously from birth to death as glandular and maturation effects occur.

What we are, then, for the most part, is the result of the interaction of hereditary material and environmental conditions. As the well-known geneticist Theodosius Dobzhansky wrote,

> Between the genes . . . and the adult phenotypes [observable characteristics] . . . there intervenes a set of developmental processes, which . . . may be exceedingly long and elaborate. This leaves ample opportunity for the uniform primary action of a gene to yield a variety of manifestations in the developing phenotypes. . . . Which potentialities will in fact be realized in a given individual at a certain stage of his development is decided by the sequence of the environments in which the development takes place (Dobzhansky, 1970, p. 33).

A gene may be perceived as potentiality. What potentiality will actually be realized, after an "exceedingly long and elaborate" developmental process, depends upon the environmental conditions. It is this interaction between biology and environment, nature and nurture, which makes us the kind of individuals we are—physically, behaviorally, and psychically. This interaction also emphasizes the point already made in the first chapter: That humans are biocultural beings.

With this introduction to the biological basis of life in mind, let us now, in the next chapter, examine how the genetic process can be applied to the process of evolution.

◇ Summary

We have dealt with two kinds of cells in this chapter—somatic cells, of which our bodies are composed, and sex cells, which are used only in the transmission of hereditary information.

Somatic cells divide by mitosis, producing two daughter cells identical to each other and to the mother cell. Sex cells divide twice by meiosis and produce four gametes. Meiosis is known as reduction division because the diploid number of chromosomes (46) is reduced to the haploid number (a complete set of 23).

There are 23 pairs of chromosomes in a human cell. Two chromosomes with similar loci, of which there are 22 pairs, are called homologous. The 23rd pair is the sex chromosomes.

Genetic information is contained in the DNA double helix. Information is taken from nucleus to cytoplasm by mRNA. Ribosomes in the cell translate the mRNA message and attract tRNA molecules. The tRNA molecules transport amino acids to the ribosomes forming a polypeptide chain. A polypeptide chain (or chains) of amino acids is a protein that makes up most of the cell structure and carries out most of the cell's metabolic functions.

A gene is not a discrete unit but is an orderly sequence of DNA codons that designates a specific chain of amino acids. The equation, one gene equals one polypeptide chain, is sometimes used as a definition of a gene.

Genes do not necessarily determine the precise nature of a physical characteristic. Genes are potentials modified by the environment, and it is the interaction of genes and environmental conditions that produces physical traits.

◇ Questions for Review

1. Name the parts of a cell discussed in the chapter.
2. List the differences between mitosis and meiosis.
3. List the steps in mitosis; in meiosis.
4. Name two important functions of meiosis.
5. Why is a pair of homologous chromosomes homologous?
6. What is a locus?
7. What is the difference between a locus and a gene?
8. Define DNA.
9. What different kinds of RNA are there?
10. What is the function of mRNA?
11. What is the function of ribosomes?
12. What is a nucleotide?
13. Name the four bases. Which bases complement each other in DNA?
14. What base is found in RNA but not in DNA?
15. What are the building blocks of a protein?
16. How is a chain of amino acids formed?
17. How are tRNA and mRNA matched?

Genetics and Evolution

CONTENTS

Twins have been objects of fascination for centuries. In our own time biologists, anthropologists, and psychologists have tested, bled, and probed them in the hope of better understanding hereditary/environmental influences on humankind. There are two varieties of twins: (1) fraternal—those conceived from two separate eggs (dizygotic)—related to each other to the same degree as siblings; and (2) identical—those conceived from a single egg (monozygotic)—and genetically identical to each other (a naturally formed clone).

Identical twins, especially, have attracted considerable interest from researchers in recent years. In an ongoing project at the University of Minnesota scientists are reuniting pairs of identical twins who were separated soon after birth. For an exhaustive week psychological, physical, and physiological testing is performed on these twins. Thus far, upwards of fifteen pairs have been studied, but the researchers hope to increase the sample to fifty pairs before completely publishing their results.

Despite this understandable caution of the researchers, a few "tidbits" of their data have leaked into the popular press. In particular, several remarkable behavioral similarities between twins have been observed. For example, the "Jim" twins (both named Jim) had been adopted into different middle-class Ohio families

Chromosome 1

Wife-naming loci. These are obviously different loci, perhaps acting in a time-sequential developmental pathway. Earlier in life the "Linda" allele is switched on, but later in life is supplanted by the "Betty" allele.

Chromosome 2

Son-naming locus. There are at least two alleles, James and Alan — which are codominant (Alan/Allan allele seems to have some slight variability in expression)

Chromosome 12

Dog-naming locus (Only one allele here; are the twins homozygous for "Toy"?)

Chromosome 15

Occupational preference locus; expression of sheriff allele must be dominant. If the brothers are heterozygous (other genes coding for ballet dancing?), these other alleles are most obviously recessive.

at four weeks of age and had not met again until they were 39 years old. A string of amazing coincidences, however, marked both their lives. Both had law enforcement training and worked part-time as deputy sheriffs; both married and divorced women named Linda and remarried women named Betty; both had dogs named Toy; both had sons respectively named James Allan and James Alan; both drove Chevrolets; and both vacationed on exactly the same stretch of beach in Florida!

The Minnesota scientists have not yet commented comprehensively on

Chromosome 19

Vacation preference loci. This must be a very large region of several closely-linked genes. A particular combination of genes coding for region of country, state, beach preference, and individual locality are being expressed identically in the two brothers.

Chromosome 20

Automobile preference locus. In American populations this is highly polymorphic — with many fairly common alleles (Buick, Ford, Plymouth, and, of course, Chevrolet). Recent massive migration has introduced an entirely new array from different populations (Datsun, Toyota, Volkswagon, etc.).

Chromosome 21

Gullibility locus. Obviously homozygous for anyone who believes this chromosome map.

these observations, but the popular press has made a great fuss over them. What exactly is being intimated? These twins were separated soon after birth, so similarities are strictly coincidental. Or are they *genetic*?

Coincidental circumstances are not all that intriguing, so the usual implication is that the similarities are somehow genetic in origin. How could this be? What genetic mechanism could possibly underlie these behavioral observations?

As we discussed earlier in the text, great progress has been made in re-cent years identifying particular genetic loci on individual chromosomes. If these behaviors seen in twins are genetic, it stands to reason that some genetic loci should exert specific influence. Perhaps in the not-too-distant future we may be able to find particular gene combinations that influence these behavioral patterns. A map of the Jim Twins' chromosomes might be imagined as shown in the accompanying figure.

SOURCE:

Holden, Constance, "Twins Reunited," *Science 80*, 1:55–59, (1980).

◇ CHAPTER FOUR

◇ Introduction

In Chapter 3, we have seen in some detail how, within the cell, genetic material is organized, packaged, distributed, and passed on to succeeding generations of cells. But when we look at the world of organisms, we see individuals who are in most cases composed of billions of cells, and our focus of organization must be shifted to a different level. In this chapter, we shall investigate the processes that allow us not only to understand, but also to predict, how genes are passed from parent to offspring. This process is the basis of the science of genetics, and its modern beginnings date to Gregor Mendel's work in the 1850s and 1860s.

◇ Early Theories of Inheritance

For ages man has been interested in the rules of heredity. We can easily imagine the early farmers of 10,000 years ago wondering how tiny grains produced wheat. Already in the fourth century B.C., Theophrastus, a Greek, had carefully studied seed germination and written a book on the subject. Some early Greeks believed that heredity among humans was a question of which sex dominated in the sex act. In the eighteenth century, Linnaeus suggested a two-layer theory, which held that "the outer layer including the vascular system is derived from the father, the inner layer including the nervous system comes from the mother."

An interesting theory dating as far back as Aristotle developed further in the seventeenth century (E. Gardner, 1965, p. 275). This theory was based on the belief, called *preformation*, that "the development of an organism is no more than the unfolding of that which is already present in miniature [Fig. 4-1]. Every organism must therefore contain in its reproductive organs an infinite series representing all of its future descendants." Ovists believed the female possessed this future of the series, and the spermists insisted it was the male.

While there were differences of opinion about the role of sex, and ignorance of the laws of animal heredity, plants were not generally discussed in these terms. That plants lacked sexuality was the conventional wisdom of the day. Not until the end of the seventeenth century was the presence of sex organs in plants demonstrated in the experiments performed in Germany by Rudolph Camerarius.

The notion that plants consisted of male and female parts came as a shock to many people. " 'What man,' exclaimed J. G. Siegesbeck, Professor of Botany at St. Petersburg, 'will ever believe that God Almighty should have introduced such confusion, or rather such shameful whoredom, for the propagation of the reign of plants. Who will instruct young students in such a voluptuous system without scandal?' " (Olby, 1966, pp. 18–19).

Figure 4-1 Some early investigators thought that they could see tiny human embryos within the sperm.

68

The discovery of sexual reproduction in plants was a notable achievement not simply because it added to our knowledge of plants, but also because it makes possible an experimental approach to plant hybridization. Once begun by Camerarius, crossing hybrids and observing what regularities might occur among the offspring became one of the most popular methods of investigating the laws of heredity.

Hybridization experiments continued in the eighteenth and nineteenth centuries. Hybrids offered an opportunity, it was believed, to work out the rules of heredity. Purebred plants produced purebreds, and there was little to learn about heredity from that kind of experiment. Among the offspring of hybrids, on the other hand, some resembled the parents, but others were quite different. If, in this apparent confusion of offspring, there were regularities of such traits as form, color, or germination patterns, they would serve as clues to the principles of heredity.

Or so it seemed. Many investigators worked on plant hybrids, but the secrets of heredity eluded them. Experimenters demonstrated, for example, that neither sex was entirely responsible for offspring but both parents contributed equally. They also demonstrated that hybrids did not breed true (as Linneaus believed they did), yet the laws of heredity remained undiscovered.

There were several reasons for this failure. The plants used were not the proper ones for the study of heredity—they were genetically too complex for the kind of observations possible at that time. Experimenters did not work with enough plants, or through sufficient generations, to find regularities. And, finally, they did not count the offspring of hybrids; that is, they failed to examine the results of their experiments from a statistical point of view. What the early experimenters saw were offspring in a confusing variety of forms and colors, which they were unable to clarify. Their conclusion was that clarification was imposible, that there probably were no universal laws of heredity.

Thus matters stood, more or less at a standstill as far as the laws of heredity were concerned, until Gregor Mendel solved the riddle in the 1860s.

Figure 4-2   Gregor Mendel.

◇ Mendel's Life

Gregor Mendel (1822–1884), shown in Figure 4-2, was born into a family of peasant farmers, in the small Silesian village of Heinzendorf in what we now Czechoslovakia. At school, he did so well in his academic studies that his teachers recommended he be transferred to a high school in a nearby town. Within a year, he had moved on to the Gymnasium (an advanced high school) at Troppau where, in 1840, he received a certificate which recognized his "great industry and all-round ability."

To continue his studies, he enrolled in the University Philosophical Institute of Olmutz. Because of lack of funds, Mendel had a difficult time, and his attempts to earn money as a private tutor failed. He wrote of this period of his life (in the third person): "The sorrow over these disappointed hopes and the anxious, sad outlook which the future offered him, affected him so powerfully at that time that he fell sick and was compelled to spend a year with his parents to recover!" (in Olby, 1966, p. 106).

Figure 4-3 Central Europe during Mendel's lifetime. The map shows the location of Brünn, now known as Brno, where Mendel conducted his plant experiments.

In 1841, Mendel returned to the university, and this time succeeded in finding part-time tutorial work, but he worked so hard his health failed again. In 1843, he discussed his future with one of his professors, Friedrich Franz, who suggested a monastery as a place that would provide the quiet kind of life Mendel required. He encouraged Mendel to apply to the monastery at Brünn and recommended him as "a young man of very solid character. In my own branch [physics] he is almost the best" (in Olby, 1966, p. 107). Mendel followed Franz' advice, was admitted as a novice on October 9, 1843, and took the name of Gregor.

Early on, it became clear that Mendel was not temperamentally suited to serve as a parish priest, since he could not witness suffering without falling ill himself. The understanding abbot of the monastery assigned him as a substitute teacher to a high school in a nearby town, and Mendel soon became known as an excellent teacher. He could not be given a permanent appointment because he lacked a teacher's certificate, and for him to obtain this document, he had to take courses at the University of Vienna.

It was at Vienna, where he came into contact with leading professors in botany, physics, and mathematics, that Mendel acquired his scientific education. His studies there helped him in his later experiments, especially in his mathematical approach, which was so different from that of other plant experimenters.

Upon completing his studies at Vienna, Mendel returned to the monastery and resumed his teaching career, as well as his work in the monastery garden. He had been experimenting for some time with the fertilization of flowers, attempting to develop new variations in colors. What impressed Mendel was the "striking regularity with which the same hybrid forms always reappeared when fertilization took place between the same species," which induced him "to follow up the development of the hybrids in their progeny."

◇ Mendel's Experiments

Mendel was well aware that no laws governing the formation and development of hybrids had yet been formulated, and he was also aware that hybridization experiments were very difficult. Nevertheless, he decided to proceed with his experiments and had definite ideas of how to go about it. He pointed out that not one experiment

> had been carried out to such an extent and in such a way as to make it possible to determine the number of different forms under which the offspring of hybrids

Figure 4-4   The monastery at Brünn (as it looks today), where Mendel spent much of his life.

appear, or to arrange these forms with certainty according to their separate generations, or definitely to ascertain their statistical relation (Mendel, 1965, pp. 1–2).

What Mendel decided to do apparently even before he began his experiments on hybrids was: (a) to determine the number of different forms of hybrids produced; (b) to arrange the forms according to generations—F_2, F_3, etc. (see terms in Box 4-1 for definitions); and (c) to attempt to evaluate the statistical relations (the proportions) of the various forms.

These three points, wrote the eminent geneticist of the early twentieth century, William Bateson, led to "the whole success of Mendel's work. . . . So far as I know this conception was absolutely new in his day" (Mendel, 1965, p. 2n) and is the basis of modern biological research.

Selection of Plants   Before discussing Mendel's actual experiments and his conclusions, one more point should be considered, for it illustrates Mendel's genius compared to other plant hybridizers. This point concerns the *kind* of plant to be used. "The value and utility of any experiment," Mendel noted in the paper he read at a meeting of the Natural History Society of Brünn in February, 1865, "are determined by the fitness of the material to the purpose for which it is used, and thus in the case before us it cannot be immaterial what plants are subjected to experiment and in what manner such experiments are conducted" (Mendel, 1965, p. 2). He went on to say that the selection of the plant "must be made with all possible care" and two qualifying conditions *must* be met: That the plant (1) possess constant differentiating characters; and (2) the hybrids of such plants be protected from foreign pollen.

Figure 4-5   Mendel's "plantation," where he conducted his genetic experiments. The garden is presently ornamental. Mendel's statue can be seen in the background.

◇ Box 4-1   Terms Used in Discussion of Genetics

Alleles   Alternative forms of the same gene. (In the ABO blood system, A, B, and O are alternative forms found at the same locus. In a population where alternative forms are available at a particular locus, they are called alleles. The gene for round seeds and the gene for wrinkled seeds are such alternative forms.)

Dominant   A trait determined by a dominant allele. A trait that is visible or measurable and which prevents the appearance of the recessive. The allele for round seeds is dominant and when present "prevents" the appearance of wrinkled seeds.

Recessive   A trait determined by the recessive allele. A trait is not visible or measurable when paired with the dominant allele. The heterozygote Rr possesses both the dominant and recessive allele, but the wrinkling is not expressed phenotypically. (R = upper case of first letter of dominant trait; used as symbol for dominant trait. r = lower case of dominant symbol, used as a symbol for recessive trait.)

Generation
P_1 The parental generation in which homozygous dominants and recessives are crossed. Parents pure or homozygous for round seeds and parents homozygous for wrinkled represent such a parental cross.

F_1 First filial generation. The offspring resulting from a parental cross of homozygotes for different alleles.

F_2 Second filial generation. The offspring resulting from a cross of F_1 individuals (or self-fertilization of F_1 individuals, where this is possible).

Genotype   The genetic makeup of a particular organism. The genes at a particular locus. The genotype for a person with A blood type may be AA or AO. The genotype of a person with O blood type is OO. The genotype for homozygous round seeds is RR, and for heterozygous round seeds it is Rr (R = round; r = wrinkled). The DNA sequence is the genotype, which is not directly ascertainable, at least at the present time.

Phenotype   The observable or measurable characteristics of an organism. Roundness in a seed is a phenotype, as is wrinkledness. These are observable. In blood types, A, B, and O are also phenotypes; they are not observable to the naked eye but they are measurable. The phenotype is an observable expression of the genotype.

Heterozygous   Having different alleles at a given locus on a pair of homologous chromosomes.

Heterozygote   A cell or individual that is heterozygous. (A hybrid is heterozygous for a particular trait.) A person who is AO is heterozygous for ABO; an F_1 round pea (Rr) is heterozygous for form.

Homozygous   Having the same allele at a given locus on a pair of homologous chromosomes.

Homozygote   A cell or individual that is homozygous. (A purebred is homozygous for a particular trait.) A pea that is RR or rr is a homozygote.

Hybrid   The progeny resulting from a cross of different parental stock.

By constant differentiating characters—a most important point—Mendel meant that the plant must possess two contrasting characters of the same trait. If color were the trait, then the plant should possess two contrasting colors; if stature, then tall and short. These conditions led Mendel to devote his attention to legumes, and experiments with several members of this group led him to the genus *Pisum*, the common garden pea.

Clearly, Mendel knew what he was doing from the very beginning. Unlike those who preceded him, he concentrated on the underlying genetic factors, what we today call genes. He proposed to follow the progress of the hybrids through a number of generations, counting the number of different types of

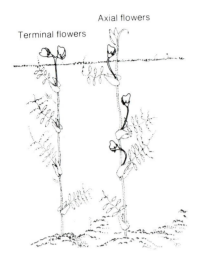

Round seed   Wrinkled seed

Figure 4-6 Contrasting characters.

Figure 4-7 Mendel cross-fertilizing his plants by hand.

hybrid progeny. He would carefully select the kind of plant that possessed the traits he considered necessary for the experiment, contrasting characters and fertility for a number of successive generations. Finally, he planned to use a large number of plants, so that the uniqueness of a small number of seeds would not bias the results.

From several nurserymen, Mendel obtained thirty-four varieties of peas, and, after checking them during a two-year trial, he selected twenty-two varieties for fertilization. Most of them belonged to the species *Pisum sativum*. As already noted, Mendel deliberately planned to use a plant that possessed at least one set of contrasting characters. With the pea he selected seven:

1. Form of the ripe seed: round/wrinkled
2. Difference in color of the seed: yellow/green
3. Difference in color of seed coat: white/gray
4. Form of the ripe pods: inflated/constricted
5. Color of unripe pods: green/yellow
6. Position of flowers: axial/terminal
7. Length of stem: tall/dwarf

THE PEA EXPERIMENTS—P GENERATION

Mendel launched his experiment in the spring of 1856. He divided the garden into sections, one for each of the seven characters of the pea. He placed contrasting characters next to each other so they would be easier to compare. Round seeds went next to wrinkled; yellow next to green; tall next to dwarf.

When the plants were ready to blossom, Mendel opened the flower buds of each plant and performed the surgery necessary to prevent the peas from fertilizing themselves in the normal manner. He then proceeded to do the cross-fertilizing himself (Fig. 4-7). Altogether, Mendel made 287 cross-fertilizations on 70 plants and then waited for the plants to mature in what the other monks called "Mendel's pea plantation."

F_1 Generation   The offspring of the P_1 cross (Fig. 4-8*a*) are designated as the F_1 generation, and when the F_1 generation matured, Mendel observed the seeds. They were all round (as in Fig. 4-8*a*). He then grew plants from these F_1 round seeds and, when the plants matured, allowed them to self-fertilize (Fig. 4-8*b*). Mendel then examined the offspring of the F_1 generation of round peas and found that in this generation (F_2) there were both round seeds *and* wrinkled seeds (Fig. 4-8*c*). When he carefully counted the numbers of each, they added up to 5,474 round seeds and 1,850 wrinkled, a ratio of 2.96 to 1. Among the other traits, the ratios were slightly over or under 3:1, and the average ratio of all the seeds of all the traits in the F_2 generation was 3:1 (Fig. 4-8). Mendel now saw clearly that when F_1 hybrids are bred, three offspring are produced that resemble one P_1 grandparent for every one offspring that resembles the other P_1 grandparent. The character that appeared three times, Mendel called *dominant*, and that which appeared once, *recessive*. (A list of definitions of terms used throughout this discussion may be found in Box 4-1).

F_2 Generation   The experiment continued through another (F_3) generation. The plants of the F_2 generation were allowed to self-fertilize, and once more Mendel carefully counted the results. He found that one-half of the F_2 plants produced round and wrinkled seeds at a ratio of 3:1; one-fourth produced only round seeds; and one-fourth produced only wrinkled seeds. Since the one-half that produced a 3:1 ratio of round to wrinkled seeds behaved in exactly the same way as the F_1 hybrids, Mendel reasoned that these must also be *hybrids*, or *heterozygotes* (Fig. 4-7).

"... it is now clear," said Mendel, "that the hybrids form seeds having one or the other of the two differentiating characters, and of these one-half develop again the hybrid form, while the other half yield plants which remain constant and receive the dominant or the recessive characters in equal numbers" (Mendel, 1965, p. 13).

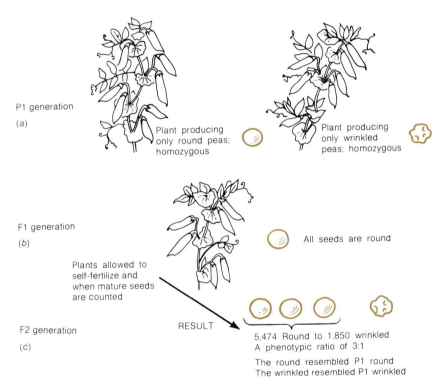

P1 generation
(a)

Plant producing only round peas; homozygous

Plant producing only wrinkled peas; homozygous

F1 generation
(b)

All seeds are round

Plants allowed to self-fertilize and when mature seeds are counted

F2 generation
(c)

RESULT

5,474 Round to 1,850 wrinkled
A phenotypic ratio of 3:1

The round resembled P1 round
The wrinkled resembled P1 wrinkled

Figure 4-8   Gregor Mendel's logic. Mendel concluded: (1) the ½ of F_2 plants that produced a 3:1 ratio of round to wrinkled were the same as the F_1 rounds that produced a 3:1 ratio—therefore ½ of the F_2 plants *must be hybrids* (heterozygous); (2) the ¼ of the F_2 plants that produced only round seeds must be homozygous for round; (3) the ¼ of the F_2 plants that produced only wrinkled must be homozygous for wrinkled; (4) hybrid forms yield a genotypic ratio of 1:2:1 (that is, 1:homozygous dominant to 2:heterozygous dominant to 1:homozygous recessive).

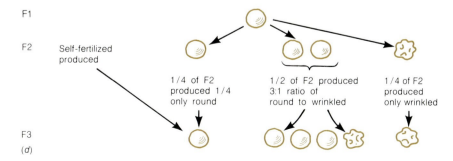

F1

F2   Self-fertilized produced

1/4 of F2 produced 1/4 only round

1/2 of F2 produced 3:1 ratio of round to wrinkled

1/4 of F2 produced only wrinkled

F3
(d)

Figure 4-9 Dominance.

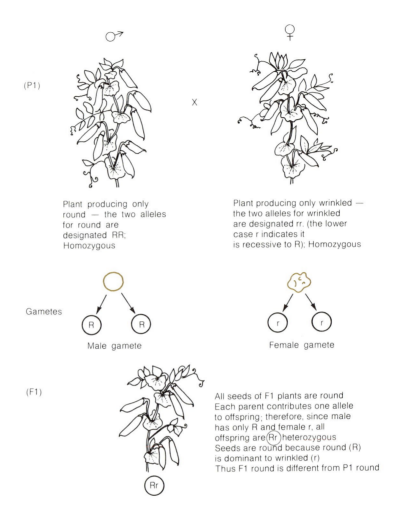

(P1)   ♂   ♀

X

Plant producing only
round — the two alleles
for round are
designated RR;
Homozygous

Plant producing only wrinkled —
the two alleles for wrinkled
are designated rr. (the lower
case r indicates it
is recessive to R); Homozygous

Gametes

R   R

r   r

Male gamete   Female gamete

(F1)

All seeds of F1 plants are round
Each parent contributes one allele
to offspring; therefore, since male
has only R and female r, all
offspring are Rr heterozygous
Seeds are round because round (R)
is dominant to wrinkled (r)
Thus F1 round is different from P1 round

Rr

EXPERIMENT RESULTS—THE RIDDLE SOLVED

Using current terminology, we would say that one-half of the F_2 generation
plants must be heterozygous, since they produced a 3:1 ratio just as the F_1
hybrids did. One-fourth of the F_2 plants produced only round seeds; therefore,
they must be *homozygous* dominant. The remaining one-fourth produced
only wrinkled seeds; therefore, they must be homozygous recessive. This led
to Mendel's conclusion that the genotypic ratio is 1:2:1 for the F_2 generation:

¼ homozygous dominant
½ heterozygous dominant =   1   : 2   : 1
¼ homozygous recessive   RR   : Rr   : rr

Mendel continued his experiments through several succeeding generations, and the results reinforced conclusions already reached. He had succeeded brilliantly where others had failed. By carefully selecting the proper
experimental plant, by using a large number of plants, and—perhaps, most
importantly—by carefully counting the numbers and kinds of offspring, Men-

del had accomplished two goals: (1) he clarified the confusion surrounding the reproduction of hybrids; and (2) he had discovered the laws of heredity. For a modest, unknown amateur this achievement was indeed remarkable.

We should point out that this method of experimental breeding was simple, but original and unique. Moreover, the experiments were *deliberately designed to test a theory*, a new idea in biology (Dunn, 1965, p. 193).

Mendel's Report   After eight years of constant work, Mendel was at long last prepared to report on his findings, and, at the February, 1865, meeting of the Natural History Society of Brünn, Mendel read his paper. Members of the society, familiar with the methodology of more traditional botanists, were confused by his ideas. The next month, when Mendel presented his algebraic equations, the lack of understanding was even greater. The idea that "heredity was the giant shuffling and reshuffling of separate and invisible hereditary factors" was so different from what had been taught that it was probably incomprehensible. When Mendel finished his report, no one rose to ask a question, and the minutes of the society record no discussion.

The society published the monograph Mendel had prepared and copies were sent, as was the custom, to cities throughout Europe, but it attracted no attention. Mendel was disappointed. He was aware of the significance of his work and decided to send his report to one of Europe's outstanding botanists, Karl von Naegeli of Munich. Naegeli obviously failed to understand the experiment and replied in a condescending letter that Mendel's work was "far from being finished." Thus, a second opportunity for science to learn the rules of heredity was lost, not to be rediscovered until 1900.

In 1868, at the age of 46, Mendel was elected abbot of the monastery and, because of heavy administrative duties, he was unable to continue his scientific work. He died January 6, 1884, a beloved figure in the town of Brünn but unknown to the world of science.

GENES, CHROMOSOMES, AND MENDEL

With this brief survey, let us now examine more systematically the rules of heredity Mendel discovered. First, it may be useful to summarize pertinent information regarding genes and chromosomes already presented in Chapter 3.

Sex cells carry two sets of chromosomes to make up a full complement (46 in humans), the diploid number. On a pair of homologous chromosomes there is a number of loci, and at each locus on the pair is genetic material (a segment of DNA—a gene) that affects a particular trait. Thus, in any individual there are two genes for each trait. There may be several loci, by the way, that affect the same trait (stature, say), but, for our purpose, it is sufficient to deal with only one locus at a time. These are called simple or Mendelian traits and follow Mendelian ratios. If at a locus there is a gene, let us say, for round seeds or a gene for wrinkled seeds, then these different forms of the gene are known as *alleles*. Alleles are similar, but slightly different, sequences of DNA that control the same trait. Normal hemoglobin and sickling hemoglobin discussed in the preceding chapter are examples of alleles for the same trait. With this review, we return to Mendel's rules.

PRINCIPLE OF SEGREGATION

Dominant and Recessive Cross   In his experiment with peas, Mendel obtained seeds that were homozygous. He tested them by planting to make sure that those intended to produce round seeds did so, and those for wrinkled seeds produced only wrinkled. The second step was to cross the plants producing only round seeds with plants producing only wrinkled seeds.* The offspring of this cross were all round even though the sex cells of the plant contained an allele for wrinkled (Fig. 4-10). They were all round, as we know, because round is dominant to wrinkled. Please note that, phenotypically, the seeds are round, but, genotypically, both alleles are present, Rr, or heterozygous. The F_1 round (Rr) are genotypically different from their P_1 round (RR) parent (Fig. 4-10).

How is the difference between the F_1 and P_1 round seeds to be explained? Both seeds are phenotypically round, but the genotypes are different. Recalling the meiotic process, we know that after cell division a gamete contains one set of chromosomes, the haploid number. Therefore, the gamete contains only one of the alleles for a particular trait. To take Mendel's example, the parent plants each contained two genes for either roundness or wrinkledness. Because of meiotic division, each parent contributes only one. Since both parents are homozygous—one for round and the other for wrinkled—one parent would have to contribute an R allele and the other an r allele (Fig. 4-10).

The offspring in the F_1 generation possess both alleles, the big R from one parent and the small r from the other. Thus, the offspring are hybrid, or heterozygous.

Heterozygous Cross—3:1 Phenotypic Ratio   In the next step of the experiment, Mendel allowed these F_1 heterozygotes to fertilize themselves (pea plants contain both male and female parts). Although fertilization occurs within one plant, the male and female sex cells may be diagrammed thus:

$$Rr \times Rr$$

The result of this self-fertilization, as we have seen, was the production of three round seeds for every wrinkled. What happened in the F_1 cross to produce a 3:1 ratio? Bearing in mind what we know of meiosis, homologous chromosomes, and alleles, it is only necessary to add one point, the element of chance.

We know that as a result of meiosis a parent can contribute, at any one time, only one of a pair of chromosomes and therefore only one of two alleles for a trait. In this case, each parent will contribute either R *or* r. There is an even chance that the male R will combine with the female R or with the female r. Similarly, the odds are even that the male r will combine with the female R or r. In other words, there are four, and only four, possible combinations. Each combination has an equal chance, a one out of four (or 25%) chance of occurring (Fig. 4-11).

*In our discussion, we shall use the round and wrinkled traits. Mendel, of course, experimented with all seven traits, and the results in every case were similar.

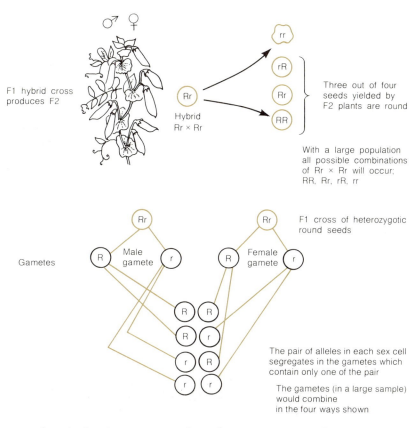

Figure 4-10 Segregation of gametes.

Since round, R, is dominant, a round seed must contain at least one gene for the characteristic "round," R. In the F_2 generation, Mendel counted three round seeds for every wrinkled, which means that three-fourths (or 75%) of the seeds contained at least one gene for round, R. A glance at Figure 4-10 indicates that this percentage is exactly correct. The fourth combination, rr, does not contain a capital R; therefore, that seed cannot be round. A seed with two alleles for wrinkled—rr—must be phenotypically wrinkled.

Statistically, that is precisely the situation with the round and wrinkled peas, and it was Mendel's insight that perceived this when none of his predecessors had done so. Perhaps it was Mendel's training in mathematics at the University that enabled him to approach his experiments from a statistical point of view.

Mendel could not have worked the statistics out had he used only a few plants. To flip a coin ten times and expect it to come up heads five times and tails five times is unreasonable. A thousand flips might average 500 heads

Figure 4-11 Gametic combinations. There are only four ways F_1 alleles can combine:

1 homozygous (RR) dominant, or round

2 heterozygous (Rr), also round

1 homozygous (rr) recessive, wrinkled

Phenotypic ratio
The ratio of phenotypes, especially from a hybrid cross. Mendel's famous F₁ hybrid cross of peas produced a 3:1 phenotypic ratio.

Principle of segregation
Genes occur in pairs. In the production of a gamete, the pair is separated so that each gamete contains only one of the pair.

Principle of independent assortment
The separation of one pair of genes does not influence the separation of other pairs of genes.

and 500 tails. Similarly, Mendel was aware, as we have seen, that a large number of plants are required to achieve a complete random assortment. When Mendel counted all the dominant and recessive characters of the seven traits, he found an average **phenotypic ratio** of 2.98 to 1, which he considered to be a 3:1 ratio.

Mendel's explanation for the 3:1 ratio solved the riddle of heredity. He suggested that the characters (genes) are paired and *segregated* when they are passed on from one generation to the next. That is, the gene on one chromosome does not normally affect the genes at the same locus on the paired chromosome. We might say each gene goes its own way. Therefore, the capital R in the male influences inheritance separately from the influence of the lower case r, and similarly with the female. (We have seen how this separation operates during meiosis.) This is Mendel's first law, called the **principle of segregation**, which states that genes, the units of heredity, exist within individuals in pairs. The pairs are segregated during the production of gametes, so that a gamete has only one of each kind.

Interestingly, Mendel was not the first to observe this 3:1 ratio. In 1820, an Englishman named John Goss carried out an experiment very similar to Mendel's, even to the extent of using peas. When the hybrids produced a mixture of dominants and recessives, he merely pointed out the facts but did not count the numbers of each. He failed to see the significance of the ratio of dominants to recessives. Perhaps even more curious is Darwin's experience with snapdragons. Darwin crossed normal and irregular snapdragons and in the F₁ generation all the offspring were normal. When he bred the F₁ normal snapdragons, the offspring were normal to irregular at roughly a 3:1 ratio. Darwin noted the F₁ uniformity and the mixture of the F₂ generation, but the significance of the 3:1 proportion escaped him also (Iltis, 1966, pp. 118–127).

Having solved the problem of the 3:1 ratio, Mendel's next task was to determine whether what he called "the law of development" also applied to a cross of two different traits (a dihybrid cross). For this experiment he used the traits of form, round/wrinkled—Rr—and color, yellow/green—Yy. He crossed round and wrinkled peas with yellow and green peas, and he found the results were the same as in the first experiment. The proportions in the F₂ generation for color and form of seeds were:

9 round and yellow—both traits dominant

3 round and green—round dominant, green recessive

3 wrinkled and yellow—wrinkled recessive, yellow dominant

1 wrinkled and green—both traits recessive

When the numbers of round and wrinkled seeds are totaled, a proportion of 12 round to 4 wrinkled, or a 3:1 phenotypic ratio, emerges. When the number of yellow (dominant) and green seeds are totaled, we find 12 yellow to 4 green, also a 3:1 phenotypic ratio.

Conclusion: Gene pairs on one set of homologous chromosomes do not influence the distribution of gene pairs on other chromosomes; they separate independently from one another during meiosis, and are randomly assorted in the gametes. This phenomenon is known as Mendel's second law, the **principle of independent assortment** (Figs. 4-12, 4-14).

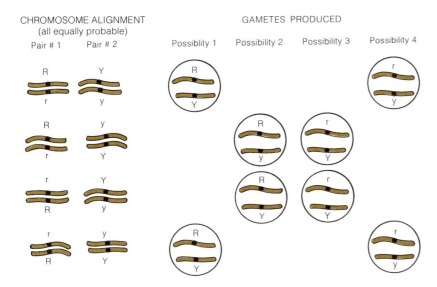

CHROMOSOME ALIGNMENT
(all equally probable)

Pair # 1   Pair # 2

GAMETES PRODUCED

Possiblity 1   Possibility 2   Possibility 3   Possibility 4

Figure 4-12   Mendel's Law of Independent Assortment.

PRINCIPLE OF INDEPENDENT ASSORTMENT

Random Assortment   Mendel was not aware of the precise cellular mechanism that caused this random assortment of one trait with respect to another. However, a brief glance at our earlier discussion of meiosis (p. 47) quickly solves the mystery. As you will recall, when homologous pairs of chromosomes align along the equator of a cell, the relative positions of one homologous pair are independent of all other pairs.

Simply stated, this is the process of *random assortment*. The independent assortment of traits observed by Mendel is the direct result of the random assortment of chromosomes that respectively carry those traits.

Figure 4-12 shows two pairs of chromosomes in an F_1 (heterozygous) pea plant, each containing one of the two traits discussed above (color of seed, shape of seed). As can be seen, the way the chromosomes align during meiosis directly affects the combination of alleles in the resulting gametes, which, in turn, combine to produce individuals exhibiting the phenotypic ratios of observed traits (round and yellow, round and green, etc.).

Possible Alignments   There are four equally possible ways the chromosomes can align, and four different kinds of gametes that can be produced in this manner in each parent. This recombination of genes—by random assortment of chromosomes—leads to all the combinations of traits we observe in different individuals in the next generation.

If Mendel had used just *any* two traits for recombination, the phenotypic ratios would quite possibly not have conformed to those expected by independent assortment (9:3:3:1). The ratio came out as he predicted, because the traits Mendel chose to observe were carried on different chromosomes. Had the two traits *both* been carried on the *same* chromosome, the alleles for the two traits would not have assorted independently but would have been transmitted together.

Figure 4-13   Crossing-over in chromosomes. Genes are more likely to cross-over and recombine when they are far apart (right) than when they are close together (left).

An exception may be produced by the process of crossing-over (see p. 51). Even if carried on the same chromosome, genes can and usually do cross-over independently of each other *if* they are not located too closely together. In this case, all four possible recombinations of alleles (CD, Cd, cD, cd) may be produced, and the expected ratios of independent assortment (9:3:3:1) may be approached (Fig. 4-14).

Figure 4-14 Dihybrid cross; Principle of Independent Assortment. Shape (round and wrinkled) has no effect on color (yellow and green). The phenotypic ratios for both shape and color are 3:1, as in the cross of a single trait. Similarly, the genotypic ratio—1:2:1—is the same for both traits.

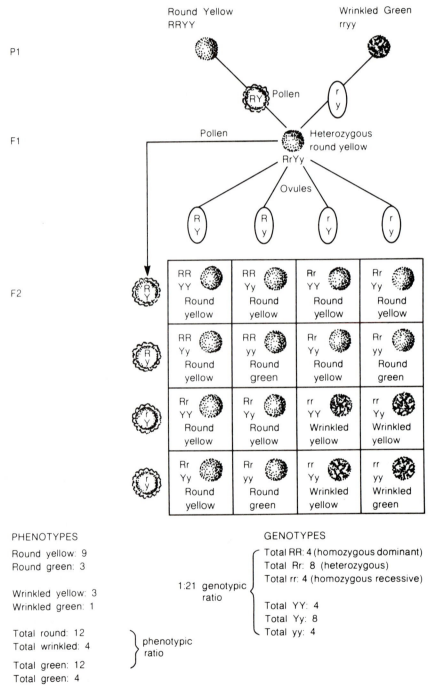

PHENOTYPES

Round yellow: 9
Round green: 3

Wrinkled yellow: 3
Wrinkled green: 1

Total round: 12
Total wrinkled: 4

Total green: 12
Total green: 4

} phenotypic ratio

GENOTYPES

Total RR: 4 (homozygous dominant)
Total Rr: 8 (heterozygous)
Total rr: 4 (homozygous recessive)

Total YY: 4
Total Yy: 8
Total yy: 4

1:21 genotypic ratio

Genotypic Ratio   Going one step further, Mendel also demonstrated that the genotypic ratio for form and color remained the same as it did in his first experiment with the contrasting characters of only one trait. The ratio of homozygous dominant, RR, to heterozygous, Rr, to homozygous recessive, rr, is 1:2:1. (The entire process from the parental generation to the F_2 generation is shown schematically in Fig. 4-14.) The proportions for color, YY, Yy, yy, are of course the same, 1:2:1.

In summary, Mendel demonstrated, and cellular biology has confirmed, that there are regularities or laws of heredity. The laws may be explained in the following manner:

1. Each individual possesses two genes for a particular trait.
2. During meiosis, the two genes from each parent segregate into different gametes (principle of segregation). This means that a parent contributes only one of the two genes to an offspring.
3. If each parent contributes a different allele for a particular trait (such as R or r), a hybrid (heterozygote) results.
4. When the two heterozygotes are crossed, or self-fertilized, there is an even chance that each of the two genes from one parent will combine with each of the two genes from the other parent. A male Rr and a female Rr can combine in four ways: RR, Rr, rR, rr. (In a large population, the result of such a hybrid cross would produce 25% RR, 25% Rr, 25% rR, and 25% rr. If we combine the two Rr, then the genotypic ratio would be 25% RR, 50% Rr, 25% rr, or 1:2:1.)
5. When two traits are crossed, each pair assorts independently of the other (principle of independent assortment).

The concept of two genes for each trait—that the two genes segregate independently of one another, that a parent contributes one of the two, that genes from parents enter into all possible combinations with each other, that genes during meiosis segregate into separate gametes—all of these made sense of what appeared to be unintelligible confusion in the process of heredity.

It would be pleasing to report that Mendel's experiments and conclusions were swiftly accepted by an eager community of scientists that immediately applied his conclusions to the development of genetic research. Unfortunately, the case was otherwise. Mendel's methods were ahead of his time. It was not until 1900, thirty-five years after he read his paper before the Natural History Society of Brünn, that three geneticists—Hugo de Vries in Holland, Erich von Tschermak in Austria, and Carl Correns in Germany—working independently of one another, discovered for themselves the laws Mendel had already formulated. Genetics had lost thirty-five years.

◇ Modern Theory of Evolution

Following the rediscovery of Mendel's work in 1900, attention quickly turned to the study of genetics in animals, particularly humans. In 1902, Archibald Garrod identified the pattern of incidence in a metabolic disorder called *alkaptonuria* as a clear example of Mendelian inheritance in humans. Since

Variation (genetic)
Inherited differences between individuals.
The basis of all evolutionary change.

Natural selection
The evolutionary factor (first articulated by
Charles Darwin) that causes changes in
gene frequencies in populations due to differential net reproductive success of
individuals.

that time the catalog of human traits known to operate in simple Mendelian
fashion has grown steadily. Recent advances in biochemical techniques have
greatly aided this research; the list now includes more than 3,300 such traits
(McKusick, 1983). In addition, great advances have been made in chromosome
mapping, and more than 500 genes have been pinpointed to specific human
chromosomes (McKusick, 1983).

By the beginning of the twentieth century, the essential foundations for
evolutionary theory had already been developed. Darwin and Wallace had
articulated the key principle of natural selection forty years earlier, and the
rediscovery of Mendelian genetics contributed the other major component—
a mechanism for inheritance. We might expect that these two basic contributions would have been joined rather quickly into a consistent theory of
evolution. However, such was not the case. For the first thirty years of this
century, geneticists (working with experimental animals, such as fruit flies)
emphasized sharp contrasts within particular characteristics of organisms.
As such, evolution was seen as a process of fairly large radical "jumps," and
this "mutationist" view came to be seen as an alternative to the "selectionist"
tradition.

A *synthesis* of these two views was not achieved until the mid-1930s, and
we owe much of our current view of the evolutionary process to this intellectual development. (See Box 4-2.)

THE MODERN SYNTHESIS

Biologists working on mathematical models of evolutionary change in the late
1920s and early 1930s came to realize that genetic and selective processes
were not opposing themes, but that a comprehensive explanation of organic
evolution required *both*. Small new changes in the genetic material—transmitted from parent to offspring by strict Mendelian principles—are, in fact,
the fuel for natural selection. The two major foundations of the biological
sciences had thus been brought together in what Julian Huxley termed the
"modern synthesis."

From such a "modern" (that is, the middle of the twentieth century on-
wards) perspective we define evolution as a two-stage process:

1. Production and redistribution of **variation** (inherited differences among
   individuals).
2. **Natural selection** acts on this variation (inherited differences, or variation,
   among individuals differentially affect their ability to reproduce successfully).

DEFINITION OF EVOLUTION

Darwin saw evolution as the gradual unfolding of new varieties of life from
previous forms over long periods of time. This depiction is what most of us
think of as "evolution," and it is indeed the end result of the evolutionary
process. But these long-term effects can only come about by the accumulation
of many small evolutionary changes occurring every generation. In order to
understand how the process of evolution works, we must necessarily study
these short-term events. Darwin attempted this kind of study in his breeding
experiments, but because the science of genetics was still in its infancy, he

◇ Box 4-2   Development of Modern Evolutionary Theory

Theodosius Dobzhansky.

Our modern understanding of the evolutionary process came about through contributions of biologists in the United States, Great Britain, and the Soviet Union.

While "mutationists" were arguing with "selectionists" about the single primary mechanism in evolution, several population geneticists began to realize that both small genetic changes and natural selection were necessary ingredients in the evolutionary formula.

These population geneticists were largely concerned with mathematical reconstructions of evolu-

tion—in particular, measuring those small accumulations of genetic changes in populations over just a few generations. Central figures in these early theoretical developments included Ronald Fisher and J.B.S. Haldane in Great Britain, Sewall Wright in the United States, and Sergei Chetverikov in the Soviet Union.

While the work of these scientists often produced brilliant insights (see particularly Fisher's *The Genetical Theory of Natural Selection*, 1930) their conclusions were largely unknown to most evolutionary biologists, especially in North America. It remained, therefore, for an individual to transcend these two worlds: the mathematical jargon of the population geneticists and the general constructs of theoretical evolutionary biologists. The scientist who performed this task (and to whom we owe the most credit as the first true synthesizer) was **Theodosius Dobzhansky**. In his *Genetics and the Origin of Species* (1937), Dobzhansky skillfully integrated the mathematics of population genetics with overall evolutionary theory. His insights then became the basis for a period of tremendous activity in evolutionary thinking that directly led to major contributions by George Gaylord Simpson (who brought paleontology into the synthesis), Ernst Mayr,[*] and others. In fact the "Modern Synthesis" produced by these scientists stood basically unchallenged for an entire generation as *the* explanation of the evolutionary process. In recent years, however, some aspects of this theory have been brought under serious question. (See the section "Recent Challenges to the Modern Synthesis," this chapter.)

*For an interesting discussion of the intellectual developments concerning the formulation of modern evolutionary theory see: Ernst Mayr and William B. Provine (eds.), *The Evolutionary Synthesis*, Cambridge, Mass.: Harvard University Press, 1980.

Population
Within a species, a community of individuals where mates are usually found.

Allele
A variant form of a gene.

Microevolution
Small, short-term changes occurring over just a few generations.

Macroevolution
Large changes produced only after many generations.

Mutation
An alteration in the genetic material (a change in the base sequence of DNA).

was not able to comprehend fully the mechanics of evolutionary change. Today, we study in various organisms (including humans) evolutionary changes occurring between generations, and are able to demonstrate how evolution works. From such a modern genetics perspective, we define evolution as *a change in gene frenquency from one generation to the next*.

Gene frequencies are numerical indicators of the genetic makeup of an interbreeding group of individuals known as a **population**. Let us illustrate the way gene frequencies change (that is, how evolution occurs) through a simplified example. First of all, we must look at a physical trait that is inherited, in this case human blood type. The best known of the human blood-type traits is ABO. There are, however, many similar blood-type systems controlled by different genes, which determine genetically transmitted properties of the red blood cells.

An inherited trait, such as human blood type, may be of slightly different form in different individuals. We call the variant genes that underlie these different forms of an inherited trait, **alleles**. The best-known blood-type alleles are A, B, and O. These different expressions of inherited traits constitute genetic variation within a population.

Let us assume that your present class of 100 members represents a population, an interbreeding group of individuals, and that we have ascertained the blood type of each member for the MN trait, a blood-group system similar to ABO (but with only two alternatives or alleles, M and N). To be a population, individuals in your class must choose mates more often from *within* the group than from outside it. Of course, the individuals in your class will not meet this requirement, but for this example's sake we will make the assumption that they do. The proportions of each of the M and N alleles are the gene frequencies for this trait. For example, suppose we find that the proportion of gene combinations in your class (population) is as follows:*

Blood Type	Number of Individuals		Percent
M	35	=	35
MN	50	=	50
N	15	=	15
	100		100%

Since the frequencies for combinations of these genes represent only proportions of a total, it is obvious that gene frequencies can refer only to whole groups of individuals, that is, populations. Individuals do not have a gene frequency, they have either M or N. Nor can individuals change gene frequency. From conception onward, the genetic composition of an individual is fixed. If you start out with blood type M, you will remain type M. Therefore, an individual cannot evolve: Only a group of individuals—a population—can evolve over time.

What happens when a population evolves? Evolution is not an unusual or a mysterious process. In fact, it is incredibly commonplace, and may occur

*This simplified example shows frequencies for the various gene combinations, what are called genotypes.

between every generation for every group of organisms in the world, including humans. Assume we measure the gene combination frequencies for the MN blood trait twenty-five years later in the children of our classroom population and find the following:

Blood Type	Number of Individuals		Percent
M	20	=	20
MN	50	=	50
N	30	=	30
	100		100%

We can see that the relative proportions have changed: M has decreased, N has increased, while MN has remained the same in frequency. Such a simple, apparently minor, change is what we call evolution. Over the short run of just a few generations, such changes in inherited traits may be only very small, but if further continued and elaborated, the results can and do produce spectacular kinds of adaptation and whole new varieties of life.

Whether we are talking about such short-term effects as our classroom population from one generation to the next, which is sometimes called **microevolution**, or the long-term effects through fossil history, sometimes called **macroevolution**, the basic evolutionary mechanisms are similar. As we will discuss below, however, they are not necessarily identical.

The question may be asked: How do gene frequencies change? Or, to put it another way, what causes evolution? The modern theory of evolution isolates general factors that can produce alterations in gene frequencies. As we have noted, evolution is a two-stage process. Genetic variation must be first produced and distributed before it can be acted upon by natural selection.

FACTORS THAT PRODUCE AND REDISTRIBUTE VARIATION

Mutation   An actual alteration in genetic material is called **mutation**. A genetic trait may take one of several alternative forms, which we have defined as alleles (M or N, for example). If one allele changes to another—that is, if the gene itself is altered—a mutation has occurred. As we have seen, a mutation is a molecular alteration—a change in the base sequence of DNA. For such changes to have evolutionary significance, they must occur in the sex cells, which are passed between generations. Evolution is a change in gene frequencies *between* generations. If mutations do not occur in sex cells (either the egg or sperm), they will not be passed to the next generation, and no evolutionary change can result. If, however, a genetic change does occur in the sperm or egg of one of the 100 individuals in our classroom (M mutates to N, for instance) the offspring's blood type also will be altered, causing a change in gene frequencies of that generation. Evolution would have occurred by mutation.

Actually, it would be rare to see evolution occurring by mutation *alone*. Mutation rates for any given trait are quite low, and, thus, their effects would rarely be seen in such a small population as our class. In larger populations mutations might be observed (one individual in 10,000, say), but would, by

Migration
Movement of genes between populations.

Genetic drift
Evolutionary changes produced by random factors.

themselves, have very little impact on shifting gene frequencies. However, when mutation is coupled with natural selection, evolutionary changes are quite possible.

Mutation is the basic creative force in evolution, and in fact is the only way to produce "new" variation. Its key role in the production of variation represents the first stage of the evolutionary process. Darwin was not aware of the nature of mutation. Only in the twentieth century, with the spectacular development of molecular biology, have the secrets of genetic structure been revealed.

Migration   The movement of genes from one population to another is called **migration**. If all individuals in our classroom population do not choose their mates from within the group, significant changes in gene frequencies could occur. For example, if four of the people who were type M married and settled outside the population, and four new individuals who were type N moved in and interbred with classroom individuals, the gene frequencies would be altered. If a change in gene frequency does take place, evolution will have occurred, this time by migration.

In humans, social rules, more than any other factor, determine mating patterns, and cultural anthropologists must work closely with physical anthropologists in order to isolate and measure this aspect of evolutionary change.

Genetic Drift   The random factor in evolution is called **genetic drift**, and is due primarily to sampling error. Since evolution occurs in populations, it is directly tied not only to the nature of the initial gene freqencies of the population, but to the size of the group as well. If, in our parent population of 100 individuals, two type M individuals had been killed in an auto accident before completing reproduction, their genes would have been removed from the population. The frequency of the M gene would have been reduced in the next generation, and evolution would have occurred. In this case, with only 100 individuals in the population, the change due to the accident would have altered the M frequency from 60% to 59%, a noticeable change. If, however, our initial population had been very large (10,000 people), then the effect of removing a few individuals would be very small indeed. In fact, in a population of large size, random effects, such as traffic accidents, would be balanced out by the equal probabilities of such events affecting N and MN individuals as well. As you can see, evolutionary change due to genetic drift is directly related to population size.

When considering genetic drift, we must remember that the genetic makeup of individuals is in no way related to the chance happenings that affect their lives. When applied to our example, this fact means that the genetic makeup of individuals has absolutely nothing to do with their being involved in automobile accidents. This is what is meant by a random event and why this factor is usually called *random genetic drift*. If, for example, a person had died in an auto accident caused by hereditary poor eyesight, such an event would not be genetic drift. If the individual, because of some such hereditary trait, dies early and produces fewer offspring than other individuals, this is not random genetic drift, it is natural selection.

Recombination   Since in any sexually reproducing species both parents contribute genes to offspring, the genetic information is inevitably reshuffled every generation. Such recombination does not in itself change gene frequencies (i.e., cause evolution). However, it does produce the whole array of genetic combinations, which natural selection can then act upon. In fact, we have shown how the reshuffling of chromosomes during meiosis can produce literally trillions of gene combinations, making every human being genetically unique.

NATURAL SELECTION ACTS ON VARIATION

The evolutionary factors just discussed—mutation, migration, genetic drift, and recombination—act to produce variation and to distribute genes within and between populations. But there is no long-term *direction* to any of these factors. What then does enable populations to adapt to changing environments? The answer is, of course, natural selection—the process so well elucidated by Darwin more than 125 years ago. Given that there is genetic variation among individuals within a population, some of these variations *may* influence reproductive success (numbers of offspring successfully raised). If, as a result of genetic variation, some individuals contribute more offspring to succeeding generations, this is natural selection. In fact, we have defined natural selection as *differential net reproductive success* see p. 38).

How then do populations adapt? A result of natural selection is a change in gene frequency relative to specific environmental factors. If the environment changes, then the selection pressures change as well. Such a functional shift in gene frequencies is what we mean by *adaptation*. If there are long-term environmental changes in a consistent direction, then gene frequencies should also shift gradually each generation. If sustained for many generations, the results may be quite dramatic.

EVOLUTION AT THE SPECIES LEVEL

A species is defined as a group of interbreeding organisms that are *reproductively isolated* and, therefore, cannot successfully interbreed with other groups. The capacity to reproduce is the critical factor in defining species. Theoretically, one can test whether two kinds of organisms are members of different species by observing their reproductive behavior under natural conditions (who mates with whom), and by observing the results (are the offspring fertile?).

Actually, a species is composed of subunits that are the breeding communities we have called populations. All members of a species can potentially interbreed, and some degree of interbreeding (migration) is theoretically possible between all populations.

The net result of all the forces of evolution (mutation, migration, genetic drift, recombination, and natural selection) acting on all populations determines the fate of the species as a whole. If sustained over a long period of time, gradual changes in gene frequencies between member populations can eventually lead to sufficient genetic differences, so that fertile reproduction is no longer possible. We then may recognize a new form of life having arisen

Speciation
The evolutionary process that produces new species from previous ones.

from one species "splitting" and producing new species, a process called **speciation**. This level of evolutionary change was the one described by Darwin and Wallace. If, on the other hand, total reproductive success is so low that all, or even most, populations become extinct, the whole species will be doomed and will disappear from the earth forever. The gross interference of natural habitats by modern industrial society has pushed numerous "endangered species" to this crucial juncture.

◇ Recent Challenges to the Modern Synthesis

In the last decade, serious reexamination has stimulated ongoing debate concerning some aspects of modern evolutionary theory.

NEUTRAL MUTATIONS

One of the premises postulated by traditional evolutionists is that natural selection is the major factor explaining most of the variation found in contemporary organisms. There is general agreement that significant aspects of variation are channeled by selection, thus leading to adaptation. But is all (or even most) of the "genetic baggage" that a species carries understandable strictly in terms of natural selection? Some scientists believe it is not. Pointing to the vast amount of variation seen in all organisms (28% of all human genes are estimated to exhibit significant population variation), these researchers argue that *much* of variation seen in natural populations is due to neutral mutations and chance factors (i.e., genetic drift).

A major aspect of this argument is that many mutations are neutral; in other words, they have no impact on reproductive success in any conceivable environment. We know, of course, that there is considerable redundancy in the DNA code, so that many point mutations will not alter the amino acid sequence whatsoever. In such a case, the phenotype is not affected at all, and selection cannot act on what it cannot see. Or as King and Jukes have put it, "Natural selection is the editor, rather than the composer of the genetic message" (King and Jukes, 1969, p. 788). These researchers, however, go far beyond postulating strictly synonymous mutations as neutral—they claim a large majority of other genetic changes are completely neutral to selective action, and are established in populations by random genetic drift.

This controversy has not yet been resolved. There is a vast store of genetic variation in all interbreeding populations. Certainly, both selection and drift have contributed, but what has been the primary architect? The consensus among most evolutionary biologists still is that natural selection is the most significant factor in explaining evolutionary change. A recent reveiw of genetic variation among humans concludes that "there is little doubt that many amino acid substitutions appear to be neutral or quasi-neutral, but neutral models do not seem to fit the distribution of most loci in the human species" (Livingstone, 1980, p. 39).

MODES OF EVOLUTIONARY CHANGE

The modern synthesis primarily explains those gene frequency changes seen over just a few generations—what is called *microevolution*. Until recently, the general consensus among evolutionary biologists was that these microevolutionary mechanisms could be translated directly into larger-scale evolutionary changes—what is called *macroevolution*, or transspecific evolution. These major evolutionary events involve the appearance of new species (i.e., speciation) as well as higher taxonomic categories (for example, genera, families, orders, etc.). A smooth gradation of changes was postulated to run directly from microevolution into macroevolution. A representative view was expressed by a leading synthesist, Ernst Mayr:

> The proponents of the synthetic theory maintain that all evolution is due to the accumulation of small genetic changes, guided by natural selection, and that transspecific evolution is nothing but an extrapolation and magnification of the events that take place within populations and species (Mayr, 1970, p. 351).

In the last decade, however, this view has been seriously challenged. Many theorists now believe that macroevolution cannot be explained *solely* in terms of accumulated microevolutionary changes. Many current researchers are now convinced that macroevolution is only partly understandable through microevolutionary models, as recently stated by two proponents of this revised view:

> We recognize that the within-population concept of adaptation via natural selection is a viable hypothesis accounting for the deterministic part of much genetic, behavioral, and morphological change in evolution. However, we strongly disagree that a smooth extrapolation of within-population (microevolutionary) processes is a logical or effective integration of such within-population mechanisms with among-species phenomena (macroevolution) (Eldredge and Cracraft, 1980).

Gradualism vs. Punctuationalism   The traditional view of evolution has emphasized that change accumulates gradually in evolving lineages—the idea of "phyletic gradualism." Accordingly, the complete fossil record of an evolving group (if it could be recovered) would display a series of forms with finely graded transitional differences between each ancestor and its descendant. The fact that such transitional forms are only rarely found is attributed to the incompleteness of the fossil record, or, as Darwin called it, "a history of the world, imperfectly kept, and written in changing dialect."

For more than a century, this perspective dominated evolutionary biology. Paleontologists searched diligently to find evidence of these gradual changes. So strong was this notion of gradualism (Darwin called it "descent with modification") that when little evidence was found to support it, researchers assumed there must be something wrong with their data—either their geological beds were inadequately dated or the paleontological record was yet too incomplete to allow a firm conclusion. Rarely did anyone suspect that the premise of gradualism itself might be flawed.

In the last decade, some evolutionary biologists have called this notion into serious question. The evolutionary mechanisms operating on species over the long run are often not continuously gradual. In a great many cases,

Punctuated equilibrium
The view that evolutionary rates are not
constant, but proceed slowly (equilibria)
until "punctuated" by rather sudden
spurts.

species persist for thousands of generations basically unchanged. Then, rather suddenly—at least in evolutionary terms—a "spurt" of speciation occurs. This nongradual process of long stasis and quick spurts has been termed **punctuated equilibrium** (Gould and Eldredge, 1977).

From a comprehensive survey of well-documented and long-ranging fossil series (including especially marine invertebrates), paleontologists Stephen Gould and Niles Eldredge conclude that:

> Most species during their evolutionary history, either do not change in any appreciable way, or else they fluctuate mildly in morphology, with no apparent change in any direction. Phyletic gradualism is very rare and too slow, in any case, to produce the major events of evolution. Evolutionary trends are not the product of slow, directional transformation within lineages; they represent the differential success of certain species ... speciation may be random with respect to the direction of a trend (Gould and Eldredge, 1977, p. 115).

What the punctuationalists are disputing concerns the "tempo" and "mode" of evolutionary change commonly understood since Darwin's time. Rather than a slow steady tempo, this new view postulates long periods of no change interspersed only occasionally by sudden bursts. From this observation, punctuationalists concluded that the mode of evolution, too, must be different from that suggested by classical Darwinists. Rather than gradual accumulation of small changes within a single lineage, advocates of punctuated equilibrium believe an additional evolutionary mechanism is required to push the process along. Accordingly, *speciation* is seen to be the major influence in bringing about rapid evolutionary change. Given new environmental opportunities, speciation events could occur in a sudden flurry—a whole array of new, fairly isolated and small incipient species would then possess a great deal of evolutionary potential. Of these, probably only a small minority would survive–through a "higher" evolutionary process sometimes called *species selection*.

How well does the paleontological record agree with this new theory? Indeed, a tremendous amount of fossil data shows long periods of stasis punctuated by occasional quite rapid changes (the transformation taking perhaps on the order of 10,000 to 50,000 years). Intermediate forms are rare, not because the record is so poor, but because the speciation events and longevity of these transitional species were so short we should not expect to find them very often.

The best supporting evidence for punctuated equilibrium has come from the fossilized remains of a variety of invertebrates, the paleontological specialty of both Gould and Eldredge. How well, then, does the human fossil record fit a punctuationalist model? Gould and Eldredge (1977, p. 115) believe "the record of human evolution seems to provide a particularly good example." When it comes to the evolution of our family, other researchers, however, are still not as convinced. Many believe punctuationalism is not all that apparent in the human evolutionary record and, alternatively, that gradualism fits the facts better (Cronin et al., 1981). Others (e.g., Tobias, 1983) believe human evolution displays periods of both punctuated *and* gradualistic changes.

It would be unreasonable to expect a single mode of evolutionary change to characterize all lineages at all times. Clearly, the rigid Darwinian belief that evolutionary change must *always* be gradual in nature is improbable. Abundant evidence shows that, in many evolutionary lines, this has not been the case. Punctuated equilibrium with change brought about by rapid speciation is another mode that now must be considered. Regarding human evolution, it is still not clear which of the two models (gradualism or punctuationalism)—or a combination of the two—provides the best approximation. As we will be discussing in great detail later in this text (Chapters 10–15), speciation was probably never very common within our particular evolutionary line since the time we diverged from other primates. As such, our lineage may not be typical, and is thus not a good example on which to base general theories of evolutionary change.

Microevolution and Macroevolution   As we have seen, gene frequencies over the span of a few generations seem to change in gradual fashion. Thus, microevolution, as conceived within the modern synthesis, conforms to the gradualistic model.

We have also seen that long-term changes (i.e., macroevolution) are not always gradual in nature; in fact, in many evolutionary lineages, the rate of change is manifestly sporadic. Are, then, microevolution and macroevolution really quite different phenomena?

While the mechanisms of microevolution and macroevolution may be partially "decoupled," that is not to say that they are unrelated. In fact, speciation can be understood as the result of accumulated genetic changes, particularly when facilitated by geographic isolation. This does not imply that the process is always gradual. Indeed, since processes affecting isolating mechanisms (for instance, mountain building, formation of island chains, etc.) are themselves irregular, we should expect speciation rates to vary as well. Species, once they have formed, are real entities. Categories of higher rank (genera, families, and so on) are merely human abstractions; they do not exist in nature. Populations evolve; species may eventually diverge and, once distinct, can only become more genetically separate. All the rest of evolutionary change is basically an extension of this process.

◇ Evolution in Modern Populations

The process of evolution acts on all species, including *Homo sapiens.* In modern populations, recombination and mutation continue to produce variation, the fuel for natural selection. Can we then see these ongoing evolutionary processes at work in human populations?

Today we find only one species of hominid represented by 4½ billion individuals widely scattered over most of the earth. However, the distribution is by no means even, since both geographical and social factors influence where people live, how many individuals collect to form a group, and who mates with whom. Moreover, there are obvious visible physical differences as well as numerous biochemically detectable variations among groups of modern human beings. How do we explain these differences?

The branch of anthropology dealing with modern human variation is centrally concerned with answering such questions in *evolutionary* terms. As discussed throughout this text, anthropology is the study of human evolution, not just in the past but in the present as well.

Human populations continue to be influenced by the forces of evolution, continue to adapt to their biocultural environments, and thus continue to evolve. Investigating the dynamic processes that mold our species is the domain of microevolutionary studies. From such work we not only develop a fuller understanding of why *Homo sapiens* varies from area to area (as well as from individual to individual), but we also can more fully comprehend how *Homo sapiens* came to be in the first place.

The following chapters tell the tale of a long succession of hominid fossils, but these are simply luckily preserved bits and pieces of earlier populations that were subject to the same dynamic evolutionary processes influencing humankind today. Over the space of several tens of thousands or millions of years small microevolutionary changes are modified into macroevolutionary ones.

THE POPULATION

The unit of evolutionary change is the *population*, which we have defined as a group of interbreeding individuals. More precisely, the population is the group within which one is most likely to find a mate. As such, a population is a genetic unit marked by a degree of genetic relatedness and sharing in a common **gene pool**. In theory, this concept is not particularly difficult. Picture a kind of giant blender into which every generation's genes are mixed (by recombination). What comes out in the next generation is a direct product of the genes going into the pool, which in turn is a direct result of who is mating with whom.

In practice, however, isolating and describing actual human populations is a very sticky business. The largest population of *Homo sapiens* that can be described is the entire species, all of whose members are at least potentially capable of interbreeding (but are incapable of interbreeding, fertilely, with members of other species). Our species is thus a *genetically closed system* and can be described quite unambiguously (human/nonhuman hybrids are not known). The problem arises not in describing who potentially can interbreed, but in isolating exactly the patterns of those individuals who are doing so.

Factors that determine mate choice are geographical, ecological, and social. If individuals are isolated into groups in an Alpine village or on an island in the middle of the Pacific, there is not much possibility of finding a mate outside the immediate vicinity. Such **breeding isolates** are fairly easily defined and are a favorite target of microevolutionary studies. Geography plays a dominant role within these isolates through influencing the range of available mates. But even within these limits cultural prescriptions can still play a powerful part in deciding who is most proper among those potentially available.

Since social factors usually play such a crucial role in human mating patterns, a cultural anthropologist is an invaluable aid in helping to decipher what is going on in the complex world of real human beings. Additional complexity (sometimes found in other cultures) is introduced when biological and social paternity are defined differently. Moreover, the physical anthropologist must always be aware of the possibility of illegitimacy; whereas marriage patterns are useful indicators, what we are ultimately after is the pattern of actual matings.

Smaller human population segments within the species are defined as groups with relative degrees of **endogamy** (marrying/mating within the group). They are not, however, totally closed systems. Migration often occurs between groups, and individuals may choose mates from distant localities. The advent of modern means of rapid transportation has greatly accelerated **exogamy** (marrying/mating outside the group), a process which always has characterized human society to some degree.

It is obvious that most humans today are not clearly members of specific breeding populations as they would be in breeding isolates. Inhabitants of large cities may seem to be members of a single population, but actually within the city borders social, ethnic, and religious boundaries crosscut in a complex fashion to form smaller population groupings. In addition to being members of these highly open local population segments we are simultaneously members of overlapping gradations of larger populations, the immediate geographical region (a metropolitan area or perhaps a whole state), a region of the country, the whole nation, the Western world, and ultimately again, the whole species.

POPULATION GENETICS

Once the microevolutionist has isolated a specific human population, the next step is to ascertain what evolutionary forces, if any, are operating on this group. In order to determine whether evolution is taking place, we measure gene frequencies for specific traits and compare the observed frequencies with a set predicted by a mathematical model: the **Hardy-Weinberg equilibrium** equation. This model provides us with a baseline set of evolutionary expectations under *known* conditions.

More precisely, Hardy-Weinberg equilibrium postulates a set of conditions where *no* evolution occurs. In other words, none of the forces of evolution is acting and all genes have an equal chance of recombining each generation (that is, random mating of individuals):

1. The *population* is assumed to be *infinitely large* (therefore no sampling error—*no random genetic drift*)
2. *No mutation* (no new genes are added by molecular alterations within gametes)
3. *No migration* (no immigration or emigration whereby new genes are added or some lost)
4. *No selection* (genes have no differential advantage relative to reproductive success)
5. *Random mating* (panmixia—no bias in who mates with whom; any female is assumed to have an equal chance of mating with any male)

If all these conditions are satisfied, gene frequencies will not change (that is, no evolution will take place) and a permanent equilibrium will be maintained as long as these conditions prevail. An evolutionary "barometer" is thus provided which may be used as a standard against which actual cir-

Gene pool
The total complement of genes in a population.

Breeding isolate
A population geographically and/or socially separate and, therefore, relatively easy to define.

Endogamy
Mating within a social unit.

Exogamy
Mating outside a social unit.

Hardy-Weinberg equilibrium
The mathematical relationship expressing—under ideal conditions—the predicted distribution of genes in populations; the central theory of population genetics.

cumstances are compared. Similar to the way a typical barometer is standardized under known temperature and altitude conditions, the Hardy-Weinberg equilibrium is standardized under known evolutionary conditions.

The relationship of the gene frequencies in populations to Mendelian genotypic proportions is a straightforward extension of simple Mendelian genetics. In fact, in 1903, very soon after the rediscovery of Mendel's work the American geneticist and animal breeder W. E. Castle developed a model showing the relationship of genes to populations. However, Castle felt the results were so obvious that he did not take the trouble to state unequivocally the conditions for genetic equilibrium nor did he actively push for acceptance of his views.

However, within just five years the English mathematician G. H. Hardy (1877–1947) and the German physician W. Weinberg (1862–1937) independently reached the same conclusion, and their formulation eventually won wide acceptance. The mathematical relationship of gene and genotype frequencies in populations is therefore usually called the Hardy-Weinberg formula or "law."

Interestingly, we note once again that the science of genetics was advancing intellectually along a broad international front. At the turn of the century three scientists in three different countries discovered Mendel's initial contribution and realized its implications. Within just another eight years the application of these principles to populations was again independently reached in three separate countries, and the discipline of population genetics was born.

Under the idealized conditions of Hardy-Weinberg equilibrium no new alleles are added and no alleles removed from the population. Moreover, every allele for a given trait has an equal chance of combining with all alleles in the gene pool.

The simplest situation applicable to a microevolutionary study is a genetic trait that follows a simple Mendelian pattern and has only two alleles (A, a). As you recall from earlier discussions, there are then only three possible genotypes: AA, Aa, aa. Proportions of these genotypes (AA:Aa:aa) are a function of the allele frequencies themselves (percentage of A; percentage of a). In order to provide uniformity for all genetic loci, a standard notation is employed to refer to these frequencies:

Gene frequency of first allele (A) = p

$$(p = \text{dominant allele—if there is dominance})$$

Gene frequency of second allele (a) = q (q = recessive allele)

Since in this case there are only two alleles, their combined total frequency must represent all possibilities. In other words:

$$\underset{\substack{\text{(Proportion} \\ \text{of A alleles)}}}{p} \quad + \quad \underset{\substack{\text{(Proportion} \\ \text{of a alleles)}}}{q} \quad = \quad 1 \text{ (unity, or all alleles)}$$

To ascertain the expected proportions of genotypes, we simply compute the chances of the alleles combining with one another into all possible combinations. Remember, they all have an equal chance of combining and no new alleles are being added.

These probabilities are a direct function of the gene frequency of the two alleles. The chances of all possible combinations occurring randomly can be simply shown as:

$$
\begin{array}{r}
p + q \\
\times \quad p + q \\
\hline
pq + q^2 \\
p^2 + pq \\
\hline
p^2 + 2pq + q^2
\end{array}
$$

(Mathematically, this is known as a binomial expansion)

What we have just calculated is simply:

Allele Combination	Genotype Produced	Expected Proportion in Population
Chances of:		
A combining with A	AA	$p \times p = p^2$
Chances of:		
A combining with a	Aa	$p \times q = 2pq$
a combining with A		$q \times p$
Chances of:		
a combining with a	aa	$q \times q = q^2$
Proportions of		
genotypes	AA: Aa: aa:	
	p^2 $2pq$ q^2	

where p = frequency of dominant allele and q = frequency of recessive allele in a population.

Calculating Gene Frequencies: An Example   How microevolutionists use the Hardy-Weinberg formula is best demonstrated through an example. Let us return to the classroom "population" of 100 individuals discussed earlier. Now that you are aware of the precise definition of a breeding population you can see that a classroom group does not meet the key prerequisite of social and/or geographic isolation. But once again let us assume that it does and thus represents a good biological population.

In addition, we will once again use the MN blood group locus as the gene to be measured. You will recall that this gene produces a blood group antigen—similar to ABO—located on red blood cells. We therefore can fairly quickly ascertain everyone's phenotype by taking blood samples and observing reactions with specially prepared antisera. From the phenotypes we can then directly calculate the gene frequencies. So let us proceed.

All 100 individuals are tested and the results are shown in Box 4-3. Although the match between observed and expected frequencies is not perfect, it is close enough statistically to satisfy equilibrium conditions. Since our population is not a large one, sampling may easily account for the small observed deviations. Our population is therefore probably in equilibrium (that is, it is not evolving).

◇ Box 4-3   Calculating Gene Frequencies in a Hypothetical Population

Observed Data:

GENOTYPE	NUMBER OF INDIVIDUALS*	PERCENTAGE	NUMBER OF ALLELES M	N
MM	40	(40%)	80	
MN	40	(40%)	40	40
NN	20	(20%)		40
Totals	100	(100%)	120 + 80 = 200	
		Proportion:	.6 + .4 = 1	

Observed allele frequencies:

M = .6(p)   p + q should = 1 (and they do)
N = .4(q)

Expected Frequencies   What are the predicted genotype proportions if genetic equilibrium (no evolution) applies to our population? We simply apply the Hardy-Weinberg formula:

$p^2 + 2pq + q^2$

p^2	= (.6) × (.6)	=	.36
2pq	= 2(.6)(.4) = 2(.24)	=	.48
q^2	= (.4) × (.4)	=	.16
Total			1.00

There are only three possible genotypes (MM:MN:NN) so the total of the relative proportions should equal 1.00; as you can see, they do.

How do these expected frequencies compare with the observed frequencies in our population?

	Expected Frequency	Observed Frequency
MM	.36	.40
MN	.48	.40
NN	.16	.20

*Each individual has two alleles; thus a person who is MM contributes two M alleles to the total gene pool. A person who is MN contributes one M and one N. One hundred individuals, then, have 200 alleles for the MN locus.

◇ Review, Genetics and Evolutionary Factors

Starting in Chapter 2 with a discussion of natural selection, we proceeded in Chapter 3 to show the molecular and cellular bases of heredity, and to illustrate in this chapter how such genetic information is passed from individuals in one generation to those in the next. It may seem that these different levels, molecular, cellular, individual, and populational, are different aspects of evolution, but they are all related and highly integrated in a way that can eventually produce evolutionary change. A step-by-step example will make this clear.

In our earlier discussion of sickle-cell hemoglobin (see p. 58), you will recall that the actual genetic information was coded in the sequence of bases in the DNA molecule. We started out with a situation where everyone in the population has the same hemoglobin type; therefore, initially no variation for this trait exists, and without some source of new variation evolution is not possible. How does this gene change? We have seen that a substitution of a single base in the DNA sequence can alter the code significantly enough to alter the protein product and ultimately the whole phenotype of the individual. Imagine that, several generations ago, just such an "accident" occurred in a single individual. For this mutated gene to be passed on to succeeding offspring, the gametes must carry the alteration. Any new mutation, therefore, must be transmitted during sex cell formation.

Once the mutation has occurred in the DNA, it will be packaged into chromosomes, and these chromosomes in turn will assort during meiosis to be passed to offspring. The results of this process are seen by looking at phenotypes (traits) in individuals, and the mode of inheritance is described simply by Mendel's principle of segregation. In other words, if our initial individual has a mutation in only one paired allele on a set of homologous chromosomes, there will be a 50% chance of passing this chromosome (with the new mutation) to an offspring.

Thus far, we have seen what a gene is, how it can change, and how it is passed on to offspring. But what does all this activity have to do with *evolution*? To repeat an earlier definition, evolution is a change in gene frequency in a *population* from one generation to the next. The key point here is that we are now looking at a whole group of individuals, a population, and it is the population that will or will not change over time.

We know whether gene frequencies have changed in a population where sickle-cell anemia is found by ascertaining the percentage of individuals with the sickling allele (Hb^s) versus those with the normal allele (Hb^A). If the relative proportions of these alleles alter with time, evolution has occurred. In addition to discovering that evolution has occurred, it is important to know why. Several possibilities arise. First, we know that the only way the new allele Hb^s could have arisen is by mutation, and we have shown how this process might happen in a single individual. This change, however, is not yet really an evolutionary one, for in a relatively large population the alteration of one individual's genes will not significantly alter gene frequencies of the entire population. Somehow, this new allele must spread in the population.

One way this could happen is in a small population where mutations in one of just a few individuals and their offspring may indeed alter the overall frequency quite quickly. This case would be representative of genetic drift. As discussed above, drift acts in small populations where random factors may cause significant changes in gene frequency. Due to small population size, there is not likely to be a balance of factors affecting individual survival, reproduction, etc. Consequently, some alleles may be completely removed from the population, while others may become established as the only allele present at that particular locus (and are said to be "fixed" in the population).

In the course of human evolution, drift may have played a significant role at times, but long-term evolutionary trends could only have been sustained by *natural selection*. The way this has worked in the past and still operates today (as in sickle-cell) is through differential reproduction. That is, individuals who carry a particular gene produce more offspring. By producing more offspring than other individuals with alternative alleles, such individuals cause the frequency of the new allele in the population to increase slowly in

Table 4-1   Levels of Organization in the Evolutionary Process

Evolutionary Factor	Level	Evolutionary Process	Science	Technique of Study
Mutation	DNA	Storage of genetic information; ability to replicate; influences phenotype by production of proteins	Molecular biology	Theoretical: from evidence of spectrophotometry, biochemistry, electron microscopy
Mutation	Chromosomes	A vehicle for packaging and transmitting genetic material (DNA)	Cytogenetics	Light, electron microscope
Recombination (sex cells only)	Cell	The basic unit of life that contains the chromosomes and divides for growth and for production of sex cells	Cytogenetics	Light, electron microscope
Natural selection	Organism	The unit, composed of cells, that reproduces and that we observe for phenotypic traits	Genetics	Visual, biochemical
Drift, migration	Population	A group of interbreeding organisms. We look at changes in gene frequencies between generations; it is the population that evolves	Population genetics	Statistical

proportion from generation to generation. When this process is compounded over hundreds of generations for numerous genes, the result is significant evolutionary change.

◇ Summary

We have now come full circle. We started our discussions of evolution (Chapter 2) by talking about populations and, indeed, this is where evolution occurs. But populations are made up of individual organisms, organisms are made up of cells, cells contain chromosomes, and chromosomes are composed of DNA. Understanding the actual mechanics of the evolutionary process comes *only* from considering all these various levels of organization.

◇ Questions for Review

1. Explain why botanists before Mendel failed to solve the problem of heredity.
2. How was Mendel's approach to the study of heredity different from those of his predecessors?
3. Why did the pea plant suit Mendel's experimental model?
4. What is the significance of contrasting characters?
5. What are the differences between P_1 and F_1 crosses?
6. Explain the principle of segregation.
7. Explain the principle of independent assortment.
8. How do these principles help us to understand evolution?

9. How is a mutation—a change in the DNA genetic code—transmitted into an actual physical change? Use sickle-cell hemoglobin as an example.

10. What are the major elements of the modern synthesis? What earlier dispute did the modern synthesis resolve?

11. Discuss two recent challenges to the modern synthetic theory of evolution.

12. Assume a mutation occurs in a small human population. What does this mutation have to do with evolution? In other words, how might gene frequencies be changed?

13. Why is it so important to study human *populations* in order to understand human evolution?

14. Why is it difficult to isolate actual populations?

15. Under what conditions does the Hardy-Weinberg equilibrium model hold true? If a deviation from expected frequencies is found, what does that suggest?

Human Diversity

CONTENTS

Note: Arthur R. Jensen is one of the leading proponents of the usefulness of IQ tests for measuring intelligence, a subject discussed in this chapter. To support his position, Jensen has cited evidence on twins gathered by British psychologist Sir Cyril Burt.

The Issue for this chapter recounts the story of Burt and his statistics. (Jensen has stated he can no longer accept Burt's evidence, but he continues to believe that IQ tests reflect intelligence.)

Did Sir Cyril cook the figures?

One of the most influential educational psychologists of this century, especially in the field of intelligence testing, was Sir Cyril Burt, who died in 1971.

Burt believed that heredity could explain the high scores achieved in intelligence tests, that mental abilities were inborn, and that intelligence was concentrated in the higher social classes. When he found an unusually high IQ among orphans or adopted children, he explained, "We commonly learned later on that the child was the illegitimate offspring of a father belonging to a superior social class." The class system, he firmly believed, was an economic reflection of a genetically determined order of human merit.

It is not surprising to learn that Burt was influenced by eugenicists, and, as a matter of fact, was acquainted with Sir Francis Galton, the principal founder of eugenics, who believed that social controls could improve or impair the qualities of future generations. Burt's explanation of differences in intelligence was invariably associated with social class. In 1912, he coauthored a paper in which Liverpool slumboys were compared with Oxford preparatory boys. He claimed the results were consistent with investigations of savage and civilized races!

Burt also conducted studies of separated pairs of identical twins.* His results showed a high correlation in the IQs of the separated twins, thus effectively reducing the significance of the environment on intelligence scores.

Burt's work influenced educational legislation in England. The British Education Act of 1944 was based explicitly on his statistical reports, which established principles of educational selectivity and segregation: three types of schools were established for different innate abilities—grammar schools, technical schools, and secondary schools.

In 1961, he published a major paper, "Intelligence and Social Mobility," which was a deadly attack against those who argued that the environment could affect

*Monozygotic twins raised from birth in separate households.

scores achieved in intelligence tests. This paper also demonstrated a remarkable correlation between intelligence and social class.

This work has been widely quoted by geneticists and psychologists, especially those involved in IQ testing, since it appeared to be the most comprehensive study ever performed on the relation of intelligence to social class and social mobility. Burt's publications had great impact on such men as Jensen, Eyesenck, and Herrnstein, staunch supporters of the importance of heredity on intelligence and intelligence scores. Burt was knighted in 1946 for his work on intelligence and his recommendations for educational reform.

Doubts about the validity and accuracy (as well as the honesty) of Burt's work surfaced just a few years after his death. Professor Leon Kamin (1971) of Princeton questioned Burt's studies of twins. Kamin pointed out that Burt's number of separated identical twin pairs increased from 15 in 1943 to 21 in 1955, to 30 in 1957, to 42 in 1958, and in 1966 reached 53, proobably the world's largest sample of an extremely rare phenomenon. Yet the correlation of intelligence of the separated twin pairs remained constant to three decimal places over this period of twenty-five years, even though the number of pairs had increased almost four times. Such a stable correlation is so unlikely that statisticians consider it impossible unless the figures were deliberately fixed.

An English journalist, Oliver Gillie (1978, 1979), tried to find the women who had collaborated with Burt in his research and publications in order to learn more of Burt's unlikely statistics. Gillie searched records at universities and psychological societies for traces of these three women associates, and he also talked to friends and employees of Burt who should have known the women and something of their whereabouts. However, he found no trace of them with the possible exception of one—a Miss Howard—who, said Gillie, if she did exist, was not the person Burt said she was. It is difficult to know why Burt would fabricate such associates, or what purpose this might have served.

The most damaging report on Burt's work is probably Professor D. D. Dorfman's examination of the statistics given in Burt's 1961 report. Burt claimed he had studied 40,000 people over a period of fifty years, comparing the intelligence of children and their fathers. He illustrated his findings in tables that showed the intelligence of fathers of six social classes and, in another table, the intelligence of their children.

In results so perfect they are too good to be true, Burt found an almost perfect normal curve of intelligence among fathers and children, and the statistics for each group were almost identical. The probability of a normal curve for intelligence is highly unlikely. The U.S. Army, for example, in the Alpha test scores for intelligence given to draftees in World War I, found a skewed, not a normal, curve. Other summaries of intelligence scores show similarly skewed results. That children's intelligence scores would be identical with their fathers', over a period of fifty years, is equally unlikely.

Dorfman concluded that Burt's results were precisely what they should have been according to a theoretical formula for such work, but, he added, such results do not occur in nature. "The almost perfect fit of Burt's adult and child distributions to the normal curve suggests that his 'actual' distributions are not actual distributions." Furthermore, "we may now say that, beyond a reasonable doubt, the frequency distributions of Burt's tables . . . were carefully constructed so as to [be] in agreement with the normal curve." And, finally, "these findings show, beyond any reasonable doubt, that Burt fixed the row and column totals of the tables in his highly acclaimed 1961 study."

We might ask, along with Gillie, "Why did psychologists, educationalists, and civil servants let him get away with it for so long?—for any reasonably careful inspection shows Burt's work to be careless, riddled with implausibilities, and inadequately documented? . . . Sir Cyril Burt, the supposed guardian of intellectual rigour, the hero of the educational conservatives, the defender of a future which was to be given over to the genetically pure, was one of the most formidable confidence tricksters British society has produced. . . . Sir Cyril takes his place alongside the manufacturers of the Piltdown Skull."

SOURCES:

Dorfman, D. D., "The Cyril Burt Questions: New Findings," *Science*, 201:1177, September 29, 1978.

Gillie, Oliver, "Sir Cyril Burt and the Great IQ Fraud," *New Statesman*, 24, November, 1978.

———, "Burt's Missing Ladies," *Science*, 204:1035, June 8, 1979.

Jensen, Arthur R., *Bias in Mental Testing*, New York: Free Press, 1980.

Kamin, Leon, *The Science and Politics of IQ*, New York: John Wiley & Sons. 1974.

◇ Introduction

We examined human variation in Chapters 3 and 4 from an adaptive point of view, in which physical differences among populations were explained largely in terms of selection pressures leading to possible adaptive responses.

This emphasis on selection and adaptation is a recent approach to human variation. In the past, scholars busied themselves constructing racial typologies, seeking the origin of races, and attributing to races a variety of personality traits.

In this chapter, we shall briefly trace the history of the scholarly and scientific approaches to human diversity. We shall question the value of racial typologies and the concept of race itself. We shall also examine the relationship—if any—between human diversity and behavior. Do physical traits determine what people do? Does pigmentation, for example, limit or aid intelligence? Is intelligence, as reflected in IQ test achievements, the result of heredity or environment, or the interaction of both?

◇ Racial Classification

As early as 1350 B.C., Egyptians recognized physical differences of populations by using four colors to distinguish various groups: red for Egyptians, yellow for those to the east, white for people from the north, and black for Africans to the south (Gossett, 1963, p. 4). In more recent times, classification of populations has been based mainly on such physical traits as pigmentation of skin, eyes, and hair; hair form, body build, and nose form. Three hundred years ago, in 1684, François Bernier, a French physician, divided the world's populations into what we call races: Europeans, Far Easterners, Blacks, and Lapps. It was "probably the first attempt in history to classify all the races of mankind" (Gossett, 1963, p. 33).

From that time until the present, scientists, including such luminaries as Linnaeus, Buffon, Huxley, and others have constructed racial classifications. In Box 5-1 are examples of racial classifications, which range from the simple fivefold division of Blumenbach to the complex schemes of Hooton and Garn.

During the sixteenth and seventeenth centuries, explorers returning from their travels to newly discovered continents brought back information about people unknown to Europeans. Scholars, like Linnaeus, attempted to fit this knowledge into an orderly arrangement, basing their classifications mainly on skin color and geography. Johann Blumenbach, a professor of medicine at the University of Göttingen in Germany, made a thorough study of numerous skulls and developed an influential racial classification. His 1781 division of

Caucasian,* Mongolian, Malay, Ethiopian, and American (which came to be popularly known as white, yellow, brown, black, and red) still persists to this day as one of the most common racial divisions of humankind. Blumenbach used the same criteria of skin color and geography as earlier scholars and added a number of others, such as shape of skull and face, hair color, nose and chin form.

Differences in races at this time were often explained by climate and environment. In the United States, the Reverend Mr. Samuel Stanhope Smith, a professor at the College of New Jersey (later Princeton) attributed color mainly to climate and believed dark skin could "be considered as a universal freckle" (Gossett, 1963, p. 39). He further believed that environment was "all that stood in the way of the advancement of Negroes and other non-white races . . ." (Gossett, 1963, p. 39).

In the latter half of the eighteenth and much of the nineteenth centuries, there was a continuing discussion of the origin of races: The **monogenists** believed all races were derived from a single pair, and credited Adam and Eve as the source. The multitudinous progeny of the original pair then spread over the world and assumed their present diversity in response to the climate and other conditions to which they were subjected. Monogenists also explained differences in human populations as deviant degeneration from the original stock.

Polygenists took the position of a multiple origin of races and ridiculed the idea that all people could have descended from Adam and Eve. In the nineteenth century, an American physician, Dr. Samuel George Morton (1799–1851), argued in favor of polygenism by pointing to his researches, which indicated that the offspring of a black and white cross, a mulatto, could bear children only with difficulty. If these women mated only with mulattoes, he maintained, their descendants would bear fewer and fewer children, and in time there would be no descendants at all! (Gossett, 1963).

In the latter part of the eighteenth century, researchers such as Blumenbach began what they considered a more scientific approach, and initiated the careful study and measurements of skulls. This practice was refined in the nineteenth century when Samuel Morton developed new ways of measuring crania by filling skulls with seed (and, later on, shot) and then weighing this material. This new science, called **anthropometry**, became the primary concern of physical anthropologists. In 1842, Anders Retzius, a Swedish anatomist, believed he had discovered a true scientific basis for racial classification: the shape of the head. This measurement, called the *cephalic index* and a refinement of Morton's technique, was a measure of the ratio of the breadth of the skull to its length. Retzius used the cephalic index to divide

Monogenists
Term applied to those who believe that all races derived from a single pair (Adam and Eve).

Polygenists
Term applied to those who believe in a multiple origin of races.

Anthropometry
anthropos: man
metric: measure
Measurement of the human body.

---

*Blumenbach was the first to use the term Caucasian for Europeans. Thomas Huxley commented that "A Georgian woman's skull was the handsomest in his collection. Hence it became his model exemplar of human skulls, from which all others might be regarded as deviations; and out of this, by some strange hocus-pocus, grew up the notion that the Caucasian man is the prototypic 'Adamic' man, and his country the primitive centre of our kind" (cited in Count, 1950, p. 119).

◇ Box 5-1　Racial Classifications

Blumenbach, 1781

Caucasian
Mongolian
Malay
Ethiopian
American

E. A. Hooton, 1946

Primary Race	Primary Subrace	Composite Race	Composite Subrace	Residual Mixed Types
White	Mediterranean	Australian	Armenoid	Nordic-Alpine
	Ainu	Indo-Dravidian	Dinaric	Nordic-Mediterranean
	Keltic	Polynesian		
	Nordic			
	Alpine			
	East Baltic			
Negroid	African Negro	Melanesian-Papuan		
	Nilotic Negro	Bushman-Hottentot		
	Negrito			
	Classic	Indonesian		
Mongoloid	Mongoloid	Mongoloid		
	Arctic Mongoloid	American Indian		

Secondary Subrace

Malay-Mongoloid
Indonesian

Dolichocephalic
dolicho: narrow
cephal: head
Narrow or long-headed; a skull in which the width is less than 75 percent of the length.

Brachycephalic
brachy: short, broad
Broad-headed; a skull in which the width is 80 percent or more of the length.

Europe into two types: a long-headed or **dolichocephalic** type and round-headed or **bracycephalic** type.

Anthropometry was enthusiastically promoted by Paul Broca, French neurosurgeon and physical anthropologist, who, in 1859, founded The Anthropological Society of Paris, the first anthropological organization in Europe. He published statistical treatises with complicated diagrams and arranged his collection of 2,000 skulls into 60 different series (Gossett, 1963, p. 76). Broca was also a resourceful, ingenious inventor of measuring instruments and devised craniometers and other gadgetry in order to discover statistical relationships of the skull. Cranial measurements proceeded with enthusiastic zeal, and the peak of anthropometry was probably reached in 1900, when A. von Törok took 5,000 measurements on a single skull (Barzun, 1965, p. 117).

Stanley M. Garn, 1969

Geographical Races:

Amerindian
Polynesian
Micronesian
Melanesian-Papuan
Australian
Asiatic
Indian
European
African

"A collection of race populations, separated from other such collections by major geographical barriers" (p. 14).

Local Races:

Northwest European
Northeast European
Alpine
Mediterranean
East African
Bantu
Tibetan
North Chinese
Extreme Mongoloid
Hindu

"A breeding population adapted to local selection pressures and maintained by either natural or social barriers to gene interchange" (p. 16).

These are examples of local races; there are many, many more.

Micro-Races:

Not well defined but apparently refers to neighborhoods within a city or a city itself since "marriage or mating, is a mathematical function of distance. With millions of potential mates, the male ordinarily chooses one near at hand" (p. 19).

Broca, as did many other anthropologists during this period, believed there was some connection between brain and race, and that measuring the shape of the skull was the best way to determine the content of the brain. He even believed it possible to identify the social class of the skulls he studied!

Despite the emphasis on anthropometry by these "scientific anthropologists," others were questioning the value of such measurements. Broca himself noted that two anthropologists rarely obtained the same figures when they measured the same skull. "The human head," he complained, "is too irregular . . . to allow accurate comparison on a statistical basis" (Gossett, 1963, p. 76), a conclusion which nevertheless did not deter his anthropometric research.

With the publication of Darwin's *Origin of Species* in 1859, there was some attempt to take evolutionary principles into consideration for racial classifi-

Typology
The science of types classifying organic or inorganic material into forms or types. In physical anthropology, the term means dividing humankind into discrete racial types.

Mongrelization
Racial mixture.

cations. But the emphasis on typology continued, as we see (Box 5-1), in the racial types suggested by Hooten as late as 1946.

However, concern with the division of the earth's human population into races was the goal of many physical anthropologists during the latter half of the nineteenth century. The assumption throughout this period was that pure races existed (sometime in the past), and it was the responsibility of anthropologists to define them. To support such a position, it was necessary to believe that races had not basically changed from whatever they were at the time of origin. And if races were fixed—a conflict with evolutionary thought, which anthropologists accepted—then there must be physical traits that remain fixed. That is, those physical traits that did not adapt to environmental conditions could be used for racial classification; those that did adapt, could not. There was, therefore, constant effort to locate *nonadaptive* traits. It was believed that once races evolved, racial traits persisted even if the people moved to another environment. Since it was obvious that pure races did not exist, certainly not in Europe, physical differences in modern populations were said to be the result of a mixture of already formed races.

The search for nonadaptive traits to serve as a basis for the classification of racial types centered on the cephalic index, although hair form, eye form, and prominence of the nose were also considered nonadaptive. W. Z. Ripley, in a book published in 1899 and widely read in the United States, summarized much of the research of European scientists. Ripley relied heavily on headform as a basis for his racial classification of Europe into three types. Not everyone agreed with the emphasis on head measurements, and Franz Boas, early in this century, criticized Ripley for "treating the cephalic index as the 'primary principle of classification'" (Stocking, 1968, p. 181). As a result of his well-known study of body form of European immigrants and their children, Boas claimed that headform was a nonadaptive trait (Boas, 1940).

Typology presents problems not readily resolved. How many divisions are there? Estimates range from as few as 3 to more than 300. There are primary divisions, major subdivisions, minor subdivisions, composite subdivisions, and so on. What is the significance of these divisions of divisions, and what is their reality? Do they represent actual living populations, or merely ideal types? What criteria are used to separate one type from another, one subdivision from another? Is one trait more important than another? Skin pigmentation, for example, is the trait most people would consider as the basic classificatory criterion; should it carry more weight than, say, head shape, nose shape, body build, or stature? If so (or if not), why? For example, in his racial classification of 1900, Deniker typed northern Europeans as tall with wavy, reddish hair, reddish white skin, and dolichocephalic skulls. What, then, shall we do with a northern European answering this description whose brother is short, not tall, with straight rather than wavy hair, and a darkish rather than reddish white skin?

There is a basic assumption in typological classification (noted above) that races existed in a pure state at some time in the past, before migrations of recent times produced the mixtures of today. **Mongrelization** is the term often used by racists. But migration has always existed; with culture, humans are capable of taking a goodly portion of their environment with them, and as Hooten has succinctly aphorized, "when groups meet they may or may not bleed, but they always breed." As Mayr has said, "To speak of 'pure races' is sheer nonsense" (1970, p. 397).

Finally, typologies tell us little if anything of human evolution. Classification, as Washburn noted, is useful if we are concerned with anatomical, genetic, and structural differences between people, "but it is useful under no other circumstances, as far as I can see" (Washburn, 1963, p. 527).

For these and other reasons, many anthropologists no longer accept the assumption that races exist and have turned away from the racial concept as biologically unrealistic. Such studies are regarded as unrewarding. Those still concerned with classification have drawn upon population genetics and consider the breeding population "the basic unit of evolutionary change . . . the unit whose structure changes in response to the action of the mechanisms of evolution" (Kelso, 1974, p. 301).

It is difficult to escape the conclusion that as a concept, race, like quicksilver, is awkward to take hold of. Just when we think we have it in our grasp, it slips through our fingers. As French anthropologist Jean Hiernaux puts it:

> To dismember mankind into races as a convenient approximation requires such a distortion of the facts that any usefulness disappears; on the contrary, only the harm done by such practices remains (Hiernaux, 1964, p. 43).

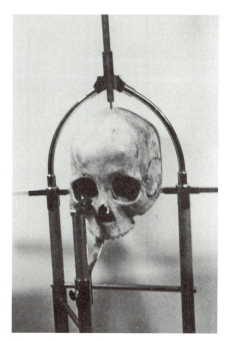

Figure 5-1   Craniometer.

◇ Definitions of Race

To understand the difficulties the concept of race presents, it may help to review briefly the process of speciation (p. 89). Species is defined as "a group of interbreeding organisms that are reproductively isolated from other such groups" (p. 89), and biologists are agreed that species is an evolutionary unit. The definition of race is more elusive, and race is not an evolutionary unit, but an arbitrary one. We see this more clearly with the process of speciation.

As the populations within a species diverge, especially between isolated groups, differences arise. When the differences become detectable, taxonomists may classify the populations as races, or subspecies. With continued isolation and divergence, the groups are known as *incipient species* (or biological races), on their way to becoming species. However, ". . . the decisions about what characteristics to emphasize in describing differences between the populations are relatively arbitrary ones" (Bodmer and Cavalli-Sforza, 1976, p. 561).

The division of the populations of any species into biological "races" tends to be arbitrary to some degree, but when it comes to human races, the situation is a quagmire. The populations of *H. sapiens* are not on their way to becoming separate species, and the reasons for this are quite clear. Human groups have been isolated in the past but never long enough to speciate. As mentioned, humans take their culture with them when they migrate, and are not entirely dependent on their environment. They can and do migrate to a considerable extent. Consequently, there has been gene exchange between groups that has kept them interfertile and, therefore, members of the same species. As communication and the means of transportation improved, and as more efficient technology developed, humans became even more independent of the environment, and the chance of speciation has become remote.

Perhaps the basic problem in defining race is to decide on the criteria. As we see from the examples on pages 108–109, these are arbitrary. A recent definition demonstrates the dilemma: A race is "... a division of a species which differs from other divisions by the frequency with which certain hereditary traits appear among its members" (Brues, 1977, p. 1). Which hereditary traits? How are they selected? On what basis? Do the same traits apply in all cases? There is no agreement on the answers. Besides, no group classified as a race differs in all its traits from another race. "... the boundaries between the races drawn on the basis of one trait will not coincide with boundaries drawn on the basis of another trait" (Bodmer and Cavalli-Sforza, 1976, p. 562). If we cannot agree on racial criteria, then defining race and classifying populations into racial groups appear impossible.

Although we question the value of the racial concept, it may be instructive to list a few definitions of race, which may delineate even further the reasons why anthropologists are dissatisfied with the concept itself.

Rudolf Virchow (1896) saw races as varieties originating from two factors, heredity and environment: "... there can be no doubt that *races are nothing more than hereditary variations* ... we must derive races also from the influence of external causes, and we may define them as *acquired deviations from the original type*" (cited in Count, 1950, p. 193). Although not the first, Virchow's view of race as hereditary variations suggests an evolutionary orientation.

As time went on, anthropologists emphasized phenotypic traits as important in racial analysis. In 1926, Hooton offered the following definition:

> A race is a great division of mankind, the members of which, though individually varying, are characterized as a group by a certain combination of morphological and metrical features, principally non-adaptive, which have been derived from their common descent.

In addition to emphasizing visible phenotypic traits (morphological features), Hooten included measurements of the body that had occupied so much of anthropological research in the latter half of the nineteenth century. He also made an attempt to construct a more precise definition by restricting it to traits that were presumably *nonadaptive*—that is, unaffected by the environment—since he considered these the most objective racial markers. Implicit in this approach is the belief that races do not change over time, that if it were possible somehow to find traits unaffected by the environment, true or pure races could be determined (see p. 110).

We now know the search for nonadaptive traits is a futile quest, that a phenotype is the result of the dynamic interaction of several genes *and* the environment.

As population genetics became important in biological research, the concept of population became part of the definition. In 1950, Boyd defined race "as a population which differs significantly from other human populations in regard to the frequency of one or more genes it possesses" (Boyd, 1950, p. 207).

Livingstone (1964, p. 49) objects to the simplistic use of gene frequencies as a criterion for race, since such a position implies that each population—

Figure 5-2   Virchow.

which probably differs in the frequency of some gene from other populations—would be a separate race.

One of the most recent modifications of the definition of race adds the concept of a *breeding*, or Mendelian, population (Garn, 1969). Livingstone again objects since the concept of breeding population may be difficult to apply. Garn, however, views race "as a breeding population, neither more nor less" (1969, p. 6). One local race (see Box 5-1), ranging from Tangier to the Dardanelles and including the Arabian Peninsula, Garn calls Mediterranean. However, this is a very unlikely breeding population, containing, as it does, wide differences in such factors as social class, religion, economy, and philosophy. Very few Christians interbreed with Muslims, or Arab Beduins with, say, Italian farmers. And even if it were possible to identify a local race, "The actual fabric of human mating behavior today is made of such a complicated and continually changing weave that not only is a simple count impossible, but even an estimate is a deception" (Kelso, 1974, p. 304).

The foregoing definitions of race and comments are not intended to discourage or confuse. The plain fact is that a great deal of confusion abounds among anthropologists, geneticists, and other researchers concerned with the concept of race. That there are physical differences among human beings is an obvious fact requiring no discussion. No one will mistake an indigenous resident of China for a European or African. But the matter is not that simple.

Topinard, writing almost 100 years ago, already recognized the problems still being discussed today:

Figure 5-3 E. A. Hooton.

> Races exist; it is undeniable; our intelligence comprehends them; our minds see them; our labors separate them out. If in thought we suppress the intermixtures of peoples, their interbreedings, in a flash we see them stand forth—simple, inevitable, with their trait-patterns and physiological systems—a compulsive consequence of collective heredity. *But nowhere can we put our fingers upon them* (emphasis ours, cited by Scheidt, 1924, p. 389).

To confuse the matter of race definition even further, the term "race," as it is popularly used, is more a sociocultural than biological concept. That is, a group of people are often designated as a race regardless of their genetic traits. Thus, children of mixed black and white parents are considered black, though genetically they are as much "white" as "black." Often classified as races are ethnic groups (Germans, French, Russians, etc.), religious groups (Muslims, Buddhists, Jews, etc.), political groups (communists, fascists). This also adds to the confusion. In wartime, when emotions run high, all manner of vices, based on "racial" traits, are attributed to the enemy (e.g., the Germans and Japanese in World War II and the Vietnamese in the Vietnam War).

If we restrict the word "race," no matter how difficult it may be to define the term, to genetic traits, it may be possible to eliminate some of the misunderstanding associated with the concept of race. However, the prognosis is not optimistic.

What, then, are we to do about the concept of race? Is race a reality? Is a breeding population a race? Are races geographic isolates? Is it even possible to study races? Is the word "race" so loaded with misconception, misunderstanding, fallacy, prejudice, and bigotry that the term itself should be changed and its study limited? Or is Dunn more perceptive when he suggests, "It seems better to define and explain its use, and to free it from its bad and false meaning, than to give up the problem by excluding the word" (Dunn, 1951, p. 12).

The validity and utility of race, as a concept, are still debated by anthropologists. Typological divisions of humankind, however, which once occupied so much anthropological effort, appear to be a phenomenon of the past. As we have indicated, there are too many problems in the construction of racial typologies, and, once a typology is developed, the nagging question remains: So what?

Instead of placing an entire population in, as it were, a racial straightjacket, many anthropologists consider the study of the distribution of single traits to be more rewarding from the point of view of evolutionary theory. This is the clinal approach to human diversity.

◇ Clinal Distribution: One Genetic Trait

A relatively recent approach* to human variation is *clinal distribution*. Just as temperatures are plotted on a weather map by means of isotherms that join points with the same temperature, so also may gene frequencies be plotted. Thus, the distribution of a particular trait is indicated on a map by zones, known as clines (Fig. 5-4). This description simply reveals the variation of that trait over a geographic area, and by itself implies no explanation, racial or otherwise. Nor does such a distribution lead to racial typologies. A clinal distribution calls for an *evolutionary explanation* of the variation: Why does the frequency of allele B, in our figure, vary as we move from east to west across Europe? Evolutionary theory—mutation, genetic drift, natural selection, migration—is one way in which clinal variation may be explained.

Human variation is perceived quite differently when approached from a clinal point of view. No attempt is made to construct a typology of traits, but rather to apply the principles of evolution. Is the variation of gene frequency due to the advantage of one gene over another? Has there been migration to or from the clinal area that may have altered the gene frequency, or perhaps an accident known genetically as drift? An advantage of a clinal study is that gene and trait frequencies can be graphically represented as they are in Figures 5-4 and 5-5. They can suggest "migratory patterns and other aspects of population history" and "observed clinal variation in a trait is particularly amenable to explanation by mathematical methods of population genetics. In this sense, there is probably no superior method by which the evolutionary mechanisms responsible for interpopulation variation in single traits can be identified" (Bennett, 1979, pp. 357–358).

An example of an evolutionary clinal approach may be seen in Dr. Joseph Birdsell's discussion of the distribution of tawny hair he found in his field work among Australian aborigines. The heaviest distribution of this blond hair is among several tribal groups in the Australian western desert (see Fig. 5-5), and the frequency then declines on a gradient outward from this center,

*J. S. Huxley introduced the clinal concept, as it applied to plants, in 1938.

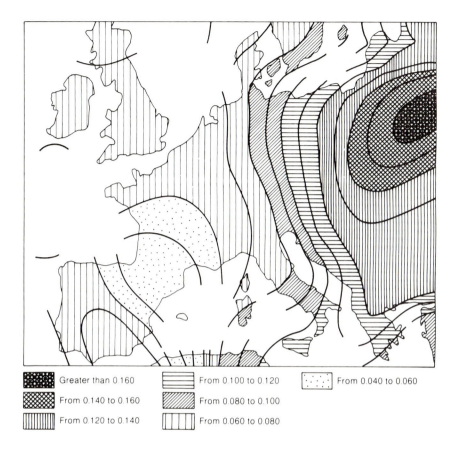

Figure 5-4 A cline frequency of the B allele. This computer-generated map shows the frequency of the B allele of the ABO blood-group system. Note the higher frequencies in Asia, and the gradual decreasing frequencies as the clines move into Europe. (Courtesy of P. E. Schreiber, IBM Research Laboratory, San Jose, California.)

Greater than 0.160	From 0.100 to 0.120	From 0.040 to 0.060
From 0.140 to 0.160	From 0.080 to 0.100	
From 0.120 to 0.140	From 0.060 to 0.080	

although not uniformly in all directions. Professor Birdsell writes (1981, pp. 352–353):

> The evolutionary significance of this clinal distribution seems apparent, even though the exact genetic basis for its inheritance has not yet been unraveled. The trait acts as though it was determined by a single codominant gene. It would appear that somewhere in the central region of high frequency, mutations, and probably repeated mutations, occurred from normal dark brown hair to this depigmented variety. The pattern of distribution indicates that it was favored by selection in some totally unknown fashion. Over considerable periods of time, through gene exchange between adjacent tribes, the new mutant gene prospered and spread outward. It seems unlikely that lightly pigmented hair in childhood should in itself have any selective advantage. Rather, it is much more probable that certain effects of this mutant gene have somehow biochemically heightened the fitness of these Aborigines in their generally desert environment. Presumably the new gene mixed well with the other genes in their pools and so *new coadaptive equlibria were produced*. The equilibria seem to have attained a plateau in the region where frequencies exceed 90 percent.

Birdsell wonders whether, if British colonization had not cut the process short, all Australian aborigines might have become blond-haired.

Figure 5-5 Gene distribution, tawny hair in Australia. Note the concentration of tawny hair in the center of distribution which can be traced by clines in a decreasing gradient. This pattern can thus be viewed on an evolutionary and genetic basis.

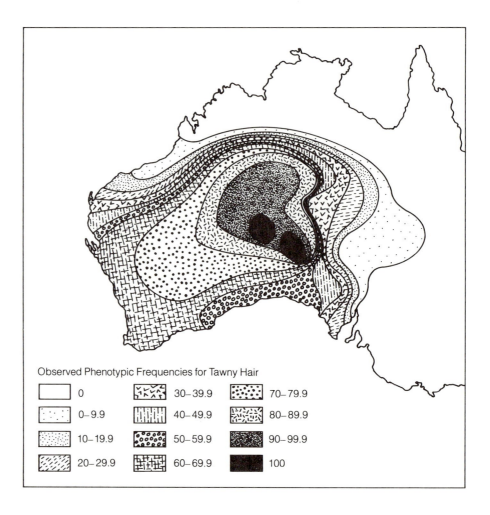

Observed Phenotypic Frequencies for Tawny Hair

0		30–39.9		70–79.9	
0–9.9		40–49.9		80–89.9	
10–19.9		50–59.9		90–99.9	
20–29.9		60–69.9		100	

◇ Multivariate Population Genetics

Whereas clinal studies isolate patterns of genetic variation one trait at a time, **multivariate** studies seek to describe the pattern for several traits simultaneously. Because the statistical manipulations of such analyses are exceedingly complex, high-speed computers have proven an invaluable tool.

An excellent example of this kind of approach to human diversity was undertaken by Harvard population geneticist R. D. Lewontin (1972), and his results are most informative. Lewontin measured the degree of population differences in gene frequencies for seventeen polymorphic traits. In his analysis, Lewontin immediately faced the dilemma: Which groups (populations) should he contrast and how should they be weighted (all equally, or bigger groups like Arabs weighted differently than smaller ones like residents of the island Tristan da Cunha)? After considerable deliberation, Lewontin decided to break down his sample into seven geographical areas (corresponding to the traditional concept of "major race") and included several (all equally weighted) populations within each. He then calculated how much of the total genetic variability within our species could be accounted for by these population subdivisions. (See Table 5-1.)

Surprisingly, only 6.3% of all variation can be accounted for at the level of major (geographic) race. In other words, close to 94% of human genetic diversity occurs *within* these gigantic groups. The large population units within races (generally corresponding to Garn's local races) account for an average of an additional 8.3%. Amazingly, the traditional concept of race (which isolates large human groups) explains about 15% of human genetic variation, leaving the remaining 85% unaccounted for.

The vast majority of genetic differences among human beings is thus explicable in terms of differences from one village to another, from one family

Multivariate
Pattern for several traits.

Table 5-1   Inclusive List of All Populations Used in Lewontin's Population Genetics Study (1972)

Caucasians

Arabs, Armenians, Austrians, Basques, Belgians, Bulgarians, Czechs, Danes, Dutch, Egyptians, English, Estonians, Finns, French, Georgians, Germans, Greeks, Gypsies, Hungarians, Icelanders, Indians (Hindi-speaking), Italians, Irani, Norwegians, Oriental Jews, Pakistani (Urdu-speakers), Poles, Portuguese, Russians, Spaniards, Swedes, Swiss, Syrians, Tristan da Cunhans, Welsh

Black Africans

Abyssinians (Amharas), Bantu, Barundi, Batutsi, Bushmen, Congolese, Ewe, Fulani, Gambians, Ghanaians, Hobe, Hottentot, Hututu, Ibo, Iraqi, Kenyans, Kikuyu, Liberians, Luo, Madagascans, Mozambiquans, Msutu, Nigerians, Pygmies, Senegalese, Shona, Somalis, Sudanese, Tanganyikans, Tutsi, Ugandans, U.S. Blacks, "West Africans," Xosa, Zulu

Mongoloids

Ainu, Bhutanese, Bogobos, Bruneians, Buriats, Chinese, Dyaks, Filipinos, Ghashgai, Indonesians, Japanese, Javanese, Kirghiz, Koreans, Lapps, Malayans, Senoy, Siamese, Taiwanese, Tatars, Thais, Turks

South Asian Aborigines

Andamanese, Badagas, Chenchu, Irula, Marathas, Naiars, Oraons, Onge, Tamils, Todas

Amerinds

Alacaluf, Aleuts, Apache, Atacameños, "Athabascans," Aymara, Bororo, Blackfeet, Bloods, "Brazilian Indians," Chippewa, Caingang, Choco, Coushatta, Cuna, Diegueños, Eskimo, Flathead, Huasteco, Huichol, Ica, Kwakiutl, Labradors, Lacandon, Mapuche, Maya, "Mexican Indians," Navaho, Nez Percé, Paez, Pehuenches, Pueblo, Quechua, Seminole, Shoshone, Toba, Utes, "Venezuelan Indians," Xavante, Yanomama

Oceanians

Admiralty Islanders, Caroline Islanders, Easter Islanders, Ellice Islanders, Fijians, Gilbertese, Guamians, Hawaiians, Kapingas, Maori, Marshellese, Melanuans, "Melanesians," "Micronesians," New Britons, New Caledonians, New Hebrideans, Palauans, Papuans, "Polynesians," Saipanese, Samoans, Solomon Islanders, Tongans, Trukese, Yapese

Austrialian Aborigines

Source: *Evolutionary Biology*, Volume 6, ed. by Dobzhansky et al. (article by R. Lewontin), p. 387. Reprinted with permission of Plenum Publishing Corporation.

to another, and to a very significant degree, from one person to another—even within the same family. Of course, when we think about the vast amount of human variation and the ways this genetic variability is rescrambled during meiosis/sexual reproduction (discussed in Chapter 3), all this individual variation should not be that amazing.

Our superficial visual perceptions tell us race does exist. But the visible phenotypic traits usually used to make racial distinctions (skin color, hair shape, nose shape, etc.) may very well be a highly biased sample, not giving an accurate picture of the actual patterns of *genetic variation*. The polymorphic traits used by Lewontin are a more objective basis for accurate biological comparisons of human groups, and they indicate that the traditional concept of race tells us very little about human variation. Indeed, Lewontin concludes with a ringing condemnation:

> Human racial classification is of no social value and is positively destructive of social and human relations. Since such racial classification is now seen to be of virtually no genetic or taxonomic significance either, no justification can be offered for its continuance (Lewontin, 1972, p. 397).

Not all population geneticists, however, are quite this critical. After all, Lewontin did find that slightly more than 6% of human variation is accounted for in the large geographic segments traditionally called major races. Whereas this is certainly a minority of all variation within *Homo sapiens*, it is not necessarily biologically insignificant. If one feels compelled to continue classifying humankind into large geographic segments, population genetics offers some aid in isolating consistent patterns of geographic variation. One such classification suggests our species can be partitioned into three major geographic groups: Africans, Caucasians, and a heterogeneous group of Easterners, including all aboriginal populations of the Pacific area (Bodmer and Cavalli-Sforza, 1976).

Whereas, to some degree, these three groups form contrasting genetic units, we must remember that the total amount of genetic variation *within* them (from one person to another, one village to another, one tribe to another, etc.) is far more than exists *between* them.

We have thus far discussed race in the abstract, as a concept, but there is a very practical aspect of race that must be considered in our modern world: the association of race and behavior, which we take up in the following section.

◇ Race and Behavior

The fact that people differ has, as we remarked at the beginning of this chapter, long been suggested. Linnaeus, for example, as far back as 1758 assigned traits to four groups: choleric, American Indians; sanguine, Europeans; melancholy, Asians; and phlegmatic, Africans.

One hundred years later, personality traits were still being attributed to race by, among others, Count de Gobineau, sometimes called the "Father of Racist Ideology" (Biddiss, 1970). We must point out that a *racial* classification differs from a *racist* one. The former attempts—usually unsuccessfully—to categorize humans into meaningful groups without making distinctions concerning the superiority of one versus another. Racist typologies, on the other hand, explicitly attempt—always unsucessfully—to impute "superior" behavioral characteristics to some races and "inferior" attributes to others.

Gobineau claimed undesirable traits for Africans, more desirable for Asiatics, and most desirable, of course, for Europeans. Needless to say, neither psychologists nor anthropologists find any validity to the correlation of personality and race. As Professor Alexander Alland, Columbia University anthropologist, points out (1971, p. 35):

> For those who have done fieldwork in Africa, there can be little doubt that behavioral and cognitive patterns in the black community in the United States bear little resemblance to those in Africa, and that, in fact, such patterns are highly variable in Africa and dependent more upon cultural differences than shared gene pools.

RACE AND INTELLIGENCE

Belief in the relationship between race and personality is popular even today, but there is no evidence that personality or any cultural trait, or any aspect of culture, such as religion or language, is in any way racial. Very likely, most scholars today would agree with this last statement, but there is an area of disagreement still being debated with surprising vehemence and emotion. That area is the question of whether race and intelligence are associated. The overwhelming majority of academic opinion (in anthropology, biology, genetics, psychology, and sociology) cannot find valid evidence that relates the two phenomena. There are, however, scientists who *do* believe in the relationship, and perhaps the best-known advocate of the proposition that race (i.e., heritability) is the *causal* factor in intelligence is Professor Arthur R. Jensen. He estimates the heritability of intelligence at about 75% (Jensen, 1980, p. 244).

Jensen, professor of educational psychology at the University of California, Berkeley, believes that intelligence is a correlate of race, that intelligence is inherited, that IQ tests measure intelligence, that racial intelligence differences can be researched from a heritability point of view, that the uncertainty of the heredity-environment problem can be reduced, and that the lower average IQ scores of blacks (about 15 points) are a function of race (Jensen, 1969a).

Jensen's views have been criticized by scientists from various disciplines. In his recent review and analysis of the literature on testing intelligence, Eckberg (1979, p. 55) is led to seriously question the degree to which the idea of a general intelligence can have usefulness in real-world pursuits. Instead, all the various lines of evidence indicate that behavior is too multiform to be encapsulated under the label of *intelligence*, unless what we intend by intelligence is something quite a bit different from that which is usually intended.

Much of the criticism of Jensen's, and other similar views, may be grouped under two headings: (1) inadequacy of the IQ test as a measure of intelligence; and (2) the failure to consider the influence of environment (in a broad sense) on ability and performance.

THE IQ TEST: UNITARY CHARACTER OF INTELLIGENCE

IQ tests, such as the Stanford-Binet, purport to give a single *general* rating of mental ability, known as "g," but many scientists have questioned whether intelligence is, in fact, a single variable. Geneticists refer to intelligence as polygenic, that is, a number of genes are involved in producing a phenotype. As Bodmer, a geneticist, says, "intelligence must be a complex characteristic under the control of many genes" (Bodmer, 1972, p. 91). If intelligence is a complex, not unitary, characteristic and consists of a combination of differing faculties, as Bodmer and others suggest, then it is questionable whether intelligence consists of a single large general factor, as Jensen claims. And it is, therefore, questionable whether an intelligence test can be constructed to test the differing mental faculties.

ENVIRONMENT AND INTELLIGENCE

Those who believe that intelligence is largely genetic and can be measured by IQ tests have probably been criticized most sharply because they have failed to consider the significance of environment in the development of intelligence. The controversy over which factor is more important, nature *or* nurture, no longer applies. Both nature *and* nurture contribute, and it is probably impossible, at this point, to separate out the percentage of each contribution.

There have been attempts to sort out environmental and genetic factors, one of the best known being the study of *monozygotic* (MZ) *twins*. MZ twins share identical genotypes, and a comparison of those who have been reared together and reared apart (that is, in different environments) should prove instructive. While such studies have been done, their reliability and applicability from one population to another (often living in very different environments) are very hotly disputed. For example, Kamin (1974) analyzed studies of separated monozygotic twin pairs. In these studies, especially those performed by Sir Cyril Burt (see Issue, p. 104)—used by Jensen to support his heritability arguments—Kamin found methodological problems serious enough to throw doubt on the validity of their conclusions. After examining Kamin's analysis of Burt's figures, Jensen conceded that Burt's studies of twins were not usable for hypothesis testing (Jensen, 1974).

That average performance on IQ exams varies among groups of schoolage children is not disputed. What causes all the furor is how to *explain* these differences. If results of twin studies, etc., do not conclusively support the Jensen, et al. argument for heredity as the clearly most dominant factor, what does that leave us with? Obviously, some form of explanation that views environmental influence as significant must be considered. The following studies reflect the view that environment must be considered as an crucial factor in IQ test results.

In 1981, Scarr reported a study, conducted by Scarr and Barker, of the cognitive differences among black and white children in Philadelphia (Scarr, 1981). These researchers found that black children performed relatively better on less culturally loaded material once the instructions were made more comprehensible to them, and also that the black environment failed to develop the skills sampled by the tests. They also noted that twins' scores were more highly correlated in the black group because family membership was more important in determining the degree to which children were exposed to the intellectual skills sampled in the tests. Their conclusion:

> The results of this study support the view that black children are being reared in circumstances that give them only marginal acquaintance with the skills and the knowledge being sampled by the tests we administered. Some families in the black community encourage the development of these skills and knowledge, whereas others do not. In general, black children do not have the same access to these skills and knowledge as white children, which explains the lower performance of black children as a group. *The hypothesis that most of the differences among the cognitive scores of black and white children are due to genetic differences between the races cannot, in our view, account for this pattern of results* (Scarr, 1981, p. 288). (Emphasis added.)

Poor nutrition may be another factor that makes for lower IQ scores. Passamanick and his associates found that a deficient maternal diet associated with low income can produce pregnancy and parturition complications followed by intellectual retardation and behavioral disorders in the children (cited in Rose, 1972, p. 139). Rose also refers to a study in which nutritional supplements were added to the deficient diets of pregnant women. This resulted in significantly raised IQs in their children at the ages of 2, 3, and 4 compared with children whose mothers did not receive the supplements.

Still other factors are the attitude toward education in some socioeconomic groups, attitude toward tests, social and economic goals, and a general **weltanschauung** (world view). All of these may combine to reduce the IQ scores of blacks; it is, therefore, difficult to reconcile the glib assertions of those who promote the genetic basis of intelligence with the environmental conditions we have just reviewed.

The core of the dispute between Jensen and the majority of scientists is whether differences in black and white IQ scores are due mainly to heredity or to environment. Most scholars are agreed that it is difficult, if not impossible, to separate the two, because (as we have just discussed) the evidence is not so clearly objective that it can be easily interpreted. IQ tests, especially, are difficult to interpret because, as many investigators have emphasized, it is not possible to construct a culture-free IQ test; that is, an IQ test that eliminates completely environmental factors.

Professor Liam Hudson, professor of educational sciences at Edinburgh University, concludes a discussion of the IQ test with the observation that:

> At the moment, and probably in principle, it is impossible to design an experiment that separates out in any neat and tidy way, the influence of hereditary and environmental factors on a human being's ability to do IQ tests (Hudson, 1972, p. 15).

Anthropologists Brace and Livingstone (1971, p. 67) suggest that *all* measured differences among major groups of humans may be explained primarily by environmental factors.

With the bulk of scientific opinion opposed to heritability as the explanation for racial intelligence, troublesome questions arise regarding the validity of IQ tests as well as the reliability of the monozygotic twin studies. We agree

Weltanschauung
welt: world
schauung: view
World view; a way of looking at the universe; a personal philosophy.

with Professor William Howells (1971, p. 8): "In all honesty, therefore, scientists must decline to see the existence of racial variation in mental ability at this stage."

RACISM

As a subject of inquiry, racism is not usually pursued by physical anthropologists. It may be surprising, therefore, that a discussion of racism is included in a physical anthropology textbook. Although racism, from a holistic and biosocial point of view, is a cultural phenomenon (based on attitudes, values, philosophies, economics, etc.), we believe it is not possible to divorce biological from cultural aspects in the study of humans.

Racism is the belief that one race is superior to another, and is associated with discriminatory acts and attitudes toward the "inferior" race(s). Belief in racism is usually based on the alleged inferior mental abilities of a people, and is often extended to the moral and ethical character of the "inferior" race. It is also assumed that mental abilities, ethics, and morals are hereditary.

The belief that a people is genetically inferior may be due to a number of factors, such as conquest, religion, family practices, moral and ethical systems, economic practices, and technology. Economic exploitation by imperialistic powers and competition for jobs, for example, have been suggested as reasons (or justification) for racist attitudes. European and American whites have frequently been singled out as practitioners of racism. However, there is evidence of racism in Japanese behavior toward the Eta (a lower social class in Japan) and the Ainu; in the historic attitude of the Chinese toward Mongols; and among the Bantu of South Africa toward the San (Bushmen).

From a physical anthropological point of view, racism is a cultural phenomenon that has no genetic basis. That one race is mentally or morally superior or inferior to another has yet to be demonstrated. Realistically, it is more likely that the basis of racism is rooted in economic, political, social, and psychological factors. Because it is cultural rather than genetic in character, it is difficult for physical anthropologists to address the problem. No matter what we say about the lack of evidence for mental inferiority or our doubts about the validity of IQ scores, racism continues in many areas of the world. People point to the "strange," "immoral," and "odious" behavior of other people, and assign this to genetic factors of the "inferior" race.

We end our discussion of race and racism with a comment from the geneticist Dobzhansky:

> The contention of racists is that cultural achievements of different races are so obviously unlike, their genetic capacities for achievement are just as different. It is, however, a matter of elementary genetics that the capacities of individuals, populations, or races cannot be discovered until they are given an equality of opportunity to demonstrate these capacities ... (Dobzhansky, 1961, p. 31).

◇ Summary

This chapter is essentially divided in two parts: (1) racial classification; and (2) race and behavior.

In the past 300 years, the trend in the study of race has moved from developing typologies based on climate and geography to the use of anthropometry to the application of evolutionary and genetic principles. At the present time, many anthropologists and other scientists believe the concept of race as a research tool is futile.

Race and behavior are discussed from the point of view of IQ tests and intelligence. Jensen and others, in recent years, have emphasized the notion that race and intelligence are correlated and support their position with IQ test results. The value of IQ tests as a measure of intelligence, without considering environmental factors, is questioned. The preponderant scientific view is that the IQ test is inadequate as a measuring instrument for intelligence, and the environment is so considerable a factor, that heredity cannot be accepted as the primary reason for racial variation in intelligence.

This controversy again serves to emphasize the dual nature of humans. Human heredity/evolution is meaningless without consideration of the relevant environmental factors, and human environments have for a long time been *cultural* ones.

Racism is discussed as a cultural phenomenon, allegedly rooted in genetics, a concept for which there is no scientific evidence.

◇ Questions for Review

1. What various criteria have been used for racial classification?
2. Why is racial typology no longer considered a useful concept in the study of human diversity?
3. Why are anthropologists dissatisfied with the concept of race?
4. Trace the definition of race from Virchow to Garn. What are the objections to the criteria used in the definitions?
5. What is a cline? What is the utility of a clinal distribution?
6. What is the value of multivariate population genetics?
7. What are the problems in correlating personality with race?
8. What are the objections to the use of IQ tests as measures of intelligence?
9. How may the environment affect IQ scores?
10. Discuss intelligence in terms of "nature or nurture."

Evolutionary Record

CONTENTS

◇ ISSUE   A Cosmic Calendar

How can we possibly conceive of the awesome stretch of time that has been flowing since, scientists inform us, our universe was first formed by the cosmic explosion called the Big Bang 15 billion years ago? In *Dragons of Eden*, Carl Sagan (1977) has condensed this prodigious period into one year he calls "The Cosmic Calendar." There are three parts to the calendar.

1. A pre-December calendar. A list of a few of the significant events in the history of the universe and earth in the first 14 billion years, represented by the 334 days from January 1 through November 30

2. A month of December calendar. Events of the last 1.25 billion years represented by the month of December

3. An evening of December 31 calendar. From 10:30 P.M. (the first humans) until midnight (now), which represents the last 2.5 million years

Examine the calendar and the place of *Homo sapiens* in a time perspective. Modern humans appeared a bit more than a minute before 12:00 midnight. You may feel humble before the immensity of time of our universe, or you may feel proud of the human achievements accomplished in such a brief speck of time.

Pre-December Dates

Big Bang	January 1
Origin of the Milky Way Galaxy	May 1
Origin of the solar system	September 9
Formation of the Earth	September 14
Origin of life on Earth	~September 25
Formation of the oldest rocks known on Earth	October 2
Date of oldest fossils (bacteria and blue-green algae)	October 9
Invention of sex (by microorganisms)	~November 1
Oldest fossil photosynthetic plants	November 12
Eukaryotes (first cells with nuclei) flourish	November 15

December 31

Origin of *Proconsul* and *Ramapithecus*, probable ancestors of apes and men [?]	~ 1:30 P.M.
First humans	~10:30 P.M.
Widespread use of stone tools	11:00 P.M.
Domestication of fire by Peking man*	11:46 P.M.
Beginning of most recent glacial period	11:56 P.M.
Seafarers settle Australia	11:58 P.M.
Extensive cave painting in Europe	11:59 P.M.
Invention of agriculture	11:59:20 P.M.
Neolithic civilization; first cities	11:59:35 P.M.
First dynasties in Sumer, Ebla and Egypt; development of astronomy	11:59:50 P.M.
Invention of the alphabet; Akkadian Empire	11:59:51 P.M.
Hammurabic legal codes in Babylon; Middle Kingdom in Egypt	11:59:52 P.M.
Bronze metallurgy; Mycenaean culture; Trojan War; Olmec culture; invention of the compass	11:59:53 P.M.
Iron metallurgy; First Assyrian Empire; Kingdom of Israel; founding of Carthage by Phoenicia	11:59:54 P.M.
Asokan India; Ch'in Dynasty China; Periclean Athens; birth of Buddha	11:59:55 P.M.
Euclidean geometry; Archimedean physics; Ptolemaic astronomy; Roman Empire; birth of Christ	11:59:56 P.M.
Zero and decimals invented in Indian arithmetic; Rome falls; Moslem conquests	11:59:57 P.M.
Mayan civilization; Sung Dynasty China; Byzantine empire; Mongol invasion; Crusades	11:59:58 P.M.
Renaissance in Europe; voyages of discovery from Europe and from Ming Dynasty China; emergence of the experimental method in science	11:59:59 P.M.
Widespread development of science and technology; emergence of a global culture; acquisition of the means for self-destruction of the human species; first steps in spacecraft planetary exploration and the search for extraterrestrial intelligence	Now: The first second of New Year's Day

*See page 485 for comment on Peking man's association with fire.

126

1 year	=	15,000,000,000 years	1 minute	=	29,000 years
1 month	=	1,250,000,000 years	1 second	=	475 years
1 day	=	41,000,000 years	1 billion years	=	24 days

DECEMBER   COSMIC CALENDAR

SUNDAY	MONDAY	TUESDAY	WEDNESDAY	THURSDAY	FRIDAY	SATURDAY
	1 Significant oxygen atmosphere begins to develop on Earth.	2	3	4	5 Extensive vulcanism and channel formation on Mars.	6
7	8	9	10	11	12	13
14	15	16	17 Precambrian ends. Paleozoic Era and Cambrian Period begin. Invertebrates flourish.	18 First Oceanic plankton. Trilobites flourish.	19 Ordovician Period. First fish, first vertebrates	20 Silurian Period. First vascular plants. Plants begin colonization of land.
21 Devonian Period begins. First insects. Animals begin colonization of land.	22 First amphibians. First winged insects.	23 Carboniferous Period. First trees. First reptiles	24 Permian Period begins. First dinosaurs.	25 Paleozoic Era ends. Mesozoic Era begins.	26 Triassic Period. First mammals.	27 Jurassic Period. First birds.
28 Cretaceous Period. First flowers. Dinosaurs become extinct.	29 Mesozoic Era ends. Cenozoic Era and Tertiary Period begins. First cetaceans. First primates.	30 Early evolution of frontal lobes in the brains of primates. First hominids. Giant mammals flourish.	31 End of the Pliocene epoch. Quaternary (Pleistocene and Holocene Period. First humans.			

SOURCE:

Sagan, Carl, *Dragons of Eden*, New York: Random House, Inc., 1977.

Calendar reprinted by permission of the author and the author's agents, Scott Meredith Literary Agency, Inc., 845 Third Avenue, New York, New York 10022.

◇ Introduction

In preceding chapters, we have discussed the mechanics of the evolutionary processes—adaptation and change through natural selection—according to concepts developed by Charles Darwin. We have also discussed the mechanisms of genetics that explain evolutionary changes between generations.

Having already dealt with the *process* of evolution, we shall now consider the *result* of that process. What actually occurred in the evolutionary record of life on earth? What were the adaptations made by living forms, and what physical changes took place in the various organisms that inhabit our globe? What evolutionary changes led to hominids, what other groups do hominids belong to, and what are the origins of these groups? We shall briefly trace invertebrate and vertebrate evolutionary history which, we believe, will help answer these questions, provide a deeper insight into evolutionary processes, and place humankind in a zoological and chronological perspective. (See Box 6-2, p. 136, Box 6-3, p. 137, and Box 6-5, p. 146, for additional views of the evolutionary processes.)

Since this book is about *Homo sapiens*, we can present only in outline the infinite number of events that occurred over the vast period of 3 billion years (Gurin, 1980), the time of life on earth. Let us then begin with the place of humans in evolutionary history.

◇ The Human Place in the Animal Kingdom

The first chapter emphasized that we are both animals and human beings. We intend, throughout the text, to discuss the relationship between both these aspects of humankind, but since we wish to trace our antecedents, we will concern ourselves first with *Homo sapiens*, the organic being.

Humans are zoologically classified as animals because they possess animal characteristics, such as:

1. Obtaining food from other organisms, not through photosynthesis
2. Mobility; most animals are mobile and can move about in one way or another at some stage of life
3. Structure and organization; tissue and organ differentiation in animals is usually more complex than in plants. Individual plant cells usually have rigid walls; animal cells usually do not
4. Nerves and muscles; most animals have nerves and muscles, which are absent in plants

This list, although incomplete, places humans in the Animal Kingdom. As multicelled animals within the Animal Kingdom, we belong to the Metazoa, a subdivision classified into more than twenty major groups called *phyla* (*sing*, phylum).

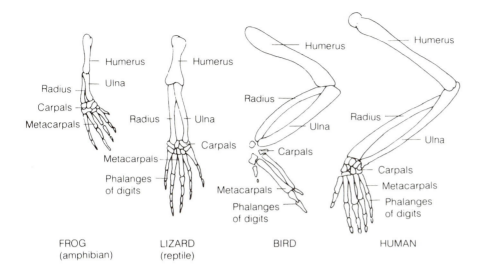

FROG
(amphibian)

LIZARD
(reptile)

BIRD

HUMAN

Figure 6-1 Homologies. The similarities in the bones of these air-breathing animals can be most easily explained by descent from a common ancestor.

TAXONOMY

Before going further it may be useful to discuss the basis of animal classification.

Organisms are classified on the basis of evolutionary relationships, that is, the degree one group is related to another through descent from a common ancestor. The extent of the relationship is determined mainly by structural similarities based on common descent, called *homologies*. Thus, the bones of the forelimb of air-breathing vertebrates are so similar (Fig. 6-1) in arrangement and number that the simplest and best explanation for the remarkable resemblances—homologies—is that all four kinds of air-breathing vertebrates ultimately derived their forelimb from a common ancestor.

Structures that are *functionally* similar, but without genetic affinity—not derived from a common ancestor—are *analogous*. The wing of a butterfly and the wing of a bird are analogous; they perform a similar function but are without genetic affinity (Fig. 6-2).

Hominids (the group to which humans belong), prosimians, monkeys, and apes are all classified as primates. Why? When the nervous system (especially the brain), teeth, limbs, digits, and other physical traits of these animals are examined, it becomes clear they share an ancestor in common. The homologies bring these animals into one group just as the homologies of lions, tigers, leopards, and the domestic cat bring these together into one group that evolved from a common ancestor.

The system of classification based on homologies is usually attributed to Linnaeus, although there were classificatory schemes before his. Linnaeus, it will be recalled, successfully instituted the binomial system of naming animals using two terms, genus and species. Thus, we are known as *Homo sapiens*, the domestic cat as *Felis domesticus*, the lion as *Panthera leo*, and the gorilla as *Gorilla gorilla*.

All people in the world today belong to one species, *Homo sapiens*, a form that has existed for at least the past 100,000 years.

Figure 6-3 is a classification chart arranged according to evolutionary

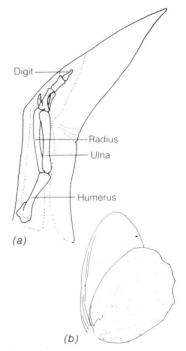

(a)

(b)

Figure 6-2 Analogies. The wings of these animals perform the same function, but their structure is quite different. Similar structure may be traced to a common ancestor; similar function represents a similar adaptive response, not necessarily a common ancestor. (a) Structure of bird wing; (b) butterfly wing.

◇ Box 6-1   Vocabulary

Analogous (ah-nal'-o-gus)   Similar in function or appearance but not in origin or development.

Homologous (hom-ol'-o-gus)   Structures that are similar in form (or function) in two or more groups of organisms related through descent from a common ancestor.

Phylum (fy'-lum; pl. phyla)   A primary division of the Animal (or Plant) Kingdom. We belong to Phylum Chordata.

Subphylum   A major division of a phylum, such as Vertebrata.

Class   A subdivision of subphylum.

Superfamily   A group of closely related families.

Family   Members of a family usually inhabit a similar environment; a category which includes genera and species.

Genus (jee'-nus; pl. genera)   A category that groups together closely related species usually inhabiting similar ecological niches.

Species (spee'shies; sing. *and* pl.)   A reproductive community; an interbreeding population (or populations) reproductively isolated from other interbreeding populations.

Dorsal (dor'-sull)   Back, pertaining to the back of an animal.

Ventral (ven'-trull)   Toward the belly; the front of an organism (as in humans) or the undersurface of an animal that does not stand erect (as a dog).

Endoskeleton (en'-doe-skeleton)   An internal bony skeleton, characteristic of vertebrates.

Exoskeleton (ex'-o-skeleton)   A hard, supporting external covering, characteristic of many invertebrates such as ants and lobsters.

Taxonomy   The theoretical study of classification, including its bases, principles, procedures, and rules (Simpson, 1961, p. 11).

Metazoa
meta: beyond
zoion: animal
Multicellular animals. A major division of the Animal Kingdom.

Kingdom
  Phylum
    Class
      Order
        Family
          Genus
            Species

The Linnaean hierarchy of zoological classification. Indentation indicates decreasing inclusiveness of the various levels (Simpson, 1961).

relationships. Observe in both Figure 6-3 and the chart in Figure 6-3a that, the closer the animals resemble one another (the more homologies they share), the smaller the group to which they are assigned. The two species (in Fig. 6-3a) *H. sapiens* and *H. erectus* belong to the genus *Homo* because they resemble each other more than either of them resembles the other three hominid species. *A. afarensis*, *A. africanus*, and *A. robustus*, which are assigned to the genus *Australopithecus*. *Homo* and *Australopithecus* resemble each other more than either one resembles apes and are, therefore, placed in the family Hominidae, and apes in Pongidae. Apes and humans resemble each other more than either resembles monkeys and are, therefore, placed in the superfamily Hominoidea, and so forth.

In summary, the more homologies two groups share, usually the more recent their descent from a common ancestor, the closer their evolutionary relationship, and the closer their position on the taxonomic chart.

To place hominids in their proper perspective in nature and to help understand human evolution, we shall glance very briefly at the evolutionary history of the Metazoa.

METAZOA

Metazoa are composed of a number of phyla, most of which are invertebrates, animals lacking a bony backbone. Invertebrates range in organization from relatively simple structures, such as sponges, to relatively complex structures,

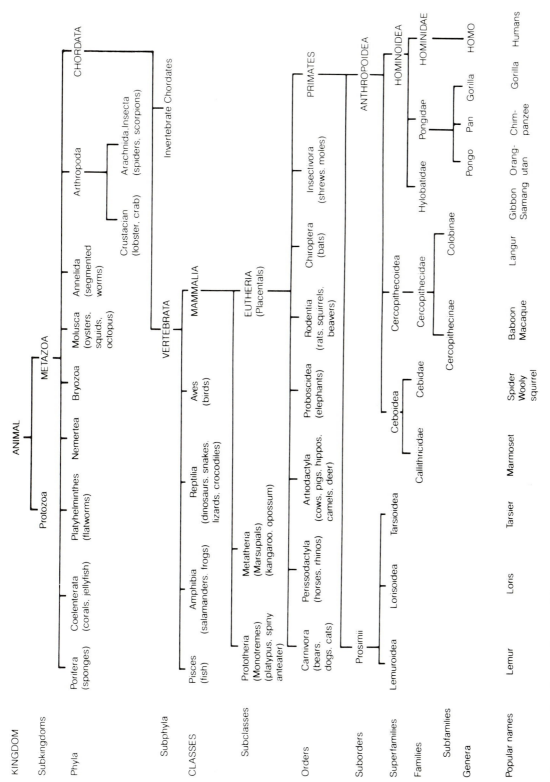

Figure 6-3 Classification chart. Modified from Linnaeus. All animals are placed in certain categories based on structural similarities. Those categories connected by a horizontal line share a common ancestor (*Pongo, Pan,* and *Gorilla,* for example).

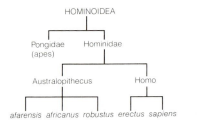

Figure 6-3a Classification of Hominoidea.

such as chordates. Chordates are important to humans because our sub-phylum, Vertebrata, belongs to this category.

Vertebrates, the most numerous of the chordates, are different in certain ways from all other Metazoa. Their primary structural feature, a vertebral column, distinguishes them from invertebrates and has given them their name. Since we belong to this group, we shall discuss vertebrates later in the chapter.

With this short discussion of the human place in nature concluded, we shall return our attention to the time dimension of evolution.

◇ Early Evolutionary History

We reviewed earlier in the chapter the place of humans in nature. We now turn to their place in the time dimension of evolution. To do this, we shall briefly review the chronology of life on earth with special reference to vertebrates. Our review will follow the outline in the Geologic Time Scale (Figs. 6-4 and 6-13). The student is encouraged to refer frequently to the Time Scale as

Figure 6-4 Geologic Time Scale. (For Cenozoic era see p. 139.

Era	Period	Time m.y.a*	Events
		65	ROCKY MOUNTAIN REVOLUTION
MESOZOIC	Cretaceous		Appearance of placental and marsupial mammals. Dinosaurs peak and become extinct. First modern birds.
		136	
	Jurassic		Great age of dinosaurs— flying and swimming dinosaurs. First toothed birds.
		190	
	Triassic		Reptiles dominant. First dinosaurs. Egg-laying mammals.
		225	
			APPALACHIAN REVOLUTION
PALEOZOIC	Permian		Reptilian radiation. Mammal-like reptiles. Many old forms die out.
		280	
	Carbon-iferous		First reptiles. Radiation of amphibia. Modern insects evolve.
		345	
	Devonian		Age of fish. Amphibians—first air-breathing vertebrates. First forests.
		395	
	Silurian		Jawed fishes appear. First air-breathing animal—scorpionlike aurypterid. Definite land plants.
		430	
	Ordovi-cian		First fishes. Trilobites still abundant. Graptolites and corals becoming plentiful. Possible land plants.
		500	
	Cambrian		Trilobites abundant, also brachiopods, jellyfish, worms, and other invertebrates.
		570	
PRE-CAMBRIAN			Various marine protozoa, mainly algae. Toward close of era, some evidence of invertebrates.

*Million years ago.

we follow the evolutionary sequence of life on earth. (See Appendix A for the complete Time Scale.)

It is possible that the earliest evidence of life comes from Greenland sedimentary rock, perhaps 3.8 billion years old (Gurin, 1980). The earliest known structurally preserved organisms may be stromatolites found near the old mining town of North Pole, Australia. Also found in the North Pole area are "fossils—a diverse collection of long, filamentous chains of cells—[that] resemble some modern bacteria, including species that are capable of performing photosynthesis" (Gurin, 1980, p. 45). This material from North Pole has been reliably dated at 3.5 billion years. This fossil material belongs to the immense segment of geologic time called the Precambrian, which goes back to the beginning of life and ends about 600 m.y.a., with the beginning of the Paleozoic era.

Abundant fossil evidence for the Precambrian is lacking, and what does exist points to different kinds of algae as the dominant life form. Toward the end of the Precambrian, there is evidence of plants, most of which are of unknown affinity, and burrows and trails of wormlike animals. It is not until the Cambrian (the first period of the Paleozoic) is reached that the rocks contain enough fossils to give a fuller view of the life forms in existence at that time.

◇ Paleozoic Era (570–225 m.y.a.)

Beginning with the Paleozoic era, fossils become more abundant and a much fuller account of life is available. During the 345 million years of the Paleozoic, evidence for members of every phylum of animals is present. Evolution continues primarily in water, but land plants appear toward the middle, and land animals toward the end, of the era. Invertebrate fossil evidence appears in the very first period and becomes a dominant form. Vertebrates evolve fairly early to become very successful aquatic animals and, toward the end of the Paleozoic, invade land habitats as well in the form of amphibians and reptiles.

The southern continents—South America, Africa, Antarctica, Australia, and India—were all closely associated into one mass known as *Gondwanaland*. The northern continents—North America, Greeland, Europe, and Asia—were known as *Laurasia*. As the Paleozoic continued, these two great land masses united during the Carboniferous and Permian periods to form an enormous land mass known as *Pangea*.

FISH

Seventy million years after the beginning of the Paleozoic, during the Ordovician, jawless fishes—**Ostracoderms**—appeared (Romer, 1959). By the Devonian (395–345 m.y.a.) fish had multiplied so rapidly in numbers and species that they became the dominant marine animal; thus, we give the name *Age of Fish* to this period.

Not as numerous or successful as the main branch of bony fish (ray-fins) were the lobe-fins, which had diverged from the others by the middle Devonian

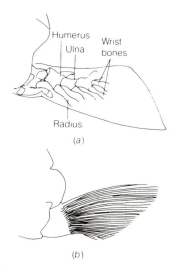

Figure 6-5 (*a*) Lobe-fin. The fin is fleshy and contains a bone structure similar to vertebrates. (*b*) Ray-fin. The fin is composed of a web of skin supported by hornlike rays.

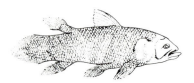

Figure 6-6   Crossopterygian. The fish that made the transition to amphibians. Long thought to be extinct. A modern survivor is the coelacanth.

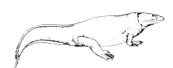

Figure 6-7   Early amphibian and lobe-finned fish. These drawings of an early amphibian and a lobe-fin illustrate the similarities of the two forms. Not a great deal of change was required to transform the fish to the air-breathing amphibian.

and went (or swam) their own way. Of importance to vertebrate evolution is the structure of their fins, which have a fleshy lobe containing bones remarkably similar to those of land vertebrates. They also possess internal nostrils (absent in ray-fins) probably useful for breathing air.

With fins containing a bony structure, nostrils, and lungs for air breathing, the lobe-finned **crossopterygians** were able to adapt to the drought conditions of the Devonian. As pools of water dried up, these fish could move across land—on their fleshy, bony fins—and, breathing air, seek a pool of water that had not yet become parched (Romer, 1959, p. 94). From this group of fish thus arose the amphibians.

AMPHIBIANS

The explosive radiation of fish in the Devonian coupled with drought conditions of that period led crossopterygians toward an amphibian body plan allowing them, as it were, to have their cake and eat it. On the one hand, they are able to spend much of their time in water; in fact, the early stages of growth have to be aquatic. On the other hand, they are able to adapt, to a certain extent, to life on land. They are, so to speak, neither fish nor land animals, but a "compromise" of both.

In terms of numbers of individuals and species, the amphibians cannot be considered as successful as other vertebrate classes. Typical amphibians are still chained to water, to which they must periodically return. As paleontologist Romer (1959, p. 101) has said: "It is, in many respects, little more than a peculiar type of fish which is capable of walking on land."

As vertebrate evolution continued, amphibians diverged into many different forms. From one of these amphibian forms another milestone in vertebrate evolution was reached with the rise of reptiles, the first true land vertebrates. These are known as *stem reptiles*, ancestors of the huge ruling reptiles of the Mesozoic and of the line leading to mammals.

Figure 6-8   Pangea. Continents at the end of the Paleozoic (*a*) and during much of the Mesozoic (*b*).

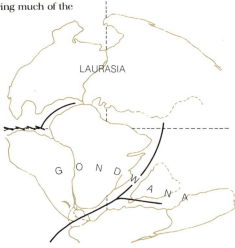

(a)

(b)

REPTILES

The reptilian strategy of adaptation was more successful than the amphibian. Developing a more efficient limb structure, an improved heart, and (perhaps most important) a self-contained, self-protected, and self-feeding egg—the *amniote* egg (Fig. 6-9)—reptiles filled many of the terrestrial econiches.

One of the results of reptilian radiation was a reptilelike mammalian form (or a mammal-like reptilian form) called *therapsids*. With a bony palate separating the oral and nasal cavities, teeth differentiated into **incisors**, **canines**, and **cheek teeth** (the latter cusped instead of cone-shaped) and limbs arranged in a fore-and-aft position under the body (see Fig. 6-10), therapsids were "on their way" to becoming mammals and are, in fact, considered to be the ancestors of mammals.

Therapsids appeared toward the end of the Paleozoic, and in the next era, the Mesozoic, reptiles and mammals continued to evolve.

◇ Mesozoic Era (225–65 m.y.a.)

Climatic conditions of the Mesozoic were not as extreme as they had been during the late Paleozoic. The great glaciers of the Permian Ice Age had disappeared, erosion had reduced many mountain ranges, and mountain building produced others. The continents, which had been joined at the end of the Permian, began to drift apart and when the Mesozoic ended, the position of the continents had approached their present locations.

In the early Mesozoic, reptiles became the dominant land animal and reigned supreme for the remainder of the era, known as the *Age of Reptiles*. Reptilian radiation (see Box 6-2) proceeded at a tremendous rate and the most well known of all reptiles—the dinosaurs—appeared in the Triassic. Not only did dinosaurs cover much of the earth, they also took to the air and water.

Dinosaurs reached their peak in the Cretaceous, but the days of these dominant beasts were numbered, and when the Cretaceous (and Mesozoic) came to a close, the enormous creatures that ruled the earth for about 150

Crossopterygians
krosso: *fringe*
pteryg: *fins*

Incisors
Front teeth used for cutting and nipping.

Canines
Usually long and pointed teeth used for piercing and grasping.

Cheek teeth
Premolars and molars used for chewing and grinding.

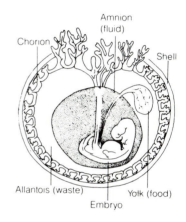

Amniote Egg

Figure 6-9 Amniote egg. Generalized diagram of the amniote egg. The embryo is surrounded by the liquid-filled amniotic chamber. The yolk sac contains food, and within the allantois enclosure (which also serves as a waste receptacle), oxygen-carbon dioxide exchange takes place.

Figure 6-10 Therapsid. Mammal-like reptiles or reptilelike mammals. Mammalian characteristics include heterodont teeth, at least some chewing instead of swallowing whole, probably a coat of hair, and perhaps incipient milk glands. The limbs are more mammalian than reptilian. (Artist's rendition.)

◇ Box 6-2   Evolutionary Processes

Adaptive Radiation   The potential capacity of an organism to multiply is practically unlimited; its ability to increase its numbers, however, is regulated largely by the available resources of food, shelter, and space. As the size of a population increases, its food, shelter, and space decrease, and the environment will ultimately prove inadequate. Depleted resources engender pressures that will very likely drive some members of the population to seek an environment where competition is considerably reduced and the opportunity for survival and reproductive success increased. This evolutionary tendency to exploit unoccupied habitats may eventually produce an abundance of diverse species.

An instructive example of the evolutionary process known as *adaptive radiation* may be seen in the divergence of the stem reptiles to the profusion of different forms of the late Paleozoic, and especially the Mesozoic. It is a process that has taken place many times in evolutionary history when a new form of life rapidly takes advantage, so to speak, of the many now available ecological niches.

The principle of evolution illustrated by adaptive radiation is fairly simple, but important. It may be stated thus: When a new form arises, it will diverge into as many variations as two factors allow—(1) its adaptive potential and (2) the adaptive opportunities of the available zones.

In the case of reptiles, there was little divergence in the very early stages of evolution, when the ancestral type was little more than one among a variety of amphibian water-dwellers. A more efficient kind of egg had already developed and, although it had great adaptive potential, there were few zones to invade. However, once reptiles became fully terrestrial, there was a sudden opening of available zones—ecological niches—accessible to the adaptive potential of the reptilian evolutionary grade.

This new kind of egg provided the primary adaptive ingredient of the reptilian form that freed reptiles from attachment to water; strengthened limbs and skeleton for locomotion on land followed. The adaptive zones for reptiles were not limitless; nevertheless, continents were now open to them with no serious competition from any other animal. The reptiles moved into the many different econiches on land (and to some extent in the air and sea), and as they adapted to these areas, diversified into a large number of species. This spectacular radiation burst with such evolutionary rapidity, it may well be termed an adaptive explosion.

Generalized and Specialized   Another aspect of evolution closely related to that of adaptive radiation involves the transition from *generalized* to *specialized characteristics*. These two terms refer to the adaptive potential of a particular trait: one that is adapted for many functions is termed generalized whereas a trait that is limited to a narrow set of ecological functions is called specialized.

For example, a generalized mammalian limb has five fairly flexible digits adapted for many possible functions (grasping, weight support, digging). In this respect, our hands are still quite generalized. On the other hand (or foot), there have been many structural modifications in our feet suited for the ecologically specialized function of stable weight support.

These terms are also sometimes used when speaking of the adaptive potential of whole organisms. For example, the aye-aye (a curious primate living in Madagascar) is a highly specialized animal structurally adapted in its dentition for an ecologically narrow rodent/woodpecker-like niche—digging out insect larvae with prominent incisors.

The notion of adaptive potential is a relative judgment and can estimate only crudely the likelihood of one form evolving into another form or forms. Adaptive radiation is a related concept, for only a generalized ancestor can provide the flexible evolutionary basis for such rapid diversification. Only a generalized organism with potential for adaptation into varied ecological niches can lead to all the later diversification and specialization of forms into particular ecological niches.

◇ Box 6-3　Superior/Inferior; Primitive/Derived

Arthropods (see p. 131) illustrate an important point in understanding the process of evolution. It is not possible to rank organisms as better or worse. Or, if we do, our criteria must be stated. One criterion is biological success, which may be said to depend on the number of species, the number of individuals, the number of adaptations to different kinds of environments and habitats, and duration of the phylum. On all these counts, arthropods are superior to vertebrates. Arthropods are

> *from ten to a hundred times more numerous than vertebrates in species, incomparably more abundant in individuals, and divergently adapted to an even wider range of environments and habits. They easily hold their own against all the attacks of man and of other animals* (Simpson et al., 1957, p. 570).

Evolution is not the process of superior animals triumphing over inferior ones but is, rather, a series of alternative adaptive strategies that have arisen in response to inconstant environments.

In this connection it may be well to add two more terms often used in discussing evolution: *primitive* and *derived*. The same point made with the terms superior/inferior may be applied here if primitive is interpreted as somehow inferior to derived. There are no backward or advanced animals, only animals that have adapted, or extinct forms that have not. Nor can modern forms be considered advanced over fossil forms. Living species have adapted to present environmental conditions; fossil species to the environments of their day.

Sometimes the word "primitive" is used for an early form from which later (called "derived") forms have arisen. Even when terms are carefully defined in this way, their use can be misleading and confusing.

million years ended their reign. Changing geographic and climatic conditions, competition from the newly evolving mammals, plus perhaps other unknown factors (either singly or in combination) may have caused their demise. No one really knows. (See Box 6-4.)

MAMMALS

Mesozoic mammals were small animals, about the size of mice, which they resembled in appearance. Since they were so small, and many of the dinosaurs so large, the primitive mammals remained inconspicuous by dwelling

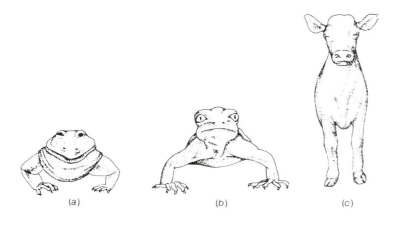

(a)　　　　(b)　　　　(c)

Figure 6-11 Evolution of body support in land vertebrates. The figures illustrate changes in land vertebrate limbs: (a) amphibian limbs project laterally from the body; (b) reptiles, with stronger pectoral and pelvic girdles, are more upright in an intermediate position; (c) in mammals, the legs project straight down.

in wooded or bushy areas and may have been **arboreal**. They are not what we would consider to be very noble creatures to have as ancestors. Romer (1959) suggests the Mesozoic may be seen as a training period during which mammalian characters were being perfected and wits sharpened. The mammalian radiation of the Cenozoic (65 m.y.a. to present) saw the rise of the ancestors of all modern mammals. Mammals replaced reptiles as the dominant terrestrial vertebrate, a position they still retain.

◇ Cenozoic Era (65 m.y.a. to present)

The modern world as we know it—geologically and geographically—assumed its present configuration during the Cenozoic era. Major continental drifting slowed considerably, and interior seas on most continents were reduced. This alteration of the topography may explain the diversity of climates, patterns of seasons, water and wind currents, and the eventual onset of the Pleistocene Ice Ages. We may view life in the Cenozoic as a process of adaptation to the climatic extremes and topographic diversity, a situation for which mammals are well equipped.

The Cenozoic is divided into two periods, the **Tertiary** (about 63 million years' duration) and the **Quaternary**, from about 1.8 m.y.a. up to and including the present. Because so much evidence of living forms is available from the Cenozoic, the two periods are further subdivided into epochs. The five epochs of the Tertiary are: Paleocene, Eocene, Oligocene, Miocene, and Pliocene. The Quaternary, the final period of the Cenozoic, is divided into two epochs: the Pleistocene, well known for its *ice ages*, and the present epoch, the Holocene, which begins with the melting of the last glaciation.

Figure 6-12   Mesozoic mammal. A speculative reconstruction of what a Mesozoic mammal might have looked like. Probably no bigger than a kitten, but with mammalian teeth, these animals were capable of attacking small lizards.

MAMMALS

Conditions in the Cenozoic were nearly ideal for mammals. They radiated so rapidly and filled the available econiches so well that the Cenozoic is known as the *Age of Mammals.*

Era	Period	Epoch	Time Years ago	Glacial Sequence Scandinavian	Alpine
CENOZOIC	QUATERNARY	HOLOCENE	10,000		
		UPPER PLEISTOCENE	40,000 75,000	WEICHSEL (glacial)	WÜRM
			100,000	EEMIAN	RISS WÜRM
			125,000		
		MIDDLE PLEISTOCENE	175,000	Cold phase	RISS
			225,000	Warm phase	
			265,000	SAALE (glacial)	
			300,000	Warm phase	MINDEL RISS
				ELSTER (glacial)	MINDEL
			380,000	HOLSTEIN	
			400,000	ELSTER glacial	
			430,000	CROMERIAN	GÜNZ- MINDEL
			500,000	MENAPIAN glacial	GÜNZ
		LOWER PLEISTOCENE	750,000 1.8 million	Uncertain Geological Sequences	
	TERTIARY	Pliocene	5 million	Hominids (Australopithecines) present	
		Miocene	25 million	Hominoidea (apelike creatures) Dryopithecines flourish . . . Probable appearance of hominids	
		Oligocene	35 million	Anthropoidea and appearance of Hominoidea	
		Eocene	53 million	Prosimians flourish; possible appearance of Anthropoidea	
		Paleocene	65 million	Appearance of Prosimii	

Figure 6-13 Geologic Time Scale: Cenozoic.

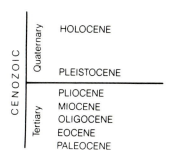

Figure 6-14 The Cenozoic. The most recent era. The two epochs, Tertiary and Quaternary, and their divisions are shown. (The Precambrian, Paleozoic, and Mesozoic are shown on p. 132.)

◇ Box 6-4   Extinction

"The theories that have been propounded (to explain the extinction of dinosaurs) are legion, and one cannot do better than quote Jepsen on this topic: 'Authors, with varying competence, have suggested that the dinosaurs disappeared because the climate deteriorated (became suddenly or slowly too hot or cold or dry or wet), or that the diet did (with too much food or not enough of such substances as fern oil; from poisons in water or plants or ingested minerals; the bankruptcy of calcium or other necessary elements). Other writers have put the blame on disease, parasites, wars, anatomical or metabolic disorders (slipped vertebral discs, malfunctions or imbalance of hormone or endocrine systems, dwindling brain and consequent stupidity, heat sterilization), racial old age, evolutionary drift into senescent overspecialization, changes in the pressure or composition of the atmosphere, poison gases, volcanic dust, excessive oxygen from plants, meteorites, comets, gene pool drainage by little mammalian egg-eaters, overkill capacity by predators, fluctuation of gravitational constants, development of psychotic suicidal factors, entropy, cosmic radiation, shift of Earth's rotational poles, floods, extraction of the moon from the Pacific Basin, drainage of swamp and lake environments, sunspots, God's will, mountain building, raids by little green hunters in flying saucers, lack of even standing room in Noah's Ark, and palaeoweltschmertz'" (Jepsen, in Halstead, 1968, pp. 146–147).

Update   In 1980, four University of California, Berkeley, scientists proposed an extraterrestrial cause for the extinction of many species of plants and animals, including dinosaurs, at the end of the Cretaceous.

They suggested that an asteroid or comet struck the earth, forming an enormous crater over 100 miles across. Dust ejected from the crater reached the stratosphere and then spread around the earth. This effectively blocked sunlight from reaching the earth's surface for about two and a half years, suppressing photosynthesis. Most food chains collapsed and extinctions resulted.

The evidence for, and acceptance of, this explanation have increased considerably in the past several years, although alternative suggestions are still presented.

SOURCES:
Alvarez, Luis W., Walter Alvarez, Frank Asaro, Helen V. Michel. "Extraterrestrial Cause for the Cretaceous-Tertiary Extinction," *Science*, 208:1095–1108, June 6, 1980.

Kerr, Richard A., "Asteroid Theory of Extinctions Strengthened," *Science*, 210:514–517, October 31, 1980.

Placental Mammalian Characters   Campbell (1974, p. 39ff) has proposed that mammalian evolution was based on a single adaptive development: The ability for constant lively activity; that is, "the maintenance of a steady level of activity in the face of basic changes in the external environment." The constant and lively activity, Campbell further points out, was made possible by "the evolution of only four great complexes, all of a homeostatic nature": homoiothermy, mastication, improved reproductive efficiency, and new ways of determining behavior. (The following discussion of these complexes is summarized from Campbell, 1974.)

Homoiothermy   A constant and appropriate body temperature regardless of external conditions is a decided advantage for an active animal. **Homoiothermy** may have evolved among mammal-like reptiles as early as the Permian and very probably was found later among at least some dinosaurs. It is difficult to know from fossil bones whether the warm-bloodedness of these forms was the same as that of mammals today. It would appear, however, that homoiothermy, as a basic characteristic, gave mammals the constant energy necessary for animals adapting to a highly active way of life. In addition, for the first time, vast forests of the temperate zone became available for exploitation by a vertebrate form.

Homoiothermy is so basic to the mammalian way of life that a number of physiological and behavioral adjustments have been developed to maintain a constant body temperature. To lower body temperature, mammals may perform one or more of the following activities: spread their limbs, lay their hair or fur flat against the skin, increase their respiration rate, dilate their capillaries, or sweat. To raise body temperature, they may curl into a ball, raise their hair/fur layer, constrict their capillaries, eat (metabolic action generates body heat), or shiver.

Mastication and Heterodontism   Except for extinct herbivorous forms, reptile teeth all have the same (**homodont**) structure. They curve inward with the jaw serving as a trap. Prey once caught cannot escape and is eaten whole without chewing. On the other hand, the mammalian jaw and **heterodont** dentition exploit various kinds of food more effectively. Different kinds of teeth—incisors, canines, premolars, and molars—evolved especially for trapping, nipping, chewing, cutting, crushing, and grinding, and the jaw was modified to make this dental activity possible. Mastication enables mammals to obtain more nutritive value from a wider variety of food by breaking up nuts, seeds, plant material, and meat, among other edibles. This is important to active homoiothermic animals, since they require more food intake.

Reproductive Efficiency   Reptiles changed the external method of amphibian fertilization by introducing internal fertilization. They lay eggs—**oviparity**—which, although not as vulnerable as amphibian eggs, are still easy prey for small carnivores.

Mammals evolved a new reproductive system. They retain copulation and internal fertilization, but the egg is kept within the mother, where it is protected and nourished until it achieves quite an advanced stage of growth. Birth is live—**viviparity**—and, because of the newborn's advanced stage, young mammals suffer fewer casualties than young reptiles.

Nevertheless, most mammalian young are born helpless although some, such as horses, cattle, and hares, are active within minutes or hours of birth. All newborn mammals, however, are unable to feed themselves and must be fed by special milk glands (mammae—modified sweat glands) of the mother. Suckling requires the young to remain close to the mother, a practice serving several functions. The young are fed, protected, and, through imitation, learn the behavior adaptive for their species.

Determinants of Behavior   In most animals activity and learning are motivated by the primary drives of hunger, sex, and self-preservation. Mammals developed a new determinant that does not satisfy these immediate needs; it is a drive, a curiosity, to investigate and explore the environment and has been termed *effectance motivation*, usually called "mammalian play." This motivation can be seen in the playful activity of young mammals, the only animals that so behave. Actually, this apparent playful activity is a means of

Homoiothermy
Homo: same
therm: heat
Same temperature.

Homodontism
homo: same
dont: teeth

Heterodontism
hetero: different
dont: teeth

Oviparity
ovum: egg
parere: to bear

Viviparity
vivus: alive
parere: to bear

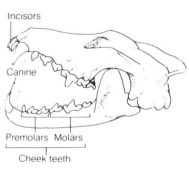

Figure 6-15   Reptilian and mammalian teeth.

Table 6-1   Mammalian Innovations (Distinguishing Mammals from Reptiles)*

Innovations	Complexes
Warm blood	Homoiothermy
Hair/fur	
Sweat glands	
Heterodontism	Mastication and heterodontism
Strong jaw	
Viviparity	Reproductive efficiency
Suckling	
Mammalian play	Effectance motivation

*There is some evidence that homoiothermy, fur, and viviparity are more common than once believed.

discovering and learning to interact with the environment. Effectance motivation evolved to provide the data input to maintain and supply a larger and more complex brain (Fig. 6-16) than had ever been known before in the organic world.

The four complexes summarized above explain a number of innovations that distinguish mammals from their reptilian ancestors: warm blood,* hair/fur, sweat glands, heterodontism, a stronger jaw, viviparity, suckling, and mammalian play.

A few more important distinguishing characteristics should be noted: an internal ear drum with an external ear flap; a four-chambered heart that generates greater energy; and more efficient limbs for improved locomotion.

*As noted earlier, some reptiles may have been warm-blooded.

Figure 6-16   Human brain. In humans the gray matter (cerebral cortex) is highly convoluted, which provides a greater surface for nerve connections and for eight billion brain cells. The cerebral cortex has also greatly expanded to cover most of the brain.

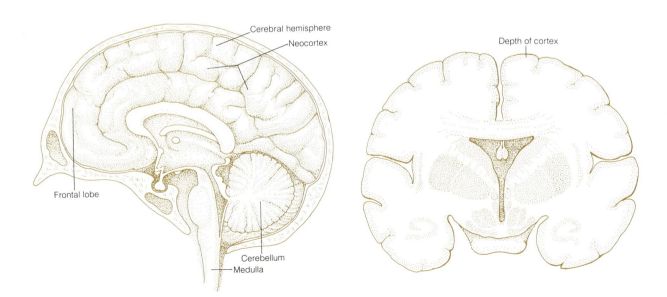

Cerebral hemisphere
Neocortex
Depth of cortex
Frontal lobe
Cerebellum
Medulla

MAMMALIAN SUBCLASSES

At the present time, placental mammals comprise most of the mammalian class; however, there still survive a few monotremes (egg-laying mammals) and marsupials (pouched mammals).

Monotremes (Prototheria)   Living in the Australasian region of Australia and New Guinea are two surviving highly specialized egg-laying mammals—the duck-billed platypus and the spiny anteater.

The platypus, a semiaquatic animal about two feet long, with a beaverlike tail, a poison barb on the heel of males, and webbed toes for swimming, lives in streams and in burrows along the banks. Instead of teeth, it has developed a ducklike bill used for burrowing in the mud in search of worms and grubs. The anteater is protected by a coat of sharp spines (recalling the porcupine), a spur on the hind legs, and the jaws—also without teeth—are formed into a long, tubular snout used for probing anthills.

Monotremes are classified as mammals since the young are nursed from teatless mammary glands. However, they are very primitive mammals and retain a number of reptilian characters. They lay eggs, have but one opening for elimination, mating, and birth (hence the term **monotreme**) and display various other reptilian traits in the shoulder girdle, skull, and vertebral column. Some authorities consider monotremes as surviving mammallike reptiles.

Marsupials (Metatheria)   At the present time, **marsupials** are found only in Australia and the New World (opossums) although they were once more widely distributed in North America, South America, and Europe. Their extermination can be laid at the hands (or claws and teeth) of the brainier placental mammals whenever these two mammals have competed. Pouched animals survived in Australia because placental mammals never reached that continent before its separation from other land masses. Marsupials entered

Monotreme
mono: one
treme: a hole

Marsupium
Pouch; pouched animals such as the kangaroo, koala, opossum.

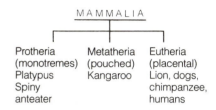

Figure 6-17   Mammalian classification chart.

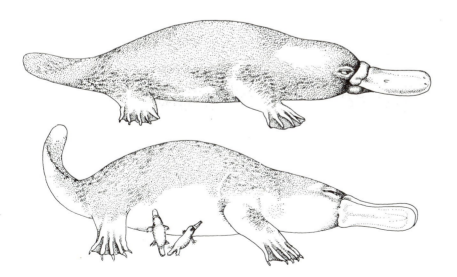

Figure 6-18   The duck-billed platypus. Offspring licking milk from mother's fur.

Figure 6-19   Spiny anteater, a monotreme.

Figure 6-20   Wallaby with infant in pouch, marsupials.

Australia before its separation and remained isolated, except for bats, which probably flew in early, and rodents, which island-hopped in. The marsupials, therefore, were protected from the onslaught of the more developed Cenozoic placental mammals.

Most South American marsupials were destroyed by placentals invading that continent at the end of the Tertiary when North and South America were joined. Only the opossums survive today.

Marsupials bear their young alive as a tiny embryo after a short gestation period. These tiny infants work their way into their mother's pouch by a swimming motion of the forelimbs over a pathway of dampened mother's hair. Once in the pouch they remain attached to nipples that line the pouch and are fed by the mother literally pumping milk into them. When they are old enough to move around, they live in and out of the pouch until they are surprisingly large.

Aside from the method of reproduction, marsupials differ from placentals in brain size and other details of the skull. Teeth are also somewhat different from those of placental mammals, but the post-cranial skeleton is generally comparable.

Placental Mammals (Eutheria)   One of the outstanding features of placental mammals (**Eutheria**) is the placenta, which gives the subclass its name. This disclike organ furnishes oxygen and nutrients from mother to developing embryo and gets rid of waste products as well. Young are born alive, as are marsupials, but in a much more advanced stage of development.

Among the many other differences distinguishing marsupials and placentals, two stand out. First, placentals possess an expanded brain, which has been suggested as the most important reason for their superiority over the pouched mammals. It may be of interest to briefly review this development.

The evolutionary history of the brain, center of the nervous system, reflects a steady growth in size and complexity as we move from fish to mammals (Fig. 6-21). The diversification of vertebrates depends largely upon the operation of the central nervous system, and the relative success of mammals

Figure 6-21   Lateral view of brain. The illustration shows the increase in the cerebral cortex of the brain. The cerebral cortex integrates sensory information and selects responses.

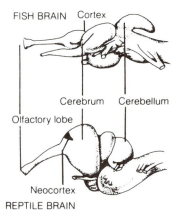

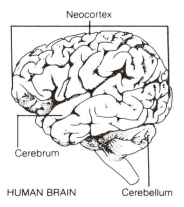

over reptiles (and perhaps reptiles over amphibians) may be largely due to greater brain efficiency.

Fish reflect the basic vertebrate brain, which is composed of three sections: forebrain, midbrain, and hindbrain. The forebrain includes the **olfactory** lobes and the cerebrum; the midbrain, the largest section in fish and the center of control and coordination, is associated mainly with the optic lobe; the hindbrain combines the **cerebellum** and medulla oblongata which act as message center and source of some autonomic and reflex actions.

The trend in brain evolution has been toward an increase in the forebrain and decrease in mid- and hindbrain. The amphibian brain is not much modified from the fish; the olfactory lobe is somewhat smaller and the cerebrum slightly larger.

Significant changes appeared in the reptile brain. The **cerebrum** is greatly enlarged but much of the forebrain is still devoted to smell. A striking innovation developed in the reptilian cerebrum. The cerebral hemispheres are coated by a pallium of neurons; in the reptile a small portion of the front part of the cerebrum is covered with a new sort of nervous tract called the **neopallium** or **neocortex**. This covering in general is what we know as "gray matter," and while the reptilian neopallium was a feeble beginning, it was a most important one.

In mammals, the neopallium dramatically expanded and spread over the cerebral hemispheres. Central control, formerly in the midbrain, passed almost entirely to the neopallium of the forebrain. The cerebrum increased in size to compose most of the brain and developed convolutions making for an even greater surface area without increasing brain size.

In humans, the growth of this section of the brain reaches its ultimate development, a fact which has made the human brain, in proportion to body size, one of the largest and most complex of any animal.

The second important difference between placentals and marsupials is *teeth*. These clearly distinguish the two forms and have been used as a basis for classification as well as the reconstruction of mammalian evolutionary history.

Eutheria
eu: good   therion: beast
All mammals except monotremes and pouched animals.

Olfactory
Smell.

Cerebellum
(sara-bell'-um)
That part of the brain concerned with coordination and balance. In humans, back of and below the cerebrum.

Cerebrum
(sar'-a-brum or se-ree'-brum)
Largest part of the human brain; the forebrain and midbrain.

Neopallium
neo: new   pallium: cloak

Neocortex
neo: new   cortex: bark, covering

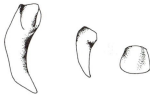

Herbivore   Carnivore   Human
(horse)

Figure 6-22 Canines.

Figure 6-23 Examples of specialization in herbivorous and carnivorous teeth. There is great variation in the size and shape of the canine in herbivorous animals, and canines are entirely lacking in many species.

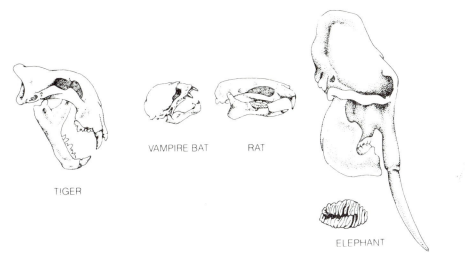

TIGER

VAMPIRE BAT   RAT

ELEPHANT

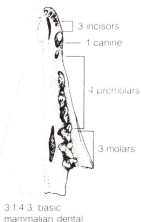

3 incisors

1 canine

4 premolars

3 molars

3:1:4:3 basic
mammalian dental
formula

◇ Box 6-5   Convergent and Parallel Evolution

Convergent Evolution   The discussion of marsupials offers an opportunity to present another evolutionary process, *convergent evolution*. We pointed out (in Box 8-2, Evolutionary Processes) that in the early stages of development, there is a tendency for newly evolved forms to become highly diversified when they invade varied environments. The diversification results from the modification of the ancestral type in adapting to new ecological niches.

Convergent evolution—a variation of adaptive radiation—is the process in which two *unrelated* groups of organisms, living in similar but separate environmental conditions, develop a similar appearance and life style. That is, similar environmental demands make for similar phenotypic responses (Mayr, 1970, p. 365). This should not be surprising since the requirements of adapting to a particular environment would require modifications of physical traits. Two similar environments would, therefore, result in similar adaptive characters.

Striking examples of convergence are the pouched mammals of Australia and placental mammals. As we have seen, Australia was isolated from South America before the great placental mammalian radiation of the Cenozoic, and marsupials survived because they were free

from the competition of the more efficient placentals. When placental mammals became prominent in the Cenozoic, only a few were able to invade Australia (via island-hopping from Southeast Asia).

Without competition, the pouched mammals spread into the varied environments of the isolated continent. There were marsupials that resembled, to a lesser or greater degree, a wolf, cat, flying squirrel, groundhog, anteater, mole, and mouse. And they occupied ecological niches similar to the placental mammals they resembled (Simpson et al., 1957, p. 470).

The variety of marsupials illustrates adaptive radiation; the resemblance in form due to similarity of econiches illustrates convergent evolution.

Parallel Evolution   A variation of both adaptive radiation and convergent evolution is *parallel evolution*. This process may be illustrated as a kind of tailed U. *Related* forms diverge as in adaptive radiation, responding to different ecological niches. Then, because of the similarity of econiches, the two or more forms respond to similar selection pressures and evolve somewhat similar phenotypes, for example, the New World and Old World monkeys (see further discussion in Chapter 7).

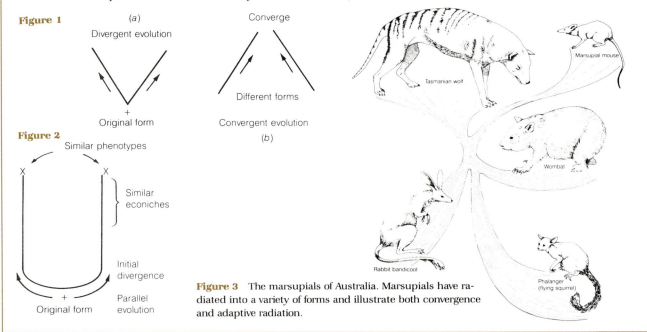

Figure 1

(a) Divergent evolution

Converge

Different forms

Convergent evolution

(b)

Figure 2

Similar phenotypes

Similar econiches

Initial divergence

Parallel evolution

Original form

Figure 3   The marsupials of Australia. Marsupials have radiated into a variety of forms and illustrate both convergence and adaptive radiation.

The structure of teeth often informs us of their use so that it is fairly easy, for example, to distinguish between the specializations of predator and herbivore teeth. Of all the teeth, it is probably the molars that are the most specialized. They perform the powerful grinding, chewing, and crushing functions, and their structure is closely associated with diet. It is difficult to exaggerate the role of teeth in studying mammalian (and especially for our purposes, primate) evolution. The student is asked to keep this in mind when we look at primate evolution, since in many cases identification, classification, relationships, and chronological placement may be based on the structure of fossil teeth. This is particularly the case for hominids because, quite often, teeth are the only fossil evidence available.

Appearing in placentals of Cretaceous age and still persisting in many modern animals, the basic pattern of placental mammalian teeth is (on each side and in both upper and lower jaws) three incisors, one canine, four premolars, and three molars (see Box 7-2, Chapter 7). Incisors tend to be pegs or blades—adapted for nipping or cutting food, as can be seen when biting into an apple.

Canines come in a variety of forms. **Carnivore** canines are spikelike and used for stabbing, piercing, and holding. In **herbivores** canines tend to be molarlike with a grinding surface, and among humans, **omnivores**, canines are spatulate, similar to incisors and utilized in a similar manner.

Premolars (called "bicuspids" by dentists) are generally complex and used for crushing and/or grinding (as are molars, which are even more complex).

Placental mammals today are found almost everywhere on earth. With sea mammals such as dolphins and seals, we find them in water, and some placentals, the bats, have taken to the air. But placentals are essentially terrestrial animals and land is where they are found in abundant numbers and species. For example, there are the even-toed ungulates (**artiodactyls**), such as cows, deer, camels, and pigs; odd-toed ungulates (**perissodactyls**), such as the horse and rhino; carnivores, such as the bear, dog, and cat; proboscids, such as elephants; insectivores, such as shrews, moles, and hedgehogs; the incredibly successful rodents, including rats, squirrels, beavers, and gophers; and, of course, the primates, including prosimians, monkeys, apes, and humans.

Of all these groups the rodents are clearly the most successful of all mammals if number of species and individuals is our criterion. In fact, they outnumber all other species of mammals combined (Romer, 1959, p. 228). Their enormous adaptive flexibility is clearly demonstrated by their ability to cope successfully with humanmade environments.

We have traced the evolution of vertebrates from fish to mammals. Mammals, as we have seen, had come a long way from the small, insignificant, insectivorelike animals of the Mesozoic to the highly diversified and very successful vertebrates of the present. We are now prepared to take up the discussion of our own order, Primates, which, like other mammals, most likely originated as shrewlike animals in the Paleocene (or possibly the late Cretaceous). Very early, they adapted to an arboreal way of life that emphasized vision, an expanded brain, and prehensible digits, as we shall see in the next three chapters.

Carnivore
carni: meat
A flesh-eating animal.

Herbivore
herba: grass
A plant-eating animal.

Omnivore
omnis: all
Plant and meat eating.

Artiodactyl
(are-tee-o-dak'-til)
artios: even
daktylos: finger, toe
Even-toed hoof.

Perissodactyl
perissos: odd
Odd-toed hoof.

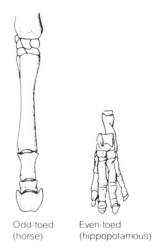

Odd-toed   Even-toed
(horse)   (hippopotamous)

Figure 6-24 Ungulates.

◇ Summary

In this chapter, we have placed humans in their natural perspective by tracing the development of evolutionary changes of invertebrates and vertebrates. We also placed humans in a temporal perspective by tracing the evolutionary development of life forms, especially vertebrates, over the immense time period of Precambrian through Tertiary.

Structural modifications of the evolutionary sequence of vertebrates—from fish to amphibians to reptiles to mammals—were included to give the very long developmental background of the hominid form. This will be continued in the chapter on primate evolution.

The basis for taxonomic classification (why animal X is placed in category Y) and several evolutionary concepts (adaptive radiation, generalized and specialized, and convergent and parallel evolution) were discussed to give a deeper understanding of "how evolution works."

◇ Questions for Review

1. What characteristics place humans in the Animal Kingdom?
2. Distinguish between homologies and analogies.
3. To what groups of the Animal Kingdom do hominids belong?
4. Explain the basis for the arrangement of the classification chart. Give several examples.
5. Outline the evolutionary history of vertebrates during the Paleozoic, Mesozoic, and Cenozoic.
6. What changes occurred in the structure of fish, amphibians, and reptiles that enables them to adapt to their econiches?
7. Define adaptive radiation and give examples.
8. Explain the evolutionary principle "generalized to specialized." Why is the reverse—"specialized to generalized"—rarely found?
9. Why are therapsids believed to be ancestors of mammals?
10. What characteristics of lobe-fins suggest they are ancestral to amphibia?
11. What "four great complexes" distinguish mammals from reptiles and contributed to mammalian success?
12. Explain the differences between convergent and parallel evolution.
13. Why are placental mammals so much more successful than marsupials?

Living Primates

CONTENTS

Today, one species of primate, *Homo sapiens*, dominates our planet. Numbering over 4 billion, we use, alter, and ultimately destroy huge hunks of the world's surface.

In the face of such an onslaught, many of the other species that share our planet are being driven to the brink of extinction. As primates ourselves, we have a special interest in the problem of preserving our primate relatives.

Even before the advent of modern technological society, primates (compared to such groups as rodents or even-toed ungulates) were not abundant. Largely restricted to forested areas in South America, Africa, and South Asia, the primates had—despite their comparative numerical inferiority—achieved a successful adaptation.

Such is no longer the case. In addition to being diminished by the dangers stemming from reduced or completely obliterated habitats, non-human primates are also easy prey for local peoples looking for food, hunters looking for scientific (mostly medical) specimens, or for poachers strictly after financial gain.

What is the future for these animals? The prospects are not hopeful. The Convention on International Trade in Endangered Species (ratified by the United States in 1973) alreadys lists *all* non-human primates as endangered or facing the prospects of soon becoming so. All of the apes—gibbons, orangutans, gorillas, and chimpanzees—are now in the convention's "most endangered" category. (All are also on the United States endangered species list: the first three as "endangered"; chimps as "threatened".)

Among the most imminently endangered of all primates is the mountain gorilla—a subspecies of the largest primate form—now restricted to an exceedingly small area of East Africa (where the borders of Rwanda, Uganda, and Zaire converge).

Mountain gorillas once ranged widely through the densely forested mountain regions bordering the great lakes of East Africa. Foraging in rough terrain, gorilla groups survived for centuries, impervious to any potential predator. In fact, the mountain gorilla was not even known to the Western world until 1903, when it was first reported by a German military expedition.

The mountain gorilla's comparative isolation from humans has been dramatically altered in recent years. It is estimated that today there are only about 220 mountain gorillas left in the wild. In the last twenty years alone, their numbers have been reduced by one-half.

Most of the deaths (perhaps as many as two-thirds) are at the hands of poachers. Gorillas are prized specimens for trophy hunters; consequently, they are often shot with high-powered rifles, after which they are decapitated, their hands cut off, and these grisly remains sold for trophies.

Gorillas also are victims of poachers in a more accidental fashion. Traps and snares are set by poachers primarily to capture antelope and buffalo, which can be sold as meat. Mountain gorillas who live in the same area step into these traps and, even if they manage to escape, usually die later from infected wounds.

Why is such reckless exploitation allowed? The answer is that, legally, it is not. Throughout the world illegal poaching of endangered species is banned, and most countries prohibit imports of products derived from such animals. Enforcement, however, is another matter. Due to political

Digit, an adult male gorilla; found after poachers had decapitated him and cut off his hands.

quently feel compelled to trap antelope and buffalo and, in the process, gorillas as well.

Despite wide publicity of the gorilla's plight in the Western world and a large influx of money from concerned conservationists, the slaughter goes on. Is there then any hope for saving the mountain gorilla? Perhaps—but time is growing dangerously short. As Dian Fossey, the leading field researcher of these primates, has ominously warned, "The mountain gorilla may become an animal which was discovered and driven extinct— in the same century."

The struggle to save the mountain gorilla eventually cost Dian Fossey her own life. Tragically, on Christmas Eve 1985, she was brutally murdered at her mountain camp in Rwanda. Following her wishes, she was laid to rest in the same graveyard where Digit and other of her treasured gorillas are also buried.

instability and periodic warfare in East Africa, central governments have been at a loss to stop the killing. In Zaire and Uganda most of the mountain gorillas are now gone. Rwanda continues to struggle with the problem, but the choices are not always easy. Among the most overcrowded and undernourished populations in Africa, Rwandans are hard-pressed to find adequate sources of animal protein. Local populations conse-

SOURCES:

Fossey, Dian. "The Imperiled Mountain Gorilla," *National Geographic*, 159:501–523, April, 1981.

Fossey, Dian. *Gorillas in the Mist*, Boston: Houghton-Mifflin Co., 1983.

◇ **CHAPTER SEVEN**

◇ Introduction

We have seen in Chapter 6 that we are a certain kind of placental mammal, a primate. This order of rather diverse animals is characterized by a set of evolutionary trends that sets it apart from other mammals. In this chapter, we will discuss what characteristics link us to our primate cousins, and we will explore some of the fascinating and unique adaptations that the non-human primates display.

◇ Primate Evolutionary Trends

Structurally, primates are not easily distinguished as a group chiefly because of the fact that, as an order, we and our close relatives have remained quite *generalized*. Unlike the specialized dentition of rodents or the specialized limbs with great reduction of digits found in artiodactyls (cows, deer, camels, pigs), primates are characterized by their *lack* of extreme structural specializations.

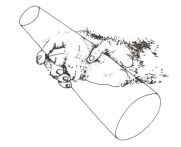

Figure 7-1 Primate (macaque) hand.

For this reason, we cannot point to a single anatomical feature that can be applied exclusively and universally to the primates. On the other hand, there is a group of **evolutionary trends** (Clark, 1971) which, to a greater or lesser degree, characterize the entire order. Keep in mind, these are a set of *general* tendencies and are not equally expressed in all primates. Indeed, this situation is one that we would expect in such a diverse group of generalized animals. In addition, trends are not synonymous with *progress*. In evolutionary terms, we are using "trend" only to reflect a series of shared common characteristics (i.e., general homologies).

Following is a list of those evolutionary trends that tend to set the primates apart from other mammals. A common evolutionary history with similar adaptations to common environmental challenges is reflected in the limbs and locomotion; teeth and diet; and in the senses, brain, and behavior of the animals that make up the order.

A. Limbs and Locomotion

1. *Retention of five digits* in the hands and feet—*pentadactyly*. As in primitive mammals, this characteristic is found in all primates, though some show marked reduction of the thumb (e.g., spider monkeys, langurs) or the second digit (e.g, lorises). In no case is reduction as extreme as that seen in such animals as cows or horses.

2. *Nails instead of claws*. A consistent characteristic on at least some digits of all contemporary primates. Unlike rodents or cats, primates must climb by wrapping their hands and feet around branches and holding on by grasping. This grasping function is further aided by the presence of tactile pads at the ends of digits.

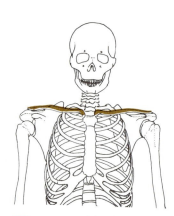

Figure 7-2 Position of the clavicle in the human skeleton.

3. *Flexible hands and feet* with a good deal of *prehensility* (grasping ability). This feature is associated directly with the lack of claws and retention of five digits.
4. *A tendency toward erectness* (particularly in the upper body). Shown to some degree in all primates, this tendency is variously associated with sitting, leaping, standing, and, occasionally, walking.
5. *Retention of the clavicle* (collarbone). Seen in all primates. The clavicle has been lost in many other quadrupedal mammals.

B. Teeth and Diet

6. *A generalized dental pattern*, particularly in the back teeth (molars). Characteristic of primates, such a pattern contrasts with the highly specialized molars seen in herbivores.
7. *A lack of specialization in diet.* This attribute is usually correlated with a lack of specialization in teeth. In other words, primates can generally be described as *omnivorous*.

C. Senses, Brain, and Behavior

8. *A reduction of the snout* and the proportionate reduction of the smell (olfactory) areas of the brain. Seen in all contemporary primates, but baboons show a secondary (coming later) increase of a *dental* muzzle.
9. *An increased emphasis on vision* with elaboration of visual areas of the brain. A trend related to the decreased dependence on smell. Binocular and stereoscopic vision is a further elaboration wherein visual fields of the two eyes overlap, transmitting both images to the brain, thus allowing depth perception. Except for some specialized nocturnal forms, color vision is most likely present in all primates.
10. *Expansion and increasing complexity of the brain.* A general trend among placental mammals and one especially true of primates. This expansion is most evident in the visual and association areas of the neopallium and to some degree in the motor cortex and cerebellum. (See p. 142.)
11. *A more efficient means of fetal nourishment*, as well as *longer periods of gestation, infancy*, and extension of the whole life span.
12. *A greater dependency on highly flexible learned behavior* is correlated with longer periods of infant and child dependency. As a result of both these trends, parental investment in each offspring is increased so that although fewer young are born, they receive more efficient rearing.
13. *Adult males often associate permanently with the group.* A behavioral trait rarely seen in other mammals, but widespread among the primates.

◇ The Arboreal Adaptation

The single most important factor influencing the evolutionary divergence of primates (with elaboration of all the trends just noted) was the adaptation to **arboreal** living. While other placental mammals were going about their business adapting to grasslands, subterranean or even marine environments,

Evolutionary trends
General structural and behavioral traits that are commonly shared by a related group of organisms.

Arboreal
Anatomy is adapted to life in the trees.

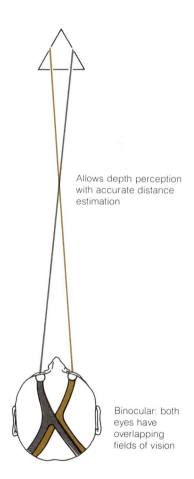

Allows depth perception with accurate distance estimation

Binocular: both eyes have overlapping fields of vision

Stereoscopic: optic nerve transmissions from each eye are relayed to *both* sides of the brain

Figure 7-3 Binocular, stereoscopic vision. Fields of vision overlap and sensory information from each eye is relayed to both sides of the brain.

Adaptive niche
The whole way of life of an organism: where it lives, what it eats, how it gets food, and so forth.

Substrate
The surface on which an animal moves or rests.

Nocturnal
Active at night.

Diurnal
Active during daylight hours.

Postorbital bar
The bony element that closes in the outside of the eye orbit—a characteristic of primates.

primates found their **adaptive niche** in the trees. Indeed, some other mammals also were adapting to arboreal living, but primates found their home (and food) mainly in the tree tops and at the ends of terminal branches. This environment—with its myriad challenges and opportunities—was the one in which our ancestors established themselves as a unique kind of animal.

Primates became primates *because* of their adaptation to arboreal living. We can see this process at work in their reliance upon vision for survival (as opposed to their depending chiefly on a sense of smell). In a complex environment with uncertain footholds, acute vision with depth perception is a necessity. Climbing can be accomplished by either digging in with claws or grasping around branches with prehensile hands and feet. Primates adopted the latter strategy, which allowed a means of progressing on the narrowest and most tenuous of **substrates**. Thus, we also see in primates pentadactyly, prehensility, and flattened nails. In addition, the varied foods found in an arboreal environment (such as fruits, leaves, berries, insects, small mammals) led to the primate omnivorous adaptation and, hence, to retention of a generalized dentition.

Finally, the long life span, increased intelligence, and more elaborated social system are primate solutions to coping with the manifold complexities of their arboreal habitat (that is, such factors as varied and seasonal food resources; and potential predators from above, below, and in the trees). This crucial development of increased behavioral flexibility may have been further stimulated by a shift from **noctural** (nighttime) to **diurnal** (daytime) activity patterns (Jerison, 1973).

A recent critique of the traditional arboreal explanation for the origin of primate structure has been proposed by Matt Cartmill (1972, 1974) of Duke University. Cartmill points out that the most significant primate trends—close-set eyes, grasping extremities, and reduced claws—may *not* have arisen from adaptive advantages in an arboreal environment.

According to this alternative theory, ancient primates may have first adapted to living in bushy forest undergrowth and only the lowest branches of the forest canopy. All these traits would have been well suited for an animal that foraged for fruits and insects. Particularly in searching for insects, early primates are thought to have relied heavily on vision, and this theory is hence called the *visual predation hypothesis*.

The close-set eyes would have allowed these primates to judge accurately the distance from their prey without moving their heads, similar to the hunting manner of cats and owls. The regression of the olfactory sense is then viewed as a necessary result of the eye orbits coming closer together. Grasping extremities may have initially been an adaptation for pursuing insects along very narrow supports (like twigs) in the forest undergrowth. Feet, as well as hands, would be prehensile to allow the animal to maintain support while snaring its prey with both hands.

The visual predation hypothesis is as internally consistent and as likely an explanation for the early evolution of primates as the arboreal theory. In fact—given the fossil record and the morphology typical of many contemporary prosimians—it may be a better explanation for the functional developments among the *earliest* primates. In particular, the small body size and insectivorous diet seen in several living prosimians and a similar adaptation

◇ Box 7-1   Primate Cranial Anatomy

Several significant anatomical features of primate skulls help us distinguish primates from other mammals. Continuing the mammalian trend of increasing brain development, primates go even further as shown by their well-expanded brain boxes. In addition, the primate trend of increased dependence on vision is shown by the generally large eye sockets; less emphasis on smell is shown in the reduced snout; the shift to using hands for grasping (instead of using the front teeth for this purpose) is revealed in the dentition; and the tendency towards more upright posture is indicated by the relationship of the head to the spinal column.

Some of the specific anatomic details seen in all modern and most fossil primate crania are:

1. Eye sockets are enclosed circumferentially by a complete ring of bone, compared to other placental mammals where the ring is incomplete (no **postorbital bar**). This bony arrangement provides protection for the eyes.
2. The entrance into the skull for the spinal column, the *foramen magnum* (Latin: "big hole") on the base of the skull, faces more downwards instead of backwards as it does in other completely quadrupedal mammals. The position of the *foramen magnum* indicates the direction of the spinal column and is related to the posturing and balancing of the head on the trunk.
3. The face of primates is reduced (snout shortened) with the axis at the base of the skull bending, thus pulling the face more underneath the brain box. This arrangement now provides a greater vertical distance in the movable lower jaw from the point of pivot (P) to the plane of the teeth (T) allowing more biomechanical action for up-and-down crushing, grinding, etc., instead of just simple back-and-forth tearing and gnashing.
4. The ear region containing the middle ear ossicles is completely encircled by a bony encasement (bulla) whose floor is derived from a particular segment of the temporal bone. Most primate paleontologists consider this feature and the formation of a postorbital bar as the structurally best diagnostic characteristics of the primate order.

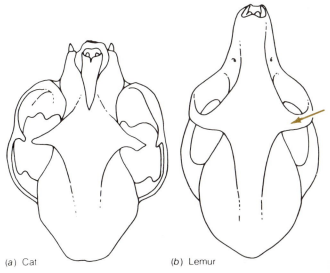

(a) Cat   (b) Lemur

Figure 1   Postorbital bar. A characteristic of primates.

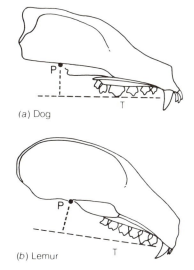

(a) Dog

(b) Lemur

Figure 2   Basi-cranial flexion relative to tooth row. In primates, the skull base is more flexed, elevating the point of pivot (P) further above the tooth row and thereby increasing the force of chewing. (© 1959 by W. E. Le Gros Clark.)

Homology
Similarities between organisms based on
common evolutionary descent.

inferred from the fossilized remains of many very early primates are consistent with the visual predation hypothesis.

The visual predation ("bug snatching") hypothesis and the arboreal theory are not mutually exclusive explanations. The complex of primate characteristics could have begun in nonarboreal settings, but would have become even more adaptive once the bug snatching was done *in the trees*.

At some point, in fact, the primates did take to the trees in earnest, and that is where the vast majority still live today. Whereas the basic primate structural complexes may have been initially adapted for visual predation, they became ideally suited for the arboreal adaptation that followed. We would say then that primates were "preadapted" for arboreal living.

◇ The Living Primates

When we apply the set of evolutionary trends under discussion here, we are able to classify a remarkable array of living forms as members of the same mammalian order, the Primates. We and our primate cousins, you will recall, share these characteristics due to **homology**. In other words, primates are part of a single evolutionary radiation, and the traits we all share derive from a common evolutionary descent.

PRIMATE CLASSIFICATION

While controversy on some minor points still exists, the living primates are traditionally categorized into subgroupings (based on increasingly similar evolutionary relationships) in the following manner:

ORDER   Primates
  SUBORDER   Prosimii
    SUPERFAMILY   Lemuroidea (lemurs of Madagascar)
    SUPERFAMILY   Lorisoidea (loris, bushbaby)
    SUPERFAMILY   Tarsiioidea (tarsier)
  SUBORDER   Anthropoidea
    SUPERFAMILY   Ceboidea (New World monkeys; e.g., spider monkey, howler monkey, capuchin)
    SUPERFAMILY   Cercopithecoidea (Old World monkeys; e.g., baboon, macaque, langur)
    SUPERFAMILY   Hominoidea
      FAMILY   Hylobatidae (gibbons)
      FAMILY   Pongidae
        GENUS   *Pan* (chimp)
        GENUS   *Gorilla*
        GENUS   *Pongo* (orangutan)
      FAMILY   Hominidae
        GENUS   *Homo* (human)

Table 7-1 shows an alternative primate classification.

Table 7-1   Alternative Classification of Living Primates—Based upon Biochemical Data (after Dene et al., 1976)

Order Primates
  Semiorder Strepsirhini
    Suborder Lemuriformes
      Superfamily Lemuroidea
        Family Lemuridae
          Genus *Lemur*   common lemur
        Family Lepilemuridae
          Genus *Lepilemur*   sportive lemur
        Family Indriidae
          Genus *Propithecus*   sifaka
      Superfamily Cheirogaleoidea
        Family Cheirogaleidae
          Genus *Microcebus*   mouse lemur
            Cheirogaleus   dwarf lemur
      Superfamily Daubentonioidea
        Family Daubentoniidae
          Genus *Daubentonia*   aye-aye
    Suborder Lorisiformes
      Superfamily Lorisoidea
        Family Galagidae
          Subfamily Galaginae
            Genus *Galago*   bushbaby
        Family Lorisidae
          Genus *Nycticebus*   slow loris
            Loris   slender loris
        Family Perodicticidae
          Subfamily Perodicticinae
            Genus *Perodicticus*   potto
              Arctocebus   angwantibo
  Semiorder Haplorhini
    Suborder Tarsioiidea
      Family Tarsiidae
        Genus *Tarsius*   tarsier

Suborder Anthropoidea
  Infraorder Platyrrhini   New World monkeys
    Superfamily Ceboidea
      Genus *Ateles*   spider monkey
        Logothrix   woolly monkey
        Alouatta   howler monkey
        Saguinus   tamarin
        Aotus   night monkey
        Callicebus   titi
        Chiropotes   saki
        Cebus   capuchin
        Saimiri   squirrel monkey
  Infraorder Catarrhini
    Superfamily Cercopithecoidea
      Family Cercopithecidae
        Subfamily Colobinae
          Genus *Colobus*   guerezas
            Presbytis   langur
            Pygathrix   douc langur
            Nasalis   proboscis monkey
        Subfamily Cercopithecinae
          Genus *Macaca*   macaque
            Papio   baboon
            Theropithecus   gelada
            Mandrillus   drill
            Cercocebus   mangabey
            Erythrocebus   patas
            Cercopithecus   guenon
    Superfamily Hominoidea
      Family Hylobatidae
        Subfamily Hylobatinae   gibbon
          Genus *Hylobates*   gibbon
            Symphalangus   siamang
      Family Hominidae
        Subfamily Ponginae
          Genus *Pongo*   orangutan
        Subfamily Homininae
          Genus *Gorilla*   gorilla
            Pan   chimpanzee
            Homo

◇ Grades of Primate Evolution

In terms of size, structure, and behavior, contemporary primates certainly represent a varied group of animals. What is even more remarkable about the living primates is that they still display in some form all the major grades of evolution that primates have passed through over the last 70 million years.

An evolutionary grade is, in Mayr's terms, "A group of animals similar in level of organization" (Mayr, 1970). We do not use the term, as some evolu-

Primitive
In evolutionary terms, an organism that is
closer to an evolutionary divergence than a
later (more derived) one.

tionary biologists have done, to imply a strict commonality of evolutionary
descent and/or an equivalent adaptive response (suggesting selection above
the species level). In fact, such processes are not now believed to be accurate
depictions of macroevolution (Eldredge and Cracraft, 1980). (See p. 91.)

You should also note that the concept of grade does not imply any inferiority
or superiority. Grades only reflect different stages of organizational levels seen
during primate evolution—from more primitive to more derived. (See p. 137.)

GRADE I: TREE SHREWS (PRIMITIVE MAMMALIAN GRADE)

Tree shrews are an enigma to the taxonomist. In classifying the natural world
into the higher taxonomic categories of family, order, etc., we are attempting
to simplify and hopefully make sense out of the complex organic continuum
that evolution has produced. Indeed, the categories are *created by us* for us.
They are symbolic devices typical of the human mind's capacity to "impose
arbitrary form on the environment." A tree shrew could care less whether it
is classified as a primate, an insectivore (another order of placental mammals),
or a whale.

It is often readily apparent that similar structural and behavioral characteristics of contemporary life forms reflect their shared evolutionary ancestry
(for example, lemurs and lorises both as prosimians; humans and apes both
as hominoids). There are, however, many organisms that do not fit neatly into
any of our categories.

The tree shrew is such an animal. Some investigators, impressed by several
structural similarities, regard tree shrews as primates (Simpson, 1945; Clark,
1971). However, most current researchers (Simons, 1972; Buettner-Janusch,
1973) view the primatelike characteristics of tree shrews as merely reflections
of their primitive mammalian heritage. As another popular alternative, tree
shrews have often been placed among the insectivores, where they do not
really fit either. As a final act of taxonomic desperation, then, most experts
now place tree shrews within their own order of placental mammals (Luckett,
1980a).

Given that tree shrews are an order unto themselves, what are their closest
relatives among the placentals? Morphological and some biochemical data
(see pp. 172–174) suggest that tree shrews, flying lemurs, and primates form
an evolutionary "cluster" and could be included together within a common
superorder (Luckett, 1980; Cronin and Sarich, 1980). However, other biochemical techniques suggest the tree shrew/flying lemur/primate cluster is not a
natural grouping, and that tree shrews, in fact, find their nearest mammalian
affinities with bats (Dene et al., 1980) or even rabbits (Goodman et al., 1983).
What makes tree shrews intriguing and relevant to a discussion of primate
evolution is that their overall anatomical structure and level of adaptation are
probably very similar to the earliest primates of 70 million years ago.

Today, tree shrews live in Southeast Asia, extending from India to the
islands of Indonesia. They are all generally small, squirrellike animals and
may not be recognized initially as primatelike in appearance. First, they have
long, projecting snouts and their eyes do not face forward (see Fig. 7-4).
Second—even more unprimatelike—they have claws (not nails) on *all* their
digits. Finally, their social behavior is most unlike primates in their "absentee"

Figure 7-4   Tree shrew.

system of mothering. (On the other hand, their tendency toward grasping definitely parallels the well-developed grasping features of the primates.) It is no wonder that the tree shrews look **primitive**, since they are not much altered from the probable general appearance and adaptive level of very early placental mammals. Since the primate adaptive radiation goes back to the roots of the placental mammal radiation at the beginning of the Cenozoic (*circa* 65 m.y.a.), living tree shrews provide an excellent structural model for the earliest primates as well as for generalized placental mammals.

GRADE II: LEMURS AND LORISES

Lemurs are found today only on the island of Madagascar off the east coast of Africa. They probably reached their island sanctuary several million years ago and were able to diversify into the many ecological niches offered on this

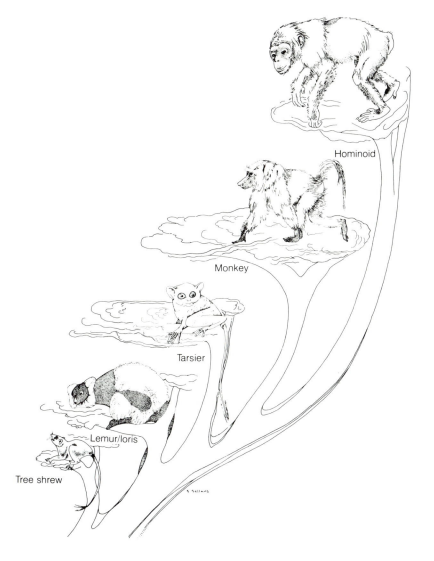

Figure 7-5 The grades of primate evolution.

Hominoid

Monkey

Tarsier

Lemur/loris

Tree shrew

Adaptive radiation
The diversification and expansion of a life form into a number of niches.

Strepsirhini
strepsi: twisted
rhini: nose
The classificatory term used to group lemurs and lorises (either suborder or semiorder).

Haplorhini
haplo: simple
rhini: nose
The classificatory term used to group tarsiers with monkeys, apes, and humans (either suborder or semiorder).

Figure 7-6   Distribution of modern lemurs.

Figure 7-7   Ring-tailed lemur.

large island of 227,000 square miles. As the *only* primates on the island, lemurs were able to survive. In continental areas, most of their prosimian cousins perished. Thus, these surviving forms represent a kind of "living fossil," preserving an evolutionary grade that has long since vanished elsewhere.

Lemurs, however, are not uniform. Some are nocturnal, others diurnal; some are completely arboreal, others are more terrestrial. In fact, the range of forms and habitats occupied before recent human interference (in the last few hundred years) reveals a remarkable evolutionary display. One unusual lemur (called the aye-aye), still living in Madagascar, suggests a rodentlike adaptation; another (indri) resembles a small monkey; and, finally, an incredible beast with extremely short hind limbs (*Megaladapis*, now extinct) weighed more than 100 pounds (Szalay and Delson, 1979).

Some forms like the aye-aye are socially solitary, whereas others primarily associate in large permanent groups (the ring-tailed lemur). All these forms evolved in the relative sanctuary that Madagascar provided. This kind of evolution, characterized by rapid diversification and expansion into varied ecological niches, is another beautiful example of **adaptive radiation**.

Lorises, very similar to lemurs, were able to survive in *continental* areas by adopting a nocturnal activity pattern at a time when most other prosimians became extinct. In this way, they were (and are) able to avoid competition with their primate descendants, the monkeys, as well as another group— including many highly successful arboreal, diurnal forms—the rodents.

Today, the geographic range of lorises is confined to tropical areas in Africa and Southeast Asia. Their nocturnal adaptation is immediately revealed structurally by their greatly enlarged eyes. Usually quite small animals, they have elongated hindlimbs, providing an adaptation for leaping and hopping. Socially, most lorises are solitary and only occasionally form sleeping pairs.

Both lemurs and lorises represent the same general adaptive level. They both have good grasping and climbing abilities and have fairly well-developed vision that is not completely stereoscopic. They all have nails on at least one of their digits (the aye-aye has a nail only on the big toe). Most of the other varieties have only one clawed digit (on the second toe). This digit is used for grooming and is called the toilet digit. Lemurs and lorises also have prolonged life spans as compared to other small mammals, averaging about fourteen years for the lorises and nineteen years for the lemurs.

However, lorises and lemurs still show many characteristics suggesting their relatively closer relationship to early placental mammals than is true for the anthropoids (monkeys, apes, and humans). For example, their faces for the most part are still quite snouty, with a markedly projecting nose. As this feature would suggest, they still rely a great deal on the olfactory sense, and some lemurs have developed specialized scent glands for the purpose of leaving "smell" messages. Dependence on olfactory cues is also shown by the naked area of moist skin—*rhinarium*—on the nose. This area is used to conduct scent efficiently. Suggestive also of their early primate ancestry are their expressionless faces, large mobile ears, and a generally unelaborated pattern of social behavior. Finally, there are some unusual specialized aspects in their dentition, particularly the projecting lower incisors and canines forming a structure used for grooming and hence called a dental comb.

Figure 7-8   Distribution of modern lorises.

GRADE III: THE TARSIER

A once widespread prosimian form, the living tarsier is today limited to one
genus (*Tarsius*) and is confined to island areas in Southeast Asia. This tiny
animal (about the size of a small kitten) has avoided competition in much
the same way as the lorises—by adapting to a nocturnal niche. The large
forward-placed eyes which dominate the face strikingly reveal this adaptation.
Another unusual feature shown by the tarsier is a greatly elongated ankle
joint (tarsus), which gives the animal its name and allows it to leap great
distances.

(a)

Like lemurs and lorises, tarsiers are also prosimians, as revealed by their
small body size, large ears, "primitive" dental pattern, and unelaborated
social behavior. However, they exhibit several physical characteristics similar
to anthropoids, placing them at a different organizational level than lemurs
and lorises. Indeed, like the tree shrew, tarsiers present somewhat of a taxonomic dilemma. Many primatologists, pointing to the numerous physical
characteristics that tarsiers share with anthropoids (which are seen as derived
states), classify tarsiers closer to anthropoids than to prosimians. Moreover,
biochemically, tarsiers are more closely related to anthropoids than to lemurs
or lorises (Dene et al., 1976). In order to accommodate this revised view,
classification schemes and classificatory labels have been changed. For example, the suborder that includes lemurs and lorises is termed the **Strepsirhini**, while tarsiers, monkeys, apes, and humans are included within another
suborder, the **Haplorhini** (Szalay and Delson, 1979). Another means of accom-
plishing the same goal is to retain the traditional subordinal nomenclature
but to distinguish lemurs and lorises from tarsiers, monkeys, apes, and
humans at a level above suborder (i.e., semiorder—see Table 7-1) (Dene et al.,
1976).

As we indicated above, tarsiers show many similarities to anthropoids.
Contrasted to those of other prosimians, tarsier eye orbits are completely

(b)

Figure 7-9   Two varieties of loris.
(a) Greater galago; (b) a Senegal galago, or
"bushbaby."

Quadrupedal
Using all four limbs relatively equally while moving.

CHINA

INDOCHINA

Malay
Peninsula   INDONESIA

Figure 7-10   Distribution of modern tarsiers.

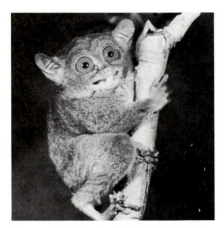

Figure 7-11   Tarsier. Note the huge eyes.

Table 7-2   Numbers of Groups of Living Primates

	Genera	Species
Lemur	12	28
Loris	5	11
Tarsier	1	3
New World monkey	16	52
Old World monkey	16	78
Hominoids	6	14
Total	56	186

Source: Data abstracted from A. Jolly, 1985, pp. 6–11.

closed *in back* by bone in the manner of the anthropoids. (Lorises and lemurs are "primitive" in this respect, having an opening between the orbit and the cranial vault, or brainbox.) You will recall that all primates have orbits that are completely encircled by bone *on the outside*. In addition, tarsier skulls are more rounded and their snouts less projecting than those of other prosimians, a situation partially explained by their small size and huge eyes. Another anthropoidlike feature is their lack of a rhinarium and a more flexible upper lip, a structure allowing for more facial expression. Finally, the bony ear canal of the tarsier is also more like anthropoids than other prosimians.

In addition to those features already pointed out, several other characteristics exist that tend to distinguish monkeys, apes, and humans from the "lower" primates. These are:

1. Generally larger body size
2. Larger brain size (in absolute terms and relative to body weight)
3. More rounded skull (seen to some degree in tarsiers also)
4. Eyes completely in front of skull, full stereoscopic vision
5. Complete back wall to eye orbit (also seen in tarsiers)
6. No rhinarium (also seen in tarsiers)
7. Only two incisors (on each side) in both jaws
8. More complex social systems
9. More parental care; often by males as well as females
10. More mutual grooming

GRADE IV: MONKEYS

The monkey grade of evolution is today the most varied group of primates (see Table 7-2). Of the 185 or so living species of primates, approximately 70% (about 130 species) are classified as monkeys. These are divided into two groups separated by geographical area (New World and Old World), as well as several million years of separate evolutionary history.

New World Monkeys   The New World monkeys (Ceboidea) exhibit a wide range of size, diet, and ecological adaptation. In size, they vary from the tiny (about twelve ounces) marmosets (family Callitrichidae) to the twenty-pound howler monkey, a member of the family Cebidae (see Table 7-3). New World monkeys are almost exclusively arboreal and will usually come to the ground only to cross spaces in order to gain access to other trees. Although confined to tree environments, New World monkeys can be found in a wide range of arboreal habitats throughout most forested areas in southern Mexico, Central America, and South America.

Nose shape is one of the characteristics distinguishing New World monkeys from those found in the Old World. New World forms have broad, widely flaring noses with a thick nasal septum, with nostrils facing outward. Conversely, Old World monkeys have narrower noses with a thinner nasal septum, and the nostrils face downward. This difference in nose form has given rise to the terms *platyrrhine* (flat-nosed) and *catarrhine* (down-nosed), the latter referring to *all* Old World anthropoids (Old World monkeys, apes, and humans). Another characteristic of New World monkeys is seen in their dentition,

Figure 7-12 (*left*) A pair of golden marmosets.

Figure 7-13 (*right*) Howler monkey. Note the expanded laryngeal apparatus used in vocalization.

which has retained three premolars. All Old World anthropoids have only two (see Box 7-2). Another feature found only in the New World, though not in all forms, is the development of a prehensile (grasping) tail that can be used like a fifth limb.

In locomotion, all New World forms are basically **quadrupedal**, but some forms (for example, the spider monkey, or the howler monkey) are able to perform considerable arm-swinging suspensory locomotion (see Box 7-3).

Old World Monkeys   After humans, Old World monkeys (Cercopithecoidea) are the most widely distributed of all living primates. They are seen throughout subsaharan Africa and southern Asia, ranging from tropical jungle habitats to semiarid desert and even to seasonally snow-covered areas in northern Japan.

The classification of Old World monkeys reveals how the same root with different endings designates the various levels (taxonomic categories) in a formal classification:

Table 7-3   New World Monkey Classification

SUPERFAMILY	Ceboidea
FAMILY	Callitrichidae (marmosets and tamarins)
FAMILY	Cebidae (howler monkey, spider monkey, woolly monkey, capuchin, night monkey, squirrel monkey)

		Ending Indicates Level of Classification
SUPERFAMILY	Cercopithecoidea (sur-ko-pith-e-koid'-ee-uh)	oidea = superfamily
FAMILY	Cercopithecidae (sur-ko-pith-ee'-si-dee)	idae = family
SUBFAMILY	Cercopithecinae (sur-ko-pith-ee'-si-nee)	inae = subfamily
	Colobinae (kol-o-bine'-ee)	
GENUS	Colobus (kol'-o-bus)	genus endings are variable, but -us is common

Figure 7-14   Distribution of modern New World monkeys.

Figure 7-15   A New World monkey prehensile tail. Shown here in a spider monkey.

The same tooth formula, 2-1-2-3 (2 incisors, 1 canine, 2 premolars, 3 molars) found in apes and humans also characterizes Old World monkeys. They are all quadrupedal and mainly arboreal, although some (baboons, for example) are adapted primarily to life on the ground. Whether in trees or on the ground, these monkeys spend a good deal of time sleeping, feeding, and grooming while sitting with their upper bodies held erect. Associated with this universal sitting posture are usually areas of hardened skin on their rear ends called *ischial callosities* that serve as sitting pads. Old World monkeys have a good deal of manual dexterity and most have well-developed tails that are never prehensile (in adults), as is true of many New World forms; the tail, however, does serve a purpose in such functions as communication and balance.

Within the entire group of Old World monkeys (superfamily: Cercopithecoidea), there is only one taxonomically recognized family, Cercopithecidae. Within this family there are in turn two subfamilies, the cercopithecines and the colobines. The former are found mainly in Africa, but some forms (the macaques) are widely distributed in southern Asia. The colobines are found mainly in Asia, but the colobus (kol′-o-bus) monkey (from which the group is named) is widely distributed in tropical Africa.

The cercopithecines are the more generalized of the two subfamilies, showing a more omnivorous dietary adaptation. The colobines, on the other hand, are more limited dietarily, specializing more on mature leaves, a behavior that has led to their designation as "leaf-eating monkeys." As a result of this behavior, structural adaptations for digestion of cellulose (a usually indigestible plant substance) have arisen. These adaptations are reflected in the high crowned molars, sacculated (divided) stomachs, and elongated intestines.

Figure 7-16   Distribution of modern Old World monkeys.

◇ Box 7-2   Tale of the Teeth

Extremely important for interpreting the relationships of *both* living and fossil forms are the number and kinds of teeth present. There are four different kinds of teeth found in a generalized placental mammal, and primates have almost universally retained all four types: incisors, canines, premolars, and molars. A shorthand device for showing the number of each kind of tooth is called a **dental formula**. This formula indicates the teeth in one-quarter of the mouth (since the arrangement of teeth is symmetrical and usually the same in upper and lower jaws). For example, the dental formula in New World monkeys for cebids is 2-1-3-3 (2 incisors, 1 canine, 3 premolars, and 3 molars in each quarter of the mouth—a total of 36 teeth); and 2-1-3-2 in marmosets, which typically lose their third molars, a situation perhaps analogous to the loss of third molars, or wisdom teeth, in modern humans. The formula in *all* Old World monkeys, apes, and humans is normally 2-1-2-3—a total of 32 teeth. Most lemur and loris dental formulae are 2-1-3-3 (total of 36), but the highly specialized aye-aye shows (for a primate) remarkable reduction in numbers of teeth

$$\frac{\text{1-0-1-3*}}{\text{1-0-0-3}}$$

for a total of only 18 teeth.

*When the formula differs in the lower jaw from that of the upper jaw, both are shown. For example, the tarsier has one less incisor in each half of its lower jaw than it does in its upper jaw:

$$\frac{\text{2-1-3-3}}{\text{1-1-3-3}}$$

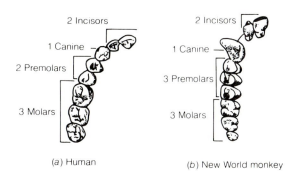

(a) Human   (b) New World monkey

Figure 1   Dental formulae. The number of each kind of tooth is given for one-quarter of the mouth.

Relative dental formulae are extremely useful indicators of phyletic relationships because they are normally under tight genotypic control. In other words, environmental influence will usually not alter the tooth formula. In making studies of primate dental phenotypes, we are quite certain, therefore, that our comparisons are based on structural homologies. Thus, similarities in structure (relative numbers of teeth) can be used as indicators of evolutionary similarity.

Dental evidence is extremely important in the interpretation of fossils, since teeth—the hardest component of the body—are the most commonly fossilized part and comprise the vast majority of fossil primate discoveries. In addition, cusp pattern and functional wear can be used to help reconstruct dietary behavior in fossil animals. The identification of diet is of central importance in any attempt to reconstruct the nature of the ecological niche, and ultimately the whole way of life of a fossil form.

The most common forms of cercopithecines include the highly diversified arboreal guenons (genus: *Cercopithecus*); the slightly larger but still arboreal mangabeys (genus: *Cercocebus*); and the more terrestrial macaques (genus: *Macaca*), baboons—both savanna and hamadryas (genus: *Papio*), forest baboon (genus: *Mandrillus*), and the gelada baboon (genus: *Theropithecus*)—as well as the patas monkey (genus: *Erythrocebus*).

The colobus monkey of Africa (genus: *Colobus*) and the various forms of Asian langurs (genus: *Presbytis*, *Rhinopithecus*, etc.) and the proboscis monkey of Borneo (genus: *Nasalis*) make up the colobine subfamily.

Dental formula
The arrangement of teeth showing the number of each type (incisors, canines, premolars, and molars).

◇ Box 7-3   Tale of the Limbs

Besides teeth (and diet), the other major functional complex most useful in describing both extant (living) and extinct primates relates to the structure of the limbs and the form of locomotion.

A meaningful functional description of locomotion among contemporary primates should include position of the body, which limbs are used, the manner and frequency they are employed, and the nature of the substrate (such as wide tree branch, narrow branch, flat ground). By understanding the locomotory behavior of contemporary primates we can analyze their respective limb structures and form meaningful *structural-functional correlations*. With such a perspective, we can then interpret fossil primates and reconstruct their probable locomotory behavior.

A common locomotory classification of contemporary primates with their typical structural correlations is shown as (after Napier and Napier, 1967):

Category	Description of Behavior	Structural Correlates	Examples
A. Vertical clinging and leaping	leaping in trees with propulsion from hind limbs, clinging with forelimbs for vertical support	elongated hindlimbs, particularly ankle area, upper body held semi-erect	tarsier, galago
B. Quadrupedalism	using all limbs relatively equally; body horizontal	front and hindlimbs relatively equal length; spine flexible	
1. Slow climbing	slow, cautious climbing; often associated with capturing insects	widely abducted (spread) thumb, reduction of 2nd digit	potto, slow loris
2. Branch running and walking	walking or running on tops of branches, also leaping	generalized quadruped; limbs equal sized; spine flexible	ringtailed lemur; all marmosets, squirrel monkey, guenons
3. Ground running and walking	quadrupedal walking and running on ground, also tree climbing	all limbs elongated, body size usually larger than strictly arboreal species	baboons, most macaques, patas monkey
4. New World "semibrachiation"*	usually quadrupedal, some arm-swinging beneath branches with use of prehensile tail; little or no leaping	forelimbs elongated; fingers often curved, thumb reduced	howler monkey, spider monkey
5. Old World "semibrachiation"*	usually quadrupedal with arm-swinging and often considerable acrobatic leaping from branch to branch	forelimbs elongated; fingers often curved, thumb reduced	colobines (colobus, langurs)

Locomotory behavior among Old World monkeys includes arboreal quadrupedalism in the guenons and mangabeys, arm-swinging and acrobatic leaping in many of the colobines, and terrestrial quadrupedalism in the baboons, macaques, and patas monkey. In the baboons particularly, adaptation to ground living has given rise to larger body size, especially in males. Such a marked difference in body form between males and females of a species is called *sexual dimorphism*. Another striking difference in baboons is canine size, which is much larger in males.

Category	Description of Behavior	Structural Correlates	Examples
C. Ape locomotion			
1. True brachiation	acrobatic swinging arm-over-arm along (under) same branch, associated with feeding on small terminal branches	small body size, greatly elongated forelimb, curved fingers, shoulder joint oriented upward, upper body held fairly erect; spine not flexible	gibbon, siamang
2. Quadrumanual climbing	slow deliberate climbing using all four limbs for grasping	large body size, hip joint flexible like shoulder, upper body held erect, spine not flexible	orang
3. Knuckle-walking	on ground semiquadrupedal, but hands supported on knuckles; while in trees considerable arm-swinging (gorillas only as subadults)	large body size, elongated fore-limbs; stable wrist joint; upper body held erect; spine shortened and inflexible	chimp, gorilla
D. Bipedalism	strictly terrestrial, standing, striding, running upright; weight alternately on single hindlimb	medium-large body size, hind-limb elongated; pelvis altered for support and muscular leverage; feet altered for stable support with little flexibility, toes shortened; upper body completely erect; head balanced on spine; spine shortened and inflexible	human**

*Semibrachiation" is a poor term, since it implies arm-over-arm suspensory locomotion. These forms are not "partial" brachiators, but are primarily quadrupedal with considerable flexibility of the upper limb.

**True bipedalism among the primates is an adaptation *only* of modern humans and our hominid ancestors. Thus the structural correlates associated with this functional complex are crucial in determining the status of our possible ancestors.

In addition, many Old World monkey females (especially baboons and many macaques) exhibit pronounced external changes, such as swelling and coloration of the genitalia, associated with the **estrous cycle**—a hormonally initiated period of sexual receptivity in female mammals correlated with ovulation.

Because of their general hardiness even under extremely trying circumstances, Old World monkeys (particularly the versatile macaques) are favorite laboratory animals for both biomedical and behavioral experiments. Indeed,

Estrous cycle
Hormonally initiated physiological changes in female primates—associated with ovulation.

Parallel evolution
The process where two life forms (that are initially related) become physically more similar through time due to adaptation to similar environments.

Hylobatidae
(Hy-lo-bat'-i-dee)

Brachiation
Arm-over-arm suspensory locomotion beneath branches.

Quadrumanual
quadru: four
manual: hand
Using all four limbs for grasping during locomotion.

Figure 7-17 A moustached guenon. An Old World monkey.

Figure 7-18 A black-and-white colobus monkey with infant.

much of what we know about the effect of infant and child deprivation has been learned from the Harlows' well-known experiments with rhesus macaques at the University of Wisconsin (Harlow, 1959). (See p. 189.)

Monkeys, Old and New World: A Striking Case of Parallel Evolution We have mentioned several differences between monkeys in the Old World compared to those in the New World. However, the striking fact remains that they are *all* monkeys. By this statement, we mean that they all are adapted to a similar (primarily arboreal) way of life. With the exception of the South American night monkey (*Aotus*), they are diurnal and all are social, usually fairly omnivorous, and quadrupedal, though with variations of this general locomotory pattern (see Box 7-3).

These similarities are all the more striking when we consider that Old and New World monkeys have gone their separate evolutionary paths for tens of millions of years. In fact, a noted primatologist, Dr. E. L. Simons (1969), suggests the split may have occurred more than 50 m.y.a. Both forms of monkey would then have evolved independently from separate prosimian ancestors. The current consensus among researchers, however, disputes this claim (Hoffstetter, 1972; Ciochon and Chiarelli, 1980) and postulates both Old and New World monkeys arose in Africa from a common monkey ancestor and later reached South America by rafting over. (Note: South America and Africa were considerably closer together earlier in the Cenozoic. In addition, migration over water barriers may have been facilitated by "island hopping" over a chain of volcanic islands.)

In either case, what is most remarkable is that the two forms of monkey have not diverged more than they have—given the time depth of separate evolutionary history in the two hemispheres. What we see today in the diverse arboreal adaptations of monkeys is then a result of **parallel evolution** (see p. 000). Similar ecological selective forces, mainly in tropical arboreal environments, led to structural evolution in different but parallel directions. The result is that the same grade of primate we today recognize as "monkey" evolved in both New and Old Worlds.

GRADE V: HOMINOIDS

The superfamily Hominoidea includes "lesser" apes (gibbons and siamangs), great apes (orangutans, gorillas, chimpanzees), and humans. Classifying humans with the apes is not an arbitrary device, for it indicates our close structural similarities, as well as shared evolutionary history. This close similarity was noted by Tyson at the end of the seventeenth century and was forcefully restated by Huxley and Darwin in the nineteenth century. As this classification indicates, we and the apes are more closely related to each other than *either* is to an Old World monkey. In fact, many primatologists feel that the relationship between humans and great apes is so close that they are often grouped within a single family (Dene et al., 1976; Szalay and Delson, 1979). (See Table 7-1.)

The structural similarities we share with the apes are numerous but most importantly include absence of a tail, generally large body size, shortened

Figure 7-19   A female baboon in estrus. Note the sexual swelling of the genitals.

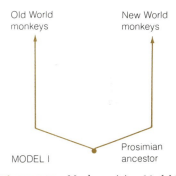

Figure 7-20   A rhesus monkey. Shown here in an isolation chamber used by NASA researchers to test the behavioral effects of long-duration space flight.

deep trunk, stable spine, and the position and musculature of the shoulder joint.

The Gibbon and Siamang   The gibbon and closely related siamang (**Hylobatidae**) are today found in the southeastern tropical areas of Asia. These animals are the smallest of the apes, with a long, slender body weighing only about thirteen pounds in the gibbon and about twenty-five pounds in the larger siamang.

The most distinctive structural feature of the hylobatids is related to their functional adaptation for **brachiation**. Consequently, they have extremely long arms, long, permanently curved fingers, and powerful shoulder muscles. This highly specialized locomotory adaptation may be related to feeding behavior while hanging beneath branches.

The Orangutan   The orang (genus: *Pongo*) is found today only in heavily forested areas on the Indonesian islands of Borneo and Sumatra. Due to poaching by humans in the past and the continuing commercial encroachment on its habitats, the orang faces imminent extinction. Such a loss would be tragic on several counts, especially because little is currently known of these mysterious red giants of the forest. Orangs are slow, cautious climbers whose whole locomotory behavior can best be described as a **quadrumanual** adaptation—a tendency to use all four limbs for grasping and support. They are large animals with pronounced sexual dimorphism (males weigh about 150 pounds and females about half that). Orangs were thought to be exclusively arboreal, but recent evidence (Galdikas, 1979) suggests they (especially males) occasionally come to the ground to traverse fairly long distances.

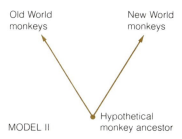

Figure 7-21   Monkey origins. Model I.

Figure 7-22   Monkey origins. Model II.

Gibbons: any area in color

Orangs: only in hatched areas

Figure 7-23 Distribution of modern Asian apes.

The Gorilla   The largest of all living primates, the gorilla (family: Pongidae; genus: *Gorilla*) today is confined to forested areas in West Africa and the great lakes area of East Africa. This species exhibits marked sexual dimorphism, with males weighing up to 400 pounds in the wild and females around 200 pounds. Due to their very large adult weight, gorillas are almost completely terrestrial, adopting a semiquadrupedal (knuckle-walking) posture on the ground. Their forelimbs are elongated, though not so much as in gibbons, their upper bodies are normally held semierect, and their arms possess considerable mobility. Consequently, there are numerous structural modifications: a flattened (front-to-back) and broadened (side-to-side) chest; a shortened, more stable spine (compared to quadrupedal monkeys); longer clavicles; and flexible, powerful shoulders. The wrist joint is also modified to support the considerable weight of the upper body during knuckle-walking. In addition, gorillas have brains more complexly organized than monkeys or gibbons, thus allowing for more learned behavior. Once considered a wild and savage beast, the gorilla has been shown by field studies to be a shy, usually gentle vegetarian (Schaller, 1963; Fossey, 1970). Recent reports, however, have shown that—like many other primates—gorillas fairly frequently attack and kill other members of their species, particularly infants (Fossey, 1981).

The Chimpanzee   Probably the best known and most loved of all the non-human primates is the chimpanzee (family: Pongidae; genus: *Pan*). Often misunderstood because of their displays within zoos and carnival sideshows, the chimps' true nature did not come to light until long hours of field work in their natural environments provided a reliable picture. Chimps are found today in equatorial Africa stretching in a broad belt from the Atlantic Ocean in the west to Lake Tanganyika in the east.

Chimpanzees are in many ways structurally quite similar to gorillas, with corresponding limb proportions and thorax (chest) shape as well as specific features of the upper limb and wrist joint. This similarity is due to the likeness in their mode of locomotion (knuckle-walking) while on the ground. Indeed, many authorities (for example, Buettner-Janusch, 1973) consider chimps and gorillas as members of a single genus (*Pan gorilla* for the gorilla; *Pan troglodytes* for the chimp). However, the ecological adaptations of the chimp and gorilla differ, since chimps spend a great deal of time arm-swinging in the trees and feeding primarily on fruit. Conversely, gorillas are almost exclusively terrestrial vegetarians, consuming such vegetative matter as roots, shoots, and bark.

Like the brain of the gorilla, the chimpanzee brain is highly developed, and the learning capabilities of these animals are well known to visitors to animal shows as well as to scientific investigators.

Humans   Humans (family: Hominidae; genus: *Homo*) belong to the one remaining genus of the superfamily Hominoidea, a genus that today consists of only one species, *Homo sapiens*. Our primate heritage is shown again and again in the structure of our body: our dependence on vision; our lack of reliance on olfactory (smell) cues; and our flexible limbs and grasping hands are all long rooted in our primate, arboreal past. Indeed, among the primates, we show in many ways the most developed set of primate characteristics.

Figure 7-24 Gibbon.

Figure 7-25   A male orangutan.

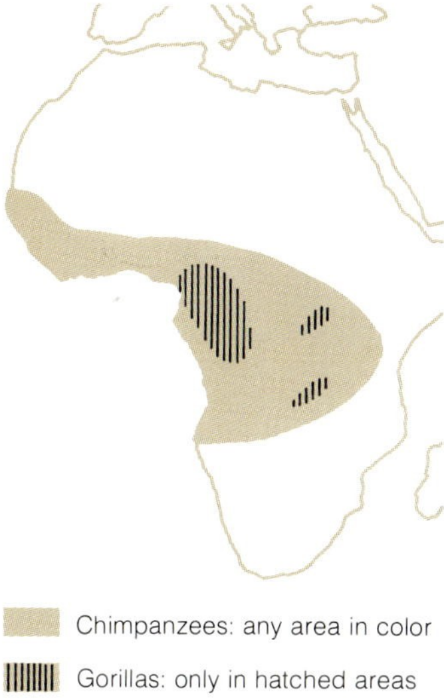

Chimpanzees: any area in color

Gorillas: only in hatched areas

Figure 7-26   Distribution of modern African apes.

Figure 7-27   A male lowland gorilla.

Figure 7-28   Chimpanzee.

For example, the development of our cerebral cortex and reliance on learned behavior with resulting complexity in social behavior are but elaborations of long-established primate trends.

The most distinct feature seen in humans is our unique manner of locomotion. The striding, bipedal gait with alternating support placed on a single hindlimb has required significant structural modifications in the pelvis and leg. By isolating similar structural modifications in the remains of fossil animals, we are able to distinguish our closely related or direct ancestors.

◇ Primate Chromosomes, Proteins, and DNA

The classification of primates used thus far in this chapter has employed the traditional approach of looking for homologies in morphological traits. However, another relatively new perspective with enormous potential for helping to clarify taxonomic problems compares **karyotypes** (chromosome numbers, shapes, banding patterns), proteins, and even roughly correlates the DNA code itself.

The usefulness of this approach is immediately obvious. When we compare outward morphology, such as limb proportions and dental formulae, we are comparing phenotypes, usually far removed from their underlying genetic basis. However, what we are really after in the construction of classification schemes are homologies, traits based on common evolutionary descent. In other words, we want to compare traits that are inherited—those coded directly in the genotype.

Direct protein products of DNA, such as hemoglobin and serum proteins (found in the blood), are excellent indicators of homologies. If two species of primates are systematically similar in their protein structure, we can infer their DNA sequences are also similar. When two species share similar DNA, that means both inherited the same blueprint (with minor revisions) from a common ancestor. Thus, we have *direct* indicators of real homologies. Two primates that superficially resemble one another (some New World and Old World monkeys, for example) may in fact not be closely related at all. Using outward morphology alone may be confusing due to unknown effects from parallel evolution. But such evidence as biochemical data and karyotype comparisons avoids these pitfalls, and indeed shows Old and New World monkeys as genetically (and evolutionarily) quite distinct.

Primatologists utilizing these techniques have, in conjunction with biochemists, in the last few years added considerable insight into our classifications of the primate order. A point worthy of mention: In most cases, biochemical evidence has reaffirmed the taxonomies constructed from comparative morphological studies (thereby supplying an extremely important independent source of data). When contradictions with traditional taxonomies have cropped up, much needed new knowledge has been gained. For example, classifying the orang with the African great apes superficially makes good sense since their outward body structures appear similar. Biochemical evidence, however, shows that both Asian apes (orangs and gibbons) are quite distinct from chimps and gorillas. Since our classifications are designed to reflect evolutionary relationships, they will have to be revised in the future to accord with this new information. (See Table 7-1.)

The way the various chromosomal and biochemical techniques are performed requires considerable technological sophistication, but their applications are straightforward. For example, two species can be compared for karotype. The more closely two species are related, the closer their karyotypes should be. When one looks at the chromosomes of the hominoids, it is readily apparent that humans and the great apes are all quite similar, with gibbons and siamangs having the most distinctive (i.e., derived) pattern (Stanyon and Chiarelli, 1982; Mai, 1983).

Among the large-bodied hominoids, the orang karyotype is the most conservative, with humans and the African apes displaying more derived features. It is interesting to note that the fossil data (which we'll take up in Chapter 10) also now suggests that orangs are probably the most conservative (i.e., primitive) of the large hominoids.

Within the human/gorilla/chimp group there are a tremendous number of similarities of the structural arrangement and banding patterns of almost all the chromosomes. A relatively small number of alterations are required to transform all three living species from a theoretical ancestor (Yunis and Prakash, 1982).

The exact sequence of evolutionary relationships among humans and the African great apes is still in some dispute. Some tentative chromosomal data have suggested that humans and chimps share a more recent ancestry after separating from gorillas (Yunis and Prakash, 1982). A more controlled study, however, with consideration of within-species variation of karyotype (Stanyon and Chiarelli, 1982), has supported the more traditional branching order, where humans and *both* African apes diverge first—followed later by a separation of chimps and gorillas.

Detailed protein structures can be compared, as between chimp and human hemoglobin, by isolating the amino acid sequences. Comparisons between humans and the African great apes for the approximately half dozen proteins analyzed in this manner show striking similarities; they are either identical or show a difference of only one or two amino acids in the entire sequence (as you will recall, the hemoglobin beta chain is 146 amino acids long).

Another method used to contrast proteins in different species is not as precise as a detailed protein analysis but is less time consuming and less costly. By measuring the strength of reaction to specially prepared antisera, similarities in proteins are calibrated on a relative scale, indicating *antigenic distance*. This approach, developed by Vincent Sarich and Allan Wilson at the University of California, Berkeley, has enabled many more proteins to be compared among a wide variety of different primate species. The results again generally tally favorably with traditional classifications.

Moreover, differences in DNA strands themselves can be compared using an elaborate technique called DNA hybridization. Scientists have recently performed some remarkable experiments in which double strands of DNA are artificially separated in two different species and then recombined into a

Karyotype
The characteristic number, size, and pattern of the chromosomes that are distinctive for particular species.

new molecule, a hybrid DNA unlike anything nature ever concocted. The genetic (and evolutionary) similarity of the two species is then calculated by measuring the number of mismatched base pairs along the hybrid sequence (in other words, places where the two sides of the molecule are not complementary: A with T, G with C, etc.).

Once again, the results of this fascinating but still fairly new technique have reaffirmed our particularly close affinities with the gorilla and chimp, a definitely less direct evolutionary link with the Asian apes, and even further genetic distinctiveness from Old World monkeys.

Finally, the revolution in molecular biology brought about by recombinant DNA research has now made it possible to directly sequence the nucleotides of humans and other organisms (Goodman, et al., 1983). As a result—when this new technique has been more widely applied—we should be able to ascertain even more unambiguously the precise genetic/evolutionary relationships among the primates.

In addition, these nucleotide sequence data will inform us concerning the frequency of "neutral" mutations and (when calibrated with fossil data) may elucidate whether primate evolution has been more characterized by "gradualistic" or "punctionalistic" modes of change (see pp. 91–93).

◇ Summary

Primates are an order of placental mammals characterized by their generalized limb structure, dependence on vision, lack of reliance on smell, developed brain (particularly cerebral cortex), and complex social organizations. All these evolutionary trends have developed, or at least have been elaborated, as a direct result of adaptation to an arboreal environment.

Living primates today represent five major grades of evolution that correspond to various stages of primate evolution over the last several million years. These grades are:

    I. Tree shrews (not really true primates)
   II. Lemurs and lorises
  III. Tarsiers
  IV. Monkeys (New World and Old World)
   V. Hominoids (apes and humans)

We are a primate and our ancestors have been primates for at least 70 million years. Only by looking at humans *as a primate* can we hope to understand the kind of animal we are and how we came to be this way.

◇ Questions for Review

1. How are primates similar to other placental mammals?
2. Discuss how binocular vision, prehensility, and an expanded cerebral cortex are adaptations for an arboreal niche.
3. What are the various superfamilies of the primate order? To which one do humans belong?
4. Discuss the geographic distribution and ecological adaptations of contemporary prosimians.
5. What are the most important differences between prosimians and anthropoids?
6. How do monkeys in the Old and New Worlds exhibit parallel evolution?
7. How do teeth reflect evolutionary relationships?
8. What are some important relationships between limb structure and locomotion in contemporary primates?
9. In what ways are humans typical primates?
10. How does biochemical evidence give indication of homologies? Why are effects due to parallel evolution more likely to cloud the picture for morphological traits than for biochemical traits?

Models for Human Behavior

CONTENTS

For years, scholars and popular writers have discussed human aggression. One of the very basic questions has been (and still is, for that matter) whether human aggression is instinctive or learned, or a combination of both. This issue is significant because, if aggression is learned, it can be unlearned; or, the learning of aggression can be modified or replaced by other attitudes. If it is instinctive, then it may be necessary to develop quite different techniques in dealing with it. Many believe that a clue to the source of human aggression might be found in nonhuman primate behavior, especially that of

the apes. Field studies have shown monkeys—especially baboons and macaques—to be quite aggressive, but since humans are more closely related to apes, the question of ape aggression is more relevant.

Until recently, field studies of apes have been infrequent, and those that were done were not nearly as thorough as those that are contemporary. While much evidence remains to be obtained, the number of field studies since 1960 has increased manyfold and data are accumulating in great quantities on chimpanzees, gorillas, and orangutans.

Dian Fossey's early reports on go-

rillas did not mention aggression, but in her recent account, Fossey writes of two kinds of gorilla aggression. One, witnessed by a student of Fossey—Peter Veit—was a violent attack by a male on a female that resulted in the female's death. The female was ill and probably would have soon perished in any event, but the male literally stomped her to death.

Fossey also reported that infanticide accounted for the deaths of 6 out of 38 infants born over a 13-year period. The killing of the infants was perpetrated by males. Fossey believes that infanticide "is the means by which a male instinctively seeks to perpetuate his own lineage by killing another male's progeny in order to breed with the victim's mother" (Fossey, 1981, p. 512). (See Sociobiology for a discussion of this theory, p. 214).

Unlike gorillas—and, as we shall see, chimpanzees—orangutans do not appear to be aggressive. At least, observers have seen very little aggression. Biruté Galdikas (1981) reported what she believes to be a case of "rape," which, however, she did not actually witness. She heard the screams of a female, heard a good deal of thrashing about, saw the male leave shortly thereafter, and then observed bruises on the female. Whether this was an isolated incident, or whether it is a common event is still not known.

In contrast to gorillas and orangs, abundant field studies of chimpanzees show evidence of frequent aggression—including killing—among these primates. Are there killer apes—apes guilty of calculated, premeditated "murder"? The case of the male gorillas mentioned above is evidence there are. More evidence comes from chimpanzees.

In the past two decades, beginning with Jane Goodall's study of chimpanzees in Tanzania's Gombe Stream National Park, intensive research on chimpanzees, gorillas, and orangutans has been conducted in Africa and Borneo. Early reports from these studies led us to believe that apes were "gentle folk," kind to their children and playing out a more or less

"live and let live" existence. The only animal that murdered its own kind, it seemed, was the human animal.

Beginning in 1974, Goodall and her colleagues at Gombe Stream observed a series of at least five unprovoked (or so it seemed to the observers) brutal, savage gang attacks by males of one group against the males of another group that had splintered off several years earlier. All seven males of the splinter group were wiped out by 1977. One attack even involved an elderly female who died as a consequence of the beating. The attackers were usually young males, using their teeth, hands, and feet, although on one occasion an older male was seen throwing a rock at a prostrate victim.

Even more disturbing, perhaps, is the cannibalism that Goodall has witnessed. She reports on a mother-daughter pair of chimps that had killed and eaten possibly up to ten newborns. Another case of cannibalism in East Africa was recently reported for the chimpanzees of the Mahale Mountains. We do not know how widespread the practice is, or what its adaptive value might be.

Because of the biochemical and genetic similarity between chimpanzees and humans, chimpanzee behavior may hold clues to human origins and even present-day human behavior. The significance of the killings and the cannibalism observed among chimpanzees remains to be worked out. Meanwhile, it is distress-

ing to find that our image of the playful, friendly chimpanzee may well be illusion rather than reality.

As Goodall observed, "It is sobering that our new awareness of chimpanzee violence compels us to acknowledge that these ape cousins of ours are even more similar to humans than we thought before."

SOURCE:

Fossey, Dian. "Imperiled Giants of the Forest," *National Geographic*, 4: 501–522, April, 1981.

Galdikas, Biruté. Public Lecture at the California Institute of Technology, May 2, 1981.

Hamburg, David A. and E. R. McCown. *The Great Apes*, Menlo Park, Ca.: The Benjamin/Cummings Publishing Co., 1979.

Goodall, Jane. "Chimp Killings: Is It the 'Man' in Them?" *Science News*, 17: 276, April 29, 1978.

———, *National Geographic*, 5: 592–620, May, 1979.

Norikashi, Kohshi. "One Observed Case of Cannibalism among Wild Chimpanzees of the Mahale Mountains," *Primates*, 23 (1):66–74, January, 1982.

◇ Introduction

How can we better understand human behavior? Observing an urbanized industrialized society such as ours will not tell us very much of our hominid heritage. After all, we have been urbanized for only a few thousand years, and the industrial revolution is merely a few centuries old, barely a flicker in evolutionary time. Consequently, to understand what behavior components may have shaped our evolution, we need a perspective broader than that which our own culture supplies. Since little is known about early hominid behavior, we study the behavior of contemporary animals adapted to environments similar to those of early hominids in the hope of gaining insight into early hominid evolution.

We shall consider as possible models for this purpose the social carnivores of the savanna (wild dogs, lions, and wolves*), as well as the nonhuman primates of the savanna (baboons) and of the forest/savanna (chimpanzees). Finally, we shall also consider modern hunting-gathering societies as a possible model for early hominid adaptation, since this may have been the hominid way of life for 99% of their existence on earth. We take, as our example, the !Kung San of the Kalahari Desert in South Africa.

In this chapter, we place nonhominid behavior in the context of its possible relationship to human behavior; that is, we address the question: Does the study of nonhuman primates serve as a window on (or model for) human behavior? Or are nonhuman primates so different in behavior from hominids that the uniqueness of the former derives little from the latter?

◇ Behavior and Human Origins

What does it mean to be human? There are several *physical* characteristics, such as adaptations for bipedal locomotion and enlarged brain, that characterize humans and—to varying extents—our hominid ancestors. But from a strictly structural point of view, we are not really that unique compared to other primates, especially when compared with the great apes. In patterns of dentition, bone development, muscle structure, and so forth, we and the other hominoids are very similar, reflecting a fairly recent shared ancestry. (Probably no more than 7 or 8 m.y. at most separate us from the African great apes.) Indeed, in the nonrepeated portions of DNA, humans and chimpanzees are 99% identical. So what, precisely, is it that distinguishes the human animal?

Quite clearly, it is behavioral attributes that most dramatically set humans

*Wolves of course are not savanna animals, but their environment—except for temperature— resembles the savanna.

apart. Human culture is our strategy for coping with life's challenges. No other primate even comes close to the human ability to modify environments. Communication through symbolic language is yet another uniquely human characteristic (see pp. 208–212 for a discussion of "language" in great apes). In addition, several other features differentiate humans from the majority of other primates. These may be summarized as follows:

Humans are bipedal.

Humans live in permanent mixed male and female groups with male/female bonding.

Humans have large brains relative to body weight and are capable of complex learning.

Partly as a consequence of neurological reorganization, humans make highly advanced use of symbolic language.

Also related to neurological developments and bipedality, *cultural* response has become the central hominid adaptive strategy.

Humans obtain food through some male/female division of labor; moreover, food is actively transported back to a base camp (home) for purposes of sharing.

Length of dependence of young has increased in humans, resulting in greater parental investment—not only by the mother, but often by adult males as well.

With more time and energy expended on each offspring, the total number raised is low in humans compared to most mammals, but, in fact, may be higher than seen in great apes (Lovejoy, 1981).

There is a relaxation of the estrous cycle and concealed ovulation in humans, so that females can be sexually receptive at any time.

These traits are fairly characteristic of all modern humans. Moreover, much of this behavioral complex is thought to be a good *baseline* for the early stages of hominid emergence. In fact, behavioral reconstructions are often central to theories explaining how hominids came to be hominids in the first place.

A recent comprehensive reconstruction of the factors influencing human origins has been proposed by C. Owen Lovejoy (1981).* The Lovejoy model attempts to integrate the behavioral and structural modifications that prevailed during the earliest stages of hominid emergence (10–5 m.y.a.). A "prime mover," according to Lovejoy, was the selective advantage of increased male parental investment.

Lovejoy sees ecological strategies of early hominids based on some *division of labor*, where males and females exploited slightly different resources. This pattern was elaborated further as males ranged farther away (particularly in search of game), while females remained closer to a central rendezvous point, which eventually became a base camp. With females staying closer to a fixed

---

*Lovejoy's model is given simply as one scholar's suggestion of human origins. Many anthropologists disagree with his interpretation and organization of the data. The authors do not necessarily agree with Lovejoy's point of view.

Polygyny
(po-lyj´-y-nee)
poly: much, many
gyn: female
One male and two or more females in a
mating relationship.

Social behavior
Exhibiting gregariousness, sociability. The
behavior of animals that live together in,
and interact as, a group consisting of
adults and young of both sexes.

base, they would avoid carrying their infants long distances, thus reducing infant mortality. While females are thought to have ranged closer to camp, gathering wild plant foods and perhaps small mammals, they alone presumably could not provide sufficient subsistence for themselves and several young. The solution, Lovejoy believes, lay in male provisioning—bringing food back to the base camp for purposes of sharing. This key aspect concerning active transport of food to a central point in order to be shared is not seen in any other primate. The same idea has also been put forth by Glynn Isaac (1976, 1978) as a significant influence on early human emergence.

With males' greater investment in the provisioning process, females could raise more young than would otherwise be the case. Thus, birth spacing could be reduced, and hominid males and females behaving in this way would consequently increase their reproductive success.

Several males returning to the females at the base camp might encourage male-male competition, but this could possibly be diffused by the development of one-to-one male/female bonding; i.e., a monogamous relationship (an idea championed by Desmond Morris, 1967).

Bipedality (probably the first major distinction of hominids) would have evolved because the male carrying food to his female would have to do so bipedally. Bipedality in the female would be adaptive because she could carry an infant in one hand, and provision herself with the other.

For this system to work, it would be necessary for the male to carry food to his female throughout the year. He would have to be permanently attracted to her, not just at the time of estrus. This could be arranged through the development of permanent features on the female's body, such as hair, skin, shape, and prominent breasts, which would permanently attract the male and keep him interested the year-round (also proposed by Morris). According to Lovejoy's model, distinctive human traits, such as bipedality, pair bonding, food sharing, and sexual and reproductive behavior, are thus explained.

The Lovejoy model proposes a comprehensive and internally consistent explanation of human origins. However, it is not a scientific theory, since it cannot be framed into testable hypotheses. More appropriately, Lovejoy's assertions (just as those of others before him—Desmond Morris, Robert Ardrey, and so forth) could be termed a *scenario*, a speculative reconstruction. Since social behavior does not fossilize (except for some tantalizing hints— see Chapter 10), it is unlikely that we will be able to fully reconstruct the details of early hominid biosocial evolution. If anything, the physical evidence of the early hominids themselves (Chapters 11 and 12) suggests that some of the central premises in Lovejoy's scenario are probably wrong.

However, the Lovejoy model is extremely useful in highlighting some of the major differences between humans and other primates. Sometime during the course of human evolution, the complex of features discussed in this scenario did emerge. We mainly disagree with Lovejoy, though, concerning the *sequence* and *timing* of these behavioral modifications. Unlike Lovejoy, we do not believe it likely (or even probable) that very early hominids were paired monogamously. The other developments—bipedalism, increased meat exploitation, food sharing, and greater parental investment (by males, too, but indirectly)—could very well all have proceeded in a **polygynously** mating early hominid society similar to the vast majority of living primates.

◇Definition of Behavior: To Be or Not To Be Social

Behavior could be generally defined as "anything an organism does." As such, it is part of a phenotype (see p. 73), which in many cases bears *some* relationship to the underlying genotype. The precise mechanisms of genotype/phenotype interaction are poorly understood—especially for the more complex animals (i.e., vertebrates). As a result, great controversies have arisen concerning the genetic contribution to behavior in such animals. (We have addressed this issue in our discussion of human intelligence on pp. 119–122.)

We are concerned, however, with those particular aspects of behavior that are most useful for informing us about human evolution. Specifically, we want to focus on **social behavior**; that is, on relationships between animals of the same species—those that associate within fairly stable groups. Most animals (such as beetles, turtles, sharks, and so forth) are not social, but pursue a solitary existence. For many species, the only social contact that occurs between individual members is when adults of the opposite sex mate.

The exceptions are what interest us. While there are many species of highly evolved colony-living social insects (termites, ants, wasps, and bees), among the vertebrates, sociality is not a blanket phenomenon. Fish, for example, are social only to a minimum, where they move together (form schools)—there is, in fish, little in the way of social differentiation (i.e., classes or castes). Nor do reptiles or amphibians exhibit much of what could be called elaborated social activity. Birds and mammals, however, *are* social, many displaying complex role development, communication, parental strategies, and learning (the latter mostly in mammals).

Of the more than 4,000 species of mammals, all are social to a degree. Most basically, there is the "bond of milk" between a mother and her dependent, unweaned young. Moreover, some contact is obviously required between adult males and females for sexual reproduction. Beyond this, however, there is not much social interaction. For example, gophers, rats, and most insectivores (moles, hedgehogs, and shrews), are solitary; that is, the mother and her unweaned young form the only longterm association. In other species, such as wild pigs, mule deer, and mountain goats, females with their young may form permanent groups, but the males remain peripheral and mostly solitary. In yet other mammals, such as sea lions, camels, and musk oxen, the males may associate with the females, but only during the breeding season.

In a few mammals, however, males associate all year long with the female groups, but it is clear that such an arrangement is the exception rather than the rule. Still, this social pattern is of great interest to us, as it is one typically seen in our own species. Some of the noteworthy mammalian examples of such integrated mixed male/female social grouping can be found among the social carnivores (i.e., members of the order Carnivora). Included here are lions and, most especially, the pack-hunting canids—wolves and wild dogs. Since these animals display a social structure in some ways roughly analogous to that of humans, and since they evolved in physical environments presumably similar to that of our ancestors, we will discuss the social carnivores in some detail later in this chapter.

◇ Box 8-1   Key Concepts

Agonistic   Hostile behavior (see pp. 200, 202).

Core Area   An area within the home range where the group habitually sleeps, feeds, and performs routine activities. The area within the home range of greatest regular use.

Display   Stereotyped behavior or series of behaviors that serves to communicate emotional states between individuals. Most often concerned with reproductive or agonistic behaviors.

Division of Labor   Activities performed only by members of a particular status, such as age or sex.

Dominance   Also referred to as *dominance hierarchy* and *status rank*. The physical domination of some members of a group by other members. A hierarchy of ranked statuses sustained by hostile, or threat of hostile, behavior, which results in greater access to resources, such as food, sleeping sites, and mates.

Grooming, Social   Cleaning the body of another by picking through the hair and fur with the fingers or teeth.

Home Range   The area utilized by an animal; the living area in which an animal performs its normal activities; the area the group is most familiar with, and which provides the group with food.

Mother-Infant Relationship   The attachment between mother and her offspring. One of the most basic themes running through primate social relations.

Presenting   A behavior, often indicating subordination or appeasement, in which an animal places itself on all fours and elevates its rear end toward another. (During estrus a female may present for purposes of copulation.)

Scent-Marking   Deposition of odoriferous substances, known as *pheromones*, on an animal or object, typically a tree, bush, or rock. The deposition may be through scent glands or urine or both.

Territory   That part of the home range used exclusively by one group. Neighbors (of the same species) do not enter, or else enter only on a brief foray. Also defined as the area defended by one group against another group of the same species.

The other major exception to the basic mammalian social order is the primates, especially the anthropoids. As Chapter 7 notes, monkeys and apes typically associate in permanent groups comprised of adult females, their young, *and* adult males. Among more than 150 species of anthropoids, there are only a few species that do not conform to this pattern (see Box 8-2, p. 185). The vast majority of anthropoids could thus be seen as displaying the "nontypical" social pattern also characteristic of human societies. Surely, this is no accident, and argues for an evolutionary background to human social behavior.

◇ Nonhuman Primates

Modern apes and humans last shared an ancestor in common somewhere between 8–14 m.y.a., according to some specialists, or 4–8 m.y.a., according to others. Researchers believe that ape behavior has changed since then, but not nearly as much as the behavior of hominids, who developed culture as their strategy of adaptation. Therefore, if we are interested in what hominid behavior might have been like before culture became a significant factor in

---

◇ Box 8-2   Types of Nonhuman Primate Social Groups

I. *Solitary Primates*   Arboreal and nocturnal, solitary in the sense that they feed alone.
EXAMPLES: mouse lemur, galago, potto, loris, aye-aye, orangutan.

II. *Family Group*   Adult male and female and their off-spring; seen only among arboreal species.
EXAMPLES: indri, titi, marmoset, gibbon.

III. *Multimale*   The most common type among primates; found in both arboreal and terrestrial forms. Several adult males and about twice as many adult females and their offspring.
EXAMPLES: ring-tailed lemur, many New World monkeys, gorilla, sifaka, chimpanzee, baboon, macaque, howler.

IV. *One-male (Harem)*   May be adaptation of multimale group to arid conditions. Since only one male is neces-

sary to procreate next generation, and since several large males would eat a disproportionate amount of scarce food, a one-male group is an efficient adaptive unit for this environment.
EXAMPLES: gelada baboon, hamadryas baboon, ground-living patas, some guenons, colobus (guereza), some langurs.

SOURCE:
After P. Napier, 1972.

ADDITIONAL SOURCES:
Bramblett, 1976 (sifaka); Jolly, 1972 (sifaka); Carpenter, 1965 (howler); Kummer, 1971 (guenon); Struhsaker and Oates, 1975 (colobus).

---

it, and if we wish to know what behaviors may have led hominids to become dependent on culture, we may find clues in the behavior of our closest relatives, the apes. Later in this chapter, we shall, then, explore chimpanzee behavior for such clues.

The social behavior of nonhuman primates may be viewed as a simplified model of human behavior. The shorter life span of nonhuman primates allows us to follow their behavior through developmental stages with more ease than a similar study of human behavior would provide. As intimated, nonhuman primate behavior provides clues to, or suggests ideas about, what early hominid behavior may have been like. This approach emphasizes correlating particular social structures of given animals with attributes of their habitats, since all living organisms must adapt to their environment (Figs. 8-1 and 8-2). Such observations may offer hints to the environmental pressures involved and may ultimately lead to comprehending the factors that led to human emergence.

Studies of nonhuman primates also assist with present human behavioral problems. Humans are *not* monkeys or apes, of course, but similarities do exist. For example, the way human infants learn to love and bond to mother and then family is reflected in the infant behavior patterns of monkeys and apes. It is, after all, possible that "The more we can learn about the evolutionary history and adaptations of other primate forms, the more we will know about the processes which shaped our own species" (Lancaster, 1975, p. 5).

Species of primates are numerous, and their behavior varies a good deal. Nevertheless, there are characteristics common to most, if not all, primates.

Figure 8-1 These baboons have adapted quadrupedally to a terrestrial savanna life.

Figure 8-2 Gibbons brachiating, an arboreal adaptation.

Most primates live in tropical or semitropical regions, but a few, such as the Japanese macaque and some langurs, have adapted to cold weather. Although they vary, primates are mainly *diurnal*, some are **crepuscular** and others, especially among prosimians, are *nocturnal*. Relatively few nonhuman primates are terrestrial—savanna baboons and gorillas are the best known; most others are arboreal. Intelligence, a difficult concept to define, is another characteristic common to primates, and it is generally conceded that all primates are more intelligent than most, if not all, other mammals.

Living in social groups is one of the major characteristics of primates, who solve their major adaptive problems within this social context. For other animals, "mating, feeding, sleeping, growth of the individual, and protection from pedators are usually matters for the solitary individual to solve, but for . . . primates they are most often performed in a social context" (Lancaster, 1975, p. 12).

Many different patterns of social groupings exist among the primates (see Box 8-2). Typically, the primate social group includes members of all ages and of both sexes, a composition that does not vary significantly during the annual cycle. As we pointed out, this situation differs from that of most mammals, whose adult males and females associate only during the breeding season, and whose young do not remain with the adults after reaching puberty.

Because they remain together over a long period of time, members of the specific primate group learn to know each other. They learn—as they must—how to respond to a variety of actions that may be threatening, cooperative, or indifferent. In such social groups, individuals must be able to evaluate a situation before acting. Evolutionarily speaking, this would have placed selective pressure on social intelligence which, in turn, would select for brains that could assess such situations and store the information. One of the results of such selection would be the evolution of proportionately larger and more complex brains, especially in the higher primates.

◇ Social Behavior

Since primates solve their major adaptive problems in a social context, we might expect that they participate in a number of activities to reinforce the integrity of the group for purposes of holding it together. The better known of these activities are described in the sections that follow.

ASPECTS OF SOCIAL BEHAVIOR

Grooming   Almost all primates groom one another. Grooming occurs in other animal species, but social grooming is a unique primate activity and plays an important role in the life of most primates. It helps remove dirt and parasites, but "it is much more than that—it is the social cement of primates from lemur to chimpanzee" (Jolly, 1972, p. 153). Grooming is often reciprocal, with roles interchanged—the groomer may become the groomee, a process resulting in the establishment of friendly social relations among the animals in the group.

Displays   A wide variety of body movements, vocalizations, olfactory signals (scent-marking, for example), and facial gestures communicate to other members of the species such emotional signals as fear, threats, greeting, danger, pain, hunger, courtship, and many other messages as well.
    Animals often display when they are excited, a state that may be brought about by such situations as the presence of an outsider, a response to the

Crepuscular
(kre-pus'-kew-ler)
creper: dark, dusty
Active at twilight or dawn.

Figure 8-3 Primate mothers and their infants.

Figure 8-4 Grooming baboons. The white eyelid of the baboon is a threat display.

Figure 8-5 (*a*) A gorilla display. (*b*) A chimp display. This old male swings his arms and then throws things at the zoo spectators.

display of another member of the group, or a need for reinforcing status relationships. The gorilla is known for its magnificent display involving such activities as hooting, throwing vegetation, and chest beating.

Displays of other primates include grunting, yawning, ground slapping, branch-shaking, head bobbing and bouncing, screams, hoots, strutting, scratching, barks, scent-marking (among prosimians), and facial gestures, such as smiling and grimacing. A display primarily communicates information that "is advantageous to the individual of the species, to the social group to which he belongs, to others of the same species, and to other species" (Buettner-Janusch, 1973, p. 307).

Dominance*   Dominance rank, or status rank, may be measured by priority access to a desired object, such as food or sex, and also by the result of threat situations. A dominant individual is given priority, and in a confrontation is the one that usually does not give way. It is believed, although not all primatologists agree, that because dominant males compete more successfully for fertile females than do subordinate males, they have greater reproductive success. Also, dominant females, because they compete for food more successfully than subordinate females, are thus provided with more energy for offspring production and have greater reproductive success than subordinate females (Fedigan, 1983).

In many primate societies males are generally dominant over females of the same age, older or stronger individuals supplant weaker ones, and each

*See Fedigan, 1983, for a review of dominance theory.

(*a*)   (*b*)

group member must learn its rank in the hierarchy, at least within its own sex and age class. "Further, the length of time spent in the group, called 'residency' or male 'tenure,' also correlates significantly with rank, positively in the case of macaques . . . and negatively with the case of baboons" (Fedigan, 1983, pp. 111–112). Dominant males are sometimes responsible for protecting the troop from predators as well as for defense against other troops if that situation should arise.

Dominance is adaptive because it operates to avoid conflict. When two individuals compete for the same scarce item, the dominant one assumes priority by threat behavior. Thus dominance serves to organize social interactions; individuals know where they belong and act accordingly, avoiding chaotic, unorganized social relations. The result is a smoothly functioning order of priority, which reduces endless quarrels for scarce resources.

Mother-Infant Relationship   The basic social unit among primates is the female and her infants. Adult males consort with females for mating purposes, but they may or may not participate as members of the social unit. Observations both in the field and in captivity suggest that this mother-offspring core provides the group with its stability.

Figure 8-6   Primate mothers and their infants. (In the photo depicting the human, a grandmother substitutes for the mother.)

The mother-infant attachment, one of the most basic themes running throughout primate social relations, begins at birth. A primate infant's first bond (in the anthropoids especially) is to its mother. After birth, the infant clings to its mother while she performs her daily activities, often without seeming regard for her offspring's success in holding on. Quite often, however, as she leaves for some activity, a mother will gather her infant protectively to her body. Unlike other social animals, in which the newborn are left in a nest or den, the clinging primate infant develops a closeness with the mother that

Figure 8-7 Wire mother and cloth mother.

does not end with weaning. This closeness is often maintained throughout life and is reflected in grooming behavior that continues between mother and offspring even after the children reach adulthood.

The crucial role played by primate mothers was clearly demonstrated by the Harlows, (1959), who raised some infant monkeys with surrogate mothers fashioned from cloth and other monkeys with no mothers at all. In one experiment, infants raised with surrogate mothers retained an attachment to their cloth mother, but those raised without a mother were incapable of forming a lasting affectional tie.

In another experiment (Harlow and Harlow, 1961), monkeys raised without a mother sat passively in their cages and stared vacantly into space. Some punished themselves by seizing one of their arms with the mouth and tearing the flesh until blood flowed. Those raised with a surrogate mother acted similarly, but somewhat less dramatically. None of the males or females raised without real or surrogate mothers ever achieved any semblance of normal sexual behavior. No motherless male ever successfully copulated and often violently assaulted the female he was paired with. Females (those raised without mothers as well as those raised with cloth mothers) that were successfully impregnated and bore young, paid very little attention to their infants. A mother often brushed away her baby "as if she were brushing off flies" or crushed her infant to the floor, and these mothers rarely held their infants or protected them as normal mothers do.

The Harlows conclude: "We only know that these monkeys without normal mothering and without peer affectional relationships have behaved toward their infants in a manner completely outside the range of even the least adequate of normal mothers" (1961, p. 55).

In more recent studies, Professor Suomi of the University of Wisconsin Primate Laboratory and a student of Harlow, has confirmed the importance of the mother-infant relationship. Even brief separations from the mother have lasting effects. He further points out that peer relationships suffer if the individual does not have a good relationship with its mother (Greenberg, 1977). His review of isolation studies has led Suomi to emphasize that social isolation initiated early in life can have devastating effects on subsequent development and behavior for many species of primates. The primate deprivation syndrome that results from early isolation is characterized by displays of abnormal self-directed and stereotypic behavior and by gross deficits in all aspects of social behavior (Suomi, 1982, p. 190).

Infants are mainly cared for by the mother, of course, but adult males are also known to take more than a casual interest. This phenomenon has frequently been noted among male hamadryas baboons, who sometimes "adopt" an infant. "He then carries it en route, allows it to sleep huddled against his belly at night, and prevents it from moving too far away" (Kummer, 1971, pp. 81–82).

What may be an extension of the mother-infant relationship has been called **allo**parent, or "aunt" behavior. This type of behavior occurs among many animal species but is most richly expressed in primates, and some researchers believe it is found among all social primates. No biological relationship is necessarily suggested by the term (although elder siblings often act as alloparents). It is just "that females are behaving like the maiden aunts of English turn-of-the-century middle-class families" (Jolly, 1972, p. 252). Usually, the alloparents crowd around the newborn infant and attempt to carry, cuddle, groom, hold, or just touch it. Some species, like the common langur, are well known for their aunts, and as many as eight females may hold the infant during its first day of life. Among patas monkeys, the mother may threaten a female that touches her baby, so the interested female resorts to a subtle maneuver. "A patas female may begin to groom a mother's arm and then slowly and cautiously transfer her grooming to the infant within it" (Kummer, 1971, p. 80).

Several functions are suggested for alloparenting. If the mother dies, the infant stands a chance of being adopted by an alloparent or other individual of the group. The practice may bind together the adults of the group, since it may be more convenient for the mother to leave her infant occasionally with another female. It may also assist the training of **nulliparous** females for motherhood.

Male-Female Sexual Bond A close sexual bond between adult males and females is not common among the higher primates, although it does occur. In the one-male group, the adult male keeps the females close to him and maintains a very alert eye for any wandering adult male. Some researchers suggest that the one-male group is adaptive in arid regions where food is scarce and widely scattered, and attack by predators a constant peril. An adult male is protection for the females and offspring, and the structure of only one male to a group diminishes the consumption of scarce food resources.

Forest monkey groups, such as the black and white colobus, are also often composed of one-male groups. Here, food is no great problem and predators

Nulliparous
null: none, not any
parous: birth
Never having given birth.

Allo
Combining form indicating different or other.

hunt by stealth. The best defense is constant vigilance by all concerned. The adult male's role, therefore, is minimal, and one male is adequate for protective and reproductive functions.

The one-male/one-female family group (not found among the great apes and probably not among the early hominids) is characteristic of gibbons and some monkeys, and can be understood in terms of adaptation to their environment. A gibbon family—one adult male, one adult female, and their offspring—controls a small patch of tropical forest, which provides enough food for a small group. Gibbons jealously protect this territory from neighbors. When a young gibbon reaches maturity, it is driven out by the adult of the same sex, thus maintaining the small size of the group and its limited food supply.

Role Separation between Adults and Young　　Among primates, especially the higher primates, there is a relatively long growth period spent in the protected environment of the social group. It is during this learning stage, when the young play and learn the skills needed in adulthood, that the brain develops the special intelligence characteristic of primates. This learning period is spent in physical and psychological safety because of the behavioral and psychological separation of roles between adults and young. The young play for many hours every day, learning many of the skills required by adults, free from anxiety because alert adults are always present. The separation of roles between adults and young enable the young to learn and practice the social, intellectual, and physical skills they will need as adults.

Figure 8-8　Hamadryas one-male groups.

Role Separation by Sex   Perhaps one of the most interesting points to be made about the separation of sex roles is that there is often very little separation. Except for the protective role played by males and the childbearing and nursing role of the mother, in many primate species both sexes perform similar functions. Females are expected to obtain their food, as are juveniles after they are weaned, and there is little sharing of food.

Among terrestrial primates, there is very often a sexual dimorphism in body size, weight, muscularity, distribution of hair on the body, and size of canines. Usually associated with separate roles, the larger size (as in baboons and gorillas) enables the male to play a dominant and protective function. In those species without sexual dimorphism, the females may be highly aggressive, as in gibbons, and join the males in defense of their territory.

Let us now examine two specific cases of primate social behavior: baboons and chimpanzees—baboons because of their well-developed social organization in a savanna environment, and chimpanzees because they are considered the primate most closely related to humans. These two species have been among the most extensively studied in the past, and are still being investigated by many observers.

EXAMPLES OF PRIMATE SOCIAL BEHAVIOR

Baboon Social Behavior   Baboons are diurnal, semiterrestrial, and (with some exceptions) open-country monkeys. There are several kinds of baboons, including the common or savanna, hamadryas, drill and mandrill, and gelada. The social behavior of each type varies. We shall describe the savanna baboon, the most widespread variety throughout Africa.

Group size among savanna baboons ranges from under 10 to as many as 200, with a mean somewhere around 40. The reason for this wide range is not clear, although the reproductive rate, death rate, emigrations and immigrations, and perhaps environmental conditions are likely factors. Food abundance does not seem to influence group size (Altmann and Altmann, 1970). Usually, the sex ratio in a troop is about even, although among adults, females outnumber males from about 2 to 4, to 1.

Home range (see Box 8-1) varies from 1.5 to 15 square miles, with the difference in area probably associated with proximity of neighbors, concentration of food and water resources, group size, and other factors. Within the home range, the group makes its daily round in the *core area* (see Box 8-1), which contains the crucial elements in the baboon world: sleeping trees, resting places, water holes, and food sources. There may be several core areas within one home range, and a troop may occasionally shift from one to the other.

Home ranges of neighboring groups overlap, which may or may not lead to hostility, but even where there is intergroup hostility, convincing evidence for territoriality is lacking.

Baboons sleep in trees.* In the morning they descend from their trees and move off to forage. They walk in a long file (not necessarily a single file) until

---

*Much of this description of baboon life is taken from the Altmann and Altmann (1970) account of baboons at the Amboseli Game Reserve in Kenya.

they reach the foraging area, where they spread out into a long, horizontal line. They continue to feed, moving forward slowly in this horizontal line and covering a total distance of roughly 3½ miles a day. By late afternoon they have reached the "sleeping" trees for that night. Some baboon troops return to the same sleeping trees on successive nights.

Baboons eat a wide variety of food. Their excellent vision, ability to climb, dig, and to cover a large area enable them to exploit many varieties of food and survive in many kinds of habitats. In the Amboseli Game Reserve in Kenya, baboon diet—grasses and acacia trees—is especially important. These baboons eat leaves, sap, cambium, blooms, seeds, seed pods, and even rotten wood. Both grass seeds and grass blades are commonly eaten. During the dry season, their special food is the rhizome and base of grass blades.

In addition to plant food, baboons eat a variety of animal food. They prey on earthworms and insects (grasshoppers, butterflies, and termites), eat bird-chicks, eggs, small frogs, lizards, and mammals (hares, young gazelles), several species of rodents, and primates (vervet monkeys and bushbabies).

The baboons at Amboseli did not share their food, although there was fighting among adult males for the meat on an infant gazelle. After the fighting ended, other baboons waited quietly, watching the one who was eating. When he finished, they walked over and picked up the scraps.

Harding and Strum (1976), observing a savanna (olive) baboon group at Kekopey, Kenya, found that, over a period of several years, the group developed rather sophisticated hunting techniques. At first their hunting was fortuitous, occasionally capturing a Thomson gazelle they happened to come across.

Figure 8-9 Baboon eating a Thomson's gazelle.

Later, they developed systematic cooperative efforts, even to the extent of pursuing the gazelles in relays. Females also began to capture prey (hares) in significant numbers. In one two-year period, 14% of all prey was caught by females and 16% by juveniles.

Adult males, females, and juveniles participated in the pursuit and capture of prey animals, but complex hunting (stalking and extended pursuit) was restricted to adult males (Strum, 1981; Hausfater, 1976).

Baboons at Kekopey also developed a form of meat-sharing and thus differed from the baboons of Amboseli. Males shared with other males and females with their young. Hausfater (1976) noted several kinds of sharing at Kekopey. Adult and juvenile baboons of both sexes all fed from a prey item, but adult males did so most frequently. Animals feeding on a carcass usually fed sequentially, but only rarely were two individuals observed to feed simultaneously from the same carcass.

While meat eating is not uncommon among baboons, and sharing of a sort occurs, it is doubtful that meat—vertebrate meat—is an important part of the diet of most baboons. As Hausfater states, "... vertebrates are probably a negligible protein source in the diet of all classes of baboons with the possible exception of adult males" (Hausfater, 1976, p. 64).

A baboon troop is organized around a male dominance hierarchy, with an *alpha male* as the most conspicuously dominant individual. In many cases, there may be several males in the central hierarchy. These co-dominants support each other in stress situations and cooperate in turning aside a threat to any one of them. Dominant males enjoy certain perquisites. They often have access to females during that time of estrus, when females are most likely to conceive. Apparently, however, this is not always the case, since recent evidence suggests that *epigamic* selection (female choice) of a mating male occurs more often than has hitherto been appreciated (Fedigan, 1983). Dominant males are less harrassed during mating, and they are assured of social space. Other less dominant animals make submissive gestures toward them, or avoid them altogether.

When predators (leopards, jackals, lions, hyenas) attack baboons, reactions are rapid, complex and variable, with a flurry of animals running in all directions. Some adult males start later and run more slowly, resulting in males interposed between the potential danger and the rest of the group. In more heavily forested areas, however, all baboons run for the trees, with the larger males usually reaching the trees first (Rowell, 1972).

There is also a female dominance hierarchy that is more stable than the male. Males change rank and groups frequently as they challenge, or are challenged by, other males. This does not occur among females, who maintain their rank for life. A baboon female infant, by observing her mother's behavior as she reacts to other female baboons, has ample opportunities to learn her mother's rank. Within a few months after birth, female infants seem to respond selectively to other individuals (J. Altmann, 1980).

High-ranking females also enjoy certain advantages. A high-ranking female can displace a low-ranking female and take over resources, such as partially dug grass corms. High-ranking females are subject to less distress interactions and have more access to newly born infants. Like less dominant males, among many primates. Ransom describes the strategy of a potential alloparent: low-ranking females make submissive gestures when approached by a high-ranking female.

Allomothering or alloparenting (p. 191) occurs among baboons as it does among many primates. Ransom (1981, p. 222) describes the strategy of a potential alloparent:

> An adult baboon may slowly approach the mother, showing various indications of friendly intent such as lip-smacking, narrowing of the eyes, and flattening of the ears, and embrace her in a variety of ways depending on the mother's posture and the sex of the other adult. During this embrace the adult will touch the infant with hand or nose several times and eventually may attempt to pull it out of the mother's arms. Such attempts for the most part appear to be intended to facilitate further investigation of the infant, but others are obviously motivated by a desire to carry it off (Ransom, 1981, p. 222).

The mother usually avoids the approach of males and will ignore or tolerate a young female. But she is permissive if the allomother is the infant's elder sibling. In an hierarchical society such as baboons, "a high-ranking female who takes an infant may refuse to return it, with the result that the infant starves to death" (Hrdy, 1981, p. 98). Sometimes a would-be allomother is insistent, even when the mother objects, and the result is a push-pull contest that may injure the infant. Among baboons, there may be a so-called nursery group composed of mothers and their infants. In such a group, a mother often interacts freely with another mother-infant pair.

Quite frequently, the most eager allomothers are nulliparous females, but because of their inexperience, they may also be incompetent. Pregnant and lactating mothers may also borrow newborns, but they tend to lose interest and, in the process of getting rid of them, may drag them along the ground or step on them. This points up the danger of allomothering, but it is useful to nulliparous females, since it provides them with the opportunity to learn mothering. Infants also gain social experience as they interact with old and young animals, both male and female. Should a mother die, the alloparent might adopt and rear her offspring. McKenna (1982) has noted that the attraction to infants and the female-female bonds established by alloparenting may contribute to group solidarity and cohesion. It may also hasten socialization, and possibly prepare the infant for a social life independent of its mother.

Grooming performed by both adults and young of both sexes is an important mechanism for maintaining peaceful social relationships and social bonding within the baboon troop. The most common grooming is female by female, but adult males groom females in estrus and often form a consort relationship. Females with infants are popular as groomees, and new mothers concentrate their grooming mainly on their newborn infants. Generally, the amount of grooming an individual receives reflects dominance rank.

With Lovejoy's model in mind, we raise the question, Does baboon social behavior offer clues to hominid evolution? Baboons adapted to the savanna with a tight social organization controlled by a highly structured dominance hierarchy. Although we do not know the structure of early hominid society, contemporary hunter-gatherers—such as the San—do not organize themselves in this way. Nor do hunter-gatherers display the aggression of the baboon troop. In hunting-gathering societies, meat sharing (distribution) is a very important activity, but it is rare among baboons. As Hausfater noted, animals fed on a carcass sequentially and only rarely were two individuals feeding simultaneously from the same carcass.

Is it possible, then, that studies of baboon behavior may suggest clues to early hunting behavior? Such studies have identified, as Strum (1981) has pointed out, a potential for primate predation, and it is quite likely that early hominids were also predators. Whether they next developed a scavenging or hunting stage is a moot point, and Strum believes nonhuman primate practices may help clarify the issue:

> The question left open for consideration is whether it is easier to develop technical and social innovations within a scavenging context, to gain a competitive edge on other predators, or within a hunting context, to allow the exploitation of larger prey. In either case non-human primate predatory behavior once again considerably clarifies the question we should ask about human evolution and the answers that will be acceptable. It also illustrates a complexity that predates the human experiment (Strum, 1983, p. 334).

Chimpanzees—apes that live in the forest and on the forest-savanna border—offer another possible model for early hominid behavior.

Chimpanzee Social Behavior   Although chimpanzee communities vary, observers are pretty well agreed that the basic social unit of chimpanzees is a fluid-membership group, within which exists a nucleus of strongly bonded adult males operating in a particular home range. Associated with these males are some females in their prime and even some past their prime. Also included in the group are other females whose membership is more variable, since they often transfer to other groups. Males rarely transfer from one community to another, but females do, temporarily, or—as in the case of many nulliparous females—permanently (Pusey, 1979).

The size of a community varies from one group to the next, and the same community varies from year to year. In a study at Kisoge, at the foot of the Mahale Mountains in East Africa, the researcher Nishida (1979) found that, during a seven-year study, the size of groups varied from 21 to 34 individuals; other estimates for community size range from 15 to 80. Nishida also noted that a community was divided into subgroups, which could be considered the actual living units.

Although not perhaps as finely structured as the baboon system, a definite hierarchy does exist among chimpanzee males. At the top of the hierarchy is the alpha male, followed by other less dominant males. However, the structure is highly flexible, as the following account suggests:

> Kasonta . . . had been an alpha male for a number of years when rivalry developed between him and Sobongo, the beta male. In this ongoing conflict, the gamma male, Kamemanfu, was pivotal. At times the gamma male joined alpha against beta; at other times he reversed his position and joined beta against alpha. When the latter occurred, Kasonta, the alpha male, lost confidence and the beta male, Sobonga, became the alpha male.
> In 1976, Sobongo, with the help of the gamma male, was threatening Kasonta and succeeded in becoming the alpha male in June. One of the rewards of the

alpha male is more frequent access to estrous females. During the months February-April, while he was still alpha, Kasonta was responsible for 85.6% of the copulations. But in months June-July, Sobongo—now the alpha male—was responsible for 87%. In May, the alpha status was unstable because gamma male Kamemanfu had switched his support to Sobongo and assisted him in attacking Kasonta. Taking advantage of the unstable situation, Kamemanfu showed the highest copulation rate.

In January, 1978, Kamemanfu threw his support back to Kasonta who reassumed his alpha status. (Nishida, 1983, p. 332).

A male's ability to dominate is related to age. As a male grows through adolescence, he becomes dominant to adolescents and then adult females. As a young adult he begins to dominante the older males, and by middle age he reaches his highest rank. At this time he can dominate most, if not all, younger and older males. As he ages and his physique deteriorates, younger individuals may begin to dominate him (Bygott, 1979).

A top-ranking male is not merely an alpha male that excels over all other males of the community. In the Kisoge study (Nishida, 1979), Kasonta, the top-ranking male of his group, was the most prominent in frequency of both aggressive behavior and threat display. Among adult males, he groomed and was groomed most frequently. Perhaps the most conspicuous characteristic of a top-ranker is the frequency with which he is followed by other adult males, and Kasonta's subgroup was usually the largest.

As we noted at Kisoge, a male's access to estrous females is directly related to his dominance rank. At Gombe, however, Goodall has not observed such a close relationship between status rank and reproductive success (personal communication). In his role as the top-ranking male, Kasonta assumed leadership in scouting and chasing, and he was the only male to defeat the male of an adjoining group without help from others.

Dominance and structural relationships are not as clearly defined among adult chimpanzee females. When a female comes into estrus, her dominance rank rises remarkably. Young adult females have been observed threatening high-ranking females, and may even snatch food from some nonconsorting adult males. Rise in dominance rank is also related to the fact that highest ranking males often monopolize estrous females. However, this high rank among estrous females is only temporary. Linear rank hierarchy may also be present, although dominance is difficult to determine because "physiological conditions of females make female relationships very complicated and unstable" (Nishida, 1979, p. 104). Generally speaking, older females are superior in rank to younger females. At Kisoge, for example, a past-prime female, Wantangwa, completely dominated all other females for the seven years of the group study (Nishida, 1979).

The relationship between a chimpanzee mother and daughter is a very close one until the daughter is at least seven years old. A newborn infant clings to the mother, holding on to her belly as she moves, and, for the first six months, the mother supports the newborn with her hand. During this time, the mother provides food, protection, transportation, and hygiene. At the end of six months, the infant begins to explore the environment without straying out of mother's sight, and eats solid food while continuing to suckle.

Figure 8-10 Flo and Flint. Flint, at the age of eight, died of "loneliness" (depression) three weeks after the death of Flo, his mother. (Baron Hugo van Lawick, © National Geographic Society.)

Weaning may begin at one year of age and continue until four or five. For the first four years, an infant is almost completely dependent on its mother. As a juvenile (ages 4–8), a daughter is still heavily dependent on her mother, but this dependency is significantly reduced during adolescence (8–10) and disappears almost completely during the daughter's subadult stage (10–12).

A similar change occurs in the close relationship between a mother and her son when he reaches about the age of ten. The young male at this time is attracted to adult males and cycling females and, again, inbreeding with female maternal kin is avoided.

Adult or adolescent females tend to disperse and form small subgroups within the home range. They travel within small areas inside the larger home range, and, where home ranges overlap, they move back and forth between the two communities.

Female-female bonds appear to be weak, and adult females usually are not seen together for any length of time. If grooming frequency is taken as an index of social bonding, we find that 46% of total grooming occurs between adult males, 39% between adult males and adult females, and 10% between adult females. Also rare among adult females are mutual greeting and sharing behavior, both of which characterize the high sociability of chimpanzees. Generally, social bonds among females may simply be due to physiologically similar activities based on similar age, maternity, and sexual receptivity.

As in baboons (see p. 196), alloparenting also occurs among chimpanzees. Mothers are often wary of females who indicate their intention of holding a neonate (newborn). Goodall observed older siblings hold a newborn with the mother's permission, but the mother rejected advances of other females (van Lawick-Goodall, 1971). Nishida (1983), however, found that among the chimpanzees of the Mahale Mountains, unrelated nulliparous females—as well as siblings, adult and adolescent males, and parous females—also took care of infants. The most frequent alloparents were nulliparous females.

The strategy of these alloparents consists of invitation, enticement, detachment from the mother, care of the infant, tickling, and rough and tumble play. The infants seem relaxed during this bout and appear at ease with any class of alloparents. Mothers, however, are often uneasy and quite solicitous of their offspring, as they carefully watch the interaction. A mother will sometimes block the advance of an alloparental candidate by drawing her infant to her chest; she may hold the hand of an alloparent and prevent contact, or she may stop the infant from leaving by placing her hand in front of it. A mother may, however, join in the playful interactions between alloparent and infant. During these bouts, mothers may sometimes rest, groom or be groomed, or supervise the alloparental care (Nishida, 1983).

Sexual attraction serves as a bond among chimpanzees, and a consort relationship frequently develops between a particular male and female. At Gombe, a male will often select a particular female as a mate, and maintain constant proximity to this female. Should another male mate with the female, the consort male interrupts the pair. The consort pair sometimes go on safari for as long as twenty-eight days. Estrous females have been observed forcing themselves between a mating pair and often present to the male.

A chimpanzee community is wary of other communities. Adult males patrol the periphery of their home range, traveling silently in close compact groups. They frequently stop to look and listen, often standing bipedally to look over the tall grass, and sometimes climb a tree to scan the area for signs of chimpanzees in the adjoining home range. When the chimpanzees return to familiar areas, they often break their remarkable silence by "an outburst of loud calling, drumming displays, and even some chasing and mild aggressive contact between individuals" (Goodall, et al., 1979).

In their patrols, chimpanzees respond to the sight or sound of neighbors with reassurance contact behavior among themselves (Fig. 8-11), such as touching, grinning, erect hair, embracing, and mounting. If the two parties are approximately of equal size, they may approach and display until one or both groups retreat. Kawanaka (1982) relates the account of an inter-unit-group encounter in which two mixed groups (adult males and females) approached each other at their territorial boundary. Although hooting from both groups could be heard, they did not meet, nor was there any agonistic behavior on either side. However, there was a good deal of stress present, evidenced by the frequent defecation of the females. If one group is outnumbered or faced with more formidable opponents, it will probably approach and then retreat. Members of different communities seldom engage in agonistic behavior because only occasionally do they come close enough for face-to-face interaction. Should a patrol party encounter a single male, however, they might attack him.

While chimpanzee males rarely cross into the home range of another community, such "trespassing" can occur. Goodall (1979) relates the account of a community at Gombe that separated, a number of adult males moving to the southern part of their home range. Over a period of three years the original group ferociously attacked and killed most of the members of the southern community by forays into their home range. Goodall could not explain this behavior except for the possibility that the northern group had

Figure 8-11 Chimp reassurance behavior. (Baron Hugo van Lawick, © National Geographic Society.)

◇ Box 8-3   Jane Goodall—Pioneer of Chimpanzee Research

It began in 1960 when a young Englishwoman, invited to visit a friend at a farm in Kenya, gave up her job and flew to Nairobi. Jane Goodall, who, at the early age of 8, had already decided to go to Africa and live with animals "when I grew up," could hardly pass up this opportunity to fulfill her childhood dream.

In Africa, a friend suggested to her that she get in touch with Louis Leakey, well-known anthropologist and at that time, curator of what is now the National Museum of Natural History (back then, Jane had never heard of Dr. Leakey!). She sought him out and introduced herself. After they conversed, Leakey offered her a job at the museum. She accepted, and ultimately joined the Leakeys on their annual paleontological expeditions to Olduvai Gorge in Tanzania. Leakey was impressed with Jane's ability and dedication, and asked if she would like to study wild chimps in the Kigoma area on the shores of Lake Tanganyika (see map). Lacking what she felt to be the necessary academic background, Jane was surprised at the offer. Leakey himself, however, believed that university training might be a disadvantage in this case. What he wanted, he said, was someone "with a mind uncluttered and unbiased by theory," someone

who had a sympathetic understanding of animals and a real desire for knowledge.

Jane happily accepted the position and waited for the funding that Dr. Leakey set out to find. With monies eventually provided by the Wilkie Foundation (of the United States), Jane prepared to leave for Kigoma. She then learned that local officials objected to a young woman living alone in a jungle uninhabited by humans. Jane arranged for her mother to join her, which satisfied the government officials, and the two Englishwomen, along with a few African assistants, went on to undertake the now-famous research effort at the Gombe Stream Chimpanzee Reserve, today known as Gombe National Park.

Jane Goodall's pioneering research—now in its twenty-fifth year—is the longest continuous study of the behavior of any animal species. As a result of her work, we have come to a better understanding of humans as primates, an understanding substantially broadened by anthropologists, zoologists, and other researchers from around the world who have followed in her historic footsteps.

Figure 8-12   Two chimpanzee research sites in Tanzania. Kigoma is Jane Goodall's area; the Mahale Mountains has been the center of research for Japanese primatologists for more than fifteen years.

been prevented from using the southern part of what had once been their home range. By eliminating the southern group, this area once more became accessible to them.

Agonistic behavior occurs between adult males, reflecting a dominance-subordinance relationship, but is also directed by males against females and immature chimps. There is little agonistic behavior between adult males and infants, probably because infants are protected by the mother, although females with infants are sometimes attacked. Adult females are dominant to juveniles, but do not attack unless provoked. Adolescent males can generally intimidate young adult and adolescent females, but might be attacked by older adult females. In the rare agonistic interaction among females, the older of the two females is usually dominant.

Among males, agonistic behavior appears to occur between four groups: alpha males, high-ranking males, middle-ranking males, and low-ranking males. Agonistic interactions between these groups is frequent, and dominance-subordinance relationships are clearly defined (Bygott, 1979).

In recent years, another form of agonistic behavior has been observed. Jane Goodall (1979) reported that, in the years 1975 to 1977, a mother and her daughter had killed and eaten at least three babies. These were deliberate cases of cannibalism. Passion, an adult female, pursued a mother holding an infant, attacked her, seized and killed the baby, and then shared the flesh with her offspring. Three males in the Mahale Mountains group were also seen sharing the flesh of an infant chimp (Nishida, et al., 1979). In 1982, still another account of cannibalism was reported for the Mahale Mountains chimpanzees: A male killed an infant and consumed the flesh (Norikashi, 1982). In all these cases, the victim appeared to be male, and in most instances little interest was shown by others, including the mother of the infants, although the presence of the highest-ranking male appears to discourage cannibalism.

It is difficult to understand this practice unless perhaps it is to change an existing mother into a reproductive-ready female. That is, when a mother loses an infant, she shortly comes into estrus and is available for conception. It should be stressed that, among chimpanzees, "cannibalism is not an exceptional accident, but is deeply rooted in the chimpanzee species society . . ." (Nishida et al., 1979, p. 19). (See Sociobiology, pp. 214–218, for a further discussion of infanticide.)

In the past, chimpanzees were considered herbivores, but recent evidence makes it clear they are capable of, and participate in, predatory behavior. More than 10 years ago, Goodall observed chimpanzees eating animals they had killed, either by fortuitous capture or deliberate hunting (van Lawick-Goodall, 1971). The chimpanzee animal diet, which supplements their predominant feeding pattern of fruits and leaves, consists mainly of the red colobus monkey and the anubis baboon, but they hunt other small mammals as well, such as bushpigs, red-tailed monkeys, and blue monkeys. In addition, chimps may gather various insects, fledgling birds, and birds' eggs. Their prey are medium to small-sized mammals and birds, always smaller than themselves. In the Mahale Mountains, chimpanzees have also been observed to kill mammals, carry away the carcasses, and eat the meat.

There is some question whether chimpanzees are cooperative hunters.

Busse (1978, p. 769) has pointed out that cooperative hunting might not be as efficient for chimpanzees as solitary hunting:

> The high level of observed competition for small kills supports the contention that over time individuals would obtain more meat by hunting alone than by hunting in groups. That chimpanzees do sometimes hunt in groups appears to be an incidental result of fortuitous encounters between chimpanzee groups and potential prey animals.

Like the baboons observed at Kekopey (p. 195), chimpanzees also share meat. Goodall observed male chimps occasionally sharing meat with other chimpanzees who begged with outstretched hands (van Lawick-Goodall, 1971). Scraps of meat left by eaters were quickly picked up by others. Some chimps attempted to take away pieces of carcass while it was being eaten by the "owner," sometimes successfully and sometimes not. Meat requesting, or begging, has several forms: by hand; peering (placing the face close to the face or meat of the meat eater); touching the meat itself, or touching the chin and lips of the meat eater; extending the hand palm up; making "soft whimper or hoo sounds while doing any of the above" (Teleki, 1973, p. 148).

Attempts to share in the meat are not always successful, and agonistic behavior during meat eating is relatively rare. Chimpanzees possessing meat portions may object to sharing and indicate this by raising the hair, waving arms, vocalizing at others, or other displays.

Other food besides meat is shared. For example, the sharing of bananas (a food provided by primatologists) occurred between all age-sex classes. Mothers pass food to their offspring regularly, and the reverse also occurs. Adult males rarely beg for bananas, and adult females seldom beg from each other (McGrew, 1979).

Chimpanzee predatory behavior has been much discussed, and indeed it is an important chimpanzee behavior. However, meat does not make up a significant portion of the chimpanzee diet, even though they appear to enjoy the taste of it. "During the many tens of thousands of hours that field researchers have observed [all] nonhuman primates, fewer than 450 sightings of vertebrate hunting and/or feeding have been reported . . ." (Butynski, 1982, p. 423). Most of these sightings have been of chimpanzees, and although they may stalk their prey, hunt cooperatively, and share meat, these behaviors are infrequent and not well developed (Butynski, 1982).

Associated with food is an interesting aspect that may be considered a sexual division of labor. Hunting by males and gathering by females have, in the past, led students of hominid evolution to assign the sexual division of labor as a uniquely hominid characteristic. However, McGrew (1979) found that male and female chimpanzees do not ingest the same kind of food. An analysis of a ten-month collection of fecal samples of chimpanzees at Gombe showed "a marked sex difference in insect eating: 45 of 81 (56%) female fecal samples contained at least one type of insect remains. Only 31 of 113 (27%) male fecal samples did so" (McGrew, 1979, p. 448). Fecal remains also showed that, in thirteen out of fourteen cases, it was the males who had eaten birds and mammals. It would appear from these data that, whereas the bulk of insects are sought and eaten by females, vertebrates are the domain of males.

Hominization
Process of becoming more human.

As a model for hominid evolution, the chimpanzees seem to be better situated than baboons. A chimpanzee community is male-dominated, but not as highly structured as the baboon community. The strongest bond is the mother-daughter relationship, and the mother never appears to become intolerant of the daughter, even after adolescence. The consort relationship—one male and one female—is quite common, and the pair may go off by themselves for as long as a month.

Behavior associated with food seems especially pertinent in this discussion. Male chimps are occasional predators, and although much of their meat is obtained fortuitously, they deliberately pursue prey, perhaps even cooperatively. What is more significant is that obtaining meat

> often involves primarily male groups roaming relatively great distances and acting cooperatively when the appropriate situation fortuitously arises—in short, *hunting*. On the other hand, female chimpanzees (predominantly) obtain ants and termites by prolonged, systematic, and repetitive manipulative sequences . . . accumulating a meal of many small units that are usually concentrated at a few known permanent sources—in short, gathering (McGrew, 1979, p. 450).

This sex difference might be considered as the basis for the hominid division of labor of female-gatherer and male-hunter that may have developed early in hominid evolution.

Food sharing is another area that was once believed to be uniquely human. There is now evidence that chimpanzees occasionally share both meat and vegetable material.

There are, of course, important differences between chimpanzee and hominid behavior: In chimpanzees, the consort relationship is not permanent, and is associated only with an estrous female; the home range is not a home base; the mother-daughter bond is not a family; chimpanzee hunting is mainly fortuitous (questions have been raised about whether this hunting is cooperative); "food sharing" may be called sharing only by stretching the meaning of the word—"distribution" is a better term (Teleki, 1973); and meat is rarely given, but it is taken, and if it is given, it is done so grudgingly and reluctantly.

Another chimpanzee activity resembling behavior once believed to be unique to hominids is the making of tools. At the present time, the evidence suggests that bipedality preceded toolmaking (stone tools) by at least a million years. Toolmaking, therefore, may not be as significant as once believed, as a factor leading to **hominization**. It is possible, however, that the object manipulation seen in chimpanzees suggests that the potential for toolmaking is primate in origin.

In additon to making simple tools, chimpanzees manipulate objects for many purposes. They throw such objects as stones, vegetation, sticks, and feces (as visitors to zoos have learned to their sorrow and their dry cleaners' profit). They also play extensively with objects, and they use leaves for cleaning the body.

The chimpanzee behavior we have described—object manipulation, food sharing, hunting, division of labor—does not mean that hominids evolved from chimpanzees. First of all, chimpanzees today evolved from an earlier form, and it is very doubtful that present-day chimp behavior is the same as that of their ancestors. Furthermore, humans developed different strategies in adapting as hunters to a savanna environment. Possibly, however, the striking morphological, biochemical, and behavioral similarities of chimpanzees and humans may point to the *kind* of ancestor that led to the hominid line.

◇ "Cultural" Behavior

At one time, anthropologists defined humans as toolmaking animals, and then modified the definition to read, "animals that make tools regularly." However, the observations of chimpanzees making and using tools by Goodall (1965) more than 20 years ago, brought such definitions into question. Many observers of chimpanzees, gorillas, orangutans, and some monkeys have verified the practice of tool manufacturing by apes and tool use by monkeys.

Probably the best-known example of nonhuman primate tool manufacture is termite fishing (Fig. 8-13). The chimpanzee inserts and probes in subterranean mounds or nests of termites with pieces of bark, vine, grass blades, or twigs. When the termites seize the probe, the chimp then withdraws the tool and eats the attached termites with its lips and teeth. Chimpanzees modify some of these objects, such as twigs, by removing the leaves—in effect manufacturing a stick from the natural material, a twig. Indeed, chimpanzees show the greatest frequency and diversity of tool using behavior of any nonhuman animal. They drag or roll branches, fallen trees, stones, cans, and camp furniture while displaying. They have been observed throwing rocks at a bushpig during predation, and throwing objects "overhead," "sidearm," and "underhand" (Beck, 1980). Chimps also make sponges from a handful of leaves, chew them for a moment, and then push them into the hollow of a tree where water has accumulated. The liquid is then sucked from this homemade sponge. Leaves are also used to dab at wounds on their bottoms, and sometimes, when a chimp has diarrhea, leaves serve as toilet paper.

At Bossou, Guinea (Africa), observers Sugiyama and Koman (1979) watched chimpanzees crack nuts with what they call a pebble tool. The striking stone weighed from 17 to 30 lb., and the platform stone on which the nut was placed weighed about 35 lb.:

> A chimpanzee who crouched in front of the platform stone chose a dry palm-seed, placed it in the cavity of the platform stone, gripped the handle side of the pebble tool, lifted it up to a height of 5-20 cm, and then struck the palm-seed. . . . When a palm-seed was broken, the chimpanzee removed the white ovule with his fingers and ate it in about 1 minute (Sugiyama and Koman, 1979, p. 515).

The authors believe this nut-cracking behavior "is highly suggestive of early man's stone-tool culture," and perhaps it is. However, it is important to note that neither the hammer stone nor the platform stone was deliberately manufactured.* Beck (1980) points out that many animals use unmodified objects

---

*Observers of nonhuman primates rarely distinguish *natural objects used as tools* from *modified objects deliberately manufactured* for specific purposes. The term tool is usually employed in both cases.

Figure 8-13   Chimp termiting.

as tools, but only apes—mainly chimpanzees—deliberately manufacture tools for specific purposes. However, we should be aware of the significant differences in toolmaking between chimps and humans. Chimpanzees usually select their material for a tool from a nearby item, and use it with little delay; humans collect material from a wide area, and may store it for a long time before using it. Although chimpanzees use and make tools, they do so comparatively rarely, whereas humans are utterly dependent on tools for their survival. Also, humans use tools to make other tools; other primates do not (Chalmers, 1980).

Like chimpanzees, Japanese macaques (a variety of Old World monkey) have also demonstrated a capacity for "cultural" behavior. In 1952, Japanese scientists embarked upon a provisioning procedure in which they supplied food at various places in Japan for groups of monkeys living in those areas. This method has proved eminently successful for purposes of observation, and the Japanese researchers have added significantly to our understanding of macaques.

Japanese monkeys have not been observed making tools, but one of them "invented" at least two methods of preparing food for eating. In 1952, sweet potatoes, a food new to the monkeys, were made available by scattering on the beach. The following year Imo, a young female, was observed using one hand to brush the sand off the sweet potatoes and the other hand to dip the potatoes in the water of a brook. The invention was picked up by juveniles through playmate relationships and was passed from juveniles to mothers, who then passed it on to their children. Within ten years, 90% of all troop members were washing sweet potatoes, except adults older than twelve years and infants less than one year.

Another invention, again by the "genius" Imo, was wheat washing. Wheat was distributed to the Koshima Island troop by scattering it on the sand, from which the monkeys could pick out single grains. Imo introduced the practice of scooping up sand and wheat, carrying a handful to the edge of the sea, and tossing the mixture onto the water. The sand sank, and Imo then skimmed the wheat grains off the surface and ate them! This practice also spread through the troop much as the sweet-potato washing habit: first juveniles, then adults—especially mothers—along family lines (Kawamura, 1959).

Defining the term "culture" may be useful, but so many definitions exist, there seems to be one for every cultural anthropologist. It would be much more valuable to note those characteristics of culture universally recognized by anthropologists.

Culture is learned behavior; that is, behavior acquired through learning, not through the genes. Culture includes nonmaterial attributes, such as language, art, religion, values, morals, etc., as well as material things, such as clothes, houses, tools, etc. Culture is social (not biological) heredity—it includes customs, traditions, attitudes. Culture is the behavioral patterns of a group, the "way of life" of a group. To sum up, culture is learned, not genetic, and has become so much the human way of life that we depend upon it for survival. It is the human strategy of adaptation.

Since primates (like all mammals) learn part of their behavior, then certainly primates are capable of cultural behavior. Chimpanzees, it appears,

Figure 8-14 Centers for Japanese macaque studies.

learn more than probably any other nonhuman primate, but the extent to which chimpanzees depend on culture for survival is another matter. It is clear they do not depend on culture completely, but to the extent that they learn to make and use tools, their behavior may be called cultural.

However, when we ask, "Can the chimpanzee way of life be called a culture?" we are on much less firm ground. Among chimpanzees, there is a good deal of genetically based behavior, as we have seen. Triggered by estrus, male responses are genetic, not learned. It is highly probable that dominance (that is, structuring social relationships based on rank) is also genetically based. Admittedly, though, it is difficult to know the extent of genetic influence upon chimpanzee behavior (and, sociobiologists might add, in human behavior as well). Nevertheless, the degree of human dependence on culture—for the human way of life—is total, or as total as we can determine. This is not the case with chimpanzees.

For one thing, cultural behavior is transmitted symbolically, and nonhuman primates do not transmit culture, or any kind of learned behavior as far as we can tell, symbolically. Chalmers points out that nonhuman primates can only learn from one another by direct observation; human beings suffer no

Figure 8-15 Macaque washing potatoes.

such limitation. Freed from this restriction, humans can make use of experience accumulated over many generations, collected over many areas, and can develop rich and complicated traditions and cultures (Chalmers, 1980, p. 224). If culture is to have meaning as the human strategy for survival, then to refer to primate behavior as culture is to blur its meaning. We do not believe that chimpanzees have a culture, nor do we believe that terms such as "protoculture" or "incipient culture" are useful in explaining their behavior. These terms suggest that chimpanzees are on their way to developing culture, a premise which is extremely doubtful. Still, the information we gain about chimpanzees and other primates is valuable, not only because we learn more about nonhuman primates, but because we gain a fuller understanding of the possible mechanisms of early hominid evolution.

This troublesome question of culture and whether or not it can be attributed to primates must take into account language, a core element in the definition of culture.

Figure 8-16 Chimpanzee facial gestures. Chimpanzees are the most facially expressive of all nonhuman primates. (From *In the Shadow of Man*, by Jane van Lawick-Goodall. Copyright © 1971 by Hugo and Jane van Lawick-Goodall. Redrawn with permission of Houghton Mifflin Company.)

◇ Language

Communication is common behavior among animals, from the smell and antenna signals of insects to the symbols of humans. Gestural and vocal signals have been observed among primates by a variety of investigators. Jane Goodall (1968a, 1971) documented numerous such signals among chimpanzees. She notes facial expressions, such as play-face and several grins, and vocal signals, including various kinds of hoots and grunts (Fig. 8-16). Expressions such as these are communication, of course, but can they be considered language?

Language, as distinct from communication, has been considered a uniquely human achievement, but work with apes has raised doubts about that position. Language has been defined in ways that would include insect communication on the one hand, or exclude everything except human speech on the other. While we prefer defining language in terms of symbolic communication, there is much disagreement on this subject. The assumption that *Homo sapiens* is the only organism capable of handling language has been brought into question by the success psychologists have achieved in teaching apes to communicate with symbols. Without attempting to settle the question of whether or not such ape ability should be called language, we shall briefly describe several successful experiments.

Washoe   In 1966, Beatrice and Allen Gardner, psychologists at the University of Nevada, decided to teach a two-way communication system to an eleven-month-old chimpanzee named Washoe. The gestures they selected were those of American Sign Language (ASL or Ameslan), a means of communication long used by the deaf.

Washoe's progress was slow at the beginning, but by the tenth month she possessed a vocabulary of a dozen words. At about this time, she began to combine signs such as "go in," "go out," and, later, produced combinations of three to five signs in sequence. At the end of four years, the Gardners claimed she had a vocabulary of over 130 signs, and it was possible for her and her trainer to engage in short, simple dialogues.

Washoe learned syntax—the proper order of words—as she demonstrated

Figure 8-17   Washoe signing "hat" when being questioned about a woolen hat.

in phrases like, "Roger you tickle." She occasionally signed to herself when alone and was seen signing "quiet" to herself before sneaking to a forbidden place, and "hurry" on the way to the potty chair.

The Gardners caution against evaluating chimpanzee linguistic ability on the basis of the Washoe data. If Washoe had been a preschool child, then her responses to the questions who? what? where? would place her at a relatively advanced level of linguistic competence. On the other hand, she would have been "a linguistically disadvantaged child." She was not exposed to American Sign Language until she was about one year old, and her trainers, learning Ameslan as a second language, were not fluent.

In a sequel to Project Washoe, the Gardners have instituted major improvements in teaching language to chimpanzees. Among the improvements are exposing chimpanzee subjects to sign language from birth and using research assistants who are fluent in Ameslan, being deaf themselves or raised by deaf parents. "Early results show that the first two new subjects are acquiring sign language much faster than Washoe did. It is highly likely that the marks set by Washoe will be surpassed under the more favorable conditions" (B. T. and R. A. Gardner, 1975, pp. 255–256).

When Washoe was pregnant in 1976, researchers were interested in whether she would transmit her Ameslan signs to her baby. Unfortuntely, the infant died a few hours after birth. Washoe was again "expecting" in January, 1979, when Dr. Roger Fouts, a former student of the Gardners, began research at the University of Oklahoma into the ability of chimpanzees to transmit their signs to other chimps. Washoe's second baby also died a few months later.

Dr. Fouts, who had moved to Central Washington University and taken Washoe with him, decided to present Washoe with a ten-month-old male chimp named Loulis. Washoe accepted the infant male and, after observing their interaction, Fouts stated that, by the spring of 1982, Loulis had acquired 32 signs from Washoe and other chimps (Friends of Washoe newsletter, Spring 1982). Fouts also claims that his experiments demonstrate that chimps can communicate with each other using Ameslan, and that they invent signs for objects that had no signs. Furthermore, not only do young chimpanzees learn signs from older ones, but older chimps learn from younger ones (Fouts, 1982, 1983).

Sarah Another chimpanzee language, specially devised by Professor David Premack (1971), was taught to his six-year-old simian student, Sarah, in an experiment initiated at the University of California at Santa Barbara in 1967. The symbols in this language system consisted of differently shaped and colored plastic pieces with a bit of metal on the back that adhered to a magnetized board.

Sarah was taught to recognize the plastic chips as symbols for various objects. The chips did not resemble the objects they represented; for example, the plastic chip for "apple" was not round and red. Sarah soon learned to correctly identify fruit, and was able to place two chips together in the proper sequence. Verbs were then introduced, and Sarah was able to place the chips properly to form a sentence, such as, "Mary give apple Sarah."

Sarah also learned to indicate which objects were the same and which different by removing the chip for question mark and replacing it with the correct chip for "same" or "different." After eighteen months, Premack believed Sarah had acquired a language competence comparable in many respects to a child of two or two and a half years.

Lana   There have been other experiments teaching language to chimpanzees, such as Rumbaugh's (1977) work with Lana at the Yerkes Regional Primate Center in Atlanta, Georgia. Lana worked with chips attached to keys on a specially built typewriter connected to a computer. After six months, Lana recognized symbols for thirty words, and was able to ask for food and answer questions through the machine.

In 1975, two young male chimps, Sherman and Austin, were added to the experiment. Because the experimenters were not certain Lana understood all the words she used, Sherman's and Austin's training emphasized the meaning of each word they encountered. This change in language training has led Rumbaugh and his colleagues to believe that Sherman and Austin (and, by extension, chimps in general) are capable of functional symbolic communication; that is, to these two chimps, words were representational, real symbols, understood and used by them. Sherman's and Austin's data demonstrate that chimpanzees can master referential use of learned symbols, the meanings of which have been arbitrarily assigned to lexigrams (words). In other words, apes are capable of mastering semantics! (Rumbaugh et al., 1982, p. 379).

Koko   The first gorilla to be taught Ameslan is Koko, a female, who is presently in her fifteenth year of instruction. Dr. Francine Patterson, in charge of the program, states that Koko knows and uses more than 500 signs. Michael, a slightly younger male, who has been in the program a few years less than Koko, also has a considerable Ameslan vocabulary. Patterson also maintains that Koko and Michael communicate with each other.

Not everyone, however, agrees that apes actually learn language. Sebeok (1980) compared the ape signals to those of a German horse named Clever Hans who appeared to be able to count by tapping his hoof in response to its owner's command. It turned out that the owner involuntarily jerked when Hans reached the correct number, and, given this clue, Hans stopped tapping at the correct answer.

Nim   Dr. Herbert Terrace, who raised a chimp (named Nim Chimpsky after the well-known linguist, Noam Chomsky) almost from birth, trained him to sign using ASL. Just like Washoe, Sarah, and other chimps, Nim was able to place the signs in sequence, but Terrace wondered whether Nim was actually fashioning proper sentences or reacting in the manner of Clever Hans to the trainer's signals.

After almost four years of working with Nim, Terrace analyzed videotapes of the training sessions. His conclusion:

> . . . it would be premature to conclude that a chimpanzee's combination [of words] show the same structure evident in the sentences of a child. The fact that Nim's utterances were less spontaneous and less original than those of a child, and that his utterances did not become longer, both as he learned new signs and as he acquired more experience in using sign language, suggests that much of the

structure and meaning of his combinations was determined, or at least suggested, by the utterances of his teachers (Terrace, 1979, p. 221).

In a provocative article titled "Why Koko Can't Talk," Terrace argued there is a tendency among experimenters to project human meaning into the imitative utterances of an ape who was simply trying to manipulate its teachers to feed it or engage in some kind of social activity (Terrace, 1982, p. 9). Criticizing some experiments, Terrace writes that the use of signs in certain instances

> suggest a type of interaction between an ape and its trainer that has little to do with human language. In each instance the sole function of the ape's signing appears to be to request various rewards that can be obtained only by signing (Terrace, 1983, p. 38).

Patterson replies (1983) to this criticism by noting that Koko and Michael invent signs for new objects and actions and can actually modulate signs by signing such adjectives as *very*, *little*, *big*. They can also, according to Patterson, modulate a statement into a question.

Other scholars have also questioned the assumptions covering the language capabilities of apes. Atherton and Schwartz (1983) believe more emphasis should be placed on whether apes understand what they are talking about. Whatever the case, these experiments are significant for the study of human evolution, since they demonstrate that ape capability is greater than once believed, and may also suggest clues to the origins of human language. One practical result from these experiments has been the development of successful techniques to help mentally disadvantaged children to express themselves (Rumbaugh et al., 1982).

Although apes have shown considerable skill and intelligence in learning and using signs—and perhaps symbols—*when taught by humans*, the fact remains that, in natural settings, chimpanzees do not use language in their social intercourse or daily activities. We believe the question of language (whether or not apes are capable of it) currently does not add any meaningful resolution to the question of apes and culture.

◇ Recent Trends in Nonhuman Primate Behavioral Research

As opposed to the psychological tradition of studying animals (including primates) in laboratory settings, the anthropological tradition has concentrated on studying primates in their native habitats. While there was some initial work of this kind before World War II (e.g., Roy Carpenter's studies of howler monkeys and gibbons in the 1930s), primatology did not come of age until the late 1950s. With the pioneering work on free-ranging groups of savanna baboons (Sherwood Washburn and Irven DeVore), mountain gorillas (George Schaller), langurs (Phyllis Dolhinow), and chimpanzees (Jane Goodall), behavioral studies of nonhuman primates became an entirely new subdiscipline of physical anthropology. Since 1960 this area of research has virtually exploded, and today there are literally hundreds of primatologists worldwide investigating scores of species.

Since primatology is indeed an infant discipline, its early stages were mostly descriptive and consisted of itemizing major ecological and behavioral components of various species. It was not until the 1970s that more rigorous theoretical perspectives came into wide use. In the last decade, two major theoretical orientations have emerged—socioecology and sociobiology. Let's review each.

SOCIOECOLOGY

Around 1970, some primatologists began to look comprehensively at the relationship between specific environmental features and the social behavior of primates (Crook, 1970). This perspective emphasizes that primate behavior is *variable* (i.e., within species as well as between species). We therefore should expect behavior to differ somewhat seasonally within a single group, and to vary from group to group within the same species (particularly if they inhabit quite different environments). Moreover, there may be some general trends of socioecological relationships that can be traced independently within different categories of primates; e.g., prosimians, New World anthropoids, Old World anthropoids. (An excellent review of socioecology can be found in Jolly, 1972.)

In order to research socioecological relationships, new methodological approaches for gathering field data were developed. Rather than brief surveys of a species' behavior, it was realized that the entire annual round should be studied, preferably for a period of several years.

Secondly, it was not possible to describe *the* behavior of a primate species on the basis of a single study in one location. Of far more interest would be contrasts between populations of the same species living under different environmental conditions. For example, Thelma Rowell's study of common baboons living in forested regions (1972) reveals a markedly different behavioral pattern than research done on the same species in more open environments.

Thirdly, it was necessary to gather detailed information on environmental factors. For example, relevant factors that might influence primate social behavior include: quantity and quality of food, the distribution of food, of water, of sleeping sites, and the kinds and distribution of predators.

Finally, socioecologists quickly realized that human interference in the observed species' food supply through artificial provisioning could be expected to severely disrupt their social behavior in largely unpredictable ways. Consequently, the massive provisioning practiced at the Japanese Monkey Centers or by Jane Goodall in the early years at Gombe Stream was avoided in later research.

Some general principles socioecologists have suggested are listed below. There are numerous exceptions to be found among the order, but these general tendencies have revealed some extremely interesting aspects of primate behavior.

1. *nocturnal forms*: Usually solitary and insectivorous (slow loris, dwarf lemur)
2. *diurnal, arboreal leaf eaters*: Often unimale groups; occasionally multimale; fewer than 30 individuals in group (langurs, howler monkeys)

3. *diurnal, arboreal omnivores*: Monogamous units (gibbons, marmosets); unimale groups (guenons); or small multimale groups (cebus monkey)
4. *partly terrestrial leaf eaters*: Unimale or small multimale (age-graded) groups (hanuman langur, gorilla)
5. *partly terrestrial omnivores*: Small multimale groups (ring-tailed lemur, vervets, some macaques) or large multimale groups (common baboon, some macaques)
6. *partly terrestrial open country forms*: Daytime foraging units almost always unimale (gelada baboon, hamadryas baboon, patas monkey).

SOCIOBIOLOGY

The second new (and highly controversial) perspective that has recently been enthusiastically applied by some researchers to the study of primates is called *sociobiology*. This approach (which is used for a wide variety of animal and insect species) seeks to find evolutionary explanations of animal social behavior in the hope of shedding light on the biological bases of human behavior.

First brought to popular attention in 1975 by Harvard zoologist E. O. Wilson, this approach can be traced to the pioneering works of R. A. Fisher (1930), J.B.S. Haldane (1932), W. D. Hamilton (1964), G. C. Williams (1966), and Robert Trivers (1971, 1972). Following publication of Wilson's monumental synthesis, vehement arguments exploded both inside and outside academia. What has caused all this furor, and what relevance does sociobiology have to understanding primates, particularly human primates?

Sociobiologists are basically classical Darwinists, postulating the evolution of behavior through operation of natural selection. Sociobiologists assume that, if any behavior has a genetic basis, its evolutionary impact will be directly measured by its effect on reproductive success. In other words, with behavioral phenotypes (just as with physical morphology), the success of genes underlying the phenotypes will be determined by their influence on reproduction. Individuals with genotypes coding for behaviors leading to higher reproductive success than other individuals will, by definition, be more fit. Consequently, they should pass on their genes at a differentially faster rate. Sociobiologists believe genotypes have evolved in this way, producing such phenomena as sterile worker castes in bees, courtship dances in birds, and scent marking in dogs. As a speculative model, this reasoning is all well and good. In fact, much of the theoretical way natural selection is discussed in Chapter 2 of this text utilizes terminology and concepts developed by sociobiologists.

When applied to relatively simple organisms—social insects, for example— sociobiological theory has proven of tremendous explanatory value. In fact, recent sophisticated molecular biological research with the DNA of marine snails has identified a family of genes that produce specific proteins whose combined action in turn governs the animal's egg-laying behavior (Scheller and Axel, 1984). This is of note because, for the first time, something that could be termed "complex" behavior has been traced to a specific genetic mechanism (i.e., DNA sequences that have been decoded).

Of course, neither insects nor snails are mammals (to say nothing of primates). The major dispute arises, then, when trying to postulate the actual mechanics of behavioral evolution in complex social animals like primates. Which specific behaviors among primates have a genetic basis, and how do these behaviors influence reproductive success?

In order to answer the first question, we will have to learn considerably more about genotype/phenotype interactions in complex traits. Such an understanding is probably decades away. To answer the second question, we will need accurate data on reproductive success in primate groups similar to that shown for birds in Chapter 2 (p. 38). As of yet, such data are almost completely lacking, but it is hoped this situation will be remedied in the near future. Thus, sociobiology as an *explanation* of primate behavior remains almost entirely a matter of open speculation. Application of evolutionary models specifically to explain human behavior are presently even more hypothetical.

Obtaining conclusive data for primates and other mammals, we will see, is no easy matter. A good starting point, however, is framing hypotheses concerning behavioral evolution on the basis of the evidence that does exist. A good example of such a perspective is Sarah Blaffer Hrdy's (1977) explanation of infanticide among langur monkeys of India.

Langurs typically live in social groups composed of one adult male, several females, and their offspring (sometimes called a "harem"). Other males without mates associate in bachelor groups. These peripheral males occasionally attack a harem, violently overthrow the previous harem master, and take over the group. Often following this admittedly bloody contest, even more gruesome behavior ensues. The infants, fathered by the previous harem master, are attacked and killed. The adult females in the group usually try to interfere with the males' infanticidal intentions, but to little avail. In the end, most or all the infants are killed.

Why should langurs behave so? Are they not dooming their species to ultimate extinction by such destructive actions? The answer, according to sociobiologists, is *not* in terms of the species. Male langurs do not know they are members of so-and-so species, nor, if they did, would they care what its future would be. Natural selection theory, as conceptualized by sociobiology, teaches us that individuals act to maximize their *own* reproductive success, no matter what its ultimate effect on the species.

Ostensibly, that is exactly what the male langur is doing. By killing the infants, he avoids a two to three year wait before the females come back into estrus. Once the infants are dead, the females stop lactating and become reproductively accessible to the newly arrived male. He can then inseminate them much earlier than would have been the case had he waited while the young (in which he had no genetic interest) were reared.

We might reasonably ask why the females should allow their infants to be slaughtered. Actually, females do attempt to resist infanticide, but their efforts in the face of large, aggressive, and determined males usually fail. Interestingly, it is not the infant's mother who assaults the attacking male, but other females in the group. Some writers suggest that these females are closely related (sisters of the mother, for example) and, if so, sociobiological theory provides an explanation for such seemingly **altruistic** behavior. Since individuals share

Altruism
Helping others without direct benefit to oneself.

Figure 8-18 Part of the large Kaukori langur group resting in mango grove.

genes with close relatives, they can contribute to their *own* reproductive
success by aiding their relatives' offspring.

In diploid species (like langurs, humans, and all vertebrates) individuals
share, on the average, ½ their genes with parents and, likewise, ½ with full
siblings. For example, when a langur defends her sister's offspring, she is
helping contribute genes to the next generation; genes she shares in common
with her nieces and nephews (on the average she shares ¼ her genes in
common with them). In this way, genes that underlie such cooperative behavior may spread in populations.

Of course, there are many possible strategies. Aiding a relative does not
always completely inhibit one's own reproduction. The success of an individual's genes (that is, one's fitness in natural selection terms) is then measured
as the sum of one's own offspring *plus* those of close relatives ("discounted"
according to how closely they are related: ¼ for her nieces and nephews,
half-siblings, or grandchildren, ⅛ for first cousins, etc.).

Langurs are, of course, not doing this consciously. As is true of the cooperative female defense efforts noted above, females are not making conscious
choices as if they *knew* the alternatives. What occurs is simply that individuals
who behave one way will have higher reproductive success than those individuals behaving in another way. Consequently, their genes (including any
that underlie this behavior) are differentially passed onto the next generation,
theoretically just another example of natural selection acting on variation.

The same phenomenon of infant killing has also been observed in mountain gorillas, accounting for 6 infant deaths over a 13-year period (Fossey,
1981; 1983) (see p. 178). In this example as well, the explanation offered has
been sociobiological—a strategy by males to increase their own reproductive
success.

Sociobiological interpretations have also been applied to a wide range of other behaviors seen in primates. For example, the extremely large testes of male chimpanzees have been explained as an adaptation to a fairly promiscuous mating pattern—where several males successfully copulate with an estrous female (a kind of "sperm competition") (Popp and DeVore, 1979). Also, the differential ranging patterns of male and female orangutans have been viewed as the result of differing reproductive strategies between sexes and maximization of food resources (Galdikas, 1979).

The Lovejoy model of human origins discussed at the beginning of the chapter is flavored with sociobiological premises. Individual reproductive success is seen as the key factor, and parental strategies were presumably shifted in hominid evolution for its greater maximization. This is all extremely interesting (and often good fun as well), but how does one go about testing such views?

In fact, all the sociobiological explanations of contemporary primate (including human) behavior, or those scenarios of hominid history, still lack the hard data on reproductive success needed to *test* such theories (in the way the value of any scientific hypothesis *must* be measured).

The difficulties in testing sociobiological theories are a major concern. To be fair, reconstruction of early hominid behavior will probably never be amenable to clear testing. In this respect, Lovejoy's theory is no weaker than many of those postulated before him. Indeed, Lovejoy does attempt to spell out some of the physical aspects of early hominids, as well as deriving specific comparisons from living primates. These points can be weighed and tested to some degree.

Testing of sociobiological theories for many living animals also poses extremely sticky methodological problems. Again, to be fair, most sociobiologists of course recognize the kinds of data that are required to establish unambiguously the validity of their claims. The obstacle is that this information is exceedingly difficult to obtain.

Mammals breed much more slowly than animals such as insects. In order to collect detailed information on individual reproductive success, life history data for entire generations would be required, perhaps for several populations. Such a pursuit would take years. In fact, to date, only one such study has been done on mammals in natural habitats—a 12-year analysis of the reproductive behavior of a red deer population on an island off Scotland (Clutton-Brock, et al., 1982). Although not in a natural setting (observations were made in a laboratory), comprehensive reproductive data have also been obtained over 6 years on an entire colony of mole rats (Jarvis, 1981).

What then of primate studies like that concerning langurs? Hrdy has proposed an interesting hypothesis, and we have suggested that the conclusions need more complete testing, but how could this be accomplished? Langurs can have active reproductive lives that easily span 10–15 years. We would need a minimum of two complete generations to get a handle on the reproductive dynamics and potentially variable strategies in this species (i.e., we could be in the field for 30 years!). Moreover, in order to generate an adequate sample size, we might well have to collect information on several populations simultaneously.

Even if all this could be done, we would still need to check which animals were actually reproducing. (For a recent discussion of this problem, see Fedigan, 1983). Maternity would obviously not be an issue, but paternity is another matter. Consequently, it would be necessary to capture animals (males and their suspected offspring) in order to compare genetic markers, such as red blood cell and white blood cell antigens. In the process of removing animals from the troop, sedating them, taking blood samples, and then returning them to the troop, we might well disrupt the very behaviors we are trying to study.

Sociobiological theories have stimulated new avenues of research and have led to some interesting insights concerning primate behavior. The vast majority of efforts thus far, however, must be regarded as theoretical. Despite the many claims either defending or attacking sociobiological postulates, it is simply too early to know how well this perspective will work. Theory is, after all, only the starting point. The field applications and testing have just begun. The discipline is still barely a newborn science!

◇ Social Carnivores

Our closest relatives, the apes, are forest animals and are mainly vegetarians. Unlike apes, our early ancestors were savanna dwellers and hunters. Early on, they probably hunted mostly small game and scavenged* larger animals; however, when they did hunt, it probably was mostly in groups. To learn more about the origins of human social systems, it may be useful to look at other savanna dwellers and group hunters, the social carnivores: lions, wolves, and wild dogs. It should be noted that social carnivores and early hominids may have adapted in somewhat analogous ways to a similar ecological situation. Phylogenetically, hominids are homologous, of course, with primates, not with social carnivores.

Lions   Like chimpanzees, a pride of lions is loosely organized. It is centered around several related adult females which may remain together for their entire lives. Chimpanzees, on the other hand (see p. 198), are organized around a core of adult *males*. The core of the pride consists of adult lion females and their young. As male offspring reach two and one-half to three and one-half years of age, they leave the pride, or are chased off.

A definite hierarchical system appears to be lacking among lions, who do, however, show dominance and rank. That males are definitely dominant to females can easily be seen, especially at feeding time. The overwhelming majority of threat behavior is directed by males against females and cubs to prevent them from approaching too closely. There is also dominance among females, and Rudnai (1973) observed a relationship among three females in which the youngest's lower status was indicated by much of the aggressive behavior directed against her, her lack of priority in obtaining food, and the greater frequency of her performing the greeting ceremony.

*There is some disagreement among paleontologists and primatologists whether hunting, scavenging, or both were the way of life of the earliest hominids.

Males may be dominant in lions, but leadership belongs to the females. An adult female leads the pride as it moves across the savanna, but in the course of a few miles, the leadership will have alternated several times among the females. Males do not lead, but move along with the pride or tag behind, and the females and cubs pay little attention to the males' movements.

Most of the hunting by lions is done by females singly or communally, but once the prey is killed, males move in and eat their fill before allowing lionesses to feed, one of the few expressions of male dominance. Single lions tend to hunt smaller game, such as Thomson's gazelle; they may also hunt larger prey—wildebeests and zebras—but their chances of success with larger animals are twice as great if two or more lionesses cooperate.

The close mother-infant relationship so typical of primates is not found among lions. Mothering ranges between care and neglect. Mothers do nurse and protect their young and snarl at males that roam too close to their cubs. On the other hand, lionesses enjoy the conviviality of other females, and if taking care of cubs means separation from the pride, the mother may abandon them. Mothers do not bring meat from a kill to their cubs. If the cubs are at a kill, they usually obtain some meat; if they are not there, then the mother must fetch them—but only after she herself has fed. However, by the time she returns with the cubs, there may be no meat left.

When the cubs are almost two years old (about the time the mother has another litter), contact with the mother decreases and she ceases to care for them. The continuing relationship between mother and offspring so marked among chimpanzees is not present in lions. The lack of a close relationship between mother and cubs, as well as the frequent neglect of cubs by the

Figure 8-19   Lioness and cub at play.

mothers, may account for the high mortality rate of cubs, estimated to be over 60% by Schaller (1972).

The social structure of the lion pride, although loosely organized, nevertheless provides them with superior hunting techniques enabling them to catch large herbivores in open terrain. Operating as a group, lions are much more successful in hunting than solitary lions. Lack of parental care and male participation in the group structure is not a good model for what we believe early hominid behavior to be; however, the lion pride has been a successful form of adaptation to a savanna environment.

In this environment, lions have developed a strategy different from early hominids. Females are the hunters, and a close mother-offspring relationship is lacking. Lion adaptations, however, help delineate early hominid strategies. Like lions, hominids also lived in social groups and most likely were social rather than solitary hunters. Like other primates, however, early hominid females were very closely associated with their offspring, which may help explain why males were most likely the primary hunters.

Wolves   Social carnivore behavior more similar to hominid adaptations may be seen in wolves. A wolf pack and a hunter-gatherer band maintain an optimal size of the group in relation to the availability of food in regions with similar ecological characteristics. Both groups tend to control births socially—wolves through rivalry between females and humans through infanticide and contraceptive taboos. Wolves and humans live well below the carrying capacity of the environment, i.e., the environment is capable of supporting more individuals than are present. Both the pack and the band have a leader or decision maker and some form of dominance hierarchy.

Children of hunting groups and wolf cubs enjoy a great deal of freedom and are usually indulged by their elders. Food sharing exists between young and old, and rituals control much aggression within the group. Pack and band allegiance appears to be maintained through rituals involving "dancing" and "music," and during a food scarcity, both groups tend to split up, nomadic one season and sedentary when food is more abundant (Fox, 1978).

A pack of wolves is formed when a mated pair leaves its parental group to produce a litter of its own. Occasionally, several families may combine to form a large pack of 7 to 10 adults of both sexes. Packs of up to 21 wolves have been sighted. Wolves are territorial and avoid using an area through which another pack has recently traveled—probably indicated by urine-marking.

Care of young pups is basically a function of the mother who suckles them; however, there is great interest in the pups evidenced by all adult pack members. Weaning takes place at six to eight weeks, and pups eat food regurgitated by the mother or other members of the pack. When the pack hunts, the mother usually remains with the pups (although other adults and yearlings may perform this function), and the male (father) and other pack members bring back food for all. The close emotional bond of a wolf pack is believed to originate in this practice of communal feeding of pups (Mech, 1966).

Hunting is a cooperative effort and, operating as a coordinated unit, the pack stalks and chases the animal it has sighted (usually a moose). If the

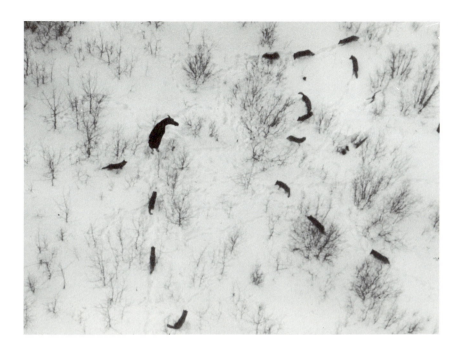

Figure 8-20 Wolves attacking moose.

moose does not run, the wolves harass it from all sides, trying to make it bolt. Should the moose run, the wolves chase it and lunge at the animal, biting and tearing in order to bring it down. If the moose stands, the wolves are more cautious, and if they cannot force it to run will abandon the moose after a few minutes.

When chasing a cow moose and calf, wolves attempt to separate them. If the wolves can keep the cow busy for thirty seconds, the calf is doomed.

Wild Dogs   Wild dogs of Africa form very amiable and closely interacting groups, which average 9 to 10 members. Schaller (1972) reports that since the young tend to remain with the adults even after the birth of a new litter, it is very likely that a pack is composed of related individuals. Most observers do not believe a dominance hierarchy exists among wild dogs, but van Lawick is certain he observed dominance and submissive behavior. Submissive behavior is shown by cringing, grinning in fear, licking and nibbling the lips of the more dominant, and presenting the neck (van Lawick, 1970). Unlike wolves, no territoriality exists among wild dogs. Ranges, which average around 240 square miles and may reach over 1,000 square miles, overlap considerably without agonistic behavior between the packs. It is not uncommon for a pack that is otherwise nonterritorial to defend the area immediately around its den.

As among wolves, care of pups is a function of all pack members, but the mother retains certain prerogatives. She suckles the young, and when the den is moved, it is her task to move the pups. When there are small young, the pack remains in the vicinity of the den, leaving for hunting and returning afterward. From about the age of two and one-half months, the young accom-

Figure 8-21 Pack of wild dogs attacking zebra.

pany adults, and the den is abandoned. Once the pups become mobile, the pack ranges much more widely in its hunting activities. Both males and females hunt, but if there are small pups, usually the mother and possibly one or two others remain at the den as guards.

While pups are still at the den, returning hunters share the kill (as do wolves) by regurgitating meat to them and to the guards as well. When pups accompany adults, they take almost complete precedence at a kill and are permitted to monopolize the carcass. Wolves and dogs take much better care of the young than lions do, especially in sharing food. Schaller (1972) mentions that even a lame dog unable to keep up with the pack was able to beg meat successfully from the hunters.

Dogs start out on a hunt by trotting along at about five miles an hour with a male in the lead. When they sight a gazelle herd, they run in a broad front and scatter the herd so they can pick out a quarry which several dogs then pursue. When a dog catches up to a gazelle, it grabs a side, rump, or thigh and pulls it down. The other dogs arrive within a few seconds and tear the animal to pieces. If a gazelle should run in a circle, the dogs hunt cooperatively. One or two dogs chase the gazelle while the rest cut across the arc and surround it.

Wild dogs hunt more successfully than lions or wolves and Schaller estimates a remarkable 89% success rate. For this reason, as well as their fierceness when attacking, they have been called "the super beasts of prey" (Wilson, 1975).

Studying social carnivores is instructive because they inhabit an ecological niche similar to that occupied by early hominids. And, like social carnivores, early hominids were also hunters. It is possible, as Schaller suggests, "that some of the same selective forces which had an influence on the social [carnivores] also had an effect on hominid societies" (1972, p. 378). Since the carnivore group, as we have seen, is superior to the solitary hunter in its success rate, there may have been selection pressures in early hominids for such cooperative methods as group hunting and encircling the prey. Living in groups makes division of labor possible as seen in the case of wild dogs, where mother guards the den while others hunt. We can conjecture that early hominids also divided their labor, shared food, and occupied a home base.

Kortlandt makes the interesting suggestion that wolves (we would include wild dogs, also) developed their cooperative hunting techniques as a result of hunting animals larger than themselves. Early hominids, he goes on, evolved similar cooperative hunting techniques since they, too, hunted game larger than themselves. Furthermore, the teamwork techniques of wolves required considerable extension of their social communication system. Kortlandt believes a similar evolutionary trend must have occurred among early hominids, but because the largely "instinctive social communication system" in hominids is poorer, they achieved an alternative evolutionary solution by extending their primarily "*noninstinctive* communication patterns," that is, speech (Kortlandt, 1965, p. 321).

◇ Hunting and Gathering Societies

We have reviewed two kinds of social animals, nonhuman primates and social carnivores, in order to gain some understanding of ourselves and our origins. Contemporary humans in an industrialized or agricultural community live far removed from ancient humans and, from an adaptive viewpoint, cannot easily be compared to nonhuman social mammals. However, there are peoples living at the present time in remote areas of the world who have maintained a way of life, to some extent at least, similar to that of early hominids. A review of these people, whom anthropologists classify as hunter-gatherers (or, as some prefer, gatherer-hunters), may give some idea of how early hominids lived 1 or 2 million years ago. We cannot claim that contemporary hunter-gatherers live identically to those ancient ones, but since adaptive problems are somewhat similar, it will be worthwhile to see how these peoples have developed adaptive strategies that enabled them to survive.

A hunting and gathering pattern (that is, hunting wild game and gathering wild plant foods) is fundamental to human behavior. More than just characteristic of early hominids, a hunting and gathering way of life has been *the* strategy used by our ancestors throughout the vast majority of human evolution.* The time span of our genus, *Homo*, has extended for about 2 million years. Of that time, our ancestors were hunter-gatherers for all but the last 10,000 years. In other words, 99.5% of the history of the genus *Homo* was spent as a hunter-gatherer.

Hunter-gatherers live today in widely divergent environments we would consider to be forbidding regions of the earth; rain forests, deserts, and the

---

*Some anthropologists believe scavenging preceded hunting and may have been the primary source of meat even for *H. erectus*.

arctic and subarctic. Such was not always the case. Before the invention of farming, hunters traversed the plains in search of food. However, with domestication, farmers pushed the hunters out of this desirable land to less hospitable areas.

Typically, hunter-gatherers live in small nomadic or seminomadic bands, in residential groups of changing composition. They usually lack the more organized forms of kinship, such as clans and lineages. There are no specialized economic, religious, or political groups since the family itself is the organization that undertakes all these roles. Depending on the season and availability of food, the size of the band expands and contracts. Bands move from one area to another within their home range according to the availability of resources in different places at different times. The food resources used by the band are communal property, and all families have equal rights to them. To protect their resources, band members may defend their territory against encroachment by strangers (Service, 1966, p. 22).

A band is not a closed group; people constantly come and go, separating when food is scarce and regrouping for collective hunts, sharing a water hole, or participating in an important ceremony. Should a conflict arise, an individual may leave his band and seek to join another.

Men do most of the hunting and women the gathering, usually in small groups, but all share their food with other members of the band. Since hunter-gatherers exercise little or no control over the plants and animals upon which they depend, they have to accommodate themselves to seasonal and annual fluctuations in resources spread over wide areas.

As an example of a hunting-gathering society, let us take a brief look at the !Kung San of the Kalahari Desert in South Africa.

!Kung San*

The !Kung San of the Dobe live on the border of Namibia and Botswana on the northern fringe of the Kalahari Desert of Southwest Africa. This area of hot, wet summers (October to May) and cool, dry winters (May to October) is a sparsely populated sand plain across which the hunting-gathering !Kung San occupy approximately 7,000 square miles. Within this area are 10 permanent water holes occupied by approximately 500 San. Some non-San people live here, also.

At the water holes, the !Kung live in camps or villages† of from 10 to 30 individuals. The type of village varies with the season. In the dry (summer) season, the village is fairly large. It is comprised of from 8 to 15 huts and 20 to 50 people, is located near a permanent water source, and is occupied for 3 to 6 months. In the rainy season, the village, from 3 to 20 huts, is located near a seasonal water and food source and is occupied for 3 weeks to 3

---

*The diacritical mark "!" indicates a click (something like the clucking sound made to a horse), which is part of the San phonetic system. Anthropologists have discarded the term "Bushmen" for these foragers living in the Kalahari and now refer to them as San, of which the !Kung are one group. Material on the !Kung is derived from Yellen (1977) and especially Lee (1984).

†Lee uses the words "camp" and "village" interchangeably.

months. In the spring and fall the camp is temporary, rarely occupied for more than 2 or 3 weeks, and no huts are built.

Until recently, each !Kung group moved every season, building and abandoning 3 to 6 villages each year. Eventually, these abandoned villages become buried in sand and were converted into archeological sites ". . . !Kung village sites of the 1960s strongly resemble the village sites of prehistoric foragers 100 to 500 or more years old . . ." (Lee, 1984, p. 33). A !Kung camp consists of kinspeople and affines (inlaws) who have found that they can live and work well together. Brothers, for example, may live together or apart, as may fathers and sons. The composition of the camp changes from day to day and month to month because the !Kung enjoy visiting. Each year about 30% of the population makes a permanent residential shift from one camp to another. There is a visiting network among camps, and during a given lifetime an

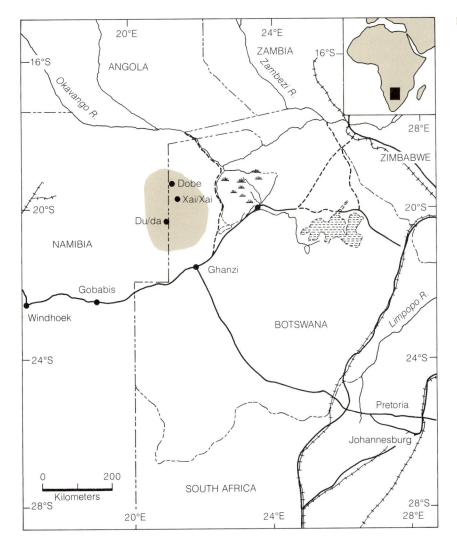

Figure 8-22   Map of San area.

individual may live for varying amounts of time at many different water holes. However, establishing residence with a camp does not require relinquishing a claim to any other camp.

This constant circulation might appear to cause residential instability. However, an entire camp may move together for at least part of the year. What gives the camp its stability is its core, which is composed of related older people, usually siblings and cousins. Generally, the core is considered to be the water hole owners. Surrounding each water hole is land that contains food resources. This forms the basic subsistence area for the residing group. The water hole and the land immediately around it is "owned" by the *k'ausi*, the core of related people, and the ownership is passed from generation to generation as long as the descendants continue to live there.

The core group is also recognized as the hosts, and anyone wishing to visit at the water hole is expected to approach the hosts for permission. The *k'ausi* are not owners in the sense that they can sell the land if they wish; they are simply the people who have lived there longer than any other. Both male and female kin and their spouses are included in the *k'ausi*. After a time the name of one member of the group becomes the name of the camp, but this leader is in no sense a headman.

A camp is built up over time by the addition of in-marrying spouses of the core siblings. A brother brings in his wife; and a sister may bring in her husband. These in-laws then bring in *their* siblings so that the camp has a relative—parent, child, sibling, or spouse—with links to the core group.

Settling at a water hole, the !Kung arrange their huts in a circle, with the entrances facing center. The huts are generally occupied by nuclear families, with husband, wife, and immature children sharing a single hut and hearth. Young, unmarried adults of the same sex usually live together in a separate hut, whereas widowers and co-wives have huts of their own.

Figure 8-23   A !Kung San camp.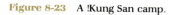

Figure 8-24   A !Kung family works at home.

People living at a water hole—residents and visitors—all share the available resources. Members of a camp, of course, have access to the resources, and, if the sharing breaks down, it ceases to be a camp. Visitors also share, and it is understood that the residents at some future time will pay a return visit to their visitors' camp and share the resources there. A fairly complex system of obligations apply between hosts and visitors.

!Kung men are excellent hunters and devote a great deal of time and effort to their pursuit of game. While snaring game is practiced, most of the hunting consists of pursuing game either singly or in twos or threes. Outstanding trackers, !Kung hunters can deduce the following information about the animal they are tracking: species, sex, age, how fast traveling, alone or with other animals, physical condition, whether and on what it is feeding, and the time of day the animal passed this way.

Known to the !Kung are some 262 species of animals, of which about 80 are eaten. Several varieties of antelopes and game birds are eagerly sought, but the species that provide the most meat are warthogs, wildebeests, gemsboks, kudus, elands, roan antelopes, and hartebeests. Although women do not hunt, men may gather when meat is scarce, and the food thus obtained accounted for 22% of all gathered food.

When a large animal is killed, it is feasting time, and great cauldrons of meat are cooked round-the-clock. People gather from far and wide, and meat is distributed to all. The distribution is made according to a set of rules, with great care, and the arranging and rearranging of the pieces may continue for an hour to ensure that each recipient is given the right proportion. Improper meat distribution can cause bitter wrangling among close relatives. Excellent distribution will be fondly recalled for months.

As in most foraging societies, women do the gathering. As a matter of fact, the foundation of !Kung subsistence depends on the 105 species of edible

Figure 8-25 !Kung hunter returns to camp.

wild plants found in their area, especially the remarkable mongongo nut, which provides up to half the !Kung vegetable diet. The wide variety of vegetable food available to the !Kung provides a cushion against changing environmental conditions.

When the !Kung establish a campsite, they eat the more desirable plant food first. When that is consumed, young members range farther afield for less desirable species, and older members collect the food closer to home. The day's foods are pooled within families and shared with other families, so that a variety of food is available to every camp member and no one goes hungry.

In his fieldwork, Dr. Lee investigated the question of how hard the !Kung San worked. He found that over a four-week period, the overall work week was 2.4 days of work per adult. During the month of this study, at least, the people appeared to spend less than half their days in obtaining food. They enjoyed more leisure time than members of many agricultural and industrial societies. And this was during the dry season of a year of serious drought!

On the days the Dobe people were not hunting or gathering, they were either at the water hole entertaining visitors, or themselves visiting other camps.

It is interesting to note that the men worked longer than the women. Men worked an average of 12 out of 28 days (providing about 45% of the food), while women worked about 9 (providing about 55% of the food), a work schedule that contradicts the view that women are the workhorses of a foraging society. Men appear to work one-third harder than the women. A day of gathering by the women produces about 68% more calories on the average than a day of hunting. Women, it seems, work fewer days, but produce more calories than the men.

At one time, it was believed that hunter-gatherers lived a hand-to-mouth existence, ever on the brink of starvation. Lee clearly demonstrated this is not the case by carefully measuring the caloric and protein intake of a group of !Kung. The daily intake of meat protein was 34.5 grams and 690 calories; from mongongo nuts, 58.8 grams of protein and 1,365 calories; and, from other vegetables, 3 grams of protein and 300 calories. This amounts to an average of 2,355 calories per person. Lee estimated their minimum daily energy requirements (given their size and activity) to be about 1,975 calories, which left a caloric surplus of 380. The !Kung, with a modest subsistence effort of 2.4 workdays per week, produced an adequate diet *and* a surplus. What makes this way of life possible, Lee believes, is sharing:

> If I had to point to one single feature that makes this way of life possible, I would focus on *sharing*. Each !Kung is not an island unto himself or herself; each is part of a collective. It is a small, rudimentary collective, and at times a fragile one, but it is a collective nonetheless. What I mean is that the living group pools the resources that are brought into camp so that everyone receives an equitable share. The !Kung and people like them don't do this out of nobility of soul or because they are made of better stuff than we are. In fact, they often gripe about sharing. They do it because it works for them and it enhances their survival. Without this core of sharing, life for the !Kung would be harder and infinitely less pleasant (Lee, 1984, p. 55).

Figure 8-26 Carrying her child, a !Kung woman gathers.

In summary, the !Kung San possess what is central to a foraging economy: sexual division of labor; simple technology; collective, nonexclusive ownership of land and resources; and widespread food sharing within and among local groups according to the principle of generalized reciprocity.

Attempting to reconstruct the situation in which early hominids evolved is speculative since so little evidence is available, especially for specific events. Evidence from social carnivores, especially wild dogs and wolves, points up the utility of cooperative hunting, which may be at least one of the reasons for their success. Additionally, reproductive success is enhanced by their home base, where the young are guarded from intruders and fed by returning hunters. Whether cooperative hunting is found among baboons and chimpanzees is presently not entirely certain, but, in any case, it is not the prevalent mode of obtaining meat. Furthermore, meat is not as important in their diet as is vegetable matter.

!Kung San are cooperative hunters, share both meat and vegetables according to an organized and formal plan, use a home base, pair bond, and the sexes divide their labor. A few of these characteristics, such as sharing and division of labor (and perhaps cooperative hunting) may be practiced by nonhuman primates, but to a very limited degree.

On the other hand—like all contemporary *Homo sapiens*—San people have a fully modern human brain. As such, they have highly elaborated capabilities for abstract thought, symbolic language, complex tool making, and so forth. They thus are not strictly comparable to very early hominids, whose brain sizes were much smaller, and who probably did not possess full language.

Moreover, the !Kung San were "disrupted" by outside civilization well before the first systematic anthropological studies were carried out (in the early 1950s). As a result, they use metal knives and arrowheads (the bow and arrow itself is probably a fairly recent import), wear cotton clothing, and employ many other introduced items. How much all of this has influenced their culture (from our point of view, specifically their ecological strategies) is difficult to say. Certainly the !Kung San (or, for that matter, any contemporary hunting-gathering group) do not have the same relationship with their environments that would have been true even a few generations ago.

Sadly, the degree of outside influence disrupting the traditional !Kung San culture has recently become overwhelming. Much of the wild game on which they had depended is either decimated or partially off-limits on protected game preserves. Pressure by governments (in South Africa and Botswana), as well as economic pressures to obtain cash resources, have led many San to settle on reservations. Here, many have become exposed for the first time to alcohol, tobacco, transistor radios, infant formula, and other modern items (Kolata, 1981).

Southern Africa today is a tinderbox of conflicting political and racial groups. The !Kung San have not been able to avoid these powerful forces and, in many cases, have been swept directly into the conflict. Since about 1970, the South African government has actively recruited !Kung San into the army, where they are used to fight insurgent groups in Namibia and also in neighboring Angola (Kolata, 1981).

◇ Conclusion: Fact and Fiction of Human Behavioral Evolution

As we have seen, no single behavioral model is adequate for reconstructing early hominid beginnings. They are all flawed in one way or another. What we must do, consequently, is to *select* those aspects from each model we think are most useful.

Certainly, early hominids were social. Moreover, we know that by at least 4 m.y.a. they were exploiting open environments and were adapted for bipedalism (although perhaps not completely—we'll discuss this in further detail in Chapter 12). By 2 m.y.a., some hominids were using stone tools, regularly exploiting meat resources, and carrying these and other items back to a central place (i.e., a base camp). As we will see in Chapter 10, this meat exploitation initially was limited mostly to small animals and probably the scavenging of larger kills brought down by other predators. Certainly, by 1 m.y.a., our ancestors were systematically going after very large animals.

Thus, the models provided by social carnivores, savanna baboons, and modern hunter-gatherers have something to tell us about how socially organized animals cope in a savanna environment. Moreover, from social carnivores (analogously) and from hunter-gatherers (homologously), we can glean some clues regarding the advantages of group hunting, food sharing, and base camps.

In addition, chimpanzees offer further insight concerning incipient tool use, complex (but mostly nonvocal) communication, and parental strategies for raising slowly developing offspring.

Beyond these generalizations, the record allows little in the way of more specific statements. Lovejoy points out that early hominids were bipedal *before* they began to systematically use stone implements. From this, he assumes that the earliest hominids were adapted for carrying something else other than tools—and suggests it was food. Moreover, the food was carried by males back to central places and shared with females to whom they were monogamously paired.

As we have indicated, hominids certainly were bipedal early on, and at a stage where as yet no definite stone tools have been recovered. It is quite possible—even probable—that these hominids did have tools made of perishable materials (wood, bone, fiber). Unfortunately, we probably will never know. It is also possible that early hominids did have marked sexual division of labor, monogamous pairs, concealed ovulation, and increased male parental investment. However, here, too, there is no way to know for certain.

In reading accounts of human behavioral evolution, particularly those aimed at the general public* we caution you to keep these concerns in mind. In so doing, it will be more possible to separate the hard evidence from speculation, and you can then draw your own conclusions.

◇ Summary

Since humans are primates and evolved from primates, anthropologists believe that the study of nonhuman primate behavior may offer insights into hominid origins and further the understanding of human behavior.

As an interpretive and organizational aid, we have presented the model of human behavioral origins proposed by Owen Lovejoy. In his model, Lovejoy emphasizes several key differences between human and nonhuman primates. These are helpful in highlighting how our primate cousins can be used to better understand human evolution. In addition, Lovejoy speculates about the sequence of certain behavioral innovations among our earliest hominid ancestors. We disagree with the implications of this, but controversies of this nature are helpful in demonstrating how various models can be used to illuminate our evolutionary history.

Although it varies a great deal, nonhuman primate behavior may be discussed under several categories: grooming, displays, dominance or status rank relationships, mother-infant relationships, male-female sexual bond, role separation between adults and young, and role separation by sex.

Baboon and chimpanzee social behavior, as a specific example of nonhuman primates, is briefly described and "cultural" behavior of chimpanzees and Japanese macaques discussed. The ability of apes—especially chimpanzees—to handle language raises interesting theoretical questions about the origin of language and the role language played in the evolution of early hominids. Whether chimpanzees who have been taught to sign can actually form sentences is also discussed.

*For example, Morris (1967); Ardrey (1966, 1976); Tiger and Fox (1974), and Morgan (1972).

Primatologists have recently begun to look at primate behavior from two new approaches: socioecology and sociobiology. Socioecology emphasizes the environmental factors that might bear on animal behavior, and sociobiology emphasizes the genetic basis of animal behavior.

Social carnivore adaptations to savanna ecological conditions are introduced as an analogy for the adaptation of early hominids to a similar environment. The way of life of contemporary hunter-gatherers (or gatherer-hunters), such as the !Kung, reflects the kind of adaptation that may have characterized early hominids.

◇ Questions for Review

1. List several reasons for studying nonhuman primate behavior.
2. What behavioral traits are common to all nonhuman primates?
3. Describe the primate social group.
4. What are the functions of grooming? displays? dominance?
5. Why is the mother-infant relationship an important one for primates?
6. Compare baboon and chimpanzee social behavior. What is the relationship between the social behavior and group structure of these primates?
7. Do baboons or chimpanzees serve as better models for hominid behavior? Why?
8. Discuss the learning achievements of chimpanzees. Why do the authors believe the concept of culture should not be applied to this behavior?
9. Chimpanzees have been taught to communicate symbolically; why is this significant?
10. What is the argument opposing the idea that chimpanzees are capable of learning language?
11. What is the basis for the sociobiological approach to animal behavior?
12. How does sociobiology explain altruistic behavior?
13. Describe the different adaptations of lions and wild dogs to a savanna ecological niche.
14. How does the study of social carnivores contribute to our understanding of hominid evolution?
15. What are the similarities in the adaptations of social carnivores and !Kung San?

Primate Evolution

CONTENTS

Ancient legends tell of Sasquatch, a strange, hairy, bipedal creature prowling the wilds of North America. In fact, Sasquatches, abominable snowmen, and other such creatures have been reported from at least 100 separate areas of the world. In North America, they have been reported most often from British Columbia, Washington, Oregon, and northern California. Various unexplained beasts, however, have also been "seen" from Alaska to Mexico and from the Pacific Coast to northern Michigan. Tales of these creatures, which are usually called *Bigfoot*, are today even further embellished as sightings, footprints, hair fragments, feces, and even photographs have been collected. Are we dealing with fact or fiction?

If Bigfoot lives, what could it be? Reports are consistent, detailing a very large (eight to twelve foot), upright animal. Its size, hair, and location (in the cold Northwest) all imply a mammal. Its body shape and locomotion further limit the possibilities. Possibly it is a bear, but the gait and footprints are not right. What is left then? A hominoid of some sort?

Is this possible? In any objective pursuit of knowledge we must admit that *anything* is possible, but some things are highly improbable. What kinds of hominoids are native to the New World? The only definite remains of indigenous hominoids in North, Central, or South America are those of *Homo sapiens* (and these are relatively recent—in the last 30,000–40,000 years or so).

If Bigfoot is a hominoid, where did it come from? The closest fossil primate matching the dimensions of the fleeting Sasquatches is *Gigantopithecus*. Remains of this extinct hominoid are well known from the Old World during the Pleistocene, but none has ever been found in the New World. Such a big animal has exceedingly large teeth, which generally have a fairly good chance of being preserved. From China alone there are more than 1,000 *Gigantopithecus* teeth, and this giant hominoid has not roamed the forests of China for half a million years. It seems very strange, indeed. If *Gigantopithecus* (or one of its supposed descendants) is still living, why have we not found any bones or teeth of this form? If such a large animal has existed for tens of thousands of years, where is the hard evidence?

What about the hundreds of sightings? Could they all have been faked? Probably not. Many of these people, no doubt, saw *something*. Perhaps often they were bears; the imagination can greatly influence our objectivity when primed with romantic tales of mythical beasts. What about footprints, photos, hairs, and fecal material? The prints (at least many of them) could have been faked, and so too with the photos (the primary evidence—a 16-mm film taken in northern California in 1967). Such a circumstance would suggest an elaborate, deliberate hoax, not a happy conclusion, but entirely possible (as you will see with Piltdown). The hairs and fecal material are from some ani-

mal, perhaps one already known, perhaps one yet to be discovered. The possibility exists that there are large terrestrial mammals in remote areas of North America unknown to science. Bigfoot may be such an animal. However, of all the possibilities, the suggestion that this creature is a hominoid is about the least likely imaginable.

The conclusion that Bigfoot is an archaic hominoid is therefore both unlikely and far from conclusively established. But it is not *completely* impossible. Perhaps descendant populations of gigantopithecines migrated from China (through thousands of miles of environments exceedingly inhospitable to such a forest-adapted form), to end up in the American Northwest. In so doing, perhaps they left nary a trace all along the way. Furthering our improbable conjectures, perhaps they have existed in North America for at least 500,000 years, without leaving a single fossil remnant. Finally, perhaps they still exist today, but deliberately conceal themselves and meticulously dispose of their dead.

SOURCES:

Napier, John. *Bigfoot; the Yeti and Sasquatch in Myth and Reality*, London: Jonathan Cape, 1972.

Sanderson, Ivan T. *Abominable Snowmen: Legend Come to Life*, New York: Chilton Co., 1961.

Shuman, James B. "Is There an American Abominable Snowman?," *Reader's Digest*, January 1969, pp. 179–186.

◇ CHAPTER NINE

◇ Introduction

In Chapters 6, 7, and 8, you were introduced to the time scale of evolution, placental mammals, and particularly the primate order. We now turn to the fossil history of primates over the last 70 million years. With what you now know of primate anatomy (teeth, limbs, etc.) and social behavior, you will be able to "flesh out" the bones and teeth that comprise the evolutionary record of primate origins. In this way, the ecological adaptations and evolutionary relationships of these fossil forms to each other (and to contemporary primates) will become more meaningful. Please note that when we look at primate evolution, we are looking at our own evolution as well.

◇ Time Scale

A brief review of the geological time scale will be helpful in understanding primate evolution during the Cenozoic.

Era	Epoch	Approximate Beginning (m.y.a.)
Cenozoic	Pleistocene	1.8
	Pliocene	5
	Miocene	25
	Oligocene	37
	Eocene	53
	Paleocene	65
Mesozoic	Cretaceous	135

Before discussing the fossil primates, we should caution that the formal taxonomic names for the various families and genera are horrendous to pronounce and even harder to remember. Unfortunately, there is no other adequate way to discuss the material. We must make reference to the standard nomenclature. As an aid, we suggest you refer to the marginal notes, pronunciation guide, and glossary for those names considered most significant.

◇ Earliest Primates

The first radiation of the primate order has its roots in the beginnings of the explosive adaptive radiation of placental mammals in general. Therefore, it is not surprising that the earliest suggestions of primates in the fossil record are difficult to discern from early members of other placental mammal groups, particularly the insectivores.

The earliest discovered traces suggesting the beginnings of our order come from the late Cretaceous and early Paleocene in the Dakota area of North America. Known only from a few teeth, this fossil form, called **Purgatorius**, exhibits the primate tendency towards a bulbous cusp pattern in the molar teeth compared to the sharper cusps seen in insectivores. Such a dental pattern apparently indicates that early primates were adapting to fruit and leaf-eating diets (Szalay, 1968), or perhaps a diet also including insects exploited in an arboreal niche (Van Valen and Sloan, 1965). Reconstructions indicate that the dental formula is still that of a generalized primitive mammal: 3-1-4-3 (Szalay and Delson, 1979). All that can be said now of this still fragmentary and mysterious animal, *Purgatorius*, is that if it was a primate, it was quite "primitive," which is not surprising considering its early date and still close ties with primitive placental mammals.

◇ Paleocene Primates (65 m.y.–53 m.y.)

During the Paleocene, the first clearly recognizable primates begin to diversify. In fact, we are able to isolate several different (at least four) families widely scattered in North America and Europe during this epoch.

One of the most widely distributed and best represented of these early primates is **Plesiadapis**, found in both North America and Europe. First known from the late Paleocene, the time range of *Plesiadapis* extends up into the early Eocene. This animal, known from a nearly complete skull plus several parts of the limb skeleton, has an estimated size range varying widely between that of a squirrel and a house cat. While these animals show definite primate tendencies, such as dependence on vision (though not completely binocular) and prehensility (though still probably with claws), they retain numerous primitive characteristics, such as lack of a postorbital bar, which serves to form a bony division between the orbit and the braincase. In addition, *Plesiadapis* and the majority of other Paleocene primates display unusual (compared to modern primates) specializations of their front teeth, which are large and procumbent (angled forward) and, in some respects, reminiscent of the specialized aye-aye.

Given these dental specializations, the possibility that any of the Paleocene forms thus far discovered are direct ancestors of later primates seems unlikely. This poses no insurmountable theoretical problem, for we must keep in mind that our meager discoveries represent only a tiny sample of the already diverse kinds of primates living at this time.

The overall anatomical plan of all these early forms could be described as prosimian or even "protoprosimian," for they are certainly more primitive than any living primate. In fact, they are more similar in evolutionary grade to the living tree shrews, which give a fairly good model of Paleocene primates (see p. 158).

◇ Ancient Landscapes and Early Primate Evolution

The distribution and the eventual fate of early primate forms is understandable only within the context of the environments in which these animals

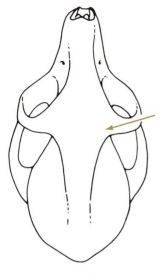

Figure 9-1   Postorbital bar.

lived. First and foremost, we must remember that 60 m.y.a. land masses were not arranged as they are today. As we discussed on p. 133, the continents have "drifted" to their present position, carried along on the shifting plates of the earth's surface.

In the late Paleozoic (*circa* 250 m.y.a.), the huge conglomerate land mass called Pangea began to break up into northern and southern continents. To the north, North America, Europe, and Asia were joined into Laurasia; to the south, Africa, South America, Australia, India, and Antarctica formed Gondwanaland (see Fig. 9-2a). Throughout the Mesozoic, the two basic land masses continued to move, with Gondwanaland breaking up into the southern continents. In the north, the continents also were separating, but North America and Europe continued to be connected through Greenland and would remain attached in this manner for several millions of years.

As we will see, this "northern connection" had a very significant influence on the geographic distribution of early primates. In fact, North America and Europe remained joined until mid-Eocene times (*circa* 45 m.y.a.) (see Fig. 9-2b). Though welded to North America, Europe was separated from Asia by a channel called the Turgai Straight. Not until the later Eocene (about 40 m.y.a.) does Europe disjoin from North America to the west and finally make contact with Asia to the east (forming an area that we today call Eurasia).

What makes all this geologic activity relevant to primate (and other paleontological) studies is that land-living animals could cross over land bridges but were effectively cut off by water barriers. Thus, we see species of *Plesiadapis* in *both* North America and Europe. On the other hand, primates are unknown in Asia until the late Eocene, when presumably they could walk in from Europe once the Turgai Strait had been closed. As far as primates go, then, from their earliest beginnings (65 m.y.a. +) up until 40 m.y.a. they were essentially limited to North America and Europe (between which free migration was still possible). With further continental movements, the "New World" and "Old World" became completely separated and thereby influenced the evolutionary histories of primates still living today (see p. 168).

Figure 9-2 Continental drift. Changes in position of the continental plates from Late Paleozoic to Late Eocene. (*a*) The position of the continents at the end of the Paleozoic (*c.* 250 m.y.a.). Pangea is breaking up into a **northern land mass (Laurasia)** and a **southern land mass (Gondwanaland).** (*b*) The position of the continents during much of the Paleocene and Eocene (up to *c.* 45 m.y.a.). Note that North America and Europe are **still joined but are separate from Asia.**

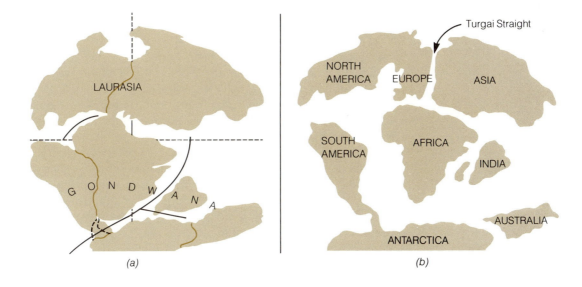

(a)   (b)

Necrolemur
(Nek-roe-lee'-mur)

As the continents moved, climatic conditions changed dramatically. In the Mesozoic and into the Paleocene, the continental masses were clustered closer to the equator, and as Laurasia in particular moved north, its climate cooled. Moreover, the fragmenting of the land masses and the consequent altering of marine flow patterns (less exchange between northern and southern seas) caused the climate to cool even further.

Finally, these climatic shifts also heavily affected plant communities. Rather than the primitive, mostly tropical flora characteristic of the Mesozoic (ferns, cycads, etc.), what we see emerging in the Cenozoic is the rapid radiation of the seed plants (including flowering plants, deciduous trees, grasses, etc.). The world was never to be the same again.

Clearly, then, it is extremely important to interpret primate evolution within the context of the earth's changing environments.

◇ Eocene Primates (53 m.y.–37 m.y.)

The first primates of modern aspect appear during the Eocene. These can now clearly be called prosimians and closely resemble the loris/lemur evolutionary grade. Primate diversification accelerates during this epoch, with four new families and as many as thirty-seven genera represented during the 16-million-year span of the Eocene.

The Eocene may be characterized as the heyday of prosimians, who attained their widest geographic distribution and broadest adaptive radiation during this period. Indeed, more than twice as many genera are found in the Eocene than are known for the whole world today (seventeen living genera, with twelve of these confined to Madagascar).

The most diversified and best-known Eocene primates are members of the lemurlike Adapidae, which includes some ten genera. The three best known of these are:

Adapis (Ad'-a-piss)	Europe
Notharctus (Noth-ark'-tus)	North America
Smilodectes (Smi-lo-dek'-teese)	North America

Some of these animals have been known from fossil evidence for a remarkably long time. In fact, the initial discovery of *Adapis* was made in France in 1821 and first described by Cuvier himself.

As mentioned, all these animals are fairly lemurlike in general adaptive level and show distinctive primate tendencies not seen in the Paleocene forms. For example, they all now have a complete postorbital bar and the eyes are rotated forward, allowing overlapping fields of perception and thus binocular vision. In the limb skeleton, further developments in prehensility are suggested, and some evidence points to the presence of an opposable large toe. In all these respects, we see the typical primate adaptive strategies allowing exploitation of an arboreal environment. Whereas these forms resemble lemurs in overall anatomical plan, they do not show the same specializations seen in contemporary lorises and lemurs, such as development of the dental comb (see p. 160).

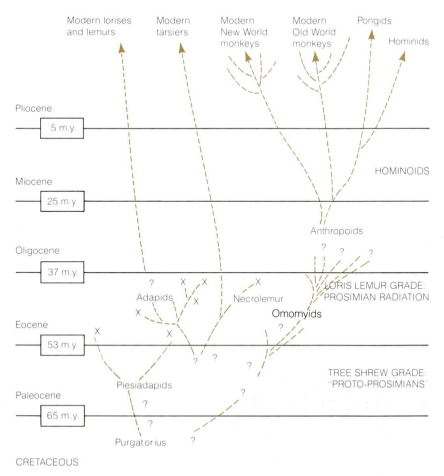

Figure 9-3 Summary, early primate evolution.

The separate evolution of the Malagasy (formerly Madagascar) lemurs may date to late Eocene times, but since this island was already isolated by a deep channel from mainland Africa, they apparently reached their island sanctuary by unintentionally floating over on drifting debris.

The evolutionary origins of the tarsiers are also indicated during the Eocene by the large-eyed and apparently noctural genus, **Necrolemur** ("dead lemur," actually a misnomer; "dead tarsier" would be more appropriate). In addition to the large size of its eyes, *Necrolemur*'s orbits are rotated completely forward, the *foramen magnum* is well forward (indicating the head was held upright over the spine), and there is some flexion in the angle at the base of the skull. All these traits reveal striking similarities with the modern tarsier. In addition, some limb bones, which may well be associated with *Necrolemur* skulls, display the distinctive tarsioid specialization of fused bones in the lower leg (see Fig. 9-4).

While *Necrolemur* almost certainly lies very close to the ancestral origins of the tarsioid line, it may not itself represent the actual ancestors. Specialization in the dental apparatus, shown by loss of some front teeth, indicates that this form could not have evolved into modern tarsiers. Such a circum-

Evolutionary reversal
The reacquisition of a structure previously lost in the evolution of a life form.

stance would necessitate an **evolutionary reversal**, which would involve the reacquisition of a structure already lost—an incredibly unlikely event.

The last group of Eocene primates we will discuss is the family Omomyidae (which some primatologists suggest show general affinities with the tarsiers; they include *Necrolemur* within this group) (Szalay and Delson, 1979). Although known mainly from bits of jaws and teeth, omomyids are the most widely distributed of known Eocene prosimians discovered in North America, Europe, and Asia. Indeed, they are the most widely distributed prosimian group ever! As we have just seen, primate migration into Asia was blocked until the late Eocene when the straits separating it from Europe were closed. Thus, some of these omomyids are the first Asian primates of which we have evidence.

The earlier members of this family are somewhat more generalized than the later ones, and may form the ancestral basis for all later anthropoids: New World monkeys, Old World monkeys, apes, and hominids. The affinities of these fossil omomyids with tarsiers (and inferentially with the anthropoids) have led many researchers to classify the entire group as one evolutionary unit—the Haplorhini—as opposed to the *true* prosimians (i.e., lemurs and lorises)—the Strepsirhini (see p. 157). The later forms are seemingly quite specialized, showing the highly unusual trait of incisor teeth in the upper and lower jaws to be larger than their canines.

Other evidence also argues for the emergence of anthropoids during the late Eocene. Fragmentary remains from Burma dating to about 40 m.y.a. suggest anthropoid affinities. In particular, a form referred to as *Pondaungia* shows several features of the dentition similar to that of Old World anthropoids (Maw et al., 1979). Another Burmese Eocene fossil known as *Amphipithecus* has also been proposed as a possible early anthropoid (Simons, 1972), but detailed consideration of dental anatomy suggests a more likely affinity with the prosimian adapids (Szalay and Delson, 1979).

Eocene Prosimians: Summary

During the Eocene epoch, a wide and highly successful adaptive radiation of prosimian forms occurred. Some, resembling modern lorises and lemurs (Adapidae), may have given rise to direct ancestors of these modern animals by late Eocene times. Others (*Necrolemur*) resemble modern tarsiers, and still others (Omomyidae) may have been the ancestral stock for all anthropoids.

By the end of the Eocene—as the continents drifted away from the equator and caused the climate to cool—tropical areas in the northern latitudes shrank, and the range of available prosimian niches therefore also began to contract. Indeed, the end of the Eocene seems to signal an end of the prosimian radiation except for small isolated areas, where some still survive. Some prosimian forms (adapids) did manage to survive for several million years in southern Asia—where perhaps they remained isolated from the "center-stage" of primate evolution (Gingerich and Sahni, 1979). What exactly brought on this evolutionary turn of events is still not completely clear. Certainly the change in climate played a part, but competition was also coming from new fronts. The remarkably diverse and successful radiation of rodents was just beginning to accelerate rapidly during this time, no doubt

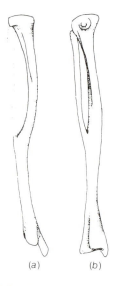

Figure 9-4 Tibio-fibula. (*a*) *Necrolemur;* (*b*) modern tarsier. Note the two fused lower leg bones—a characteristic feature of tarsiers. (© 1959 by W. E. Le Gros Clark.)

bringing some of them into direct competition with prosimians. With their highly specialized teeth, large litters, short generation spans, and flexible adaptive potential, the rodents were more than a match for the prosimians.

Competition may have come from still another quarter, for some prosimians (omomyids) probably had already evolved into early monkeys by late Eocene times. Monkeys (with their larger brains, more flexible social behavior, and more varied exploitation of arboreal niches) probably also were more than a match for their prosimian cousins.

◇ New World Monkeys

The center of action for primate evolution after the close of the Eocene is confined largely to the Old World, for only on the continents of Africa and Eurasia can we trace the evolutionary development of apes and hominids.

However, the New World, while geographically separated from the Old World, was not completely devoid of anthropoid stock, for here the ceboids evolved in their own right.

Any discussion of ceboid evolution and its relation to Old World anthropoid developments must consider crucial geological events, particularly continental drift (see pp. 236–238). By late Eocene times, Europe and North America had separated, and South America and Africa, though closer together than at present, were also drifting apart.

In such a geological context, the introduction of monkeys into South America poses a certain problem. Some authorities have postulated that, because the distance between South America and Africa was still not very great, monkeys, originating in Africa, could then have rafted to the New World (Gavan, 1977; Ciochon and Chiarelli, 1980). This point, however, is disputed. Others suggest a separate origin followed by parallel evolution of monkeys in the two hemispheres (Simons, 1969).

In any case, that Old and New World primates shared any evolutionary history since at least the late Eocene (some 40 m.y.a) is unlikely. There is no trace of any ancestor of our lineage anywhere in the New World following this time until fully modern *Homo sapiens* walked in during the late Pleistocene.

While primate fossils abound in the Western Hemisphere (particularly North America) during the early Cenozoic, the record is extremely sparse later on. For the entire span of Oligocene to late Pleistocene, we have only a few bits and pieces, a jaw fragment from Bolivia, a nearly complete skull from Texas, another quite complete cranium from Argentina, and a few other small fragments from Colombia and Jamaica. Together, all the evidence comprises less than a dozen individuals. Thus, tracing the evolutionary heritage of New World monkeys with any degree of certainty is a difficult task.

◇ Old World Anthropoids

The focus of our attention will henceforth exclusively be the Old World (Europe, Asia, Africa), for this area is where our ancestors have lived for the past 40 million years. This evolutionary and geographic fact is reflected in the

Figure 9-5 Location of the Fayum, an Oligocene primate site in Egypt.

grouping of Old World anthropoids (Old World monkeys, apes, and humans) into a common infraorder (Catarrhini) as opposed to the infraorder for New World monkeys (Platyrrhini).

◇ Oligocene (37 m.y.–25 m.y.)

It is apparent that during this epoch a great deal of evolutionary action was taking place; by the end of the Oligocene, Old World monkeys and hominoids were probably evolving along their separate evolutionary pathways. No doubt, diverse species of anthropoids were adapting to varied ecological niches in Africa and probably Asia and Europe as well. Unfortunately, the fossil record for the entire period is limited to only one locality in Egypt, sixty miles southwest of Cairo. This site, called the *Fayum*, is today an extremely arid region 100 miles inland, but, in Oligocene times, it was located close to the Mediterranean shore and was traversed by meandering streams crisscrossing through areas of tropical rain forest. The upper fossil beds have been dated by potassium/argon at approximately 25–27 m.y.a., and a series of lower beds were probably deposited 33–35 m.y.a.

Much of the Fayum fossil material is quite fragmentary. Consequently, evolutionary interpretations are not as unambiguous as we would like. Given the nature of the material, the classification of the fossils into recognized genera and species (always a difficult task; see p. 262) is somewhat disputed.

Apidium (Two Species)

A well-known 30-million-year-old fossil animal from the Fayum is **Apidium**, represented by about 80 jaws or partial dentitions and over 100 postcranial elements. This animal, about the size of a squirrel, had several anthropoid-like features, but also shows quite unusual aspects in its teeth. *Apidium*'s dental formula (see p. 165) is 2-1-3-3 which, as you can easily see, reveals an extra premolar not found in any contemporary Old World anthropoid. For that matter, extremely few fossil anthropoids in the Old World have this extra premolar. Another unusual Old World anthropoid form, which has been suggested as possibly related to *Apidium*, is called *Oreopithecus* from the late Miocene (10–12 m.y.a.) of Italy. Since they are separated by some 18 million years, the *Apidium–Oreopithecus* phylogenetic relationship is a most tenuous one. The similarities between the two forms may be explained by convergence, which would account for the presence of apparently independently *derived* characteristics in both (Szalay and Delson, 1979).

Propliopithecus (Two Species)*

Among the first fossils found at the Fayum, an incomplete *Propliopithecus* mandible was recovered in 1907. Unfortunately, since detailed geological and

*Some primatologists have suggested a third species of *Propliopithecus (P. markrafi)* at the Fayum (Fleagle and Kay, 1983). This species, however, is also known from only a single specimen.

paleontological methods were not yet developed, the stratigraphic position of this form is not known.

Morphologically, this fossil is a quite generalized Old World anthropoid, displaying a 2-1-2-3 dental formula. In most every relevant respect, this early (?) *Propliopithecus* form is quite primitive, not showing particular derived tendencies in any direction. To date, only this one specimen represents this *Propliopithecus (haeckeli)* species.

The second *Propliopithecus* species is considerably better known, with several new specimens discovered at the Fayum between 1977 and 1979. Stratigraphically, this species (*P. chirobates*) comes from the upper beds (*circa* 27–28 m.y.a.) and is, therefore, probably later in time than the isolated *haeckeli* specimen. Consequently, it is not surprising that *chirobates* is more derived in several anatomical features. Still, this form is a remarkably primitive Old World anthropoid. Considerably more evolutionary change would be required to transform this animal into anything distinctively recognizable as either an ape or a monkey.

Earlier interpretations of fragmentary remains of this fossil suggested affinities with gibbons (Simons initially proposed a separate genus rank, "Aeolopithecus"). However, more complete recent discoveries have shown that such an evolutionary relationship is not likely (Kay et al., 1981).

Aegyptopithecus

The most complete and probably evolutionarily most significant fossil from the Fayum is **Aegyptopithecus** (*circa* 28 m.y.a.), which is known from a nearly complete skull found in 1966, as well as numerous jaw fragments and several limb bones (most of which have been found quite recently). The largest of the Fayum anthropoids, *Aegyptopithecus* is roughly the size of a modern howler monkey, 13 to 18 pounds (Fleagle, 1983). *Aegyptopithecus* is important because, better than any other fossil, it bridges the gap between the Eocene prosimians on the one hand and the Miocene hominoids on the other.

With a dental formula of 2-1-2-3, *Aegyptopithecus* shows the familiar Old World anthropoid pattern. More detailed aspects of the dentition possibly align this Oligocene form with the Miocene hominoids (which we shall discuss shortly), but the evolutionary affinities are not presently well established. In most respects, the dentition is primitive for an Old World anthropoid without specifically derived features in either the hominoid or Old World monkey direction. Recently, there has been a change in interpreting Old World monkey dental evolution. It was previously believed that the dental patterns (particularly, the molar cusp pattern) seen in Old World monkeys were the more primitive and, conversely, those seen in hominoids were more derived from the ancestral **catarrhine** condition. Reevaluation of the fossil materials now suggests that, if anything, the Old World monkey pattern is more derived, and the hominoid cusp arrangement is the more primitive.

The establishment of the "polarities" of primitive/derived characteristics is crucial to making sound evolutionary interpretations. However, the trajectories of evolutionary change are not always easy to ascertain. The determination of the ancestral catarrhine molar cusp pattern is only one example. In the subsequent section on Miocene hominoids, we will encounter several further dilemmas in sorting out such issues.

Apidium
(A-pid'-ee-um)

Catarrhine
The group (infraorder) comprising all Old World anthropoids, living and extinct.

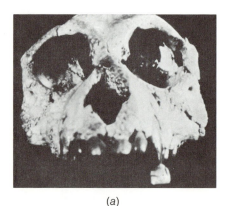

(a)

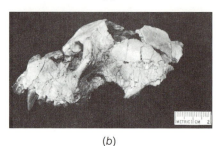

(b)

Figure 9-6 *Aegyptopithecus* skull from the Fayum, Egypt. Oligocene, *circa* 28 m.y.a., discovered in 1966. (*a*) Front view; (*b*) side view.

Even more primitive than the teeth of *Aegyptopithecus* is the skull, which is small and resembles the skull of a monkey in some details. Brain size and relative proportions can be reconstructed from internal casts of the one well-preserved cranium thus far discovered (see Fig. 9-6). It appears that the brain was somewhat intermediate between that of prosimians and anthropoids. The visual cortex was large compared to prosimians, with concomitant reduction of the olfactory lobes, but the frontal lobes were not especially expanded. Even considering the relative small size of this animal, the brain—estimated at only 30 to 40 cm³ (Radinsky, 1973)—was by no means large.

Evidence from the limb skeleton also revealed nothing particularly distinctive. From analysis of limb proportions and muscle insertions, primatologist John Fleagle (1983) has concluded that *Aegyptopithecus* was a short-limbed, heavily muscled, slowly moving, arboreal quadruped.

Further detailed study of *Aegyptopithecus'* anatomy has even allowed primatologists to speculate about the social behavior of this ancient primate. For instance, dental remains from different individuals vary greatly in canine size. This fact implies male/female differences (sexual dimorphism), which apparently were quite marked. Comparisons with living primates further suggest that males may have been competing for females and that the mating pattern was probably polygynous.

All in all, *Aegyptopithecus* presents somewhat of a paleontological enigma. In most respects, it is primitive for an Old World anthropoid, and could thus be potentially an ancestor for *both* Old World monkeys and hominoids. There are some slight yet suggestive clues in the teeth that have led some researchers (most notably, E. L. Simons of Duke University) to already place *Aegyptopithecus* on the hominoid line. Primarily because of the primitive aspects of this creature, other researchers (e.g., Fleagle and Kay, 1983) are not as convinced.

There remains, then, the problem of how to classify *Aegyptopithecus*. Even though they recognize that this fossil may well have lived before the major evolutionary split between Old World monkeys and hominoids (see Fig. 9-3), John Fleagle and Richard Kay still opt to call *Aegyptopithecus* a hominoid. Accordingly, they recognize that the superfamily Hominoidea then becomes what they term a "wastebasket" category (i.e., it is used for convenience, but does not reflect phylogenetic reality). This is one solution, although it will not satisfy all researchers. Perhaps, for the moment, it would be best to regard *Aegyptopithecus* (as well as the other Fayum anthropoids) as "primitive catarrhines," without referring them to particular superfamilies.

OLIGOCENE FOSSIL ANTHROPOIDS: SUMMARY

The spectacular array of fossils from the Fayum in the period between 32 m.y. and 28 m.y. demonstrates that anthropoids were radiating along several evolutionary lines. As with the earlier primate fossil material from the Paleocene and Eocene, the fragmentary nature of the Oligocene fossil assemblage makes precise reconstruction of these evolutionary lines risky.

Given the primitive nature of these fossil forms, it is wise, for the present, not to conclude specifically how these animals relate to later primates. In earlier primatological studies (as well as earlier editions of this book), such conclusions were indeed made, but reanalysis of the fossil material from the perspective of primitive/derived evolutionary modifications has cast serious doubt on many of these interpretations. The new interpretations, however, are still far from certain. As we have mentioned, untangling the polarity of primitive versus derived evolutionary states is a most difficult task. What many paleontologists would dearly like to establish is a clear link between these Oligocene fossils (particularly *Propliopithecus* and *Aegyptopithecus*) and the unambiguously hominoid forms of the Miocene. Unfortunately, as the following quote argues, this is not yet possible:

> In light of current knowledge about the very primitive dental, cranial, and skeletal morphology of the *Oligocene* hominoids, *Propliopithecus* and *Aegyptopithecus*, there is no reason to believe that any single group of extant hominoids (either hylobatids, hominids, or pongids) can be traced back to an Oligocene divergence (Fleagle and Kay, 1983, p. 190).

◇ Miocene (25 m.y.–5 m.y.)—Hominoids Aplenty

If the Eocene was the age of prosimians and the Oligocene the time of great diversity for early anthropoids, the Miocene was certainly the epoch of hominoids.

A great abundance of hominoid fossil material has been found in the Old World from the time period 23 m.y.—7 m.y. The remarkable evolutionary success represented by this adaptive radiation is shown in the geographic range already established for hominoids during this period. Miocene hominoid fossils have been discovered in France, Germany, Spain, Czechoslovakia, Greece, Hungary, China, India, Pakistan, Turkey, Egypt, Uganda, and Kenya.

Interpretations of this vast array of fossil material (now including more than 500 individuals, and perhaps as many as 1,000) were greatly complicated

Figure 9-7 Miocene hominoid distribution—fossils thus far discovered.

for several decades due to inadequate appreciation of the range of biological variation that a single genus or species could represent. As a result, the taxonomic naming of the various fossil finds became a terrible muddle, with more than 20 genera and over 100 species proposed. The biological implications of such taxonomic enthusiasm were unfortunately not seriously considered. In such an atmosphere, it was possible for two genera to be named—one with only upper jaws represented, the other with only lower jaws, each matching the other!

It is not difficult to understand why such confusion arose if we consider that discoveries of these fossils spanned more than 100 years (the earliest find came from France in 1856) and took place on three continents. Not until the early 1960s did scientists systematically study *all* the material, the result being a considerable simplification of the earlier confusion. As a result of this research, E. L. Simons and David Pilbeam "lumped" the vast majority of Miocene forms into only two genera: one presumably quite "pongidlike" and the other "hominidlike." In just the last few years, however, a tremendous amount of new data has come to light from both new field discoveries and finds in museum collections of previously unrecognized material. Consequently, it is now apparent that the Simons-Pilbeam simplification went too far. Hominoid evolutionary radiation during the Miocene produced a whole array of diverse organisms, many of which have no living descendants (and thus no clear analog among living higher primates).

As these new discoveries are analyzed, many of the perplexing problems concerning Miocene hominoids should be solved. For the moment, it is possible to make only general interpretive statements regarding Miocene hominoid adaptive patterns.

PALEOGEOGRAPHY AND MIOCENE HOMINOID EVOLUTION

As they were to early primate evolution (see p. 236), the factors of changing geography and climates (at work as well in the Miocene) are also crucial to interpretations of the later stages of primate evolution. The Oligocene revealed a proliferation of early Old World anthropoid forms from one area in North Africa. In the Early Miocene, the evidence is also restricted to Africa, with fossils coming from rich sites in the eastern part of the continent (Kenya and Uganda). It would thus appear, on the basis of current evidence, that hominoids originated in Africa and experienced a successful adaptive radiation there before dispersing to other parts of the Old World.

The hominoids would maintain this exclusive African foothold for some time. The earliest of these East African hominoid fossils is slightly more than 20 m.y. old, and later fossil finds extend the time range up to about 14 m.y.a. For most of this period, East Africa is thought to have been more heavily forested, with much less woodlands and grasslands (savannas) than exist today (Pickford, 1983).

As in the earlier Cenozoic, the shifting of the earth's plates during the Miocene played a vital role in primate evolution. Before about 16 m.y.a., Africa was cut off from Eurasia; consequently, once hominoids had originated there in the Early Miocene, they were isolated. However, around 16 m.y.a. the African plate "docked" with Eurasia (Bernor, 1983) through the Arabian Peninsula, a contact that was to revolutionize mammalian faunas of the later Miocene. Many forms, such as proboscideans, giraffoids, and pigs, that had originated in Africa now migrated into Eurasia (van Couvering and van Couvering, 1976). Apparently, included among these mid-Miocene intercontinental pioneers were some hominoids. Since they had evolved in the mainly tropical setting of equatorial Africa, most of the earlier hominoids probably remained primarily arboreal. Accordingly, it has been suggested that a relatively continuous forest would have been necessary across the Afro-Arabian-Eurasian land bridge.

Ecological changes were, however, already afoot in Africa. By 16 m.y.a., the environment was getting drier, with less tropical rainforest and, conversely, more open woodland/bushland and savanna areas emerging (Bernor, 1983; Pickford, 1983). In other words, the environments in East Africa were being transformed more into their contemporary form. With the opportunities thus presented, some African hominoids were almost certainly radiating into these more open niches about 16 to 17 m.y.a. Part of this adaptation probably involved exploitation of different foods and more ground-living than practiced by the arboreal ancestors of these hominoids. Some partly terrestrial, more open-country adapted hominoids were probably thus on the scene and fully capable of migrating into Eurasia, even through areas that were not continuously forested.

The environments throughout the Old World were, of course, to alter even more. Later in the Miocene, some of these environmental shifts would further influence hominoid evolution and may have played a part in the origin of our particular evolutionary lineage, the hominids. More on this later.

MIOCENE HOMINOIDS—CHANGING VIEWS AND TERMINOLOGY

So, throughout the Miocene, environmental and geographic factors imposed constraints on hominoids as well as opened new opportunities to them. Over a time span of close to 15 m.y., hominoids in the middle two-thirds of the Miocene were successful indeed. Once they migrated into Eurasia, they dispersed rapidly and diversified into a variety of species. After 14 m.y.a., we have evidence of widely distributed hominoids from Pakistan, India, Turkey, Greece, Hungary, China, and Western Europe. Much of this material has only recently been uncovered and is incredibly abundant. For example, from Lufeng in southern China alone, 5 partial skulls and more than 1,000 teeth have been found in the past decade (Wu and Oxnard, 1983). The other areas have also yielded many paleontological treasures in the last ten years. Moreover, recent searches of museum collections in East Africa, as well as resurveys of fossil sites, have uncovered yet more fossils.

Given this quantity of new information, it is not surprising that heretofore existing theories of early hominoid evolution have been reevaluated. In fact, it would not be unfair to describe the last five years as a "revolution" in paleontological views of Miocene hominoid evolution. With a great deal of this recent fossil material still unanalyzed, all the answers are not presently at hand. In fact, the more fossils found, the more complicated the situation seems to become. However, two major subgroups of Miocene hominoids have been described. These correlate nicely with the relevant ecology and geology:

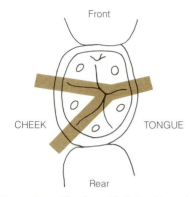

Figure 9-8 The dryopith Y-5 pattern. A characteristic feature of hominoid molars.

1. A forest living, primarily arboreal set of species, which early on are limited to Africa but later are found in Europe. This group we will call "dryopiths," a simple descriptive term and nontaxonomic (so as to avoid the pitfalls of making hasty evolutionary judgments).*
2. A more open-country (woodland or woodland/bushland/savanna mosaic) and probably more ground-living set of species. This group, mostly Eurasian in distribution, we will call "ramapiths."

DRYOPITHS

These fossil forms are best known during the earlier Miocene from East Africa, where a diverse array of species has been recognized. Some researchers also believe some dryopiths may have lived in southern Asia during the Middle-Late Miocene, but this has not been conclusively demonstrated. Certainly, in the later Miocene, there are some fragmentary dryopithlike hominoids in Western Europe, but their relationship to the earlier forms in Africa is, presently, still unclear. Our discussion will thus emphasize the more complete and better-known East African varieties.

In East Africa, the first dryopiths are the earliest hominoids we have evidence of during the Miocene. Indeed, except by broadly expanding the definition of the hominoids (see p. 244), these are the first *definite* hominoids we have from anywhere.

No doubt, these forms occupied a wide range of niches. It is therefore not surprising that they also exhibit a great deal of morphological variation, with overall sizes ranging from that of a medium-sized monkey to that of a good-sized chimp. Accurate reconstructions of overall body size are, however, quite difficult, since most of the fossil material consists only of jaws and teeth. Interpretations of this important series of fossil animals must therefore be based almost exclusively on dental criteria.

When we look at the teeth of the dryopiths, we see in all of them a definite hominoid pattern, but with a great deal of variation in specific traits. Dryopith teeth are characterized first of all by the Y-5 pattern, an arrangement of cusps in the lower molars also seen in modern hominoids (see Fig. 9-8). Most of the Miocene forms also have fairly large canines that overlap, the upper one occluding with a sectorial (cutting) first lower premolar. However, we must keep in mind that, while the features of canine size and shape of the first lower premolar are diagnostic in separating later hominids from pongids, they do not apply consistently in the Miocene; the fossil sample is too variable for the uniform application of such simplistic criteria. We also must remember that it is crucial to distinguish those characteristics that are found in a

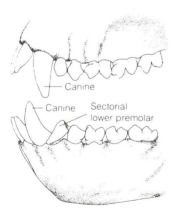

Figure 9-9 Overlapping canines and sectorial lower first premolar. (Shown here in a macaque.)

*What to call the Miocene hominoids? A proliferation of names has been suggested for group 1: Dryopithecidae, Dryopithecinae, Dryopithecini, dryopithecines, dryomorphs, and dryopiths; and, for group 2: Sivapithecinae, Sivapithecini, sivapithecines, Ramapithecidae, Ramapithecinae, Ramapithecini, ramapithecines, ramamorphs, and ramapiths. In two earlier editions of this book, in fact, we have used two different sets of terms. Not everyone at this point is going to be completely satisfied with any of these terms. Here we follow the suggestion of Russell Ciochon (1983) and use "dryopith" and "ramapith" as descriptive, short, and taxonomically unloaded referents.

primitive state in an evolutionary lineage (and, therefore, potentially representative of common ancestral stock of forms that diverge later) from *derived* characteristics found only in particular offshoots (and, therefore, representative of forms that have already diverged).

Many of the presumed distinguishing features argued as evidence of "pongid" or "hominid" affinities for Miocene fossils are, in fact, primitive characteristics of hominoids in general. Whereas dryopith cranial remains are known from only a few discoveries, there is fortunately one splendidly preserved skull found in 1948 by Mary Leakey on an island in Lake Victoria, Kenya. Quite generalized in structure, it is monkeylike in many ways. In any case, this skull does not exhibit any of the structural specializations (such as large jaws, face, and muscle attachment areas) found in modern pongids.

A few pieces of dryopith limb skeleton have also been found, including several parts of the postcranial skeleton of an individual found in Kenya (Walker and Pickford, 1983). Including most of the limb bones, several cranial and jaw fragments, and a few vertebrae and ribs, these remains from Rusinga Island are the most complete of any Miocene hominoid individual (and among the most complete for the entire primate fossil record until fairly recent times). From that well-preserved skeleton, it is possible to accurately estimate the body size of the animal, which turns out to be about that of a male colobus monkey (i.e., around 24 pounds). Detailed analysis of the forelimb and preliminary study of other skeletal parts suggest this was a fairly generalized quadruped. Earlier interpretations have indicated that this dryopith was a brachiator, potential knuckle-walker, a ceboidlike quadruped, or a cercopithecoidlike quadruped (Greenfield, 1980). The most reasonable inference is that this small hominoid was probably an arboreal quadruped (Morbeck, 1975) with some suspensory abilities (Fleagle, 1983).

Such attempts to reconstruct the feeding or locomotory behavior of fossil animals like the dryopiths are made through comparisons with modern primates and their observed structural/functional relationships (see p. 166). However, we must be extremely cautious in applying such models too grossly to fossil animals, for they may not closely resemble the behavior of *any* contemporary primate. In our attempts to reconstruct the behavior of earlier primates, therefore, we must be careful not to obscure the uniqueness of the very animals we seek to understand.

A lack of appreciation of the structural (and presumably ecological) uniqueness found in many fossil primates has characterized recent interpretations of Miocene hominoids. It was once thought that dryopiths were clearly pongid and therefore in a direct evolutionary line leading to modern great apes and separate from that leading to hominids. While dryopiths resemble pongids in a few dentral traits, they are all in all a quite varied lot, in most characteristics unlike *any* living hominoid (hominid or pongid). We should remember that using modern hominoids as models for those in the Miocene does not really provide a broad basis for comparison—only three genera of great apes (with perhaps only four species) and only one genus and one species of hominid now exist. It might well be that none of these provide a valid model for the behavior of the whole array of ecologically diverse hominoids of the Miocene. To look at these fossil animals and expect to assign them into neat categories, such as hominid and pongid, is much too simplistic. Our fossil

(a)

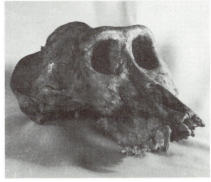

(b)

Figure 9-10 (a) *Proconsul africanus* skull. Discovered by Mary Leakey in 1948. (From early Miocene deposits on Rusinga Island, Kenya.) (b) A modern gorilla skull. By way of contrast, note the more projecting face, larger teeth, and more robust muscle attachments in the modern pongid.

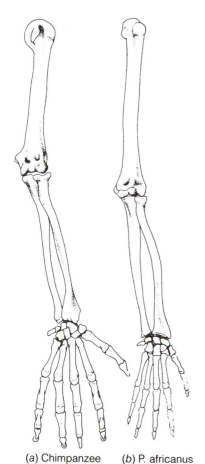

(a) Chimpanzee   (b) P. africanus

Figure 9-11 Reconstructed upper limb of
P. africanus compared to modern chimpanzee. (a) Chimpanzee; (b) *P. africanus.*
(© 1959 by W. E. Le Gros Clark).

sample almost certainly includes members of several evolving **lineages**; some
of these are probably closely related to ancestors of living primates, but most
of them are probably on extinct sidebranches of hominoid evolution. The
complexity of the evolutionary process demands that we not think in overly
simple terms, and we should thus conceive of our evolutionary history as an
intricate "bush" instead of a simple "ladder" (Gould, 1976b).

Only in terms of this more complex framework can we understand the
Miocene dryopiths. For example, anthropologists once postulated that dryopiths were pongids on the basis of shape of their dental arcade. Unlike
hominids, and resembling modern great apes, they presumably possess *parallel* tooth rows, and, in fact, some dryopiths do seem to have such a dental
arcade. But most of them have tooth rows that diverge in back, unlike the
parallel rows of modern great apes or the parabolic row of modern humans.
The shape of the dental arcade in modern chimps and gorillas is an obvious
derived characteristic seen primarily in relatively recent pongids. The same
can be said of the *parabolic* row for hominids. Therefore, neither kind of tooth
row tells us much about dryopith relationships.

Much of the variation seen in dryopiths can be accounted for by time (15
million years of evolution) as well as geography. The earliest and most generalized dryopiths are found in East Africa. Many primatologists, recognizing
that these East African forms lack many of the derived characteristics seen
in later dryopiths, have referred them to a separate genus (*Proconsul* for the
early East African forms, contrasted to *Dryopithecus* for the later, more derived
ones from Europe).

One general set of ecological adaptations does appear, however, to tie the
dryopiths together: all are forest-adapted, primarily arboreal, and probably
mostly fruit-eating (frugivorous) (Pilbeam, 1979). Given this type of adaptation,
migration from area to area would require a relatively continuous forest.
Ecological reconstructions of the Miocene world prior to 17 m.y.a. suggest
that forests were quite widespread, thus providing the opporunity for migration within East Africa. How dryopiths were able to cross the Afro-Eurasian
land bridge once climatic cooling began is still a mystery.

During the Middle Miocene, with this climatic cooling, considerable shrinkage of forested areas occurred. Consequently, further isolation of regional
dryopith populations would have been promoted. The next time we pick up

Figure 9-12 Dental rows: Ape parallel arcade compared to human parabolic pattern. (a) Gorilla; (b) human.

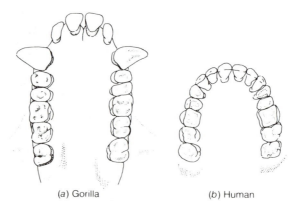

(a) Gorilla   (b) Human

the threads of dryopith evolution is in Western Europe (Germany, Austria, France, Spain) several million years later (after 15 m.y.a.). We still do not know how these later, as-yet-fragmentary fossils are linked to the earlier, primitive dryopiths from East Africa.

On the other hand, as we have pointed out, with the shrinkage of forests, more open kinds of environments expanded, particularly woodland/forest fringe niches. Those hominoids already preadapted for exploitation of these environments would then have had considerably more evolutionary opportunities than was true previously.

Interestingly, it is at about this time (14–10 m.y.a.) that varieties of more ground-living hominoids began to diversify in several parts of the Old World. It is to this group, the ramapiths, that we now turn.

RAMAPITHS

The other major subgrouping of Miocene hominoids is the ramapiths, a highly successful and widely distributed group of species. In fact, except for later species of the genus *Homo* (in the last million years only), ramapiths were the most widely distributed hominoids that ever existed. The time range for these forms goes back at least 14 m.y. in East Africa, and they probably are also that old in Pakistan and Turkey.

The evidence for the earliest ramapith may go even further back. A newly discovered 16–18 m.y. old fossil, including pieces of the jaws and face, was uncovered in 1983 at Buluk in northern Kenya by Richard Leakey and Alan Walker (Lewin, 1983). The animal, apparently the size of a male chimp, is thought by Walker to be closely aligned with the Asian varieties of ramapiths we are about to discuss. If so, this would be the earliest representative of this group. Somewhat later (around 14 m.y.a.), again from Kenya, is another site (possibly there is a third as well) that also has some fragmentary pieces similar to ramapiths. In any case, these do not conform to the dryopith pattern we have described.

The prime evidence for the ramapith group, however, comes from Eurasia. Geographically, then, we have an interesting dichotomy: While dryopiths are mostly known from Africa, ramapiths are better known from Eurasia.

In recent years, these Eurasian ramapiths have been uncovered in several areas in remarkable abundance. As we noted on p. 247, Lufeng in southern China (*circa* 8 m.y.a.) has yielded over 1,000 teeth as well as 5 partial crania. In addition, upwards of 50 individuals have been recovered from the Potwar Plateau (7–13.5 m.y.a.) in the Siwalik Hills of Pakistan (plus several more individuals recovered over several years from the Indian side of the Siwaliks). Included in the superb Pakistani collection is a multitude of mandibles (15 in all, some of which are nearly intact) many postcranial remains, and a recently discovered partial cranium, including most of the face (Pilbeam et al., 1977; Pilbeam, 1982). While not as productive as those in China and Pakistan, other sites in Western Asia and Europe have also recently added to the harvest. More than 20 individuals have been recovered from 3 sites in Turkey (12–13 + ? m.y.a.), and a similar yield has been excavated from the **Rudabánya Mountains of Hungary** (less than 11 m.y.a.?) (Morbeck, 1983). Finally, at least 12 or possibly 13 individuals have been found in northern Greece near Salonika (10–12 m.y.a.).

Lineage
An evolutionary line of phylogenetically related forms.

Dental arcade
The shape of the tooth row.

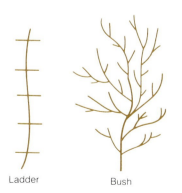

Ladder   Bush

Figure 9-13 Two phylogenetic models: A simple ladder versus a complex bush.

The earliest firmly dated ramapiths in Eurasia are from the lower beds at the Potwar Plateau, estimated minimumly at 13 m.y.a. (Raza, et al., 1983). The earliest sites in Turkey *may* also be this old, or even older (Kay and Simons, 1983). In any case, it is quite clear that no ramapiths (or any hominoid) are found anywhere in Eurasia until after the docking of the African plate with the Eurasian land mass around 16 m.y.a. (see p. 246). Once established, the ramapiths apparently lasted quite a long time, surviving in Pakistan up until about 7 m.y.a.

Dispersed over thousands of miles and over at least 7 million years of time, it is no wonder that ramapiths are quite variable. Indeed, several different species have been suggested, some in just the last few years. As we'll see later in this chapter, such interpretations can be a biological minefield. Here, then, we will primarily concentrate on the more general morphological and ecological characteristics and limit our taxonomic conclusions to some genus-level considerations.

The ramapiths differ morphologically from the dryopiths in their dentition and facial anatomy. The front teeth, especially the central incisors, are often quite large, while the canine is fairly good-sized (low-crowned and robust) (Andrews, 1983). In general, the canines are large compared to what we see in humans (and earlier hominids) but are not as big as they are in the large (male) extant apes (Kay and Simons, 1983). There are, however, large discrepancies in canine size among different ramapith individuals, partly because some species were bigger overall, but also because there was apparently considerable variation (sexual dimorphism) within the same species. In fact, in body size, some ramapiths were apparently as dimorphic as modern gorillas and orangs (Andrews, 1983).

The first lower premolar is also quite variable in shape. Usually, it is fairly sectorial; that is, it shows the shearing surface typical in most catarrhines (consequently, this is most likely to be the primitive condition). In some cases, however, an accessory cusp displays enlargement, perhaps either as a precursor to the derived condition seen in hominids (Kay and Simons, 1983) or as a separate evolutionary parallelism between these ramapiths and our line (Ciochon, 1983).

The most distinctive part of the dentition of ramapiths may be seen in the back tooth row, where the molars are large, flat-wearing, and thick-enameled (in some species, the enamel is heavily wrinkled as well). The thickness of the enamel cap has played a most significant role in recent interpretations of Miocene hominoid evolution. Among living hominoids, relative to body size, humans have by far the thickest molar caps. Gorillas and chimps have thin enamel, *but* orang molars could be described as moderately thick (Ward and Pilbeam, 1983). Thick (in fact, very thick) enamel is also seen in early hominids (in the period 1–4 m.y.a.).

As a characteristic, thick enamel in the ramapiths could then be seen as a derived feature linking them specifically with either orangs or hominids. A third possibility is that thick enamel is the *primitive* condition in large-bodied hominoids, with orangs and humans maintaining a more primitive expression, while chimps and gorillas are more derived.

Again, we have a thorny problem in attempting to establish the direction (polarity) of primitive-derived character transformation. Since our evolutionary reconstructions are ultimately based on such interpretations, the conclusions are less than clearcut. More on this presently.

Probably, the most characteristic anatomical aspects of the ramapiths are seen in the face, especially the area immediately below the nose (Ward and Kimbel, 1983). Facial remains from Pakistan, Greece, and Hungary have concave profiles and projecting incisors (and, overall, remarkably resemble the modern orang). In particular, the partial cranium discovered in 1980 at the Potwar Plateau (Pakistan, *circa* 8 m.y.a.) and published two years later (Pilbeam, 1982) bears striking similarities to the orangutan (see Fig. 9-14). The published description of this specimen, with illustrations similar to those shown here, had a tremendous impact on paleoanthropology. As we have seen (p. 173), biochemical evidence demonstrates the distinctiveness of the orang from the African apes and humans; here, then, was fossil evidence suggesting some ancient Asian traces of the orang lineage. As a result, the views of biochemists and paleoanthropologists agree more closely (pp. 259–260).

Many earlier fossil-based interpretations of ramapith evolutionary affinities had, of course, to be reevaluated. As we hinted at the beginning of our discussion of Miocene hominoids (p. 246), in the 1960s E. L. Simons and David Pilbeam suggested a Middle Miocene ramapith hominoid as the first hominid (i.e., clearly diverged on our particular line and separate from that leading to

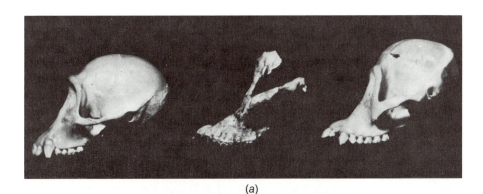

(a)

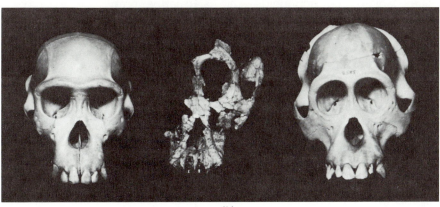

(b)

Figure 9-14 Comparison of *Sivapithecus* cranium (center) with modern chimpanzee (left) and orangutan (right). The *Sivapithecus* fossil is specimen, GSP 15000 from the Potwar Plateau, Pakistan, *c.* 8 m.y.a. (*a*) lateral view; (*b*) frontal view.

Sivapithecus
(Shiv'-ah-pith-eh-kus)

any extant ape). According to this view, this early hominid was *Ramapithecus*—known at that time mostly from India, with some bits from East Africa.

We have already illustrated some of the dramatic new discoveries of the 1970s and early 1980s. As a consequence of these new discussions, the earlier suggestion that *Ramapithecus* was a definite hominid was seriously questioned, if not rejected altogether. One primary advocate of this revised view is David Pilbeam (1977; 1982), an initial architect of the earlier widely accepted theory. Pilbeam, who has led the highly successful paleoanthropological project at the Potwar Plateau, has been swayed by the new fossils recovered there and elsewhere. These more complete specimens (like that shown in Fig. 9-14) have been placed in the genus Sivapithecus.

A variety of other generic terms have also been put forward for other ramapiths (see Table 9-1) but, except for *Gigantopithecus* (discussed shortly), most of these can easily be accommodated within *Sivapithecus*. What about *Ramapithecus*? The strong consensus among primatologists is that this genus is also really part of *Sivapithecus*, although most probably a separate species (Greenfield, 1979; Ward and Pilbeam, 1983; Kay and Simons, 1983; Corruccini and Ciochon, 1983).

If *Sivapithecus* can be placed in—or at least close to—the lineage of modern orangs, what becomes of the assertion that "Ramapithecus" (now part of the same evolutionary group, or "clade") is an early hominid? Many researchers, seeing distinctive oranglike derived features in these Miocene fossils, would now reject this claim (Ward and Pilbeam, 1983; Cronin, 1983; Andrews, 1983).

Paleontologists are far from unanimous in this determination. The other primary exponent of the "Ramapithecus as hominid" hypothesis, E. L. Simons (with his colleague Richard Kay), believes that *Sivapithecus*—into which they have "sunk" *Ramapithecus*—shows many derived hominid features. They point particularly to aspects of the dentition they consider hominidlike and argue that other dental/facial similarities with orangs resulted from evolutionary parallelisms. They conclude that *Sivapithecus* is already a hominid (basically, this is the same theory proposed much earlier; however, where before we had *Ramapithecus*, we now read *Sivapithecus*).

A third alternative also exists: *Sivapithecus* may not already have diverged in the orang *or* the hominid direction. Perhaps it was a common ancestor for all later large-bodied hominoids—the Asian forms (orang) and the African ones (gorilla, chimp, and human). This view would then emphasize that

Table 9-1 Some Suggested Names for Miocene Ramapith Forms

Name	Locality
Ramapithecus	India/Pakistan
Sivapithecus	India/Pakistan
Kenyapithecus (usually sunk into *Ramapithecus*)	Kenya
Bodvapithecus	Hungary
Rudapithecus	Hungary
Ouranopithecus	Greece
Gigantopithecus	India/Pakistan (Pleistocene species from China)

many features of ramapith (and probably also orang) morphology, such as enamel thickness, lower face morphology, etc., are simply primitive expressions of the ancestral hominoid condition. The African hominoids would then be seen as the more derived forms (Wolpoff, 1983; Greenfield, 1983).

We have, then, three possible alternatives for interpreting the evolutionary relationships of most of the Miocene ramapiths (i.e., *Sivapithecus*):

1. *Sivapithecus* is already on the orang line, not specifically related to any of the other hominoids. This suggests that the Asian/African hominoid divergence occurred prior to 14 m.y.a. From this assertion, no direct claim is made on when hominids originated from African hominoid stock, but the implication is considerably after 14 m.y.a. (quite comfortably, after 10 m.y.a., in fact).
2. *Sivapithecus* is specifically on the hominid line. This suggests that orangs must have diverged considerably earlier than 15 m.y.a., while hominids and African apes (gorillas and chimps) must have been diverging at about that time (or a little earlier).
3. *Sivapithecus* is a possible common ancestor of all large-bodied hominoids—orangs, chimps, gorillas, and humans. The split leading to orangs is thus seen as occurring within the ramapith "complex," somewhere between 10–15 m.y.a. The hominid/African ape split, then, is later yet (5–6 m.y.a.?).

Among knowledgeable primate paleontologists familiar with the original fossil material, one can find support for each of these three interpretations. It is thus easy to say, "more fossil material is needed to decide." However, one can *always* say that. Thanks to the spectacular successes of the last decade, we now have a wealth of hominoid fossils, including hundreds of teeth, several partial crania, dozens of jaws, etc. More fossil evidence is not likely to add substantially to the picture already emerging. In fact, more concrete interpretations of the Miocene hominoids have not come solely from additional fossils; sophistication of analysis, especially the sorting out of primitive/derived character states, has also contributed. We still have a way to go, though, in order to establish precisely which are the primitive, and which the derived, characteristics of hominoids.

For now, the first alternative on our list seems to us to be the best-supported interpretation, with the third somewhat less likely. New fossil material (especially facial remains), along with biochemical findings, indicate the second alternative to be the least probable.

Paleoecology of Sivapithecus   Of course, what *everyone* would like to know about *Sivapithecus* is: To whom is it related? We have just taken our best shot at that difficult question. Another fascinating research effort involves reconstructing the way of life of this early hominoid and speculating upon factors that influenced its evolution.

For example, what were these ramapiths eating? By referring to certain structural/functional analogs seen in modern primates, investigators have postulated a diet that correlates with ramapith dental structure. This diet is thought to chiefly include tough hard morsels, such as seeds, which some believe were exploited primarily on the ground (Jolly, 1970).

Figure 9-15 Ramapith distribution during the Miocene, 14–7 m.y.a.—fossils thus far discovered.

A more comprehensive comparison of a wide variety of living primates, however, reveals ramapith dental parallels (especially larger, flat-wearing, more thickly enameled molars) among several arboreal species eating nuts, seeds, and hard fruits found in the trees (Kay, 1981). Thus, ramapith dental features quite possibly could have originated in an arboreal setting. Most researchers attempting to reconstruct the paleoecology of the ramapiths, however, assume that, eventually, ramapiths did take greater advantage of terrestrial environments than their dryopith cousins. Evidence from Eurasian sites (Potwar Plateau, Lufeng, Rudabánya) suggests that ramapiths lived in environments exhibiting greater seasonality than the tropics (where most dryopiths lived). Consequently, fruits would not have been available all year long, and ramapiths could not have been primarily frugivorous (i.e., fruit-eaters) (Andrews, 1983).

Moreover, within these environments, there was less continuous forest vegetation, with more woodland/bushland mosaic niches. These changes

Figure 9-16 Two ramapith mandibles from the Potwar Plateau, Pakistan. Discovered in 1976 and 1977. Approximate age, 9 m.y.

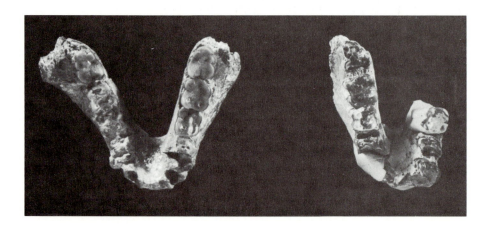

were further stimulated by a general cooling of the earth's climate, after about 16 m.y.a. (see p. 247). Such a niche, being ecologically poor, is no place to find a primate. It is hypothesized, therefore, that ramapiths may have been environmental "opportunists," analogous to bears and pigs, exploiting below-ground resources, such as roots and tubers.

Utilization of nonarboreal resources would, of course, require some ground-living. Ramapiths are generally larger-bodied than dryopiths, a fact which could argue for greater terrestriality. Of course, body size varied greatly (some individuals may have exceeded 150 pounds) largely as a result of marked sexual dimorphism (Andrews, 1983).

Some such environmental adaptation did, indeed, prove successful for the ramapiths—witness their longevity and geographic dispersal. If ramapiths were such successful opportunists, what spelled their doom? No single answer suffices. Perhaps heightened competition from the extremely successful Old World monkeys (some of these were also becoming partly terrestrial) played a part. Also, in the later Miocene, recall that the environment continued to change. Further cooling and drying probably isolated some groups and may often have critically reduced effective breeding population size (see p. 94). As a part of this ongoing dessication process, the Mediterranean and Black Seas dried up (very late Miocene—approximately 6.5 m.y.a.) and there was further cooling in adjacent seas. To the north, in Eurasia, the challenges must have been harsh. With the exception of pockets in the more tropical areas of southern Asia, no hominoids (except *Gigantopithecus*—see the following section) apparently survived here beyond the Miocene.

To the south, in Africa, things were to be different. The African apes and hominids had diverged (or were about to), and within the still-changing (and probably more seasonal) environments of Africa, our family—the hominids—originated. The story that followed comprises the remainder of this book.

Gigantopithecus   Evidence exists for another and very distinctive ramapith that can trace its origins back into the Miocene. This highly unusual primate, called *Gigantopithecus*, came to the attention of scientists in a most unusual way. For centuries, Chinese folk medicine has prescribed the use of ground "dragon bones" in the concoction of various potions. The source of many of these bones was fossil sites and, from there, these dragon bones often found their way into Chinese apothecaries (drugstores). It was in such an establishment that the first *Gigantopithecus* teeth were recognized in 1935 by Ralph van Koenigswald, a young German paleontologist on the lookout for important fossil remains.

Since the 1930s, more than 1,000 individual teeth have been collected (largely from apothecaries). Three lower jaws were archeologically excavated in China in the 1950s, and one was recovered in northern India in 1968. The Indian specimen is clearly the oldest of the lot, falling in the late Miocene (5 m.y.–9 m.y.), while the Chinese material belongs to the Middle Pleistocene (500,000 y.a.–1 m.y.a.).

Truly an animal to titillate the imagination, *Gigantopithecus* was apparently a huge hominoid. It was named for the enormous proportions of its teeth and jaws (all that is preserved of the animal), and estimates place its weight in excess of 600 pounds and its stature somewhere between 6 and 9

Figure 9-17   A Chinese apothecary, or drugstore.

Figure 9-18 *Gigantopithecus* III mandible (left) compared to modern gorilla. This *Gigantopithecus* mandible is by far the largest hominoid jaw ever discovered.

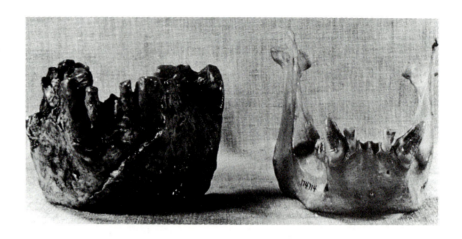

Allometric growth
The process of differential growth whereby some parts of the body grow proportionately more than others.

feet! (Simons and Ettel, 1970). Such estimates may, however, be somewhat exaggerated. Differential patterns of growth (called **allometric growth**) probably produced different body proportions in this extinct animal from those seen in living hominoids (Johnson, 1979). Some postcranial bones found in the Potwar Plateau (Miocene), which may belong to a *Gigantopithecus* form, support a smaller size estimate. From these data, it has been suggested that *Gigantopithecus* weighed about the same as a small female gorilla (equivalent to 150 pounds) (Pilbeam, 1979).

Numerous dental characteristics clearly establish *Gigantopithecus* as a ramapith hominoid, and some superficial features even appear hominidlike. However, these similarities are apparently functional analogies associated with heavy back tooth grinding and do not represent particularly close evolutionary relationships (that is, homologies). In fact, *Gigantopithecus* exhibits some rather unusual features, such as flat-worn canines, apparently heavily used as grinding teeth. Such a situation is unusual among primates (a similar pattern may also be present in *Sivapithecus*), and even the peglike incisors may have been used in mastication of heavy vegetation. Although some investigators have speculated that *Gigantopithecus* may be closely related to our particular evolutionary line (Weidenreich, 1946; Frayer, 1973; Gelvin, 1980), sophisticated statistical analysis has confirmed the unique status of this fossil form (Corruccini, 1975a).

Despite these findings, rather bizarre notions concerning this fossil still abound. Indeed, Soviet scientists have gone so far as to speculate the unsubstantiated "abominable snowman" as a descendant, and newspaper accounts tell of Soviet-led expeditions into the frozen heights of the Himalayas to find proof!

More conservative research has centered on reconstructions of what *Gigantopithecus* ecologically was "doing for a living." Apparently, its niche was a mixed one in China, probably consisting primarily of forest-type environments, while the earlier species lived in a more open environment in India (Simons and Ettel, 1970). Just what *Gigantopithecus* was chewing in its huge jaws is still a mystery, but apparently it consisted of enormous amounts of vegetable foods. There are many structural analogies between the teeth of

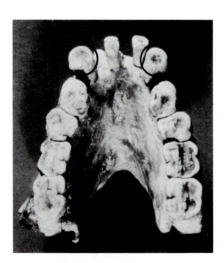

Figure 9-19 *Gigantopithecus* mandible, occlusal view. Note that the canines (circled) are worn flat.

◇ Box 9-1   Timing the Hominid-Pongid Split

One of the most fundamental of all questions in human evolution is: When did the hominid line originate? Or, to put it another way: When did we last share a common ancestry with our closest living relatives, the pongids?

Scientists have taken different perspectives in attempting to answer this question. The traditional approach of paleontology is still the most common. Recent years have produced considerably more paleontological sophistication through a vast new array of fossil material, more precise chronometric dating, and more rigorous interpretation of primitive-derived characteristics. Still, the fossil record remains incomplete, and significant gaps exist for some of the most crucial intervals. So the question still persists: How old is the hominid line?

Data drawn from a completely different perspective have also been applied to this problem. Popularized by Vincent Sarich and Allan Wilson of the University of California, Berkeley (1967), this perspective utilizes comparisons of living animals. By calibrating the overall immunological reactions of proteins from different species, by sequencing the amino acids within proteins, or by doing DNA hybridization (see pp. 173–174), living species can be compared to each other.

Certainly, such data are immensely valuable in demonstrating *relative* genetic distances among contemporary organisms (as we discussed in Chapter 7). However, proponents of this view go considerably further and postulate that biochemical distance can be used directly to calculate evolutionary distance. In other words, a "molecular clock" is thought to provide unambiguous divergence dates for a host of evolutionary lineages, including hominids/pongids (Sarich, 1971).

Several hotly disputed assumptions are required, however, to perform this feat. Most importantly, the rate of molecular evolution must be constant over time. Such regularity could be accomplished if mutations were strictly *neutral* (see p. 90) or if selection pressures remained constant. Since environmental changes are decidedly not constant through time, the latter assumption is not valid. As for the first point, while neutral mutations certainly do occur (and perhaps do so quite frequently), many researchers are not convinced that most mutations are neutral (e.g., see Livingstone, 1980). Moreover, even if mutation was mostly neutral, major evolutionary shifts may still be quite nongradual in tempo—given the suggested punctuated mode of change (see p. 91).

Another possible complicating factor concerns generation length. Those species that reproduce in shorter periods of time should (according to strict application of the molecular clock) show, for the same period of time, greater amounts of molecular evolution than more slowly reproducing forms (Vogel, et al., 1976). Given the variation in generation lengths, it is not justifiable to make strict linear reconstruction for divergence times among prosimians, monkeys, and hominoids.

Another problem is that there is no certain indicator of molecular evolutionary rates; different proteins yield significantly different rates of evolution and thus greatly influence inferences about divergence times (Corruccini et al., 1980). In fact, the *greatest* margin of error would occur in attempting to calculate relatively recent evolutionary events—for example, the hominid-pongid split.

Analysis of amino acid sequences of proteins by another group of biochemists (at Wayne State University in Detroit) has confirmed that, indeed, rates of molecular evolution are not constant, but are rather characterized by periods of acceleration and deceleration (the latter being particularly true in the last few million years). Thus, these researchers conclude: "For proteins demonstrating striking shifts in rates of amino acid substitutions over time, it is not possible to calculate accurate divergence dates within Anthropoidea using the molecular clock approach. Our analysis of amino acid sequence data of several proteins by the clock model yields divergence dates, particularly within the Hominoidea, that are far too recent in view of well-established fossil evidence" (Goodman et al., 1983, p. 68).

As a result of such criticisms of the "clock," some paleontologists have been skeptical of its claimed applications. For example, Milford Wolpoff (of the University of Michigan) argues that, "Probably the best way to summarize the very disparate points raised is that the 'clock' simply *should not* work" (Wolpoff, 1983a, p. 661).

Naturally, not everyone takes so negative a view of the clock approach. Vincent Sarich continues to believe firmly in its basic accuracy (when applied correctly) and, justifiably, feels vindicated by recent recalibrations of theories derived from fossil evidence, which bring them closer to the biochemically derived hypotheses.

The fossils themselves are not going to provide the whole answer. The paleontological record is usually too

(*continued on next page*)

◇ Box 9-1   Timing the Hominid-Pongid Split, continued

incomplete to provide clearcut ancestor-descendant associations. More fossils will always help, of course, but the way we think about them (i.e., the questions we raise about them) is also crucial in framing workable theories.

The biochemical perspective has been important in that it has articulated key issues for evolutionary consideration (for example, the place of the orang in relation to other large-bodied hominoids). The interplay between the paleontological and biochemical perspectives has thus been most productive. In fact, these viewpoints agree more now on several aspects of hominoid evolu-

tion than they did just a few years ago. The greatest furor has been raised from overly strong claims for the unique validity of either approach. We have shown in this chapter that more fossil evidence *and* more controlled analyses have forced previous views to be reconsidered. Moreover, it is equally unfair to portray the clock approach as a complete answer. As one of the leading advocates of this method has recently stated, "The clock is one of an approximate, not metronomically perfect nature" (Cronin, 1983, p. 116).

Gigantopithecus and that of the bamboo-shoot-eating giant panda. An animal having the bulk of *Gigantopithecus* would have required a huge masticatory apparatus with large, grinding teeth and heavy jaws. And this picture is exactly the one that we envision, even to the extreme point of including the front teeth in this functional complex.

In addition to the apparent specialization of this animal, *Gigantopithecus* would seem an unlikely close relative of hominids, for it survived so late—up to the Middle Pleistocene in China. Long before this time, definite hominids had been diverging, and by the Middle Pleistocene they were already closely approximating modern humans in such features as body size and teeth.

Therefore, it seems likely that *Gigantopithecus* diverged from other hominoids in the middle-late Miocene, set out on a specialized evolutionary path, and eventually became extinct in the Middle Pleistocene.

MIOCENE HOMINOIDS: SUMMARY

Firm judgments concerning the diverse array of Miocene hominoids cannot yet be made, but it is apparent that the evolutionary picture is a good deal more complex than previously thought. In this regard, it is interesting to note that David Pilbeam, a proponent of the earlier simplistic view, has recently altered his opinions. Many of his current views are reflected in the interpretations given here.

There are probably at least three distinct genera of hominoids by mid-Miocene times, with a multitude of species. Most, if not all, of these forms are filling niches not strictly analogous to any living hominoid, and our interpretation must not obscure the evolutionary uniqueness these animals no doubt possessed.

Ideally, we would like to draw conclusions concerning how these Miocene hominoids are related to extant apes and to ourselves. The earlier, quite uncomplicated suggestions just have not worked out, as Pilbeam has noted: "We know enough now to realize that our earlier and simple scenarios were too simple, though not enough yet to choose among a variety of more complex ones" (Pilbeam, 1977, p. 3).

Presently, we cannot trace with any certainty the hominid lineage or that of the African apes back to any of these Miocene forms. The orang, however, may well share close relationship with some of the Asian ramapiths.

It would thus be fair to say, on the basis of current evidence, that not all possible evolutionary scenarios are equally probable. The placement and frequency of question marks in Figure 9-20 reflect this fact.

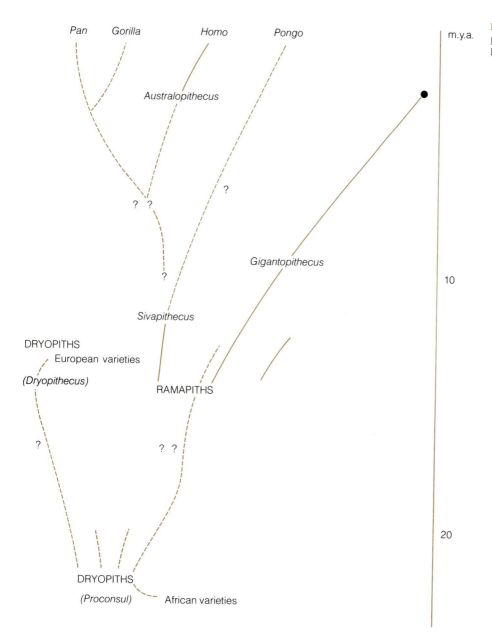

Figure 9-20 A provisional model showing possible relationships of Miocene and later hominoids.

◇ The Meaning of Genus and Species

Our discussion of fossil primates has introduced a multitude of cumbersome taxonomic names. We should pause at this point and reasonably ask: Why use so many names like *Sivapithecus*, *Ramapithecus*, and *Gigantopithecus*? What does such naming mean in evolutionary terms?

Our goal when applying genus, species, or other taxonomic labels to groups of organisms is to make meaningful biological statements about the variation that is present. When looking at populations of living or long extinct animals, we are assuredly going to see the presence of variation. This situation is true of *any* sexually reproducing organism due to the factors of recombination (as independent assortment and crossing-over—see Chapter 3). As a result of recombination, each individual organism is a unique combination of genetic material, and this uniqueness is usually reflected to some extent in the phenotype. In addition to such *individual variation*, we see other kinds of systematic variation in all biological populations. *Age changes* certainly act to alter overall body size, as well as shape, in many animals. One pertinent example for fossil hominoid studies is the great change in number, size, and shape of teeth from deciduous (milk) teeth (only twenty present) to the permanent dentition (thirty-two present). It obviously would be a great error to assign two different fossil hominoids to different species *solely* on the basis of age-dependent dental criteria. If one were represented only by milk teeth and the other only by permanent teeth, they easily could be differently aged individuals of the *same* population.

Variation due to sex also plays an important role in influencing differences among individuals observed in biological populations. Differences in structural traits between males and females of the same population are called *sexual dimorphism*, and we have seen that great variation does exist between the sexes in some primates (for example, gorillas and baboons) in such elements as overall body size and canine size.

As we have seen when looking at body size differences, as well as differences in tooth size, among the ramapiths, a reasonable assumption is that what we are really viewing is simply the variations between males and females of the same species.

Keeping in mind all the types of variation present within interbreeding groups of organisms, the minimum biological category we would like to define in fossil primate samples is the *species*. As previously defined in Chapter 4, the species is biologically described as a group of interbreeding or potentially interbreeding organisms that are reproductively isolated from other such groups. In modern organisms, this concept is theoretically testable by observations of reproductive behavior. In animals long dead, such testing is obviously impossible. Therefore, in order to get a handle on the interpretation of variation seen in fossil groups like the ramapiths we must refer to living animals.

We know without doubt that variation is present. The question is: What is its biological significance? Two immediate choices occur: Either the variation is accounted for by individual, age, and sex differences seen within every biological species—**intraspecific**—or the variation present represents differences between reproductively isolated groups—**interspecific**. How do we judge between the alterntives intra- or interspecific? We clearly must refer to already defined groups where we can observe reproductive behavior; in other words, contemporary species.

If the amount of morphological variation observed in fossil samples is comparable with that seen today *within species of closely related forms*, then we should not "split" our sample into more than one species. We must, however, be careful in choosing our modern analogs, for rates of morphological evolution vary widely among different groups of mammals. In interpreting past primates, we do best when comparing them with well-known species of modern primates.

Our evolutionary interpretations of the vast array of variable Miocene hominoids is greatly simplified by adhering to relevant biological criteria:

1. First we must look at *all* relevant material. We are not justified in splitting fossil groups into several species on the basis of only presumed differences in the sample (Simons' and Pilbeam's contribution was a major step in rectifying this situation for Miocene hominoids).
2. We must statistically reconstruct the variation observed in our often very small fossil *samples* to realistic dimensions of actual biological *populations*. Every piece of every bone found is part of an individual, who in turn was part of a variable interbreeding population of organisms.
3. We then refer to known dimensions of variation in closely related groups of living primates, keeping in mind expected effects of age, sexual dimorphism, and individual variation.
4. Our next step is to extrapolate the results to the fossil sample and make the judgment: How many species are represented?
5. Since fossil forms are widely scattered in time, we also must place the different species within a firm chronology.
6. Finally, we would like to make interpretations (at least, educated guesses) concerning which forms are related to other forms as ancestors-descendants. To do this, we must pay strict attention to primitive as opposed to derived characteristics.

Following the above steps will greatly reduce the kind of useless confusion that has characterized hominoid studies for so long. We do not, however, wish to convey the impression that the biological interpretation of fossils into taxonomic categories is simple and unambiguous. Far from it! Many complexities must be recognized. Even in living groups, sharp lines between populations representing only one species and populations representing two or more species are difficult to draw. For example, a chain of integrating subspecies in gulls exchange genes at overlapping boundaries. However, at the terminal ends of the chain, two subspecies (species?) live side-by-side along the coasts of Europe with little or no hybridization. In practice, isolating exactly where species boundaries begin and end is exceptionally difficult, especially in a dynamic situation like that represented by gulls.

In contexts dealing with extinct species, the uncertainties are even greater. In addition to the overlapping patterns of variation *over space*, variation also

Intraspecific
Within one species.

Interspecific
Between two or more species.

Figure 9-21 Circular overlap in gulls. A, B, C are subspecies of *Larus argentatus*. D (*L. glaucoides*) is a separate species. All along the chain subspecies interbreed (C1 with C2; C3 with C4, etc.) but at the terminal ends A2 lives side-by-side with B3 and B4 and does *not* interbreed. Where does one then draw species designations?

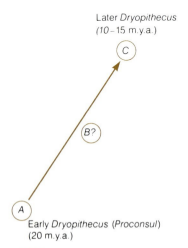

Later *Dryopithecus*
(10–15 m.y.a.)

Early *Dryopithecus (Proconsul)*
(20 m.y.a.)

Figure 9-22 Evolution in a continuing evolving lineage. Where does one designate the different species?

occurs *through time*. In other words, even more variation will be seen in such **paleospecies**, since individuals may be separated by thousands or even millions of years. Applying strict Linnaean taxonomy to such a situation presents an unavoidable dilemma. Standard Linnaean classification, designed to take account of the variation present at any given time, describes a static situation. However, when dealing with paleospecies we are often involved in great spans of time and thus with much additional variation.

Where do we establish meaningful species boundaries in such a dynamic situation? Often, our task is made easier because of the incompleteness of the fossil record. Quite frequently, fossil samples are separated by great gaps of time (as between A and C) and the morphological differences may therefore also be clearcut. In such a case, we feel quite comfortable calling these different species. But what about fossil populations (B, for example) that are intermediate in both time and morphology? This question has no easy answer. Any taxonomic designation in such a continuously evolving lineage is by necessity going to be arbitrary.

Such a line, which has no speciation events (see p. 89), is referred to as **monophyletic**. For such a lineage, many evolutionary biologists see no point in making separate species designations—that is, the entire line is seen as a single paleospecies (Eldredge and Cracraft, 1980). Many biologists believe, in fact, that long, gradual transformations of this type are not the rule, but that branching (i.e., speciation) is much more typical of evolutionary change. (Once again, the view of the punctuationalists—see p. 91.)

Moreover, it is imperative in evolutionary interpretation to understand ancestor-descendant relationships. Most paleontologists have traditionally made anatomical comparisons and then immediately constructed evolutionary trees (also called *phylogenies*). Recently, another perspective has been advanced. In this approach, a detailed interpretation of primitive versus derived states must first be explicitly stated. Only then can patterns of relationships be shown.

These are best interpreted in the form of a *cladogram* (a set of relationships shown as a hypothesis). In fact, usually several cladograms can be constructed from the same set of data. Those that are seen as most economically explaining the patterns of derived characteristics are then provisionally accepted, while less adequate ones are rejected. Such a perspective has been termed **cladistics**, and has injected a good deal more objectivity into paleontology (Eldredge and Cracraft, 1980). It must be pointed out, however, that not all paleontologists have accepted this approach. A basic assumption of cladistic analysis is that trait *patterns* are developed as the result of ancestor-descendant relationships and, conversely, that parallelism and convergence (see p. 146) have little import. In primate evolution, this assumption may not hold true; an analysis of morphological features in lemurs and lorises showed that 80% of the traits studied displayed some parallelism (Walker et al., 1981).

The next level of formal taxonomic classification, the *genus*, presents another problem. In order to have more than one genus, we obviously must have at least two species (reproductively isolated groups), and, in addition, the species must differ in a basic way. A genus is therefore defined as a group of species composed of members more closely related to each other than they are to species from another genus.

Grouping contemporary species together into genera is largely a subjective procedure wherein degree of relatedness becomes a strictly relative judgment. One possible test for contemporary animals is to check for results of hybridization between individuals of different species—rare in nature but quite common in captivity. If two normally separate species interbreed and produce live, though not necessarily fertile, offspring, this process shows genetically that they are not too distant and that they probably should be classified into a single genus. Well-known examples of such interspecific crosses within one genus are horses with donkeys (*Equus caballus* × *Equus asinus*) or lions with tigers (*Panthera leo* × *Panthera tigris*). In both these cases, the close morphological and evolutionary similarities between these species are confirmed by their occasional ability to produce live hybrids.

As mentioned, we cannot perform breeding experiments with animals that are extinct, but another definition of genus becomes highly relevant. Species that are members of one genus share the same broad adaptive zone or, in Sewall Wright's terminology (Mayr, 1962), a similar "adaptive plateau." What this represents is a general ecological life style more basic than the particular ecological niches characteristic of species. This ecological definition of genus can be an immense aid in interpreting fossil primates. Teeth are the most

Paleospecies
A group of organisms from different time periods classified within the same species.

Monophyletic
mono: one
phyletic: line of evolutionary descent

Cladistics
The school of evolutionary biology that seeks to make ancestral-descendant hypotheses through interpreting patterns of primitive/derived characteristics.

Figure 9-23 Cladograms. Three alternative statements representing ancestral-descendant relationships among three taxa. (*a*) C diverges earliest, with A and B sharing a more recent common ancestor; (*b*) B diverges earliest, with A and C sharing a more recent common ancestor; (*c*) A diverges earliest, with B and C sharing a more recent common ancestor.

often preserved parts, and they are usually excellent general ecological indicators.

Therefore, if among the Miocene hominoids some animals appear to inhabit different adaptive/ecological zones (for example *Proconsul* vs. *Sivapithecus* vs. *Gigantopithecus*), we are justified in postulating more than one genus present.

Operationally, then, categorization at the genus level becomes the most practical biological interpretation of fragmentary extinct forms. While species differences necessarily were also present (probably in great complexity), these are usually too intricate to recognize in incomplete material.

As a final comment, we should point out that classification by genus is also not always a clearcut business. Indeed, the argument among primate biologists over whether the chimp and gorilla represent one genus (*Pan troglodytes*, *Pan gorilla*) or two different genera (*Pan troglodytes*, *Gorilla gorilla*) demonstrate that even with living, breathing animals the choices are not always clear.

◇ Summary

In this chapter, we have traced the evolutionary history of our primate origins between 70 and 10 m.y.a. Beginning in the late Cretaceous, the earliest primate ancestors are probably little more than arboreally adapted insectivores. In the Paleocene, we begin to see more definite primate trends in such animals as *Plesiadapis*, but there are still numerous "primitive" characteristics present in these forms. In the following epoch, the Eocene, we begin to see an abundant diversification of primates of modern aspect. During this epoch, the lemurlike adapids and early ancestors of tarsiers begin their evolutionary radiation. Early anthropoid origins probably also date to sometime in the late Eocene. In addition, Old and New World primates apparently shared their last common ancestry in the Eocene or early Oligocene and have gone their separate ways ever since.

In the Old World, the Oligocene reveals a large number of possible early anthropoid ancestors at the Fayum. By and large, all these are primitive Old World anthropoids, and none of the modern lineages (Old World monkeys, gibbons, large-bodied hominoids) can definitely be traced into the Oligocene.

The Miocene reveals an abundant and complex array of hominoid forms that sort into an early African group (the dryopiths) and a later, mostly Asian group (the ramapiths). The best known of these Miocene hominoids—at least through abundance of recent discoveries—is the ramapith *Sivapithecus*. While again there is little firm evidence tying these fossil forms to extant apes or ourselves, some tentative evidence suggests that *Sivapithecus* is closely related to the ancestors of the orang. Where, then, are the ancestors of the African apes or, even more relevantly, of ourselves? In the next six chapters, we will seek to answer this question.

◇ Questions for Review

1. Why is it difficult to distinguish the earliest members of the primate order from other placental mammals? If you found a nearly complete skeleton of an early Paleocene mammal, what structural traits might lead you to believe it was a primate?

2. Compare the fossil primates of the Paleocene and Eocene with living members of the primate order.

3. Why did so many prosimians become extinct at the end of the Eocene? Discuss the alternative explanations critically.

4. If you (as an expert physical anthropologist) were brought remains of a purported 30 m.y. fossil hominoid from South America, why might you be skeptical?

5. What kinds of primates were evolving at the Fayum in Oligocene times? What is meant by saying they are primitive catarrhines?

6. Compare and contrast the anatomical features of dryopiths and ramapiths.

7. Discuss the three alternative interpretations of the evolutionary affinities of *Sivapithecus*.

8. How did the shifting of the earth's plates, as well as climatic changes, affect hominoid evolution in the Miocene?

9. What kind of primate was *Gigantopithecus*, and why is it an unlikely hominid ancestor?

10. If two fossil groups are classified as *Sivapithecus indicus* and *Sivapithecus sivalensis*, at what taxonomic level is the distinction being made? What are the biological implications of such a classification?

11. If two fossil groups are classified as *Dryopithecus* and *Sivapithecus*, at what taxonomic level is this distinction? What are the biological implications?

Paleoanthropology

CONTENTS

Has our evolution, both cultural and biological, been systematically and deliberately tampered with by beings from other worlds? Popularized by Erich von Däniken in a series of fantastically successful books (1968, 1970, 1973), this bizarre theory has been further promulgated in movies and television. Is it possible?

Scientific inquiry cannot "prove" *anything* impossible, but it can attempt to demonstrate what is probable. Von Däniken is correct in asserting that, given the vast number of stars (and planets) in the universe, there is a high probability of intelligent life out there *somewhere*. Of all these life forms, however, how many are capable of efficient interstellar travel (necessitating speeds approaching that of light)? Furthermore, even if some life forms possessed this technology, where would they look for other intelligent life? If they randomly sampled all "inhabitable" planets in the universe, their probability of finding us would be low indeed. Perhaps, however, they are watching or listening for signs. They might assume, as we have, that an intelligent life form with even a modest degree of technological sophistication could produce radio waves. In the hopes of hearing such an intergalactic message, we have recently turned our own ears to the heavens.

If creatures "out there" have done likewise, they may *eventually* hear our radio signals. However, we have been producing such communications for only the last fifty years or so (and these radio waves have only traveled about fifty light-years). Special frequency signals aimed specifically at distant worlds have only been initiated in the last few years. Consequently, on the basis of simple logical deduction, it would seem unlikely that we have even been detected, to say nothing of actually playing host to extraterrestrial travelers.

Remember, however, that whereas such a postulation is exceedingly improbable, it is not completely impossible. What, then, of evidence?

Von Däniken has audaciously postulated that extraterrestrial beings have visited earth dozens of times. Nor did they *just* visit; they helped construct huge monuments (presumably to themselves—what a being capable of building spaceships would see in a stone edifice is a mystery). They even assisted with the writing of tablets and making of maps, and let themselves become deified by the masses of humble *H. sapiens* in the bargain.

Surely mysteries abound in the archeological record, which is incomplete and, thus, far from perfect. However, that fact does not justify postulating the unlikely, the bizarre, or the ridiculous when a much more probable (but admittedly, less exciting) explanation is easily found. Indeed, much of von Däniken's primary "hard" evidence has been debunked. The huge pyramids of Egypt and Mesoamerica, the mysterious geometric designs of Nazca, Peru, and the formidable stone monuments of Easter Island have all been demonstrated as *human* achievements using relatively simple technological principles and good old-fashioned human labor.

If, in 100,000 years, future generations of archeologists were to excavate some of the "wonders" of our world, they would (in the absence of written records) be struck by the seeming incongruities and mysteries. The incredible Gothic cathedrals of Europe, built during a period of economic and intellectual disorganization, would appear a giant paradox. Did space beings build them? Or, even closer to home, the massive vaults excavated into the Rockies housing the genealogical records of the Mormon Church might also confuse and befuddle our descendants. Yet, the architects and engineers in Utah clearly did not require or receive extraterrestrial assistance in constructing this marvel.

Human beings routinely achieve the incredible, the fantastic, the inexplicable, and they do it on their own. After all, the New York Mets did win the World Series back in 1969!

SOURCES:

von Däniken, Erich. *Chariots of the Gods?*, New York: G. P. Putnam's Sons, 1968.

———. *Gods from Outer Space*, New York: G. P. Putnam's Sons, 1970.

———. *Gold of the Gods*, New York: G. P. Putnam's Sons, 1973.

◇ Introduction

In the last three chapters, we have seen how humans are classed as primates, both structurally and behaviorally, and how our evolutionary history coincides with that of other primates. However, we are a unique kind of primate, and our ancestors have been adapted to a particular kind of life style for several million years. Some kind of ramapith may have begun this process more than 10 m.y.a., but, beginning about 5 m.y.a., evidence from Africa reveals much more definite hominid relationships. The hominid nature of these remains is revealed by more than the morphological structure of teeth and bones; we know these animals are hominids also because of the way they behaved— emphasizing once again the *biocultural* nature of human evolution. In this chapter, we will discuss the methods scientists use to explore the secrets of early hominid behavior. We will then demonstrate these through the example of the best-known early hominid site in the world: Olduvai Gorge in East Africa.

◇ Definition of Hominid

If any ramapith fossils represent the earliest stages of hominid diversification, our definition of them as hominid must then primarily be a *dental* one. Teeth and jaws are most of what we have of these Miocene forms. However, dentition is not the only way to describe the special attributes of our particular evolutionary radiation and is certainly not the most distinctive of its later stages. Modern humans and our hominid ancestors are distinguished from our closest living relatives (the great apes) by more obvious features than proportionate tooth and jaw size. For example, various scientists have pointed to other hominid characteristics, such as large brain size, bipedal locomotion, and toolmaking behavior, as being most significant in defining what makes a hominid a hominid (as opposed to a pongid, a cercopithecoid, or anything else for that matter). This last definition—humans as toolmakers—is the one that we wish to discuss in this chapter. The important structural attributes of the hominid brain, teeth, and locomotory apparatus will be discussed in the next chapter, where we investigate early hominid anatomical adaptations in greater detail.

BIOCULTURAL EVOLUTION: HUMANS AS TOOLMAKERS

Although other primates do occasionally make tools (see Chapter 8), only hominids depend on culture for their survival. We and our close hominid ancestors alone have the ability to "impose arbitrary form on the environment" (Holloway, 1969). For example, chimps who use termite sticks have a direct and immediate relationship with the raw material and purpose of the

Artifacts
Traces of hominid behavior; very old ones are usually of stone.

tool. Such is not the case in most human cultural behavior, which usually involves several steps often quite arbitrarily removed from a direct environmental context.

We are defining culture primarily as a mental process. The human mind—presumably the minds of our hominid ancestors as well—has the unique capacity to *create* symbols. When a chimp sees water, it probably sees only the immediate environmental setting plus any learned experiences that are directly associated. Humans, however, can introduce all kinds of additional meanings, such as "holy water," physically identical to all other water but with symbolic value. A chimp can see water and know from experience it is wet, drinkable, etc. However, the chimp will never be capable of grasping the superimposed, arbitrary ideas invented and understood only by humans.

Obviously, we cannot "get inside the head" of a chimpanzee to know exactly what it is or is not thinking. The assumptions we have made are derived from behavioral observations in natural habitats, as well as results of learning experiments. However, as discussed in Chapter 8, among scientists there is still considerable dispute concerning the behavioral capacities of chimpanzees; the assumptions expressed here reflect the views of the authors. Humans, of course, also have the capacity to manipulate their environments in infinitely more complex ways than other animals. The simple human invention of a watertight container, such as a hollowed-out gourd or an ostrich egg, is several orders of magnitude more complex than chimp or rhesus monkey "cultural" behavior.

Culture as a complex adaptive strategy has become central to human evolution and has acted as a potent selective force to mold our anatomical form over the last several million years. In the archeological record, early cultural behavior is seen in the preserved remains of stone implements, traces of a uniquely human activity. "The shaping of stone according to even the simplest plan is beyond the behavior of any ape or monkey" (Washburn, 1971, p. 105).

Thus, when we find stone tools made to a standardized pattern, we know we have found a behavior indicator of a hominid, and *only* homind, adaptation. We are justified, then, in defining hominids as habitual toolmakers, *culturally dependent* animals, distinct in this respect from all other primates.

Figure 10-1   Early stone tools. Traces of hominid behavior, from Olduvai Gorge, East Africa, about 1.6 m.y.a.

◇ The Strategy of Paleoanthropology

In order to understand human evolution adequately, we obviously need a broad base of information. The task of recovering and interpreting all the clues left by early hominids is the work of the paleoanthropologist. Paleoanthropology is defined as "the science of the study of ancient humans." As such, it is a diverse *multidisciplinary* pursuit seeking to reconstruct every possible bit of information concerning the dating, structure, behavior, and ecology of our hominid ancestors. In just the last few years, the study of early humans has marshalled the specialized skills of many diverse kinds of scientists. Included primarily in this growing and exciting adventure are the geologist, archeologist, physical anthropologist, and paleoecologist (Table 10-1).

Table 10-1   Subdisciplines of Paleoanthropology

Physical Sciences	Biological Sciences	Social Sciences
Geology	Physical Anthropology	Archeology
Stratigraphy	Ecology	Cultural Anthropology
Petrology	Paleontology	Ethnography
(rocks, minerals)	(fossil animals)	Psychology
Pedology	Palynology	
(soils)	(fossil pollen)	
Geophysics	Primatology	Ethnoarcheology
Chemistry		
Geomorphology		
Taphonomy*		

*Taphonomy (taphos: dead) is the study of how bones and other materials come to be buried in the earth and preserved as fossils. A taphonomist studies such phenomena as the processes of sedimentation, action of streams, preservation properties of bone, and carnivore disturbance factors.

The geologist, usually working with an anthropologist (often an archeologist) does the initial survey work in order to locate potential early hominid sites. Many sophisticated techniques can aid in this search, including aerial and satellite photography. Paleontologists may also be involved in this early search, for they can help find fossil beds containing faunal remains; where conditions are favorable for the bone preservation of such specimens as ancient pigs and elephants, conditions may also be favorable for the preservation of hominid remains. In addition, paleontologists can (through comparison with known faunal areas) give fairly quick estimates of approximate age of fossil sites without having to wait for the more expensive and time-consuming chronometric analyses. In this way, fossil beds of the "right" geologic ages (that is, where hominid finds are most likely) can be isolated.

Once potential areas of early hominid sites have been located, much more extensive surveying begins. At this point, the archeologist takes over in the search for hominid "traces." We do not necessarily have to find remains of early hominids themselves to know they consistently occupied a particular area. Behavioral clues, or **artifacts**, also inform us directly and unambiguously about early hominid occupation. Modifying rocks according to a consistent plan, or simply carrying them around from one place to another (over fairly long distances), are behaviors characteristic of no other animal but a hominid. Therefore, when we see such behavioral evidence at a site, we know absolutely that hominids were present.

No doubt, early hominids sometimes utilized implements of wood or bone, and probably began doing so several million years ago (6–4 m.y.a.?). It is not altogether clear, however, just how many of these potential tools were available without *first* processing them with stone. Naturally pointed pieces of wood could probably have been utilized as digging sticks or perhaps for puncturing an ostrich egg (to make a watertight container). Beyond this, it probably would have been quite difficult to make much use of wood resources without some modification; yet, how could this have been done without something harder with which to cut, scrape, or sharpen (i.e., stone tools)? Bone is even

Paleoecological
paleo: old
ecological: environmental setting
The study of ancient environments.

more intractable and would seem also to have been "off-limits" to hominids without some stone implement to crush, cut, etc. Probably the only bone sources available were splinters left behind at kills by large carnivores. This all remains, of course, speculative, since *direct* evidence is not available. Unfortunately, these organic materials usually are not preserved, and we thus know little about such early tool-using behavior.

On the other hand, our ancestors at some point showed a veritable fascination with stones, for these provided not only easily accessible and transportable weights (to hold down objects, such as skins and windbreaks) but also the most durable and sharpest cutting edges available at that time. Luckily for us, stone is almost indestructible, and early hominid sites are virtually strewn with thousands of stone artifacts. The earliest artifact site now documented is from the Omo region of Ethiopia, dating from at least 2.4 m.y.a. Another contender for the "earliest" stone assemblage is from the Hadar area, farther to the north in Ethiopia—dated 2.0–2.5 m.y.a.

If an area is clearly demonstrated as a hominid site, much more concentrated research will then begin. We should point out that a more mundane but very significant aspect of paleoanthropology not shown in Table 10-1 is the financial one. Just the initial survey work in usually remote areas takes many thousands of dollars, and mounting a concentrated research project takes several hundred thousand dollars. Therefore, for such work to go on, massive financial support is required from governmental agencies and/or private donations. A significant amount of the paleoanthropologist's efforts and time are necessarily devoted to writing grant proposals or to speaking on the lecture circuit to raise the required funds for this necessary work.

Once the financial hurdle has been cleared, a coordinated research project can commence. Usually headed by an archeologist or physical anthropologist, the field crew will continue to survey and map the target area in great detail. In addition, they will begin to search carefully for bones and artifacts eroding out of the soil, take pollen and soil samples for ecological analysis, and carefully recover rock samples for chronometric dating. If, in this early stage of exploration, the field crew finds a fossil hominid, they will feel very lucky indeed. The international press usually considers human fossils the most exciting kind of discovery, a situation that produces wide publicity, often working to assure future financial support. More likely, the crew will accumulate much information on geological setting, ecological data, particularly faunal remains, and, with some luck, archeological traces (hominid artifacts).

After long and arduous research in the field, even more time-consuming and detailed analysis is required back in the laboratory. The archeologist must clean, sort, label, and identify all the artifacts, and the paleontologist must do the same for all faunal remains. The kinds of animals present, whether forest browsers, woodland species, or open-country forms, will greatly help in reconstructing the local **paleoecological** settings in which early hominids lived. In addition, analysis of pollen remains by a palynologist will further aid in a detailed environmental reconstruction. All of these paleoecological analyses can assist in reconstructing the diet of early humans (see p. 301). Many complex kinds of contributions go into assembling and interpreting the relevant data in such analyses (see Table 10-2).

Table 10-2   Elements of Hominid Paleoecology

Physical Environment:

Altitude	Mean wind speed
Temperature	Degree of wind gusting
Rainfall	Mean cloud cover
Relative humidity	Surface water availability
Insolation	Surface water salinity
Soil:	
Development	
Physical composition	
Chemical composition	
Tree and shrub density	Habitat selectivity
Shade cover	Herbaceous basal cover
Degree of clumping of woody plants	Grass and forb height

Diet:

Content:	Metabolic energy requirements
Animal	Energy intake
Vegetable	Digestibility
Soil (geophagy)	Time of feeding
Manner obtained	Season of feeding
Manner eaten	
Drinking	

Population:

Numbers	Mortality
Weights	Birth spacing
Growth	Sexual maturity
Natality	

Interspecific Relations:

Grouping	Division of labor
Group interaction	Distances between group sleeping sites
Sexual relations	Grooming
Dominance interactions	

Interspecific Relations:

Cooperation with other species	Prey
Competition with other species	Predators
Tolerance of other species	

Other Behavior:

Extent of daily movement	Group activity at various times of the day:
Tool use and manufacture:	Feeding intensively and/or moving rapidly
material, source, use	Feeding leisurely and/or resting
Sleeping place	Resting
Vocalizations	
Diurnality/nocturnality	

Source: Reprinted by permission of the Kroeber Anthropological Society from Kroeber Anthropological Society Papers No. 50, ed., Noel T. Boaz and John E. Cronin (Berkeley: Kroeber Anthropological Society, 1977), p. 56, © 1977 by the Kroeber Anthropological Society.

Pedologist
pedon: ground, soil

Petrologist
petr: rock

More information will be provided by analysis of soil samples by a **pedol-ogist**, and rock and mineral samples by a **petrologist**. A geomorphologist may also be asked to reconstruct the sequence of past geologic events, including volcanics, mountain building, earth movements, such as faulting, and changes in the orientation of the earth's magnetic pole.

As work progresses in later field seasons with more laboratory analyses, even more experts from other scientific specialties may be consulted. If a hominid bone or tooth is eventually recovered, a physical anthropologist will clean it, reconstruct it if necessary, describe it in minute anatomical detail, and attempt to relate it to other fossil hominid finds. The archeologist may decide that a particularly well-preserved location or the site of a hominid discovery calls for precise archeological excavation. In order to recover and record all relevant information in such an undertaking, thousands of work-hours are required to excavate even a relatively small area (a few dozen square feet). An extensively detailed *microstratigraphic analysis* may also be useful in recreating the precise conditions of sedimentation, thus calling for the specialized skills of a taphonomist (see Table 10-1).

In the concluding stages of interpretation, the paleoanthropologist will draw together the following essentials:

1. *Dating*
   geological
   paleontological
   geophysical
2. *Paleoecology*
   paleontology
   palynology
   geomorphology
3. *Archeological traces of behavior*
4. *Anatomical evidence from hominid remains*

From all this information, the paleoanthropologist will try to "flesh out" the kind of animal that may have been our direct ancestor, or at least a very close relative. In this final analysis, still further comparative scientific infor-mation may be needed. Primatologists may assist here by showing the de-tailed relationships between the structure and behavior of humans and that of contemporary nonhuman primates (see Chapters 7 and 8). Cultural anthropologists may contribute ethnographic information concerning the varied nature of human behavior, particularly ecological adaptation of those groups exploiting roughly similar environmental settings as those found at our hominid site (for example, the San or Australian aborigines—see p. 224). Ethnoarcheologists can assist further by demonstrating how observed be-havioral patterns (as implement manufacture and meat eating) actually end up in the ground as artifacts. Finally, neuroanatomists, psychologists, and linguists may aid physical anthropologists in the reconstruction of physio-logical/behavioral information suggested by the fossil hominid remains, such as brain dimensions and their relationship to language capacities.

The end result of years of research by dozens of scientists will (we hope) produce a more complete and accurate understanding of human evolution—

how we came to be the way we are. Both biological and cultural aspects of our ancestors pertain to this investigation, each process developing in relation to the other.

◇ Paleoanthropology in Action—Olduvai Gorge

Several paleoanthropological projects of the scope discussed above are now in progress in diverse places around the globe. The most important of these include: David Pilbeam's work in the Miocene beds of the Potwar Plateau of western Pakistan (*circa* 13–7 m.y.a.); Don Johanson's project in the Hadar area of Ethiopia (*circa* 3.7–1.6 m.y.a.); a now completed research project along the Omo River of southern Ethiopia (*circa* 4–1.5 m.y.a.) directed by F. Clark Howell (both the Howell and Johanson projects have sometimes been forced to cease work due to warfare in Ethiopia); Richard Leakey's fantastically successful research around the shores of Lake Turkana (formerly Rudolf) in northern Kenya (*circa* 2.0–1.5 m.y.a.); and Mary Leakey's famous investigations at Olduvai Gorge in northern Tanzania (*circa* 1.85 m.y.a.–present).

Of all these early hominid localities, the one that has yielded the finest quality and greatest abundance of paleoanthropological information concerning the behavior of early hominids has been Olduvai Gorge.

First "discovered" in the early twentieth century by a German butterfly collector, Olduvai was soon thereafter scientifically surveyed and its wealth of paleontological evidence recognized. In 1931, Louis Leakey made his first trip to Olduvai Gorge and almost immediately realized its significance for

Figure 10-2 Major paleoanthropological projects.

Figure 10-3 Olduvai Gorge. A sketch map showing positions of the major sites and geologic localities.

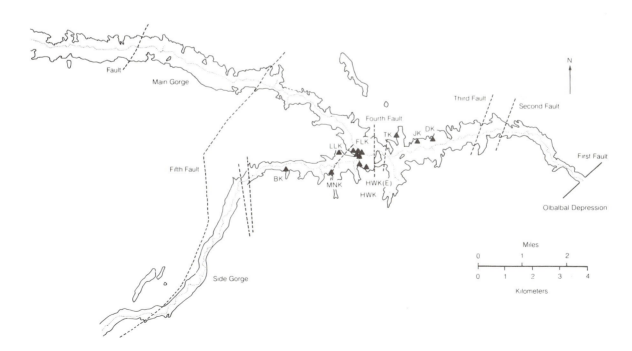

◇ BIOGRAPHY   Louis S. B. Leakey 1903–1972

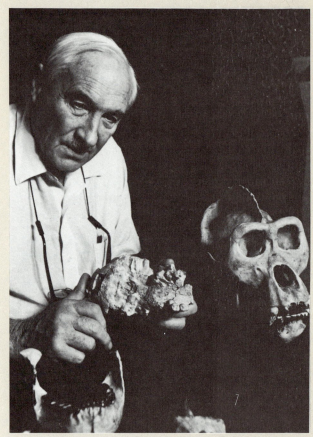

Louis Leakey. Shown displaying casts of fossil hominid discoveries from East Africa. To the right is the skull of a male gorilla.

Called the "Charles Darwin of prehistory," Louis Leakey was truly a man for all seasons. Blessed with a superior intellect and an almost insatiable curiosity, Leakey untiringly quested after knowledge, which to him included everything there was to know about everything. His interests encompassed not just prehistory, archeology, and paleontology but modern African wildlife, African peoples, languages, and customs. He once stalked, killed, and butchered a gazelle with just his bare hands and stone tools he had fashioned himself. He had previously attempted to use only his teeth and hands to dismember dead animals, but found it impossible, leading him to the conclusion that early hominids also *must* have used stone tools for butchering. Leakey also was a leading authority on handwriting, a skill he put to good use as the chief of British military intelligence for Africa during World War II.

The child of British missionary parents, Louis was born in a Kikuyu village in 1903—probably one of the first white children born in East Africa. His upbringing was to be as much African as European, and he was actually initiated into the Kikuyu tribe. Sworn to a sacred oath of silence, Louis never revealed the secret rites of initiation, even to his wife Mary.

Following his early training in the African bush, Louis was dispatched to England for a more formal education, eventually receiving his degree from Cambridge. His consuming interest, however, was focused on Africa, where he returned to begin exploration of prehistoric sites— leading his first expedition in 1926 at the age of 23! In 1931, Leakey made his first trip to Olduvai Gorge with the German paleontologist Hans Reck. Louis liked to relate years later how he found the first stone tool in context at Olduvai within an hour of his arrival there!

In the next forty years, the fantastic discoveries at Olduvai by Louis and his archeologist wife, Mary, as well as their extensive work at other sites all around the Rift Valley, were to make them famous to professional and layman alike.

However, perhaps Louis' greatest contribution was not the many discoveries he made himself, but his ability to stimulate and involve others. The definitive research on all the great apes was initiated by Louis Leakey, who personally recruited Jane Goodall to work with chimpanzees, Dian Fossey to investigate the mountain gorilla, and Biruté Galdikas to learn the secrets of the orang. Louis' greatest legacy is probably that all these projects continue today,* and, of course, Mary carried on the work at Olduvai while their son, Richard is involved in numerous research expeditions in central and northern Kenya.

*Despite Dian Fossey's tragic death in December, 1985, the work on mountain gorillas continues.

Figure 10-4 Aerial view of Olduvai Gorge. Volcanic highlands are visible to the south.

studying early humans. Beginning in 1935, when she first worked there, Mary Leakey directed archeological excavations at Olduvai until she retired in 1983.

Located in the Serengeti Plain of northern Tanzania, Olduvai is a steep-sided valley resembling a miniature version of the Grand Canyon. Indeed, the geological processes that formed the gorge are similar to what happened in the formation of the Grand Canyon. Following millions of years of steady accumulation of several hundred feet of geological strata (including volcanic, lake, and river deposits), faulting occurred 70,000 years ago to the east of Olduvai. As a result, a gradient was established, causing a rapidly flowing river to cut through the previously laid strata, eventually forming a gorge 300 feet deep—similar to the way the Colorado River cut the Grand Canyon.

Olduvai today is a deep ravine cut into an almost mile high grassland plateau of East Africa, and extends more than twenty-five miles in total length. In fact, if one were to include all the side gulleys and ravines, the area of exposures would total more than seventy miles with potentially hundreds of early hominid sites. Climatically, the semiarid pattern of present day Olduvai is believed to be similar to most of the past environments preserved there over the last 2 million years. The surrounding countryside is a grassland savanna broken occasionally by scrub bushes and acacia trees. It is a note-worthy fact that this environment presently (as well as in the past) supports a vast number of large mammals (as zebra, wildebeest, and gazelle), repre-senting an enormous supply of "meat on the hoof."

Geographically, Olduvai is located on the western edge of the eastern branch of the Great Rift Valley of Africa. The geological processes associated with the formation of the Rift Valley makes Olduvai (and the other East African sites) extremely important to paleoanthropological investigation. Three re-sults of geological rifting are most significant:

1. Faulting, or earth movement, exposes geological beds near the surface that are normally hidden by hundreds of feet of accumulated overburden
2. Active volcanic processes cause rapid sedimentation and thus often yield excellent preservation of bone and artifacts that normally would be scat-tered by carnivore activity and erosion forces

Figure 10-5   The East African Rift Valley
system.

Figure 10-5   The East African Rift Valley system.

3. Volcanic activity provides a wealth of radiometrically datable material

The results of these geological factors at Olduvai are the superb preservation of ancient hominids and their behavioral patterns in datable contexts, all of which are readily accessible.

The greatest contribution Olduvai has made to paleoanthropological research is the establishment of an extremely well-documented and correlated *sequence* of geological, paleontological, archeological, and hominid remains over the last 2 million years. At the very foundation of all paleoanthropological research is a well-established geological picture. At Olduvai, thanks to two decades of work by Dr. Richard Hay, the geological and paleogeographic situation is known in minute detail. Olduvai is today a geologist's delight, containing sediments in some places 350 feet thick accumulated from lava flows (basalts), tuffs (windblown or waterlain fine deposits from nearby volcanoes), sandstones, claystones, and limestone conglomerates, all neatly stratified. A hominid site can therefore be accurately dated relative to other sites in the Olduvai Gorge by cross-correlating known marker beds. The stratigraphic sequence at Olduvai is broken down into four major beds (Beds I–IV), with other, more recent, beds usually referred to by specific local place names (Masek, Ndutu, Naisiusiu). Moreover, careful recording of the precise context of gelogical samples also provides the basis for accurate radiometric dating.

Paleontological evidence of fossilized animal bones also has come from Olduvai in great abundance. More than 150 species of extinct animals have been recognized, including fish, turtle, crocodile, pig, giraffe, horse, and many birds, rodents, and antelopes. Careful analysis of such remains has yielded voluminous information concerning the ecological conditions of early human habitats. In addition, precise analysis of bones directly associated with artifacts can sometimes tell us about the diets and hunting capabilities of early hominids. (There are some reservations, however—see Box 10-1.)

The archeological sequence is also well documented over the last 2 million years. Beginning at the earliest hominid site in Bed I (1.85 m.y.a.), there is already a well-developed stone tool kit, including chopping tools as well as some small flake tools (Leakey, 1971). Such a tool industry is called *Oldowan* (after Olduvai) and continues into Bed II with some small modifications, after which it is called *Developed Oldowan*. In addition, around 1.6 m.y.a., the first appearance of a new tool kit, the *Acheulian*, occurs in the Olduvai archeological record. This industry is characterized by large bifacial (that is, flaked on both sides) tools commonly known as hand-axes and cleavers. For several hundred thousand years, Acheulian and Developed Oldowan are *both* found side-by-side at Olduvai, and the relationship between these parallel tool kits remains to be determined.

Finally, remains of several fossilized hominids have been found at Olduvai, ranging in time from the earliest occupation levels (*circa* 1.85 m.y.a.) to fairly recent *Homo sapiens*. Of the more than forty individuals represented, many are quite fragmentary, but a few (including four skulls and a nearly complete foot) are excellently preserved. While the center of hominid discoveries has now shifted to other areas of East Africa, it was the initial discovery by Mary Leakey of the *Zinjanthropus* skull at Olduvai in July, 1959, that focused the world's attention on this remarkably rich area. "Zinj" provides an excellent example of how financial ramifications directly result from hominid bone discoveries. Prior to 1959, the Leakeys had worked sporadically at Olduvai on

Figure 10-6 View of the Main Gorge at Olduvai. Note the clear sequence of geological beds. The discontinuity to the left is a major fault line.

◇ BIOGRAPHY   Mary Leakey 1913–

Mary Leakey. At the site of the "Zinj" find on the thirteenth anniversary of its discovery.

Mary Leakey, one of the leading prehistorians of this century, spent most of her professional life living in the shadow of her famous husband. But to a considerable degree, Louis' fame is directly attributable to Mary. Justly known for his extensive fieldwork in Miocene sites along the shores of Lake Victoria in Kenya, Louis is quite often associated with important hominoid discoveries. However, it was Mary who, in 1948, found the best-preserved dryopith skull ever discovered.

The names Louis Leakey and Olduvai Gorge are almost synonymous, but here, too, it was Mary who made the most significant single discovery—the "Zinj" skull in 1959. Mary has always been the supervisor of archeological work at Olduvai while Louis was busily engaged in traveling, lecturing, or tending to the National Museum in Nairobi.

Mary Leakey did not come upon her archeological career by chance. A direct descendant of John Frere (who, because of his discoveries in 1797, is called the father of Paleolithic archeology), Mary always had a compelling interest in prehistory. Her talent to illustrate stone tools provided her entry into African prehistory, and was the reason for her introduction to Louis in 1933. Throughout her career, she has done all the tool illustrations for her publications, and has set an extremely high standard of excellence for all would-be illustrators of Paleolithic implements.

A committed, hard-driving woman of almost inexhaustible energy, Mary conducted work at Olduvai, where she lived most of the year. Busily engaged seven days a week, she supervised ongoing excavations, as well as working on the monumental publications detailing the fieldwork already done.

Since Louis' death in 1972, Mary, to some degree, has had to assume the role of traveling lecturer and fund raiser. Today, she lives outside Nairobi, where she energetically continues her research and writing.

a financial shoestring, making marvelous paleontological and archeological discoveries. Yet, there was little support available for much needed large-scale excavations. However, following the discovery of "Zinj," the National Geographic Society funded the Leakeys' research, and within the next year, more than twice as much dirt was excavated than during the previous thirty!

◇ Dating Methods

As we have discussed, one of the key essentials of paleoanthropology is putting sites and fossils into a chronological framework. In other words, we want to know how old they are. How, then, do we date sites—or, more precisely, the geological strata in which sites are found? The question is both reasonable and important, so let us examine the dating techniques used by paleontologists, geologists, paleoanthropologists, and archeologists.

Scientists use two kinds of dating for this purpose—relative and **chrono-metric** (also known as *absolute dating*). Relative dating methods tell you that something is older, or younger, than something else, but not how much. If, for example, a skull were found at a depth of fifty feet, and another skull at seventy feet at the same site, we usually assume the skull discovered at seventy feet is older. We may not know the date (in years) of either one, but we would know that one is older (or younger) than the other. Whereas this may not satisfy our curiosity about the actual number of years involved, it would give some idea of the evolutionary changes in skull morphology (structure), especially if a number of skulls at different levels were found and compared.

This method of relative dating is called **stratigraphy** and was one of the first techniques to be used by scholars working with the vast period of geologic time. Stratigraphy is based upon the law of superposition, which states that a lower stratum (layer) is older than a higher stratum. Given the fact that much of the earth's crust has been laid down by layer after layer of sedimentary rock, like the layers of a cake, stratigraphy has been a valuable aid in reconstructing the history of earth and life on it.

Stratigraphic dating does, however, have a number of problems connected with it. Earth disturbances, such as volcanic activity, river activity, and mountain building, among others, may shift about strata of rock or the objects in them, and the chronology of the material may be difficult or even impossible to reconstruct. Furthermore, the time period of a particular stratum is not possible to determine with much accuracy.

Another method of relative dating is *fluorine analysis*, which applies only to bones (Oakley, 1963). Bones in the earth are exposed to the seepage of groundwater, usually containing fluorine. The longer bones lie in the earth, the more fluorine they incorporate during the fossilization process. Therefore, bones deposited at the same time in the same location should contain the same amount of fluorine. The use of this technique by Professor Oakley of the British Museum in the early 1950s exposed the Piltdown (England) hoax by demonstrating that the human skull was considerably older than the jaw found with it (Weiner, 1955). Lying in the same location, the jaw and skull should have absorbed approximately the same quantity of fluorine. But the skull contained significantly more than the jaw, which meant that it (the skull) had lain in the ground a good deal longer than the jaw. It was unlikely that the skull had met an untimely demise while the jaw lingered on for thousands of years. The discrepancy of fluorine content led Oakley and others to a closer examination of the bones, and they found that the jaw was not that of a hominid at all but of a young adult orangutan! (See p. 306.)

Unfortunately, fluorine is useful only with bones found at the same location. Because the amount of fluorine in groundwater is based upon the local river system and local conditions, it varies from place to place. Also, some groundwater may not contain any fluorine. For these reasons, comparing bones from different localities by fluorine analysis is impossible.

Chronometric
chrono: time
metric: measure
A dating technique that gives an estimate in actual numbers of years.

Stratigraphy
Sequential layering of deposits.

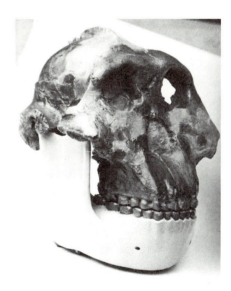

Figure 10-7 *Zinjanthropus* skull. Discovered by Mary Leakey at Olduvai Gorge in 1959. The skull and reconstructed jaw depicted here are casts at the National Museum of Kenya, Nairobi.

◇ GREAT MOMENTS IN PREHISTORY   Discovery of Zinjanthropus July 17, 1959

That morning I woke with a headache and a slight fever. Reluctantly I agreed to spend the day in camp.

With one of us out of commission, it was even more vital for the other to continue the work, for our precious seven-week season was running out. So Mary departed for the diggings with Sally and Toots [two of their dalmatians] in the Land-Rover, and I settled back to a restless day off.

Some time later—perhaps I dozed off—I heard the Land-Rover coming up fast to camp. I had a momentary vision of Mary stung by one of our hundreds of resident scorpions or bitten by a snake that had slipped past the dogs.

The Land-Rover rattled to a stop, and I heard Mary's voice calling over and over: "I've got him! I've got him! I've got him!"

Still groggy from the headache, I couldn't make her out.

"Got what? Are you hurt?" I asked.

"Him, the man! *Our* man," Mary said. "The one we've been looking for [for 23 years]. Come quick, I've found his teeth!"

Magically, the headache departed. I somehow fumbled into my work clothes while Mary waited.

As we bounced down the trail in the car, she described the dramatic moment of discovery. She had been searching the slope where I had found the first Oldowan tools in 1931, when suddenly her eye caught a piece of bone lodged in a rock slide. Instantly, she recognized it as part of a skull—almost certainly not that of an animal.

Her glance wandered higher, and there in the rock were two immense teeth, side by side. This time there was no question: They were undeniably human. Carefully, she marked the spot with a cairn of stones, rushed to the Land-Rover, and sped back to camp with the news.

The gorge trail ended half a mile from the site, and we left the car at a dead run. Mary led the way to the cairn, and we knelt to examine the treasure.

I saw at once that she was right. The teeth were premolars, and they had belonged to a human. I was sure they were larger than anything similar ever found, nearly twice the width of modern man's.

I turned to look at Mary, and we almost cried with sheer joy, each seized by that terrific emotion that comes rarely in life. After all our hoping and hardship and sacrifice, at last we had reached our goal—we had discovered the world's earliest known human.

From: "Finding the World's Earliest Man," by L.S.B. Leakey, *National Geographic Magazine*, 118:431, September 1960. Reprinted with permission of the publisher.

In both these methods—stratigraphy and fluorine analysis—the age of the rock stratum and the objects in it is difficult to calculate. To determine the absolute number of years of age, scientists have developed a variety of chronometric techniques based on the phenomenon of radioactive decay. The theory is quite simple: Certain radioactive isotopes of elements are unstable, disintegrate, and form an isotopic variation of another element. Since the rate of disintegration is assumed to be constant, the radioactive material forms an accurate geological time clock. By measuring the amount of disintegration in a particular sample, the number of years it took for the amount of decay is then known. Chronometric techniques have been used for dating the immense age of the earth as well as artifacts less than a thousand years old. Several techniques have been employed for a number of years and are now quite well known.

Uranium 238 (^{238}U) decays to form lead with a half-life of 4.5 billion years. That is, one-half of the original amount of ^{238}U is lost in 4.5 billion years and through various processes becomes lead. Therefore, if a chunk of rock is measured and one-half of the uranium has been converted to lead, the age of that piece of rock is 4.5 billion years. In another 4.5 billion years, half the remaining ^{238}U would have decayed. The isotope ^{238}U has proven a useful tool in dating the age of the formation of the earth.

Another chronometric technique involves potassium 40 (^{40}K)—which produces argon 40 (^{40}Ar)—with a half-life of 1.3 billion years. Known as the K/Ar, or potassium-argon method, this procedure has been extensively used by paleoanthropologists in dating materials in the 1 to 5 million year range, especially in East Africa. Organic material, such as bone, cannot be measured, but the rock matrix in which the bone is found can be. K/Ar was used to date the deposit containing the Zinjanthropus skull (it actually dated a volcanic layer above the fossil).

Rocks that provide the best samples for K/Ar are those rich in potassium and heated to an extremely high temperature, such as that generated by volcanic activity. When the rock is in a molten state, argon 40, a gas, is driven off. As the rock cools and solidifies, potassium (^{40}K) continues to break down to ^{40}Ar, but now the gas is physically trapped in the cooled rock. In order to obtain the date of the rock, it is reheated and the escaping gas measured. Potassium-argon has been used for dating very old events, such as the age of the earth, as well as those less than 100,000 years old (Dalrymple, 1972).

A well-known chronometric method popular with archeologists is carbon 14 (^{14}C), with a half-life of 5730 years. It has been used to date material from less than 1,000 years to as much as 75,000 years,* although the probability of error rises rapidly after 40,000 years. The ^{14}C technique is based upon the following natural processes: Cosmic radiation enters the earth's atmosphere, producing neutrons, which react with nitrogen to produce a radioactive isotope of carbon, ^{14}C. As the ^{14}C is diffused around the earth, with the earth's rotation, it mixes with carbon 12 and is absorbed by plants in their life processes. It is then transferred to herbivorous animals that feed on plants and to carnivores that feed on herbivores. Thus, ^{14}C and ^{12}C are found in all living forms at a fixed ratio. When an organism dies, it no longer absorbs ^{14}C, which then decays at a constant rate to ^{14}N (and a beta particle). It takes 5370 years for half the amount of ^{14}C to become ^{14}N.

Let us say that charcoal, the remains of a campfire, is found at an archeological site and measured for the ^{14}C/^{12}C proportions. Suppose the findings are that the proportion of the ^{14}C to ^{12}C shows only 25% of the original ^{14}C remaining. Since it takes 5730 years for half the ^{14}C atoms to become ^{14}N, and another 5730 years for half the remaining ^{14}C to become ^{14}N, the sample must be about 11,460 years old. Half the remaining ^{14}C will become ^{14}N in the next 5730 years, leaving 12.5% of the original amount. This process continues, and as you can see, there would be very little ^{14}C left after 40,000 years, when measuring becomes difficult.

Other absolute dating techniques that do not involve radioactive elements are *dendrochronology*, or dating by tree rings, especially developed for the American Southwest, and *varve chronology* (annual glacial deposit), particu-

---

*Grootes' studies (1978) suggest 75,000 years. A new technique using ^{14}C is being worked out at the University of California's Lawrence Berkeley Lab and at the University of Rochester. Scientists involved in the project believe it will extend the dating to 100,000 years (Thomsen, 1978). This technique using a cyclotron ("atom smasher") requires a much smaller sample—"as little as one thousandth of a gram"—than the conventional method and directly counts the number of ^{14}C atoms themselves.

Figure 10-8   Carbon-14 dating. Cosmic rays bombard the upper atmosphere, producing neutrons. When these collide with nitrogen, small amounts of ¹⁴C are produced. The ¹⁴C combines with oxygen to form carbon dioxide. The carbon dioxide containing ¹⁴C is absorbed by plants, and eventually animals feeding on the plants add ¹⁴C to their bodies. When the plant or animal dies, it ceases to absorb ¹⁴C and the ¹⁴C changes back to nitrogen at a regular rate.

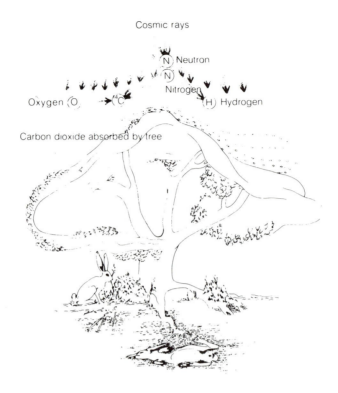

larly useful for the late Pleistocene and the post-Pleistocene in northern Europe. Although neither of the techniques has a direct bearing on dating early human fossils, they are both ingenious dating methods with important regional applications.

We should stress that none of these methods is precise, and that each method is beset with problems that must be carefully considered during laboratory measurement and in the collection of material to be measured. Because the methods are imprecise, approximate dates are given as probability statements with a plus or minus factor. For example, a date given as 1.75 ± .2 million years should be read as a 67% chance that the actual date lies somewhere between 1.55 and 1.95 million years.

There are, then, two ways in which the question of age may be answered. We can say that a particular fossil is *x* number of years old, a date determined usually either by K/Ar or ¹⁴C chronometric dating techniques. Or, we can say that fossil X lived before or after fossil Y, a relative dating technique.

DATING METHODS AT OLDUVAI

Olduvai has proven a rich and varied source for numerous dating techniques, and as a result it has some of the best-documented chronology for any hominid site in the Lower or Middle Pleistocene.

Potassium-argon dating had its birth as a paleoanthropological tool in the early 1960s with its application to the dating of the "Zinj" site at Olduvai. To everyone's amazement, including Louis Leakey's, the chronometric age was determined at more than 1.75 million years—more than twice the age depth previously assumed for the *whole* Pleistocene. As a result of this one monumental date (Leakey, et al., 1961), the entire history of the Pleistocene and our corresponding interpretations of hominid evolution had to be rewritten.

Potassium-argon (K/Ar) is an extremely valuable tool for dating early hominid sites and has been widely used in areas containing suitable volcanic deposits (mainly in East Africa). At Olduvai, K/Ar has given several reliable dates of the underlying basalt and several tuffs in Bed I, including the one associated with the "Zinj" find (now dated at $1.79 \pm .03$ m.y.a.). When dating relatively recent samples (from the perspective of a half-life of 1.3 billion years for K/Ar, *all* paleoanthropological material is relatively recent), the amount of radiogenic argon is going to be exceedingly small. Experimental errors in measurement can therefore occur as well as the thorny problem of distinguishing the atmospheric argon normally clinging to the outside of the sample from the radiogenic argon. In addition, the initial sample may have been contaminated or argon leakage may have occurred while it lay buried.

Due to the potential sources of error, K/Ar dating must be cross-checked using other independent methods. Once again, the sediments at Olduvai (particularly in Bed I) provide some of the best examples of the use of many of these other dating techniques.

Fission-track dating is one of the most important techniques for cross-checking K/Ar determinations. The key to fission-track dating is that ^{238}uranium (^{238}U) decays regularly by spontaneous fission so that, by counting the fraction of uranium atoms that have fissioned (shown as microscopic tracks caused by explosive fission of ^{238}U nuclei), we can ascertain the age of a mineral or natural glass sample (Fleischer and Hart, 1972). One of the earliest applications of this technique was on volcanic pumice from Bed I at Olduvai, giving a date of 2.30 ($\pm$ .28 m.y.a.)—in complete accord with K/Ar dates.

Another important means of cross-checking dates is called **paleomagnetism**. This technique is based on the constantly shifting nature of the earth's magnetic pole. Of course, as anyone knows, the earth's magnetic pole is now oriented in a northerly direction, but this situation has not always been so. In fact, the orientation and intensity of the geomagnetic field have undergone numerous documented changes in the last few million years. From our present ethnocentric point of view, we call a northern orientation "normal" and a southern one "reversed." Major epochs of geomagnetic time are:

    Normal
0.7 m.y.a.
    Reversed
2.5 m.y.a.
    Normal
3.4 m.y.a.
    Reversed
    '
    '
    '
    '
    ?

Paleomagnetism
Dating method based on shifting magnetic poles.

Figure 10-9 Paleomagnetic sequences. Correlated for major East African sites—Olduvai, East Turkana, Omo. (After Isaac, 1975.)

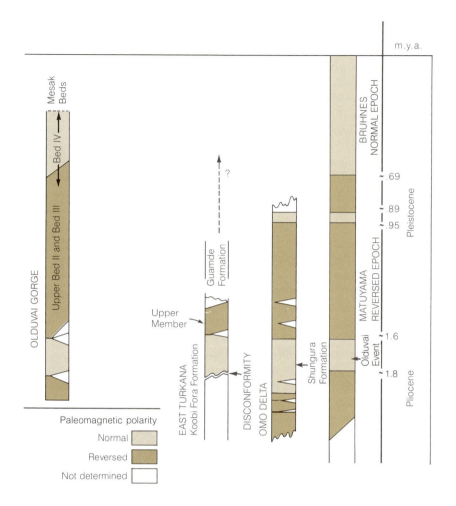

Figure 10-9 Paleomagnetic sequences. Correlated for major East African sites—Olduvai, East Turkana, Omo. (After Isaac, 1975.)

Paleomagnetic dating is accomplished by carefully taking samples of sediments that contain magnetically charged particles. Since these particles maintain the magnetic orientation they had when they were consolidated into rock (many thousands or millions of years ago), we have a kind of "fossil compass." Then the paleomagnetic *sequence* is compared against the K/Ar dates to check if they agree. Some complications can arise, for during an epoch a relatively long period of time can occur where the geomagnetic orientation is the opposite of what is expected. For example, during the reversed epoch between 2.5–1.7 m.y.a. (Matuyama Epoch) there was a time period called an *event*, lasting about 160,000 years, where orientations were normal. As this phenomenon was first conclusively demonstrated at Olduvai, it is appropriately called the *Olduvai Event*.

However, once these oscillations in the geomagnetic pole are well worked out, the sequence of paleomagnetic orientations can provide a valuable cross-check for K/Ar and fission-track age determinations.

A final dating technique employed in the Lower Pleistocene beds at Olduvai and other East African sites is based in the regular evolutionary changes in well-known groups of mammals. This technique, called faunal correlation or biostratigraphy, provides yet another means of cross-checking the other methods. Two groups of animals that have been widely used in biostratigraphical analysis in East Africa are fossil pigs (suids) and fossil elephants (proboscids). From areas where dates are known (by K/Ar, for instance) approximate ages can be extrapolated to other less well-known areas by noting which genera and species are present and by measuring specific evolutionary trends, such as length of the third molar in *Mesochoerus* (a giant fossil pig found at Olduvai and several other Plio-Pleistocene East African sites). In this well-documented evolutionary lineage, back teeth gradually become larger from earlier to later representatives.

All these methods, potassium-argon, fission-track, paleomagnetism, and biostratigraphy have been used in dating Beds I and II at Olduvai. So many different dating techniques are necessary because no single one is perfectly reliable by itself. Sampling error, contamination, and experimental errors can all introduce ambiguities into our so-called "absolute" dates. However, the

Biostratigraphy
Dating method based on evolutionary changes within an evolving lineage.

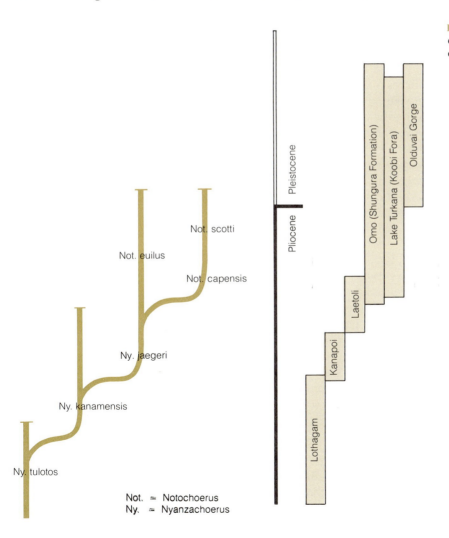

Figure 10-10 Partial biostratigraphic sequence of pigs. Used to correlate East African sites. (After White and Harris, 1977.)

Not. = Notochoerus
Ny. = Nyanzachoerus

Figure 10-11 Excavations in progress at Olduvai. This site is more than one million years old. It was located when a hominid ulna (armbone) was found eroding out of the side of the gorge.

Figure 10-11 Excavations in progress at Olduvai. This site is more than one million years old. It was located when a hominid ulna (armbone) was found eroding out of the side of the gorge.

sources of error are different for each technique, and therefore cross-checking between several independent methods is the most certain way of authenticating the chronology for early hominid sites.

We should mention that still other dating techniques have been used at Olduvai in the upper beds where different methods are applicable. [14]C dating has been employed to date a 17,000-year-old site in the upper part of the Gorge, and this date has been further corroborated by a relatively new dating method called *amino acid racemization* (based on regularly shifting optical properties of amino acids). (See also Chapter 17.)

◇ Excavations at Olduvai

Because the vertical cut of the Olduvai Gorge provides a ready cross-section of 2 million years of earth history, sites can be excavated by digging "straight-in" rather than finding them by having first to remove tons of overlying dirt. In fact, sites are usually discovered by merely walking the exposures and observing what bones, stones, etc. are eroding out.

Several dozen hominid sites (at a minimum, they are bone and tool scatters) have been surveyed at Olduvai, and Mary Leakey has extensively excavated close to twenty of these. An incredible amount of paleoanthropological information has come from these excavated areas, data which can be generally grouped into three broad categories depending on implied function:

1. *Butchering sites*. Areas containing one or only a few individuals of a single species of large mammal associated with a scatter of archeological traces. An elephant butchering site and another containing a *Deinotherium* (a

large extinct relative of the elephant) have been found at levels approximately 1.7 m.y.a. Both sites contain only a single animal, and it is impossible to ascertain whether the hominids actually killed these animals or exploited them (presumably for meat resources) after they were already dead. A third butchering site dated at approximately 1.2 m.y.a. shows much more consistent and efficient hunting of large mammals by this time. Remains of 24 *Pelorovis* (a giant extinct relative of the buffalo, with horn spans more than ten feet across!), have been found here, and Louis Leakey suggested they were driven into a swamp by a band of hominids and then systematically slaughtered (Leakey, 1971).

2. *Quarry sites*. Areas where early hominids extracted their stone resources and initially fashioned their tools. At such sites, thousands of small stone fragments are found of only one type of rock usually associated with no or very little bone refuse. At Olduvai, a 1.6 m.y.–1.7 m.y. old area was apparently a chert factory site, where hominids came repeatedly to quarry this material.

3. *Living sites*. Also called campsites. General purpose areas where hominids ate, slept, and put the finishing touches on their tools. The accumulation of living debris, including broken bones of many animals of several different species and many broken stones (some complete tools, some waste flakes) is a basic human pattern. As the late Glynn Isaac, probably the foremost prehistoric archeologist who has worked in Africa, noted, "The fact that discarded artifacts tend to be concentrated in restricted areas is itself highly suggestive. It seems likely that such patches of material reflect the

Figure 10-12 A living floor at Olduvai. From a site approximately 1.6 m.y.a.

◇ Box 10-1   Are the Sites at Olduvai Really "Sites"?

The generally agreed-upon interpretation of the bone refuse and stone tools discovered at Olduvai has been that
most, if not all, of these materials are the result of hominid activities. Recently, however, a comprehensive reanalysis of the bone remains from Olduvai localities has
challenged this view (Binford, 1981; 1983). Archeologist
Lewis Binford criticizes those drawn too quickly to the
conclusion that these bone scatters are the remnants of
hominid behavior patterns while simultaneously ignoring
the possibility of other explanations. For example, he
forcefully states:

> All the facts gleaned from the deposits interpreted as
> living sites have served as the basis for making up
> "just-so stories" about our hominid past. No attention
> has been given to the possibility that many of the facts
> may well be referable to the behavior of nonhominids
> (Binford, 1981, p. 251).

From specifics concerning the kinds of animals present, which body parts were found, and the differences in
preservation among these skeletal elements, Binford concluded that much of what is preserved could be explained by carnivore activity. This conclusion was
reinforced by certain details observed by Binford himself
in Alaska—details on animal kills, scavenging, the transportation of elements, and preservation as the result of
wolf and dog behaviors. Binford describes his approach
thus:

*I took as "known," then, the structure of bone assem-
blages produced in various settings by animal predators and scavengers; and as "unknown" the bone
deposits excavated by the Leakeys at Olduvai Gorge. Using mathematical and statistical techniques I considered to what degree the finds from Olduvai Gorge
could be accounted for in terms of the results of predator behavior and how much was "left over" (Binford,
1983, pp. 56–57).*

In using this uniquely explicit approach, Binford arrived at quite different conclusions than those previously
suggested by other archeologists:

*For instance, the very idea of a site or living floor as-
sumes conditions in the past for which there is no
demonstration. In fact, it assumes the very "knowledge" we would like to obtain from the archeological
remains. Site and living floor identifications presup-
pose that concentrations and aggregations of archeological and other materials are only produced by man.
Are there not other conditions of deposition that could
result in aggregations of considerable density found on
old land surfaces? The answer must be a resounding
yes.*

And, later, he concludes:

*It seems to me that one major conclusion is justified
from the foregoing analysis: The large, highly publi-*

organization of movement around a camp or home base, with recurrent
dispersal and reuniting of the group at the chosen locality. Among living
primates this pattern in its full expression is distinctive of man. The
coincidence of bone and food refuse with the artifacts strongly implies
that meat was carried back—presumably for sharing" (Isaac, 1976, pp. 27–
28). (See Box 10-1 for a different interpretation.)

Several campsites have been excavated at Olduvai, including one that is
over 1.8 m.y. old (DK 1—see Box 10-2). This site has a circle of large stones
forming what may have been the base for a windbreak or, as Mary Leakey,
who dug the site, has suggested, may have been the foundation for a primitive
structure. Without the meticulous excavation and recording of modern archeological techniques, the presence of such an archeological feature would
never have been recognized. This point requires further emphasis. Many

cized sites as currently analyzed carry little specific information about hominid behavior . . . arguments about base camps, hominid hunting, sharing of food, and so forth are certainly premature and most likely wildly inaccurate (Binford, 1981, pp. 281–282).

Binford is not arguing that *all* of the remains found at Olduvai have resulted from nonhominid activity. In fact, he recognized that "residual material" was consistently found on surfaces with high tool concentrations "which could *not* be explained by what we know about African animals" (Binford, 1983).

Support for the idea that at least some of the bone refuse was utilized by early hominids has come from a totally different tact. Recently, researchers have analyzed (both macroscopically and microscopically) the cutmarks left on fossilized bones. By experimenting with modern materials, they have further been able to delineate clearly the differences between marks left by stone tools as opposed to those left by animal teeth (or other factors) (Bunn, 1981; Potts and Shipman, 1981). Analysis of bones from several early localities at Olduvai showed unambiguously that these specimens were utilized by hominids, who left telltale cutmarks from stonetool usage. The sites thus far investigated reveal a somewhat haphazard cutting and chopping, apparently unrelated to deliberate disarticulation. It has thus been concluded (Shipman, 1983) that hominids scavenged carcasses

(probably of carnivore kills) and did *not* hunt large animals themselves. Materials found at later sites (postdating 1 m.y.a.), on the other hand, do show deliberate disarticulation, indicating a more systematic hunting pattern, with presumably meat transport and food-sharing as well (Shipman, 1983).

If early hominids (close to 2 m.y.a.) were not hunting consistently, what did they obtain from scavenging the kills of other animals? One obvious answer is, whatever meat was left behind. However, the positioning of the cutmarks suggests that early hominids were often hacking at nonmeat-bearing portions of the skeletons. Perhaps they were simply after bone marrow, a substance not really being exploited by other predators (Binford, 1981).

The picture that emerges, then, of what hominids were doing at Olduvai around 1.8 m.y.a. hardly suggests consistent big game hunting. In Binford's words:

. . . this is evidence of man eating a little bit of bone marrow, a food source that must have represented an infinitesimally small component of his total diet. The signs seem clear. Earliest man, far from appearing as a mighty hunter of beasts, seems to have been the most marginal of scavengers (Binford, 1983, p. 59).

people assume archeologists derive their information simply from analysis of objects (stone tools, gold statues, or whatever). However, it is the **context** and **association** of objects (that is, precisely where the objects are found and what is found associated with them) that give the archeologist the data required to understand the behavioral patterns of ancient human populations. Once pot hunters or looters pilfer a site, proper archeological interpretation is never again possible.

Other living sites at Olduvai include the large occupation area at the "Zinj" site (FLK = 1.75 m.y.a.) and a very thin (perhaps occupied just a few days) **living floor** (HWK East = 1.7 m.y.a.). Preservation of occupational debris along one relatively narrow horizon is what is meant by a living floor, and the extraordinary conditions at Olduvai have preserved many of the bones and stones almost exactly as the hominids left them more than 1 m.y.a.

Another kind of living site is MNK (Lower Middle Bed II = 1.6 m.y.a.) where

Context
The environmental setting where an archeological trace is found.

Association
What an archeological trace is found with.

Living floor
A narrow horizon of archeological remains; corresponds to brief period of occupation.

◇ Box 10-2   Olduvai Site Names

The naming of sites at Olduvai is a marvelous wonder concocted from fascinating combinations of the English alphabet. Sites are designated with such shorthand abbreviations as FLK, MNK, LLK, etc. The K stands for Korongo, Swahili for gully (Olduvai is made up of dozens of side gullies). The first initial(s) is usually, though not always, that of the individual who made an important discovery at that locality. For example, FLK stands for Frida Leakey Korongo (Louis' first wife), MNK is Mary Nicol Korongo (Mary Leakey's maiden name), and LLK is Louis Leakey Korongo (where Louis found a hominid cranium in 1961). When more than one site is found in the same gully, those discovered later are given directional orientations relative to the initial site. For example, FLK is the main site name where "Zinj" was found in 1959. FLK N (that is, 'FLK North," where the elephant and *Deinotherium* butchering sites occur at slightly different levels) is just north of the main site, and FLK NN ("FLK North North," the location of yet another important hominid discovery) is just a bit farther north up the gully.

occupational debris is scattered through more than six feet of earth, suggesting hominids periodically reoccupied this area—perhaps seasonally.

The detailed excavations of all these different hominid occupation areas are of tremendous importance, since the dispersal pattern of the remains of ancient human behavior can yield great insight into the biocultural evolution of humankind.

ARTIFACTS

While context, association, and ecological information are of paramount interest to the prehistoric archeologist, detailed analysis of the stone artifacts themselves can yield much additional information about the behavior of early hominids. Mary Leakey has been the pioneer in the study of Plio-Pleistocene African artifacts, and her classification system and description of some of the artifacts found at Olduvai are discussed in Box 10-3.

◇ Experimental Archeology

Classifying artifacts into categories and types is scientifically insufficient. We can learn considerably more about our ancestors by understanding how they made and used their tools. It is, after all, the artifactual traces of prehistoric tools of stone (and to a lesser degree, bone) that comprise our primary information concerning early human behavior. Millions of tons of stone debris litter archeological sites worldwide. A casual walk along the bottom of Olduvai Gorge will be interrupted every few seconds by prehistoric tools that could be easily tripped over!

Archeologists are thus presented with a wealth of information revealing at least *one* part of human material culture. What do these artifacts tell us about our ancestors? How were these tools made? In which ways were they used? To answer these questions contemporary archeologists have attempted to reconstruct prehistoric techniques of stone toolmaking, butchering, and so forth. In this way, experimental archeologists are, in a sense, trying to recreate the past.

STONE TOOL (LITHIC) TECHNOLOGY

Since stone is by far the most common residue of prehistoric cultural behavior, archeologists have long been keenly interested in this material.

When struck properly, certain types of stone will fracture in a controlled way. The smaller piece struck off is called a **flake**, while the larger remaining chunk is called a **core**. The obvious useful result is that both core and flake now possess sharp edges useful for cutting, sawing, or scraping. The earliest hominid cultural inventions probably employed nondurable materials that did not survive archeologically (such as a digging stick or an ostrich egg shell used as a watertight container). Still, a basic human invention was the recognition that stone can be fractured to produce sharp edges. In fact, the earliest stone tools (over 2 m.y.a.) show that both flake and core implements were already being fashioned.

Breaking rocks by bashing them together is one thing. Producing consistent results is quite another. It takes years of practice before stone **knappers** learn the intricacies of the type of rock to choose, the kind of hammer to employ, the angle and velocity with which to strike, etc. Such experience allows us to appreciate how skilled in stoneworking our ancestors truly were.

Flakes can be removed from cores in a great variety of ways. The object in making a tool, however, is to produce a usable surface. By reproducing results similar to those of earlier stoneworkers, experimental archeologists can infer which kinds of techniques *might* have been employed.

For example, the choppers found in sites in Beds I and II at Olduvai (*circa* 1.85–1.2 m.y.a.) are flaked on one side only (that is, unifacially). It is possible, although by no means easy, to produce such implements by hitting one stone—the hammerstone—against another—the core—in a method called **direct percussion** (see Fig. 10-14).

In Bed IV sites (*circa* 400,000 y.a.), however, the majority of tools are flaked on both sides (that is, bifacially) and have long sinuous edges. Such a result cannot be reproduced by direct percussion with just a hammerstone. The edges must have been straightened ("retouched") with a "soft" hammer, such as bone or antler.

In order to reproduce implements similar to those found in later stages of human cultural development, even more sophisticated techniques are required. Tools such as the delicate **microliths** found in the uppermost beds at Olduvai (*circa* 17,000 y.a.), the superb Solutrean blades from Europe (*circa* 20,000 y.a.), and the expertly crafted Folsom projectile points from the New World (*circa* 10,000 y.a.) all require a mastery of stone matched by few, if any, knappers today.

Reproducing implements such as those mentioned above requires removal

Lithic
lith: stone

Flake
Thin-edged fragment removed from a core.

Core
Stone reduced by flake removal.

Knapping
Flaking stone tools.

Direct percussion
Striking core or flake with a hammerstone.

Microliths
Small stone tools usually produced from narrow blades punched from a core. Found especially in Africa during the latter part of the Pleistocene.

Core   Flake

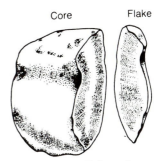

Figure 10-13   Flake and core.

Figure 10-14   Direct percussion.

Figure 10-15   Pressure flaking.

◇ Box 10-3   Classification of Artifacts

Stone artifacts, depending on context, shape, flake scars, and inferred function, fall into four broad categories:

1. *Manuports.* Rocks that are not modified but are found out of their natural context; that is, rocks that have been manually carried, a definite hominid behavior. The stone circle at DK I perhaps consisted of manuports, and much of the occupational debris at MNK is made up of unmodified manuports. Their functions remain unknown.

2. *Utilized material.* Stones used to modify other stones but not used as tools themselves. Under this category, Mary Leakey includes hammerstones and anvils.

3. *Debitage.* Very small flakes, either waste material struck off while making tools or perhaps used themselves as very small cutting implements.

4. *Tools.* A broad category of intentionally modified stones that have been shaped according to a preset, consistent pattern. Mary Leakey classifies the stone tools found at Olduvai primarily on the basis of shape and size. As yet no definite conclusions on their functions have been reached. Tools are thus classed as spheroids, discoids, polyhedrons, bifaces, etc. Occasionally, function is inferred with such terms as chopper, scraper, burin, and awl.

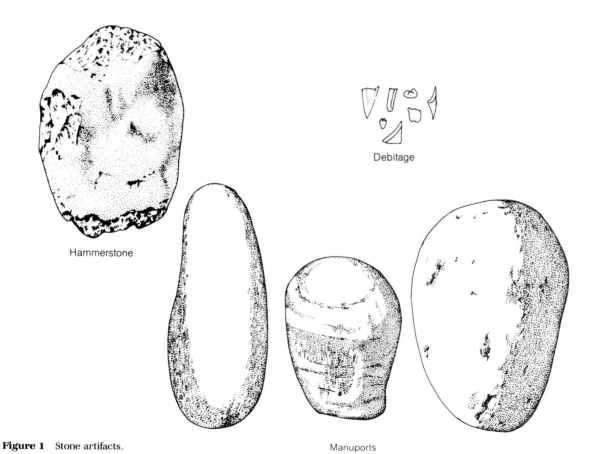

Debitage

Hammerstone

Manuports

Figure 1   Stone artifacts.

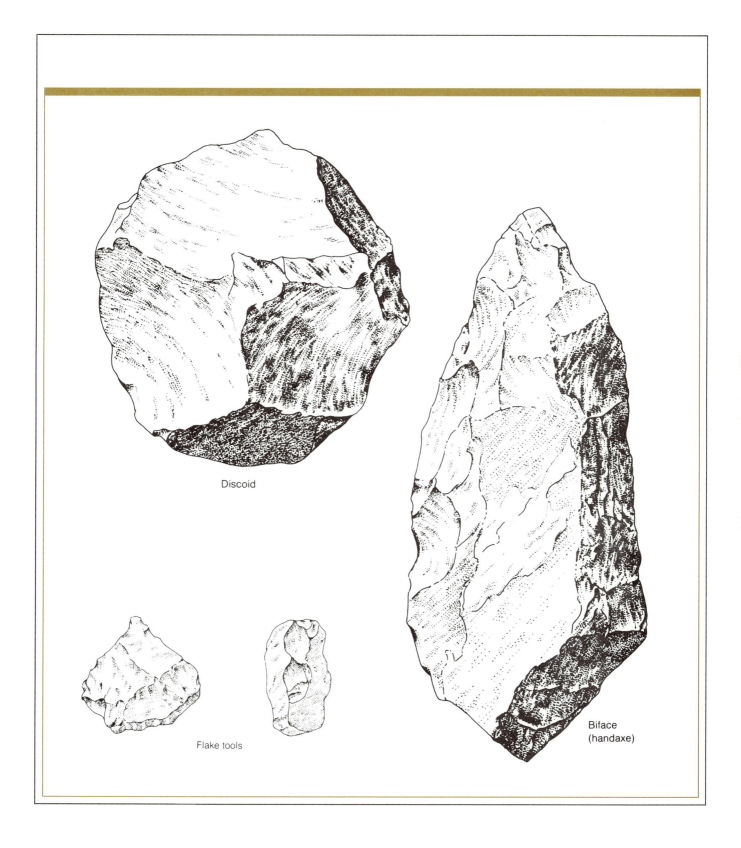

Discoid

Flake tools

Biface
(handaxe)

Pressure flaking
A method of removing flakes from a core by pressing a pointed implement (e.g., bone or antler) against the stone.

Microwear
Polishes, striations, and other diagnostic microscopic changes on the edges of stone tools produced during use.

Phytolith
Microscopic silica structures formed in the cells of many plants, particularly grasses.

Figure 10-16 Microwear: The polish left on an experimental flint implement by scraping wood for ten minutes. Bright, smooth areas are the microwear polish; dark, grainy areas are the unworn flint surface. Arrows indicate implement edge. (Magnification, 200×)

of extremely thin flakes, possible only through **pressure flaking**—for example, using a pointed piece of bone, antler, or hard wood and pressing firmly against the stone (see Fig. 10-15).

Once the tools were manufactured, the ways our ancestors used them can be inferred through further experimentation. For example, archeologists from the Smithsonian Institution successfully butchered an entire elephant (which had died in a zoo) using stone tools they had made for that purpose (Park, 1978). Others have cut down trees using stone axes they had made.

Ancient tools themselves may carry tell-tale signs of how they were used. Lawrence Keeley, in his graduate work at Oxford University, performed a series of experiments in which he manufactured flint tools and then used them in diverse ways—whittling wood, cutting bone, cutting meat, and scraping skins (Keeley, 1980). The implements were next viewed under a microscope at fairly high magnification to reveal patterns of polishes, striations, and other kinds of **microwear**. What is most intriguing is that these patterns vary depending on how the implement was used and which material was worked. For example, Keeley was able to distinguish among implements used on bone, antler, meat, plant materials, or hides. In the latter case, he was even able to determine if the hides were fresh or dried! In addition, orientations of microwear markings are also indicative of the way in which the tool was used (e.g., for cutting or scraping). Evidences of microwear poliish have been examined on even the extremely early hominid stone tools from Koobi Fora (East Lake Turkana) Kenya (Keeley and Toth, 1981).

Recent advances in tool-use studies include the application of scanning electron microscopy (SEM). Working at 10,000 × magnification, researchers have found that the working edges of stone implements sometimes retain vegetal fibers and amino acids, as well as nonorganic residues, including **phytoliths**. Because phytoliths produced by different plant species are morphologically distinctive, there is good potential for identifying the botanical materials that came in contact with the tool during use (Vaughan, 1985; Rovner, 1983). Such work is most exciting, since for the first time we may be able to make definite statements concerning the uses of ancient tools.

ANALYSIS OF BONE

Experimental archeologists are also interested in the ways bone is altered by human and natural forces. We saw previously how ethnoarcheologists are able to trace the events that lead from human use of animal resources to archeological deposition of bony material.

Other scientists are also vitally concerned with this process; in fact, an entire new branch of paleoecology—taphonomy—has emerged (see p. 273). In recent years taphonomists have carried out comprehensive research on how natural factors influence bone deposition and preservation. In South Africa, C. K. Brain has collected data on Hottentot butchering practices, carnivore (dog) disturbances, and so forth, and has correlated these factors with the kinds and numbers of elements usually found in bone accumulations (Brain, 1981). In this way, he has been able to account for the accumulation of most (if not all) of the bones in South African cave sites. Likewise, in East African game parks, observations have been made on decaying animals to measure the effects of weathering, predator chewing, and trampling (Behrensmeyer et al., 1979).

Further insight into the many ways bone is altered by natural factors has come from experimental work in the laboratory by N. T. Boaz and A. K. Behrensmeyer (1976). In an experiment conducted at the University of California, Berkeley, human bones were put into a running-water trough. Researchers observed how far different pieces were transported and how much damage was done. Application of such information is extremely useful in interpreting early hominid sites. For example, the distribution of hominid fossils at Olduvai suggests that less active water transport was prevalent there than in the Omo River Valley.

Detailed examination of bones may also provide evidence of butchering by hominids, including cutmarks left by stone tools. Great care must be taken to distinguish scars left on bone by carnivore or rodent gnawing, weathering processes, or even normal growth. High magnification of a cut made by a stone tool may reveal a minutely striated and roughened groove scored into the bone's surface. Many such finds have been recognized at early hominid sites, including Olduvai Gorge (Potts and Shipman, 1981). (See p. 293.)

RECONSTRUCTING BEHAVIOR FROM GARBAGE

Since most of what we find littering archeological sites is the debris of earlier societies, an understanding of the ways behavior may be indicated via study of material refuse is essential. Since 1972 a major study of exactly this nature has been carried out in Tucson by William Rathje of the University of Arizona (Rathje and McCarthy, 1977). Rathje maintains that, by demonstrating the archeologist's ability to learn something about our present culture through the study of modern refuse, his project has helped to reinforce the claim that the past can be revealed through archeology (Rathje, 1979).

Over a three-year period more than 1,000 households were sampled and more than 70,000 items were collected, weighed, and classified into 200 categories of food and other household goods. In addition, census data were used to select representative samples in order to correlate information about garbage with family size, income, and ethnicity.

The project has encouraged some rethinking about the assumed relationships between artifacts and the people and cultures who produce, use, and discard them. In the Tucson study, for instance, the correlations between demographic factors and discard behavior were not always the expected ones. Evidence from garbage provided substantially different (and, no doubt, more accurate) information concerning alcohol consumption than people admitted in questionnaire surveys. Moreover, since the data have been carefully sampled and quantified, we can get a far better idea of exactly how many usable items are thrown away. The middle-class households in the survey accounted for a higher percentage of wasted food (nearly 10% of the food purchased) than either the poor or the wealthy. But such patterns did not extend to nonfood waste. Despite the popular image of Americans as "conspicuous consumers," the archeologists encountered few usable household items in garbage or trash dumps. There seemed to be a widespread practice of recycling furniture and appliances through yard sales and charities. Higher-

(a) Knapper, Alan Leventhal, starts with hammerstone and nodule of obsidian.

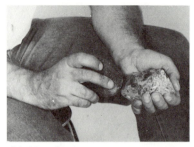

(b) Manufacturing technique: hard hammer direct percussion—applied force on striking platform.

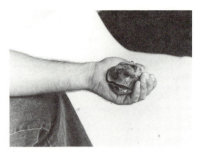

(c) Removal of a large primary flake.

(d) Ventral side of flake (removed above) and striking platform for removal of next flake.

(e) Removal of second large flake (to be used as primary flake blank).

(f) Platform preparation on primary flake blank.

(g) Manufacturing technique: soft hammer percussion. Bifacial shaping and thinning.

(h) Removal of thinning flake.

(i) Further straightening of edge by soft hammer percussion.

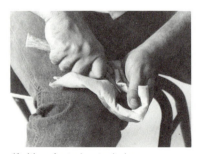

(j) Manufacturing technique: pressure flaking with sharpened antler tip.

(k) Removal of pressure flakes for final straightening and sharpening of edge.

(l) Finished product. A bifacial knife.

Figure 10-17 Stone tool technology. Reduction sequences of an obsidian core to a finished product.

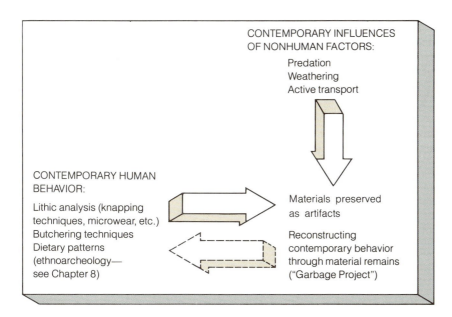

income households tended to replace items at a somewhat higher rate, thus replenishing the supply of goods entering the system (Schiffer, Downing, and McCarthy, 1981).

◇ Diet of Early Hominids

Paleoanthropological research is concerned with more than the recovery and recording of bones and artifacts. What we are trying to obtain is a reconstruction of the kind of animal our ancestor was. Paleoanthropology must therefore be centrally concerned with interpretation of the behavioral patterns of early hominid populations.

One of the most important questions we would like to answer about early hominid behavior is: What did they eat? Scattered broken bone debris associated with artifacts *may* provide direct evidence concerning one important aspect of early human dietary behavior. However, we must not forget that modern analogs like the San of South Africa clearly show us that vegetable foods, which usually leave little trace in the archeological record, probably made up a large part (even a majority) of the caloric intake of early hominids. As Glynn Isaac noted, reconstructing dietary behavior is like navigating around an iceberg—four-fifths of what is of interest is not visible (Isaac, 1971, p. 280).

Postulated diets available to hominids 1–2 m.y.a. with use of only a simple digging stick as a tool include: berries, fruits, nuts, buds, shoots, shallow-growing roots and tubers, most terrestrial and smaller aquatic reptiles, eggs and nesting birds, some fish, molluscs, insects, and all smaller mammals (Bartholomew and Birdsell, 1953).

Olduvai has shown that the range of postulated meat resources was indeed exploited in Beds I and II (1.85–1.0 m.y.a.). Fossils of turtles, rodents, fish, birds, pigs, horses, and small antelopes are all fairly common at many Olduvai sites. Of course, exactly how much of these remains were eaten—as opposed to having just "dropped dead" there or having been preyed upon by other animals—is still undetermined (see Box 10-1). Evidence for fish eating has also come from a comparably aged site in southern Ethiopia (the Omo), where fish bones have been found in human coprolites (fossilized feces).

Moreover, as the elephant and *Deinotherium* butchering sites indicate, occasional exploitation of large mammals also occurred more than 1.5 m.y.a. By 1 m.y.a., systematic hunting of large mammals apparently provided important meat resources, as shown by the *Pelorovis* butchering site.

Thanks to the extraordinary dedication of Louis and Mary Leakey, just one relatively small area of northern Tanzania has provided a continuous record of the development of hominids and their behavior for almost 2 million years. Without Olduvai we would know much less than we do about the emergence of human culture prior to 1 m.y.a.

◇ Summary

The biocultural nature of human evolution requires that any meaningful study of human origins examine both biological and cultural information. The multidisciplinary approach of paleoanthropology is designed to bring together varied scientific specializations in order to reconstruct the anatomy, behavior, and environments of early hominids. Such a task is centered around the skills of the geologist, paleontologist, paleoecologist, archeologist, and physical anthropologist.

Much of what we know about the origins of human culture between 1 and 2 m.y.a. comes from archeological excavations by Mary Leakey at Olduvai Gorge in East Africa. Olduvai's well-documented stratigraphic sequence, its superior preservation of remains (often as living floors), and the varied dating techniques possible there have made it an information bonanza for paleoanthropologists. Excavated sites have yielded a wealth of bones of fossil animals, as well as artifact traces of hominid behavior. Ecological reconstructions of habitat and dietary preferences are thereby possible and inform us in great detail concerning crucial evolutionary processes affecting early hominid populations.

Archeologists are better able to interpret the "bones and stones" of earlier populations through experimentation. In recent years much new light has been shed on the techniques of making stone tools as well as the factors affecting preservation of bone. In addition, anthropologists are using archeological techniques to help illuminate our understanding of contemporary behavior through systematic analysis of garbage.

In the next three chapters, we will survey the fossil hominid evidence in South and East Africa that inform us directly about human origins during the Plio-Pleistocene.

◇ Questions for Review

1. Why are cultural remains so important in the interpretation of human evolution?
2. How are early hominid sites found, and what kind of specialist is involved in the excavation and analysis of paleoanthropological data?
3. What kinds of paleoanthropological information have been found at Olduvai Gorge? Why is this particular locality so rich in material?
4. What kinds of dating techniques have been used to date early hominid sites at Olduvai? Why is more than one technique necessary for accurate dating?
5. Why are context and association so important in the interpretation of archeological remains?
6. What different activities can be inferred from the different kinds of sites at Olduvai? Discuss alternative views in the interpretation of these "sites."
7. How do archeologists determine the functions of ancient stone tools?
8. How do archeological techniques contribute to understanding contemporary behavior?
9. How do we infer what early hominids were eating? Give a brief list of the kinds of food that were probably exploited.

Plio-Pleistocene Hominids: South Africa

CONTENTS

When first announed to the world in 1912, *Eoanthropus dawsoni* ("Dawson's Dawn Man") created an anthropological sensation. Found during 1911 in Sussex in the south of England by Charles Dawson, a lawyer and amateur geologist/antiquarian, this "fossil" was to confuse, bewilder, and befuddle two generations of anthropologists. "Piltdown man," as he popularly came to be called, was comprised of a fragmented skull and parts of a lower jaw. The enigma of the fossil from the very beginning was the combination of a large *sapiens*-like skull (initially estimated at 1,070 cm³, but later shown to be more like 1,400 cm³) with an apelike lower jaw.

Most tantalizing of all, Piltdown was apparently extremely ancient, associated with long extinct fauna, such as mastodon, hippo, and rhino, all suggesting a date of early Pleistocene. A puzzling feature was the presence of these early fossils mixed in with clearly late Pleistocene fauna. The prevailing consensus, however, was that Piltdown was indeed ancient, "the earliest known representative of man in Western Europe."

Despite its seeming incongruities, Piltdown was eagerly accepted by British scientists, including Keith, Elliot Smith, and Smith Woodward (all later knighted). What made the fossil such a delectable treat was that it confirmed just what had been expected, a combination of *modern* ape and *modern* human characteristics— a true "missing link." We, of course, now know that no ancestral fossil form is a fifty-fifty compromise between modern ones, but represents its own unique adaptation. In addition to mistaken enthusiasm for a missing link, the fossil also represented a "true" man as opposed to the obviously primitive beasts (Java

Figure 1   The Piltdown skull.

man, Neandertals) found elsewhere. Such a fervently biased desire to find an "ancient modern" in the human lineage has obscured evolutionary studies for decades and still causes confusion in some circles.

While generally accepted in England, experts in France, Germany, and the United States felt uneasy about Piltdown. Many critics, however, were silenced when a second fragmentary find came to light in 1917 (actually found in 1915) in an area two miles away from the original site. The matter stood in limbo for years, with some scientists as enthusiastic supporters of the Piltdown man and others remaining uneasy doubters. The uneasiness continued to fester as more hominid material accumulated in Java, China, and particularly the australopithecines in South Africa. None of these hominids showed the peculiar combination of a human cranium with an apelike jaw seen in Piltdown, but actually indicated the reverse pattern.

The final proof of the true nature of the Dawn Man came in the early 1950s, when British scientists began an intensive reexamination of the Piltdown material. In particular, fluorine analysis (see Chapter 10), performed by Kenneth Oakley showed both the skull and jaw were relatively

recent. Later, more extensive tests showed the jaw to be younger than the skull and *very* recent in date. Now a much more critical eye was turned to all the material. The teeth, looking initially as though they had been worn down flat in the typical hominid fashion, were apparently ape teeth filed down deliberately to give that impression. The mixed bag of fauna was apparently acquired from all manner of places (a fossil elephant came from Tunisia in North Africa!), and the jaw was deliberately stained with chromate to match the older fossils in color. Finally, some "tools" found at Piltdown also met the hand of a forger for the bone implements showed modifications that apparently could only have been made by a metal knife.

The "fossil" itself was probably purchased from local dealers. The skull probably came from a moderately ancient grave (a few thousand years old), and the jaw was a specially broken, filed, and stained mandible of a fairly recently deceased adolescent orang! The evidence was indisputable: a deliberate hoax. But who did it?

Just about everyone connected with the "crime" has, at one time or another, been implicated—beginning with Piltdown's discoverer: Charles Dawson. Yet, Dawson was an amateur; and, thus, may have lacked the expertise to carry out the admittedly crafty job of anatomical modification.

In addition, at various times, suspicions have been cast towards neuroanatomist Sir Grafton Elliot Smith, geologist W. J. Sollas, and French philosopher/archaeologist Father Pierre Teilhard de Chardin. Still, for none of these people has a conclusive case been made.

Recently, however, another intriguing possibility has been raised:

Figure 2 The Piltdown committee. The individuals central to the "discovery" and interpretation of the Piltdown "fossil." Back row, standing, left to right: Mr. F. O. Barlow (maker of the casts), Prof. G. Elliot Smith (anatomist), Mr. C. Dawson ("discoverer"), Dr. A. Smith Woodward (zoologist). Front row, seated: Dr. A. S. Underwood (dental expert), Prof. A. Keith (anatomist), Mr. W. P. Pycraft (zoologist), Sir Ray Lankester (zoologist). From the painting by John Cook.

. . . there was another interested figure who haunted the Piltdown site during excavation, a doctor who knew human anatomy and chemistry, someone interested in geology and archeology, and an avid collector of fossils. He was a man who loved hoaxes, adventure and danger; a writer gifted at manipulating complex plots; and perhaps most important of all, one who bore a grudge against the British science establishment. He was none other than the creator of Sherlock Holmes, Sir Arthur Conan Doyle (Winslow and Meyer, 1983, p. 34).

Doyle, as a medical doctor, certainly possessed the anatomical knowhow to craft the forgery. His other avocations—chemistry, geology, and especially, anthropology—would have been useful to him, *if* he were the forger.

In a remarkable piece of detective work (worthy of the master sleuth Sherlock Holmes himself), John Winslow has assembled a convincing array of *circumstantial* evidence against Doyle. Doyle, first of all, is the only suspect that can be shown to have had ready access to all the elements of the forgery. He was friendly with collectors or dealers who easily could have provided him with the cranium, the orang jaw, and the stone tools. As far as the animal fossils are concerned, Doyle also could have acquired many of the local (English) fossils from collector friends, but some of the odd bits obviously are from elsewhere (most likely, Malta and Tunisia). And, interestingly enough, Doyle had traveled to Malta a few years before Piltdown came to light, and may have been in Tunisia as well. At the very least, he was closely acquainted with people who had been to this part of North Africa.

But what of motive? As rich and as successful a figure as Doyle would seem an unlikely candidate for such a ruse. Winslow, however, has also found some clues that suggest Sir Arthur *may* indeed have had a motive.

Doyle was a longtime spiritualist who believed firmly in the occult and in extrasensory powers. He bore little patience with scientific critics of such views, whom he regarded as closed-minded. In particular, he had a special rival, Edward Ray Lankester, one of the most renowned evolutionists of the early twentieth century. Perhaps, as Winslow speculates, Doyle invented the whole scheme as farce to embarrass the scientific establishment and, most especially, Lankester.

"So the case against Doyle is made. Besides the necessary skill, contacts, knowledge, and opportunity to qualify as the hoaxer, Doyle also had sufficient motive and an inviting target, Lankester" (Winslow and Meyer, 1983, p. 42).

Fascinating as it all is, we may never know whether the creator of Sherlock Holmes was also the Piltdown forger. Seventy years after the crime, the trail has grown stone cold—the forger covered his tracks very well indeed!

SOURCES:

Weiner, J. W., *The Piltdown Forgery*, London: Oxford University Press, 1955.

Winslow, John Hathaway and Alfred Meyer, "The Perpetrator at Piltdown," *Science '83*, September, 1983, pp. 33–43.

◇ Introduction

We have seen in the last two chapters that hominids can be defined on the basis of dental adaptations and/or toolmaking behavior. In this chapter, we will review a series of remarkable discoveries in South Africa that persuaded paleoanthropologists to radically reassess their theories on human evolution.

◇ Early Hominids in the Plio-Pleistocene

The beginnings of hominid differentiation almost certainly have their roots in the late Miocene (*circa* 5–10 m.y.a.). Sometime during the period between 8 and 4 m.y.a., hominids began to adapt more fully to their peculiar ground living niche, and evolutionary evidence from this period would be most illuminating. However, scant information is presently available concerning the course of hominid evolution during this significant 4-million-year gap. But beginning around 4 m.y.a., the fossil record picks up considerably. We now have a wealth of fossil hominid material from the Pliocene and the earliest stages of the Pleistocene (5–1 m.y.a.), and this whole span is usually referred to as the Plio-Pleistocene.

◇ Earliest Discoveries

The first quarter of this century saw the discipline of paleoanthropology in its scientific infancy. Informed opinion considered the likely origins of the human family to be in Asia, where fossil forms of a primitive kind of *Homo* had been found in Indonesia in the 1890s. Europe was also considered a center of hominid evolutionary action, for spectacular discoveries there of early populations of *Homo sapiens* (including the famous Neandertals) and millions of stone tools had come to light, particularly in the early decades of this century.

Few knowledgeable scholars would have given much credence to Darwin's prediction (see Box 11-1) that the most likely place to find early relatives of humans would be on the continent of Africa. It was in such an atmosphere of preconceived biases that the discoveries of a young Australian-born anatomist were to jolt the foundations of the scientific community in the 1920s. Raymond Dart arrived in South Africa in 1923 at the age of 30 to take up a teaching position in anatomy at the University of Witwatersrand in Johannesburg. Fresh from his evolution-oriented training in England under some of the leading scholars of the day (especially, Sir Grafton Elliot Smith), Dart had developed a keen interest in human evolution. Consequently, he was well prepared when startling new evidence began to appear at his very doorstep.

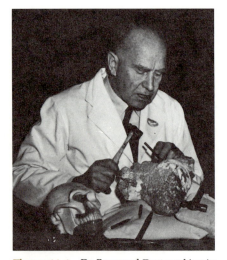

Figure 11-1 Dr. Raymond Dart working in his laboratory.

◇ Box 11-1   Hominid Origins

"In each great region of the world the living mammals are closely related to the extinct species of the same region. It is, therefore, probable that Africa was formerly inhabited by extinct apes closely allied to the gorilla and chimpanzee, and as these two species are now man's nearest allies, it is somewhat more probable that our early progenitors lived on the African continent than elsewhere."

SOURCE:
Charles Darwin. *The Descent of Man*, 1871.

The first clue came in 1924 when one of Dart's students saw an interesting baboon skull on the mantelpiece while having dinner at the home of the director of the Northern Lime Company, a commercial quarrying firm. The skull, that of a large baboon, had come from a place called Taung about 200 miles southwest of Johannesburg. When Dart saw the skull, he quickly recognized it as an extinct form and asked that any other interesting fossil material found be sent to him for his inspection.

Soon thereafter he received two boxloads of fossils and immediately recognized something that was quite unusual, a natural endocast of the inside of the braincase of a higher primate, but certainly no baboon. The endocast fit into another limestone block containing the fossilized front portion of skull, face, and lower jaw. However, these were difficult to see clearly, for the bone was hardened into a cemented limestone matrix called *breccia*. Dart patiently chiseled away for weeks, later describing the task: "No diamond cutter ever worked more lovingly or with such care on a priceless jewel—nor, I am sure, with such inadequate tools. But on the seventy-third day, December 23, the rock parted. I could view the face from the front, although the right side was still imbedded. ... What emerged was a baby's face, an infant with a full set of milk teeth and its permanent molars just in the process of erupting. I doubt if there was any parent prouder of his offspring than I was of my Taung baby on that Christmas" (Dart, 1959, p. 10).

As indicated by the eruption of the first permanent molars, the Taung child was probably about 5 to 6 years of age at death. Dart's initial impression that this form was a hominoid was confirmed when he could observe the face and teeth more clearly. However, as it turned out, it took considerably more effort before the teeth could be seen completely, since Dart worked 4 years just to separate the upper and lower jaws.

But Dart was convinced long before he had an unimpeded view of the dentition that this discovery was a remarkable one, an early hominoid from South Africa. The question was, what kind of hominoid? Dart realized it was extremely improbable that this specimen could have been a forest ape, for South Africa has had a relatively dry climate for many millions of years. Even though the climate at Taung was not as arid as was previously believed (Butzer, 1974), it was an unlikely place to find an ape!

If not an ape, then, what was it? Features of the skull and teeth of this

Endocast
An endocast is a solid (in this case, rock) impression of the inside of the skull showing the size, shape, and some details of the surface of the brain.

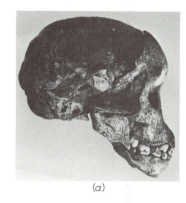

(a)

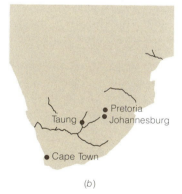

(b)

Figure 11-2 (a) The Taung child discovered in 1924. The endocast is in back with the fossilized bone mandible and face in front; (b) Taung. Location of the initial australopithecine discovery.

◇ GREAT MOMENTS IN PREHISTORY
Raymond Dart and the Discovery of the Taung Child, November, 1924

On his return Young told me that at Taungs he had met an old miner, Mr. M. de Bruyn, who for many years had taken a keen interest in preserving fossils. Only the previous week he had brought quite a number of stone blocks containing bone fragments to Mr. Spiers' office. When Young mentioned my interest to Mr. Spiers, Spiers gave instructions for them to be boxed and railed to me.

I waited anxiously for their arrival, reasoning that if fossilized baboon skulls were such a common feature at Taungs many other, more interesting specimens might be found there. Of course, the packages turned up at the most inappropriate time.

I was standing by the window of my dressing room cursing softly while struggling into an unaccustomed stiff-winged collar when I noticed two men wearing the uniform of the South African Railways staggering along the driveway of our home in Johannesburg with two large wooden boxes.

My Virginia-born wife Dora, who was also donning her most formal outfit, had noticed the men with the boxes and rushed in to me in something of a panic.

"I suppose those are the fossils you've been expecting," she said. "Why on earth did they have to arrive today of all days?" She fixed me with a business-like eye. "Now Raymond," she pleaded, "the guests will start arriving shortly and you can't go delving in all that rubble until the wedding's over and everybody has left. I know how important the fossils are to you, but please leave them until tomorrow."

At the time, however, this seemed of little importance when I considered the exciting anthropological bits and pieces that the boxes from Taungs might contain. As soon as my wife had left to complete her dressing I tore the hated collar off and dashed out to take delivery of the boxes which meanwhile obstructed the entrance to the *stoep*. I was too excited to wait until my African servants carried them to the garage, and ordered them to leave the crates under the pergola while I went in search of some tools to open them.

(Later on that momentous day, my wife told me that she had twice remonstrated with me but had been ignored. I had no recollection of any interruptions.)

I wrenched the lid off the first box and my reaction was one of extreme disappointment. In the rocks I could make out traces of fossilized eggshells and turtle shells and a few fragmentary pieces of isolated bone, none of which looked to be of much interest.

Impatiently I wrestled with the lid of the second box, still hopeful but half-expecting it to be a replica of its mate. At most I anticipated baboon skulls, little guessing that from this crate was to emerge a face that would look out on the world after an age-long sleep of nearly a million years.

As soon as I removed the lid a thrill of excitement shot through me. On the very top of the rock heap was what was undoubtedly an endocranial cast or mold of the interior of the skull. Had it been only the fossilized brain cast of any species of ape it would have ranked as a great discovery, for such a thing had never before been reported. But I knew at a glance that what lay in my hands was no ordinary anthropoidal brain. Here in lime-consolidated sand was the replica of a brain three times as large as that of a baboon and considerably bigger than that of any adult chimpanzee. The startling image of the convolutions and furrows of the brain and the blood vessels of the skull was plainly visible.

I stood in the shade holding the brain as greedily as any miser hugs his gold, my mind racing ahead. Here, I was certain, was one of the most significant finds ever made in the history of anthropology.

SOURCE:
Adventures with the Missing Link by Raymond Dart, 1959. Reprinted with permission of the author.

small child held clues that Dart seized upon almost immediately. The entrance of the spinal column into the brain (the *foramen magnum* at the base of the skull) was further forward in the Taung child than in modern great apes, though not as much as in modern humans. From this fact Dart concluded that the head was balanced *above* the spine, indicating erect posture.

In addition, the slant of the forehead was not as receding as in apes, the milk canines were exceedingly small, and the newly erupted first molars were large, broad teeth. In all these respects, the Taung fossil looked more like a hominid than a pongid. There was, however, a disturbing feature that was to confuse and befuddle many scientists for several years: the brain was quite small. Recent studies have estimated the Taung's child brain size at approximately 405 cc. (cubic centimeters), which translates to a fully adult size of only 440 cc., not very large when compared to modern great apes, as the following tabulation (Tobias, 1971; 1983) shows:

	Range	Mean
Chimpanzee	282–500 cc.	394 cm³
Gorilla	340–752 cc.	506 cm³
Orang	276–540 cc.	411 cm³

As the tabulation indicates, the estimated cranial capacity for the Taung fossil falls within the range of all the modern great apes, and gorillas actually *average* about 10% greater. It must, however, be remembered that gorillas are very large animals, whereas the Taung child represents a population whose average adult size may have been less than sixty pounds. Since brain size is partially correlated with body size, comparing such differently sized animals cannot be justified. A more meaningful contrast would be with the pygmy chimpanzee (*Pan paniscus*), whose body weight is more comparable. Pygmy chimps have adult cranial capacities averaging 356 cm³ for males and 329 for females, and thus the Taung child versus a *comparably sized* pongid displays a 25% increase in cranial capacity.

Despite the relatively small size of the brain, Dart saw that it was no pongid. Details preserved on the endocast seemed to indicate that the association areas of the parietal lobes were relatively larger than in any known pongid. However, recent reexamination of the Taung specimen has shown that the sulcal (folding) pattern is actually quite pongidlike (Falk, 1980; 1983).

We must emphasize that attempts to discern the precise position of the "bumps and folds" in ancient endocasts is no easy feat. The science of "paleoneurology" is thus often marked by sharp differences of opinion. Consequently, it is not surprising that the other leading researcher in this field, Ralph Halloway (1981), disagrees with the conclusion by Falk (just cited) and suggests, alternatively, that the Taung endocast has a more hominidlike sulcal pattern.

Realizing the immense importance of his findings, Dart promptly reported them in the British scientific weekly *Nature* on February 7, 1925. A bold venture, since Dart, only 32, was presumptuously proposing a whole new view of human evolution! The small-brained Taung child was christened by Dart **Australopithecus africanus** (southern ape of Africa), which he saw as a kind of halfway "missing-link" between modern apes and humans. The concept of a single "missing link" between modern apes and humans was a fallacious one, but Dart correctly emphasized the hominidlike features of the fossil.

A storm of both popular and scholarly protest greeted Dart's article, for it ran directly counter to prevailing opinion. Despite the numerous hominid

Australopithecus
(Os-tral-oh-pith'-e-kus)

Africanus
(af-ra-kan'-us)

Figure 11-3 Pygmy chimpanzee. A modern pongid probably similar in body size to many of the australopithecines.

Figure 11-4 The human brain. Schematic diagram of surface showing major functional areas and surface features.

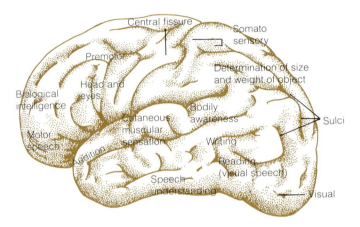

fossils already discovered, widespread popular skepticism of evolution still prevailed. The year 1925 was, after all, the year of the Scopes "monkey trial" in Tennessee. The biggest fly in the ointment to the leading human evolutionists of the day—Arthur Keith and Grafton Elliot Smith—was the small size of the brain compared to the relatively large proportions of the face and jaws. At that time, anthropologists generally assumed that the primary functional adaptation distinguishing the human family was an immense increase in brain size, and that dental and locomotory modifications came later. This view was seemingly confirmed by the Piltdown discovery in 1911, which displayed the combination of a large brain (estimated at 1400 cm³, well within the range of modern man) with an ape-like jaw (see pp. 306–307). Keith even went so far as to postulate a "Cerebral Rubicon" of 750 cm³ below which—by definition—no hominid could fall. Most scientists in the 1920s thus regarded this little Taung child as an interesting aberrant form of ape.

Hence, Dart's theories were received with indifference, disbelief, and scorn, often extremely caustic. Dart realized more complete remains were needed. The skeptical world would not accept the evidence of one fragmentary, immature individual no matter how highly suggestive the clues. Clearly, more fossil evidence was required, particularly more complete crania of adults. Not an experienced fossil hunter himself, Dart sought further assistance in the search for more **australopithecines** (the colloquial name referring to the members of genus *Australopithecus*).

◇ Hominids Aplenty

Soon after publication of his controversial theories, Dart found a strong ally in **Dr. Robert Broom**. A Scottish physician and part-time paleontologist, Broom's credentials as a fossil hunter had been established earlier with his highly successful paleontological work on early mammallike reptiles in South Africa.

Although interested, Broom was unable to participate actively in the search for additional australopithecines because of prior commitments and did not seriously undertake explorations until 1936. However, soon thereafter he met with incredible success. From two of Dart's students, Broom learned of

Figure 11-5 Dr. Robert Broom. Shown with one of his paleontological discoveries from South Africa. This photo was taken earlier in Dr. Broom's career; it would be almost thirty years later before he would even begin his search for australopithecines.

◇ GREAT MOMENTS IN PREHISTORY
Dr. Broom and the Discovery of the Kromdraai Ape-Man

On the forenoon of Wednesday, June 8, 1938, when I met Barlow, he said, "I've something nice for you this morning"; and he held out part of a fine palate with the first molar-tooth in position. I said, "Yes, it's quite nice. I'll give you a couple of pounds for it." He was delighted; so I wrote out a cheque, and put the specimen in my pocket. He did not seem quite willing to say where or how he had obtained it; and I did not press the matter. The specimen clearly belonged to a large ape-man, and was apparently different from the Sterkfontein being.

I was again at Sterkfontein on Saturday, when I knew Barlow would be away. I showed the specimen to the native boys in the quarry; but none of them had ever seen it before. I felt sure it had not come from the quarry, as the matrix was different. On Tuesday forenoon I was again at Sterkfontein, when I insisted on Barlow telling me how he had got the specimen. I pointed out that two teeth had been freshly broken off, and that they might be lying where the specimen had been obtained. He apologized for having misled me; and told me it was a schoolboy, Gert Terblanche, who acted as a guide in the caves on Sundays, who had picked it up and given it to him. I found where Gert lived, about two miles away; but Barlow said he was sure to be away at school. Still, I set out for his home. There I met Gert's mother and sister. They told me that the place where the specimen was picked up was near the top of a hill about half a mile away, and the sister agreed to take me up to the place. She and her mother also told me that Gert had four beautiful teeth at school with him.

The sister took us up the hill, and I picked up some fragments of the skull, and a couple of teeth; but she said she was sure Gert had some other nice pieces hidden away. Of course, I had to go to school to hunt up Gert.

The road to the school was a very bad one, and we had to leave the car, and walk about a mile over rough ground. When we got there, it was about half-past twelve, and it was play time. I found the headmaster, and told him that I wanted to see Gert Terblanche in connection with some teeth he had picked up. Gert was soon found, and drew from the pocket of his trousers four of the most wonderful teeth ever seen in the world's history. These I promptly purchased from Gert, and transferred to my pocket. I had the palate with me, and I found that two of the teeth were the second pre-molar and second molar, and that they fitted on to the palate. The two others were teeth of the other side. Gert told me about the piece he had hidden away. As the school did not break up till two o'clock, I suggested to the principal that I should give a lecture to the teachers and children about caves, how they were formed, and how bones got into them. He was delighted. So it was arranged; and I lectured to four teachers and about 120 children for over an hour, with blackboard illustrations, till it was nearly two o'clock. When I finished, the principal broke up the school, and Gert came home with me. He took us up to the hill, and brought out from his hiding place a beautiful lower jaw with two teeth in position. All the fragments that I could find at the spot I picked up.

SOURCE:
Finding the Missing Link by Robert Broom (2nd Ed.), 1951. By permission of C. A. Watts/Pitman Publishing Ltd., London.

---

another commercial limeworks site, called **Sterkfontein**, not far from Johannesburg. Here, as at Taung, the quarrying involved blasting out large sections with dynamite, leaving piles of debris that often contained fossilized remains. Accordingly, Broom asked the quarry manager to keep his eyes open for fossils, and when Broom returned to the site in August 1936, the manager asked, "Is this what you are looking for?" Indeed, it was, for Broom held in his hand the endocast of an adult australopithecine—exactly what he had set out to find! Looking further over the scattered debris, Broom was able to find most of the rest of the skull of the same individual.

Australopithecine
(os-tral-oh-pith'-e-seen)

Sterkfontein
(Sterk'-fon-tane)

Figure 11-6 Australopithecine sites in South Africa.

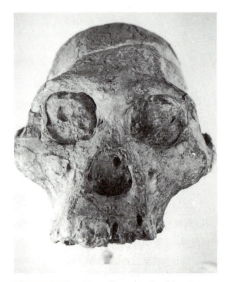

Figure 11-7 A gracile australopithecine skull from Sterkfontein (Sts. 5). This specimen is the best preserved gracile skull yet found in South Africa. Discovered in 1947.

Such remarkable success, just a few months after beginning his search, was not the end of Broom's luck, for his magical touch was to continue unabated for several more years. In 1938, he learned from a young schoolboy of another australopithecine site at **Kromdraai** about one mile from Sterkfontein, and, following World War II (1948), he found yet another australopithecine site, **Swartkrans**, in the same vicinity. A final australopithecine site, **Makapansgat**, was excavated in 1947 by Raymond Dart, who returned to the fossil-discovering bandwagon after an absence of over twenty years.

Numerous extremely important discoveries came from these five sites, discoveries that would eventually swing the tide of intellectual thought to the views Dart expressed back in 1925. Particularly important was a nearly perfect skull and a nearly complete pelvis, both found at Sterkfontein in 1947. As the number of discoveries accumulated, it became increasingly difficult to simply write them off as aberrant apes.

Although Robert Broom was an absolute wizard at finding fossils, his interpretations of them were clouded by an irresistible urge to give each new discovery a different taxonomic label. Consequently, in addition to Dart's *A. africanus* from Taung, a disconcertingly large number of other names have been used at various times for the South African australopithecines (see Table 11-1). The problem with all this taxonomic splitting was a lack of appreciation for the relevant biological principles underlying such elaborate interpretations (see Chapter 9 for a discussion of the meaning of taxonomic statements).

By 1949, at least thirty individuals were represented from the five South African sites. That year represents an important turning point, since it marks the visit to South Africa and the resulting "conversion" of W. E. Le Gros Clark. As one of the leading human evolutionists of the day, Sir Wilfrid Le Gros Clark's unequivocal support of the australopithecines as small-brained early hominids was to have wide impact. But the tides of wisdom had begun to turn even before this. Writing in 1947, **Sir Arthur Keith** courageously admitted his earlier mistake:

"When Professor Dart of the University of Witwatersrand, Johannesburg, announced in *Nature* the discovery of a juvenile *Australopithecus* and claimed for it human kinship, I was one of those who took the point of view that when the adult was discovered, it would prove to be nearer akin to the living African anthropoids—the gorilla and chimpanzee. . . . I am now convinced of the evidence submitted by Dr. Robert Broom that Professor Dart was right and I was wrong. The Australopi-

Table 11-1 Taxonomic Labels Applied to South African Australopithecines

	Site	Discovered and named by
Australopithecus africanus	Taung	Dart
Plesianthropus transvaalensis	Sterkfontein	Broom
Paranthropus robustus	Kromdraai	Broom
Paranthropus crassidens	Swartkrans	Broom
Australopithecus prometheus	Makapansgat	Dart
Telanthropus capensis	Swartkrans	Broom

thecinae [formal designation of the australopithecines as a subfamily of the hominids] are in or near the line which culminated in the human form" (Keith in Le Gros Clark, 1967, p. 38).

With the exposé of the Piltdown forgery in the early 1950s, the path was completely cleared for the nearly unanimous recognition of the australopithecines as early hominids. With this acceptance also came the necessary recognition that hominid brains had their greatest expansion *after* earlier changes in teeth and locomotory systems. In other words, the rates of evolution in one functional system of the body vary from other systems, thus displaying the **mosaic** nature of human **evolution**.

Even today, the evidence from South Africa continues to accumulate. The search continues at Sterkfontein, Swartkrans, and Makapansgat. An important portion of pelvis was found at Swartkrans in 1970, and a partial skull was found at Sterkfontein (west pit) in 1976. Indeed, discoveries are now coming faster than ever. In the year 1984 alone more than 150 *new* specimens have come to light at Sterkfontein—exceeding the total for any previous year (see Table 11-2). A truly remarkable feast of early hominids, the total number of remains from South Africa exceeds 1,500 (counting all teeth as separate items), and the number of individuals is estimated to be close to 190 individuals (Tobias, 1983).

Of all the hominid remains from South Africa, less than 10% are postcranial (that is, below the head), but this evidence, nevertheless, is crucially significant in revealing the all-important locomotory function of these animals. As of 1972, this extremely informative evidence included twenty-two remains representing the shoulder girdle and upper limb, thirteen from the pelvic girdle and lower limb, and thirty-four from the rib and vertebral areas (Tobias, 1972).

From an evolutionary point of view, the most meaningful remains are those from the australopithecine pelvis, which now includes portions of nine **innominates** (Fig. 11-11). Remains of the pelvis are so important because, better than any other area of the body, this structure displays the unique requirements of a bipedal animal, such as modern humans *and* our hominid forebears.

Kromdraai
(Kromm'-dry)

Swartkrans

Makapansgat
(Mak-ah-pans'-gat)

Mosaic evolution
Rate of evolution in one functional system varies from other systems.

Innominate
The fused half-portion of a pelvis; contains three bones—the ilium, ischium, and pubis.

Figure 11-8   Sir Arthur Keith.

Table 11-2   Sterkfontein Hominid Specimens, 1936–1984*

	Number in Calendar Year	Cumulative Total
1936–1979	—	145
1979	10	155
1980	5	160
1981	7	167
1982	69	236
1983	44	280
1984 (to 24 August)	164	444

*These are totals for specimens, not individuals. A single individual may be represented by several teeth in a given sample, each tooth of which counts as a different specimen. Data provided courtesy of Professor Phillip Tobias.

Figure 11-9 A partial hominid skull from Sterkfontein (Stw. 53). Discovered during recent excavations (August 1976).

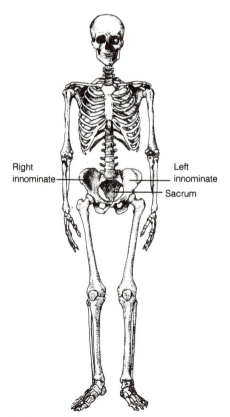

Right innominate

Left innominate

Sacrum

Figure 11-10 The human pelvis. Various elements shown on a modern skeleton.

◇ Hominids on Their Feet

As we discussed in Chapter 7, there is a general tendency in all primates for erect body posture and some bipedalism. However, of all living primates, efficient bipedalism as the primary form of locomotion is seen *only* in hominids. Functionally, the human mode of locomotion is most clearly shown in our striding gait, where weight is alternately placed on a single fully extended hindlimb. This specialized form of locomotion has developed to a point where energy levels are used to near peak efficiency. Such is not the case in nonhuman primates, who move bipedally with hips and knees bent and maintain balance in a clumsy and inefficient manner.

From a survey of our close primate relatives, it is apparent that, while still in the trees, our ancestors were adapted to a fair amount of upper body erectness. Prosimians, monkeys, and apes all spend considerable time sitting erect while feeding, grooming, or sleeping. Presumably, our early ancestors also displayed similar behavior. What caused these forms to come to the ground and embark on the unique way of life that would eventually lead to humans is still a mystery. Perhaps natural selection favored an animal such as *Sivapithecus* coming occasionally to the ground to forage for food on the forest floor and forest fringe. In any case, once it was on the ground and away from the immediate safety offered by trees, bipedal locomotion became a tremendous advantage.

First of all, bipedal locomotion freed the hands for carrying objects and for making and using tools. Such early cultural developments then had an even more positive effect on speeding the development of yet more efficient bipedalism—once again emphasizing the dual role of biocultural evolution. In addition, in the bipedal stance, animals have a wider view of the surrounding countryside, and, in open terrain, early spotting of predators (particularly the large cats, such as lions, leopards, and saber tooths) would be of critical importance. We know that modern ground-living primates, such as the savanna baboon and chimpanzee, will occasionally adopt this posture to "look around" when out in open country. Certainly, bipedal walking is an efficient means of covering long distances, and when large game hunting came into play (several million years after the initial adaptation to ground living), further refinements in the locomotory complex may have been favored. Finally, it has been suggested that bipedalism was initially most adaptive for carrying—particularly food brought by provisioning males to females and young (Lovejoy, 1981). (See pp. 181–182.) Exactly what initiated the process is difficult to say, but all these factors probably played a role in the adaptation of hominids to their special niche through a special form of locomotion.

Our mode of locomotion is indeed extraordinary, involving as it does a unique kind of activity in which "the body, step by step, teeters on the edge of catastrophe" (Napier, 1967, p. 56). The problem is to maintain balance on the "stance" leg while the "swing" leg is off the ground. In fact, during normal walking, both feet are simultaneously on the ground only about 25% of the time, and, as speed of locomotion increases, this figure becomes even smaller.

In order to maintain a stable center of balance in this complex form of locomotion, many drastic structural/functional alterations are demanded in the basic primate quadrupedal pattern. Functionally, the foot must be altered to act as a stable support instead of a grasping limb. When we walk, our foot is used like a prop, landing on the heel and pushing off on the toes, particularly the big toe. In addition, the leg must be elongated to increase the length of the stride and lower the center of gravity. The lower limb must also be remodeled to allow full extension of the knee and to allow the legs to be kept close together during walking, thereby maintaining the center of support directly under the body. Finally, significant changes must occur in the pelvis to permit stable weight transmission from the upper body to the legs and to maintain balance through pelvic rotation and altered proportions and orientations of several key muscles.

The major structural changes that are required for bipedalism are all seen in the australopithecines. In the pelvis, the blade (ilium—upper bone of the pelvis) is shortened top to bottom, which permits more stable weight support in the erect position by lowering the center of gravity. In addition, the pelvis is bent backwards and downwards, thus altering the position of the muscles that attach along the bone. Most importantly, the gluteus medius (glue-tee'-us meed'-ee-us) now becomes a very large muscle acting to stablize the trunk and keep it from slumping to the unsupported side while the body is supported on one leg. The gluteus maximus (glue-tee'-us max'-a-mus) also becomes important as an extensor—pulls the thigh back—during running, jumping, and climbing.

Other structural changes shown by australopithecine postcranial evidence further confirm the morphological pattern seen in the pelvis. The vertebral column, known from a beautifully preserved specimen from Sterkfontein, shows the same forward curvature as in modern hominids, bringing the center of support forward and allowing rotation of the bottom of the vertebral column (sacrum) below, thereby getting it out of the way of the birth canal. In addition, the lower limb is elongated and is apparently proportionately about as long as in modern humans. Fossil evidence of a knee fragment from Sterkfontein also shows that full extension of this joint was possible, thus allowing the leg to be completely straightened, as when a field goal kicker follows through.

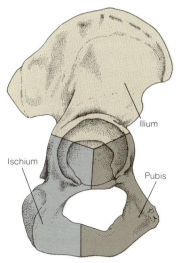

Figure 11-11 The human innominate. Composed of three bones (right side shown).

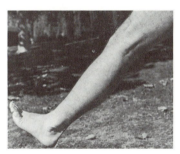

Figure 11-12 The knee in full extension.

Figure 11-13 Innominates, (a) *Homo sapiens*; (b) australopithecine (Sts. 14); (c) chimpanzee. Note especially the length and breadth of the iliac blade.

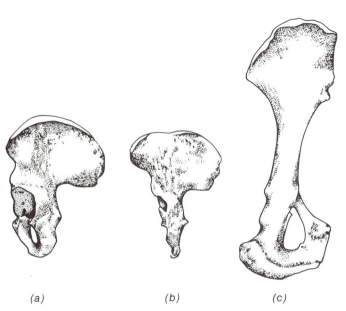

(a)   (b)   (c)

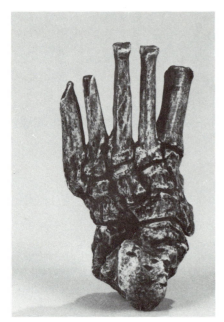

Figure 11-14 A nearly complete hominid foot (OH 8). From Olduvai Gorge, East Africa.

Structural evidence for the foot is not abundant in South Africa, but one ankle bone from Kromdraai shows a rather mixed pattern. This particular foot probably belonged to an animal that was a well-adapted biped but still retained considerable climbing ability. More complete evidence for evolutionary changes in the foot skeleton comes from Olduvai Gorge in East Africa, where a nearly complete hominid foot is preserved, and from the Afar region in Ethiopia, where numerous foot elements have been recovered. As in the ankle bone from Kromdraai, the East African fossils suggest a well-adapted bipedal gait. The arches are developed and the big toe is pulled in next to the other toes, but some differences in the ankle also imply that considerable flexibility was possible (for climbing?). As we will see in the next chapter, some researchers have recently concluded that the early forms of australopithecine probably spent considerable time in the trees. Moreover, they may not have been as efficient bipeds as has previously been suggested (see p. 343).

◇ Australopithecines: How Many Forms?

All the australopithecines in South Africa are clearly hominid as shown in the morphological details of their pelvis, limbs, dentition, and skull. However, a dichotomy exists among the fossils between larger, more heavily built (robust) individuals and smaller, more lightly built (gracile) ones. There is also a dichotomy in the sites of occupation of these two forms, with graciles found at Sterkfontein and Makapansgat and robusts at Swartkrans and Kromdraai (the Taung child remains somewhat of an enigma).

Accurate size and weight estimates are extremely difficult to ascertain from fragmentary evidence, but the best guess for the graciles is a stature of 4–4½ feet with a weight of about 60 pounds. Estimates by different investigators, however, vary considerably (stature, 42–57 inches; weight, 40–61 pounds). The robusts are definitely larger, standing approximately 4½–5 feet and weighing around 100 pounds. (Range of estimates: stature, 57–65 inches; weight, 70–200 pounds.)

In addition to overall size differences, gracile and robust forms may be contrasted in their respective cranial and dental anatomy. The robust skull is generally larger with a cranial capacity (sample size, or $N = 1$) estimated at 530 cm³ compared to a mean of 450 cm³ ($N = 7$) for the graciles. Since, of course, brain size is partially correlated with body size, we would expect larger skulls in the bigger animals. In addition to size, however, there are also differences in shape. The graciles have a more rounded braincase, which rises more vertically above the eyes, yielding a well developed forehead, as compared to the flattened-out appearance of the robust skull.

The face structure of the graciles is also more lightly built and somewhat dish-shaped compared to the more vertical configuration seen in robust specimens. In robust individuals, a raised ridge along the midline of the skull, called a **sagittal crest**, is occasionally observed. This structure provides additional attachment area for the large temporal muscle, which is the primary

Figure 11-15 A nearly complete cranium from Swartkrans (Sk. 48). The best preserved skull of a robust australopithecine from South Africa.

muscle operating the massive jaw below. Such a structure is also seen in some modern apes, especially male gorillas and orangs; however, in australopithecines, the temporal muscle acts most efficiently on the back of the mouth and is therefore not functionally equivalent to the front tooth emphasis seen in pongids (see Fig. 11-16).

The most distinctive difference observed between gracile and robust australopithecines is in the dentition. Compared to modern humans, they both have relatively large teeth, which are, however, definitely hominid in pattern. In fact, more emphasis is on the typical back-tooth grinding complex among these early forms than the forms of today; therefore, if anything, australopithecines are "hyperhominid"! Robust forms emphasize this trend to an extreme degree, showing deep jaws and much-enlarged back teeth, particularly the molars, severely crowding the front teeth (incisors and canines) together. Conversely, the graciles have proportionately larger front teeth compared to the size of their back teeth. This contrast is seen most clearly in the relative sizes of the canine compared to the first premolar: in robust individuals, the first premolar is clearly a much larger tooth than the small canine (about twice as large) whereas, in gracile specimens, it only averages about 20% larger than the fairly goodsized canine (Howells, 1973).

These differences in the relative proportions of the teeth and jaws best define a gracile, as compared to a robust, form. In fact, most of the differences in skull shape we have discussed can be directly attributed to contrasting jaw function in the two forms. Both the sagittal crest and broad vertical face of the robust form are related to the muscles and biomechanical requirements of the extremely large-tooth chewing adaptation of this animal.

◇ South African Australopithecines: Intepretations

Clearly, variation among the South African Plio-Pleistocene hominids defines two fairly distinct groups: gracile and robust australopithecines. The question that now must be addressed is: How do we interpret this variation in biologically meaningful terms? In order to answer, we must keep certain biological principles clearly in mind (see Chapter 9).

We know, of course, that our australopithecine fossils are samples of what were once interbreeding populations. We also know that all such populations show variation. Our task is to interpret this variation in a biologically realistic manner, assign appropriate taxonomic labels, and, in the end, hopefully gain some insight into the nature of human evolution.

We have noted that, even in living forms, biological interpretations, such as those suggested by genus and species designations, are often a complex and risky endeavor. To assign genus and species names to long-dead fossil groups (whose adaptations must be indirectly inferred from usually small samples of fragmentary skeletal remains) is a considerably more difficult task.

As a means of reconstructing realistic dimensions of expected biological variation due to sexual dimorphism, age, and other factors, we refer to living

Sagittal crest
Raised ridge along the midline of the skull where the temporal muscle (used to move the jaw) attaches.

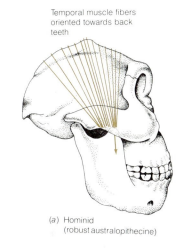

Temporal muscle fibers oriented towards back teeth

(a) Hominid
(robust australopithecine)

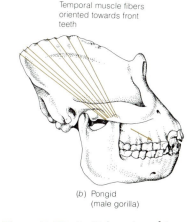

Temporal muscle fibers oriented towards front teeth

(b) Pongid
(male gorilla)

Figure 11-16 Sagittal crests and temporal muscle orientations. Hominid compared to pongid.

populations of primates. Yet even this kind of analysis provides no easy, unambiguous answer to the question of how best to interpret the differences between robust and gracile australopithecines. Variation in modern primates can match the observed differences in the australopithecines either *within*

Figure 11-17 Intraspecific variation: sexual dimorphism—(*a*) male (left) and female gelada baboons. Interspecific variation: two species of macaque—(*b*) *Macaca mulatta* (Rhesus monkey); (*c*) *Macaca nemistrina*.

(a)

(b)

(c)

one species (*intraspecific*, as in gelada baboons) or *between two different species* (*interspecific*, as between some species of macaques).

Given these complexities, it is no wonder that considerable controversy surrounds the detailed interpretation of variation in australopithecine fossil material.

THE SINGLE SPECIES HYPOTHESIS

The most straightforward and economical interpretation of the australopithecines, both gracile and robust, is that they are members of one species, *A. africanus* (this name takes precedence according to the rules of the International Code of Zoological Nomenclature).

This theory—accounting for all South African australopithecine material—is usually referred to as the *single species hypothesis*. In this view, the variation among the australopithecines is explained by simple sexual dimorphism; the robust specimens are the males, and the graciles are females. Certainly, such variation is present in early hominids, and proponents of this theory point out that considerable sexual dimorphism is displayed today in other terrestrial primates, particularly baboons and gorillas (Brace, 1973). Moreover, advocates of the single species hypothesis have also correctly emphasized that it is not legitimate to describe the differences between robust and gracile on the basis of isolated individuals. Unfortunately, this has often been done using the best-preserved specimens, Sts. (Sterkfontein) 5 and Sk. (Swartkrans) 48, but these two fossils may not be representative of their respective populations. For example, Sts. 5 may be a female (therefore the popular name, "Mrs. Ples") and Sk. 48 may well be a male. To compare a male from one population with a female from the other overemphasizes the real biological differences. Clearly, what must be done then is to use *all* the relevant fossil material, and abundant samples, especially teeth, are known from both Sterkfontein and Swartkrans. When all the material is compared, it becomes apparent that considerable overlap in physical traits occurs between robust and gracile groups of australopithecines.

Whereas the single species hypothesis is attractive, and theoretically is an excellent starting point for *any* interpretation of biological variation, it does not completely explain the situation for South African australopithecines. First of all, there is the problem that robust individuals seemingly come just from Swartkrans and Kromdraai, while graciles are confined to Sterkfontein and Makapansgat. Secondly, as we will see later in the chapter (p. 325), the graciles from Sterkfontein and Makapansgat are considerably earlier in time (perhaps a million years or more) than the robusts from Swartkrans and Kromdraai. Moreover, the great amount of variation between robust and gracile australopithecines can occasionally be matched within species of some modern primates (for instance, baboons and gorillas), but are these necessarily good models for hominids? In addition, the *pattern* of variation in the teeth is not matched between sexes in any living primate.

Apparently, then, the variation among South African australopithecines is greater than can be explained by sexual dimorphism (or, for that matter, any kind of *intraspecific* variation). We are then left with the most likely conclusion

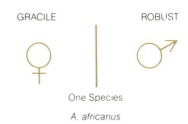

Figure 11-18 The single species hypothesis.

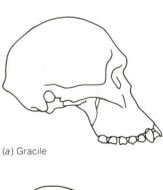

(a) Gracile

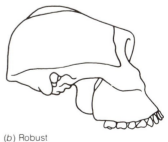

(b) Robust

Figure 11-19 Two varieties of South African australopithecines.

Table 11-3 Summary of Morphological Differences, Gracile versus Robust Australopithecines

Gracile	Robust
smaller, more lightly built	larger, more heavily built
height: 4–4½ ft.	height: 4½–5 ft.
weight: 60 lbs.	weight: 100 lbs.
skull more rounded, more vertical forehead	skull flattened out
sagittal crest never seen*	occasional sagittal crest
face usually dish-shaped and narrow	face broad and more vertical
front teeth (incisors and canines) reasonably good size; back teeth large	front teeth, quite small; back teeth, very large

*One specimen from Makapansgat may have had a sagittal crest. In many respects the Makapansgat material is transitional in nature between robust and gracile features.

that more than one species of australopithecines existed; but how do we interpret this conclusion in an evolutionarily meaningful way?

THE DIETARY HYPOTHESIS

Another school of thought not only draws a species-level difference between gracile and robust australopithecines but a genus-level one as well. In this theory, usually called the *dietary hypothesis*, graciles are called *Australopithecus* and robusts, **Paranthropus**.

The central aspect of the dietary hypothesis concerns dentition and what it may tell us about diet. As we have discussed, robust australopithecines have proportionately larger back teeth and smaller front teeth than have the gracile form. From this fact, Robinson (1972) has inferred that the robust had a specialized vegetarian diet contrasted with a more omnivorous one for the graciles. All the modifications of skull and face of the robust group are then seen as directly related to the mechanical demands of chewing large amounts of vegetable foods.

Initially suggested by J. T. Robinson, once Broom's assistant and now at the University of Wisconsin, this theory has three primary biological and evolutionary implications:

1. The two groups were not interbreeding; speciation had already occurred.
2. More than speciation, genus-level differences due to variable ecological life styles had also occurred. (The direct implication here is that speciation had occurred a good deal earlier, and these two forms are thus not particularly closely related.)
3. Since only *one* species of hominid (*H. sapiens*) is now living, only *one* species at any given time could be our direct ancestor. The robust group (*Paranthropus*) is seen here as the more specialized form, whereas the gracile form (*Australopithecus*)* is usually viewed as the more likely ancestor (even this suggestion has recently come into question—see Chapter 12).

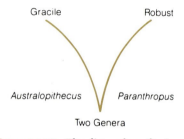

Figure 11-20 The dietary hypothesis.

While this theory explains the observed variation and the site distribution of fossil discoveries, it may be somewhat overzealous. It is often quite difficult to reconstruct diet on the basis of tooth proportions (Clark, 1967), and many of the observed dental and cranial differences may in fact be simply a function of the larger body size in the robust form (Pilbeam and Gould, 1974).

Paranthropus
(Par-an'-throw-pus)

ONE GENUS, TWO SPECIES

Most anthropologists advocate a somewhat middle position between the two theories just described. They agree with points 1 and 3 of the dietary hypothesis, namely, that speciation (and thus reproductive isolation) had occurred, and that the robust form was probably on an extinct sidebranch. However, advocates of this more moderate point of view (Clark, 1967; Tobias, 1967; Pilbeam, 1972) are not willing to go so far as to postulate a sufficiently major difference in ecological adaptation to justify a genus-level distinction. Moreover, they see the two species as quite closely related. Therefore, proponents of this theory postulate one genus, *Australopithecus*, with two species: gracile, *africanus*; and robust, *robustus*.

Another modification of this interpretation views the differences between graciles and robusts as the result of temporal evolution within a single evolutionary lineage (Johanson and White, 1979). In other words, gracile australopithecines simply evolved into robust ones, who then went extinct.

We feel that, on the basis of present evidence, some version of this last theory is the most probable, and explains the variation among South African australopithecines in the most biologically reasonable manner. However, as the varied opinions themselves indicate, no clear conclusion is possible given the kind and amount of evidence available.

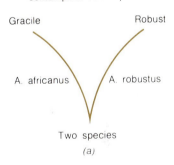

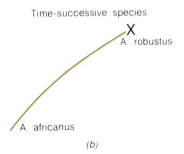

Figure 11-21 One-genus, two-species interpretation. (*a*) Two at least partially contemporaneous species. (*b*) Time-successive species: *A. africanus* evolves into *A. robustus*.

◇ Geology and Dating Problems

The five South African australopithecine sites are extremely complex geologically. All were discovered by commercial quarrying activity, which greatly disrupted the geological picture and, in the case of Taung, completely destroyed the site.

The australopithecine remains are found with thousands of other fossilized bones embedded in limestone cliffs, caves, fissures, and sinkholes. The limestone was built by millions of generations of shells of marine organisms during the Pre-Cambrian—more than 2 billion years ago—when South Africa was submerged under a shallow sea. Once deposited, the limestones were cut through by percolating ground water from below and rain water from above, forming a maze of caves and fissures often connected to the surface by narrow shafts. Through these vertical shafts and horizontal cave openings, bones

*J. T. Robinson (1972) has included genus *Australopithecus* within *Homo*, what taxonomists call "sinking" one genus into another.

Figure 11-22 Swartkrans, geological section. The upper (reconstructed) part has been removed by erosion since the accumulation of the fossil-bearing deposit. (After Brain, 1970.)

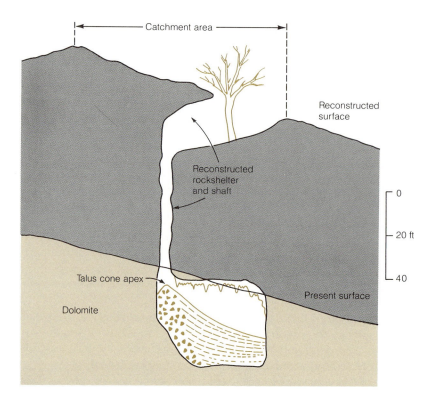

either fell or were carried in, where they conglomerated with sand, pebbles, and soil into a cementlike matrix called *breccia*.

As the cave fissures filled in, they were constantly subjected to further erosion forces from above and below, so that caves would be partially filled, then closed to the surface for a considerable time, and reopened again to commence accumulation thousands of years later. All this activity yields an incredibly complex geological situation that can only be worked out after the most detailed kind of paleoecological analysis.

Since bones accumulated in these caves and fissures largely by accidental processes, it seems likely that none of the South African australopithecine sites are *primary* hominid localities. In other words, unlike East Africa, these are not areas where hominids organized activities, scavenged food, etc.

Just how did all the fossilized bone accumulate and, most particularly, what were the australopithecines doing there? In the case of Swartkrans, Sterkfontein, and Kromdraai, the bones probably accumulated through the combined activities of carnivorous leopards, sabre-toothed cats, and hyenas. However, the unexpectedly high proportion of primate (baboon and hominid) remains suggests that these localities were the location (or very near the location) of primate sleeping sites, thus providing ready prey for the predators (Brain, 1981).

Raymond Dart has argued enthusiastically for an alternative explanation, suggesting the australopithecines camping at Makapansgat regularly used bone, tooth, and horn remains as *tools*, which he has grandly called the osteodontokeratic culture complex. Analogies with modern Hottentot food habits indicate the bone accumulation at Makapansgat may be accounted for simply by hominid and carnivore eating practices. Recent paleoecological work at Makapansgat has thrown Dart's assertions into even greater doubt. Apparently, remains accumulated here primarily in a similar fashion to Sterkfontein and Swartkrans—through a narrow shaft entrance. Therefore, large animals could have entered but not departed the deep subterranean cavern. Makapansgat, like Sterkfontein and Swartkrans, probably also represents the accumulated debris of carnivore activity (perhaps hyenas) outside the cave entrance.

So little is left of the final site, Taung, that accurate paleoanthropological reconstructions are not feasible.

Due to the complex geological picture, as well as lack of appropriate material such as volcanics for chronometric techniques, dating the South African australopithecine sites has posed tremendous problems. Without chronometric dating, the best that can be done is to correlate the faunal sequences in South Africa with areas such as East Africa where dates are better known (this approach is called "biostratigraphy"—see p. 289). Faunal sequencing of this sort on pigs, bovids such as antelopes, and baboons has provided the following tenuous chronology:

Osteodontokeratic
osteo: bone
dento: tooth
keratic: horn

	1 m.y.	
Kromdraai		
Swartkrans		Taung?*
	2 m.y.	
Sterkfontein		
Makapansgat	3 m.y.	

Recent attempts at paleomagnetic dating (see p. 287) suggest an age of 3.3–2.8 m.y.a. for Makapansgat (Brock et al., 1977), thus pushing the estimates to the extreme limits of those provided by biostratigraphy. In fact, some researchers believe the paleomagnetic results are ambiguous and continue to "put their money" on the biostratigraphic data, especially those dates determined by analysis of pig fossils. From such considerations, they place the South African australopithecine sites as much as one-half million years later (i.e., for Makapansgat, around 2.5 m.y.a.) (White et al., 1981).

◇ Summary

Between 2 and 3 m.y.a., bipedal but small-brained hominids occupied South Africa. The fact that the tremendous expansion of the brain was a *late* development in hominid evolution came as a surprise to most scholars in the early part of this century. However, the discoveries of Raymond Dart and Robert Broom eventually were to demonstrate convincingly the mosaic nature of human evolution. Bipedal animals, the australopithecines are clearly hom-

*Some (Butzer, 1974; Tobias, 1976) have suggested Taung may be very late, even Middle Pleistocene (*circa* 700,000–800,000 y.a.), but this conclusion remains a matter of active dispute.

inid, as repeatedly shown in the details of their pelvis, limbs, feet, and vertebral column. In addition, the structure of their skull and teeth also confirm the hominid affinities of these forms. While hominids, all australopithecines are not identical and fall into two major groups, robust and gracile, distinguished primarily on the basis of body size and tooth proportions.

Interpretations of the variation between these two groups have engendered several theories, three of which are discussed in this chapter: the single species hypothesis; the dietary hypothesis; and the one-genus/two-species explanation. All these theories have something to offer, but consideration of the relevant biological principles make the one-genus/two-species explanation the most reasonable at this time. Thus, there are probably at least two species of hominids in South Africa during the Plio-Pleistocene—*Australopithecus africanus* (gracile) and *Australopithecus robustus* (robust).

Just how these fossil hominids fit into a comprehensive scheme of human evolution is difficult to answer in the absence of a reliable chronology. For this kind of reliability we must turn to East Africa where discoveries in the last twenty years have demanded a total reappraisal of the earlier finds in South Africa.

◇ Questions for Review

1. Why was Raymond Dart's announcement of a small-brained bipedal hominoid greeted with such skepticism in 1925?
2. What led Dart to suggest the Taung child was *not* an ape?
3. What was Robert Broom's contribution to revealing the hominid nature of the South African australopithecines?
4. (a) Why is postcranial evidence (particularly the lower limb) so crucial in showing the australopithecines as definite hominids? (b) What particular aspects of the australopithecine pelvis and lower limb are hominidlike?
5. What are the most important morphological distinctions between gracile and robust australopithecines?
6. How might the variation between the gracile and robust forms be interpreted (in a biologically meaningful manner)? Critically evaluate:
   (a) the single species hypothesis
   (b) the dietary hypothesis
   (c) the one-genus/two-species model
7. Why is it so difficult to obtain accurate dates for the South African australopithecine sites?

Plio-Pleistocene Hominids: East Africa

CONTENTS

Are we preprogramed gene-machines designed to behave in an instinctively aggressive manner toward our fellow creatures? Some researchers, popular writers, and even movie producers would have us believe so. Raymond Dart, the discoverer and namer of the first australopithecine, has long advocated such a view. From fragmented fossil remains from South Africa, Dr. Dart has characterized our australopithecine forebears as a "bone-club-wielding, jaw-bone-cleaving Samsonian phase of human emergence" (Dart, 1954). Playwright-turned-popular-science-writer Robert Ardrey popularized Dart's views, proclaiming that "man is a predator whose natural instinct is to kill with a weapon" (Ardrey, 1961). Desmond Morris, a full-time zoologist, has gone even further, claiming our whole evolution has been shaped as the "naked ape" became a "killer ape" (Morris, 1967).

Such overwrought imagery has even permeated the film industry. Anyone who has seen Stanley Kubrick's *2001: A Space Odyssey* must

Reconstruction showing how the observed change to the skull of a Swartkrans australopithecine child could have been caused by a leopard. The leopard's lower canines are thought to have penetrated the skull of the dead child while it was being dragged to a feeding place. (After Brain, 1970.)

be struck (hopefully, not too hard) by the club-wielding, apish protohominid depicted as our ancestor.

In many ways, this view of ourselves is psychologically satisfying (it seems to explain so much about the inhumanity of human beings), but it

has no basis in fact. Indeed, all such reconstructions are founded solely on speculation. No evidence from the Plio-Pleistocene shows conclusively that *any* hominid met with a violent end at the hands of a fellow creature. Most, no doubt, did die violently, but large carnivores were probably the agents responsible (such as leopards at Swartkrans). At Zhoukoudian (*circa* 500,000 y.a.) skull smashing seems to have been in fashion, but such evidence does not necessarily indict *Homo erectus* on several counts of murder. Similar cultural practices have been recorded among several modern groups and usually involve some sort of ritualistic cannibalism—for example, eating the brains of one's *already* dead relatives to carry on their spirit, power, etc. (Montagu, 1976). By around 100,000 y.a. (at the Krapina site in Yugoslavia) hominids were apparently systematically bashing each other's heads, but again the reasons may be more ritualistically rather than aggressively or nutritionally motivated.

Where does this leave us in terms of a comprehensive behavioral picture of *Homo sapiens*, the animal? Several relevant points can be made:

Point 1: Any animal capable of complex behavior (i.e., all vertebrates) is also capable of aggression.

Point 2: All social animals (primates in particular) must have efficient means of channeling such aggression, since they usually live in complex groups (composed of several adults—often including more than one male); therefore, we should expect aggression-mediating behavior to be deeply ingrained in our evolution (going back perhaps 60 million years).

Point 3: Observation of behavior in many "primitive" human groups shows they are patently *nonaggressive* (for example, the Tasaday—a small, isolated group discovered in the Philippines in 1971); in fact, given population densities and the frequency of interpersonal contacts in all human groups, it is obvious that the vast majority of human behavior is nonaggressive.

Point 4: While aggression is *usually* channeled, it can be and often is displayed by humans under a wide variety of circumstances—such aggressive behavior (individual fighting, but not warfare, which is usually much more ideologically motivated)

is readily mobilized using neurological equipment adapted for this function.

What is humankind? We are neither fallen angels nor risen apes; we are a complex social mammal and most of all, a primate. We retain the *capacity* for aggression, but the *social* necessities of primate life and the *cultural* necessities of hominid life have added a great deal of behavioral flexibility as well as the ability to control such behavior.

SOURCES:

Ardrey, Robert. *African Genesis*, New York: Atheneum, 1961.

Dart, Raymond. "The Predatory Transition from Apes to Man," *International Anthropological and Linguistic Review*, 1:207–208, 1954.

Montagu, Ashley. *The Nature of Human Aggression*, New York: Oxford University Press, 1976.

Morris, Desmond. *The Naked Ape*, New York: McGraw-Hill, 1967.

◇ CHAPTER TWELVE

◇ Introduction

For many years after their initial discovery, the South African australopithecines remained in an anthropological vacuum. Without a firm chronology, the best that anthropologists could do was to make educated guesses concerning their dates. Most scientists, therefore, placed all the South African material between 1,000,000 y.a. and 500,000 y.a. Few would have suspected the remarkable discoveries waiting to be made in East Africa, finds that would completely alter the chronology and interpretation of hominid evolution in the Plio-Pleistocene (5–1 m.y.a.)

◇ The East African Rift Valley

Stretching along a more than 1,200-mile trough extending through Ethiopia, Kenya, and Tanzania from the Red Sea in the north to the Serengeti Plain in the south is the eastern branch of the Great Rift Valley of Africa. This massive geological feature has been associated with active mountain building, faulting, and vulcanism over the last several million years.

Because of these gigantic earth movements, earlier sediments (normally buried under hundreds of feet of earth and rock) are literally thrown to the surface, where they become exposed to the trained eye of the paleoanthropologist. Such earth movements have exposed Miocene beds at sites in Kenya, along the shores of Lake Victoria, where remains of dryopiths and ramapiths have been found. In addition, Plio-Pleistocene sediments are also exposed all along the Rift Valley, and paleoanthropologists in recent years have made the most of this unique opportunity.

More than just exposing normally hidden deposits, rifting has stimulated volcanic activity, which in turn has provided a valuable means of chronometrically dating many sites in East Africa. Unlike the sites in South Africa, those along the Rift Valley are *datable* and have thus yielded much crucial information concerning the precise chronology of early hominid evolution.

Figure 12-1 East African Plio-Pleistocene hominid sites and the rift system.

◇ East African Hominid Sites

The site that focused attention on East Africa as a potential paleoanthropological gold mine was Olduvai Gorge in northern Tanzania. As discussed in great detail in Chapter 10, this site has offered unique opportunities because of the remarkable preservation of geological, paleontological, and archeological records. Following Mary Leakey's discovery of "Zinj," a robust australopithecine, in 1959 (and the subsequent dating of its find site at 1.75 m.y.a. by the K/Ar method), numerous other areas in East Africa have been surveyed and several intensively explored. We will briefly review the geological and chronological background of these important sites beginning with the earliest.

EARLIEST TRACES

For the period preceding 4 million years ago only very fragmentary remains possibly attributable to the Hominidae have been found. The earliest of these fossils comes from the Lake Baringo region of central Kenya and the Lake Turkana Basin of northernmost Kenya.

In the Lake Baringo region possible hominid fossils have been found within the following geological areas:

1. Ngorora Formation (age approximately 10 m.y.–11 m.y.)—one partial upper molar. Not much can be said about this tooth, except that it is "hominoidlike."
2. Lukeino Formation (age approximately 5.4 m.y.–7 m.y.)—one lower molar. While some authorities believe this tooth has "distinct hominid resemblances" (Howell, 1978), detailed metrical analysis indicates this tooth is clearly more pongidlike than hominidlike (Corruccini and McHenry, 1980).
3. Chemeron Formation (age approximately 4 m.y.)—one isolated temporal bone from the side of a skull. While not yet completely described, this bone appears quite hominidlike and has been provisionally referred to genus *Australopithecus* (Howell, 1978).
4. Tabarin (4–5? m.y.)—a newly discovered site west of Lake Baringo, where a partial hominid lower jaw was found in February 1984. The find—a small fragment containing two molar teeth—has not yet been described, and the dating for the site also is still quite provisional.

Figure 12-2 Early hominid localities in East Africa: The Baringo and Turkana Basins.

Abundant fossil-bearing beds spanning the period 10–4 m.y.a. are now known in the Lake Baringo area. Further explorations in this region may well contribute to filling that currently vexing gap in hominoid prehistory between 7 m.y.a. and 4 m.y.a.

Samburu Hills   To the north and west of Lake Baringo, some other early and potentially highly productive fossil-bearing beds have recently been explored. In the Samburu Hills of north-central Kenya, a team led by Hidemi Ishida of Osaka University discovered a partial hominoid jaw in August 1982. Consisting of the left half of an upper jaw with five teeth in place, this find has been *very* provisionally estimated as 8 million years old. Detailed descriptions are not yet available, but are eagerly awaited by paleoanthropologists.

Lothagam (Loth'-a-gum)   Located on the southwest side of Lake Turkana in northern Kenya, this site was first explored by a Harvard University team in the middle 1960s. No radiometric dates exist for this site, but faunal correlation suggests a date of around 5.5 m.y.a. While surveying the area in 1967, the Harvard team found one hominoid fossil, the back portion of a mandible with one molar in place. Although this specimen is too fragmentary for any firm decision to be based on it, the mandible does appear hominid. As such, it would be the earliest definite hominid discovery. (Some, in fact, have suggested a resemblance to *Australopithecus africanus* in South Africa.) Only surface surveys were done at Lothagam and no cultural material was found.

Kanapoi (Kan'-a-poy)   Located close to Lothagam on the southwest side of Lake Turkana, Kanapoi was also surveyed by members of the Harvard University research project. In 1965, they found one hominid bone at this site, the lower end of an upper arm bone, or humerus.

Dating of Kanapoi, also by means of faunal correlation, gives a date of approximately 4 m.y.a. Like Lothagam, the hominid material is too fragmentary to allow much elaboration, except to note that it appears hominid and resembles *A. africanus*. Also like Lothagam, surface surveys at Kanapoi revealed no archeological traces.

LAETOLI (LYE'-TOLL-EE)

Thirty miles south of Olduvai Gorge in northern Tanzania lie beds considerably older than those exposed at the Gorge. While Laetoli was first surveyed back in the 1930s, intensive work did not begin there until 1974, when Mary Leakey decided to reinvestigate the area.

With numerous volcanic sediments in the vicinity, accurate K/Ar testing is possible and provides a provisional date of 3.77–3.59 m.y.a. for this site. This date must still be considered provisional, since it has been calibrated by only one type of dating technique (K/Ar) and only on one kind of mineral (mica) (Curtis, 1981). As we will see shortly, it is crucial to corroborate dates through use of several different techniques in order to have confidence in the results.

Since systematic fossil recovery began at Laetoli in 1974, twenty-four fossil hominid specimens have been found, consisting almost exclusively of jaws and teeth with fragmentary postcranial remains of one immature individual (Johanson and White, 1979; White, 1980).

In February, 1978 Mary Leakey announced a remarkable discovery at Laetoli: fossilized footprints embossed into an ancient volcanic tuff more than 3.5 m.y.a.! Literally thousands of footprints have been found at this remarkable site, representing more than twenty different taxa (Pliocene elephants, horses, pigs, giraffes, antelopes, hyenas, and an abundance of hares). Several hominid footprints have also been found, including a trail more than 75 feet long, made by at least two—and perhaps three—individuals (Leakey and Hay, 1979) (See Fig. 12-3.)

Figure 12-3 Laetoli hominid footprint trail, northern Tanzania. The trail on the left was made by one individual; the one on the right seems to have been formed by two individuals, the second stepping in the footprints of the first.

Such discoveries of well-preserved hominid footprints are extremely important to furthering our understanding of human evolution. For the first time we can make *definite* statements regarding locomotory pattern and stature of early hominids. Initial analysis of these Pliocene footprints compared to modern humans suggests a stature of about 4 feet, 9 inches for the larger individual and 4 feet 1 inch for the smaller individual, who made the trail seen in Figure 12-3 (White, 1980). Studies of these impression patterns clearly show that the mode of locomotion of these hominids was fully bipedal, and, further, *very* similar to modern humans (Day and Wickens, 1980). Some researchers, however, have concluded that these early hominids were not bipedal in quite the same way that modern humans are (see p. 343). From detailed comparisons with modern humans, estimates of step length, cadence, and speed of walking have been ascertained, indicating that the Laetoli hominids moved in a "strolling" fashion with a rather short stride (Chateris et al., 1981).

HADAR (HA-DAR′) (AFAR TRIANGLE)

Potentially one of the most exciting areas for future research in East Africa is the Afar Triangle of northeastern Ethiopia, where the Red Sea, Rift Valley, and Gulf of Aden all intersect. A joint American-French team led by Don Johanson and the French geologist Maurice Taieb began intensive field work in this area in 1973. Concentrating on a 42 km² area in the central Afar called the Hadar, paleoanthropologists have found remarkably well-preserved geological beds 400–460 feet thick. Initial K/Ar dating has suggested an age of up to 3.6 m.y.a. for the older hominid fossils and 2.5 m.y.a. for the upper artifactual-bearing beds (Johanson and Edey, 1981). These dates, too, must be considered provisional until systematically corroborated by other laboratories and other dating techniques (Curtis, 1981).

Some of the chronology at the Hadar appears clearcut. For example, there is general agreement that the Lucy skeleton (see below) is about 3 million years old. Analysis of the older beds, however, has led to some ambiguity regarding their precise dating. Study of one of the volcanic tuffs at Hadar has suggested a correlation (i.e., the result of the same volcanic eruption) with well-defined tuffs at Omo in southern Ethiopia and East Lake Turkana in northern Kenya (see below for discussion of these areas). On the basis of this chemical fingerprinting of tuffs (Brown, 1982), the paleomagnetic data, and biostratigraphic interpretations (Boaz et al., 1982), some researchers have concluded the 3.6 m.y. date for the earlier beds at Hadar is too old; accordingly, they suggest a basal date for the hominid-bearing levels of around 3.2–3.3 m.y.a.

However, opinion still varies. The proposed correlation of the volcanic tuffs across northeastern Africa is not accepted by all researchers (e.g., Aronson et al., 1983). Moreover, the biostratigraphy is also subject to differing interpretations (White, 1983).

A 300,000 to 400,000 year discrepancy may not seem all that important, but it is a most significant time period (10% of the total *known* time range of hominids). The evidence from the South African australopithecine sites has shown us the monumental problems when a sound chronology is lacking, and the dating complexities at the Hadar point up the inadequacy of even relatively accurate estimates. To form a consistent theory of exactly what was going on in the Plio-Pleistocene, we need precise chronological controls.

The chronologies, however, often take years of study to sort out. Most crucially, cross-correlations between different dating techniques (K/Ar, biostratigraphy, paleomagnetism, fission-track) must be determined. As we will see presently, it took several years of this kind of cross-checking to establish the chronology of the important hominid locality of East Lake Turkana in northern Kenya.

Due to the excellent preservation conditions in the once-lakeside environment at Hadar, an extraordinary collection of fossilized bones has been discovered—6,000 specimens in the first two seasons alone! Among the fossil remains, at least thirty-six hominid individuals (up to a maximum of as many as sixty-five) have been discovered (Johanson and Taieb, 1980).

Two extraordinary discoveries at Hadar are most noteworthy. In 1974, a partial skeleton called "Lucy" was found eroding out of a hillside. This fossil is scientifically designated as Afar Locality (AL) 288-1, but is usually just called Lucy (after a popular Beatles' song, "Lucy in the Sky with Diamonds"). Representing almost 40% of a skeleton, this is one of the most complete individuals from anywhere in the world for the entire period before about 100,000 years ago.

The second find, a phenomenal discovery, came to light in 1975 at AL 333. Johanson and his amazed crew found dozens of hominid bones scattered along a hillside. These bones represented at least thirteen individuals including four infants. Possibly members of one social unit (a family?), this group apparently all died at the same time, perhaps during a flash flood. Considerable cultural material has been found in the Hadar area—mostly washed into stream channels, but some stone tools recently have been reported in context at a ?2.5 m.y.a. site, potentially making it the oldest cultural

Figure 12-4   Hadar deposits, northeastern Ethiopia.

◇ GREAT MOMENTS IN PREHISTORY
Discovery of the Hadar "Family," November to December, 1975

On November 1, I set out for the new area with photographer David Brill and a visiting scientist, Dr. Becky Sigmon.

Climbing into my Land Rover, David asked, "When do we find our next hominid?"

"Today," I replied.

In less than an hour, anthropology student John Kolar spotted an arm-bone fragment. From some distance away, Mike Bush, a medical student, shouted that he had found something just breaking the ground surface. It was the very first day on survey for Mike.

"Hominid teeth?" he asked, when we ran to him. There was no doubt.

We called that spot Afar Locality 333 and scheduled full excavation for the next day.

Morning found me at 333, lying on my side so that I could wield a dental pick to excavate the upper-jaw fragment Mike had found. Michèle Cavillon of our motion-picture crew called to me to look at some bones higher up the hill.

Two bone fragments lay side by side—one a partial femur and the other a fragmentary heel bone. Both were hominid.

Carefully, we started scouring the hillside. Two more leg bones—fibulae—showed up, but each from the same side. The same side? That could only indicate two individuals.

Then from high on the slope came a cry, "Look at the proximal femur—it's complete!" Turning I saw, outlined against the blue sky, the top end of a thigh bone. Even from a distance I could tell that it was not Lucy-size; it was much larger. Slowly I groped up the hillside and held the femur.

Mike wanted to come look but was distracted by finding two fragments composing a nearly complete lower jaw. The entire hillside was dotted with the bones of what were evidently at least two individuals.

We held a strategy meeting. Maurice established that the bones we found on the surface had originally been buried several yards up the slope. Mike chose a crew of seven workers to survey carefully every inch of the area and collect all bone material, sifting even the loose soil.

Time was of the essence. Rainstorms during the months of our absence could wash away fragments that would be lost forever down the ravines. I felt I was moving through a dream: Each day produced more remains.

The picture became tangled. Another upper jaw of an adult came to light. The wear pattern on the lower jaw we'd found did not match either of the uppers. At least three individuals had to be represented. More mandible fragments appeared that could not be definitely fitted to either upper jaw. Extraordinary! We had evidence of perhaps as many as five adults of the genus *Homo*.[*]

Apart from teeth and jaws, we recovered scores of hand and foot bones, leg bones, vertebrae, ribs, even a partial adult skull. A baby tooth turned up, suggesting the presence of a sixth hominid at the site. Then a nearly complete lower jaw of a baby appeared, as well as an almost intact palate with baby teeth. Not heavily worn, the teeth suggested that their possessor was only about 3 years old.

So we had evidence of young adults, old adults, and children—an entire assemblage of early hominids. All of them at one place. Nothing like this had ever been found!

SOURCE:
"Ethiopia Yields First 'Family' of Early Man" by Donald C. Johanson, *National Geographic Magazine*, Vol. 150, pp. 790–811, December 1976. Reprinted with permission of the publisher.

[*]Johanson and his colleagues later assigned all this material to *Australopithecus afarensis* (see p. 343).

evidence yet found. Most unfortunately, political unrest and sporadic warfare in Ethiopia forced a halt to further investigations at the Hadar in 1977. As the situation settled somewhat, hopes for further fieldwork were rekindled. In fact, initial survey work in the Afar Triangle (Middle Awash Valley) in 1981 uncovered fragments of a hominid femur and cranium (dated provisionally, 3.5–4.0 m.y.a.) (Clark et al., 1984). Plans were thus made for full-scale investigations in 1982, but Ethiopian authorities initiated a temporary moratorium on research that, for the moment, has stalled all efforts.

OMO (OH'-MOH)

The thickest and most continuous Plio-Pleistocene sequence in East Africa comes from the Omo River basin in southern Ethiopia just north of Lake Turkana. This site was also worked jointly by French and American scientists with F. Clark Howell of the University of California, Berkeley, leading the American team.

Total deposits at the Omo are more than one-half mile thick, and the area surveyed extends over more than 200 km². These exceedingly thick sediments are composed largely of lake and river deposits, but more than 100 volcanic ash deposits have also been recognized. These ash deposits provide an excellent basis for accurate K/Ar determinations. This dating technique, supported by paleomagnetic and biostratigraphic results, has placed the hominid-bearing levels at the Omo between 2.9 and 1.0 m.y.a.

A fantastically rich paleontological sample, more than 40,000 mammal specimens alone, has been collected at the Omo. This site, with its well-documented chronology and huge paleontological series, has become the basis for extrapolation to other East African and some South African sites.

Several cultural remains have come to light in the Omo area dating from around 2 m.y.a. Most of this cultural material consists of fragments of flakes struck from stone pebbles and chunks. Only one primary site, where archeological traces retain their original context, has been excavated, and it has revealed a large quantity of these rather crude-looking flakes. What hominids were doing at this location 2 m.y.a. is still somewhat of a mystery. Apparently, it was not a multi-purpose area like those at Olduvai, since no animal bones were found with the tools.

Hominid discoveries at the Omo come from 87 different localities and include more than 200 teeth, 9 lower jaws, 4 partial or fragmentary skulls, and a complete ulna (a lower-arm bone).

EAST LAKE TURKANA (TUR-CAN'-AH)

Richard Leakey, the second oldest son of Louis and Mary Leakey, has greatly benefited from the fossil-hunting training given him by his parents. In fact, in the huge, remote, arid area encompassing more than 400 square miles on the eastern side of Lake Turkana,* he and his field crew have found more

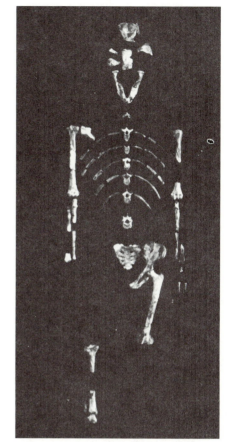

Figure 12-5 "Lucy," a partial hominid skeleton. Discovered at the Hadar in 1974.

---

*Lake Turkana was formerly called Lake Rudolf, and the naming of specimens reflects the earlier name: KNM-ER 406 = Kenya National Museum—East Rudolf specimen #406.

Figure 12-6   Excavations in progress. East Lake Turkana, northern Kenya.

than twice as many hominid remains since 1968 as his parents found at Olduvai in more than forty years of searching!

Geologically, the situation at East Lake Turkana is exceedingly complex, with deep sections of lake and river deposits crisscrossed by the effects of **tectonic movements**, stream action, and volcanic activity. While the latter is useful in providing material for radiometric dating, the geological complexities have made the precise chronology of the area a matter of dispute.

The latter sediments have been securely dated at 1.3–1.6 m.y.a., and consensus on this part of the chronology has existed for several years. However, there has been considerable dispute regarding the earlier levels, particularly a key volcanic bed called the KBS tuff.

Initially, conventional K/Ar was attempted, but frequent contamination of samples made results unreliable. Thus, a modification of this procedure* was performed, giving estimates of about 2.6 m.y.a. Later, on the basis of fission-track results and paleomagnetic interpretations, this date was moved down to 2.4 m.y.a.

Since, as we pointed out in Chapter 10, there are built-in errors in each of these different dating techniques, several methods must be used for cross-checking. Analysis of the faunal components at Turkana associated with the KBS tuff did not correlate with the 2.4 m.y. age when compared to fossil

---

*This technique is called the $^{40}Ar/^{39}Ar$ stepheating method and measures the steady decay of the ^{39}Ar isotope to that of ^{40}Ar.

materials from the Omo and Olduvai, but, in fact, suggested a date 600,000 years later. Further radiometric tests (using conventional K/Ar) corroborated these findings, and yet further analyses confirmed them: The lower hominid-bearing levels at Turkana are around 1.8 m.y. old.

Once again, then, as in our example of the dating of Hadar (see p. 334), the cross-correlation of different techniques is crucial to establishing a firm chronology for these ancient fossil sites. The sampling, testing, evaluation, comparison, and reconsideration of the Turkana dating materials took more than ten years before general agreement was reached.

As noted, numerous hominids have been discovered at East Lake Turkana in the last decade. The current total exceeds 150 hominid specimens, probably representing at least 100 individuals, and this fine sample includes several complete skulls, many jaws, and a fine assortment of post-cranial bones.

Next to Olduvai, Turkana has yielded the most cultural information concerning the behavior of early hominids. More than twenty archeological sites have been discovered, and excavation or testing has been done at ten localities. Two sites are of particular interest and are both directly associated with the KBS tuff (age, therefore, 1.8 m.y.a.). One is apparently a habitation site (base camp), whereas the other is the butchering site of an extinct form of hippopotamus. The stone tools from these earlier sediments at Turkana are in many ways reminiscent of the Oldowan industry in Bed I at Olduvai (with which they are contemporaneous).

OLDUVAI GORGE

The reader should by now be well acquainted with this remarkable site in northern Tanzania, particularly with its clear geological and chronological contributions. Hominid discoveries from Olduvai now total forty-eight individuals ranging in time from 1.85 m.y.a. to Upper Pleistocene times less than 50,000 years ago.

◇ East African Hominids

From the time period between 4 and 1 m.y.a., East African sites have thus far yielded close to 300 hominid individuals. This huge collection of material (much of it in well-dated contexts) has allowed paleoanthropologists to formulate (and reformulate) their interpretations of human evolution. At present, it appears that at least three groups (which we will refer to as "sets") of hominids are distinguishable in East Africa during the Plio-Pleistocene. The first of these sets was distinctly earlier and more primitive, while the other two appeared later and apparently lived contemporaneously for at least 1 million years.

SET I. EARLY PRIMITIVE AUSTRALOPITHECINES (A. afarensis)

Prior to 4 m.y.a. the fossil hominid (or "hominoid") remains from East Africa (which is all there is anywhere) are extremely scrappy, represented by only two molars, one cranial bone, two fragmentary jaws, and one arm bone (see

Tectonic movement
Movements of the earth—for example, along fault lines, during mountain building, and so forth.

Tuff
A solidified sediment of volcanic ash.

pp. 331–332). The best that can be said about this material is that it is hominoid, and in some cases, "hominidlike."

It is not until 4–3 m.y.a. that we get the first *definite* collection of hominid fossils. These crucial remains come from two sites explored within the last decade: Laetoli in northern Tanzania and Hadar in northeastern Ethiopia. From these two sites together several hundred hominid specimens have been recovered, representing a minimum of 60 individuals and perhaps close to 100. In addition, there are of course those fascinating hominid footprints from Laetoli.

Interpretation of fossil hominids is a laborious and highly technical undertaking. Finding the fossils is only the first step. They then have to be cleaned (often of intractable matrix), measured, described, reconstructed, and then measured again. It is thus not surprising that, although the first hominid specimens were recovered from Hadar and Laetoli in 1973 and 1974 respectively, their taxonomic affinity was not published until 1978 (Johanson et al., 1978); a systematic reappraisal of *all* hominids from the Plio-Pleistocene appeared soon thereafter in early 1979 (Johanson and White, 1979), and comprehensive descriptions were published in April, 1982, in the *American Journal of Physical Anthropology*.

Certainly, the announcement of a new species always raises considerable professional and public interest. The proposal of *A. afarensis* by Johanson and his colleagues was no exception. Predictably, not all the reaction was favorable. In science, this is a healthy attitude; hypotheses *always* need to be scrutinized and tested against further evidence.

What exactly is *A. afarensis*? Without question, it is more primitive than any of the australopithecine material from South Africa (discussed in the previous chapter) or any of the later hominid material from East Africa (discussed subsequently). In fact, *A. afarensis* is the most primitive of any definitely hominid group thus far found anywhere. By "primitive," we mean that *A. afarensis* is less evolved in any particular direction than is seen in later species of *Australopithecus* or *Homo*. That is to say, *A. afarensis* shares more primitive features with other early hominoids (such as *Dryopithecus*, *Sivapithecus*, etc.) and with living pongids than is true of later hominids, who display more derived characteristics.

For example, the teeth are quite primitive. The canines are often large, pointed teeth that slightly overlap; the first lower premolar is semisectorial, and the tooth rows are parallel or even posteriorly convergent (see Fig. 12-7a).

The pieces of crania that are preserved also display several primitive hominoid characteristics, including a compound sagittal/nuchal crest in the back (see Fig. 12-8), as well as several primitive features of the cranial base (involving the tubular appearance of the external ear canal, as well as an open-appearing articulation for the lower jaw). Cranial capacity estimates for *afarensis* show a mixed pattern when compared to later hominids. A provisional estimate for the one partially complete cranium (see Fig. 12-8b)—apparently a large individual—gives a figure of 500 cm³, but another, even more fragmentary, cranium is apparently quite a bit smaller and has been provisionally estimated at less than 400 cm³ (Holloway, 1983). Thus, for some individuals (males?), *afarensis* is well within the range of other australopithe-

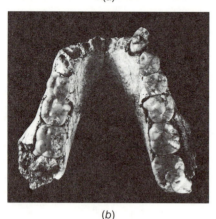

(a)

(b)

Figure 12-7 Jaws of *Australopithecus afarensis*. (a) Maxilla, AL-200-1a, from Hadar, Ethiopia. (Note the parallel tooth rows and large canines.); (b) mandible, L. H. 4, from Laetoli, Tanzania. This fossil is the type specimen for the new species, *Australopithecus afarensis*.

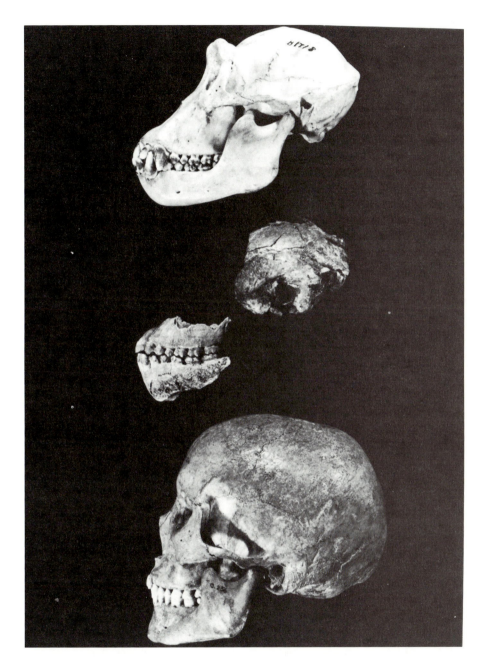

Figure 12-8 Comparison of hominoid crania. (*a*) Chimpanzee; (*b*) *Australopithecus afarensis* composite cranium assembled from three individuals—AL 333-45, 200-1a, and 400-1a; (*c*) human.

cine species, but others (females?) may be significantly smaller. An overall depiction of cranial size for *A. afarensis* as a species is not possible at this time—this part of the skeleton is unfortunately too poorly represented.

A host of postcranial pieces have been found at Hadar (mostly from the partial skeleton "Lucy," and from individuals of the "family" at AL 333). Initial impressions suggest that the upper limbs are long relative to the lower ones (also a primitive hominoid condition). In addition, the wrist and hand bones show several differences from modern humans. Stature can now be confidently estimated: *A. afarensis* was a short hominid. From her partial skeleton, Lucy is figured to be only about 3½ to 4 feet tall. However, Lucy—as demonstrated by her pelvis—was a female, and at Hadar and Laetoli, there is evidence of larger individuals as well. The most economical hypothesis explaining this variation is that *A. afarensis* was quite sexually dimorphic—the larger individuals are male and the smaller ones such as Lucy are female. Estimates of male stature can be approximated from the larger footprints at Laetoli, inferring a height of about 5 feet.

Without question, *A. afarensis* was a quite sexually dimorphic form. In fact, for overall body size, this species may have been as dimorphic as *any* living primate (i.e., as much as gorillas, orangs, or baboons). The elaborate behavioral reconstruction proposed by Lovejoy (1981) (see pp. 180–182) is based upon a *lack* of dimorphism in this species. Lovejoy points particularly to the relatively small degree of canine dimorphism between presumed males and females, but, even here, there are some reasonably good-sized differences apparent. Indeed, in the original description of *A. afarensis* (Johanson et al., 1978), a feature noted to define this form was "strong variation in canine size."

Beyond the claimed lack of canine size dimorphism (which has not been presented as *quantifiable* data compared to known ranges in living primates), there are even more serious problems with the Lovejoy model. In those few nonhuman primates that are monogamous (e.g., marmosets, gibbons) there is clearly little body size dimorphism. Yet, in *A. afarensis*, males may be twice as big as females, and thus rival the amount of dimorphism in the most dimorphic living primates. Clearly, these highly dimorphic primates are uniformly polygynous, and many less dimorphic species of monkeys also follow mostly polygynous mating strategies.

In conclusion, the physical evidence of sexual dimorphism within *A. afarensis* could hardly be used to argue for monogamous mating patterns. Indeed, it could be quite forcefully used to argue against it!

Behavioral debates such as these are certainly stimulating, but what is most interesting about *A. afarensis* is the distinctive physical morphology it displays. In a majority of dental and cranial features *A. afarensis* is clearly more primitive than are later hominids. This should not come as too great a surprise, since *afarensis* is at least 1 m.y. older than other East African finds and perhaps .5–.7 m.y. older than the oldest South African hominid. In fact, from the neck up, *A. afarensis* is so primitive, that without any evidence from the limb skeleton, one would be hard-pressed to call it a hominid at all (although the back teeth are large and heavily enameled, unlike pongids). In the teeth particularly, *A. afarensis* is in some ways reminiscent of Miocene hominoids (e.g., *Sivapithecus*) (Greenfield, 1979).

What then makes *A. afarensis* a hominid? The answer is revealed by its manner of locomotion. From the abundant limb bones recovered from Hadar and those beautiful footprints from Laetoli we know unequivocally that *afarensis* walked bipedally when progressing on the ground. Whether Lucy and her contemporaries still spent considerable time in the trees, and just how efficiently they walked, have recently become topics of major dispute.

Locomotion of Australopithecus afarensis A recent comprehensive analysis of the postcranial anatomy of *A. afarensis* by Jack Stern and Randall Susman of the State University of New York at Stony Brook has challenged the view that this early hominid walked bipedally, much as you or I (Stern and Susman, 1983). Their interpretation is based upon many parts of the skeleton (limbs, hands, feet, pelvis, etc.), which they have compared with other hominids (fossil and modern), as well as with great apes.

Such features as long, curved fingers and toes, long upper limbs but short lower limbs (Jungers, 1982), the positioning of the hip and knee joints, and pelvic orientation have led these researchers to two conclusions: (1) *A. afarensis* was capable of efficient climbing and probably spent considerable time in the trees (sleeping, feeding, escaping from predators, etc.); and (2) while on the ground, *A. afarensis* was a biped, but walked with a much less efficient bent-hip, bent-knee gait than that seen in modern humans.

As might be expected, these conclusions themselves have also been challenged. While pointing out some slight differences from modern humans in postcranial anatomy, Owen Lovejoy (1983) and his associates (e.g., Latimer, 1984) see nothing that suggests these hominids were arboreal or, conversely, that precluded them from being *very* efficient bipeds. Moreover, Lucy's "little legs" may not really be that small, considering her small body size (although her arms were apparently rather long) (Wolpoff, 1983b).

Other researchers have also noted differences between the postcranium of *A. afarensis* and later hominids. Interestingly, however, in many respects the hand and pelvis of *A. afarensis* are extremely similar to *A. africanus* from South Africa (Suzman, 1982; McHenry, 1983).

From all this debate, little has yet emerged in the way of consensus, except that all agree the *A. afarensis* did exhibit some kind of bipedal locomotion while on the ground. In searching for some middle ground between the opposing viewpoints, several researchers have suggested that *A. afarensis* could have been quite at home in the trees *as well as* being an efficient terrestrial biped (Wolpoff, 1983; McHenry, 1983). As one physical anthropologist has recently put it:

> One could imagine these diminutive early hominids making maximum use of *both* terrestrial and arboreal resources in spite of their commitment to exclusive bipedalism when on the ground. The contention of a mixed arboreal and terrestrial behavioural repertoire would make adaptive sense of the Hadar australopithecine forelimb, hand, and foot morphology without contradicting the evidence of the pelvis (Wolpoff, 1983, p. 451).

Challenges to Australopithecus afarensis Following the formal naming of *Australopithecus afarensis* in 1978 (Johanson et al., 1978) and its systematic interpretation a year later (Johanson and White, 1979), some questions have been raised concerning the status of this fossil hominid. In general, these challenges have taken two forms:

1. Is there more than one taxon represented at Hadar and Laetoli?
2. Can *afarensis* simply be included as an earlier member of *A. africanus* (i.e., the same species as at Sterkfontein and Makapansgat)?

Regarding the first question of possible multiple taxa (i.e., more than one species) at Hadar and Laetoli, some of the initial analyses by the primary researchers at Hadar did indeed suggest this possibility (Johanson and Taieb, 1976). Once *all* the Hadar material was evaluated, as well as comparisons made with the Laetoli fossils, this view was rejected (in favor of simply grouping all the fossils into one obviously variable, sexually dimorphic species).

Not all paleoanthropologists, however, are convinced of this latter interpretation. Two French paleoanthropologists, Brigett Senut and Christine Tardieu of the University of Paris, have suggested from analyses of postcranial remains (especially the elbow and knee) that early members of genus *Homo* may also have been present at Hadar and Laetoli (Senut, 1981).

While possible, of course, these claims have yet to be substantiated. Moreover, on the basis of detailed dental comparisons (White, et al., 1981), there appears to be no reason to "split" the samples into different taxa. Accordingly, *A. afarensis* is seen as a quite variable and most certainly sexually dimorphic form. As we have pointed out in Chapters 9 and 11, it is most prudent to assume a minimum number of species to be represented by any given fossil sample, unless *conclusive* evidence can be presented to suggest otherwise. For the present, anyway, most paleoanthropologists are comfortable regarding *all* the Hadar and Laetoli fossils as part of one species.

More troublesome, though, is the second question concerning the status of *A. afarensis*: Is it part of *A. africanus*? Phillip Tobias, the world's leading authority on the morphology of *A. africanus* in South Africa, believes that "the Laetoli and Hadar hominids cannot be distinguished at specific level from *A. africanus*" (Tobias, 1980, p. 1).

This assertion is also entirely possible, and, on the basis of Tobias's familiarity with the South African material, it requires serious consideration. Of all the other hominids to which *A. afarensis* could be compared, it is morphologically and chronologically closest to *A. africanus*. Yet, there are still some important differences in the face, cranial vault, mandible, and teeth, all of which consistently show *A. afarensis* to be more primitive than *A. africanus* (or, for that matter, any other known hominid) (White et al., 1981). More detailed comparisons will have to be done, but, given the overall primitive morphology of these early fossil hominids from Hadar and Laetoli, they are presently best considered within their own species, *A. afarensis*, and thus separate from *A. africanus*.

SET II. LATER AUSTRALOPITHECINES—EAST AFRICAN ROBUST FORMS (*A. boisei*, ALSO CALLED *A. robustus*)

After its discovery in 1959, the beautifully preserved cranium and upper dentition of "Zinj" was classified by Louis Leakey into a new and separate genus and species, *Zinjanthropus boisei* (boy'-see-eye). You may well ask, What biological basis was Leakey using to justify such a distinction? As it turned out, there was not much ground for postulating a totally separate genus, and most scientists (later including Leakey himself) have included this specimen in *Australopithecus*.

"Zinj" is a very robust young male australopithecine with enormous back teeth, a large broad face, and a sagittal crest atop the skull. In addition, the

Figure 12-9 *Australopithecus afarensis* re-constructed cranium—using evidence from several individuals and filling in portions for which no fossil data exist (shown in white).

skull displays considerable postorbital constriction and has a cranial capacity of 530 cm³, the same as the only South African robust australopithecine that can be measured. "Zinj's" third molars are newly erupted and unworn, suggesting his age at death was probably around 18 years.

When compared with material from South Africa, "Zinj" does show some differences in detail, but these are apparently due to one functional special-ization, the massive increase in cheek tooth size. While sufficient grounds do not exist to justify assigning this East African australopithecine to a genus distinct from those in South Africa, separate specific rank may well be called for. Therefore, "Zinj" is now usually referred to as *Australopithecus boisei*, specifically distinct from *A. africanus* and *A. robustus*. The direct biological implication is that the East African variety of robust australopithecine, re-moved by 2,000 miles from South Africa, were reproductively isolated from their contemporaries, *A. robustus*, to the south.

We must, however, remain cautious about unnecessarily splitting these fossil populations into biologically meaningless categories. We have chastised such splitting in the early interpretations of South African australopithecines (for example, Robert Broom's classification, see p. 314), and we should not be guilty of making the same error in East Africa. In fact, many authorities believe there is not a specific difference between *A. robustus* in the south and its robust contemporary in the eastern part of the continent. Since these inves-tigators feel there is not sufficient evidence to show that *A. boisei* falls *outside* the range of *A. robustus*, they call *both A. robustus* (the earlier name takes precedence).

In our ensuing discussion we will refer to the East African robust group as *A. boisei*, but this reference should not be interpreted as an ironclad biological conclusion. It simply provides, for the moment, a shorthand means of referring to the East African robust australopithecines.

Figure 12-10   Two mandibles discovered at East Lake Turkana. Note the difference in proportions of jaws and teeth; KNM-ER 818 (right) is one of the largest hominid mandibles ever found. KNM-ER 992 (left) is thought to be an early *Homo*. (Photographs of casts.)

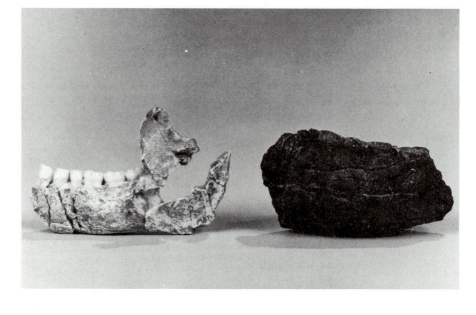

Figure 12-11   A robust australopithecine mandible from East Lake Turkana (KNM-ER 729). Note the enormous proportions of the molars and premolars.

Figure 12-12   The "demicranium" discovered at East Lake Turkana (KNM-ER 732). A female robust australopithecine?

A. boisei is a well-defined group in East Africa, not only at Olduvai, but at several other sites as well. From East Turkana, particularly, several fossils have been found that are clearly members of this species, including some mandibles of gigantic proportions. In addition, a few skulls from Turkana also belong to *A. boisei*. One of these, a nearly perfect skull (KNM-ER 406), is very much like "Zinj" and is also apparently a robust male australopithecine. Cranial capacity, estimated at 510 cm³, is a little smaller for the Turkana male, compared to the 530 cm³ figure for "Zinj."

Of course, *A. boisei* populations were variable, and one kind of variation we should expect to see is due to sexual dimorphism. In fact, another East Turkana fossil cranium shows this phenomenon exactly. The specimen KNM-ER 732 is a partial cranium, much like 406 and "Zinj" but smaller, particularly in the face and muscle attachment areas of the skull. Cranial capacity at around 500 cm³ for this **demicranium** is also slightly smaller than that approximated for the males. Comparison with modern populations of primates suggests that the pattern of variation seen between the larger and smaller skulls may well represent differences between males and females of one interbreeding species.

Postcranial bones at Turkana that are definitely attributable to *A. boisei* are difficult to ascertain exactly, for none has been found directly associated with a skull. However, one upper arm bone (humerus), ER 739, is very robust and quite uniquely shaped. Biomechanical reconstructions show it to be unlike *any* living hominoid. If this arm bone does indeed belong to *A. boisei*, it suggests that, postcranially, they may have been quite unusual compared to other hominids.

Further evidence along the same line comes from the Omo, where several teeth and three mandibles are, because of their size, attributed to *A. boisei*. In addition, an unusual ulna has been found which, like the Turkana humerus, also suggests that the forelimb of *A. boisei* is quite unlike other hominids.

Remains of *A. boisei* are also known from a nearly complete mandible 1 million years old from Peninj, a site near Lake Natron about seventy miles from Olduvai and also from a partial skull of about the same age (1.5–1.2 m.y.a.) from the Chesowanja site in central Kenya (in the Lake Baringo region).

Apparently, *A. boisei* does not appear anywhere in East Africa until about 2 m.y.a., and until about 1 m.y.a. lived basically unchanged. It is interesting to note that South African robust australopithecines (*A. robustus*) at Swartkrans and Kromdraai also do not appear until about this same time. Quite clearly, all varieties of robust australopithecines are much later than the more primitive *afarensis*—up to 1.0 m.y.–1.5 m.y. later. It is thus easier to understand the obviously more *derived* physical characteristics of robust australopithecines.

Many anthropologists speculate that these robust forms had a specialized vegetarian diet consisting mostly of small, hard objects (seeds, etc.). As a result of the rigorous demands of masticating these kinds of foods, robust forms gradually adopted a large back tooth chewing complex. Accompanying this change, structural modifications also occurred in the jaw and in rearrangements of cranial architecture, eventually producing that highly derived hominid form we recognize as a robust australopithecine.

First appearing at around 2 m.y.a., robust forms lived contemporaneously for 1 million years in East Africa (and perhaps South Africa also) with another, quite different, kind of hominid.

SET III. EARLY *Homo* (ALSO CALLED *Homo habilis*)

The first hint that another hominid was living contemporaneously in East Africa with *boisei* came at Olduvai Gorge in the early 1960s. Louis Leakey named a new form of hominid *Homo habilis* on the basis of remains, some a little older than "Zinj," others somewhat more recent (Leakey et al., 1964). Unfortunately, the remains at Olduvai attributable to this **taxon** are all either fragmentary or distorted in one way or another. The initial *habilis* material included a fragmentary skull with a distorted juvenile mandible (OH 7) and a partial skull with a complete upper and lower dentition (OH 13), called "Cinderella" by the Leakeys. A third *habilis* specimen, a severely fragmented skull, discovered after being trampled by local Masai cattle (OH 16), is known popularly as "Olduvai George." A final *habilis* skull, found in 1968, is a nearly complete cranium (OH 24) that was severely crushed. It required extensive restoration. This fossil, thought to be female, is called "Twiggy."

The *habilis* material at Olduvai ranges in time from 1.85 m.y.a. for the earliest to about 1.6 m.y.a. for the latest. Due to the fragmentary nature of the fossil remains, interpretations have been difficult and much disputed. The most immediately obvious feature distinguishing the *habilis* material from the australopithecines is cranial size. The six partial *habilis* skulls, although difficult to measure accurately, have an estimated average cranial capacity of 646 cm³ compared to 504 cm³ for all measurable robust australopithecines and 450 for graciles (Tobias, 1983). *Habilis*, therefore, shows a 26–42% cranial size increase respectively over both forms of australopithecine.

In their initial description of *habilis*, Leakey and his associates also pointed to differences from australopithecines in cranial shape (less postorbital con-

Demicranium
demi: half

Taxon (pl. taxa)
A population (or group of populations) that is judged to be sufficiently distinct and is assigned to a separate category (such as genus or species).

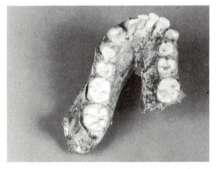

(*a*)

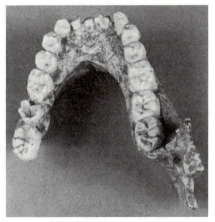

(*b*)

Figure 12-13 Two mandibles. Initially assigned to "*H. habilis*," from Olduvai Gorge. (*a*) OH 7; (*b*) OH 13, "Cinderella." These specimens are now usually referred to as "early *Homo*." (Photographs of casts.)

Figure 12-14 A nearly complete skull from Olduvai Gorge. Initially assigned to "H. habilis," OH 24, "Twiggy." This specimen may be an "early *Homo*" or perhaps, a gracile australopithecine. (Photograph of cast.)

striction) and in tooth proportions (larger front teeth relative to back teeth and narrower premolars).

The naming of this fossil material as *Homo habilis* (handy man) was meaningful from two perspectives. First of all, Leakey inferred that members of this group were the early Olduvai toolmakers. If true, how do we account for a robust australopithecine like "Zinj" lying in the middle of the largest living floor known at Olduvai? What was he doing there? Leakey has suggested he was the remains of a *habilis* meal! Excepting those instances where cutmarks are left behind (see pp. 292–293), we must point out that there is no clear way archeologically to establish the validity of such a claim. However, the debate over this assertion serves to demonstrate that cultural factors as well as physical morphology must be considered in the interpretation of hominids as biocultural organisms. Secondly, and most significantly, by calling this group *Homo*, Leakey was arguing for at least *two separate branches* of hominid evolution in the Plio-Pleistocene. Clearly only one could be on the main branch eventually leading to *Homo sapiens*. Labeling this new group *Homo* in opposition to *Australopithecus*, Leakey was guessing he had found our ancestors.

Since the initial evidence was so fragmentary, most paleoanthropologists were reluctant to accept *habilis* as a valid taxon distinct from *all* australopithecines. Differences from the hyperrobust East African variety (*A. boisei*) were certainly apparent; the difficulties arose in trying to distinguish *habilis* from *A. africanus*, particularly for dental traits that considerably overlap. Moreover, the ambiguous dating of the South African forms made it difficult to interpret the relationship between *A. africanus* and *habilis*.

Recent discoveries, especially from Lake Turkana, of better-preserved fossil material have shed new light on early *Homo* in the Plio-Pleistocene. The most important of this new *habilis* material is a nearly complete cranium (ER 1470) discovered at East Lake Turkana in 1972. With a cranial capacity of 775 cm³, this individual is well outside the known range for australopithecines and actually overlaps the lower boundary for *Homo*. In addition, the shape of the skull vault and face are in many respects unlike that of australopithecines.

Figure 12-15 Skull profiles (seen from above).

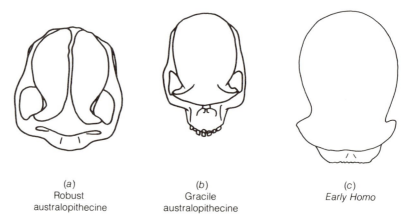

(a)
Robust
australopithecine

(b)
Gracile
australopithecine

(c)
Early Homo

Figure 12-16 The Kenyan team at East Lake Turkana. Kamoya Kimeu (driving) is the most successful fossil hunter in East Africa. He is responsible for dozens of important discoveries.

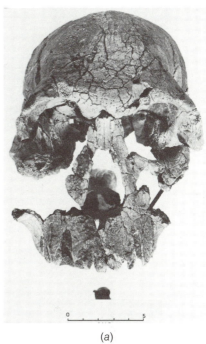

(a)

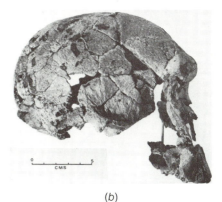

(b)

Figure 12-17 A nearly complete "early *Homo*" skull from East Lake Turkana (KNM-ER 1470). One of the most important single fossil hominid discoveries from East Africa. (a) Frontal view; (b) lateral view.

However, the face is still quite robust (Walker, 1976), and the fragments of tooth crowns that are preserved indicate the back teeth in this individual were quite large.

Additional discoveries at Turkana also strongly suggest the presence of a hominid lineage contemporaneous with and separate from australopithecines. Another skull discovered in 1972 (ER 1590) is similar to 1470 and may even be larger! Moreover, several mandibles, including two nearly complete specimens (ER 820 and 992), have tooth proportions (relatively larger front teeth) characteristic of our genus. Finally, several postcranial remains discovered at Turkana show a taller, more gracile group than that inferred for australopithecines. The dating of all this crucial early *Homo* material from Turkana is tied to the dating of the KBS tuff. As we discussed on p. 338, the dating of this key bed has recently been established at around 1.8 m.y.a. Thus, the earliest *Homo* materials at Turkana *and* Olduvai are contemporaneous (i.e., 1.8–2.0 m.y.a.).

Other Plio-Pleistocene sites also have revealed possible early members of the genus *Homo*. From the Omo in southern Ethiopia scattered remains of a few teeth and small cranial fragments are similar in pattern to other comparable early *Homo* material.

If the discussion of *Australopithecus* versus *Homo* seems confusing, do not despair. The distinction is not yet well formulated and causes much confusion even in professional ranks. It is true that the *A. boisei* group of australopithecines in East Africa is quite distinctive, characterized by an enormous back-tooth grinding complex. It is equally true that another whole set of gracile fossil hominids in East Africa usually called early *Homo* does not fall into this group. The thorny problem comes in trying to distinguish these gracile individuals (*Homo sp.*) from the South African gracile variety of australopithe-

Figure 12-18 An "early *Homo*" mandible from East Lake Turkana (KNM-ER 820). Note the relatively even proportions of back teeth to front teeth.

Table 12-1 *Australopithecus* Compared to Early *Homo*

Australopithecus	Early *Homo*
Cranial:	
Face large relative to vault size	Face small relative to vault size

Absolute size of cranium smaller:
    gracile $= 450$ cm³ ($N = 7$)
    robust $= 504$ cm³ ($N = 5$)
	Cranium–larger
	    average $= 646$ cm³ ($N = 6$)

Cranial bone thinner	Cranial bone thicker
More postorbital construction	Less postorbital construction
Mandible large, more massive Ramus of mandible, higher	Mandible smaller, not as thick Ramus not as high
Shape of mandible: Narrow in front diverges in back, as:	Mandible more open in front, not as divergent in back; shaped more as:
 -shaped	 -shaped
Front teeth relatively quite small to very small compared to back teeth	Front teeth are larger relative to size of back teeth—which, in some cases (ER 1470), are still very large
Postcranial:	
Differences not yet well worked out, but some apparent differences in femur: Upper (proximal) end; smaller head, flatter, longer neck	Head larger, neck more round in cross-section and not as relatively long

After Leakey et al., 1964; Walker, 1976; Wood, 1976; Tobias, 1976; Howell, 1978; Tobias, 1983.

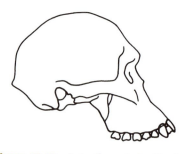

Figure 12-19 A gracile australopithecine.

cines, *A. africanus*. Since much overlap exists in physical traits (and probably chronology as well) between these two forms, this will never be an easy task. (For a summary of the current perspectives regarding the distinction between *Australopithecus* and *Homo* in the Plio-Pleistocene see Table 12-1.)

On the basis of evidence from Olduvai and particularly from Lake Turkana we can reasonably postulate that *Homo* was present in East Africa by *at least* 2 m.y.a., developing in parallel with at least one line (*A. boisei*) of australopithecines. These two hominid lines lived contemporaneously for a minimum of 1 million years, after which the australopithecine lineage apparently disappears forever. At the same time, the *habilis* line was emerging into a later form, *Homo erectus*, which, in turn, developed into *H. sapiens*.

In the next chapter, we will take up in detail several alternative theories dealing with evolutionary relationships of these fossil hominids in the Plio-Pleistocene.

◇ Summary

The East African Rift Valley contains several Plio-Pleistocene hominid sites ranging in time from slightly more than 5 m.y.a. up to about 1 m.y.a. The list that follows is a summary of these sites, their location, estimated ages, and a tentative designation of the kinds of hominids found:

Site Name	Location	Age (m.y.a.)	Hominids
Peninj	N. Tanzania	1	1 individual; australopithecine
Olduvai	N. Tanzania	1.85–1	48 specimens; australopithecines; early *Homo*
Turkana	N. Kenya (eastern side of Lake Turkana)	1.9–1.3	More than 150 specimens; many australopithecines; several early *Homo*
Omo	S. Ethiopia	2.9–1	215 specimens; several dozen individuals? australopithecines; some early *Homo*
Hadar	N.E. Ethiopia	?3.7–2.6	Minimum of 36 individuals (maximum of 65); early australopithecine (*A. afarensis*)
Laetoli	N. Tanzania	3.77–3.59	24 hominids; early australopithecine (*A. afarensis*)
Kanapoi	N. Kenya (S.W. Lake Turkana)	4	1 hominid = australopithecine??
Lothagam	N. Kenya (S.W. Lake Turkana)	5.5	1 hominid = australopithecine??

◇ Questions for Review

1. Why are the early hominid sites in East Africa so much better dated than those in South Africa (discussed in Chapter 11)?
2. In East Africa all the early hominid sites are found along the Rift Valley. Why is this significant?
3. Compare the various East African Plio-Pleistocene sites for the kinds of cultural information uncovered.
4. How does the dating problem of the KBS tuff at Lake Turkana illustrate the necessity for cross-correlation of several dating techniques?
5. What hominid sites have yielded remains of *A. afarensis*? In what ways is the fossil material more primitive than other hominids from South and East Africa?
6. What kinds of robust australopithecines have been found in East Africa? How do they compare with South African australopithecines?
7. Why are some Plio-Pleistocene hominids from East Africa called "early *Homo*"? What does this imply for the evolutionary relationships of the australopithecines?

8. What did Louis Leakey mean by using the specific name, "habilis" for a fossil hominid from Olduvai?

9. Compare the morphological features of early *Homo* with *Australopithecus*. Is it easier to draw a clear distinction between *Homo* and robust australopithecines (*A. robustus; A. boisei*) or gracile (*A. africanus*) ones? Why?

CONTENTS

Plio-Pleistocene Hominids: Organization and Interpretation

Anthropologists have long been concerned with the behavioral evolution of our species. Accompanying changes in anatomy (locomotion, dentition, brain size and shape) were changes in mating patterns, social structure, cultural innovations, and, eventually, language. In fact, changes in these behavioral complexes are what mostly *explain* the concomitant adaptations in human biological structure.

We are, then, vitally interested in the behavioral adaptations of our early hominid ancestors. In seeking to reconstruct the behavioral patterns of these early hominids, anthropologists use inferences drawn from modern primates, social carnivores, and hunting-gathering people (see Chapter 8). In addition, they derive information directly from the paleoanthropological record (see Chapter 10).

Despite numerous detailed and serious attempts at such behavioral reconstructions, the conclusions must largely remain speculative. In point of fact, behavior does not fossilize. Accordingly, researchers must rely considerably upon their imaginations in creating scenarios of early hominid behavioral evolution. In such an atmosphere, biases often emerge; these biased renditions, in turn, stimulate heated debates and alternative scenarios—often as narrow as those being attacked.

Probably no topic has stimulated more controversy (or has been more riddled with implicit biases) than the debate concerning origins of hominid sex-role differences. Did early hominid males have characteristically different behavioral adaptations than their female counterparts? Did one sex dominate the frontier of early hominid cultural innovation? And if one sex did lead the way, which one?

A now well-known rendition of early hominid behavioral development was popularized in the 1960s and 1970s. According to this "man, the hunter" theory, the hunting of large animals by males was the central stimulus of hominid behavioral evolution. According to such widely read works as Desmond Morris' *The Naked Ape* (1967) and several books by Robert Ardrey (including *The Hunting Hypothesis*, 1976), early apish-looking forms *became* hominids as a result of a hunting way of life. As Ardrey states, "Man is man, and not a chimpanzee, because for millions upon millions of evolving years we killed for a living" (1976, p. 10).

In this reconstruction, the hunting of large, dangerous mammals by co-operating groups of males fostered the development of intelligence, language, tools, and bipedalism. Increased intelligence accompanied by the development of weapons is also blamed in this scenario for the roots of human aggressiveness, murder, and warfare. (See Issue, Chapter 12.)

This "man, the hunter" scenario further suggests that while the males are leading the vanguard in hominid evolution, females remain mostly sedentary, tied to the home base by the burden of dependent young. Females may have contributed some wild plant foods to the group's subsistence, but this is not seen as a particularly challenging (and certainly not a very noble) endeavor. In this situation of marked division of labor, sexual relationships quickly changed. Males, constantly away from the home base (and, thus, away from the females too) could not keep a watchful eye over their mates. In order to better insure fidelity (and to reduce the risk of cuckoldry), monogamy came into being. In this way, a male would be assured that the young in

which he invested was his own. This important factor of male-female bonding as a product of differential foraging patterns has recently been forcefully restated by Owen Lovejoy (1981). (See p. 181.)

From the female's point of view, it would be beneficial to maintain a close bond with a provisioning male. Consequently, she would want to appear "attractive," and thus, through time, the female breasts and buttocks would become more conspicuous. Besides rearing their young and being attractive sex objects, females were useful to males in another way. Groups of male hunters living in the same area might occasionally come into potentially dangerous competition for the same resources. As a means of solidifying political ties between groups, the males would thus routinely exchange females (by giving or "selling" their daughters to neighboring bands).

Thus, in a single stroke, this complex of features accounts for human intelligence, sexual practices, and political organization.

As might be expected, such a male-centered scenario did not go unchallenged. Ignoring females or relegating them to a definitely inferior role in human behavioral evolution drew sharp criticism from several quarters. As one anthropologist noted:

So, while the males were out hunting, developing all their skills, learning to cooperate, inventing language, inventing art, creating tools and weapons, the poor dependent females were sitting back at the home base having one child after another and waiting for the males to bring home the bacon. While this reconstruction is certainly ingenious, it gives one the decided impression that only half the species—the male half—did any evolving. In addition to containing a number of logical gaps, the argument becomes somewhat doubtful in the light of modern knowledge of genetics and primate behavior (Slocum, 1975, p. 42).

In fact, such a rigid rendering of our ancestors' behavior does not stand up to critical examination. Hunting is never defined rigorously. Does it include only large, terrestrial mammals? What of smaller mammals, sea mammals, fish, and birds? In numerous documented human societies, females actively participate in exploiting these latter resources.

Moreover, nonhuman primates do not conform to predictions derived from the "man, the hunter" model. For example, among chimpanzees, females do most of the toolmaking, not the males. Finally, in most nonhuman primates (most mammals, for that matter), it is the females—not the males—who choose with whom to mate.

Granting that the hunting hypothesis does not work, what alternatives have been proposed? As a reaction to male-centered views, Elaine Morgan (1972) advanced the "aquatic hypothesis." In this rendition, females are seen as the pioneers of hominid evolution. But rather than having the dramatic changes of hominid evolution occur on the savanna, Morgan has them take place on the seashore. As females lead the way to bipedal locomotion, cultural innovation, and intellectual development, the poor males are seen as splashing pitifully behind.

Unfortunately, this theory has less to back it up than the hunting hypothesis. Not a shred (even a watery one) of evidence has ever been discovered in the contexts predicted by the aquatic theory. Little is accomplished by such unsubstantiated overzealous speculation. Chauvinism—whether male or female—does not elucidate our origins and only obscures the evolutionary processes that operated on the *whole* species.

Can nothing then be concluded about differential male-female sex roles? While the pattern is not as rigid as the hunting hypothesis advocates would have us believe, in the vast majority of human societies hunting of large, terrestrial mammals is almost always a male activity. In fact, a comprehensive cross-cultural survey shows that of 179 societies, males do the hunting exclusively in 166, both sexes participate in 13, and in *no* group is hunting done exclusively by females (Murdock, 1965).

In addition, as we noted in Chapter 8, there is some incipient division of labor in foraging patterns among chimpanzees. Females tend to concentrate more on termiting, while hunting (though it is only occasional) is done mostly by males. Early hominids, expanding upon such a subsistence base, eventually adapted a greater sexual division of labor than found in any other primate. Two points, however, must be kept in mind. First, both the gathering of wild plant foods and the hunting of animals would have been indispensible components of the diet. Consequently, *both* males and females always played a significant role. Secondly, the strategies must always have been somewhat flexible. With a shifting, usually unpredictable resource base, nothing else would have worked. As a result, males probably always did a considerable amount of gathering and in most foraging societies still do. Moreover, females—while not usually engaged in the stalking and killing of large prey—nonetheless contribute significantly to meat acquisition. Once large animals have been killed, there still remain the arduous tasks of butchering and transport back to the home base. In many societies, women and men participate equally in these activities.

A balanced view of human behavioral evolution must avoid simplistic and overly rigid scenarios. As recently stated by a researcher concerned with reconstructing early hominid behavior:

Both *sexes must have been able to care for young, protect themselves from predators, make and use tools, and freely move about the environment in order to exploit available resources widely distributed through space and time. It is this range of behaviors—the overall behavioral flexibility of both sexes—that may have been the* primary *ingredient of early hominids' success in the savanna environment (Zihlman, 1981, p. 97).*

SOURCES:

Ardrey, Robert. *The Hunting Hypothesis*. New York: Atheneum, 1976.

Dahlberg, Frances (ed.). *Woman the Gatherer*. New Haven: Yale University Press, 1981.

Lovejoy, C. Owen. "The Origin of Man," *Science*, 211:341–350, 1981.

Morgan, Elaine. *The Descent of Woman*. New York: Stein and Day, 1972.

Morris, Desmond. *The Naked Ape*. New York: McGraw-Hill, 1967.

Murdock, G. P. *Culture and Society*, Pittsburgh: University of Pittsburgh Press, 1965.

Slocum, Sally. "Woman the Gatherer: Male Bias in Anthropology," In: *Toward an Anthropology of Women*, R. R. Reiter, ed., New York: Monthly Review Press, pp. 36–50, 1975.

Zihlman, Adrienne L. "Women as Shapers of the Human Adaptation," In: *Woman the Gatherer, op. cit.*, pp. 75–120, 1981.

◇ Introduction

We have seen in the last two chapters that a vast and complex array of early hominid material has been discovered in South and East Africa. In just the past few years, particularly in the eastern part of the continent, a great number of new discoveries have been made. We now have Plio-Pleistocene hominid collections totaling close to 200 individuals from South Africa and probably more than 300 from East Africa. Given the size and often fragmentary nature of the sample, along with the fact that a good deal of it is so recently discovered, we should not be surprised that many complications arise when it comes to interpretation. In addition, both popular enthusiasm and the strong personalities often connected with fossil hominid discoveries have generated even more confusion.

In this chapter, we will look at several *theories* that attempt to organize the huge amount of Plio-Pleistocene hominid material. We ask you to remember that these are only theories and must remain so, given the incomplete nature of the fossil record. Even considering the seemingly very large number of fossils there is a *great* deal of time over which they were distributed. If we estimate about 500 total individuals from all African sites recovered thus far for the period 4–1 m.y.a., we still are sampling just one individual for every 6000 years! Until much of the new material from East Africa has been properly analyzed and detailed reports published, we cannot form even reasonably secure hypotheses without extreme difficulty. At the present time, only a very few East African hominids have been thoroughly studied; all the rest are thus far described in preliminary reports.

It will no doubt appear that many opposing and conflicting theories attempt to describe exactly what is going on in human evolution during the crucial period between 5 and 1 m.y.a. And, indeed, there are many theories. Hominid fossils are intriguing to both scientists and nonscientists, for some of these ancient bones and teeth are probably those of our direct ancestors. Equally intriguing, some of these fossils are representatives of populations of our close relatives that apparently met with extinction. We would like to know how these animals lived, what kinds of adaptations (physical and cultural) they displayed, and why some continued to evolve while others died out.

◇ More Hominids—More Complications

In our review of hominid evolution in the Plio-Pleistocene, we have discussed two varieties of australopithecines in South Africa, probably representing two separate species (*A. africanus* and *A. robustus*). In East Africa, three forms are known: an early primitive australopithecine (*A. afarensis*); a later, hyperrobust form (*A. boisei*); and one smaller but brainier than any of the other forms and therefore called an early member of genus *Homo* (*H. habilis*). The vast majority

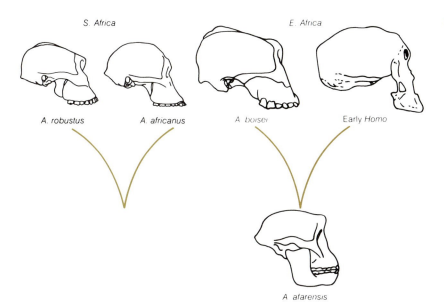

Figure 13-1　Plio-Pleistocene hominid evolution—a simple reconstruction.

of hominid discoveries from the Plio-Pleistocene can be assigned to one of these groups. However, a few fossils do not fit neatly into this scheme. As noted, most of this material is quite new and conclusions must, therefore, remain highly speculative at this stage. Following are three more considerations drawn from this newly discovered fossil material. We will eventually work them into our interpretations of early hominid evolution.

A. africanus IN EAST AFRICA?

We have discussed in detail (Chapter 11) the gracile form of australopithecine from South Africa called *A. africanus*. This form combines small brain size and relatively small back teeth (premolars and molars, compared to the massive ones seen in the robust forms) and is well known in South Africa at about 3–2 m.y.a. But what about East Africa? From here we have after 2 m.y.a. a very robust form with massive jaws and back teeth (*A. boisei*), and a smaller form with scaled down tooth proportions and a large brain (*Homo habilis*). Until recently, a hominid with the combination of a small brain and moderately sized teeth (i.e., *africanus*) was not recognized in East Africa. As already noted, it is sometimes extremely difficult to distinguish the individuals assigned to early *H. habilis* from the smaller gracile australopithecines (*A. africanus*).

The major differences most often underscored are in brain size and tooth proportions, but these distinctions are often impossible to define in fragmentary remains. Since both gracile australopithecines and early populations of genus *Homo* have considerable within-group variation (individual, sexual dimorphism, etc.), they may also have considerable overlap of structural traits, such as tooth and brain size. Operationally, then, in East Africa it becomes a tortuous task to distinguish early members of genus *Homo* on one hand and gracile australopithecines on the other. The East African evidence of a third

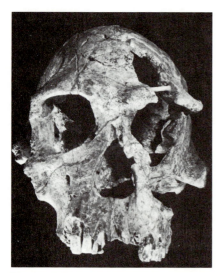

Figure 13-2 A nearly complete cranium (ER 1813) discovered at East Lake Turkana, 1973. Evidence of *A. africanus* in East Africa 1.3–1.6 m.y.a.?

kind of hominid, in addition to robust *A. boisei* and *H. habilis* is tenuous, but some suggestive clues do exist.

A fossil skull found at East Turkana in 1973 (ER 1813) dated 1.6–1.3 m.y.a. led Richard Leakey (1974) to suggest the presence of *A. africanus* in East Africa contemporaneous with *A. boisei* and *Homo*. Additional finds (at the Omo) of mandibular fragments, one upper arm bone, and about twenty teeth (from around 2.5 m.y.a.) may also belong to members of *A. africanus*. Some of the remains from Olduvai initially attributed to "*habilis*," particularly the skull called "Twiggy," may again be a gracile australopithecine.

As yet, this issue is unresolved. Most researchers, for the moment, prefer to keep the evolutionary picture as uncomplicated (parsimonious) as the evidence permits. Consequently, the potential *africanus* individuals noted above are simply regarded as small representatives of *H. habilis*. In fact, within the samples used to estimate cranial capacities for *H. habilis* (cited on p. 347), both ER 1813 (513 cm³) and OH 24 ("Twiggy"—597 cm³) were included (following Tobias, 1983b). It should be noted, however, that if these two specimens were deleted from the *habilis* sample, the average cranial size for the species (using the four other specimens) would be significantly larger.

Homo habilis IN SOUTH AFRICA?

Some recently discovered evidence suggests that, as in East Africa, early *Homo* lived contemporaneously with australopithecines in South Africa.

The first recognition of a more advanced hominid already present in australopithecine times was made by Broom and Robinson in the early 1950s. Fossil finds from Swartkrans, the site yielding most of the remains of *A. robustus*, also contained fragments (perhaps close to 2 million years old) initially called "Telanthropus capensis" (Robinson, 1953). While suggestive, "Telanthropus" remains were too fragmentary to generate much excitement. More complete evidence came to light in a museum twenty years later by simply joining pieces of previously discovered fossils.

Ron Clarke, a physical anthropology student and expert in fossil reconstruction, was looking at hominid material in the Transvaal museum in Pretoria. While comparing fragments of two "different" individuals, one supposedly "Telanthropus" and the other a robust australopithecine, he noted they fitted together perfectly! With the additon of yet another piece, a composite cranium was assembled making up a good part of the face and the left side of the skull of the same individual (Clarke and Howell, 1972). Presto, a "new" find, much more complete than anything previously attributed to an advanced hominid lineage in South Africa! Thus, we can say a good deal more about it than was true for the original "Telanthropus" fossils.

The shape of the brow as well as the front part of the vault of the composite skull (SK 80/846/847) are more *Homo*-like than are australopithecine skulls. While cranial capacity cannot accurately be determined from this partial cranium, the relatively higher forehead and shallower postorbital constriction indicate a larger brain size than that of australopithecines. The key diagnostic feature of size of face relative to skull vault is apparently similar for this Swartkrans composite cranium and the East African representatives of *H. habilis*.

Figure 13-3 The composite cranium (Sk. 847) from Swartkrans. Evidence of *Homo habilis* in South Africa?

◇ Box 13-1   A Visit to the Plio-Pleistocene: East Lake Turkana, Late One Afternoon

If an observer could be transported back through time and climb a tree in the area where the Koobi Fora Formation was accumulating, what would he see?

As the upper branches are reached, the climber would find himself in a ribbon of woodland winding out through open areas. A kilometer or so away to the west would be seen the swampy shores of the lake, teeming with birds, basking crocodiles, and *Euthecodons*. Here and there are schools of hippos. Looking east, in the distance some ten or twelve kilometers away lie low, rolling hills covered with savanna vegetation. From the hills, fingers of trees and bush extend fanwise out into the deltaic plains. These would include groves of large *Acacia*, *Celtis*, and *Ficus* trees along the watercourses, fringed by shrubs and bushes. Troops of colobus move in the tree tops, while lower down are some mangabey. Scattered through the bush, the observer might see small groups of waterbuck, impala, and kudu, while out in the open areas beyond would be herds of alcelaphine antelope and some gazelle (*Megalotragus* and *Antidorcas*). Among the undergrowth little groups of *Mesochoerus* pigs rootle, munching herbiage.

Peering down through the branches of the tree, the climber would see below the clean sandy bed of a watercourse, dry here, but with a tidemark of grass and twigs caught in the fringing bushes and showing the passage of seasonal floods. Some distance away down the channel is a small residual pool.

Out beyond the bushes can be seen large open floodplains, covered with grasses and rushes, partly dry at those seasons of the year when the lake is low and when the river is not in spate. Far across the plains, a group of four or five men approach; although they are too far off for the perception of detail, the observer feels confident that they are men because they are striding along, fully upright, and in their hands they carry staves.

To continue the reconstruction in a more purely imaginative vein: as the men approach, the observer becomes aware of other primates below him. A group of creatures has been reclining on the sand in the shade of a tree while some youngsters play around them. As the men approach, these creatures rise and it becomes apparent that they too are bipedal. They seem to be female, and they whoop excitedly as some of the young run out to meet the arriving party, which can now be seen to consist mainly of males. The two groups come together in the shade of the tree, and there is excited calling, gesturing and greeting contacts. Now the observer can see them better, perhaps he begins to wonder about calling them men; they are upright and formed like men, but they are rather small, and when in groups they do not seem to engage in articulate speech. There are a wealth of vocal and gestural signals in their interaction, but no sustained sequential sound patterns.

The object being carried is the carcass of an impala, and the group congregates around this in high excitement; there is some pushing and shoving and flashes of temper and threat. Then one of the largest males takes two objects from a heap at the foot of the tree. There are sharp clacking sounds as he squats down and bangs these together repeatedly. The other creatures scramble around picking up the small sharp chips that have been detached from the stones. When there is a small scatter of flakes on the ground at his feet, the stone worker drops the two chunks, sorts through the fragments and selects two or three pieces. Turning back to the carcass, this leading male starts to make incisions. First the belly is slit open and the entrails pulled out; the guts are set on one side, but there is excited squabbling over the liver, lungs, and kidneys; these are torn apart, some individuals grab pieces and run to the periphery of the group. Then the creatures return to the carcass; one male severs skin, muscle and sinew so as to disengage them from the trunk, while some others pull at limbs. Each adult male finishes up with a segment of the carcass and withdraws to a corner of the clearing, with one or two females and juveniles congregating around him. They sit chewing and cutting at the meat, with morsels changing hands at intervals. Two adolescent males sit at the periphery with a part of the intestines. They squeeze out the dung and chew at the entrails. One of the males gets up, stretches his arms, scratches under his arm pits and then sits down. He leans against the tree, gives a loud belch and pats his belly. . . . *End of scenario.*

SOURCE:

"The Activities of Early Hominids" by Glynn Ll. Isaac. In *Human Origins. Louis Leakey and the East African Evidence*, G. Isaac and E. R. McCown, eds. The Benjamin/Cummings Publishing Company, Inc. © 1976. Reprinted with permission of the publisher.

Figure 13-4 Hominid skull from Sterkfontein (Stw. 53).

Further evidence along these same lines was found in August, 1976, at Sterkfontein. New excavations in the west pit area of Sterkfontein uncovered a partial cranium and part of an associated lower jaw. This skull is fairly complete, including a good part of the face with most of the upper dentition and parts of the cranial vault. Like the Swartkrans composite skull, this new find from Sterkfontein is also *Homo*-like, with a higher forehead and shallower postorbital constriction. The cranial capacity has not yet been approximated, but it is probably larger than that of australopithecines.

Thus it seems reasonable to postulate, at least tentatively, that *H. habilis* was living contemporaneously with australopithecines in South Africa as well as East Africa between 2 and 1.5 m.y.a. We must remember that dating in South Africa is far from clear. It seems apparent, however, that at both Swartkrans and Sterkfontein, the fossils provisionally referred to here as genus *Homo* are demonstrably younger than the australopithecines at these sites (Howell, 1978). How much younger they are nobody knows. If these fossils prove to be closer to 1 m.y.a. than to 2 m.y.a., they might most accurately be considered representatives of *Homo erectus*. (See the following section.)

Homo erectus IN THE PLIO-PLEISTOCENE

Homo habilis in East Africa and probably South Africa appears well on its way in human evolution by 2 m.y.a. Well on its way where? As we shall see in the next chapter, the fossil hominid group that succeeded early *Homo* and preceded *Homo sapiens* is called *Homo erectus*. For several years, *Homo erectus* was thought to have appeared long *after* the australopithecines, coming on the scene as late as 500,000 years ago. However, a fossil skull found at Olduvai by Louis Leakey in 1960 pushed this date back to at least 1 m.y.a., and recent calibration of dates in the upper beds at Olduvai may push this back even further—to about 1.2 m.y.a.

Yet another important fossil hominid discovery from Lake Turkana was uncovered by Richard Leakey's remarkably successful crew in September, 1975. A nearly perfectly preserved skull (ER 3733), looking much like well-known members of Asian *erectus*, was recovered from beds dating 1.6–1.3 m.y.a. What is more, from these same beds come undisputed fossils of robust australopithecines (*A. boisei*) plus perhaps members of *A. africanus*. Consequently, it appears undeniable that *Homo erectus* was living contemporaneously in East Africa with australopithecines, perhaps as much as 1.6 m.y.a.*

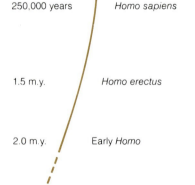

250,000 years	*Homo sapiens*
1.5 m.y.	*Homo erectus*
2.0 m.y.	Early *Homo*

Figure 13-5 The "main line" of hominid evolution over the last 2 million years.

◇ Hominids in the Plio-Pleistocene Outside Africa?

To date, the vast majority of hominid fossils and artifactual material predating 1 million years ago have been found on the African continent. There are, however, some claims (although still unconfirmed) that hominids may have dispersed from Africa earlier than had previously been believed (perhaps well before 1 m.y.a.).

*In addition, the mostly complete skeleton of a *Homo erectus* child (age, 12 years) was found on the west side of Lake Turkana in 1984 (date, approximately 1.6 m.y.a.).

JAVA

As we will see in the next chapter, there are abundant *Homo erectus* remains known from Java that are almost certainly Middle Pleistocene in date (i.e., after 700,000 B.P.*). Some fragmentary finds from earlier beds in Java are also known; their chronological placement, however, is a matter of dispute.

Initial K/Ar dates for these early Javanese hominids place them as far back as 2 million years ago, but these dates still lack confirmation by other techniques and thus are still open to question (see p. 381).

ISRAEL

A site on the western side of the Jordan River Valley in Israel, called Ùbeidiya, has been thought for some time to be quite ancient. Little has come from this site in the way of fossil hominids (just some nondiagnostic fragments), but artifacts are abundant. A recent biostratigraphic attempt at aging this site has yielded a provisional date (presumably associated with the ancient artifacts) of 2 million years (or even more!) (Repenning and Fejfar, 1982).

Obviously, the stratigraphic context at Ùbeidiya will have to be completely established, and further cross-correlation of this initial date will have to be performed. At present, it is intriguing to speculate about early hominids (*H. habilis*; very early *H. erectus*??) in southwestern Asia. We can reasonably postulate that *when* hominids first did emigrate from Africa, they passed through this region. Whether they already had done so by 2 m.y.a. remains to be seen.

FRANCE

Several sites in France (especially Vallonet Cave) have been suggested as potentially predating 1 m.y.a. No hominid fossils have been found at any of these sites, but stone tools have been discovered in what some researchers thought to be very early contexts. Systematic paleontological and geological work is still going on at several localities in south-central France, and attempts to establish a firm chronology are progressing. The most recent results (from paleomagnetic calibrations) indicate that all the potential hominid localities, in fact, postdate 1 m.y.a., although some of them perhaps not by much (Thouveny and Bonifay, 1984).

◇ Interpretations: What Does It All Mean?

By this time, it may seem anthropologists have an almost perverse fascination in finding small scraps buried in the ground and then assigning them confusing numbers and taxonomic labels impossible to remember. We must realize that the collection of all the basic fossil data is the foundation of human evolutionary research. Without fossils, our speculations would be

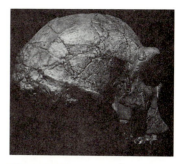

Figure 13-6   A nearly complete *Homo erectus* cranium (ER 3733) from East Lake Turkana. Dated approximately 1.3–1.6 m.y.a.

---

*B.P. indicates Before Present.

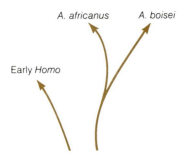

Figure 13-7 Phylogenetic interpretation. Early *Homo habilis* genetically distinct from australopithecines.

completely hollow. Several large, ongoing paleoanthropological projects discussed in Chapter 10 are now collecting additional data in an attempt to answer some of the more perplexing questions about our evolutionary history.

The numbering of specimens, which may at times seem somewhat confusing, is an attempt to keep the designations neutral and to make reference to each individual fossil as clear as possible. The formal naming of finds as *Australopithecus*, *Homo habilis*, *Homo erectus*, etc., should come much later, since it involves a lengthy series of complex interpretations. The assigning of generic and specific names to fossil finds is more than just a game, although some paleoanthropologists have acted as if it were just that. When we attach a particular label, such as *A. boisei*, on a particular fossil, we should be fully aware of the biological implications of such an interpretation (see p. 262).

Even more basic to our understanding of human evolution, the use of taxonomic nomenclature involves interpretations of fossil relationships. For example, two fossils such as "Zinj" and ER 406 are both usually called *A. boisei*. What we are saying here is they are both members of one *interbreeding* species. These two fossils can now be compared with others, like Sts. 5 from Sterkfontein, which are usually called *A. africanus*. What we are implying now is that "Zinj" and ER 406 are more closely related to each other than *either* is to Sts. 5. Furthermore, that Sts. 5 (*africanus*) populations were incapable of successfully interbreeding with *boisei* populations is a direct biological inference of this nomenclature.

We can carry the level of interpretation even further. For example, fossils such as ER 1470 are called early *Homo* (*Homo habilis*). We are now making a genus-level distinction, and two basic biological implications are involved:

1. *A. africanus* (Sts. 5) and *A. boisei* ("Zinj" and ER 406) are more closely related to each other than either is to ER 1470
2. The distinction between the groups reflects a basic difference in adaptive level (see Chapter 9)

From the time that fossil sites are first located to the eventual interpretation of hominid evolutionary events, several steps are necessary. Ideally, they should follow a logical order, for if interpretations are made too hastily, they confuse important issues for many years. A reasonable sequence is:

1. Selection and surveying of sites
2. Excavation of sites; recovery of fossil hominids
3. Designating individual finds with specimen numbers for clear reference
4. Detailed study and description of fossils
5. Comparison with other fossil material—in chronological framework if possible
6. Comparison of fossil variation with known ranges of variation in closely related groups of living primates
7. Assigning taxonomic names to fossil material

The task of interpretation is still not complete, for what we really want to know in the long run is what happened to the populations represented by the fossil remains. Indeed, in looking at the fossil hominid record, we are looking for our ancestors. In the process of eventually determining those populations that are our most likely antecedents, we may conclude some hominids are on evolutionary sidebranches. If this conclusion is accurate, they necessarily must have eventually become extinct. It is both interesting and relevant to us as hominids to try to find out what caused some earlier members of our family to continue evolving while others died out.

PUTTING IT ALL TOGETHER

The interpretation of our paleontologic past in terms of which fossils are related to other fossils and how they are all related to us is usually shown diagramatically in the form of a *phylogeny*. Such a diagram is a family tree of fossil evolution. This kind of interpretation is the eventual goal of evolutionary studies, but it is the final goal, only after adequate data are available to understand what is going on. For example, the phylogeny of horse evolution for the last 60 million years is well known (see Fig. 13-8).

Whereas hominid fossil evidence has accumulated in great abundance, the fact that so much of the material has been discovered so recently makes any firm judgments concerning the route of human evolution premature. However, paleoanthropologists are certainly not deterred from making their "best guesses," and thus diverse speculative theories have abounded in recent years. The vast majority of more than 300 fossils from East Africa are still in the descriptive and early analytical stages. At this time, the construction of phylogenies of human evolution is analogous to building a house with only

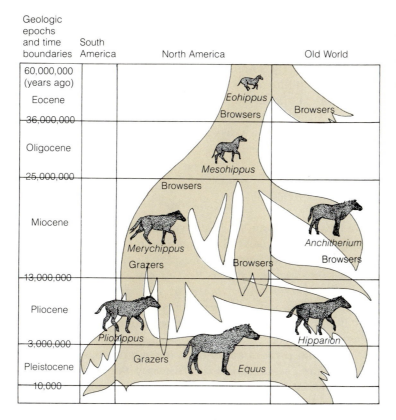

Figure 13-8 Schematic diagram (phylogeny) of horse evolution over the last 60 million years. (From *Heredity, Evolution and Society*, Second Edition, by I. Michael Lerner and William J. Libby. W. H. Freeman and Company. Copyright © 1976.)

a partial blueprint. We are not even sure how many rooms there are! Until the existing fossil evidence has been adequately studied, to say nothing about possible new finds, speculative theories must be viewed with a critical eye.

In the following pages, we will present several phylogenies representing different and opposing views of hominid evolution. We suggest you do not attempt to memorize them, for they *all* could be out of date by the time you read this book. It will prove more profitable to look at each one and assess the biological implications involved. Also, note which groups are on the main line of human evolution leading to *Homo sapiens* and which are placed on extinct sidebranches.

INTERPRETING THE INTERPRETATIONS

There are two basic interpretations of hominid evolution in the Plio-Pleistocene: the single lineage theory and the double lineage theory. The single lineage theory, derived from the single species hypothesis, states that only *one* hominid species lived at any one time. Therefore, only a single line without branching leads directly from all fossil hominid ancestors to *Homo sapiens*.

The double lineage theories postulate a major division in hominid evolution, with one main branch leading to *Homo erectus* and *sapiens* and another line with various offshoots eventually dying out.

The various double lineage theories fall into two basic categories:

1. *A. africanus-Homo* line versus *robustus-boisei* line
2. *All* later australopithecines versus *Homo*.

The first double lineage interpretation sees *A. africanus* as ancestral to *erectus* with "early *Homo*" transitional between the two. The *robustus-boisei* line diverges, ultimately becoming extinct. The second theory postulates that early *Homo* (i.e., *habilis*) and then *erectus*, forming one line, lived at the same time as australopithecines (which had already diverged) forming another line. This australopithecine sidebranch then died out during the Plio-Pleistocene.

◇ Conclusions

As we have often stated, it is still simply too early to draw firm conclusions. We can, however, suggest which possibilities seem most likely. While the single lineage theory is an economical explanation, the amount of variation during a given time—particularly in East Africa—throws doubt on this view. The finds of *H. erectus* and *A. boisei* in the same beds at East Turkana have demonstrated two very different yet contemporary forms. If we accept two or more hominid forms living contemporaneously, we are left with some double lineage explanation.

We feel that present evidence best fits a phylogeny resembling Phylogeny VI (or a more recent variation, Phylogeny IX). Such an explanation, *for the moment* at least, adequately accounts for variation in the hominid fossil record during the Plio-Pleistocene. The earliest definite hominids of which we have evidence are found in sites dating between 4 and 3 m.y.a. These fossils are

(a)   PHYLOGENY I
      Single-Lineage Theory
      (Brace, 1967)

H. sapiens

H. erectus

A. robustus

A. africanus

Note: Only one hominid at any one
time = direct implication of single
species hypothesis.

(b)   PHYLOGENY II
      Modified Single-Lineage Theory
      (Brace and Montagu, 1977)

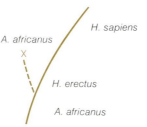

A. africanus
      X

H. sapiens

H. erectus

A. africanus

Note: Postulates possible
coexistence of A. africanus with
descendant H. erectus populations.

(c)   PHYLOGENY III
      Double Lineage Theory
      (Le Gros Clark, 1967)

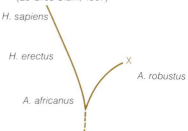

H. sapiens

H. erectus
                                    X
A. africanus   A. robustus

Note: One minor sidebranch.
A. africanus on main line

(d)   PHYLOGENY IV
      Paranthropus
      Double Lineage Theory
      (Robinson, 1972)

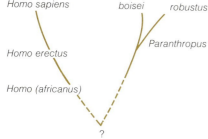

Homo sapiens   X   X
                    boisei   robustus

Homo erectus   *Paranthropus*

Homo (africanus)

                         ?

Note: One major sidebranch.
Both robust species seen as
very distinct. A. africanus
seen as same as early Homo.

(e)   PHYLOGENY V
      Boisei
      Double Lineage Theory
      (Campbell, 1976)

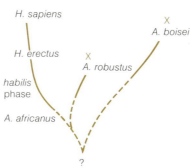

H. sapiens   X
                            A. boisei

H. erectus   X
                 A. robustus
habilis
phase

A. africanus

                  ?

Note: A. boisei seen as very
distinct with very early
split = Miocene? Early Homo
("habilis") = transitional.

(f)   PHYLOGENY VI
      Early *Homo*
      Double Lineage Theory (Leakey,
      1974: Pilbeam and Gould, 1974)

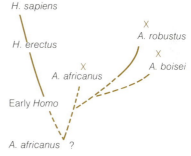

H. sapiens   X
                            A. robustus
H. erectus   X
                 X   A. boisei
             A. africanus
Early *Homo*

A. africanus   ?

Note: A. africanus as possible common
ancestor in Pliocene? Early Homo
already distinct from australopithecines
by Late Pliocene.

(g)   PHYLOGENY VII
      Triple Lineage Theory
      (L. Leakey, 1966)

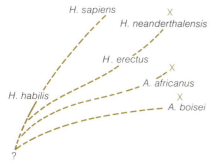

H. sapiens   X
               H. neanderthalensis

               H. erectus
                            X
                         A. africanus
H. habilis   X
                      A. boisei

?

Note: Only "habilis" on main line
before sapiens. Louis Leakey first
advocated this theory and it was
recently proposed again as a possibility
by Tattersall and Eldredge (1977).

(h)   PHYLOGENY VIII
      Nonhominid Double Lineage
      Theory (Oxnard, 1975)

H. sapiens

X   *Australopithecines*
     africanus
     robustus
     boisei
     habilis (Olduvai)   H. erectus

                    Early *Homo*
                    (Late Turkana)

                 ?

Note: All australopithecines classified
as nonhominids comprising long-separate
line of hominoid evolution. Extinct
sidebranch includes Olduvai "habilis"
finds; Turkana early Homo on main line.

(i)   PHYLOGENY IX
      Afarensis Common Ancestor Theory
      (Johanson and White, 1979)

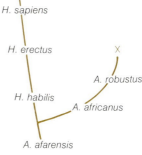

H. sapiens

H. erectus   X

                            A. robustus
H. habilis
                         A. africanus

A. afarensis

Note: *Afarensis* postulated as
common ancestor to all Plio-Pleistocene
hominids.

Figure 13-9   **Phylogenies of hominid evolution.**

Table 13-1   Dates for Early *Homo*

East Lake Turkana	*1.8 m.y.a.*
Olduvai	*1.8 m.y.a.*
Omo	*1.85 m.y.a.*
Sterkfontein	*1.5–2.0 m.y.a.*
Swartkrans	*1.5–2.0 m.y.a.*

also the most primitive of any hominid known, particularly as seen in the conformity of the cranium as well as numerous dental characteristics. Since these early forms combine a small brain with an already completely efficient bipedal adaptation, they are best considered members of the genus *Australopithecus*. However, they are not like the more specialized australopithecines seen later in both South and East Africa. Consequently, we believe the designation of these early australopithecines as a separate species (*A. afarensis*) is justified.

In addition to calling attention to a different morphology, a separate species name also can be used to make phylogenetic inferences. In this case, it appears that *afarensis*—particularly as seen in the dental complex—makes a good *potential* common ancestor for all the later australopithecines and genus *Homo*. In the later australopithecines, the relatively large front teeth are much reduced, while the back teeth become considerably larger. This trend towards a large, grinding tooth specialization is seen most dramatically in the robust australopithecines.

Meanwhile, in the evolutionary line that diverged into genus *Homo* the front teeth are also reduced, but the back teeth do not undergo the specialized development such as that of the later australopithecines. In addition, as compared to their smaller-brained australopithecine cousins, the *Homo* line displays a progressive increase in cranial capacity. Certainly, by about 2 m.y.a., the early *Homo* line is becoming larger-brained and probably more culture-dependent; these two factors obviously interact with one another as a primary determinant of human biocultural evolution. Evidence such as the 1470 skull from Turkana clearly shows us that such a large-brained lineage was evolving in East Africa in the Plio-Pleistocene. Some fragmentary remains at about the same time from South Africa suggest a similar process, since tantalizing evidence from Swartkrans and Sterkfontein implies a large-brained lineage was evolving there as well.

The other lineage (later *Australopithecus*) seems to have remained in an evolutionary backwater perfecting its already specialized adaptation, probably involving a heavy vegetarian diet with only minimal cultural dependence. By about 1.6 m.y.a., the *Homo* line—in East Africa anyway—had reached the level of *erectus*, the larger-brained, culturally more developed ancestor of our species. (For the story of *erectus*, see Chapter 14.)

A reasonable, though for now still extremely tenuous, hypothesis of the course of hominid evolution in the Plio-Pleistocene is shown in Figure 13-10.

◇ Summary

The huge amount of fossil hominid material from the Plio-Pleistocene of South and East Africa has generated a great deal of interest. As more evidence is found, more questions rather than answers seem to arise. Some possible additional complexities discussed in this chapter include: (1) the continued existence of *A. africanus* in East Africa contemporaneous with *A. boisei* and early *Homo*; (2) early *Homo* living contemporaneously with australopithecines

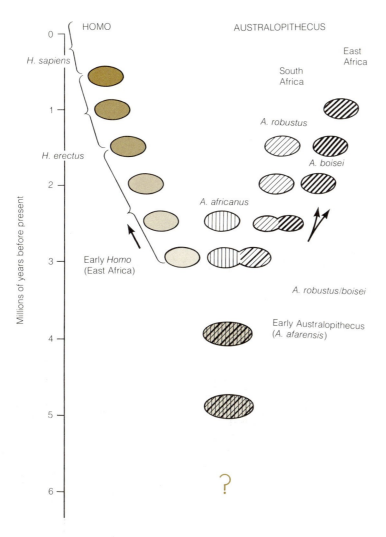

Figure 13-10 Phylogeny of hominid evolution in the Plio-Pleistocene: A provisional view.

in South Africa; (3) early appearance by 1.6 m.y.a. in East Africa of *Homo erectus*; and (4) Plio-Pleistocene hominids outside Africa?

Attempts to explain all the variation observed in fossil hominid material in the Plio-Pleistocene have yielded many alterntive theories. None of these is yet reasonably secure, and new evidence probably will force major reassessments in the next decade. What is significant in all this current debate is the way fossil hominids are utilized to make general biological inferences concerning the mechanics of human evolution.

◇ Questions for Review

1. What evidence suggests the presence of early *Homo* in South Africa in the Plio-Pleistocene?
2. What is a phylogeny?

3. Why have so many phylogenies been proposed for hominid evolution covering the last 5 million years?
4. Compare and contrast the biological implications of a single-lineage phylogeny with a double-lineage phylogeny.
5. Why is it important to be aware of within-species variation (sexual dimorphism, age, individual variation) when assessing the evolutionary relationships of fossil hominid populations?

Homo Erectus

CONTENTS

In the summer of 1941, war between the United States and Japan appeared inevitable to the officials at the Cenozoic Research Laboratory of Peking Union Medical College. To prevent the priceless Peking Man bones from falling into the hands of the Japanese, already in Peking, the officials packed them into boxes and shipped them to a warehouse at Camp Holcomb, a Marine Corps base not far from Peking. The marines, scheduled to leave China on December 8 aboard the *S.S. President Harrison*, were to take the bones with them on their return to the United States.

On December 7, 1941, Pearl Harbor was attacked, and war declared against Japan. Instead of leaving, the marines were arrested by the Japanese and interned for the duration of the war. What happened to the bones has remained a deep mystery ever since.

One account is that in the fall of 1941, Col. Ashurst, Commander of the Marine Corps Headquarters at Camp Holcomb, ordered the boxes of bones sent to Lt. Wm. E. Foley, a Marine Corps physician, who was to take the boxes with him aboard the *President Harrison*. When he received the boxes, Dr. Foley, realizing arrest and internment were imminent, distributed them to institutions and reliable Chinese friends in Tientsin, a city near Camp Holcomb. Dr. Foley has steadfastly refused ever since to divulge the names of these Chinese friends without guarantees for their safety from the Chinese government. Since he did not open the boxes when they arrived, it is not known for certain whether they even contained the bones.

In 1972, more than twenty-five years after the war ended, another chapter unfolded in the case of the missing bones. Mr. Christopher Janus, an American businessman, became interested in locating the bones after a visit to China and offered a reward of $5,000 for information leading to their recovery. Soon afterward, in New York, Janus received a telephone call from a woman who claimed her husband, a former marine now deceased, had left her a footlocker of what he believed were stolen Peking Man bones. Janus requested a meeting, which the so-called "mystery woman" insisted be held on the observation deck high atop the Empire State Building. At the meeting, the woman, who refused to give her name, showed a photograph of the footlocker's contents to Janus, who later checked the photo with Dr. Harry Shapiro, a physical anthropologist at the American Museum of Natural History. Shapiro, long interested in Peking Man and the missing bones, thought a skull in the photograph resembled that of Peking Man, and with that assurance Janus opened negotiations with the mystery woman's lawyer. The woman wanted $500,000 and guarantees that the United States government would not prosecute for possession of stolen property or confiscate the bones. Later, when these conditions were met, she raised her price to $700,000 and demanded a letter from the Chinese government stating they would not prosecute. The Chinese did not reply to the request for such a letter, and negotiations were never resumed.

Many rumors of the bones' location came to Mr. Janus, who eagerly investigated a number of them. He heard they were in Taiwan; they were not, but while there he increased the reward to $150,000. He also heard they were in Hong Kong—they were not; in Bangkok—not there, either. He was told they were in Burma, Tokyo, and Manila; but by this time he thought it was a waste of time and money to follow up these leads. Since then, 1975, Janus has not reported any further activity, and in November, 1977, withdrew his offer of reward.

The fate of the Peking bones remains unknown. The New York mystery woman might have a skull; Dr. Foley's friends in China may have all the bones; the bones might have been found in the Camp Holcomb warehouse by Japanese soldiers who, not realizing what they had, destroyed or abandoned them. They may have found their way to Burma, Bangkok, or—though very unlikely— the United States. Whoever has them—if anyone—is not telling.

The New York Times reported (May 11, 1980) that a former marine, Roger Ames, telephoned from his hospital bed in Dallas recently and told Janus the following story:

While on guard duty the night before Pearl Harbor he saw two marine officers, carrying a footlocker and shovels, dig a hole and bury the footlocker.

Urged on by the ex-marine's message, Janus decided to resume his investigation of the missing bones. He is going to attempt to locate the buried footlocker at the Peking site, where it may have been buried for safekeeping.

SOURCES:

Janus, Christopher G. with William Brashler. *The Search for Peking Man*, New York: Macmillan Publishing Co., Inc., 1975.

Shapiro, Harry L. "The Strange, Unfinished Saga of Peking Man," *Natural History,* 80:8 (No. 9), 1971.

———. *Peking Man*, New York: Simon and Schuster, 1974.

The New York Times, Sunday, May 11, 1980.

◇ CHAPTER FOURTEEN

◇ Introduction

In the preceding several chapters, we introduced an early grade (see Box 14-1) of hominid evolution, the australopithecines of the Plio-Pleistocene. We discussed at some length the confusion surrounding them, confusion brought about by the various interpretations of the number of australopithecine species or lineages. Furthermore, recently discovered hominid remains in East Africa—designated as *Homo sp.* (or *H. habilis*) and apparently contemporary with australopithecines—have added to the muddle. These problems were discussed in Chapter 13 and though it is unfortunate that a clear and uncomplicated picture of early hominid evolution cannot yet be presented, we fervently hope that future discoveries will provide evidence to bring the scenario into focus.

The next grade of hominid evolution, *Homo erectus*, is much clearer, although some aspects remain murky. *H. erectus* inhabited a wider geographic area than australopithecines. We find their remains in Africa, Europe, and Asia, but not in Australia or the New World. They were taller, larger-brained, more culture-dependent, and more skillful toolmakers. Unlike australopithecines, who lived in much of the Pliocene and early Pleistocene, *H. erectus* is mainly a Pleistocene hominid. In our discussion of *H. erectus*, therefore, we must necessarily refer to the Pleistocene—its climate, **biosphere**, geological events, and dates.

Biosphere
The entire area inhabited by organisms.

Interstadial
Temperate period during the phases of a glacial period.

◇ The Pleistocene (1.8 m.y.a.–10,000 y.a.)

During much of the Pleistocene (also known as the Age of Glaciers), large areas of the northern hemisphere were covered with enormous masses of ice, which advanced and retreated as the temperature fell and rose. Until recently, European glaciers were considered to be four in number—Günz, Mindel, Riss, and Würm (to use the Alps Mountain glacial terminology). In reconstructing the history of the Pleistocene, scholars attempted to work out the dates of these glacial advances. Then they further attempted to develop the hominid history of Europe and Asia by correlating hominid fossil bones and artifacts found in association with animals indicative of the glacial advances or retreats. For example, if human bones were found with those of a warm-weather animal, the researchers assumed that this was an interglacial or interstadial period. This procedure may appear straightforward enough, but one of the problems was that the Alpine glaciers have not been chronometrically dated.

In addition, the glacial story has many more complications to it than had been realized (Turner, 1975). There were not four but probably eight or more glacial advances. Also, within a given major advance, there were numbers of short retreats and advances. Furthermore, the northern European (Scandi-

371

1. *Australopithecus*
2. *Homo erectus*
3. *Homo sapiens* (including transitional forms, Neandertals, and modern populations)

navian) continental glaciations were found to be more suitable for study, and palynologists have arrived at what they consider to be more acceptable dates for the northern European glacial stratigraphy. However, paleoanthropologists and archeologists tend to use Alpine glacial terminology more often than Scandinavian, and we shall follow that procedure in this chapter. In Figure 14-2 we show both schemes, so that references to one or the other can easily be reconciled.

A long-standing problem in the study of the Pleistocene involves its dating. At one time, the Plio-Pleistocene boundary was defined by the appearance of certain mammals believed to identify the beginning of the Pleistocene. Since the appearance of these mammals—modern cow, modern horse, Indian elephant—occurs at different times on different continents, this criterion

Figure 14-1 A partial listing of *Homo erectus* sites. *H. erectus* inhabited areas of Europe, Africa, and Asia, a much wider distribution than australopithecines.

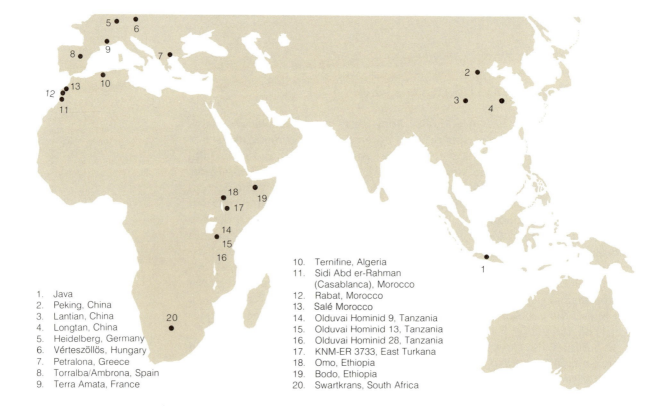

1. Java
2. Peking, China
3. Lantian, China
4. Longtan, China
5. Heidelberg, Germany
6. Vérteszöllös, Hungary
7. Petralona, Greece
8. Torralba/Ambrona, Spain
9. Terra Amata, France
10. Ternifine, Algeria
11. Sidi Abd er-Rahman (Casablanca), Morocco
12. Rabat, Morocco
13. Salé Morocco
14. Olduvai Hominid 9, Tanzania
15. Olduvai Hominid 13, Tanzania
16. Olduvai Hominid 28, Tanzania
17. KNM-ER 3733, East Turkana
18. Omo, Ethiopia
19. Bodo, Ethiopia
20. Swartkrans, South Africa

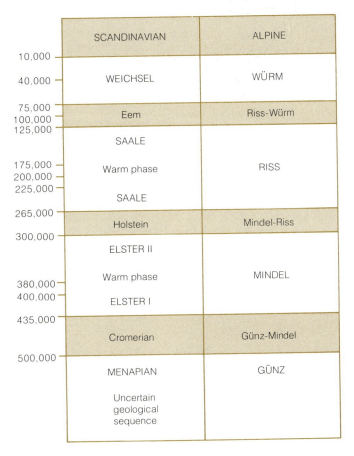

SCANDINAVIAN	ALPINE
WEICHSEL	WÜRM
Eem	Riss-Würm
SAALE	
Warm phase	RISS
SAALE	
Holstein	Mindel-Riss
ELSTER II	
Warm phase	MINDEL
ELSTER I	
Cromerian	Günz-Mindel
MENAPIAN	GÜNZ
Uncertain geological sequence	

(Scale at left, top to bottom: 10,000 · 40,000 · 75,000 · 100,000 · 125,000 · 175,000 · 200,000 · 225,000 · 265,000 · 300,000 · 380,000 · 400,000 · 435,000 · 500,000)

Figure 14-2 Glacial sequence. With the exception of the Würm, dates for glacial and interglacial periods have not been well worked out yet. The Scandinavian sequence refers to the northern European glacier; the Alpine to the region at the Alps Mountains. Scholars use both sequences in discussing Pleistocene events.

could not be used on a worldwide basis. What was needed was an event that occurred everywhere on earth at the same time, and just such an event has recently been found in the reversal of the earth's magnetic field (Dalrymple, 1972).

We have known for a long time that the earth's magnetic field has frequently been reversed. During the reversal period, what we consider to be the North Pole became the South Pole, and a compass needle would have pointed south instead of north as it does now. In recent years, earth scientists have succeeded in dating these reversals, which are worldwide events. The reversals now serve as markers to correlate geophysical activity in different parts of the world.

For example, as we noted in Chapter 10, paleomagnetism has been widely applied in East Africa for the dating of early hominid sites. About 2.2 m.y.a., a "lasting" reversal occurred (except for intermittent shifts) until about 700,000 years ago. This long reversal is known as the Matuyama Reversed Epoch. Within the Matuyama Epoch are periods of "normal" magnetism, and experts agree that one of these—the Olduvai Event (occurring about 1.8 m.y.a.)—can be considered the boundary between the Pliocene and Pleistocene. The Matuyama Reversed Epoch ended about 700,000 years ago, and a "normal"

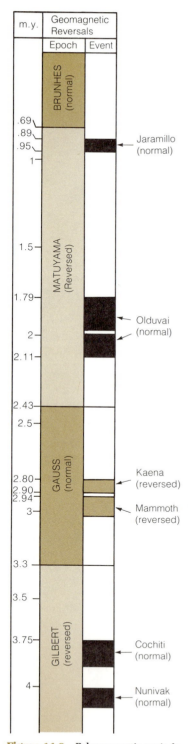

Figure 14-3 Paleomagnetic periods.

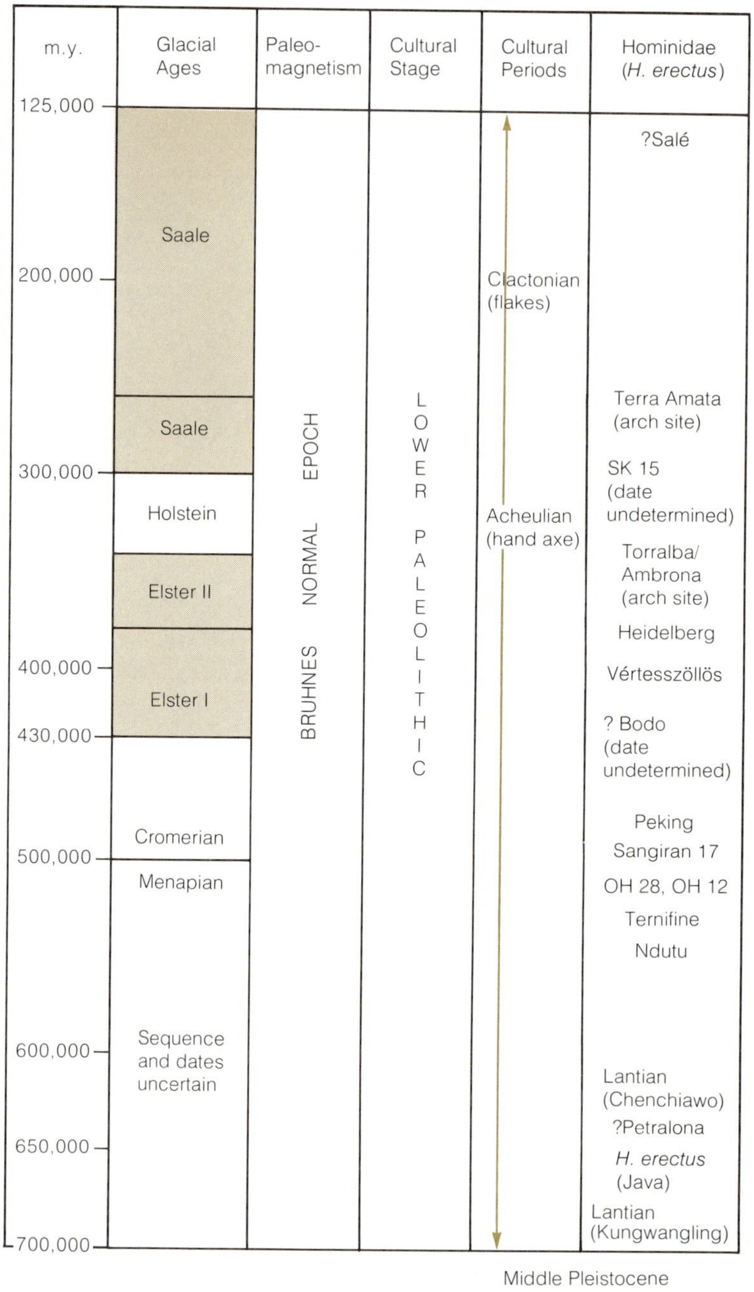

m.y.	Glacial Ages	Paleo-magnetism	Cultural Stage	Cultural Periods	Hominidae (*H. erectus*)
125,000	Saale				?Salé
200,000				Clactonian (flakes)	
	Saale		L O W E R P A L E O L I T H I C		Terra Amata (arch site)
300,000		EPOCH			SK 15 (date undetermined)
	Holstein				Torralba/ Ambrona (arch site)
	Elster II	NORMAL		Acheulian (hand axe)	Heidelberg
400,000					Vértesszöllös
	Elster I	BRUHNES			? Bodo (date undetermined)
430,000					
	Cromerian				Peking
500,000					Sangiran 17
	Menapian				OH 28, OH 12
					Ternifine
					Ndutu
600,000	Sequence and dates uncertain				Lantian (Chenchiawo)
650,000					?Petralona
					H. erectus (Java)
700,000					Lantian (Kungwangling)

Middle Pleistocene

Figure 14-4   The Middle Pleistocene.

magnetic field period (the Brunhes Normal Epoch) was established and has continued until the present time. Professionals in the field commonly agree that the period from the beginning of the Pleistocene at 1.8 m.y.a. to 700,000 y.a. (the Matuyama-Brunhes boundary) be defined as the Lower (or Early) Pleistocene and the period beginning at 700,000 years as the Middle Pleistocene.

Although differences of opinion exist concerning the boundary between the Middle and Upper (or Late) Pleistocene, we shall use the widely accepted figure of 125,000 years, correlated with the beginning of the Riss-Würm interglacial. Figure 14-4 correlates Pleistocene, paleomagnetic periods, and Alpine glacial periods.

The Pleistocene, which lasted almost 2 million years, was an important time in hominid evolutionary history. *Homo erectus* appears. From their brain size and tools, we can clearly see that this form, using culture as their strategy of adaptation, should be called human. By the time the Pleistocene terminated, modern humans had already appeared, dependence on culture as the human way of life had dramatically increased, and domestication of plants and animals—one of the great cultural revolutions of human history—was either about to commence or had just been invented. With this background of the time span in which *H. erectus* evolved and developed, let us examine more closely the hominid to whom we owe so much.

◇ Homo Erectus

We have already observed that *H. erectus* was taller, larger-brained, and more dependent on culture than australopithecines. These statements are general, and it will therefore be necessary to discuss the characteristics of *H. erectus* in more detail. Since we are dealing with the evolution of hominids from something resembling an australopithecine stage to the modern stage, what we shall see in the modifications of hominids, for the most part, are relative changes. That is, *H. erectus* is taller than australopithecines, but shorter than *H. sapiens*; larger-brained than australopithecines, but smaller-brained than *H. sapiens*, etc. *Homo erectus*, in both physical and cultural characteristics, is intermediate between the australopithecine and *sapiens* stages.

From a time perspective, *H. erecutus* is usually associated with the Middle Pleistocene (which we have dated from 700,000 to 125,000 years ago). However, as we shall see, there are African, Javanese, and Chinese remains that may go back an additional million years. Nevertheless, the evolution of *H. erectus* proceeded most rapidly during the Middle Pleistocene.

The cranial capacity of *H. erectus* ranges widely from 775 to 1,225 cm³, with a mean of 1020 cm³. In terms of averages, this would make the skull of *H. erectus* roughly twice the size of australopithecines, 50% larger than early *Homo*, and 75% as large as *H. sapiens*.

When we look at the skull of *H. erectus* in profile, several characteristics are immediately apparent. Overhanging the orbits is a pronounced bony ledge, the supraorbital torus, and, just behind it, is a marked depression

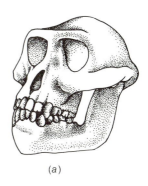

(a)

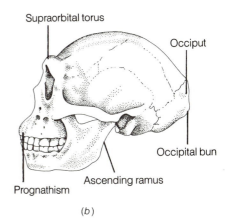

(b)

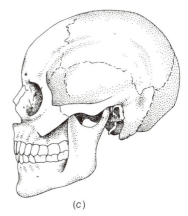

(c)

Figure 14-5 (a) *Australopithecus* (*afarensis*); (b) *H. erectus* (Peking); (c) *H. sapiens* (anatomically modern). Note the changes in prognathism, ascending ramus, slope of foreheads, vault height, and development of occiput. (Not to scale.)

◇ Box 14-2   Vocabulary

Alveolar prognathism   Forward projection of the maxilla

Ascending ramus   Rear upright portion of the mandible

Callote or *calva*   Uppermost portion of the braincase

Calvarium   The skull minus the face and mandible

Cranium   The complete skull; bones of the head, face, and mandible

Cervical   Pertaining to the neck, as in cervical vertebrae

Clavicle   Collar bone

Condyle   A rounded protuberance of bone which articulates (forms a joint, moves against) with another bone. The ball in a ball and socket joint (humerus and femur)

Coronal suture   The suture running transversely across the skull joining the frontal and parietal bones

Femur   Thigh bone

Fibula   The narrow long bone on the outside of the lower leg (see tibia)

Frontal bone   The front bone of the skull including the forehead

Humerus   Upper arm bone

Lambdoid suture   The transverse suture at the back of the top of the skull joining the parietal and occipital bones

Maghreb   An area in Northwest Africa

Mandible   Lower jaw

Maxilla   Upper jaw

Occiput, occipital bone   The rear bone of the skull

Paleolithic   (Paleo: old; lithic: stone) Old Stone Age. The culture period preceding food-producing (farming, herding)

Parietal   The right and left side bones on top of the skull; joined by the sagittal suture

Platycephaly   (platy: flat; cephaly: head) Flatheadedness as opposed to dome shape of anatomically modern human beings

Sagittal suture   The suture joining the left and right parietals; bounded by coronal suture in front and lambdoidal suture behind

Scapula   Shoulder blade

Supraorbital torus   (supra: above; orbital: eye opening; torus: ridge) Ridge above the orbits on a skull, very pronounced in *H. erectus*, Neandertals, and some australopithecines

Tibia   The large long bone of the lower leg; the shin (see fibula)

Zygomatic bone   Outer portion of orbit forming parts of its floor; and the cheekbone

Zygomatic arch   The bony arch below the orbit

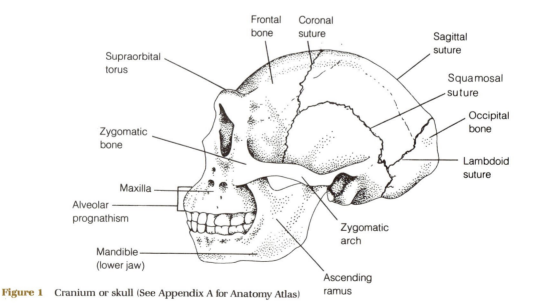

Figure 1   Cranium or skull (See Appendix A for Anatomy Atlas)

known as postorbital constriction. The forehead recedes instead of rising sharply as it does in modern humans, and the long, low skull is reminiscent of a deflated football. At the end of the skull is the occiput, a bone forming the back and part of the base of the skull. The occipital bone angles sharply down and forward, unlike the rounded profile of *H. sapiens*. The rear end of the skull profile also points up a ridge of bone—**nuchal** crest or line—for the attachment of neck muscles that hold up the head. Protruding beyond the occiput is an extension of bone called an *occipital bun*.

Returning to the front of the profile, we see the **alveolar** prognathism, receding chin, and teeth similar to but slightly larger than modern populations. Such traits reflect heavy chewing, and there is, indeed, a number of indications of well-developed **masseter** muscles. Heavy muscles require bony attachments, and these can be seen in the ridges on the mandible, the "buttresses on the facial skeleton—such as the broad nasal root, the thick supraorbital torus, the thick frontal process of the zygomatic bone—and the well-marked temporal lines" (Jacob, 1975, p. 314).

From the rear, we can see the most important feature that distinguishes an *H. erectus* skull: its pentagonal shape, with maximum breadth at or near the base. In later hominids, maximum breadth is higher up on the skull. (See Figs. 14-7, 14-13, and 14-20.)

Differences in size and structure of teeth occur among the various *H. erectus* forms. In several of the Javanese upper jaws, a surprising **diastema** exists between the lateral incisor and canine, and the canine projects a bit beyond the margin of the other teeth. These are nonhominid primate characteristics that are not found among most australopithecines. What their adaptive function might have been is difficult to know. Characteristic of pongids and many australopithecines, too, is that the molar teeth increase in size from front to back. This sequence varies among *H. erectus*, but in most cases the 3rd molar is *smaller* than the second, a design that is typical of the later hominid pattern.

Two other dental traits may be mentioned. First, **shovel-shaped** incisors (Fig. 14-8). The edges of both sides of the teeth have raised ridges of enamel, and the incisors resemble a tiny scoop or coal shovel. It has been suggested that shovel-shaped incisors are an adaptive response in hunting and gathering societies, such as the Eskimo, in which a great deal of chewing takes place with the front teeth. The additional enamel may serve as structural support that enables the teeth to last longer.

The second trait is known as **taurodontism**, or enlarged pulp cavity. If roots of the molars (and sometimes premolars) should fail to grow to their adult length, a tendency of the pulp cavity in the center of the tooth to become enlarged occurs. This characteristic is an advantage among hard-chewing humans and such grazing animals as horses and cows that require high crowns on their teeth. In time, the pulp hardens and more wear is possible than in ordinary teeth.

In the past, it was believed that the locomotor skeleton of *H. erectus* was practically indistinguishable from *H. sapiens*. However, more recent analyses suggest that there are a number of morphological differences. "Nonetheless, the functional locomotor capabilities appear to have been generally similar

Alveolar
(al-vee′-lar)
Tooth-bearing portion of upper or lower jaw.

Masseter
Chewing.

Nuchal
Pertaining to the neck.

Diastema
(dye-a-stee′-ma)
Gap, space.

Shoveling
Raised ridges of enamel on the tongue (lingual) side of the incisors.

Taurodontism
taurus: bull
dont: tooth
Characteristic of molars of grazing animals.

Figure 14-6   *H. erectus* (Peking Man), From this view, the supraorbital torus, low vault of the skull, and angled occiput can be clearly seen.

Figure 14-7   *H. erectus* (Peking Man). Note that the widest part of the skull is toward the bottom, giving the skull a pentagonal form.

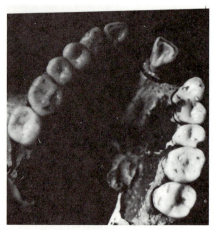

Figure 14-8 Shovel-shaped incisors.

to adaptations in *H. sapiens* for habitual erect posture and efficient striding bipedal gait" (Howell, 1978). These adaptations include a pelvic tilt mechanism, a hip extensor mechanism for raising the trunk, a pelvic rest mechanism, center of gravity behind the hip joints, transfer of body weight to the pelvis through the sacral suspensory mechanism, and powerful hip flexion and knee extension (Howell, 1978). Similarly, the forelimb morphology also diverges in distinct ways from *H. sapiens*, but, overall, *H. erectus* approximate *H. sapiens* more closely than it does *Australopithecus*.

◇ Asia

JAVA

Scientific discoveries are normally the result of careful planning, hard work, and thorough knowledge of the subject. In addition, they are frequently tales of luck, adventure, and heartbreak, which brings us to the story of Eugene Dubois, a Dutch anatomist.

The latter half of the nineteenth century was a period of intellectual excitement. In England, Darwin's *Origin of Species* (published in 1859) provoked scientists and educated laymen to take opposing sides, often with great emotion. In Germany, for example, the well-known zoologist Ernst Haeckel eagerly supported Darwin's statement that man descended from apes and even suggested the name for the missing transitional link between the two: *Pithecanthropus alalus*, "the ape man without speech." He was criticized by Rudolf Virchow, one of Europe's most famous scientists and Haeckel's one-time zoology professor, who publicly and scornfully disagreed with these speculations. In 1856, a strange skull had been recovered near Dusseldorf, Germany. This specimen is what we today recognize as a Neandertal skull, but, when a description of it was published, scientific opinion was again divided and feelings ran high. "The opinions and counter-opinions about the Neandertal skull and other odd skulls, jaws, and bones that turned up in Europe kept science and the keenly interested lay public in something of an uproar for many years" (Moore, 1961, p. 235).

This stimulating intellectual climate surrounded the youthful Eugene Dubois, born in Holland in 1858, the year before Darwin's *Origin* and two years after the discovery of the Neandertal skull. As a young man, Dubois took up the study of medicine at the University of Amsterdam, and we can imagine how much these debates about human ancestors engaged the interest of an anatomy student. When Dubois graduated, he was appointed lecturer in anatomy at the University in 1886, but his heart was not in it. Visions of finding our fossil ancestors were more exciting than a stodgy academic career, and Dubois made up his mind to resign his university post and search for "Early Man." He was the first person ever to deliberately set out on such a venture. But where did one search in the 1880s?

Haeckel had reasoned that the missing link might be found in the Indonesian Islands under the mistaken notion that gibbons, native to that area, belonged in human ancestry. Virchow had pointed out that tropical habitats

Figure 14-9 Eugene Dubois.

◇ Box 14-3   Portion of a Complete Definition of *Homo Erectus*

Homo erectus (Dubois) 1894   A species (extinct) of the genus *Homo*, known from Eurasia and Africa, distinguished by very substantial enlargement of the brain size, mean (1,020 cc) nearly twice that of large *Australopithecus* species and substantially above that of antecedent species of genus *Homo*; endocranial cast with essentially (modern) human fissuration pattern; generally low, flattened frontal region and prominent frontal keel; expanded (unilaterally) inferior frontal region, with wide separation from anterior temporal lobe; expanded precentral cortical area; exposed anterior insular area, in whole or part related to substantial development of Sylvian crest; lack of approximation between temporal lobe and cerebellum; absolutely and relatively narrow temporal lobe, tapering anteromedially, with poorly expanded inferior temporal area, salient superior temporal area, and posteriorly expanded posterior part of middle temporal convolution, expanded (unilaterally) inferior parietal region (supramarginal area); cerebellum with ipsilateral asymmetry, and cerebrum largely symmetrical, but with contralateral asymmetry expressed particularly in parieto-occipital and inferior frontal regions.

Cranial length greater than *Australopithecus*; vault bones of substantial to massive thickness, as expressed in outer and inner tables, cranial suture closure apparently earlier than in *H. sapiens*, and with coronal preceding sagittal suture closure; maximum breadth of vault at or toward the cranial base, usually coincident with biauricular breadth, with lesser bitemporal and biparietal dimensions; substantial postorbital constriction; low to more moderately arched vault, with low receding frontal (with or without notable frontal tuberosity), longitudinally flattened parietal, and occipital with marked to substantial angulation between upper (squama) and lower (nuchal) scales; usually distinct sagittal thickening, especially in bregmatic area, often associated with marked parasagittal depression; parietal smaller, more rectangular and transversely more curved than in *H. sapiens*, usually with sub-. . . .

SOURCE:
F. Clark Howell, "Hominidae." In: V. J. Maglio and H.B.S. Cooke (eds.). *Evolution of African Mammals*, Cambridge: Harvard University Press, 1978.

of anthropoid apes were still totally unexplored. Indonesia seemed a judicious choice, especially since it was Dutch colonial territory. Dubois secured an appointment as a surgeon in the Royal Dutch Army and sailed for Sumatra in November, 1887, on the beginning leg of his journey to discover the first "apeman."

Dubois started digging in several caves in Sumatra and, except for teeth of extinct orangutan, found nothing of a hominoid nature. Hearing the digging was more favorable on Java, Dubois transferred his operations to that island. While there, he was sent a skull from a rock shelter at Wadjak, Java. Dubois then managed to be transferred to Java and immediately went to Wadjak, where, in 1889, he found a skull known as the Wadjak skull (discussed in Chapter 15).

Moving on, Dubois continued searching, and reached the small village of Trinil in August, 1891. On the banks of the Solo River near the village, he found a molar he thought might belong to a chimpanzee, and this find spurred him to even greater effort. A month later, he discovered what he had come halfway round the world to find. Lodged in the dirt was a dark, bowl-like fossilized bone, which Dubois immediately recognized as the top of a

Figure 14-10 The Indonesian area.

Tektite
A round, glassy body of unknown origin.

Kabuh
Middle Pleistocene geologic formation.

Figure 14-11 Skullcap (Pithecanthropus I, found by Eugene Dubois). Femur, also found by Dubois, led him to name this form *Pithecanthropus erectus*, now known as *H. erectus*. The abnormal spur of bone on the femur is known as an *exostosis*. It has no bearing on the identification of the femur. (Photograph of casts.)

skull. He worked feverishly and carefully to extract the bone "until a fine cranium emerged, a cranium like that of no living creature. Almost the whole skullcap was there, harder than marble and heavy in weight and portentiousness" (Moore, 1961, p. 237). Dubois' dream had become reality!

Or had it? The skullcap was low with a very pronounced supraorbital torus, and Dubois thought it might, like the molar, also belong to a chimpanzee. Digging stopped for the rainy season and, soon after resuming work the following year, Dubois recovered a femur fifteen yards upstream in the same level, the Trinil horizon, as the skullcap. He discerned at once that it resembled a human femur and belonged to an individual with an upright posture. But he was convinced he was dealing with a chimpanzee, or something like it, and that the molar, skullcap, and femur belonged not only to the same kind of creature, but to the same individual.

After studying his discoveries for a few years, Dubois startled the world in 1894 with a paper sensationally entitled, "*Pithecanthropus erectus*, a Human Transitional Form from Java." The name, *Pithecanthropus*, was adopted in honor of Haeckel, who had suggested the name *Pithecanthropus alalus* for the "missing link." A scientific uproar reminiscent of Darwin's time greeted Dubois' publication. Virchow, who did not seem to believe in the existence of fossil humans, rejected Dubois' views; Haeckel, of course, was overjoyed, since he believed his views had been vindicated.

The contrary opinions announced by scientists, and the outrage expressed by the public, especially the clergy, hurt and discouraged Dubois. He locked the bones in strongboxes and steadfastly refused permission to anyone, including scientists and public, to view them. Von Koenigswald, whom we shall meet shortly, gives a painful account of Dubois during this time:

> *Pithecanthropus* became Dubois' destiny. It was his discovery, his creation, his exclusive possession; on this point he was as unaccountable as a jealous lover. Anyone who disagreed with his interpretation of *Pithecanthropus* was his personal enemy. When his ideas failed to win general acceptance he sullenly withdrew, growing mistrustful, unsociable and eccentric. He showed his finds to hardly anyone, and at night he used to hear burglars prowling around the house, bent on stealing his *Pithecanthropus*. If anyone came to his door in whom he scented a colleague, he was simply not at home (von Koenigswald, 1956, p. 32).

Dubois was finally persuaded to open the strongboxes, in 1923, to the inspection of Dr. Aleš Hrdlička, an American anthropologist at the Smithsonian Institution. By 1930, the controversy had faded, especially in light of important new discoveries near Peking, China, in the late 1920s (discussed subsequently). These finds clearly demonstrated that Peking Man was human, an early form no doubt, but human nevertheless. Resemblances between the Peking skulls and Dubois' *Pithecanthropus* were obvious, and scientists pointed out that the Java form was not an apeman, as Dubois contended, but a true human.

One might expect that Dubois would welcome Peking Man and the support it provided for the human status of *Pithecanthropus*, but the eccentric Dutchman refused to recognize any connection between Peking and Java and described Peking "as a degenerate Neanderthaler" (von Koenigswald, 1956,

◇ Box 14-4   Reference List for Important People Mentioned in Chapter 14

NAME	IDENTIFICATION	ASSOCIATED WITH
Andersson, J. Gunnar	Swedish geologist	Zhoukoudian, China
Black, Davidson	Canadian anatomist	Zhoukoudian, China
Bohlin, Birgir	Swedish geologist	Zhoukoudian, China
Dubois, Eugene	Dutch anatomist	Java
Haeckel, Ernst	Nineteenth-century German zoologist	
Howell, F. Clark	Physical anthropologist, University of California, Berkeley	Torralba/Ambrona, Spain
Isaac, Glynn	Archeologist, Harvard University	East Turkana, Kenya
Von Koenigswald, G.H.R.	German paleontologist	Java
Leakey, Louis	Physical anthropologist	Olduvai Gorge, Tanzania
Leakey, Mary D.	Archeologist	Olduvai Gorge, Tanzania
Leakey, Richard E. F.	Paleoanthropologist	East Turkana, Kenya
De Lumley, Henry	French archeologist	Terra Amata, France
Pei, W. C.	Chinese geologist and archeologist	Zhoukoudian, China
Poulianos, Ari	Greek paleoanthropologist	Petralona, Greece
Schoetensack, Otto	German paleontologist	Heidelberg, Germany
Virchow, Rudolf	Nineteenth-century German zoologist and pathologist	
Weidenreich, Franz	German, later American, anatomist and paleoanthropologist	Zhoukoudian, China

p. 55). Even more sadly, at about this time, Dubois changed his mind and declared his *Pithecanthropus* was not after all a transitional form between ape and human, but a giant gibbon, a position he tenaciously held until his death in 1940 (Wendt, 1955).

The story of *Homo erectus* does not, of course, end with the death of the beleaguered Dr. Dubois. Others, notably a younger paleontologist born in Germany, G. H. R. von Koenigswald, took up the search for ancient humans in Java in the 1930s.

Before reviewing the bone material found in Java, a cursory account of the island background will allow us to place its hominid evolutionary history in proper perspective.

The Lower Pleistocene of Java is associated with the geological Putjangan Beds and the faunal period known as Djetis. A recent K/Ar date has established the Putjangan Beds at 2.1–1.9 m.y.a. (Ninkovich and Burckle, 1978). The geological **Kabuh** Beds and Trinil fauna are associated with the Middle Pleistocene. The dating for the beginning of this period is poorly established, but there is a definite K/Ar date for **tektites** from the Kabuh Beds near Sangiran of 700,000 y.a. to 1 m.y.a. If we define the beginning of the Middle Pleistocene

Trinil fauna
Animal remains associated with the Middle Pleistocene Trinil period.

as we have, at the Matuyama-Brunhes Reversal 700,000 years ago, then the Kabuh Beds and **Trinil fauna** are somewhere in that neighborhood.

The geological strata of the Upper Pleistocene are known as the Notopuro Beds and the faunal period as the Ngandong. Again, the dating is not well established for the beginning of this period, but this need not concern us at this point, since *Homo erectus* proper probably did not survive into the Upper Pleistocene.

Most of the Javanese *H. erectus* material (summarized in Table 14-1) has been found in three areas: Modjokerto, Sangiran, and Trinil.

With this information of time, place, and stratigraphy, we are prepared for the fossil hominid material. From the Putjangan Beds of the Lower Pleistocene, dated at 1.9 m.y., von Koenigswald and his workers recovered three important finds:

1. An infant *H. erectus* skull (Perning) from the Modjokerto site
2. Portions of a heavy adult skull including occipital bone and maxilla: Sangiran 4, or *Pithecanthropus robustus*, from Sangiran
3. A mandible, Sangiran 16, from Sangiran

Another important find often referred to as *Meganthropus* (Sangiran 8) also comes from this Djetis faunal period at Sangiran. First identified by von

Table 14-1 *Homo erectus* Fossil Sites[a]

Age[b]	Name[c]	Country	Site	Material		Discovery	
				Skeletal	Cranial capacity (cc.)	Scientist associated with find	Year
Middle Pleist. (700,000–500,000)	*H. erectus* Pithecanthropus I	Java	Sangiran	calva, femur	940[d]	Dubois	1891 1892
Middle Pleist. (700,000–500,000)	*H. erectus* Sangiran 2, 3, 10, 12	Java	Sangiran	bones of the skull	775–900	von Koenigswald, Jacob, Sartono	1937–1973
Middle Pleist. (500,000)	*H. erectus* P. VIII Sangiran 17	Java	Sangiran	almost complete cranium	1,029	Sartono	1969
Lower Pleist. (1.9–1.5 m.y.) (1.9–1.5 m.y.)	Sangiran 4	Java	Sangiran	portions of adult skull	900	von Koenigswald	1939
Lower Pleist. (1.9–1.5 m.y.)	*H. modjokertensis* Perning	Java	Modjokerto	infant calvarium	650	von Koenigswald	1936
Lower Pleist. (1.9 m.y.)	Meganthropus Sangiran 16	Java	Sangiran	mandible fragment	—	von Koenigswald	1952
Upper Pleist. (200,000)	*H. solensis* Solo Man Ngandong	Java	Ngandong	portions of eleven skulls	1,100 (avg.)	ter Haar, Oppenoorth	1931–1933

a. Only better-known fossils are included.

b. These are best estimates—authorities differ.

c. These are either the names given by the finder (or scientist associated with the find) or the name commonly used by anthropologists.

d. Holloway, 1981.

Koenigswald, and perhaps close to 2 million years old, it has been compared to robust australopithecines. However, it is most likely an early *H. erectus*.

Dubois recovered his famous skullcap, *Pithecanthropus* I, from the Trinil faunal level near the village of Trinil. Also from these Kabuh Beds, but from the productive nearby Sangiran site, came remains of Sangiran skulls 2, 3, 10, 12, and 17. These fossils are considered to be in the range of 1 million to 500,000 years.

Several fossil hominid remains have also been recovered from the Notopuro Beds containing Ngandong fauna of the Upper Pleistocene. Found along terraces of the Solo River, these hominids are called Solo Man or Ngandong. Since there is some question whether they are *H. erectus* or *H. sapiens*, we shall leave the matter for later discussion.

In summary, the material found by Dubois, von Koenigswald, Jacob, Sartono, the Geological Survey for Java, and others consist of the remains of eight skulls, several mandibles or mandible fragments, at least one complete femur and portions of others, and a number of loose teeth. The cranial capacity of those skulls suitable for measurement range from 775 to 1,029 cm³, with an average of 900 cm³. The femora found at these sites are similar (though not identical) to those of modern *H. sapiens*, and indicate the Java population was roughly the same size as (or a few inches shorter than) humans today. Java *erectus* lived, if the dates recently suggested are correct, from almost 2 million to about 500,000 years ago.

When we compare the skulls of the Lower and Middle Pleistocene of Java, we find a pattern of what Sartono (1975) has called small-brained and large-brained pithecanthropines. In the Lower Pleistocene, the evidence from Sangiran 4 suggests characteristic *H. erectus* traits, only more so. The brain is smaller, bones thicker, skull flatter, and there is that unexpected diastema in the upper jaw and the projecting canine.

By Middle Pleistocene times in Java, *H. erectus* had changed, but not a great deal. A slight increase occurred in the height of the vault (see craniograms in Fig. 14-13), and the diastema and projecting canine had disappeared. The small brain continues in the Trinil (Sangiran) 2, 3, 10, 12, and 17 specimens, which are all remarkably similar. There seems to have been very little evolutionary change within the Middle Pleistocene until the upper levels of the Kabuh Beds are reached. Here, a recent significant find, Sangiran 17, estimated at about 500,000 years, represents a decided break in the similarity of Javanese Middle Pleistocene *erectus* forms.

Although this almost complete skull retains the basic morphologic pattern of Java *erectus*, it is longer, broader, and higher. The dental arch is remarkably similar to *H. sapiens*, and the forehead is higher than any other Javanese *H. erectus* of the Middle Pleistocene. These modifications of skull size are reflected in the cranial capacity of Sangiran 17, which measures 1,029 cm³. We do not presently know what processes might have occurred in the short time represented in the 30 feet of strata separating Sangiran 12 (900 cm³) from Sangiran 17 (1,029 cm³) that could have produced this increase in cranial capacity.

Solo, or Ngandong, a problem Javanese form, should be mentioned here.

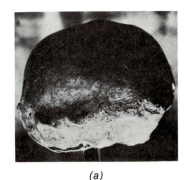

(a)

(b)

Figure 14-12 (*a*) Sangiran 12. Rear view illustrates pentagonal shape of skull. (*b*) Sangiran 17.

Figure 14-13   Craniograms.

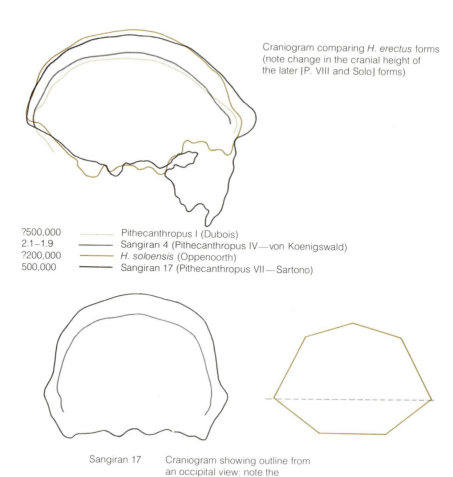

Craniogram comparing *H. erectus* forms (note change in the cranial height of the later [P. VIII and Solo] forms)

?500,000	⸺⸺⸺	Pithecanthropus I (Dubois)
2.1–1.9	⸺⸺⸺	Sangiran 4 (Pithecanthropus IV—von Koenigswald)
?200,000	⸺⸺⸺	*H. soloensis* (Oppenoorth)
500,000	⸺⸺⸺	Sangiran 17 (Pithecanthropus VII—Sartono)

Sangiran 17

Sangiran 2

Craniogram showing outline from an occipital view: note the widest area is toward base of skull giving a pentagonal form

Figure 14-14   Craniograms.

Peking man

Pithecanthropus I, Sangiran 2, 3, 4, 12

Sangiran 17

⸺⸺⸺ Sangiran 4 (robustus)
⸺⸺⸺ Sangiran 17

Actually, there are two problems: (1) Is Ngandong *H. erectus* or *H. sapiens*? and (2) when did it live? Estimates range from 300,000 y.a.–60,000 y.a.

Similarities to *H. erectus* include the thickness of the skull bone, thick brow ridges, and sharply angled occiput. On the other hand, the vault is higher than *H. erectus*, and the forehead rises more vertically. Also, the occiput seems more filled out, the nuchal ridge for the neck muscles is lower down (a *H. sapiens* trend), and the angulation of the occiput is not as sharp. The skull is larger than *H. erectus*, ranging from 1,035 to 1,255 cm³ (the mean is 1,154 cm³) for the eleven calvaria that have been found.

Ngandong has long been considered a relative of the earlier Javanese *H. erectus* forms. This belief receives further support from a skullcap found not far from Sangiran and known by its site name, Sambungmachen. This is a larger skull than the earlier fossils from Java, probably over 1,000 cm³, and possesses some typical early *H. erectus* traits, with changes especially in the occipital area that foreshadow the Ngandong material.

Like some of the European fossils of the Middle Pleistocene, Ngandong is difficult to place because of the mixture of *H. erectus* and *H. sapiens* traits. It is possible, of course, that like Swanscombe, Steinheim (p. 510), and some others, Ngandong is a transitional form between *H. erectus* and *H. sapiens*. Coming in the latter portion of the Middle Pleistocene, this is entirely possible.

We can say little about the hominid way of life in Java during the Lower and Middle Pleistocene. Tools have been found, but not in their original strata nor in direct association with faunal, including human, assemblages. Apparently they date from the Middle Pleistocene, and consist mainly of crudely made choppers and chopping tools similar to those found in Burma, Northwest India, and northern China.

Like other *H. erectus* populations, the Java *H. erectus* was most likely a systematic hunter, a life style made possible by the striking increase in brain size over australopithecines. The relatively large Java *H. erectus* brain may be explained by the selective pressures of a hunting society. In hunting "the abilities to learn from the past, plan for the future, and communicate one's ideas are at a premium for a creature who, alone and unarmed, is unable either to out-spring or out-fight its potential prey" (Brace and Montagu, 1977, p. 314).

PEKING

The story of Peking Man is another saga filled with excitement, hard work, luck, and misfortune. It began in 1911, when J. Gunnar Andersson, a Swedish geologist, accepted an appointment as adviser to the Chinese Government to arrange a survey of its coalfields and ore resources. In his investigations, Andersson became interested in the mammals of Tertiary and Pleistocene deposits, and he and his colleagues collected many specimens. Europeans had known for a long time that the "dragon bones" (like the *Gigantopithecus* teeth mentioned in Chapter 9), so important to the Chinese for their healing and aphrodisiac power, were actually mammal bones. In 1917, the Geological Survey of China resolved to find the sites where these dragon bones were collected by local inhabitants and sold to apothecary shops. In 1921, An-

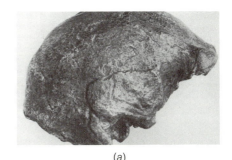

(a)

(b)

Figure 14-15 (a) Lateral view of Solo skull; (b) rear view of Solo skull.

Figure 14-16 Zhoukoudian Cave. Grid on wall drawn for purposes of excavation.

dersson and a few other scientists were investigating a place called Chicken Bone Hill near the village of Zhoukoudian, about thirty miles southwest of Beijing.* While laying plans to excavate the hill, they were approached by a local resident who told the scientists that much larger and better dragons' bones could be obtained not far away.

The new discovery lay in an abandoned quarry 500 feet west of the railway station at Zhoukoudian. The villager showed them a fissure in the limestone wall, and in a few minutes they found the jaw of a pig, which indicated that the site was a more important one than Chicken Bone Hill. "That evening we went home with rosy dreams of great discoveries" (Andersson, 1934, pp. 97–8).

Andersson assigned a colleague, Dr. Otto Zdansky, to excavate the site, and told him, "I have a feeling that there lie here the remains of one of our ancestors and it is only a question of your finding him. Take your time and stick to it till the cave is emptied, if need be" (Andersson, 1934, p. 101). Zdansky worked the site for several summers and took the material he excavated back to Sweden. In 1926, he wrote Andersson that after carefully cleaning and preparing the material, he had found a premolar and molar, which he cautiously identified as belonging to a creature resembling *Homo* sp. Andersson, not nearly so cautious, jubilantly exclaimed, "The man I predicted has been found" (Andersson, 1934, p. 103).

Andersson's enthusiasm and the discovery of the remarkable teeth led to a more organized effort to excavate the Zhoukoudian cave under the direction of Dr. Birgir Bohlin of Sweden. Work began in April, 1927, and continued until October 18 of the same year. Two days before the season ended, Bohlin found a hominid tooth, which he immediately took to **Dr. Davidson Black**, anatomist at the Peking Union Medical College, and responsible for the study of hominid material recovered from the cave. Of this episode, Black wrote to Andersson:

*Beijing is now widely accepted as the spelling for Peking. Peking will continue to be used in the text when referring to the fossils associated with that name.

On October 19th at half-past six in the evening Bohlin came to my institution in field dress, covered with dust, but beaming with pleasure. He had finished the season's work . . . and on October 16th he had discovered the tooth. . . . Certainly I was overjoyed! Bohlin came to me before he told his wife he was in Peking. . . . (Andersson, 1934, p. 107).

After carefully examining the tooth, Black decided it belonged to the same species as the two teeth found by Dr. Zdansky. He thus set up a new genus, *Sinanthropus*, with the species name, *pekinesis*. To designate a new genus and species on the basis of three teeth was a bold move, but Black felt he was fully justified in doing so. It was an exciting discovery, and *Sinanthropus pekinensis*, which we know today as *Homo erectus pekinensis*, immediately acquired worldwide fame. Shortly after this, Black went on leave to visit America and Europe:

Figure 14-17 Dr. Davidson Black.

He had a large gold watch chain made for him in Peking with a small receptacle hanging from it, into which the tooth exactly fitted. In this way he travelled about the world with his precious fossil, showing it to colleagues and asking their opinion (von Koenigswald, 1956, p. 45).

Bohlin resumed working in 1928, and recovered more than a score of teeth, as well as parts of skulls of both young and adult individuals, but a complete skull evaded his efforts. A young Chinese geologist, W. C. Pei, took over direction of the excavation in 1929, and concentrated in what is called the lower cave. On December 1 of that year, he began digging out the sediment in one branch of the lower cave, and at 4 P.M. of the following day found one of the most remarkable fossil skulls to be recovered up to that time. One of the Chinese workers tells the story:

We had got down about 30 metres deep. . . . It was there the skull-cap was sighted, half of it embedded in loose earth, the other in hard clay. The sun had almost set. . . . The team debated whether to take it out right away or to wait until the next day when they could see better. The agonizing suspense of a whole day was felt to be too much to bear, so they deciced to go on (Chia, 1975, pp. 12–13).

Pei brought the skull to Dr. Black, but because it was embedded in hard limestone, it took Black four months of hard, steady work to free it from its tough matrix. The result was worth the labor since the skull, that of a juvenile, was thick, low, and relatively small, but in Black's mind there was no doubt it belonged to early man. The response to this discovery, quite unlike that which greeted Dubois almost forty years earlier, was immediate and enthusiastically favorable. Peking Man became one of the more famous of fossil human skulls.

Work at Locality 1, as the Zhoukoudian cave is known, continued. Dr. Black maintained a killing schedule, working at night so he would not be interrupted at his desk. His health was not robust, and he probably should not have remained in Peking's harsh climate. As von Koenigswald related it:

He tried to stick it out but it was too much for him. When his secretary entered his room on March 15, 1934, she found him slumped over his desk, dead from a heart attack, with the beloved skull of Peking Man in his hand (von Koenigswald, 1956, p. 48).

◇ Box 14-5   Subspecies

Populations of a species are often designated by a subspecific term. Here are three examples of *H. erectus* populations with their subspecific designations.

H. erectus erectus	Java, Trinil Bed
H. erectus pekinensis	China, Zhoukoudian
H. erectus heidelbergensis	Germany, Mauer

Dr. Franz Weidenreich, distinguished anatomist and well known for his
work on European fossil hominids, succeeded Black. Weidenreich left his
native Germany because of the academic repression and preposterous "racial" policies of the Nazi regime. He was a visiting professor of anatomy at the
University of Chicago when he was appointed, in 1935, to be a visiting professor of anatomy at the Peking Union Medical College, and honorary director
of the Cenozoic Research Laboratory, Geological Survey of China. Excavations
at Zhoukoudian ended in 1937, with Japan's invasion of China, but the Cenozoic Research Laboratory continued.

As relations between the United States and Japan deteriorated, Weidenriech
decided he had better remove the fossil material from Peking to prevent it
from falling into the hands of the Japanese. Weidenreich left China in 1941,
taking beautifully prepared casts, photographs, and drawings of the Peking
material with him. After he left, the bones were packed in November, and
arrangements made for the U.S. Marine Corps to take the bones with them
when they left Peking to return to the United States. The bones never reached
the United States and have never been found. No one to this day knows what
happened to them, and their location remains a mystery (see p. 370).

Zhoukoudian Material   According to a recent account (Wu and Lin, 1983),
the total fossil remains of Peking Man unearthed at the Zhoukoudian cave
amount to:

6	complete or almost complete skulls
12	skull fragments
15	pieces of mandibles
157	teeth
3	humerus fragments
7	femur fragments
1	clavicle
1	tibia fragment
1	lunate (wrist) bone

(and over 100,000 artifacts)

Figure 14-18   Dr. Franz Weidenreich.

These belong to upwards of 40 male and female adults and children. This is a respectable amount of evidence, the most and the best of any *H. erectus* specimens, and (with the meticulous work by Dr. Weidenreich) has led to a good overall picture of the northern Chinese *H. erectus*.

Dating caves is not always a simple matter; in some cases, the roof of the cave has fallen in and not only is the stratigraphy disturbed, but fossil bones may have been washed into the cave. After a five-year comprehensive investigation of the Zhoukoudian site by more than 120 Chinese scientists (including paleoanthropologists, archeologists, geologists, climatologists, palynologists, and speleologists, who study caves), the researchers came to the following conclusions about Peking Man dates in the Zhoukoudian caves: There were three cultural stages beginning 460,000 y.a. and ending 230,000 y.a., when the people were forced out as the cave filled with rubble and sediment. These Middle Pleistocene dates place Peking Man considerably later than their conspecifics in Java, a time lapse that probably explains why the Zhoukoudian population had moved a bit further along the hominid trail than most of their Javanese relatives.

That Peking and Java hominids are related is clearly demonstrated by a comparison of the bones. The postcranial material is very similar, except that Peking's leg bones suggest he was shorter (at 5 feet 2 inches) than Java.

Peking, like Java, possesses the typical *erectus* fore and aft bulges—the supraorbital torus in front and the occipital ridge behind; the skull is keeled by a sagittal ridge, the face protrudes in alveolar prognathism, the incisors are shoveled, and molars contain large pulp cavities. Again, like the Java forms, the skull is vintage *H. erectus*, showing its greatest breadth near the bottom.

Table 14-2 *Homo erectus* Fossil Sites—China[a]

Age[b]	Name[c]	Country	Site	Material		Discovery	
				SKELETAL	CRANIAL CAPACITY (CC.)	SCIENTIST ASSOCIATED WITH FIND	YEAR
Middle Pleist. (500,000–400,000)	Peking Man, *Sinanthropus pekinensis*; *H. erectus pekinensis*	China	Zhoukoudian (Locality 1)	bones of skull, mandibles, teeth, limbs from more than forty persons	1,040 (avg.)	Bohlin Pei	1927–present
Middle Pleist. (400,000)	Longtan	China	Longtan	skull	?	Jia	1980
Lower Pleist. (800,000)	Lantian Man[d]	China	Gong Wang	calva, facial bones, teeth	780	Woo	1964
Middle Pleist. (650,000)	Lantian Man[d]	China	Chengjiawo	mandible (female)	—	Woo	1963–1965

a. Only better-known fossils are included.
b. These are best estimates—authorities differ.
c. These are either the names given by the finder (or scientist associated with the find) or the name commonly used by anthropologists.
d. See Wu, 1982.

Table 14-3   Zhoukoudian Material (Middle Pleistocene)

Material	Discovered		Cultural Material
	Year	By	
Premolar, molar	1923	O. Zdansky	choppers, scrapers, points, hammerstones, anvils, worked deer skulls (?drinking cups), bone "knives," traces of fire—ash layers, charred stone and wood.
Molar	1927	B. Bohlin	
Teeth and skull fragments	1927–28	B. Bohlin	
Skullcap	1929	W. C. Pei	
Portions of skulls, mandibles, teeth, limbs, 6 complete calva, 9 skull fragments, 6 pieces of facial bone, 15 mandibles, 152 teeth, 7 fragmented limb bones; 45 persons represented.	1929–37	W. C. Pei, D. Black, F. Weidenreich	
1 calvarium, 5 teeth, 1 mandible	1960s	Pei and others	

Locality 13 (one-half mile from Peking Cave) older than Locality 1; no human skeletal material; some stone tools and traces of fire.

Locality 15 (225 feet from Peking Cave) more recent than Locality 1; no human skeletal material, stone implements and traces of fire.

These similarities were recognized long ago by Black and Weidenreich; at one time, in fact, it was suggested that Peking's nomen be changed from *Sinanthropus* to *Pithecanthropus pekinensis*. However, the similarities of European and African Middle Pleistocene forms to those of Asia, and the resemblance of all these to the genus *Homo*, persuaded taxonomists that the correct name was *Homo erectus*.

What mainly distinguishes Peking from Java is cranial capacity. In their recent investigation (Wu and Lin, 1983), the Chinese scientists found that the cranial capacity of the earliest Peking individuals measured "some 900 cubic centimeters." When Peking Man emerged, the average capacity had reached 1054 cubic centimeters (Wu and Lin, p. 90). Had a juvenile skull been omitted from the measurements, the average would have been larger—1088 cc. As the craniogram illustrates (Fig. 14-14), the larger Peking skull is reflected by a higher vault of the skull, a higher forehead, and a longer and broader cranium. What accounts for the larger brain? Possibly, Peking represents a later period in the evolution of *Homo erectus*. With greater dependence on culture and selective pressures associated with that dependence, brain size assuredly increased. It is probably no accident that Peking Man (460,000–230,000 years ago in China) and Sangiran 17 (500,000 years ago in Java), both late in Asiatic *H. erectus* evolution, are relatively "large-brained."

More than 100,000 artifacts were recovered from this site that was occupied for almost 250,000 years, which, according to the Chinese (Wu and Lin, p. 86) "is one of the sites with the longest history of habitation by man or his ancestors...." The occupation of the site has been divided into three culture stages.

Earliest stage (460,000–420,000 y.a.)*   The tools were large, close to a pound in weight, and made of soft stone, such as sandstone.

Middle Stage (370,000–350,000 y.a.)   Tools become smaller and lighter (under a pound) and these smaller tools comprise 68% of the total; the large tools make up only 12%.

Final Stage (300,000–230,000 y.a.)   Tools are still smaller, and the tool materials were of better quality. The coarse quartz of the earlier periods was replaced by a finer quartz, sandstone tools had almost disappeared, and flint tools increased as much as 30%.

The early tools were crude and shapeless but become more refined over time, and, toward the top of Locality 1, there are some finely made tools. Common tools at the site are choppers and chopping tools, but retouched flakes were fashioned into scrapers, points, burins, and awls. Handaxes, found in abundance in Europe and Africa, are absent from Zhoukoudian.

Stone was not the only material selected by Peking hominids; they also utilized bone and horn. Found in the cave were antler fragments, which had been hacked into pieces. Antler roots might have served as hammers and the sharp tines as digging sticks. Many skulls of sika and thick-jaw deer minus facial bones as well as antlers and crania bases leaving only the braincase were also found. Chia suggests that since the skulls show evidence of repeated whittling and over 100 specimens were discovered, all similarly shaped, "it is reasonable to infer they served as 'drinking bowls.'" He goes on to conjecture that the brain cases of Peking Man "retain similar characteristics and probably served the same purpose" (Chia, 1975, p. 31).

Animal residue—nearly ninety species of mammals—has been identified, including deer, wild boar, bison, bear, leopard, and horse, all attesting to the ability of Peking hunters. Not all the animal bones were necessarily the remains of hunting expeditions; the animals may have wandered into the cave when it was uninhabited by *H. erectus*. But many of the animals were no doubt hunted, especially the sika deer, whose remains were found in great abundance. The animal bones were scraped and split to get at the marrow, and many of them were charred, indicating they had been cooked.

Further evidence for Peking's vocation as hunter comes from the skulls themselves. We have already mentioned that the human skulls found in the cave, like many of the other mammalian skulls, were badly broken, faces removed, and the base of the skull surrounding the foramen magnum broken away. It is possible they served as "drinking bowls," but it is also possible that enlarging the foramen magnum enabled living Peking people to extract the brain. Also, the fact that relatively few postcranial bones were recovered would suggest that Peking hunted, killed, and ate his human prey elsewhere, usually bringing the skull back to the cave where he could snack at leisure.

Other suggestions for the mutilated human skulls are their use as ritual items or trophies. Eating the brains may not have been dietary, but a magical ritual to take on properties—the intelligence of the owner, for example. Pos-

*These dates should be considered tentative until more precise chronometric techniques are available.

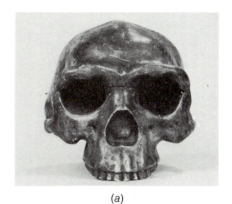

(a)

(b)

(c)

Figure 14-19   Peking Man (reconstructed cranium). (*a*) Frontal view; (*b*) lateral view; (*c*) rear view. The widest part of the skull is toward the bottom.

Figure 14-20 Views of: (*a*) *Homo erectus erectus* and (*b*) *Homo erectus pekinensis*; (*c*) the Solo XI skull; (*d*) the Rhodesian skull; (*e*) the Saccopastore skull; and (*f*) the skull of La Chapelle-aux-Saints. Note the pentagonal shape of skulls in upper row compared to those of the Neandertal and Rhodesian skulls in the lower row. (From Weidenreich, 1951.)

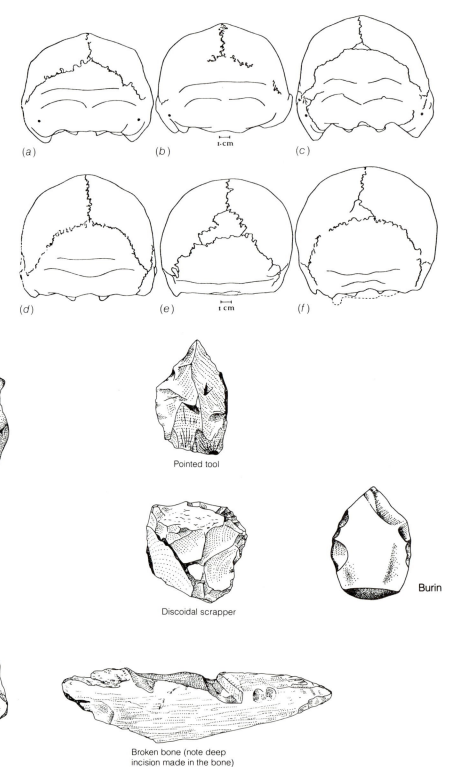

(*a*)   (*b*)   1 cm   (*c*)

(*d*)   (*e*)   1 cm   (*f*)

Chopper

Pointed tool

Discoidal scrapper

Burin

Chopper

Broken bone (note deep incision made in the bone)

Figure 14-21 Tools used by Peking Man.

sibly, the skull may have been hung about the neck as a trophy, or a symbol of the prowess of the hunter. Unfortunately, there is insufficient evidence to demonstrate any of these suggestions.

From the flourishing plant growth surrounding the cave, we can assume the inhabitants of Locality I supplemented their meat diet by gathering herbs, wild fruits, tubers, and ostrich eggs. Fragments of charred ostrich eggshells and copious deposits of hackberry seeds were unearthed in the cave.

In addition to charred eggshells and bones, charred stones and bits of charred wood have also come from the cave. All of this is evidence of fire, of course, and it is obvious that the Peking people controlled fire, although it is doubtful whether they were capable of making it themselves. The main evidence of fire comes from layers of ash over eighteen feet deep at one point. Hearths were also found, demonstrating that Peking could confine fire within a specific area and keep it burning for long periods of time.

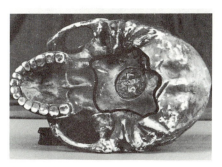

Figure 14-22 Cannibalism at Zhoukoudian. The area around the foramen magnum has been cut out to enable Peking Man to get at the brain. Whether this was for ritual or dietary purposes is not known.

Peking Man, who seems to have lived later than *H. erectus* of Java, also enjoyed a more developed culture. With a large brain, the Zhoukoudian hominids were accomplished hunters, cooked their food, fashioned stone and bone tools, and even made ornaments. Wu and Lin (1983) state that "Peking Man was a cave dweller, a fire user, a deer hunter, a seed gatherer and a maker of specialized tools" (p. 94). This leads them to suggest three social adaptations for the Peking population:

1. Living in a group. Hunting large animals is "complicated, difficult, and hazardous," and cooperation of many individuals would be required; therefore, it is likely that Peking Man lived in a group when he began to hunt deer. (See pp. 405–408 for a discussion of this "hunting hypothesis.")

2. Sexual division of labor. Because of women's physiological constraints, it would be difficult for them to engage in hunting activities, which would then be left to the men. "The pattern of male hunters and female gatherers, which is common in hunting-and-gathering societies today, may have already been established" (p. 94).

3. Education. Tools during the more than 200,000 years that Peking Man lived in Zhoukoudian became more sophisticated. This "suggests that the earliest practice of education may have taken place in Peking Man's cave" (p. 94). Each generation could not have developed new technological skills without having learned existing ones taught by the older generation.

Could they speak? Their hunting and technological skills would suggest they possessed some kind of symbolic communication. If the skull was, in fact, used as a symbol as speculated above, then symbolic communication is even more suggestive. (See Box 14-6 for Wolpoff's neurological evidence.) Did they wear clothing? Perhaps, since they manufactured awls, and one of the bone tools may be a needle. How long did they live? Studies of the fossil remains reveal that almost 40% of the bones belong to individuals under the age of 14, and only 2.6% are estimated in the 50 to 60 age group (Chia, 1975, p. 43).

To sum up, the Zhoukoudian *H. erectus* was an excellent hunter and forager with a diet composed of a wide range of meat, vegetables, fruit, berries, and seeds. Controlling fire, they cooked their food and may also have used fire to keep marauding animals out of the cave. We can imagine that living

◇ Box 14-6   Speech

Human speech capacity is an extremely complicated behavior, involving the development of tracts between the motor and associated speech areas and between the frontal and posterior parietal portions of the brain. The basis for speaking would seem to lie more in neurological structures than in morphological ones. The importance of the frontal-posterior parietal tract is that it allows the frontal area to "make sense" out of the crossmodal associations of the posterior parietal area, while the motor-associational speech area tract provides a pathway for this information to reach the motor-speech area.

The evolution of language ability seems tied to the appearance of hemispheric dominance and asymmetry. The marked bilateral asymmetry in size and morphology in the newly discovered Zhoukoudian cranium 5* provides one of the few direct morphological correlates with the ability to speak in humans. Thus, there is every reason to believe that *Homo erectus* was capable of human vocal language (Wolpoff, 1980a).

*Cranial parts found in 1966 fit the temporal fragments discovered and described by Weidenreich in the 1930s.

Table 14-4   *Homo erectus* of the Lower Pleistocene

Million Years	Hominids
.9	Lantian (Gong Wang)
	Sangiran 8
1.2	OH 9
1.5	OH 13
	ER 3733
1.8 (?)	Perning (Java)
Pliocene (?)	Sangiran 4

conditions—in a climate of very cold winters and hot summers similar to Beijing today—were harsh, and few people lived much beyond thirty years. They made tools skillfully and used them effectively. There is even a possibility of supernatural beliefs and—primitive though it may have been—of symbolic communication.

Lantian   Somewhat older than Zhoukoudian and contemporary with material from the Trinil (Kabuh levels) of Java are hominid bones from the villages of Chengjiawo and Gong Wang, near the town of Lantian, in Shaanxi province of central China. A mandible, skullcap with facial bones and teeth, stone artifacts, and some bones of other fossil vertebrates were found there in 1963–1965.

The skullcap found at Gong Wang (800,000 y.a.–750,000 y.a.) is small, with an estimated capacity of around 778 cm³, almost identical to Sangiran 4 of Java. Also, in the same manner as the early Java hominids, the vault bones are very thick and the supraorbital torus well pronounced.

The well-preserved Chengjiawo mandible (about 650,000 y.a.) possesses most of its teeth and is believed to be an old female. Interestingly, neither of the 3rd molars (wisdom teeth) had erupted; not even a tooth germ is present—the earliest known case of missing 3rd molars. This poor Lantian old woman also suffered a bad case of **periodontal** disease, not unusual among hunter-gatherers.

Longtan   On November 4, 1980, a complete skull was found in Longtan (Dragon Pool) Cave, south China. A few human teeth and a mandible fragment were also excavated, and at least twenty-five species of mammal bones. The material is presently being analyzed at the Institute of Vertebrate Paleontology and Paleoanthropology. Although a complete description is not yet available,

Figure 14-23   The Longtan skull (rear view).

Chinese scientists believe it is *Homo erectus* about 400,000 years old, but somewhat different from both Zhoukoudian and Lantian. This is the first *H. erectus* skull found in south China (*China Pictorial*, 1981).

Periodontal
peri: around
dontal: teeth
Gum and jaw disease.

◇ Europe

HEIDELBERG (MAUER)

Only a jaw was found here, near the village of Mauer and not far from Heidelberg University (see Box 14-7) in 1907. The mandible is more massive than those from early (Djetis) Java, but the teeth, though not small, are not proportionate to the size of the jaw. No diastema or projecting canines are seen, and the chin recedes in the fashion of other Middle Pleistocene jaws. Dating, as in so many cases, is uncertain, and estimates range from 600,000 y.a.–250,000 y.a. Some believe Heidelberg may be the oldest human bones ever discovered in Western Europe, and that may well be the case. However, the "earliest ever" is a frequent claim for European *H. erectus* finds.

The classification of Heidelberg as an *H. erectus* has been questioned. Like the majority of European Middle Pleistocene forms, the situation is not clear-cut because the skulls possess both *H. erectus*-like traits and archaic* *sapiens* traits. As more data are made available, it is possible that classification may become clearer. However, as Wolpoff (1980b) points out, if the evolution in Europe was a continuous one, from *H. erectus* to *H. sapiens*, it is going to be difficult to draw an absolute line separating the two grades.

VÉRTESSZÖLLÖS

In 1965, at the small town of Vértesszöllös, thirty miles west of Budapest, Hungary, Dr. Laszlo Vértes unearthed an adult occiput and a few fragments of infant teeth. Extrapolating from the occiput, it is estimated that the skull may have been as large as 1,300 cm³ (Wolpoff, 1980a).

The occiput, with a well-developed nuchal torus, is noted for its thickness, greater than the *H. erectus* average. However, the bone is quite large, approximating modern size, which is remarkable for a skull that may be as much as 400,000 years old. Although it is considered to fall within *H. erectus* measurements, the large and rounded occipital bone may presage the beginnings of a *H. sapiens* trait. Overall, the occiput suggests a large-brained, heavily muscled *H. erectus* specimen. Pebble tools, recalling the Oldowan industry of Africa, were also found at the site.

The controversy surrounding the placement of Vértesszöllös is another example of the problem of classifying specimens having what appear to be both *H. erectus* and archaic *sapiens* traits. In this case, the problem is aggravated by the presence of only one adult bone—the occiput.

Figure 14-24   Cast of the Heidelberg (Mauer) jaw.

*"Archaic" is the term now commonly applied to early *H. sapiens*. It is not intended as a precise term or taxonomic designation. Middle Pleistocene skulls that possess *erectus*-like and *sapiens*-like traits are now often referred to as archaic *sapiens*.

◇ Box 14-7   Finding Heidelberg

For a number of years Professor Otto Schoetensack, a Heidelberg University paleontologist, had been observing the commercial operations at a sandpit near the village of Mauer, six miles southeast of the university town. Because of the Tertiary and Pleistocene strata, Schoetensack had arranged with the owner of the sandpit that all bones uncovered in the ancient strata during the operation be donated to the University. The sandpit had yielded hundreds of mammalian bones, but for twenty years Schoetensack waited in vain for a human fossil. It was not until October 21, 1907, that Herr Rosch, the sandpit owner, sent a thrilling message to the patient professor:

For twenty years you have been making efforts to find traces of primitive men in my sandpit in order to prove human beings lived in this district at the same time as the mammoth. Yesterday we came across this proof. Sixty-five feet below ground level at the bottom of my sandpit the lower jawbone of a prehistoric man was found, in a very good state of preservation (in Wendt, 1963, p. 442).

Schoetensack named the jaw *Homo heidelbergensis*, which raised the hackles of many European scientists who were either still opposed to the idea of evolution or did not believe the Mauer jaw belonged to the genus *Homo*. However, the furor lacked the passionate spirit of Dubois' time and may have helped justify Dubois' views.

PETRALONA

Just south of the northern Greek capital of Salonika lies Petralona where, in 1959, villagers digging for water fell into a cave that had lain sealed and unknown. Near a stalagmite, practically on the surface of the soil, they found a fossil hominid skull about 1200 cm³ in size. It is one of the largest of any *H. erectus* skulls and may be the largest of any of the European Middle Pleistocene hominids. It is an important find, since there is relatively little hominid material from Europe during the range of time when Petralona lived.

However, Petralona is a perplexing find. While almost complete (the mandible is missing) and quite well studied, one of the problems is its date, which has been estimated by various researchers from 250,000 y.a. to 750,000 y.a. Faunal remains and the geology suggest a glacial period (the Mindel) or an interglacial period, either the Cromerian (500,000 y.a. or more) or Holsteinian (around 300,000 y.a.). Furthermore, since there are differences of opinion precisely where in the cave the skull was found, the dating becomes even more difficult.

Another puzzle is determining Petralona's affiliation—to which subspecies should it be assigned? He (it is considered to be male) lived during the *H. erectus* period, if the older date is valid; if the later date is correct, then Petralona lived on the verge of *H. sapiens* origins. Dating aside, what about Petralona's morphology? What does he *look* like, or perhaps more properly, what does he *measure* like? At this point, we run into inconsistencies. In size, Petralona resembles archaic *sapiens*; the frontal bone relates him to *H. erectus* and archaic *sapiens*; the supraorbital torus is unique in some ways, in others similar to archaic *sapiens*, and in still others approximates the neandertals; the face aligns him with early neandertals; the overall facial form

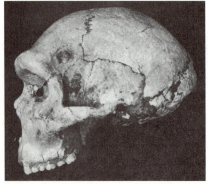

Figure 14-25   The Petralona skull.

to archaic *sapiens*; and the occipital bone resembles *H. erectus* and archaic *sapiens* in some respects.

Without going into more detail, the morphology of the Petralona skull associates it here with *H. erectus*, there with archaic *sapiens*, occasionally with neandertals and even anatomically moderns, and some of its features are unique and relate the skull to no other subspecies. With Petralona's measurements, it could be considered ancestral to neandertals or to archaic *sapiens*; or to African forms, such as Broken Hill and Bodo; or to none of these. Dr. Milford Wolpoff (1980b), who examined the skull several years ago, believes it is more like *H. erectus* than some other early Europeans (e.g., Steinheim and Swanscombe, pp. 414–416), but on the whole concludes it belongs in the *H. sapiens*, rather than *H. erectus*, grade.

Figure 14-26   The Petralona (Greece) site and the Vértesszöllös site (Hungary).

Figure 14-27 *H. erectus* in Western Europe and North Africa.

It can be seen from the foregoing that it is difficult to assign Petralona to a definite subspecies. It has been suggested that hominids of this time period not be assigned to a subspecies, but rather to *H. sapiens* grades, without implying "that members of any grade were automatically regarded as ancestral to members of the succeeding grade" (Stringer et al., 1977, p. 250).

For the present, because of the confusion of dates and its remarkable variation in morphology, we shall leave Petralona in this *H. erectus* chapter. However, it should be noted that it could well fit into the next chapter as a transitional form, an archaic *sapiens* ancestral (or not ancestral) to neandertals or to anatomically moderns, or to both, or neither.

From a cultural point of view, the fauna found in the cave suggest that the Petralona people were hunter/gatherers and probably led a life not too different from that described for Peking Man. Unfortunately, relatively few artifacts were found, and it would be difficult to reconstruct Petralona life on the basis of their technology.

TORRALBA/AMBRONA

Probably the best-known Middle Pleistocene site associated with *H. erectus*, but minus its bones, is in the Rio Ambrona-Masegar Valley, 100 miles northeast of Madrid, at Torralba and Ambrona, in central Spain. These sites, two miles apart, were dug by F. Clark Howell during the summers of 1961 through 1963 (Howell, 1966; 1982). Excavations were resumed in 1980 and continued in the summers of 1981, 1982, and 1983.

In this grassy valley lived a group of *H. erectus* during a mild recession of the Mindel Glaciation, sometime between 400,000 and 300,000 years ago. The evidence of their occupation comes from the remains of butchered elephants and other animals, and many tools consisting of handaxes, cleavers, and scrapers characteristic of the Middle Pleistocene industry known as Acheulian. Evidence of charcoal and worked wood and bone were also found.

Unfortunately for purposes of positive identification, no human bones or teeth have so far been discovered. Nevertheless, the number of broken animal bones, especially elephant, and the pattern of breakage and deliberate fashioning and trimming leave no doubt of humans at work. Little question remains that people were working together in a cooperative effort. Armed with wooden spears and stone tools, they evidently drove a herd of elephants along the valley into the swamps. (For vivid accounts of the Torralba/Ambrona excavations and how these populations lived and hunted, the student is encouraged to read the Time-Life books and Pfeiffer, listed at the end of the chapter. See Freeman, 1975, for a more technical discussion.)

TERRA AMATA

Another occupation site lacking human bones, dated about 300,000 y.a. during the Holstein interglacial, was located by French archeologist Henry de Lumley in the heart of the city of Nice on the opulent French Riviera. The site is now situated on a hillside, an ancient sloping sand dune, below the imposing Chateau de Rosemont, once the residence of the king of Yugoslavia, and has been recently converted into a museum of paleontology. In an alley called **Terra Amata**, not far from the port of Nice, builders, in 1966, began the construction of luxury apartments closely monitored by de Lumley, who was aware of the archeological possibilities. When bulldozers cut away several feet of earth, de Lumley spotted some pebble tools and succeeded in stopping construction for several months. Collecting a digging crew of 300, de Lumley and his archeologist wife spent 40,000 hours excavating 144 square yards 70 feet deep. They uncovered 21 separate living floors and removed 35,000 objects. (See de Lumley, 1969.)

Although this French site failed to yield human skeletal material, an imprint of a right foot 9½ inches long was found preserved in the sand. De Lumley estimated the stature of this individual at about 5 feet 1 inch.

Many of the 35,000 objects consisted of pebble tools, but there were Acheulian tools, such as cleavers, scrapers, projectile points, and choppers. Bone had also been worked. Like their Spanish neighbors, the Terra Amata people were also hunters, as indicated by the tools and remains of hunting game.

One of the most fascinating finds was evidence of huts, 21 of them at three different locations. The evidence comes from holes in the ground where stakes had been driven to form the walls, and a line of stones paralleling the stake imprints that apparently served as wall braces. The imprints suggest oval huts, and de Lumley estimated they were fairly good-sized, from 26 to 49 feet long and 13 to 20 feet wide, and may have housed ten to twenty people. The huts, he believes, were constructed of sturdy branches bent to interlock at the top. In the center of the hut was a hearth, a smoke hole above it, and an entrance at one end.

Less than fastidious, the Terra Amata hut dwellers used part of their home as a bathroom, and pollen analysis of the **coprolites** suggests the huts were occupied in spring and early summer. Since the earth of the living floors was

Terra Amata
terra: land
amata: beloved

Coprolites
Fossilized feces.

Figure 14-28 Shelter at Terra Amata. Evidence of habitation at Terra Amata enabled de Lumley to reconstruct what a hut might have looked like. (Courtesy California Academy of Sciences.)

not compacted, the occupants must have been transients, staying only for a few days at a time, much like their present-day successors who vacation at this famous resort area.

Reviewing the Middle Pleistocene, we find that remains in Europe are scarce (and Lower Pleistocene lacking) compared to Asia and Africa. The dating is presently approximate at best, but the more serious problem is the mixture of early and late physical traits.

The specimens discussed in the preceding sections are not decisively *H. erectus* or *H. sapiens*. Some of the skull bones reflect the ruggedness of *H. erectus*, while others are more subdued, tending toward a *H. sapiens* character. It is possible to argue that these hominids had already evolved beyond the *erectus* grade but were not decisively sapient. If earlier specimens are found, they may prove to belong to the *erectus* grade—in the strict sense.

Professor Howells (1980), in his survey of *H. erectus*, suggests that some evidence of earlier European inhabitants may exist. Tools found in Western Europe have been provisionally dated at almost a million years. Fossil remains associated with this material are absent, unfortunately, and it is not possible to say what hominid grade they belong to.

Homo erectus, then, as far as faunal comparison can tell us, inhabited Europe from about 700,000 (or longer) to 300,000 years ago. They hunted large game and gathered plant food, utilized caves, and may have built shelters. They may have been capable of speech, and used fire (as their Asiatic contemporaries did). Once again, though, we find it impossible to say whether they knew how to *start* a fire. Wood and bone were both worked, but their principal tools were made of stone characteristic of the Acheulian industry. The likelihood is that family units, perhaps several of them, cooperated in their economic pursuits, and from the remains at Torralba/Ambrona we may infer they were capable of deliberately planning their activities.

◇ North Africa

We have found *H. erectus* in Southeast Asia, eastern Asia, and Europe. With a more sophisticated culture than their predecessors, we might expect that *H. erectus* would spread to all the possible niches they could manage. North Africa is one of these and is represented by sites in Algeria and Morocco, all of which contain skeletal material (see Fig. 14-29).

Remains from Algeria (Ternifine) and Morocco (Rabat, Temara, and Casablanca) consist of mandibles—and a partial skull from Salé—which reflect *H. erectus* characteristics. Ternifine, the oldest North African site (?500,000 +), shows some resemblances to Asian mandibles.

A find of special interest, recovered by the French scientist Jean Jacques Jaeger, is Salé (Morocco), the only reasonably complete North African *erectus* skull. Jaeger dates the skull in the 100,000 year range and estimates the cranial capacity at 930–960 cm³, surprisingly small for this time period. According to Jaeger, the front part of the skull—teeth and frontal bone (the

Figure 14-29 The Salé skull. The most complete *erectus* skull discovered in North Africa.

face is missing)—shows the characteristics of *Homo erectus*. The occipital area, on the other hand, "gives a fairly modern impression," but all things considered, Jaeger would place the skull in the *erectus* grade of evolution (Jaeger, 1975).

The fossil evidence from North Africa appears to fit into the *erectus* stage, but the material is sadly incomplete. The recently discovered incomplete calvarium from Salé gives a provocative glimpse of what Middle Pleistocene humans in the Maghreb of North Africa looked like. But placing the fossils in their proper time period is a problem yet to be resolved. No chronometric dates are at hand, and estimates from faunal associations for the various sites range from as much as 800,000 y.a. to as late as 100,000 y.a. We have assigned the late remains to *H. erectus*, but they might also possibly be transitional to *H. sapiens*.

Table 14-5 *Homo erectus* in East Africa

Olduvai Hominid 9 (OH 9, Chellean Man)

Olduvai Hominid 13 (OH 13, Cinderella, *H. habilis*)

Olduvai Hominid 28 (OH 28)

KNM-ER 3733

Bodo

◇ East Africa

Since 1959, with the discovery of "Zinj," East Africa has become the El Dorado of the search for ancient humans. A prodigious quantity of fossil hominid remains, most of them australopithecines, have been recovered, but an increasing number of *Homo* specimens have been excavated in recent years.

It is not feasible in an introductory text to describe, or even list, all fossils from East Africa. We shall discuss a few and mention others in order to give a summary report of *H. erectus* evolution in this area.

OLDUVAI (TANZANIA)

As far back as 1960, Dr. Louis Leakey unearthed a skull at Olduvai (OH 9) that he identified as *H. erectus* (and referred to as Chellean Man). The skull OH 9 from Upper Bed II has a massive cranium; it is faceless and has the largest capacity (1,067 cm³) of all the early *H. erectus* specimens. Dated at 1.2 m.y., this is indeed a large skull for that time period. The browridge is huge, the largest known for any hominid in both thickness and projection. The cranial base is heavily buttressed where muscles attach, yet the vault bones are fairly thin, an australopithecine feature.

Another Lower Pleistocene skull recovered from Olduvai by the Leakeys is OH 13, called "Cinderella" by Louis Leakey and identified by him as a *Homo habilis*. The skull is small with thin walls (australopithecine traits), but Tobias and von Koenigswald (1965) believe the mandible resembles early *H. erectus* from Java. If their analysis is correct, OH 13—estimated to be about 1.5 m.y.— is one of the oldest African *H. erectus* forms. Is Cinderella an *A. africanus*, *H. habilis*, or *H. erectus*? Perhaps a glass slipper somewhere in the Olduvai volcanic ash may provide the answer.

Later at Olduvai, from Bed IV of the Middle Pleistocene (dated at about 500,000 years), are two finds of some significance. The skull OH 12, probably female, has a cranial capacity of 735 cm³ and resembles OH 9 from Bed II. It is interesting that similarities in skull morphology would endure for three-

Figure 14-30 *H. erectus* sites in East Africa.

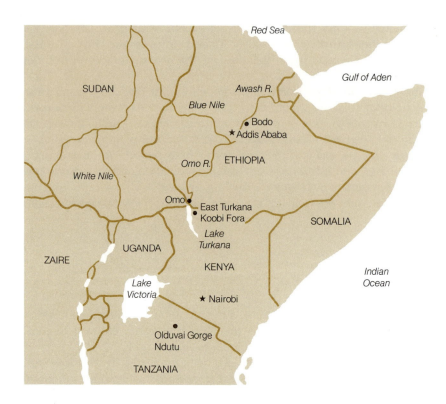

quarter million years. These similarities may reflect a regional clade (see p. 265 for a discussion of clade).

The other finds are rare postcranial remains—a left femoral shaft and an innominate bone belonging to the same individual, a female found by Mary Leakey in 1970. These bones are important evidence of postcranial morphology of hominids living at this time, since they shed light on how East African *H. erectus* stood and walked (which was very much as we do). Acheulian tools were found in association with the bones.

Not far from Olduvai Gorge is Lake Ndutu, where an incomplete skull was uncovered when the lake waters receded during the 1971 dry season. Associated with the skull were spheroids, hammerstones, and a few flake tools all "rather nondescript and of an indeterminate industry" (Mturi, 1976). A date of 500,000 years has been suggested for Ndutu.

The cranium has been compared to Zhoukoudian with some advanced features, and Clarke (1976) believes Ndutu may form an evolutionary link between the Peking forms and *H. sapiens*.

LAKE TURKANA (KENYA)

Some 400 miles north of Olduvai Gorge, on the northern boundary of Kenya, is the finger lake—Lake Turkana. Excavated by Richard Leakey since 1969, the eastern shore of the lake has been a virtual gold mine for australopithecines, early *Homo*, and *H. erectus* fossil remains.

One of the oldest* of *H. erectus* forms (1.5 m.y.) is a remarkably well-preserved skull, KNM-ER 3733 (Fig. 16-32), found by Bw. Bernard Ngeneo during the 1974–1975 field program in the highly productive Koobi Fora Formation (Leakey and Walker, 1976). Consisting of an almost complete calvarium with typical *H. erectus* characteristics and resembling OH 9 on a smaller scale (Rightmire, 1979), the skull is estimated at 850 cm³, falling in the middle range of *Homo erectus* cranial measurements.

A puzzling aspect of the ER 3733 skull is that it was found in the same geological bed with robust australopithecines (*A. boisei*) and perhaps *A. africanus* as well. This raises the single- versus multiple-species question, which anthropologists have been debating for years. Is it possible for two (or more) hominid species to live side by side contemporaneously, or is there a limit of one species to one niche at one time? The evidence of the ER 3733 and australopithecine "bedmates" appears to decide the issue in favor of the multiple-species argument.

ETHIOPIA

Continuing north to Ethiopia, we find several sites that have been excavated during the past fifteen years. Just across the Kenya border, in the Lower Omo River Basin, are parietal and temporal fragments dated at 1.2–1.0 m.y.a.

In northeast Ethiopia, north of Addis Ababa, is the Afar Depression, where Lucy was found (Chapter 12). It was in the Awash River Valley area of Afar that a fairly complete skull was found, at Bodo D'Ar, during the 1976 and 1978 excavating seasons. This skull shows many typical *H. erectus* features. The vault bones are extraordinarily thick; in fact, one part of it is the thickest hominid bone ever reported. There is also some evidence of more advanced features, such as less postorbital constriction. Bodo's overall morphological pattern may be closest to the Rhodesian skull (p. 435), and may possibly be assigned to archaic *sapiens*.

The site appears to be one of butchering, where cut-up hippos and stone tools were found associated with the skull. Indeed Bodo himself appears to have been scalped—as seen in telltale cutmarks on the skull. Unfortunately, the dating is extremely ambiguous and is "estimated" somewhere between 700,000 y.a.–125,000 y.a. (Conroy et al., 1978).

A number of kill sites and butchering sites confirm that *H. erectus* was a hunter in Africa as well as in Europe and Asia. Supporting these data is the more than 1 million-year-old BK *Pelorovis* kill site at Olduvai (see Chapter 10). We also find that during this Lower Paleolithic period (Box 14-8) stone tools continued to be developed as reflected in the change from early to late Acheulian industries.

In East Africa, *Homo erectus* appeared sometime around 1.6 m.y.a. and disappeared as a species roughly 500,000 y.a. From Tanzania to Kenya to Ethiopia (and Chad, west of Ethiopia), this thick-boned, heavy brow-ridged,

*In November, 1984, Richard Leakey announced the find, on the western shore of Lake Turkana, of an almost complete skeleton of a 12-year-old male: *H. erectus*, 1.6 m.y. old (the oldest African *H. erectus* known) and 5 feet 5 inches tall. As an adult, the boy would have reached a height of 6 feet.

(a)

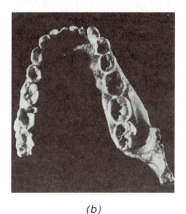

(b)

Figure 14-31 *(a)* OH 9; *(b)* OH 13 ("Cinderella" mandible—cast).

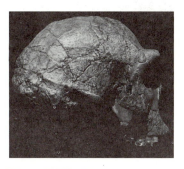

Figure 14-32 ER 3733.

◇ Box 14-8   The Paleolithic and Plio-Pleistocene

Pliocene and Pleistocene are geologic and zoologic epochs. Culture periods are known by other terms: Paleolithic, Mesolithic, Neolithic, Bronze Age, and so on. Beginning about 2.5 m.y.a. with the first evidence of culture, mainly stone tools, is the Paleolithic or Old Stone Age. Divided into Lower, Middle, and Upper Paleolithic,

each period is assigned its own criteria based on the kinds of tools made, the style of manufacture, the material used, and other such factors. Within each period are industries that identify the types of stone tools.

The table* you see here correlates the Plio-Pleistocene and the Paleolithic.

Geologic Subdivisions	Absolute Age	Cultural Subdivisions	
		PALEOLITHIC	INDUSTRIES†
Holocene	10,000		
Upper Pleistocene		Upper	Magdalenian Solutrean Gravettian Aurignacian
	40,000		Chatelperronian
	125,000	Middle	Mousterian
Middle Pleistocene	700,000		Acheulian
Lower Pleistocene	1,000,000		
	1,800,000	Lower	
Pliocene			Oldowan
	5,000,000		

*Not to scale.

†These industries are not necessarily sequential and may overlap in time.

muscular human lived for 1 million years along rivers or streams and on the shores of the ocean or lakes.

Three kinds of sites have been found: family or multifamily living camps, kill sites, and gathering sites. Archeological material tells us that *H. erectus* hunted medium- and large-sized mammals, including giant baboons. This kind of activity suggests cooperative groups of people capable of organizing for large-game hunting.

◇ South Africa (Swartkrans)

Homo erectus is entirely lacking in South Africa except possibly for a relatively small mandible (probably female), two molars, and a radius fragment, all belonging to the same individual (SK-15), found at Swartkrans, the site of earlier australopithecine fossils. It has been dated as most likely late Middle Pleistocene, and the bones were found in association with a Developed Oldowan industry. Originally, this jaw was designated "Telanthropus" by its discoverers (Broom and Robinson). Later research has suggested it fits well into the genus *Homo*.

Figure 14-33　SK-15 site, Swartkrans.

◇ Human Emergence: Australopithecus to Homo Erectus

Hominid evolution from australopithecines to *H. erectus* is marked by: (1) The physical modifications already described—*H. erectus* is the taller, larger-brained with thick skull bones, a heavily buttressed skull evidenced by the thick and projecting supraorbital torus and nuchal torus, spongy bone toward the base of the skull that developed its greatest width along the nuchal area, reduction of the posterior teeth, and increase in the anterior teeth; (2) cultural modifications, such as more skillful toolmaking, a wider variety of tools, and a specialized tool kit, accomplished big-game hunting, organized and planning groups, regular use of fire, and perhaps speech. While these cultural modifications reflect a more sophisticated culture for *H. erectus*, it is interesting that for the hundreds of thousands of years of the Acheulian industry, there was relatively little change in the tools over time and space. There is a remarkable similarity in the tools found in Africa, Europe, and southwest Asia. Is it possible that this cultural stasis might be related to the limitations of *H. erectus'* brain size and organization and their economic adaptations?

To account for at least some of these physical and cultural changes, Wolpoff (1980a) offers a suggestive hypothesis. It should be emphasized that Wolpoff's explanation is hypothetical; direct evidence is often lacking. His hypothesis is based on the shift from the australopithecine scavenging/gathering adaptation with some small-scale hunting to a hunting/gathering adaptation characteristic of *H. erectus*.

As hunting developed into a more important source of food, it was organized and planned. Meat became a regular and dependable (rather than opportunistic) part of the diet, replacing some of the more difficult-to-chew plant foods that had been dietary staples. Improved technology produced more hunting-efficient and food-processing tools as well as more skillful manufacturing techniques. Archeological evidence shows an increasing number of tool types, such as crudely pointed chopperlike tools and small scraping tools. Spheroids, a round ball-like stone tool—usually showing evidence of battering—greatly increased in frequency, and it is thought the battering resulted from pounding foods to make them easier to chew:

> Every increase in the amount of cutting, chopping, or smashing that took place before food was chewed would have decreased the need to maintain a chewing complex that produced powerful forces (Wolpoff, 1980a, p. 168).

This combination of changes in diet and food preparation probably accounts for the reduction in the postcanine teeth.

The change in diet, from tough foods to meat and softer foods, produced further changes in the skull (Box 14-9). The load on posterior teeth decreased,

◇ Box 14-9   Forces on the Teeth and Skull

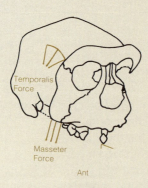

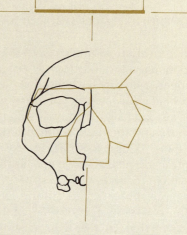

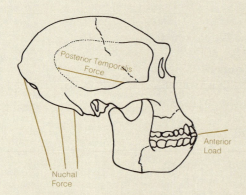

(a) Drawing of the later Indonesian *Homo erectus* cranium Sangiran 17 showing the positions of the main jaw-associated muscles that resist a force on the front teeth and the combined horizontal and vertical components that such a force must have (unless the force is completely vertical).

(b) Side view of F. Weidenreich's reconstruction of the Indonesian late Lower Pleistocene cranium Sangiran 4 and the Sangiran 1 mandible. The drawing shows a load between the anterior teeth exerting force in the *horizontal* direction, and indicates the positions of the two main muscles that can resist it. The nuchal (neck) muscles bring the cranium backward, and the posterior temporalis brings the mandible backward. Both of these muscles are well developed in *Homo erectus*.

(c) A simplified model of the reaction of the face to *vertical* anterior loads, based on a drawing of the ER-3733 face. The model is derived from B. Endo's facial stress analysis. In the face below, the upward-pointing arrow represents the force of an object between the teeth. This force is provided by the force of the mandible on the object. Therefore, the muscles closing the mandible also produce forces on the face. These are represented by the arrows on the right, and the main lines of facial resistance to these forces are represented by a simple beam model. The lower (downward-pointing) arrow represents the masseter force, and the upper ones the anterior temporalis force. The actions of these forces meet in the area above the eyes. Their effects in this area can be reduced to a simpler model by representing the region above the eyes by a beam (shown above). On this beam, a central force acts upward, and the forces to the sides act to bend the beam downward and pull it outward. It is the concentration of bending and tensile (producing tension) forces in the beam (supraorbital region) that creates the necessity of strengthening. In early hominids with low foreheads, the strengthening takes the form of a buttress, or torus, called the *supraorbital torus* or the browridge.

making for smaller back teeth, and the load on front teeth increased, resulting in their somewhat larger size. However, not only did tooth size change, but the muscles operating the jaw and the forces operating on the skull developed front and back buttressing, i.e., the supraorbital torus and the nuchal torus, where chewing and neck muscles attach. (Although the use of fire came in after hunting had become an important food source, it would also have served to make chewing easier and would have affected the load on posterior and anterior teeth.)

Unlike other carnivores (see pp. 193–205), when primates hunt they depend largely on vision, and early hominids were, therefore, diurnal (daytime) hunters. For diurnal hunting in the tropics it would be a great advantage if the hunter were heat-adapted in order to get rid of excess heat. One of the ways of doing this is by sweating, during which drops of sweat evaporate and cool the skin. Body hair, which makes drop formation and dripping easy, reduces the amount of sweat that evaporates. Adaptation to the tropics, therefore, involved reducing the number and size of hair follicles (loss of body hair) and development of sweat glands all over the body.

Water loss through sweating makes for a thirsty hominid, and it is not surprising that most major early hominid sites are found close to water. But hunting is not always possible near water, so carrying water became very important:

> Carrying water depends on one of the most basic human inventions . . . the container. The innovation of containers was one of the most important human cultural adaptations, and probably one of the critical factors that led to the development of effective organized hunting (Wolpoff, 1980a, p. 169).

It is also possible that the invention of containers may have resulted in increased body size, and to some extent, therefore, brain size. Without suffi-

---

Table 14-6   *Homo erectus* Sites

ASIA

Java	Trinil, Modjokerto, Sangiran
China	Zhoukoudian, Lantian, Longtan

EUROPE

	Heidelberg (Mauer), Germany
	Vértesszöllös, Hungary
	Petralona, Greece
	Torralba/Ambrona, Spain
	Terra Amata, France

AFRICA

North Africa	Ternifine, Algeria
	Sidi abd er-Rahman, Morocco
	Rabat, Morocco
	Salé, Morocco
	Temara, Morocco
East Africa	Olduvai Gorge, Tanzania
	East Turkana, Kenya
	Omo, Ethiopia
	Afar, Ethiopia
South Africa	Swartkrans, Republic of South Africa

cient water, a small body is advantageous since skin surface is proportionately greater and heat loss (by sweating) is improved. Carrying containers of water would remove the small-size limitation.

Another possible result of heat adaptation, suggests Wolpoff, is darker skin color as protection against ultraviolet rays of the tropical sun. However, there is currently little concrete evidence to support this.

SOCIAL CHANGES

In addition to these physical and physiological modifications, there were also social innovations. Hunting gives a group more free time, since less meat (compared to plants) is required for the same food value. Also, assuming hunting and gathering activities were planned and cooperatively executed, there was opportunity for more complex social interaction within and between populations.

With a division of labor (males hunting and females gathering), males assumed responsibility for protecting females and young. Not only was food shared within the band, but the sharing was ritualized; strategies were developed requiring cooperation between males, and attempts made at long-range planning.

Whether or not this scenario proposed by Wolpoff did, in fact, occur, when we look back at the evolution of *H. erectus*, we realize how significant were this early human's achievements toward **hominization**. It was *H. erectus* who completed striding bipedalism and erect posture; who embraced culture wholeheartedly as a strategy of adaptation; whose brain was reshaped and increased in size to within *sapiens* range; who became a proficient hunter with greater dependence on meat (which in turn reduced jaw and posterior teeth size); who apparently established more or less permanent living sites, probably some sort of social organization, such as family and band; and who used fire extensively. We salute *Homo erectus*, the first human beings.

◇ Summary

Homo erectus (also known as pithecanthropines) represents the second grade of human evolution and is usually associated with the Middle Pleistocene, although they appear much earlier. The beginning of the Middle Pleistocene has been set at the Matuyama-Brunhes paleomagnetic boundary, 700,000 years ago.

Differences from australopithecines are notable in *H. erectus*' larger and reproportioned brain, taller stature, and changes in facial structure and skull buttressing.

Remains of *H. erectus* come from three continents. In Asia, there are two locations: Java and China. Europe contains three sites that have produced hominid skeletal material: Heidelberg, Vértesszöllös, and Petralona. Two European sites with cultural material, but lacking bones, are also discussed: Torralba/Ambrona in Spain and Terra Amata in France. There are three *H. erectus* areas in Africa: North Africa, East Africa, and South Africa.

A hypothetical reconstruction of evolutionary change from australopithe-cines to pithecanthropines is presented, suggesting evolution was due to changes in diet, from plant material to greater dependence on meat. Adaptation to tropical diurnal hunting/gathering was perhaps responsible for loss of body hair, sweat glands, and increased body size. Dependence on meat changed chewing habits and, therefore, facial and skull structure. Cultural flexibility required for hunting big game (giving rise to organized and cooperative groups) selected for a larger and reproportioned brain and hastened the process of hominization.

◇ Questions for Review

1. Describe the Pleistocene in terms of (a) temperature and (b) the dating of fossil hominids.
2. Why is paleomagnetism more useful than other methods in dating the earth's history?
3. Describe *H. erectus*. How is *H. erectus* anatomically different from australopithecines?
4. What are the significant features of *H. erectus*' cultural life?
5. What was the intellectual climate in Europe in the latter half of the nineteenth century, especially concerning human evolution?
6. Why was there so much opposition to Dubois' interpretation of the hominid fossils he found in Java?
7. Why do you think Peking Man was enthusiastically accepted whereas Java Man was not?
8. Describe the life of Peking Man.
9. Compare the three European *H. erectus* remains. What physical and cultural characteristics justify designating them *H. erectus*?
10. What do the Torralba/Ambrona and Terra Amata sites tell us of Middle Pleistocene culture?
11. *Homo erectus* is called the first human. Why?
12. What is the *H. erectus* evidence from Africa, and what questions of human evolution does the evidence raise?
13. Summarize the evolutionary events (physical and cultural) of the Middle Pleistocene.
14. What events, according to Wolpoff, led to loss of body hair and increased body size?
15. Why do we "owe so much" to *H. erectus*?

Homo Sapiens

CONTENTS

The world is full of wonders! Ivan T. Sanderson, a well-known writer on the subject of primates and a science editor of *Argosy*, wrote an article in the May 1969 issue of that magazine on an adventure he had recently experienced. If we take Sanderson at his word, he was completely serious.

Early in 1969, Sanderson decided to investigate a report concerning a strange-looking corpse encased in a 6,000-pound block of ice that had been placed on display at the annual Stock Fair in Chicago. Accompanying him was Dr. Bernard Heuvelmans of the Belgium Royal Academy of Sciences and a longtime student of matters like the Abominable Snowman and similar singularities.

On a remote Minnesota farm, they met the frozen Neandertal along with a Mr. Frank Hansen who owned it or rented it, or was at least in charge of it. The body was indeed encased in ice (which made examination and measurement difficult), but the two men did their best.

Sanderson described "Bozo," as they nicknamed it, as a very sturdy, approximately six-foot "human" covered with hair over almost the entire body. Its fingers and toes had nails, not claws, and it had practically no neck. Its torso was "barrel-shaped and it tapers down, not to a waist, but to rather narrow hips" (Sanderson, 1969, p. 26). And, although its legs were about the right length, its arms were longer than average. Its most outstanding characteristic was its enormous, spatulate hands, but the thumbs were surprisingly slender and long. The eyeballs were the most bizarre features of Bozo's face—both eyes had been "blown out" of their sockets, and the nose was distinctly pugged, like that of a Pekingese dog. It was also very obviously male.

"Let me say, simply," wrote Sanderson, "that one look was actually enough to convince us that this was—from our point of view, at least—'the genuine article.' This was no phony Chinese trick, or 'art' work" (1969, p. 26).

Whence cometh this Iceman? Several stories purport to explain the presence of the Iceman in the United States and on the carnival circuit. In one tale, Bozo was found floating in a block of sea ice in the Bering Sea by a Soviet whaling ship. When the Soviets put in at a Chinese port, the authorities seized the specimen, which then disappeared into Red China. It finally turned up, no one knows how, in Hong Kong, still in 6,000 pounds of ice, which had apparently not melted even one ounce worth.

An alternate story is that the original discoverers were not Soviet, but Japanese whalers, and that the find occurred somewhere off the coast of Kamchatka, not the Bering Sea. The creature was taken to Japan and then sold to a Hong Kong exporter.

Once in Hong Kong, the ice and the creature were wrapped in a sort of super plastic bag and stored in a deep freeze by an exporter who sold all kinds of curios. An agent for a wealthy American associated with the movie industry heard that the Iceman was for sale and bought it for his client. It was then rented by Mr. Hansen, who took it about, still in the ice block, from carnival to carnival, fair to fair, and sideshow to sideshow, exhibiting it to the public throughout the country.

In his book *Bigfoot*, primatologist Dr. John Napier (1973)—who had originally apparently been taken in by all of this—exposed the Iceman for what it really was. After some investigation, Napier concluded that the entire affair was a publicity stunt initiated by Mr. Hansen, who really owned the object, and not the mysterious Hollywood multimillionaire. It also appeared that the "body" was made of latex rubber and hair and had been put together on the West Coast. In 1970, Hansen "confessed" in *Saga* that the story he told Sanderson was simply a showman's spiel. What actually happened, he wrote, was that in 1960, while on a hunting trip in Minnesota, he shot a doe. When he came up to it, three hairy creatures were tearing the animal apart with their bare hands and drinking its blood. One of the creatures sprang screeching at him. Panicked, Hansen fired his rifle point blank, blowing out the creature's eyes and killing it instantly. Terrified, Hansen ran off, but returned a few days later to find the creature frozen stiff. He carried it back to his home, cautioned his wife not to say a word about it, and deposited it in their deep freeze, where it spent the next seven years until Hansen decided to take it on the road.

A different thrilling story was carried in the *National Bulletin* on June 30, 1969, under the heading, "I Was Raped by the Abominable Snowman!" A young woman, Helen Westring by name, alleged that while hunting alone in Minnesota, she met an Abominable Snowman. The monster ripped off her clothes, glared at her lustfully, and proceeded to rape her. Luckily, Helen fainted during the action, as a proper maiden should, but when she regained consciousness, she shot the brute through the right eye (which dislocated the left eye). And that was how the Iceman lost his eyes—at the hands of a heroic girl avenging her honor in the Minnesota woods!

Sanderson was convinced Bozo was real and a Neandertal (he—Sanderson—died before Napier completed his investigations). However, Sanderson and Heuvelmans are not the only believers in the presence of Neandertals living in remote areas of the world. Several Soviet paleoanthro-

pologists at the Darwin Museum in Moscow have developed a theory on the origin of *Homo sapiens*, part of which is that "relic hominoids," such as Bigfoot, Yeti, and others of native folklore, are really Neandertals or their descendants (Proshnev, 1974; Bayanov and Bourtsev, 1974, 1976).

The Soviets write persuasively of relic hominoids, but hard, convincing evidence remains surprisingly lacking. Sightings of relic hominoids (much like sightings of UFOs) have been widespread, and the evidence appears to be of about the same caliber. Why all this interest in relic hominoids that propels men to the isolated woods of the Pacific Coast, the mountaintops of Himalaya, and assorted lonely steppes and deserts? Perhaps Napier's cogent comments may help explain this strange phenomenon:

Man has an insatiable appetite for ghouls and bogles, and large sections of the entertainment business make it their concern to see that his tastes are well catered for. Horror-films, horror-comics, horror-exhibits are big business. . . . This determination of mankind to frighten itself to death can perhaps be regarded as an endearing trait, an expression of a touching, child-like naiveté in the face of the monstrous Forces of the Unknown. On the other hand, perhaps it is just a cult that owes nothing to na-

ture, religion, philosophy or the mainstream of folklore, but is simply another form of self-indulgence (Napier, 1973, p. 193).

UPDATE

Myra Shackley's archeological research in Mongolia led her to believe ("half sceptically") in the possibility of Neandertal survivals in the Altai ranges of central Asia. Local inhabitants know of people living in the Altai Mountains who are quite different from themselves and, Shackley says, may be surviving Neandertals.

Until careful studies are made, we withhold judgment.

SOURCES:

Bayanov, Dmitri and Igor Bourtsev. "Reply [to comments on Proshnev's article]," *Current Anthropology* 15(4):452–56, 1974.

———. "On Neanderthal vs. Paranthropus," *Current Anthropology* 17 (2):312–18, 1976.

Napier, John. *Bigfoot.* New York: E. P. Dutton & Co., Inc., 1973.

Proshnev, B. F. "The Troglodytidae and the Hominidae in the Taxonomy and Evolution of Higher Primates," *Current Anthropology* 15 (4):449–50, 1974.

Sanderson, Ivan T. "The Missing Link," *Argosy*, May, pp. 23–31, 1969.

Shackley, Myra. "The Case for Neanderthal Survival: Fact, Fiction or Faction?" *Antiquity* 56:31–41, 1982.

CHAPTER FIFTEEN

◇ Introduction

Evolution does not proceed by hops, skips, or jumps (although the rate of change may increase or decrease), but by a gradual modification that eventually produces a new species.* This period of modification may be thought of as a transition between species. We find such a transitional period somewhere in the 400,000 y.a. to 100,000 y.a. range, between the old species, *Homo erectus*, and the new, *Homo sapiens*. (See Box 15-1.)

Because the transition between species is so gradual, it is often difficult to clearly separate transitional fossil forms from the species that precede or follow them. In this chapter, several such difficult cases will be presented, such as *H. sapiens* with lingering *H. erectus* traits, or *H. erectus* with emerging sapient traits. "You pays your penny and you takes your choice."

The chapter is divided into three sections: transitional forms, Neandertal forms, and Upper Paleolithic (anatomically modern) forms. This scheme is somewhat simplistic, given the problems of gradually evolving hominids, but it will serve as an adequate device for dealing with the emergence of the *H. sapiens* grade of evolution.

◇ Transitional Forms

The term "transitional forms" as it is used in this section refers to those fossil forms that have changed too much to be definitely *H. erectus* but not enough to be considered—*without quibble*—completely *H. sapiens*. It is not necessary that a line be drawn between the two; nor is it necessary that any fossil, for that matter, be classified absolutely one way or the other.

STEINHEIM

Just as Professor Schoetensack waited so many years at the sandpit before the Mauer mandible was exposed, so Dr. F. Berchkhemer, chief curator of the Natural History Museum of Württemberg, waited with hope over twenty-five patient years for a hominid discovery at a gravel pit at Steinheim, Germany, twelve miles north of the city of Stuttgart. His patience was finally rewarded on July 24, 1933, when Herr Sigrist, owner of the gravel pit, excitedly reported the recovery of a highly petrified primitive human skull minus the jaw.

Under the heavy weight of twenty-three feet of wet earth, the Steinheim skull was warped and the left side unfortunately crushed behind the left eye. Much like the Peking skulls, the foramen magnum was cut away, allowing access to the brain, perhaps for cannibalistic or ritualistic purposes; never-

---

*Gould and Eldredge have recently suggested that evolution does indeed proceed by rapid "jumps" what they have called "punctuated equilibrium" (see pp. 91–93).

◇ Box 15-1   Comparison of *H. sapiens* and *H. erectus*

Homo sapiens differs from *H. erectus* in a number of characteristics.* In *Homo sapiens*:

1. The skull is larger with a 1,350 cm³ mean cranial capacity
2. Muscular ridges in the cranium are not strongly marked
3. The forehead is rounded and vertical
4. The supraorbital ridges are not well developed and do not form a continuous and uninterrupted torus

5. The occipital region is rounded and the nuchal area is relatively small
6. Mastoid process is prominent and of a pyramidal shape
7. The calvaria is of maximum width, usually in the parietal region
8. Jaws and teeth are relatively small
9. Maxilla has concave surface including a canine fossa
10. The chin is distinct
11. Limb bones are relatively slender and slight

*For a fuller definition see Howell, 1978, pp. 201ff.

---

theless, much of the cranium was intact, especially the face. Unfortunately, artifacts were not found associated with the skull.

The skull is believed to be that of a young woman, who lived between 300,000 y.a.–200,000 y.a., with a cranial capacity between 1,150 and 1,175 cm³. Though the brain is small, it is larger than most *H. erectus* forms and is within the lower range of *H. sapiens*.

Figure 15-1   Sites of transitional forms and Neandertals.

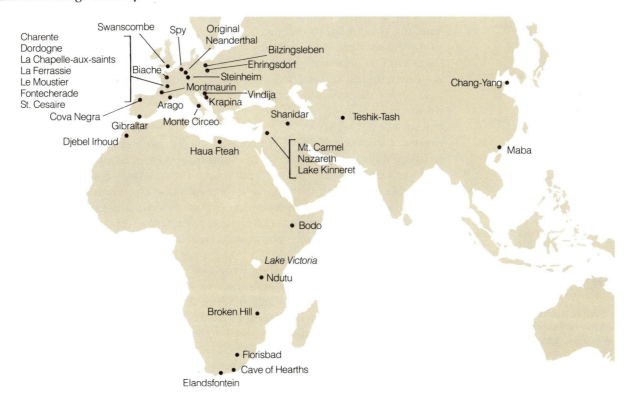

Figure 15-2 Steinheim site.

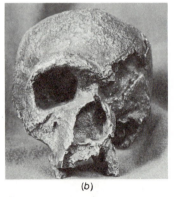

Figure 15-3 (continued below)

Figure 15-3 Cast of Steinheim skull. (a) Basal view, showing how the foramen magnum was enlarged, apparently for removal of the brain—for dietary or ritualistic purposes; (b) frontal view showing warped skull.

Steinheim's face, except for its height, is remarkably like *H. erectus*, and the supraorbital torus is heavier than that of any Neandertal (Wolpoff, 1980b). The overall shape of the skull and its reduced bone thickness approaches *H. sapiens*. The nose is apparently broad, but the face is relatively straight (with some midfacial prognathism) and hangs nicely underneath the brows, compared to *H. erectus*. The teeth tend to be smaller than those of *H. erectus*.

This melange of *H. erectus*-like and *sapient*-like characters (Fig. 15-2) places Steinheim in the middle of the evolutionary modification, between the two hominid grades. We have, for better or worse, included Steinheim in the *H. sapiens*, rather than *H. erectus* chapter, since she seems to be definitely on her way to becoming *H. sapiens*.

SWANSCOMBE

Watching and waiting at probable sites for the appearance of human artifacts and fossil human bones are incurable pursuits for both professional and amateur archeologists. A likely site well known to a generation or more of watchers and waiters was Swanscombe, located not far from London. This site yielded remains of Pleistocene mammals and several hundred thousand Acheulian artifacts, especially handaxes, but also some flake tools.

A dentist and amateur archeologist, A. T. Marston, in June 1935, was the man who first noticed that local cement workers had uncovered an occipital bone. Marston, encouraged by his find, maintained his vigil, and in March of the following year, eight yards from where the occipital had been found, he caught sight of a left parietal which, it turned out, belonged to the same skull as the earlier bone. Like a Ripley "Believe It or Not" item, twenty years after the occipital was found, a right parietal was discovered seventy-five feet from the original find, and it fitted the other two bones exactly!

It is clear that the mammals associated with the skull, such as elephant, rhino, and red deer, were warm-weather animals and, therefore, the gravel bed in which they were found was laid down during an interglacial period. General agreement holds this period to be the second (Mindel-Riss or Holsteinian) interglacial. Dating by the uranium-thorium technique gives a date of over 300,000 years (Butzer and Isaac, 1975), which conforms with the mammals of the period. It appears, therefore, that the hominid bones belong where they were found, and are as old as the radiometric date indicates. Nevertheless, there remains considerable speculation on the age of the gravel bed deposits. Still, Swanscombe may well be honored as the first known Englishman (or woman).

Since the remains are fragmentary and lack those elements used most accurately in estimating sex and age (see Appendix A), it is not possible to know whether Swanscombe was male or female, or how old he/she was at death; the best that can be stated is: "adult." Unfortunately, the frontal bones and face are missing, and it is not known whether Swanscombe, with an occipital similar to Steinheim, also possessed Steinheim's heavy supraorbital torus. If it does, and there is some reason to believe this is the case, Swanscombe apparently is not as modern as once believed and would fit very nicely into the Steinheim population—transitional between *H. erectus* and *H. sapiens*.

ARAGO (TAUTAVEL MAN)

Fieldwork at the Arago cave, near the village of Tautavel (which is near the Spanish border in southeastern France) began in 1964 under the supervision of the same husband and wife team who excavated Terra Amata—Henry and Marie-Antoinette de Lumley. They were attracted to the site by materials collected over the years by prehistorians and amateurs, and they believed the site to be an early one and well worth excavating (de Lumley, H., and de Lumley, M., 1973).

Abundant faunal remains reflect a cold climate, and the Mindel glaciation has been suggested for the date of Arago (Cook et al., 1982). Radiometric measurements—including several very recently developed methods—have failed to agree on a date. We are left, therefore, with a Mindel date, perhaps 400,000 y.a., but really nothing solid in numbers of years. At that time, prehistoric hunters occupied the site, and the de Lumleys located more than twenty occupation levels, each separated by two to seven feet of sterile sand. More than 100,000 Acheulian artifacts have been recovered from the site.

Over 50 cranial and postcranial remains of at least four adults and three children have been recovered. Most important of the specimens are a partial cranium, mostly face and frontal bone (Fig. 15-6), two mandibles, a parietal bone, an almost complete innominate, and various other cranial and postcranial fragments.

The cranium is apparently that of a young male, and the face is especially useful because there are so very few available from this period. It gives a pretty good idea of what these Middle Pleistocene Europeans might have looked like. The supraorbital torus is very prominent, the forehead is relatively long, flat, and narrow, and the cranial capacity is estimated to be in the 1050 to 1150 cm³ range.

The mandibles, neither of which fit the cranium, belong to a young adult male (Arago 13) and a female of around 40 to 55 years of age (Arago 2). These are massive mandibles; the size of the female's teeth fall within the range of Neandertals and anatomically moderns, but those of the male are huge, exceeding those of Heidelberg and matching the largest of Ternifine. The mandibles display *H. erectus*, as well as archaic *sapiens*, characters.

Arago, like Swanscombe and Steinheim, is difficult to assign to a definite species. It could fit *H. erectus* or archaic *sapiens*, and scholars have classified it in both categories.

BILZINGSLEBEN

In East Germany, about twenty-five miles north of Weimar, near the village of Bilzingsleben, four hominid skull fragments and a single molar tooth were found in 1971 and over the next few years. The dating is uncertain, although it appears to be second interglacial (Mindel-Riss). The brow ridges are similar to *H. erectus*, heavy and not arched, and the skull bones are quite thick. Vlček

Figure 15-4 Cast of Swanscombe skull.

Figure 15-5 Sites for Swanscombe; Arago.

Figure 15-6 Partial Arago skull.

Figure 15-7 Gilzingsleben site.

(1978) has pointed out the similarity to Olduvai Hominid 9 (p. 401), who lived close to a million years earlier and is assigned to *H. erectus*. However, the forehead and occipital areas of Bilzingsleben appear to be moving in a sapient direction.

It would be entirely possible to place Bilzingsleben in the preceding chapter along with Petralona and Vértesszöllös. This is the kind of problem to be expected during a period of change, when physical traits of a specimen reflect, as they do here, traces of different grades or species.

In addition to these fossil remains, there are a few other transitional forms dating from the Middle Pleistocene:

Montmaurin—Toulouse, southern France. A mandible that resembles Heidelberg in some features, and the Arago and Neandertal jaws in others.

Abri Suard—Charente, southern France. A number of skull and mandible fragments and teeth.

Cova Negra—Spain. A parietal.

Lazaret Cave—Nice, southern France. Remains of three hominids associated with Acheulian industry.

Biache-Saint-Vaast—France. Cranial fragments similar to Swanscombe.

Chang-yang—Cave of Dragons near Chang-yang, Hupei, China. A left maxilla with some teeth.

Overall during this period of transition in the second (Holsteinian) interglacial and third (Riss) glacial, there were changes in crania and postcrania that reflect the evolutionary trend from *H. erectus* to what we recognize as *H. sapiens*. While it is not always easy to attribute causes of physical modifications, it is not unreasonable to assume they were due to changing behavioral patterns.

Humans were improving their technology and intensifying their social interactions. Greater dependence on culture—more efficient technology—may have begun to reduce stress on anterior teeth with resultant changes in mandible, forehead, supraorbital torus and occipital area (see Box 14-9, p. 406). Improved technology also suggests dependence on a more efficient brain, resulting in selection for a larger brain, and/or reorganization of the brain. This may well have intensified the feedback relationship of behavior and technology that produced the physical changes.

The cranial capacity average of 1,166 cm³ for these transitional forms represents an 11% expansion in volume from the later *H. erectus* sample. The occipital region was reduced in robustness, spongy* bone at the base of the skull was reduced, and, while posterior teeth were reduced, anterior teeth continued to increase in size. There is also a tendency for the canine to be incisiform (more spatulate). Increase in anterior tooth size suggests continued use of these teeth for functions other than chewing, such as gripping, holding, or pulling. These activities may account for the prominent midfacial prognathism and the development of puffiness of the maxillary sinuses on both sides of the nose.

*Spongy (pneumatization). This refers to "a type of bone growth where air sacs or air cells are incorporated within the center of the bone tissue" (Kennedy, 1980, p. 220). If the air cells are very large, they are called *sinuses*; if very small, the bone assumes a "spongy" appearance.

Behaviorally, technological improvement suggests that these people may have had a clear mental image of the tool to be made before manufacturing it. Standardization of various tool types increased, and new shapes (ovoid and triangular) appear. A wide variety of handaxes of many different forms and sizes were probably special-purpose tools. At Bilzingsleben, East Germany, an elephant bone was set up on an anvil and smashed by using large cobbles. Also at Bilzingsleben, red deer antlers were used for axes and cleaverlike tools. Retouched bone may also have been present (Cook et al., 1982).

Although artificial structures may have been built before this period, the evidence now appears more clearly. A shelter, about 11 by 4 feet, is known from Lazaret Cave of southern France. Inside the shelter, there are remains of two hearths. Outside the cave, traces of a series of tents were found, and just inside the door of each tent was a wolf skull. The exact significance of the wolf skulls may never be known, but they were surely symbolic and possibly indicative of a ritual of some kind. At Bilzingsleben, outlines of two possible structures were recognized during recent excavations, so it is possible that artificial structures were more common than the archeological record has previously suggested.

During the Riss, it is possible that geographic differences appeared among human beings as they adapted to different environmental conditions. It was also during this time that humans first began to occupy caves extensively (seasonally, in some cases), as well as open sites. Archeological evidence makes it clear that many different food sources were being utilized, such as fruits, vegetables, seeds, nuts, and so forth, each in its own season. Marine life was exploited: from Orgnac, in southern France, comes evidence for freshwater fishing (trout, char), perch from Lazaret, and tench (carp family) from Bilzingsleben.

Although art does not become well developed until the Upper Paleolithic, beginning signs are already in evidence. At Terra Amata (p. 398) red ochre remains were found, and intentional engraving on an ox rib, dating back to the Riss glacial, is evidenced from southern France.

During the Middle Pleistocene, humans were becoming more aware of ecological opportunities, and changes in life styles appear. Shelters were becoming more common, a greater variety of food was being eaten, and changes in stone technology were made, as well as at least a beginning in the use of new materials. Not many hunting tools have been found, which suggests the possible use of wooden weapons, or perhaps the practice of netting or trapping. It is also possible that scavenging from carcasses, killed by other carnivores or natural events, has been underestimated. In any case, it does appear that the pace of change was increasing.

From an evolutionary point of view, two points should be kept in mind concerning these remains from the Holsteinian interglacial and Riss glacial: first, there is a great deal of variation in these populations, with differences in many if not all features of the skull; second, as we pointed out at the beginning of this section, some characteristics recall the preceding *H. erectus* forms and others mark a trend toward *H. sapiens*.

It should also be pointed out that chronological placement of the European hominid sample is very difficult and, at the present time, not yet possible.

Figure 15-8 Sites of Orgnac, Lazaret, Terra Amata.

Mousterian
(moo-stair'-ee-en)
A cultural tradition of the Upper Pleisto-cene associated with Neandertals.

Dating fossil finds is the problem and, until reliable dating is established, the course of human evolution in the latter Middle Pleistocene remains unresolved.

◇ Neandertals (125,000 y.a.–40,000 y.a.)

Despite their apparent disappearance 35,000 y.a.–40,000 y.a., Neandertals continue to haunt the best laid theories of paleoanthropologists. They fit into the general scheme of human evolution, and yet they are misfits. Classified as *H. sapiens*, they are like us and yet different, and some of those in Western Europe are even more different yet. It is not an easy task to put them in their place.

These troublesome hunters are the cave man of cartoonists, walking about with bent knees, dragging a club in one hand and a woman by her hair in the other. They are described as brutish, dwarfish, apelike, and obviously of little intelligence. This image is more than somewhat exaggerated.

While cartoonists' license is not to be denied, the fact remains that Neandertals walked as upright as any of us, and, if they dragged clubs and women, there is not the slightest evidence of it. Nor are they dwarfish or apelike, and, in the light of twentieth-century human behavior, we should be careful of whom we call brutish.

As far as intelligence is concerned, Neandertals produced excellent **Mousterian** implements and, in fact, invented a new technique, the disc-core

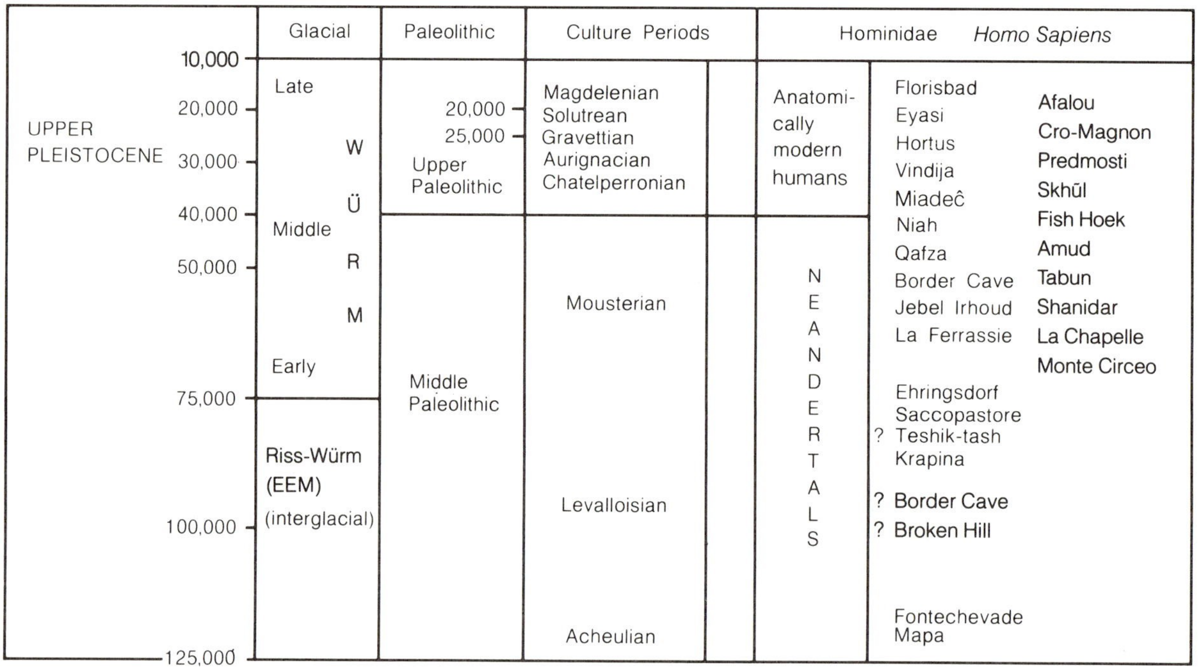

Figure 15-9 The Upper Pleistocene. The correlations of fossil finds with culture periods and dates are approximations and sometimes speculative. There is no intent to indicate that this depiction is validated by evidence. The culture periods of the Upper Paleolithic are not necessarily sequential as shown. This figure is simply meant to assist the student in organizing Upper Pleistocene data.

		Glacial	Paleolithic	Culture Periods		Hominidae	*Homo Sapiens*	
UPPER PLEISTOCENE	10,000	Late	20,000 — Upper Paleolithic	Magdelenian Solutrean Gravettian Aurignacian Chatelperronian		Anatomically modern humans	Florisbad Eyasi Hortus Vindija Miadeĉ Niah	Afalou Cro-Magnon Predmosti Skhūl Fish Hoek
	20,000 —	W	25,000 —					
	30,000 —	Ü						
	40,000 —	R					Qafza	Amud
	50,000 —	M		Mousterian		N E A N D E R T A L S	Border Cave Jebel Irhoud La Ferrassie	Tabun Shanidar La Chapelle Monte Circeo
		Middle	Middle Paleolithic				Ehringsdorf Saccopastore ? Teshik-tash Krapina	
		Early						
	75,000 —							
	100,000 —	Riss-Würm (EEM) (interglacial)		Levalloisian			? Border Cave ? Broken Hill	
	125,000 —			Acheulian			Fontechevade Mapa	

technique (Campbell, 1976, p. 328). This method is a highly productive one in which a nodule of stone is trimmed around the edges to make it disc-shaped. Then flakes are removed from the core by rapping the edges, knocking off flakes until the core becomes too small and is thrown away. The flakes are then further trimmed to provide the edges necessary for whatever kind of work was needed on wood, carcasses, or hides.

Neandertals were also clever enough to cope with the cold weather of the glacial period. In addition to open sites, they lived in caves, wore clothing, built fires, gathered in settlements (some of which extended right up to the Arctic Ocean), hafted some of their tools, and hunted with a good deal of skill. They had to be skillful hunters in order to survive by subsisting off herds of reindeer, wooly rhinoceros, and mammoth. There was very little vegetable food available on the cold tundra.

Finally, the brain size of Neandertals is, on the average, at least that of *H. sapiens sapiens* and probably larger. Estimates for Neandertal skulls range from approximately 1,200 to 1,800 cm^3.

For many years, the question of what to call hominids from the Middle Paleolithic (the cultural period, including the Riss-Würm or Eemian inter-glacial and the early Würm glacial) has been debated by paleoanthropologists. We shall refer to all those who more or less fit the pattern of Western Europeans and Near Easterners of this period as Neandertals. For others (in Africa and Eastern Asia) who lived at about the same time, but do not fit this pattern, we shall use the term contemporaries.

Neandertals lived from about 125,000 y.a. until roughly 40,000 y.a. Although they show considerable physical variability over this 85,000-year period, there is a characteristic morphology that includes both the earlier forms of the Eemian and the *classic* Neandertals of the early fourth glacial.

The following description (after Howells, 1973) applies more strictly to the classic Neandertals of the fourth glacial rather than those of the Eemian, who did not completely develop the extreme traits of the classical forms:

> The skull is large, long, low, and bulging at the sides. At the rear of the skull a bun protrudes, but the occiput is rounded without the angulation of *erectus*. There is less spongy bone at the base of the skull, and the greatest breadth is higher up on the skull.
>
> In front, the forehead rises though not as steeply as in modern *sapiens*, and the brow ridges, not quite as pronounced as *H. erectus*, arch over the orbits instead of forming the straight bar of *H. erectus*. Variability found among Neandertals may be seen in the almost complete lack of these ridges in some specimens.
>
> Compared to moderns, the Neandertal face stands out. Facial length is considerably greater for Neandertals than for Upper Paleolithic *sapiens* and even more so compared to ourselves. Alveolar prognathism is noticeable and, in fact, the entire face projects as if it had been pulled forward.
>
> Neandertal's nose was high, angled, and prominent. "Many of the unique features of Neandertal facial morphology center about the nose. A fully fleshed Neandertal nose must have been a phenomenal object" (Wolpoff, 1980a, p. 280). On both sides of the nose the maxillary sinuses expand outward, giving the maxilla a puffy look and convex shape.

Anatomically modern H. sapiens (or human beings)
Population of the Upper Paleolithic who physically resemble populations of today.

Classic Neandertals
Western Europe and Near Eastern Neandertals who lived during the early Würm.

The teeth were larger than both Upper Paleolithic and present-day populations, but posterior teeth continued to decrease in size from earlier forms. Anterior teeth in the early Würm increased then reversed growth and began to decrease in size, a process that continued with *H. sapiens sapiens*.

Our description of Neandertals has stressed the differences between them and those **anatomically modern H. sapiens** appearing in the Upper Paleolithic. Actually, the resemblances of Neandertals and anatomically moderns are significant, and Neandertals belong in the taxon, *H. sapiens*. There are probably no Neandertal traits that are totally outside the variation range of modern humans. However, taken as a group, Neandertal characteristics form a constellation of traits unlike any modern population.

NEANDERTALS AND UPPER PALEOLITHIC MODERNS

One of the many puzzling questions about human evolution is that of the ancestry of Neandertals and Upper Paleolithic *sapiens*. Upper Paleolithic humans appear in Europe about 40,000 y.a.,* at about the time Neandertal physical traits are no longer prevalent in human populations. For decades, paleoanthropologists have been vehemently arguing whether or not:

1. There are divergent lines leading to Neandertals on the one hand and Upper Paleolithic *sapiens* on the other
2. There is only one line of descent, with Neandertals evolving from transitional forms, and Upper Paleolithic *sapiens* from Neandertals
3. Neandertals disappear, to be replaced by Upper Paleolithic *sapiens*
4. These two groups represent populations isolated within their econiches or intermingled
5. *H. erectus* populations in various parts of the world evolved into separate *H. sapiens* populations (or did this occur only once, or only in a few places?)

These questions have been disputed for years, and no answers have been widely accepted; nor shall we present any. We hope, however, that the following discussion may throw some light on the matter.

Paleoanthropologists have organized the Neandertal-Upper Paleolithic *sapiens* relationship under three hypotheses:

1. Pre-*sapiens*
2. Pre-Neandertal
3. Neandertal phase of man

Pre-Sapiens Hypothesis   According to this view, the ancestors of anatomically modern humans are to be found back in the Middle Pleistocene. Neandertals are considered a side branch, too specialized to be ancestral to Upper Paleolithic *H. sapiens*; consequently they are placed in a separate species from *H. sapiens* and become extinct somewhere at the end of the early Würm. Swanscombe, of the second interglacial, and Fontechevade (discussed sub-

(a)

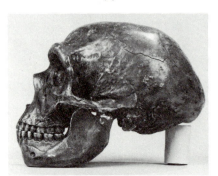

(b)

Figure 15-10   Cast, La Chapelle-aux-Saints. The best-known classic Neandertal. (*a*) Frontal view; (*b*) lateral view.

*Evidence appears to be accumulating that anatomically modern humans may have evolved considerably earlier than previously considered. The evidence comes especially from South Africa, and may go back more than 100,000 years. There are still questions about the dating, and the next few years may settle the matter. (See Kennedy, 1980; Rightmire, 1983.)

sequently), of the third interglacial, are believed by the adherents of the pre-*sapiens* hypothesis to display cranial morphology suggestive of the anatomically modern humans and are, therefore, proposed as the direct ancestors of Upper Paleolithic *H. sapiens*.

Unfortunately for this scheme, more recent analyses of Swanscombe and Fontechevade do not support the thesis of anatomically modern humans in the making (Sergi, 1967).

Pre-Neandertal Hypothesis   In this plan, Neandertals are said to have evolved from *H. erectus* through Swanscombe and Steinheim in the Eemian interglacial and spread throughout Europe, North Africa, and Asia. Then, at the beginning of the last (Würm) glaciation, Neandertals of Western Europe are isolated by the advance of both the Scandinavian and Alpine glaciations. Cut off from contact with other humans by glacial barriers, selection pressures of the cold environment created a breeding isolate that produced the specialized features characteristic of the **classic Neandertals** of Western Europe. At the same time, Neandertals and their contemporaries in other areas, adapting to different environmental pressures, were evolving into anatomically modern populations.

This plan presents two problems. First, the evidence is not conclusive that the physical characteristics of these specialized Neandertals (and there is general agreement they *are* specialized) are the result of adaptation to cold climate. Second, this hypothesis does not tell us what happened to the classic Neandertals. Did they also evolve into anatomically modern populations? Were they assimilated into, or destroyed by, an Upper Paleolithic population that migrated into Western Europe from Eastern Europe or Africa? (For a novelist's imaginative account of what might have happened, the reader is referred to William Golding's *The Inheritors*.)

The destruction of the Neandertals by a better-adapted contemporary population has long been suggested as an explanation for their "sudden" disappearance. This notion has received further support in recent years from two theories. First, that Neandertals were unable to speak fluently and thus would have been at a disadvantage in competition with anatomically modern humans who had appeared on the scene at about the time Neandertals "disappeared." As noted later (see p. 440), few paleoanthropologists have accepted Neandertal's inability to speak.

The second theory uses disease as the explanation for extinction. Studies of the Fore of New Guinea have shown that kuru, a severely debilitating disease often resulting in death, is associated with cannibalism (when cannibalism was prohibited in the 1950s, the incidence of this disease became rarer). It is argued that since Neandertals practiced cannibalism, they were infected with the kuru virus, which would have led to their ultimate annihilation, or to their easy destruction by a noncannibalistic population (Wolbarsht, 1975). This idea is interesting, but there is no way of proving the prevalence or absence of the disease among Neandertals. And, of course, many paleoanthropologists do not believe Neandertals "suddenly disappeared" at all. Supporters of the Pre-Neandertal hypothesis believe classic Neandertals in Europe were too specialized to have evolved into anatomically moderns (although they may have contributed genes), nor was there enough time. (See Wolpoff, 1980a, pp. 289–291, for a critique of this argument.)

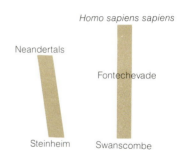

Figure 15-11 Pre-*sapiens* hypothesis. Neandertals evolve from Steinheim. They are too specialized and become extinct in the Würm. The *Homo sapiens sapiens* line originates with Swanscombe and evolves through Fontechevade to anatomically moderns of the Upper Paleolithic.

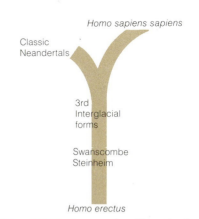

Figure 15-12 Pre-Neandertal hypothesis. The hominid line evolves from *Homo erectus* to Swanscombe/Steinheim to third interglacial forms. The fourth (Würm) glaciation isolates the population of Western Europe in a cold environment and produces specialized classic Neandertals. Third interglacial forms elsewhere evolve to anatomically modern *sapiens*.

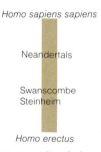

Figure 15-13 Neandertal phase of man hypothesis. This is a straight-line evolutionary scheme that considers Neandertals not as a separate branch, but as the ancestors of the Upper Paleolithic anatomically modern humans.

The Neandertal Phase of Man Hypothesis This scheme, first advanced by Hrdlička in 1927, is linear: *H. erectus* to Neandertals to *H. sapiens sapiens*. The hypothesis assumes that Neandertal populations in various parts of the world evolved into anatomically modern populations in their respective areas. No distinction is made between classic and early Neandertals, who are explained in terms of a variable population.

Such an economical hypothesis is attractive, but it does not explain what most authorities consider the specialized traits of the Western European classics. Why should these specializations be so localized? Also, whereas evidence in some areas of the world points to the evolution from Neandertals to anatomically modern human beings, no solid evidence from Western Europe suggests that classic Neandertals evolved into Upper Paleolithic *sapiens*. Perhaps they did, but the fossil remains from Western Europe supply abundant evidence of classic Neandertals, then comes a period of a few thousand years with practically no hominid remains, and then anatomically modern humans seem to suddenly appear.

This rapidly evolving change, from Neandertal to anatomically moderns in Europe—if, in fact, it did occur—might be explained in terms of punctuated equilibrium (see p. 91). However, there are several reasons why punctuation may not explain what appears to be a sudden change:

1. Forms intermediate between Neandertals and Upper Paleolithic *sapiens* have been found (see pp. 432–436)
2. Dates for Middle and Upper Pleistocene are still vague for many of the fossils; therefore, it is entirely possible that intermediate forms may fit between the time Neandertals are supposed to have disappeared and anatomically moderns appeared
3. Neandertals may not have disappeared when moderns came on the scene. The Neandertal skeleton found a few years ago at St. Cesaire (p. 429) has been dated at 32,000 years. It was found in association with tools considered to be Upper Paleolithic; therefore, it would seem that Neandertals were still living during the early Upper Paleolithic. The Middle/Upper Paleolithic transition is a hotly debated period today. (See White, 1982; Stringer, 1982.)

If we now turn to examine the evidence from the Eemian interglacial and the Würm glacial, it may help us understand the anthropological dilemma posed in the preceding discussion.

◇ The Eemian (Third or Riss-Würm) Interglacial (125,000 y.a.–75,000 y.a.)

FONTECHEVADE

Archeologist Mlle. Germaine Henri-Martin broke through the cave floor at Fontechevade in southern France in 1947. Above the floor are occupation levels of people who lived there during the Upper Paleolithic. Below the floor she found evidence of a Tayacian (that is, pre-Mousterian) industry associated with warm-weather Eemian interglacial fauna. In the same deposits are portions of two human skulls, Fontechevade I and II. Fluorine analysis of the human and mammalian bones indicate they are about the same age—estimated to be about 110,000 y.a.

Fontechevade I consists of a small piece of forehead (including the critical area above the nose) belonging to an immature individual perhaps under 10 years of age. This fragment would be insignificant except that this area is where the supraorbital torus should be, but is not. The lack of a supraorbital torus has led to much discussion about the modern look of this specimen. Did it possess a heavy brow ridge? If so, then the bone fits rather well into what might be expected at this time; if it did not, then it is possible that a smooth-forehead, modern type had evolved, and could be the ancestor of Upper Paleolithic *sapiens*. Unhappily for the argument on both sides, the bone fragment of one immature individual does not settle the matter. Neandertal children do not always possess brow ridges, and had this young person lived, he or she might have developed brow ridges—or perhaps not!

Furthermore, a more recent study (Corruccini, 1975) of the parietals of Fontechevade II, with an estimated cranial capacity of about 1,400 cm³, notes the presence of features similar to later classic Neandertals and to the much earlier Steinheim. If this is the case, then Fontechevade cannot be considered more modern than the later Neandertals and thus as *the* ancestor of Upper Paleolithic *sapiens*.

OTHERS

Other fossil remains of the Eemian interglacial are similarly inconclusive. At Ehringsdorf, near Weimar in what is now East Germany, researchers found a variety of skull bones that reflect archaic traits resembling Steinheim, and others that look quite modern. From Saccopastore, just outside Rome, come two skulls that also appear both archaic and modern. The small size of the brain, around 1,200 cm³, low vault, and prognathism of the upper face recall *erectus* traits, but the morphology of the brain, rounded occiput, and smooth area of neck muscle attachment are modern.

In Yugoslavia, from a rock shelter at Krapina, come 649 pieces of bones, many of them broken at the time of death. Evidence of charred bone, and long bones apparently split for their marrow, suggest cannibalism. The group—at least fifteen individuals have been identified and five skulls partially reconstructed—varies widely in physical traits. Krapina, like Saccopastore, Ehringsdorf, and Fontechevade, has been pointed up as possessing modern traits and, therefore, ancestral to anatomically modern humans of the Upper Paleolithic (pre-Neandertal hypothesis). However, the variable pattern of these forms raises serious questions about this evolutionary sequence.

The cultural material from these sites is essentially Mousterian, an industry usually associated with Neandertals. At Ehringsdorf, the tools include scrapers, small handaxes, drills, and burins, a variety that may be due to a mixture of several related populations. Over one thousand flint implements were recovered at Krapina, most of them unanalyzed. In addition to Mousterian artifacts at Krapina, there may also be Acheulian tools and possibly

Figure 15-14 Fontechevade II fragment. View of left side. The forehead is at the left. (Courtesy of N. Vallois.)

Figure 15-15 Sites of Fontechevade, Ehringsdorf, Krapina.

Pressure-flaking
A stoneworking technique in which flakes
are removed from the edges by pressure
rather than percussion.

In situ
(sigh'-too)
In its original or natural position.

some flakes, such as blades and microliths, similar to those from the Upper Paleolithic. This—as the Ehringsdorf assemblage—may also represent a possible mixture of different people, or cultural evolution in process, or both.

Both physical and cultural traits of the Eemian interglacial display a mixture of old and new. Physically, the population appears to be intermediate between *H. erectus* and *H. sapiens*, but tending toward the *sapient* end of the range. This is what we should expect in the course of human evolution if adaptive pressures were selecting for those traits that characterize anatomically modern humans.

The variety in technology of the Eemian may be due to adaptation to local conditions. The standardized tools of the Middle Pleistocene, especially the handaxe, were giving way to a more specialized technology. The improved technology of the Eemian may be seen in the use of flakes rather than cores, the techniques of **pressure-flaking**, and the variation in the types of tools.

◇ The Würm (Fourth) Glaciation (75,000–40,000 y.a.)

EARLY STAGES

For 300,000 years, more or less, *Homo sapiens* has been in existence and evolving from more *erectus*-like forms to Upper Paleolithic anatomically modern *sapiens* forms.

With the onset of the Würm, about 75,000 years ago, we encounter the complicated situation concerning the Neandertals in Western Europe. For the relatively short period of 30,000–35,000 years, from about 75,000 y.a.–40,000 y.a., a fairly homogeneous population lived in Western Europe. That population has engendered controversy and aroused more emotions, hypotheses, and theories than any other hominid group. As Howells has said: "Neandertal man has served to launch, to enhance, and to mar anthropological careers. Perhaps he is like the Tar Baby—each time Brer Rabbit hit him another lick, he got stuck faster" (Howells, 1975, p. 390).

It is generally accepted that fourth-glacial Neandertals are different from the *H. sapiens* preceding and following them. The question is: *How different?* Are they different enough to be considered a group apart from what was going on in Eastern Europe, the Near East, and North Africa? Or are they simply a variation of these populations? This may seem like unnecessary academic quibbling, but detailed considerations of human evolutionary theory are complicated. Most anthropologists place classic Neandertals as a side branch to the evolutionary flow from *H. erectus* to Upper Paleolithic *H. sapiens* but include the probability of gene exchange between these early fourth-glacial populations and the developing *H. sapiens sapiens* populations.

In the following section we shall describe several of these "classics" whose morphology has aroused such unprofessional emotions and academic discussion.

Neandertal Beginnings   Neandertal takes its name from the Neander Valley near Düsseldorf, Germany. In 1856, workmen quarrying limestone caves in

Years ago	Temperature C W	Stratigraphy
10,000		Late I
13,000		
20,000		
25,000		
29,000		Middle II
40,000		
50,000		
60,000		Early II
65,000		
75,000		

Figure 15-16   The Würm glaciation. During a glacial period, such as the Würm, the temperature—and the presence of ice—varies. The 65,000 years of the Würm was not simply one long cold period.

the valley blew up the entrance to one of the caves and came across fossilized bones. The owner of the quarry believed they belonged to a bear and gave them to Johann Karl Fuhlrott, teacher of natural science in the local high school. Fuhlrott knew his subject, and when he saw the bones he realized they were not the remains of a cave bear. He believed they must be those of an ancient human, something between the gorilla (first discovered a few years earlier) and *Homo sapiens*. Exactly what the bones represented became a *cause célèbre* for many years, and the fate of Neandertal Man, as the bones were named, hung in the balance for years until later finds were made.

What swung the balance in favor of accepting the Neander Valley specimen as a genuine hominid fossil were other nineteenth-century finds similar to it. What is more important, the additional fossil remains brought home the realization that a form of human different from nineteenth-century Europeans had in fact existed.

Some of these nineteenth-century finds include a skull, which no one understood, found at Gibraltar in 1848. A decade later, the Neander Valley find placed the Gibraltar skull in a more accurate perspective as a Neandertal. In 1866, in the La Naulette Cave, Belgium, a mandible and a few odd bones were discovered and were attributed to the same species as Neandertal. In 1880, a child's mandible from Sipka, Czechoslovakia, demonstrated that large Neandertal teeth were not pathological, since this young mandible possessed large and normal teeth. Whereas there were cries of pathology and abnormality, voiced especially by Virchow (see Chapter 16), most scientists were impressed by the two skeletons recovered in 1886 from a cave at Spy, near the town of Namur, Belgium. These two skeletons were carefully observed in situ by scientists, and the site and excavation were carefully recorded. Similarities between these remains and those of earlier Neandertals were so extensive there could be no doubt that there really was a Neandertal Man.

In the post-Darwinian period, following the publication of *Origin* in 1859, the evolution controversy continued to rage, as we already have discussed in Chapters 2, 14, and elsewhere. Not even all scientists were persuaded that evolution was a valid concept; and more to the point, many scientists were very skeptical of the existence of hominid fossils. Cuvier's dictum, *"L'homme fossile n'existe pas"* (free translation: there is no such thing as fossil man), was still accepted by many Europeans, both laypeople and scientists. Virchow, for example, claimed to be a follower of Darwinian evolution, but was apparently unable to accept any of the hominid fossils discovered during his lifetime (he died in 1902) as honest-to-goodness hominid fossils. He described them as moderns, pathological in one way or another; and we have already alluded to the argument between Virchow and Haeckel about the evolution of hominids from pongids.

The discovery, in 1908, of La Chapelle-aux-Saints (discussed in the following section) settled the issue of the existence of fossil hominids once and for all. Unfortunately, by this time Cuvier was long since dead and, we assume, no longer in a position to change his mind. Virchow, too, had died a few years before, although the subsequent description of La Chapelle, written by Professor Marcellin Boule, seems to have followed in the footsteps of his predecessors, Cuvier and Virchow.

Figure 15-17 Sites: Gibraltar, Spy, La Naulette, Neandertal.

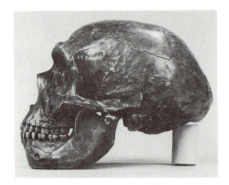

Figure 15-18   Cast, La Chapelle-aux-Saints.

La Chapelle-aux-Saints   One of the most important Neandertal discoveries was made in 1908 at La Chapelle-aux-Saints, near Correze in southwestern France. Found in a Mousterian cultural layer by three French priests, the Abbes A. and J. Bouysonnie and L. Bardon (already known for their archeological researches), was a nearly complete human skeleton. The body had been deliberately buried in a shallow grave and fixed in a ritual position, a bison leg placed on his chest, and the trench filled with flint tools and broken animal bones. This attitude suggests respect toward death, and the tools included with the body may very well indicate a belief in an afterlife where such implements could be used.

The skeleton was turned over for study to a famous French paleontologist, Marcellin Boule, who published his analysis in three volumes from 1911 to 1913. It was his exhaustive, and no doubt biased, publication that set the tone for the description of prehistoric man that survives to this day.

Why did Boule describe Neandertal as the slouching, brutish, apelike, unintelligent creature that became the staple of the cartoonist's prehistoric man? Professor Brace suggests the reason was that Boule, trained in France in the traditions of Cuvier's catastrophism, did not really believe in evolution. He could not deny, as Cuvier had, the existence of fossil humans, but he could reject the notion that Neandertals were ancestral to anatomical moderns, especially if Neandertal looked noticeably different. "With the over-emphasis of the nonmodern features of the La Chapelle-aux-Saints skeleton it became a much less likely candidate for the forefather of the succeeding Upper Paleolithic forms" (Brace, 1977, p. 219).

The skull of the old man, at least forty years of age—old for that time—is very large, with a cranial capacity of 1,620 cm³ (Day, 1977). The vault is low and long, the supraorbital ridges immense, with the typical Neandertal arched shape, and the forehead is low and retreating. Prognathism in the alveolar area is pronounced, and the face is long and projecting. At the rear of the skull, the occiput is protuberant and bun-shaped.

La Chapelle is not typical of classic Neandertals, but is a very robust male and "evidently represents an extreme in the Neanderthal range of variation" (Brace et al., 1979, p. 117). Unfortunately, this skeleton, which Boule claimed did not even walk completely erect (he walked as erect as any other elderly human with spinal arthritis), has been widely accepted as "Mr. Neandertal." That other classic Neandertals are not as extreme is shown by La Ferrassie, a contemporary of La Chapelle.

Figure 15-19   Sites of La Chapelle-aux-Saints, La Ferrassie, St. Césaire, Vindija.

La Ferrassie   Between 1909 and 1912, in Dordogne, southern France, French archeologist D. Peyrony excavated two adult skeletons and portions of skeletons of four children associated with Mousterian artifacts. Trenches had been dug for the skeletons in what has been described as a "family" cemetery. Flint flakes and bone splinters were placed in the male skeleton's grave, and over his shoulders and head was set a flat stone slab, perhaps to protect him, or could it have been to restrain him from coming back to life? (Constable, 1973, p. 98).

La Ferrassie resembles La Chapelle in the extraordinary long face and pronounced arched supraorbital ridges, but La Ferrassie's chin is relatively well marked, the forehead is not as sloping, and the occiput lacks the pro-

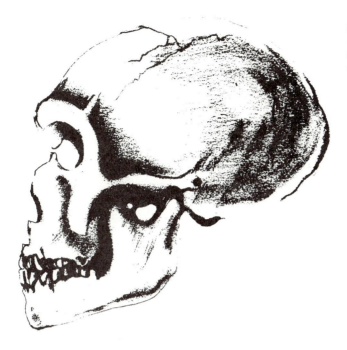

Figure 15-20 La Ferrassie. A classic Neandertal that varies from La Chapelle-aux-Saints. The forehead is higher, the chin less receding, and the occiput more rounded.

tuberant bun. The differences between La Chapelle and La Ferrassie have led Brose and Wolpoff (1971) to define the latter as a transitional form evolving from classic Neandertals to anatomically modern *H. sapiens*, a claim denied by Professor Howells (Howells, 1974, p. 28). Whether or not La Ferrassie may be classified transitional is a matter for continued study by the experts; what is very clear, however, is that the classic Neandertal population of Western Europe is variable, as we would expect of *any* human population.

Vindija   Some thirty-five specimens from a lower level (G₃) of this Yugoslavian site are associated with a late Mousterian (Middle Paleolithic) assemblage and the Lower Würm glaciation. Although in some respects approaching anatomically moderns, the skeletal material is considered to be definitely Neandertal.

St. Cesaire   An incomplete skeleton, believed to be that of an adult woman, was found in 1979 at St. Cesaire (Charènte-Maritime, France), by Professor Bernard Vandermeersch of the University of Paris. From the evidence of limbs, and especially the skull—receding forehead, low cranial vault, supraorbital torus, midfacial prognathism—Vandermeersch defined the skeleton as Neandertal (Vandermeersch, 1981, p. 286).

St. Cesaire, the most recent Neandertal known from Europe, was recovered from a bed of discarded chipped blades, hand axes, and other stone tools of a type called "Chatelperronian."

Several questions immediately arise: Did the Neandertals really disappear at about 40,000 y.a., as we have believed for so many years, or did the Neandertals and Upper Paleolithic moderns live side by side, at some social distance (without interbreeding)? Were Neandertals relegated to an inferior status by the more sophisticated moderns? Did they become fugitives in remote areas and survive there? (Some say they still survive today—see Issue at the beginning of this chapter.) How do we explain the existence of St. Cesaire, this Middle Paleolithic individual, in the Upper Paleolithic, long after Neandertals were supposed to have become extinct? At present, there is no answer to any of these questions that is widely accepted.

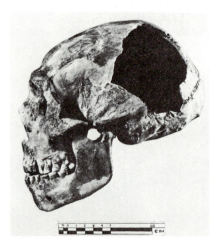

Figure 15-21 Shanidar.

◇ Neandertals Outside Europe

Tabun Neandertals very similar to those of Western Europe are found in other parts of the world. From south of Haifa, Israel, about 50,000 y.a. (Jelinek, 1982) comes Tabun, with a low vault, prognathism, heavy brow ridges, but a nicely rounded occiput. The cranial capacity of Tabun 1, a female, is estimated at 1271 cm³.

Shanidar A most remarkable site is Shanidar, in the Zagros Mountains in northeastern Iraq, where partial skeletons of nine male and female individuals—seven adults and two infants—were found, four of them deliberately buried. These are quite typically classic, although the nuchal torus is weak, the occiput is fairly well rounded, and an incipient chin is present on at least one of the jaws. Several skulls look deformed, as if their foreheads had been bound as children (Trinkaus, 1984). Cranial deformation is known from several areas of the world in very recent times.

One of the more interesting individuals is Shanidar 1, a male who lived to a fairly old age for his time, between 35 and 50. His stature is estimated at 5 feet 7 inches, with a cranial capacity of 1600 cm³, a bit over the European Neandertal mean of 1510 cm³. The right side of his body suffered a crushing injury that affected his right arm, clavicle, scapula, and lower right limb. The injury may have been due to a rockfall, or it is possible that the atrophy of the right arm was the result of nerve injury suffered from severe damage to his left eye. It is also possible that his right arm was amputated at the elbow, which, if true, is the first evidence of deliberate human surgery (See Trinkaus, 1982, 1983; Stringer and Trinkaus, 1981).

Another individual, Shanidar 4, was deliberately buried on his left side, legs drawn up against his chest in a flexed position. Pollen analysis of the soil associated with the skeleton indicates the presence of a number of spring flowers (hyacinths, daisies, hollyhocks, and bachelor's buttons) that had apparently been placed on the grave at the time of death (Solecki, 1971).

Neandertals must have lived dangerously, if the Shanidar evidence has been interpreted correctly. An atrophied arm, a crushing eye fracture resulting in blindness in that eye, arm and foot fractures, skull scars, and various rib injuries were found on several of the adult male skeletons. Shanidar 3 suffered a rib injury that may have been caused by a stabbing. One of his ribs was damaged by a sharp instrument that probably caused his death. If this were a deliberate stabbing, it would be the oldest known case of interpersonal violence; however, there is no way of knowing whether it was deliberate or

Figure 15-22 Sites: Tabun, Shanidar.

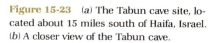

Figure 15-23 (a) The Tabun cave site, located about 15 miles south of Haifa, Israel. (b) A closer view of the Tabun cave.

(a)

(b)

Upper Paleolithic
Culture period noted for technological, artistic, and behavioral innovations. Also known for appearance of anatomically modern human beings. (See p. 431.)

accidental. No matter how it happened, Shanidar 3 was taken care of for at least several weeks and intentionally buried when he died (Trinkaus and Zimmerman, 1982).

Since many of the injuries were serious and the men survived for a time, some for years, it suggests that their social system was organized, that cooperation and care of the sick and disabled were an important value of their culture. Intentional burials and flowers placed on a grave are evidence of a special attitude toward death and perhaps a belief in a future life and the supernatural.

Teshik-Tash   In Soviet Uzbekistan, in a cave at Teshik-Tash, we find another deliberate burial. A nine-year-old boy, with a cranial capacity of 1,490 cm³, was buried in a shallow grave surrounded by five pairs of wild goat horns, suggesting a burial ritual or perhaps a religious cult. Like many other Neandertals, Teshik-Tash is a mixture of Neandertal traits (heavy brow ridges and occipital bun) and modern traits (high vault and definite signs of a chin).

Maba*   Finally, extending the range of Neandertals from Western Europe across Asia to southeastern China is Maba, Qujiang County, Guangdong. The characters of this middle-aged male are similar, yet different, from those of Western Europe. "The browridge is robust and protruding" and the skull bones are about the same thickness as Neandertal. "The height of the skull and the angle of the forehead are also similar to those of Neanderthal [but] obviously different from the typical Neanderthal of Western Europe" (Wu, 1982, p. 475).

◇ Contemporary Upper Pleistocene Forms

Living at about the same time as Neandertals are forms we have called contemporaries of Neandertal. These forms do not fit the physical pattern of Neandertals, nor are they quite **Upper Paleolithic** *H. sapiens* (see Box 15-2, p. 433). Contemporaries exhibit what appear to be both Neandertal and anatomically modern traits that seem to represent an evolutionary trend toward Upper Paleolithic moderns. Some of these, in fact, may well be considered transitional between Neandertals and *H. sapiens sapiens* of the Upper Paleolithic. Examples of such contemporaries who may be transitional have been found in Europe, the Near East, and Africa.

EUROPE

Hortus   Found by the de Lumleys, Hortus combines archaic and modern features, seen especially in mandibles and teeth.

Vindija   At middle levels of Vindija, in Yugoslavia, higher up in the sequence than the Neandertals from this same site, are remains dated at somewhat

Figure 15-24   Sites: Teshik-Tash, Maba.

*Formerly spelled Mapa. Chinese paleoanthropologist Wu uses Maba spelling.

◇ Box 15-2   Characteristics of Anatomically Moderns
and Their Differences from Neandertals

THE CRANIUM

1. Cranial capacity, ranging from about 1,000–2,000 cm³ with a mean of 1,400 cm³, is only slightly higher than the Neandertal average
2. The forehead is more vertical, brow ridges are absent to moderate and never continuous across the orbits; ridges are slightly separated over the middle of each orbit
3. The skull vault is higher
4. There is little prognathism and the face hangs more or less vertically below the forehead
5. Alongside the nose is a canine fossa

6. A chin is always present
7. The occiput is rounded with little or no bun or strong torus
8. Maximum breadth of the skull is high on the parietals
9. Skull bones are thinner

POSTCRANIUM

1. Bone thickness throughout the entire body is reduced
2. Musculature is reduced
3. Marked curvature of long bones is lacking

---

less than 27,000 y.a. and associated with Aurignacian (Upper Paleolithic) artifacts. These later Vindija fossils have been compared to both Neandertals and Upper Paleolithic populations, and appear to indicate an evolutionary trend from Neandertals to anatomically moderns (Smith, 1982).

ISRAEL

Skhūl   Also from south of Haifa, close to the Tabun site (p.430), comes Skhūl, dated between 35,000 and 40,000 y.a. Skhūl is represented by at least ten individuals with remarkable variability. The brow ridges are prominent on one skull, but less so on others; the chin is also variable, as is the occipital bun. The skull vault is higher and the anterior teeth a bit smaller (both of these are modern traits). The variability of this sample has been explained as a process of evolutionary change leading to anatomically moderns, although not all paleoanthropologists agree.

Qafzeh   South of Nazareth and about the same age as Skhūl, Qafzeh is quite similar to Skhūl in its combination of older and more modern traits.

Amud   Of uncertain date, Amud was found north of Lake Kinneret and, like Skhūl, also shows a mixture of Neandertal and anatomically modern traits. For example, Amud is platycephalic (flat-headed) like Neandertal, the supraorbital torus is large, the maxilla inflated, and the facial area prognathous. However, paralleling the modern features of the skulls discussed above, Amud's skull vault is high and the occiput lacks a nuchal torus. The brow ridges tend to separate into two parts above the middle of each orbit as they do in

Figure 15-25   Neandertal and contemporary sites in the Near East.

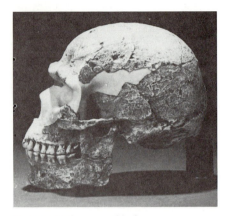

Figure 15-26   Cast, Skhūl V.

Figure 15-27   The Skhūl cave.

modern skulls. Amud had a very large cranial capacity, 1,740 cm³, and at 5 feet 8 inches was one of the tallest Near Eastern individuals.

NORTHWEST AFRICA

Djebel Irhoud (Morocco)   Perhaps in the range of 50,000 y.a., Skull II from this site in northwest Africa can be compared to Skhūl from Israel as a mixture of Neandertal and anatomically modern characters.

EAST AFRICA

Omo (Ethiopia)   Omo I comes from the Kibish Formation of the Omo site in southern Ethiopia, where very old hominid remains were also found (p. 337). The Kibish formation has been given a date of 130,000 years, but there are serious doubts about this. Parts of a calvarium and some postcranial fragments, including pieces of femur, were excavated. Kennedy (1984) studied the reconstructed femur and concluded that it should be classified as anatomically modern. Because of the unresolved questions about the date and the fragmentary nature of the skull, we have placed Omo in this archaic rather than fully anatomically modern, stage. Omo II, also found in the Kibish formation, is considered more archaic than Omo I.

Ndutu   This specimen was also originally assigned to *H. erectus* (see p. 402), but a recent reexamination by Rightmire (1983) notes that the occipital and temporal areas point in the direction of *H. sapiens*. Rightmire also sees similarities with Kabwe and Bodo.

Laetoli Hominid 18   In 1976, in the Ngaloba beds overlying the area where Mary Leakey found the now famous footprints of early australopithecines (p. 333), and recovered a well-preserved skull with resemblances to Omo, Kabwe, Bodo, and Ndutu. L.H. 18, like these, shows a combination of *H. erectus* and *H. sapiens* characteristics, probably more like the latter than the former. The skull is small, 1,200 cm³, and has been dated to about 120,000 y.a. (Day et al., 1980; Kennedy, 1980).

SOUTH AFRICA

Kabwe (Broken Hill)   A complete skull and some skeletal fragmentary material were recovered in 1921 from a shallow mine shaft in Kabwe, Zambia (formerly Northern Rhodesia). Kabwe has been a puzzle from the day it was found. It has been called Neandertal and neandertaloid, but conformation of the massive brow ridges (among the largest known), small brain (1,200 cm³), neck muscle attachments, and large teeth raise doubts about its affiliation with Western European Neandertals. Characteristics of the occiput, frontal bone, and parietals have led Rightmire (1976) to refer it to archaic *sapiens* and give it a formal designation as *Homo sapiens rhodesiensis*. The dating for Kabwe is uncertain, but faunal association and amino acid racemization analysis suggest it is at least 110,000 years old.

Elandsfontein (Hopefield, Saldanha)   Skeletal material found at Elandsfontein near Hopefield, Saldanha Bay, on the west coast of South Africa, is quite similar to Kabwe. Dating is uncertain, although a Middle Pleistocene date has been suggested.

Florisbad   In 1932, T. F. Dreyer found a partial skull near Florisbad, about thirty miles north of Bloemfontein, South Africa. The skull includes portions of parietal, frontal, and facial bones. In the past, Florisbad was considered anatomically modern and similar to the present-day San people (p. 224). However, Rightmire (1978) restudied the original fossil material and concluded that Florisbad is not as modern as once believed. Florisbad, he states, resembles archaic (*sapiens*) hominids like Kabwe and Elandsfontein, and he places it roughly intermediate between archaic *sapiens* and recent *Homo sapiens*. Dating this material has been difficult, but Rightmire gives it a date much older than 42,000 years ago.

Summarizing the evidence from the early Upper Pleistocene (third interglacial and early fourth glacial), we find two aspects of human evolution occurring at the same time. First, there is a trend toward anatomically modern *H. sapiens*, attributed to changes in diet, improved technology, or adaptations to local ecological conditions. This trend culminates in the appearance of the modern forms about 40,000 years ago. Second, there is a specialized *sapiens*, the classic Neandertals, who inhabit the Near East, central and eastern Asia, and especially Western Europe. Exactly what their relationship is to those evolving into anatomically moderns is still a matter of dispute. Finally, the specialized form of classic Neandertal has never been explained, although a number of anthropologists lean toward F. Clark Howell's theory of adaptation to cold weather.

One of the serious problems in working out the Neandertal evolution and their relationship to other hominid populations (both *H. erectus* and *H. sapiens sapiens*) is the lack of chronometric dates. Most Neandertal remains were discovered before ¹⁴C and K/Ar techniques were developed. (Also, the sites were excavated before the more rigorous archeological methods of recent years were developed, and material that might have been invaluable for dating purposes was ignored or discarded.) Furthermore, most Neandertals lived between the outer limits of both dating methods—too long ago for ¹⁴C and too recently for K/Ar, although some Neandertals have been ¹⁴C dated. Therefore, much of Neandertal dating has been based on stratigraphy and correlated with associated faunal remains. Many of these dates are uncertain, and it is not always possible to know which fossil is older and which younger. Consequently, the place of Neandertal in human phylogenetic schemes and the trends of Neandertal evolution are still frustratingly vague.

It should be emphasized that much of the discussion and research regarding Neandertals and Middle/Upper Paleolithic transitional forms has centered on Near Eastern and Western European fossils. In the past fifteen years or so, there has been a resurgence of interest in African material for this equivalent period. New finds (such as Bodo, Ndutu, Laetoli Hominid 18, and others) and restudy and reinterpretation of earlier finds (such as Kabwe, Elandsfontein, Omo, and Florisbad) have given rise to rethinking of human evolution in Africa.

Figure 15-28   Neandertal contemporary sites in Africa.

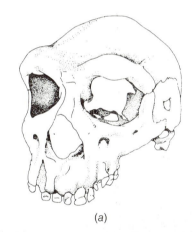

(a)

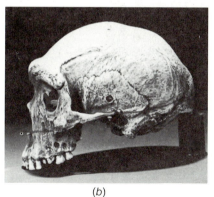

(b)

Figure 15-29   Kabwe (also known as Rhodesian man and Broken Hill). (*a*) Note very heavy supraorbital torus. (*b*) Photograph of cast.

Figure 15-30   Mousterian tools (after Bordes).

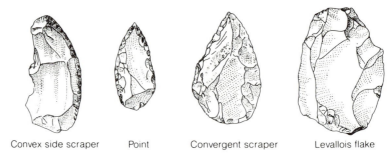

Figure 15-30   Mousterian tools (after Bordes).

Convex side scraper   Point   Convergent scraper   Levallois flake

Similarities in East and South African skulls have suggested placing these individuals in the *H. sapiens rhodesiensis* subspecies, an evolutionary lineage separate and somewhat different from the Eurasian populations. It is also significant that dates (over 100,000 y.a.) provisionally assigned to these finds are earlier than the Neandertal and early Upper Paleolithic dates of Europe/Near East.

If these dates are found to be accurate, then it could be argued that a more sapient form evolved in Africa (probably South Africa) earlier than in Europe. Furthermore, if the early dates are valid, then there is the possibility that Neandertals in Europe were replaced by the more advanced sapient forms who immigrated from Africa. (But Smith, 1982, makes a strong case for gradual evolution from Neandertals to anatomically moderns in South-Central Europe.)

A number of paleoanthropologists have seriously considered these possibilities; however, until the nagging problem of dates, which are not at all clear, can be determined, the whole matter of human evolution in Africa for the Middle and Upper Pleistocene cannot be settled.

◇ Culture of Neandertals

Neandertals, who lived in the culture period known as the Middle Paleolithic, are usually associated with the Mousterian industry (although the Mousterian industry is not always associated with Neandertals), which had its roots in the Eemian interglacial, or even the Riss glacial. In the early Würm, Mousterian culture extended from the Atlantic Ocean across Europe and North Africa to the Soviet Union, Israel, Iran, and as far east as Uzbekistan and, perhaps, China.

Technology   Mousterian people specialized in the production of flake tools based on the Levallois method, a prepared core technique that originated perhaps as much as 200,000 y.a. A chunk of flint was chipped all the way round and on top, resembling a turtle in form, and then rapped on the side to produce a flake ready for use (Fig. 15-30).

Neandertals improved on the Levallois technique by inventing a variation. They trimmed the flint nodule around the edges to form a disc-shaped core.

Each time they struck the edge, they produced a flake until the core became too small and was discarded. Thus, the Neandertals were able to obtain more flakes per core than their predecessors. They then trimmed (retouched) the flake into various forms like scrapers, points, knives, and so on.

Neandertal craftsmen elaborated and diversified traditional methods, and there is some indication of development in the specialization of tools used in skin and meat preparation, hunting, woodworking, and perhaps hafting (attaching handles to tools). They may have made some use of new materials, such as antler and bone, but their specialization and innovation cannot be compared to the next culture period, the Upper Paleolithic. Nevertheless, the Neandertals advanced their technology, which tended to be similar in typology, over great geographic distances, far beyond that of *H. erectus*. It is quite likely that their modifications in technology laid the basis for the remarkable changes of the Upper Paleolithic.

Nodule

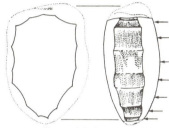

The nodule is chipped on the parameter.

Settlements   People of Mousterian culture lived in a variety of open sites, caves, and rock shelters. Living in the open on the cold tundra suggests the erection of shelters, and there is some evidence of such structures, although the last glaciation must have destroyed many open sites. At the site of Moldova I, in the Ukraine region of the Soviet Union, archeologists found traces of an oval ring of mammoth bones, enclosing an area of about 26 by 16 feet, which may have been used to weigh down the skin walls of a temporary hut or tent. Inside the ring are traces of a number of hearths, hundreds of tools, thousands of waste flakes, and many bone fragments of animals probably brought home for comfortable dining around the fireplace.

Evidence for life in caves is abundant, and Mousterians must have occupied them extensively. Windbreaks of poles and skin were probably erected at the cave mouth for protection against the weather. Fire is in general use by this time, of course, and no doubt used for cooking, for warmth, and for keeping dangerous animals at bay.

How large were Neandertal settlements, and were they permanent or temporary? These questions are not yet answered, but Binford (1982) believes the settlements were short-term occupations used over and over again.

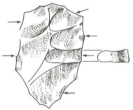

Flakes are radially removed from top surface.

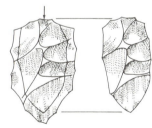

A final blow at one end removes a large flake.

Figure 15-31   The Levallois method.

Religion   An important innovation of the Middle Paleolithic is deliberate burial, often with indications of funerary ritual. Deliberate burials are common, as we have seen, at La Chapelle, La Ferrassie, Shanidar, and Teshik-Tash, and there are many others. At Teshik-Tash, we find an interesting ring of goat horns surrounding a child's grave, an arrangement that would certainly seem to indicate ritualism of some sort. Shanidar IV was buried with flowers, an act which may or may not suggest ritual, but which certainly does suggest a special attitude toward death. A remarkable burial occurs at the La Ferrassie rock shelter perhaps as much as 60,000 years ago. It looks like a family cemetery; the presumed parents are buried head to head and four children are interred neatly nearby. A short distance beyond, a small mound contains the bones of a newly born infant, and a bit further under a triangular stone is the grave of a six-year-old child.

Figure 15-32 Neandertal ritual and hunt. Neandertals are cutting up a wooly rhinoceros. The men to the left are offering pieces of meat to the rising sun. It is not known for certain whether this ritual was actually performed, but Neandertals did perform burial rituals. (Courtesy California Academy of Sciences)

Besides ritual burials, Neandertals also practiced a bear cult. At the back of the cave of Drachenloch, high up in the Swiss Alps, a stone chest was found containing seven bear skulls. Still farther back in the cave, six bear skulls had been set in niches along the walls, and limb bones placed next to them. At another site at Regourdu, in southern France, a pit covered by a heavy stone slab contained the bones of more than twenty bears, estimated to be nine feet tall and outweighing a grizzly.

From this extraordinary treatment of bear remains, Neandertals must have felt that bears were special. Perhaps they held these formidable foes in great respect, and the care taken with bear skulls and bones was an attempt to propitiate or soothe the ferocious spirits of these giant beasts. Some Siberians, Ainu of northern Japan, and a number of American Indian tribes, among others, also show a special ceremonial regard for bears.

Bears may not have been the only animals treated in a ritualistic manner. Ralph Solecki, who excavated Shanidar Cave (p. 430), found evidence of a deer ceremony in another cave in Lebanon. Neandertals had cut up a deer, placed the meat on a bed of stones, and sprinkled it with red ochre. The red ochre may have symbolized blood, and this ritual could have been a magical attempt to control deer, an animal the Neandertals hunted (Constable, 1973).

We mentioned earlier (p. 391) Peking Man's practice of cutting away the base of a human skull to remove the brain. Deep in the Guattari Cave, sixty miles south of Rome, Neandertals performed a similar ritual. Explorers found a human skull—the right side crushed and the foramen magnum area cut out—in the center of a circle of stones. Near the circle were several piles of deer, cattle, and pig bones. Apparently, the man had been killed (sacrificed?)

outside the cave, by a smashing blow to the right side of his head. His head was then taken into the cave and placed within the circle of bones.

What is the meaning of this remarkable activity? For the first time in human history, we find people who are concerned with more than the material aspects of life. Deliberately burying a corpse and depositing objects that belonged to him alongside his body reflects attitudes and values different from the ordinary. Death had meaning, perhaps mystical, something unknown, and Neandertals recognized that they had to come to terms with what they didn't understand.

Similarly with animal cults. Instead of earlier hunting practices of catch-as-catch-can, Neandertals were beginning to single out certain animals for game. Did they believe they could control their game animals? (If so, did these rituals serve as forerunners of Upper Paleolithic cave art that also may have been a form of hunting magic?) Were they attempting to help the animals multiply, improve their own hunting success, or increase the chances of their own safety? Do these rituals signify that Neandertals were becoming aware of their distinctiveness—they were something more than simply animals?

Figure 15-33   La Ferrassie burial.

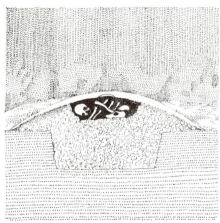
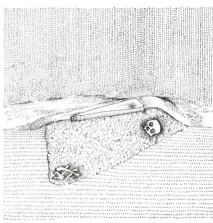

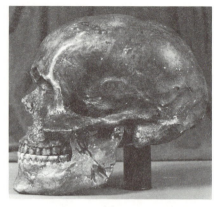

(a)

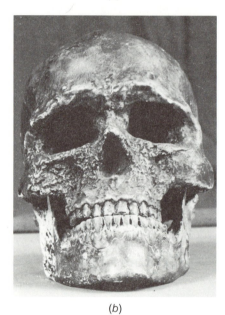

(b)

Figure 15-34 Cast, Cro-Magnon. (a) Lateral view; (b) frontal view.

Did the rituals reflect, as they do for many hunting peoples, that killing an animal leaves a void in the universe, and it is necessary to propitiate the animal's spirits to prevent an imbalance in the physical and spiritual universe?

No one, of course, knows the answers to these questions, and we don't even know for certain whether Neandertals believed in spirits, a future life, and the supernatural, but the evidence is irresistably suggestive.

Economy   Neandertals were successful hunters, as the abundant remains of animal bones at their sites demonstrate. As the evidence from Shanidar suggests, they probably gathered berries, nuts, and other plants. It does not appear that they sought more exotic foods, such as seafood or birds.

It is assumed that, in the freezing weather of the fourth glacial, Neandertals must have worn clothing to survive the winters—and they may have developed methods of curing skins. But since there is no evidence of sewing equipment, the clothing was probably of simple design. Nor is there evidence of personal ornaments or individual adornment, although these might be difficult to recognize.

Abstract Thought   Neandertal behavior, as deduced from the archeological and osteological evidence, is complex enough to reflect abstract ideas. Braidwood points to the "variety of combinations of the different basic habits or traditions of tool preparation" signifying "mixtures and blends of many of the other ideas and beliefs of these small groups" (Braidwood, 1975, p. 62). Therefore, there was not *one* Neandertal culture but "a great variety of loosely related cultures at about the same stage of advancement." For the first time in hominid history, we can see that humans have the ability to develop a variety of cultural adaptations to a variety of ecological conditions.

With the complexity of Neandertal life comes the question of communication, and scholars are not agreed that Middle Paleolithic people could communicate fluently on a symbolic basis (that is, via language). A controversial paper published a few years ago claims that Neandertals were unable to articulate easily because of the anatomical structure of their throats (Lieberman and Crelin, 1971). Given Neandertal brain size, their success in hunting, adaptation to severe weather, their technological improvements, and probably a well-developed social organization, most anthropologists would probably disagree.

◇ Upper Paleolithic and Homo Sapiens Sapiens

In Europe, during a warm break in the Würm glaciation, about 40,000 years ago, and elsewhere in the world at about the same time, two impressive events occurred in human evolution. Modern humans very similar to ourselves appear, and a remarkable change occurs in culture, especially in stone/bone tool technology. We shall attempt to deal later with the reason for the simultaneous appearance of these two events, but before opening that "can of worms," let us look at a sample of these early anatomically modern *sapiens*.

CRO-MAGNON

One of the first Upper Paleolithic hominids to be discovered (in 1868) comes from a rock shelter in the village of Cro-Magnon, near Les Eyzies, in the Dordogne of southern France. During the construction of a railway, workmen found the remains of five human skeletons that had been buried there between 20,000–30,000 y.a. Associated with the burials were faunal remains, worked flint, and other artifacts of the Aurignacian tradition. The best known of the five skeletons is the famous "Old Man of Cro-Magnon," who was between forty and fifty years of age when he died.

With a large brain (cranial capacity estimated at 1,590 cm³, larger than the average European today) the "Old Man" had a high forehead, protruding chin, nicely rounded occiput, and some development of the supraorbital ridges. He was an anatomically modern human being, and walking down the street dressed in modern clothes, he probably would be difficult to distinguish from a present-day European.

The term "Cro-Magnon" is often used synonymously with Upper Paleolithic moderns. However, considerable population variation was evident in Europe and elsewhere during this time. The following examples illustrate this variation.

Figure 15-35 Upper Paleolithic European sites.

OTHERS

A neighbor of Cro-Magnon, who lived at approximately the same time, is Combe Capelle. This fossil reflects variability (which we have repeatedly emphasized) even within the same environment. Combe Capelle retains some Neandertal characteristics, such as facial prognathism, prominent brow ridges, and a considerably less developed chin than Cro-Magnon.

Some of the twenty-nine individuals of various ages and both sexes from Předmosti, Czechoslovakia, illustrate a European variation more like Combe Capelle than Cro-Magnon. A few skulls show strikingly pronounced supraorbital arches (modern), others have occipital buns, and one has a surprising amount of basal spongy bone.

Mladeč, also from Czechoslovakia, was found in association with an Aurignacian industry. Like Předmosti, the skulls possess neandertal-like traits.

During the late Pleistocene, anatomically modern *H. sapiens* appear in several regions of Africa. In North Africa, fragments of more than fifty skeletons were uncovered at Afalou-bou-Rhummel, Algeria. Except for rugged brow ridges, the skulls are completely modern. Other sites in North Africa have been found in Algeria, Morocco, the Sudan, and Egypt.

Anatomically moderns have also been found at sites in East Africa—at Lake Turkana and Olduvai, where early hominids were also found, and at Lukenya Hill in Kenya. In South Africa, remains have been found at Boskop, Fish Hoek, Springbok Flats, and Border Cave. Recently, Dr. Rightmire (1979) suggested that the Border Cave cranium is not only anatomically modern (similar to present-day Hottentots), but perhaps as much as 115,000 years old. This would mean, as discussed on p. 436, that anatomically moderns evolved earlier in Africa than in Europe or elsewhere. However, it has not been

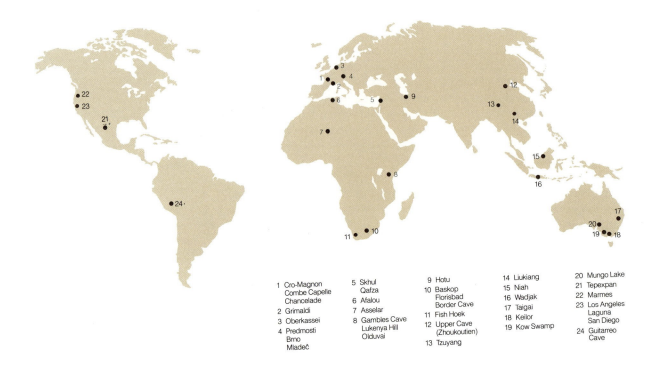

1 Cro-Magnon
  Combe Capelle
  Chancelade
	5 Skhul
	  Qafza
		9 Hotu
		10 Baskop
		  Florisbad
		  Border Cave
			14 Liukiang
			15 Niah
			16 Wadjak
			17 Taigai

2 Grimaldi	6 Afalou	11 Fish Hoek	18 Keilor
3 Oberkassei	7 Asselar	12 Upper Cave (Zhoukoutien)	19 Kow Swamp

4 Predmosti
  Brno
  Mladeč
	8 Gambles Cave
	  Lukenya Hill
	  Olduvai
		13 Tzuyang	20 Mungo Lake
			21 Tepexpan
			22 Marmes
			23 Los Angeles
			  Laguna
			  San Diego
			24 Guitarreo
			  Cave

Figure 15-36 Upper Paleolithic hominid fossil sites. Only better-known fossils are listed on the map. Note that for the first time humans lived on all continents.

an easy task to arrive at an acceptable Border Cave date, which remains debatable.

In the Far East, modern humans appeared as early as they did in Europe. In fact, the Niah Cave of North Borneo has yielded one of the earliest *H. sapiens sapiens* so far discovered. A ^{14}C date of 40,000 years has been assigned to the skull of this teenage female. In China, from the site of Peking Man at Zhoukoudian, seven or eight individuals were found higher up in the cave, known as Upper Cave. Farther south, at Liukiang, a female cranium and postcranial material were discovered, and from Tzuyang, in Szechuan province, comes another female skull.

Modern skulls have also been found in Java and Australia. From Wadjak, Java, come two skulls excavated in the 1890s by Dubois in his search for the "missing link," and which are said to resemble (and are perhaps ancestral to) present-day Australian aborigines. A skull found at Keilor, ten miles north of Melbourne, Australia, has been carbon-dated at about 15,000 years and resembles the two modern skulls Dubois recovered from Java. From south Queensland comes the Talgai skull and, from Victoria, the Cohuna skull.

An important site recently excavated at Mungo Lake, New South Wales, may be 35,000 years old or more. This site contains tools, cremations (probably the earliest known), and anatomically modern human remains reflecting a gracile form. At Kow Swamp in Central Victoria, over 40 burials of robust, big-boned individuals, reminiscent of Java Solo Man, were excavated and dated at about 10,000 y.a. As in the manner of the Shanidar people of Iran, head deformation may have been practiced at Kow Swamp. It is interesting that the much earlier Mungo Lake people appear more modern-looking than the robust Kow Swamp population.

Studies are presently being conducted to determine where in Indonesia the early Australians came from, and when. However, native Australians are demanding the return, for reburial, of all bones and artifacts that have been excavated, and government agencies are sympathetic. Paleoanthropologists and archeologists hope they will have sufficient opportunity to complete their study of bones and artifacts before this occurs.

◇ The New World

Anthropologists generally agree that modern *H. sapiens* entered the New World across the Bering Strait some time in the past 40,000 years. Most likely this movement would have occurred during the last glaciation (Wisconsin in New World terminology) when a land bridge some 1,300 miles from north to south joined Asia to North America. The newcomers settled in central Alaska, which was free from ice, and later made their way east, into present-day Canada, and, later, into what is now the United States, Mesoamerica, and South America. The two ice sheets that covered Canada during the last (Wisconsin) glaciation must have separated to let the wanderers travel south, but geologists are not quite sure when the separation(s) occurred. A great deal of research and discussion has been going on for years by geologists, paleontologists, archeologists, and paleoanthropologists to solve the riddle of when these treks into Alaska and continental areas of the New World were made.

There are (at least) two schools of thought on the matter: (1) Those who believe that these hunters came across the Bering Strait at least 40,000 y.a. and (2) others who claim there is no *solid* evidence beyond about 12,500 y.a. Archeological evidence is abundant for the more recent date, and this evidence is quite common in the western United States, where the early projectile points known as Folsom and Clovis were found. However, there are a number of sites that may be considerably older than 12,000 years, and it is possible that human occupation in the New World may prove to be 40,000 years old or more.

The earliest people of the New World are known as big game hunters, the big game being mammoths and other large animals, which they hunted with spears or lances and also by driving them into a surround or over a cliff.

All of the excavated bone material (which is scarce) indicates these early inhabitants were anatomically modern humans. As a matter of fact, there is little acceptable osteological evidence that can be dated much more than 12,000 years or so ago. Tepexpan in Mexico and Marmes in Washington State are dated at 11,000 y.a., and Guitarrero Cave in Peru* at 12,500 y.a. California specimens from Laguna, Los Angeles, and San Diego are sometimes given older dates, but these are debatable. No hard evidence at all exists for any type of human in the New World except anatomically modern *H. sapiens*— no Neandertals, no Bigfoot!

*See Ch. 17 for a more detailed account of South American prehistory.

Figure 15-37   The punch blade technique.

◇ Upper Paleolithic Culture

TECHNOLOGY

About 40,000 years ago (perhaps more) anatomically modern humans begin to appear (although they may not have been present in Europe until several thousand years later). Associated with these newly evolved moderns are new technological techniques and new tools, quite different from the Mousterian of the Neandertals. The major technological difference between the earlier Mousterian and the Upper Paleolithic is the shift from flake to blade tools. A blade is a parallel-sided flake, at least twice as long as it is wide, with sharp cutting edges that make an excellent knife. The contribution of Upper Paleolithic peoples to blade manufacture was the introduction of the punch technique, in which numerous identical blades from a core of flint were punched out.

Using the blades as blanks, anatomically moderns produced a wide variety of tools, one of the characteristics of Upper Paleolithic technology. It is interesting to note that, while the variety of tools and the materials they were made from increased, Neandertals were more efficient in their use of flint. Not only did the Mousterians use fewer strokes manufacturing a tool, but they produced more cutting edges from a pound of flint, as we can see in a comparison of the following industries (the Mousterian increase is *five* times the Acheulian; the anatomically modern is *three* times the Mousterian).

	Inches Per Pound of Flint
Upper Paleolithic	120
Mousterian	40
Acheulian	8
Oldowan	2

Much regional variability existed in the Mousterian, but in the Upper Paleolithic the variation seems to be more evolutionary. That is, contemporaneous assemblages are very similar, though they change quickly over time. French archeologist F. Bordes, a specialist in Paleolithic tools, identified 62 tool types for Lower and Middle Paleolithic typologies, which together cover about 2 million years. M. Denise de Sonneville-Bordes has identified 112 types for the 30,000 years of the Upper Paleolithic, a period of much more variability among tool types.

The shaping of bone, antler, and teeth prevails in the Upper Paleolithic. In the Mousterian, bone tools were scarce, although unshaped bone fragments were probably used as tools. But even the earliest Upper Paleolithic displays large bone assemblages.

Also prominent in the Upper Paleolithic tool kit is the *burin* (or graver) used for (*a*) engraving on bone and stone and (*b*) making grooves in wood and bone that could then be used as handles or shafts for other tools. The cutting edge at the end of a burin is transverse like a chisel, and, as a matter of fact, the burin may be considered the first chisel.

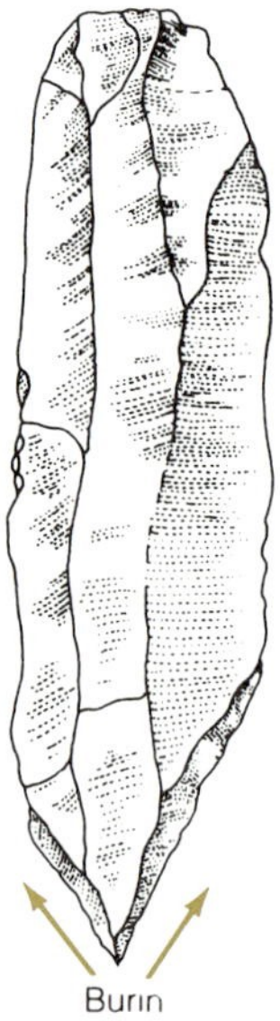

A bewildering variety of rapidly changing tool types was available to these

Burin

Figure 15-38   A burin.

hunters, especially in Europe: knives, many kinds of points, notched blades used as spokeshaves (to prepare shafts for spears, for example), awls, drills, borers, scrapers of various types, spear-throwers (the first artificial propulsive devices invented by humans), throwing sticks, clubs, shaft straighteners—and this list is only a partial one. They were clearly a technologically oriented people.

Personal ornaments—pendants and decorated objects—made of antler, shell, and bone suggest that Upper Paleolithic people were developing an increasing awareness of personal, and perhaps group, identity. For whatever reason or reasons, Upper Paleolithic populations produced a culture that is noted for its rapid change, variety, artistic achievement, and comparative sophistication.

Since much of what is known about the Upper Paleolithic is based on European sites, it may be beneficial to discuss this period in Europe in more detail.

The Upper Paleolithic of Europe must focus on sites known in France. Archeological investigation began here in the 1850s, and the country produced the first Cro-Magnon and Neandertal major finds. Much of the Upper Paleolithic technology and typologies has been worked out based on the extremely rich area east of Bordeaux along the Dordogne River. In this approximately twelve-square-mile region over 200 Paleolithic sites have been found, some with 20–25 feet of deposit.

In addition to the previously mentioned shift from flakes to blades, there is also a shift in the faunal exploitation patterns. The Middle Paleolithic is characterized by a generalized exploitation, with one species (out of fifteen present), usually accounting for a maximum of 50% of the animals. In the Upper Paleolithic, a single species (reindeer) usually makes up 80% of the animals. Fishing and hunting of waterfowl and other birds become common. The fifteen to twenty large herbivores present at the time were often not hunted, since reindeer were preferred.

Middle Paleolithic (Mousterian) sites are seldom larger than 300–400 square yards and are fairly restricted. The Upper Paleolithic witnessed a population explosion of sorts, with sites of over 7,000 square yards as well as many small sites.

Not until the Upper Paleolithic does one find frequent evidence of habitation structures in France. At Pincevant, careful excavations of an occupation site were conducted so that none of the workers touched the floor but were suspended overhead. An interesting feature of these habitation structures was that they almost always faced to the south or southwest.

The Upper Paleolithic introduced many exotic raw materials into the material culture. For example, shells were present 300 miles from the Mediterranean Sea, but are never found this far inland in Mousterian sites.

In the approximately 30,000 years of the Upper Paleolithic (from roughly 40,000 y.a. to 10,000 y.a.) a sequence of cultural traditions may be traced in Europe (see Table 15-1). During this time the weather in Europe was warm, beginning with an interstadial, then fluctuating warm and cool and becoming cold around 30,000 years ago. After a brief interstadial about 20,000 years ago, the ice returns with the final Würm stage climaxing at about 18,000 years ago. Sometime around 10,000 years ago, we enter the **Holocene**, or Present.

Holocene
Entirely recent; the epoch following the Pleistocene; the Present.

Figure 15-39 Upper Paleolithic economy. A common method of hunting used in recent times in North America. This method involves driving a herd over a cliff where they could be easily killed by the hunters. (Courtesy California Academy of Sciences)

Table 15-1   Upper Paleolithic Cultures*

Glacial	Time (YEARS AGO)	Culture Periods	Hominids
	10,000		Anatomically
	17,000	Magdalenian	
LATE	20,000–	Solutrean	Modern
	25,000	Gravettian	
WÜRM	30,000–	Aurignacian	Human
	32,000	Chatelperronian	
	40,000		Beings

*Times are not necessarily precise, and culture period sequence is only suggestive.

Figure 15-40   Pincevant.

The innovative Upper Paleolithic peoples developed surprisingly sophisticated cultures compared to the Neandertals. We shall briefly discuss these cultures as they developed in southwestern France, where so much archeology has been accomplished.

Chatelperronian   We may not be certain of the fate of classic Neandertals, whether they were eliminated or assimilated by, or evolved into, the ancestors of anatomically moderns, or whether they met some unimaginable end. But their Mousterian technology lingered on, at least for a time. The Chatelperronian of 32,000 years ago, the earliest of Upper Paleolithic industries, is located directly above Mousterian levels and contains numerous and varied scrapers, Mousterian points, and other evidence of Mousterian features. This period is probably a transitional one between Middle and Upper Paleolithic industries.

Aurignacian   In the Europe of 30,000 years ago, the weather becomes colder and a venturesome group of people from the central and eastern parts of Europe migrate into the culturally backward country of Western Europe. Excellent hunters (well known as Cro-Magnons), they brought with them the industry known as Aurignacian. Bone and antler, worked by splitting, sawing, and rubbing down, were the primary tool materials.

Cro-Magnons of the Aurignacian were artists and may have sculpted the female figurines, known as Venuses or mother-goddesses, which emphasize female sexual traits and could have been fertility symbols.

Aurignacian sites are more frequent and larger than those of Chatelperronians, suggesting Cro-Magnons lived in more populous groups and with good sense selected shelter in deep valleys where they would be protected from the severe cold.

Gravettian   For some reason, Aurignacian culture ebbs as another culture, the Gravettian, becomes more prominent in southern France. It begins about 25,000 years ago, a time of relatively mild climate which then becomes extremely cold.

Figure 15-41   Chatelperronian tool.

Gravettian tools continue the Chatelperronian style. Bone becomes more common as a tool material and is used for the manufacture of awls, punches, and simple points. The great art of the Upper Paleolithic, seen in Lascaux Cave, begins during this period.

Solutrean Both Gravettian and Aurignacian, two separate traditions, apparently disappear around 20,000 years ago to be replaced by the Solutrean. Who the Solutreans are and where they came from is another Upper Paleolithic mystery. Pfeiffer suggests their ancestors may have been Neandertals who had been isolated in the rugged mountain country of southeast France (Pfeiffer, 1978). It is possible they may be the Upper Paleolithic equivalent of Bigfoot, but rumors of surviving Neandertals have excited the imagination of credulous people for thousands of years.

In any case, this tradition did not endure for long, a few thousand years at most. It is best known for remarkable flintwork expressed in magnificent, pressure-flaked lanceheads.

Magdalenian The "brilliant Solutrean culture, which carried flintworking to one of its highest levels, suddenly disappeared in somewhat mysterious circumstances" (Bordes, 1968, p. 159). Replacing it is the Magdalenian, which directly overlies the Solutrean levels. Since the implements of the two traditions are so different, Solutrean representing one of the great achievements in stone-chipping and Magdalenian one of the poorest (at least at first), it is impossible the latter could have evolved from the former.

Although its origins are obscure, the Magdalenian is a spectacular period of technological growth that developed during the last major advance of the final Pleistocene glaciation. Large herds of reindeer that roamed the tundra of Western Europe are a major game animal, and mammoth, wild horse, bison, and a host of smaller animals are also hunted. It is a time of affluence; Magdalenians spread out over Europe, living in caves and open-air camps, and achieve a higher density of population than any of their predecessors.

They excel in the use of bone and antler in fashioning a variety of tools, weapons, and miscellaneous objects, which they often decorated beautifully. Upper Paleolithic art, already well advanced in Gravettian times, reaches its peak in the Magdalenian, and the cave art of this period in southwest France and northeast Spain is one of the world's great artistic achievements.

THE PROBLEM OF NEANDERTALS AND ANATOMICALLY MODERN HUMANS

With this review of the Upper Paleolithic, we are ready to address the question posed earlier: How is it possible to explain the sudden appearance of Upper Paleolithic (1) anatomically modern humans and (2) their sophisticated culture, especially in Western Europe? Both culture and anatomically moderns appear so suddenly (or so it seems) about 40,000 years ago that many scholars in the past have been reluctant to credit Neandertals with any part of the cultural achievements or genetic development of Upper Paleolithic peoples. (For further discussion see Brace, 1964.)

Actually, Upper Paleolithic moderns did not appear suddenly; there were

Figure 15-42 Venus of Willendorf.

Figure 15-43 Solutrean blade. This is the best-known work of the Solutrean tradition. Solutrean stone work is considered the best of the Upper Paleolithic.

already indications of modern traits in some of the classic Neandertals of the Würm, such as La Ferrassie, and in contemporaries, such as Qafzeh and Jebel Irhoud. Furthermore, the Upper Paleolithic populations themselves display some Neandertal traits. A recent discovery at St. Césaire, France, nicely illustrates this point. An incomplete skeleton, morphologically Neandertal both in skull and limb bones, was found in a Chatelperronian level of the Upper Paleolithic. According to Vandermeersch, this find is evidence that Neandertals did not become extinct at the end of the Middle Paleolithic. "Some of them were still extant at the beginning of the Upper Paleolithic and were contemporaneous with the first European *Homo sapiens sapiens*" (Vandermeersch, 1981, p. 286).

To account for the change from Neandertal to modern, Brace suggests that Upper Paleolithic technology reduced the adaptive significance of the huge Middle Paleolithic dentition and the facial structure that supported it (Brace and Montagu, 1977, p. 335). The result was smaller teeth, smaller jaws, and less bone for the attachment of the smaller muscles of the masticatory apparatus. Thus, the Upper Paleolithic skull.

There remains the second part of the question: Why the sudden appearance of the superior Upper Paleolithic culture? Again, we find that this appearance was *not* sudden. Early Upper Paleolithic industry (Chatelperronian) included much Mousterian (Neandertal) influence, and industries that followed were influenced to some extent by the Chatelperronian. It has also been suggested that Upper Paleolithic peoples possessed a fully articulated

Figure 15-44 Magdalenian material. During this last period of the Upper Paleolithic artistic expression reached its greatest height.

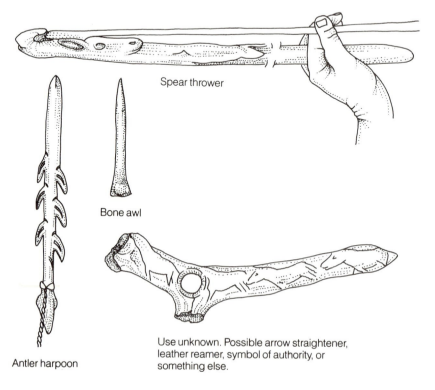

Spear thrower

Bone awl

Antler harpoon

Use unknown. Possible arrow straightener, leather reamer, symbol of authority, or something else.

Figure 15-45 Cave painting. A fine painting of a bison bellowing.

language that would have given them a decided advantage over their predecessors, who lacked this ability. However, we have already pointed out that the claim of Neandertal inability to articulate fully has been frequently disputed. Marschack (1972) believes Upper Paleolithic superiority may have been due to the people's ability to make notational counts. Keeping track of references to past and future events would be of some advantage, and it may possibly account for the rapid development of Upper Paleolithic technology, but the connection is not an easy one to perceive.

These are not fully satisfactory answers, and the problem remains unsettled.

◇ Summary

Archaic *Homo sapiens* first appear about 300,000 years ago and, possessing both *H. erectus* and *H. sapiens* traits, is considered transitional between the two forms.

Early Neandertals are present in the Eemian interglacial, followed by transitional forms apparently evolving in the direction of anatomically modern *H. sapiens* (who are definitely present in the Upper Paleolithic by about 40,000 years ago). During the early Würm glacial, Neandertals, more specialized than other *H. sapiens*, appear in Western Europe and areas of the Near East. Hominids contemporary with Neandertals are found in northwestern, eastern, and southern Africa. Several of the African forms, according to some paleoanthropologists, are considered to be anatomically modern and considerably older than the date usually given for the appearance of anatomically moderns. Questions have been raised about both their dates and their modern morphology.

Neandertals introduced technological innovations, changes in settlement patterns, and ways of obtaining food. They may have been the first humans to practice some form of religious ceremonies. Mousterian industries, associated with Neandertals of the Middle Paleolithic, are succeeded by Upper Paleolithic industries associated with anatomically modern *sapiens*. In Europe, especially, anatomically moderns are known for the variety of new tools and toolmaking techniques, new food sources, more permanent shelters, artistic achievements, and a generally more sophisticated culture.

Recent finds in Australia suggest movements of gracile moderns from Indonesia as early as 35,000 years ago. The problem of entrance of human populations into the New World remains unsolved.

Several questions are raised in this chapter: What is the phylogenetic line from *H. erectus* to *H. sapiens sapiens*? Was this transition rapid (punctuated equilibrium) or gradual? What is the role of classic Neandertals in the evolution of anatomically modern humans? Is there a relationship between Africans believed to be anatomically modern and Upper Paleolithic populations of Europe? Did anatomically moderns migrate to Europe and displace, in some fashion, the Neandertals? How is Upper Paleolithic technology related to that of the Middle Paleolithic?

Possible solutions to most of these questions have been suggested. Unfortunately, however, entirely satisfactory answers are still unavailable.

◇ Questions for Review

1. Define "transitional forms."
2. List the physical traits that characterize *Homo sapiens*.
3. Why are Steinheim, Swanscombe, and Arago considered transitional?
4. How do Neandertals differ from *H. erectus* on the one hand and anatomically modern humans on the other?
5. What are the differences between the pre-*sapiens*, pre-Neandertal, and the Neandertal phase of man hypotheses?
6. What does the evidence of the Eemian interglacial tell us about human evolution?
7. What is the "Neandertal problem"?
8. Why is La Chapelle-aux-Saints considered an important fossil?
9. Describe Mousterian culture.
10. What does the evidence suggest for the intellectual (including communication) ability of Neandertals?
11. What is meant by contemporary forms?
12. Describe the variation of physical characteristics of Upper Paleolithic peoples.
13. What technological innovations were introduced in the Upper Paleolithic?
14. Summarize the development of culture from the Chatelperronian to the end of the Upper Paleolithic.
15. How may the "sudden" appearance of anatomically modern humans and the rich Upper Paleolithic culture be explained?

Post-Pleistocene Adaptations in the Old World

CONTENTS

Stonehenge is probably the best known archeological site in the world. As a British tourist attraction, it ranks second only to the Tower of London. Yet, the only thing about Stonehenge that people can agree on is its location on the Salisbury Plain, Wiltshire, in southcentral England.

Stonehenge is the most elaborate of the surviving prehistoric stone circle sites. Stone circles, in turn, are the most complex form of ancient megalithic (or large stone) construction, the others being single standing stones, stone alignments, and burial chambers. Stone circles are confined to Great Britain, whereas the other styles are common throughout western Europe.

There is more to Stonehenge than simply a ring of large stones. Jacquetta Hawkes has characterized it as a "composite structure," built in three phases between 2800 and 1100 B.C. The monument comprises a circular earthen embankment of 320 feet in diameter, within which a circle of 56 small pits encloses 2 semicircular arrangements of larger pits. The dominant central features of the site are its two circles of large standing stones and two horseshoe-shaped stone arrangements. The larger stone circle and horseshoe are formed of immense sandstone blocks having an average weight of 28 tons and a length of up to 30 feet. These stones were obtained from Marlborough Downs, at a distance of 15 to 20 miles. Though smaller in scale, the inner circle and horseshoe are even more intriguing. Their stones, weighing about 8,000 pounds apiece, were derived from the Presely Mountains in Wales, at a distance of some 300 miles by the shortest practical land and water route. One estimate places the cost of building Stonehenge at 30 million work-hours.

How were these stones quarried, transported, and set into place without benefit of metal tools? What people designed and erected the monument? And, the greatest mystery of all: Why was Stonehenge built?

Stonehenge today guards her secrets closely. One might almost say there is a "stony silence" about the place. Not that there has been any lack of speculation applied to all these questions. Even in medieval times, Stonehenge was an object of fascination. Geoffrey of Monmouth, a twelfth-century chronicler, maintained that the monument was built by Merlin the Magician as a tomb for the father of King Arthur. Through the ages, alternate views have favored giants, dwarfs, Atlanteans, and extra-terrestrials as the architects of Stonehenge. In his recent book *Megalithomania*, John Michell cites some of the other groups who have at various times received credit: Phoenicians, Romans, Danes, Saxons, Celts, aboriginal Britons, Brahmins, Egyptians, Chaldeans, and even American Indians.

The most persistent association, however, is the Druid connection. More than 2000 years ago, Julius Caesar described Druid priests in Britain and noted their interest in astronomy and divination. While Caesar's account does not mention Stonehenge, the temptation to view the monument as a Druidical observatory has proven irresistible to some. John Aubrey, a seventeenth-century Stonehenge researcher, was the first modern writer to make the case, and the idea gained currency in the subsequent 200 years. In the late nineteenth century, the Druid hypothesis temporarily lost ground as scientific excavations at monuments like Stonehenge seemed to promise the ultimate answers. But, to quote John

Michell's assessment of decades of archeological work on the megalithic sites, "the sum total of all their labours has contributed scarcely at all to resolving the problem obviously presented by the substantial presence of the megalithic monuments, the problem of why they were built."

Since the mid-1960s, a different approach to solving the riddle has gained followers. Researchers calling themselves "archeoastronomers" are endeavoring to prove that prehistoric societies in many parts of the world had the interest and capacity to make careful observations of major heavenly bodies. The information these ancients gathered was then applied to practical purposes that ranged from planting to prophecy. Stonehenge seemed to be a fruitful site for archeoastronomers, since there is little question that its builders aligned it with the position of the midsummer sunrise.

Astronomer Gerald Hawkins, whose book *Stonehenge Decoded* helped launch the study of archeoastronomy, believes that the site is literally a Stone-Age computer. He argues that the stones provided sight lines for precisely calculating important solar, lunar, and planetary

events. Alexander Thom, a retired Oxford engineering professor, is likewise convinced that many of the megalithic constructions found throughout the British Isles were used for similar purposes. His careful surveys suggest that distant uprights were often linked by lines of sight to form a network of astronomical observation points.

Some archeologists, such as Glyn Daniel, an eminent authority on megaliths, are not so sure. Daniel finds archeoastronomy "an all too clear demonstration of the imagination, wishful thinking and credulousness of many authors, and the abysmal ignorance of many alleged archeologists who can only be described, if uncharitably, as fantasy buffs." The case for ancient astronomers, he maintains, "has never been proved." Christopher Chippindale considers recent enthusiasm for the idea of Stonehenge as a computer/observatory to be merely another "scientific myth devised in a scientific age."

While he is unsympathetic to the hard-line position taken by these archeologists, John Mitchell cautions that even the archeoastronomers may not have all the answers. "Anyone who pretends to have 'decoded'

Stonehenge has seriously underestimated the magnitude of that task and the quality of learning, imagination and understanding that would be required to accomplish it." Stonehenge and other megalithic sites may "touch on such fundamental matters as the origins of human culture and the first principles behind the development of modern civilization and science."

SOURCES:

Chippindale, Christopher. "Stonehenge Astronomy: Anatomy of a Modern Myth," *Archaeology*, 39:1, 48–52, January, 1986.

Daniel, Glyn. "Megalithic Monuments," *Scientific American*, 243:15, 78–81, July, 1980.

Hawkes, Jacquetta. "Stonehenge," *Scientific American*, 188:14, 25–31, June, 1953.

Hawkins, Gerald. *Stonehenge Decoded*, New York: Souvenir Press, 1966.

Michell, John. *Megalithomania*, Ithaca, N.Y.: Cornell University Press, 1982.

Renfrew, Colin. "The Social Archaeology of Megalithic Monuments," *Scientific American*, 249:5, 152–163, May, 1983.

Thom, Alexander. *Megalithic Sites in Britain*, Oxford: Oxford University Press, 1967.

◇ CHAPTER SIXTEEN

◇ Introduction

Scientists have dated the end of the Pleistocene or Ice Age period to around 10,000 years ago. Few climatologists or geologists are really convinced that large-scale glaciation will never occur again, but all will agree that many major changes took place after the most recent glacial period. In recognizing these developments, they use the term *Holocene* to designate the Recent, or postglacial, period.

During the early phases of the Holocene, the climate continued to warm slowly, until only the polar regions and Greenland today have permanent ice sheets. Land areas formerly covered by ice became available for colonization by plants, animals, and *Homo sapiens sapiens*. As meltwater returned to the seas, some coastlines were inundated to a depth of 100 meters or more (over 300 feet). In other areas, the flooding was offset by the uplift of land that had been compressed under the ice masses. These transformations most directly affected the middle latitudes, including northern and central Europe and North America. The major climatic and topographic shifts were sufficient to alter conditions of life for flora and fauna, presenting new opportunities for some species while forcing others to extinction. In northwestern Europe, for example, as forests expanded across the open landscape, red deer, elk, and **aurochs** replaced the reindeer, horse, and bison of Pleistocene times. Anatomically modern people, armed with more efficient tools and weapons, also contributed to the success or decline of various species as they ranged into new regions.

Food collecting, along with specialized hunting (now supplemented by an increased exploitation of fish and shellfish), persisted during the Holocene period in northern latitudes as the primary subsistence economy. This pattern formed the basis of the **Mesolithic** way of life. In more temperate zones to the south, post-Pleistocene human adaptations soon included some preliminary farming activities, which ultimately resulted in the domestication of selected plant and animal species. In these areas, and later in some adjoining regions as well, Mesolithic foraging yielded to **Neolithic** lifeways based on the new food-producing strategies and other technological innovations. A secure economic base in some instances permitted further cultural elaboration and expansion, giving rise to the early civilizations found in Mesopotamia, Egypt, the Indus valley, northern China, and the Mediterranean world. Of course, more conservative cultures persisted in marginal areas until much later times.

◇ Mesolithic Hunter-Fisher-Gatherers

The environmental changes of the Pleistocene/Holocene transition were associated with a number of cultural changes that are represented in the archeological record. Major portions of northern Europe had undergone radical climatic, biological, and even topographic alterations. New economic patterns and technologies aided people in adjusting to their changing world.

Mesolithic is the term used to characterize those cultures in which an intensive hunting, fishing, and gathering routine served as an adaptation to post-Pleistocene conditions. The relative importance of each of these activities varied from region to region, and even from season to season within any given area. It is the fact that people were obtaining their primary subsistence from a wide variety of localized resources, rather than from a small number of wide-ranging species, which is of importance here. The Mesolithic focus on new kinds of food resources, particularly more plants, fish, and shellfish, corresponds to a de-emphasis on large game after the end of the Pleistocene. Many of the former prey animals were already extinct, and the accompanying habitat changes and the behavioral differences of some of the replacement species probably adversely affected the hunters' success. Moreover, foraging presents high prospects for good returns, especially since anyone—young or old, male or female, experienced or not—may participate and so contribute to the general food supply. These varied resources were obtained most effi-

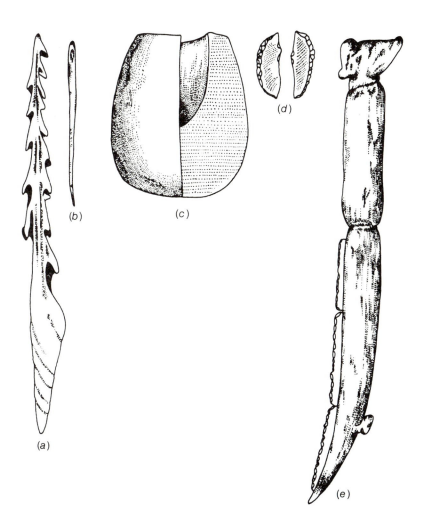

Figure 16-1 Mesolithic tool kit. (*a*) Barbed bone harpoon head; (*b*) bone needle; (*c*) stone mortar, showing section; (*d*) two views of flint knife; (*e*) horn reaping knife with inset flint blades.

Composite
Made of several parts.

Weir
(weer)
A brush or stone obstruction for trapping fish.

Nomadism
Lifeway of wandering in search of food.

Midden
A refuse heap marking a Mesolithic campsite.

Burin
A chisel-ended stone blade used for working bone and antler.

ciently with the invention and use of new weapons and tools, many of them manufactured from raw materials not previously used to any great extent. Mesolithic people commonly crafted not only stone, but also bone and antler, leather, bark, and other plant materials into new kinds of implements. Many of these items were much more sophisticated than the tools of the Ice Age hunters. **Composite** weapons, made up of several elements, were in wide use by the early Mesolithic period of some nine or ten thousand years ago. The bow and arrow and the harpoon are good examples. Each is comprised of a blade or point, a foreshaft, main shaft, bindings, and other parts, all expertly combined into an efficient weapon system.

With the spread of forests in the mid-latitudes, wood became more generally available. It replaced bones and tallow and dung as the primary fuel, and it also served as a useful raw material for making dugout canoes, house posts, weapons, bowls, and smaller items. The tough antlers of the red deer or elk were used as picks in quarrying flint for chipped and polished stone tools. Some of the new technologies were adapted to the exploitation of new resources. Nets, woven basketry traps, and cleverly contructed stone or brushwood **weirs** (or fish-dams), placed across the mouths of small tidal streams, enabled people to obtain large quantities of fish. Shellfish beds offered an abundance of easily obtained food as well. The honey of wild bees was a prize obtained from hollow trees with the aid of axes and containers.

Given the increased environmental complexity in the mid-latitudes, usually including a wider diversity of potentially exploitable plant and animal species, Mesolithic foragers faced a somewhat different prospect than their Pleistocene predecessors. In addition to more specific-purpose tools, they also required an intimate knowledge of their local environment and its assets in order to predict when each resource should have reached its period of highest productivity or desirability. Then, by making a conscious and well-formed decision, the people could schedule their movements so as to appear on the scene at the proper time to take fullest advantage of that particular resource at its peak. This concept of "seasonality and scheduling" is a key to understanding the success of Mesolithic peoples. The often misused term **nomadism**—a more or less random wandering existence—cannot properly be applied to most hunting-gathering groups.

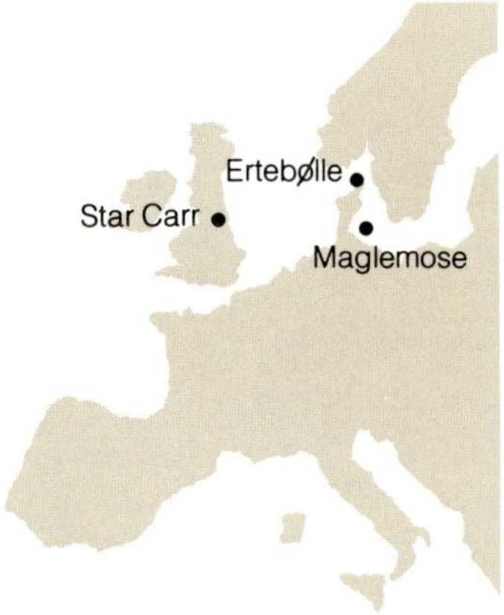

Variety of Mesolithic Adaptations

Northern Europe   The northern fringes of Europe must have presented great challenges to the people who tried to maintain themselves as hunters and foragers. Following the withdrawal of the continental ice, much of the depressed land surface of northern Europe was inundated by the rising water that created today's North and Baltic seas. The gently sloping plains that formed the broad shores of these shallow seas were covered at first by grasses, but forests took over as the climate continued to warm. As grazing animals were displaced, human populations must have dwindled. Only those cultures that were prepared to adapt by utilizing the less obvious resources could have been successful. Sites such as Star Carr, near Scarborough in Yorkshire, England, and Maglemose, near Copenhagen, Denmark, are well-known examples of Mesolithic campsites (Clark, 1972, 1979). These and other locations show us that people were using stone axes and adzes to fell trees and to

Figure 16-2   Mesolithic sites of northern Europe.

make useful objects from their wood. The bow had been developed by the end of the Ice Age as an effective weapon for hunting, and the domesticated dog was in use at Star Carr by at least 9500 y.a. Along the coasts of northern Europe, the British Isles, and even the Mediterranean, people were turning to the collection of shellfish as a productive food source. The Mesolithic Ertebølle culture of northern Denmark is well known for its huge shellheaps, called **middens.** But the countless shells piled along these shores should not disguise the fact that one red deer carcass may represent the caloric equivalent of 50,000 oysters (Bailey, 1975). Shellfish rarely contributed as much as 10 percent of the Mesolithic diet.

Star Carr is a key archeological site that has provided many clues to understanding the habitat and economy of northern Mesolithic peoples. Excavated by the British prehistorian Graham Clark and collaborators some thirty years ago, the site still represents a milestone in archeological technique and interpretation.

The Star Carr settlement area covered about 200 square meters, which was large enough to accommodate perhaps fifteen to twenty individuals. Hunting appears to have been their primary activity, with red deer, elk, wild ox, and roe deer serving as the major prey. Many animals were hunted with long arrows tipped by *microliths*—small flint blades of geometric shape—which were set into slots along the end of the shaft and then held in place by resin. Barbed bone and antler spear points, butchering implements, and stone **burin** blades for working antler were among the other common artifacts (Clark, 1972).

The stage of antler development of the animals killed for food revealed that Star Carr was occupied for only part of the year. Since deer grow and shed their antlers annually, on a species-specific cycle, it was possible to determine

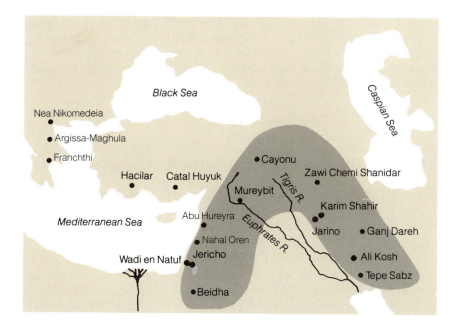

Figure 16-3 Mesolithic and early Neolithic sites in the "Fertile Crescent" and the eastern Mediterranean.

that the animals had been killed from about late fall to early spring. During the remainder of the year, the hunters apparently exploited upland territories at some distance from Star Carr and the moors.

Southwest Asia   Star Carr and other Maglemosian sites of northern Europe represent the most dramatic phase of the Mesolithic, since people in these areas had to devise new lifeways in order to adapt to the significant postglacial changes. But farther south, in central and southern Europe and Asia Minor, other peoples found themselves in less marginal circumstances. For example, residents at the Mesolithic cave site of Franchthi on the southern tip of Greece exploited a rich assortment of species ranging from large mammals (wild horses, deer, pigs, and goats), to fish and shellfish, and a number of prominent plant resources (among them wild barley and oats, three kinds of legumes, and two species of nuts). Several of these resources may already have been coming under human control before 8000 y.a. at this site (Dennell, 1983). Likewise, the Natufian culture of southwestern Asia, which was roughly contemporary with the northern European foragers of about 9500 y.a., was making use of a wealth of local resources, including herds of gazelle and lush stands of wild seed-grasses (Redman, 1978). Their residence in small clusters of semipermanent pit houses with stone foundations and their nearby cemeteries, like those excavated at Nahal Oren in Israel and Abu Hureyra in Syria, indicate that they were able to rely upon local species with little need of moving from place to place. Horn sickles with inset flint blades and an abundance of grinding stones and mortars testify to the importance of wild grains in the Natufian diet. Bone and stone points and bone fish hooks demonstrate the diversity of Natufian subsistence activities. By about 9000 y.a., a number of the people in this region were already preserving both plant and animal domestication.

In summary, the Mesolithic period was a time of economic and cultural transformation from the Paleolithic hunting stage to the food-producing Neolithic stage. But if we consider the Mesolithic foragers to be transitional between Paleolithic hunters and Neolithic farmers, then we must also indicate that only the more southerly of the Mesolithic cultures actually effected this transition. Those in the northern latitudes long remained marginal to the process, although they are of interest to us because of their specialized adaptation to a difficult environment.

◇ The "Neolithic Revolution" and Its Consequences

A famous European archeologist, V. Gordon Childe, proposed the term "Neolithic Revolution" to express the fundamental importance of food production in human history. While we now recognize that Neolithic lifeways did not develop and spread rapidly from a single Near Eastern center, as Childe apparently believed, we should acknowledge that the Neolithic was truly revolutionary in a broader sense. The emergence of food production eventually transformed most of the world's cultures, and, in the process, prompted changes in the natural world as well.

The Neolithic revolution, as it is now recognized, consists of at least three dimensions: domestication, new settlement patterns, and new technologies.

Why Did Domestication Occur?

Domestication refers to an interdependency between humans and one or more selected plant or animal species. Archeologists had once hoped to locate the very site where some genius had first planted a seed or harnessed an animal. Today, we understand that domestication is really a process, not an event. How the process was initiated is a matter for debate. There have been several important approaches to this question. However, we may safely assume that people had observed the role of the seed in plant reproduction long before they turned to farming as a way of life.

Environmental Explanation   Childe himself proposed the idea that a radical climatic shift occurred at the end of the Ice Age, resulting in increased rainfall for Europe and widespread dessication throughout southwestern Asia and North Africa (Childe, 1952). Humans, animals, and plants in these latter areas found themselves forced to congregate in the relatively small areas where permanent water existed. In these oases, intensive interaction among humans and certain other species resulted in the domestication of some of them, including wheat, barley, sheep, and goats. Today, the oasis theory of domestication, along with environmental determinism in general, is not very popular. Moreover, climate experts argue that the climatic changes hypothesized by Childe did not actually occur.

Demographic Explanation   Another viewpoint on the origins of domestication suggests that societies finally committed themselves to farming only when no other alternatives appeared sufficient to feed a human population that had outgrown the capacity of its environment (Boserup, 1965). For example, the failure of a once-reliable natural resource, or, alternatively, the movement of the group into a marginal area, might have stimulated foragers to take up farming or herding activities to enhance the productivity of their environment. Such experiments would most likely be successful in areas where potential domesticates naturally occurred.

Marginal Zone Hypothesis   The emphasis on population pressures as the stimulus for agriculture spurred Lewis Binford (1968) to devise a model that incorporated this concept. Looking back at the situation in the Near East after about 10,000 B.C., Binford speculated that (a) humans had moved into almost every available ecological niche, and (b) the population had reached a state of equilibrium with the environment. In other words, the environmental niche was filled. Expansion of the population would have been possible only in the marginal zones on the frontiers of the optimal areas. Since even these areas were already occupied (probably by semisedentary hunter-gatherers), a zone of tension was established. In order to compete, according to Kent Flannery (1973), the incoming population may have attempted to artificially reproduce the stands of wild cereal grasses they knew from their previous home. Likewise, the original inhabitants may have been compelled to try new ways of obtaining sufficient food.

Symbiosis
syn: together
bios: life
Mutually advantageous association of two
different organisms.

Rachis
The stem of a plant, to which individual
seeds attach.

Symbiosis and Domestication   The preceding theories attempt to explain why domestication occurred, without addressing the issue of how it may have occurred. Domestication involves a changing relationship between humans and selected plant and/or animal species. This relationship may be characterized by the word **symbiosis**, meaning a mutually beneficial association between individuals of different species. For example, we now know that the domestication of many plants involved genetically based biological changes that ultimately made the species more useful to people, while often and at the same time resulting in the plant's increased dependency on human intervention in dispersing its seeds (Rindos, 1984). In the case of wheat, the domesticated plants average more grains per head than their wild relatives, and the **rachis**, or stem, which attaches the seed to the stalk, is less brittle in the domesticated variety. While the tough rachis makes it easier for people to harvest the grain with less loss, the plant is unable to scatter its own seed. In the same way, we find that individual seed coats or husks become less tough. Also, over time, the plants eventually became adapted to new environments well beyond their ancestral range. Such changes may have resulted from long-term pressure by human gatherers, who consistently selected for those traits that improved the plant's productivity and quality, but they may also have resulted without any conscious tampering (Flannery, 1973).

Archeological Evidence for Domestication

Although ancient plant remains are uncommon on archeological sites, evidence of domestic grains may be preserved in several ways. Sometimes the charred kernels themselves are found, but more often they are represented only by the impressions of individual seeds that once adhered to wet plaster, mud brick, or pottery surfaces. Generally, domesticated grains average larger in size than their wild progenitors, and may show other morphological differences as well. Such evidence seems to show that plant domestication took place in several regions at about the same time, including Southwest Asia, Southeast Asia, and Mexico and Peru in the New World. The suggestion that the idea derived from a single center is dramatic but not supported by any evidence. On the contrary, most of the involved species differ from area to area, and the process of domestication itself requires substantial changes, which must have occurred over a fairly long transitional period.

It is more appropriate to examine the issue of concurrent domestication from a cultural and ecological standpoint. Within several thousand years after the close of the Pleistocene ice ages, when modern climatic and biotic conditions had become established, people were already using a relatively advanced Upper Paleolithic or Mesolithic technology to exploit those species they encountered in local econiches. Gathering seeds may have become a more efficient and intensive activity than ever before, given the use of the special sickles, basketry containers, and substantial processing tools we associate with such cultures. Under these conditions, people may have begun to have a greater impact on the species they were exploiting, so that the kinds of changes outlined above soon developed. It should then be no surprise to find evidence of plant domestication in widely scattered locations.

The precise course of plant domestication may never be fully traced, given the scarcity of ancient plant specimens. Most likely, the process was not only

◇ Box 16-1   Against the Grain

Archeologists have long acknowledged that several areas of the Near East exhibit some of the earliest evidence for agriculture. But few were prepared for the announcement of *Late Paleolithic* plant domestication in the Nile Valley! Fred Wendorf and Romuald Schild, excavating prehistoric fishing camps in Wadi Kubbaniya (not far from Aswan, Egypt) in 1978 discovered a buried hearth containing several carbonized grains of barley and einkorn wheat. When numerous charcoal samples from the hearth were radiocarbon dated to between 17,000 and 18,500 y.a., the associated grains suddenly took on great significance. Another kernel found on the living floor, and still more barley discovered on a comparable site nearby in 1981, increased the researchers' confidence. The barley was a six-row variety, apparently a domesticate. An abundance of milling stones further supported the idea that the site's ancient inhabitants had made use of domesticated cereals more than 9000 years earlier than their first known appearance elsewhere.

   People probably had been attracted to Wadi Kubbaniya because it was an area where huge Nile catfish might become stranded in low water adjacent to the river after each year's inundation. The excavators reasoned that grain seeds were deliberately planted in the wet mud at the conclusion of the fishing season, as the pools began to dry up. Months later, the people would return to the same camps to hunt waterfowl and harvest their crops.

   To put their theories to the test, the archeologists made use of recent advances in radiocarbon-dating techniques, which require only minute samples for analysis. Now, the tiny cereal grains themselves could be submitted for direct dating. If their ages matched that of the hearth from which they were recovered, then the idea of early Nile Valley fisher-farmers would be difficult to dismiss.

   But the outcome did not favor this scenario. On the contrary, the application of improved dating methods

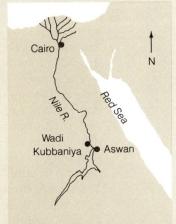

Figure 1   Location of Wadi Kubbaniya.

Figure 2   Carbonized barley from Wadi Kubbaniya, Egypt.

brought results favorable to the more conservative and generally accepted view of a post-Pleistocene Neolithic adaptation in the region. Though varied (presumably because of contamination from substances applied to the kernels in earlier laboratory studies), the carbon dates for the Wadi Kubbaniya grains suggest an age of less than 5000 years. In other words, the seeds must have gotten into the older levels of the site long after its abandonment by the mobile fishing people who had lived there some 18,000 y.a. What about the milling stones? The researchers now assume they were used to process starchy wild tubers that grew plentifully along the banks of the Nile.

SOURCES:
Wendorf, Fred, and Romuald Schild. "The Earliest Food Producers," *Archaeology*, 34(5):30–36, 1981.
——— et al. "New Radiocarbon Dates on the Cereals from Wadi Kubbaniya," *Science*, 225:645–646, 1984.

lengthy but somewhat casual as well. Since at least the last ice age, people were utilizing a number of plant and animal resources that eventually emerged as domesticates. In the case of cereal grains, for instance, it would be difficult to decide when harvesting activities may have extended to the scattering of selected wild seeds in new environments. These activities could have induced genetic changes in the plants due to selection and isolation from other plants of the same species, and perhaps even stimulated further environmental and human behavioral modifications. From there, the steps to full domestication would have been small ones.

Animal domestication in the Old World involved many economically and technologically important species. The cultures of Asia, Europe, and Africa domesticated and came to rely heavily upon a large number of animals. Even those that may have been most important for food usually had additional value as sources of manure, leather, horn, or even social status. Some animals conveyed tremendous technological advantages to their owners' culture, including traction, transportation, or power for milling grain. Conversely, the few animal species domesticated by the New World's native inhabitants—llama, guinea pigs, and fowls—were of relatively minor importance beyond their localized distribution.

The process of animal domestication differed from plant domestication to a certain extent, and probably varied even from one species to another. The dog appears to have been our first domesticated animal and may have accompanied hunters even during the Ice Age. Its relationship with humans differed (and still does) from that of most subsequently domesticated species. Less important for its meat or hide, the dog's oldest role was as a ferocious hunting weapon under at least a modicum of human control and direction. These early hunting dogs probably extracted substantial payments of fresh meat before their human allies succeeded in retrieving the carcass. As other animals were domesticated, the dog's behavior had to be further curbed for service as a herder, and later even as an occasional form of transportation among such people as the American Plains Indians. In return, the tamer canids of later times were extended the privilege of scavenging for scraps and other camp waste.

Of course, animals are more mobile than plants, and may have been no less so than the early people who exploited them. Therefore, it is unlikely that hunters could have induced useful genetic changes in wild animals

Table 16-1 Early Cereal Production and Animal Husbandry*

		Barley	Einkorn	Emmer	Bread-wheat	Sheep	Goats	Cattle	Pigs
The Aegean									
Argissa	8500 y.a.	+	+	+		+	+	+	+
Knossos	8100 y.a.	+		+	+			+	
Anatolia									
Hacilar	9000–7000 y.a.	+	+	+	+				
Levant									
Tell Ramad	9000 y.a.	+	+	+	+				
Jericho	9000–7500 y.a.	+	+	+					
Deh Luran									
Ali Kosh	8750–8000 y.a.	+	+	+		+	+	+	
Tepe Sabz	7500–7000 y.a.	+			+	+	+	+	
Kurdistan									
Karim Shahir	10,900 y.a.					+			
Jarmo	8750–8500 y.a.		+	+		+	+		+
									(also dogs)

*Blank spaces indicate that the grain or animal in question was not present.

SOURCE: Personal communication, Robert Redden.

merely by stocking them in new environments or by selective hunting alone. Animals such as gazelle or reindeer might be managed to a degree even in the wild state, perhaps by establishing a "rapport" with the herds and encouraging them to graze in harvested areas in the winter, or perhaps by restricting hunting activities to a few quick raids, during which the herd might be selectively harvested or thinned. There is evidence in the Near East that wild sheep, goats, and gazelle were being managed in this manner some eight or nine thousand years ago. The gazelle never achieved complete domestication. Nor are reindeer herds in Lapland even today really comprised of truly domesticated or even fully "tame" animals. The herds and herders exist in a state of mutual toleration and interdependency.

Full domestication, involving dramatic genetic changes, might be reached only by more direct steps. To attain this degree of domestication in animals such as cattle, sheep, goats, pigs, horses, or camels, people would have to first restrain the animals somewhat or maintain them in captivity and then selectively breed for those traits deemed most useful or desirable, such as meat, fat, milk or wool production, strength, speed. This process might begin with young animals spared by hunters for that purpose. Captive animals not suitable for breeding represent meat on the hoof, a convenient method of storing food against spoilage or future want.

Archeological evidence for animal domestication is difficult to assess. In most species there seems to have been no significant increase in body size. Attempts have been made to compare the bone structure and allometric proportions of wild and domestic members of the same species, with some apparent success (Herre, 1969). Other persuasive arguments have been based on observed changes in herd demography. For example, an increase in the number of skeletal elements from mature rams may indicate that humans had an opportunity to deliberately select these animals for slaughter, while reserving most females and young for breeding purposes (Bökönyi, 1969). The population curve for animals hunted from a wild population would more likely reflect a normal distribution, with more equal age and sexual representation. None of these indicators is definitive, however, and large samples of faunal remains must be studied to verify domestication.

Again, we should emphasize that domestication is not an event, but a process. As such, it is nearly impossible to say precisely when a species has become domesticated, for the process involves much more than an indication of "tameness" in the presence of humans. Of much greater significance are the changes in gene frequences that result from selective breeding and long isolation from wild relatives. Once people consistently select seed or breeding stock according to some desirable trait (size, hardiness, fecundity, etc.) and succeed in perpetuating those characteristics through succeeding generations, then domestication has clearly occurred. These "artificial" (as opposed to "natural") selection pressures constitute an evolutionary force in their own right. The rate of divergent evolution from the wild ancestral forms of the species accelerates as humans continue to exercise control. Moreover, we should acknowledge that, because of the interdependent relationship inherent in domestication, humans also sustained major changes in their culture and behavior—and even in their biology—as a result of resource domestication. Those consequences are what the term "Neolithic Revolution" should connote.

Most domesticated animals were maintained solely for their meat at first. Richard J. Harrison's insightful analysis of faunal collections from Neolithic sites in Spain and Portugal concludes that meat remained the primary product only until about 4000 y.a., when subsequent changes in herd composition (age and sex ratios), slaughter patterns, and popularity of certain breeds all point to new uses for some livestock (Harrison, 1985). Oxen pulled plows, horses provided transport, cattle and goats contributed milk products, and sheep were bred for wool. Animal waste, too, became a valued fertilizer in agricultural areas.

Consequences of Food Production

Domestication and food production were the driving forces of the Neolithic revolution, but the consequences were much more far-reaching. Once food production was established as a reliable subsistence base, many other changes followed.

Increased Population Density and Permanent Settlements   Population size and density both tended to increase as farming activities began to produce large and steady yields. People often clustered in more permanent villages and towns, surrounded by their fields and pastures. A number of early Neolithic settlements, such as Jericho in the Jordan river valley and Catal Hüyük in Turkey, attained considerable size.

New Technologies   Changes in material culture accompanied food production and the development of permanent settlements. For example, Neolithic people soon replaced most of their basketry and skin containers with bulkier but more versatile ceramic vessels. They used looms to weave cloth from wool and plant fibers. Some items, such as grinding **querns** and axeheads, were still being made from stone, but with greater care and crafting. (Early archeologists considered polished stone tools to be the hallmark of this era, hence the term *Neolithic*—"new stone.") The use of copper increased as people found ways to refine and process the ore into a variety of implements and ornaments. Specialized tasks of this type required the attention of full-time craftsworkers, who could exchange the products of their skill for food produced by others. As agricultural techniques and the resulting harvests continued to improve, still other segments of the population could be relieved of the obligation of producing food in order to fill roles as priests, merchants, administrators, and the like.

New Economic and Social Relations   Food surplus in the form of stored grain or herds of animals served as a kind of capital that allowed for new kinds of economic transactions. Barter and exchange were promoted, as was credit, or lending against future productivity. The necessity of keeping accurate accounts inspired some of the earliest forms of writing, which sometimes have been preserved on baked clay tablets. Because land itself was the source of potential capital, its possession became the basis for a new social order that distinguished between landowners and tenants. A social and economic hierarchy consisting of productive peasants, nonfarming specialists of many kinds, and an elite frequently emerged. In many early societies, all or much of the arable land was reserved for the king or royal family. It was worked by the peasants, but the produce was collected and later redistributed to all elements of the society, although usually in proportions that varied according to social rank rather than need alone.

New Views of Environment   Unlike hunters and gatherers, who extract their livelihood from the available natural resources, Neolithic farmers found it necessary to alter their environment by removing existing species and substituting their own domesticated plants and animals. Plowing, terracing, and digging irrigation ditches were other Neolithic activities that contributed to deforestation, erosion, and the decline of many native species.

Development of Science and Religion   Disciplines such as botany, zoology, astronomy, meteorology, and mathematics can probably trace their origins back to attempts by Neolithic peoples to improve their agricultural techniques, to predict or ameliorate the weather, and to divide land. Most of these early "sciences" were undoubtedly understood and practiced by a select group of priestly specialists.

Promotion of Culture Change   We should also consider that Neolithic societies had a tremendous impact on other cultures. In seeking new farmlands to feed ever-increasing populations, they often overwhelmed nearby hunting and gathering groups. They involved other societies in exchange networks, whereby the surplus products of agriculture, animal husbandry, or the new technologies were traded for raw materials, wild produce, and even slaves. Exchange and communication among Neolithic societies and between them and their non-Neolithic neighbors promoted a great deal of culture change.

Not all the consequences of food production were beneficial. We noted above that rapid environmental degradation accompanied many Neolithic activities, resulting in deforestation, soil loss, and silted streams. Some areas associated with early farming societies were so damaged that they remained unproductive thousands of years later. One example is the lower Tigris-Euphrates valley, where high levels of soluble salts carried by irrigation waters poisoned the soil. People experienced negative effects as well. Hunter-gatherer societies were often displaced or even eradicated altogether as a result of habitat changes and direct competition from farmers. Neolithic diets tended to be starchy and lacking in protein, resulting in decreased stature, increased dental disease, and susceptibility to other nutritional disorders. Outright starvation was the not infrequent result of crop failures due to drought, blight, or insects. Farmers' long-term settlement in one location brought about overcrowding, poor sanitation, and a host of epidemic diseases. And, agricultural activities often required long periods of hard labor! Clearly, as an adaptive mechanism, the Neolithic way of life has been a mixed blessing for humankind, one that promoted a dramatic worldwide population explosion at the cost of many environmental and health-related problems.

Examples of Early Neolithic Cultures

Near Eastern Farmers   Charles A. Reed has noted that "the first postglacial period of environmental change following the evolution of anatomically modern man (*Homo sapiens sapiens*) was accompanied by, or followed shortly by, the appearance of agriculture in several areas on several continents" (Reed, 1977, p. 941).

In the Near East, the transition to agriculture may have been accomplished slowly, perhaps even reluctantly, among hunting-gathering cultures such as the Natufians, whom we met previously. Their use of stone-bladed sickles by some 12,000 y.a. suggests a greater efficiency in gathering wild grass seeds, including the ancestral forms of wheat and barley that were native to the region. Improved efficiency may have promoted better yields, which in turn may have resulted in greater reliance upon seed supplies that could be stored for weeks or months after the short harvest period. Stone- or clay-lined pits or "silos" appear on Natufian sites by about 9500 y.a. and are accompanied by more substantial stone-based houses that seem to indicate longer residence in one area. The process of genetic selection that we considered as a possible explanation of domestication itself may have gotten under way at this juncture.

According to evidence that has been accumulating in the Near East, wheat and barley were domesticated first, with sheep and goats being the earliest domesticated herd animals, probably followed by pigs, then cattle and camels (Reed, 1977). By about 9000 y.a., agriculture and herding were well established in a broad arc across the Near East, from the Red Sea to western Iran. Neolithic villages or towns had already sprung up throughout this region. Among them is Ali Kosh on the Deh Luran plain of Iran. Early Neolithic people here grew several varieties of wheat, barley, and lentils, and herded sheep and goats. Yet, the seeds of wild cereals, fruits, nuts, and the meat of wild game continued to make up about two-thirds of their diet even after domesticated resources were available (Flannery, 1971). Similar proportions of wild and cultivated species are common in early Neolithic sites of many areas.

Asian and African Farmers   A long history of archeological research in the Near East has produced an impressive and detailed account of agricultural development. While much less complete, archeological data from several areas of the Far East indicate that several independent Neolithic societies were emerging there at about the same time. Because the domesticates were native to Asia, it has been reasoned that, at least initially, there was no stimulation from Near Eastern centers.

Southeast Asian sites have produced some tantalizing but very fragmentary evidence for early farming practices. Wilhelm Solheim, citing remarkable finds made by the late Chester Gorman at Spirit Cave, Thailand, claims that farmers in that area had domesticated bottle gourds, cucumbers, water chestnuts, and various legumes by as early as 14,000 y.a. (Solheim, 1972). Other archeologists, however, remain skeptical of this chronology and are unconvinced that the recovered plant remains represent true domesticates. More persuasive data exist for early rice farming in Southeast Asia. The initial stages of rice agriculture seem to be represented at two other northern Thailand localities, Ban Chiang and Non Nok Tha. Here, domesticated plant remains may date back to 6000 y.a. (Reed, 1977).

Available data from China suggest the existence of an early farming phase in the Huang Ho (or Yellow River) valley at about the same period. Farmers here selected well-drained locations for their fields of **millet**, a small-seeded but productive cereal grass native to the region. Domesticated pigs and dogs are also represented at these sites (Chang, 1977).

Other areas, such as the Sahara region, India, and Europe, received their first Neolithic impulses through diffusion from the Near East. Excavations in India, for example, have yielded no evidence of agricultural activities prior to about 5000 y.a., when wheat, barley, sheep, and goats appeared on the scene as domesticated transplants from the Near East.

Sub-Saharan Africa presents a more complex picture. There is a strong possibility that yam **horticulture** existed in the tropical forest clearings for centuries prior to the diffusion of the standard Near Eastern farming complex based on grain cultivation and animal husbandry. The success of cereal crops and cattle herding was restricted primarily to the margins of the rainforest environment and the savanna grasslands, where several indigenous cereals, including millet and **sorghum**, were locally domesticated. About 2000 y.a., yet another set of domesticates appeared. This time, shifting horticulturalists using slash-and-burn techniques introduced bananas and coconuts into the tropical forests of Africa. The ultimate source of these crops was probably Southeast Asia (Murdock, 1959).

It is evident from some of the foregoing discussion that farming has been "invented" at least several times in various parts of the Old World. Independent invention best accounts for the diversity of domesticates and the distinctiveness of Neolithic lifeways in Southeast Asia, sub-Saharan Africa, and the Near East.

Apart from independent invention, there are two other ways to account for the appearance of Neolithic lifeways in new regions. In some cases, people migrated and colonized areas that had been beyond their original ranges, bringing their culture and their domesticates with them. The other method was for people on the margins of Neolithic societies to borrow selected traits and perhaps even pass them along to yet other cultures. It is often difficult to determine satisfactorily the explanation that best fits the facts in any given archeological setting, for the end results were usually much the same—the diffusion of Neolithic lifeways.

European Farmers   We have already suggested that cereal farming and animal breeding eventually spread out of Southwest Asia into sub-Saharan Africa and eastward into India. But even earlier, around 8000 y.a., farmers had already appeared on Europe's Balkan Peninsula. During the next couple of millennia, they penetrated into the eastern and central parts of the continent.

Nearly all the available evidence suggests that these earliest European farming cultures had probably spread from Asia Minor and the Near East. This relationship is indicated most strongly by the sudden appearance of fully domesticated sheep, goats, wheat, and barley in the Balkans, accompanied by a host of other Near Eastern cultural traits, including burial types, clay figurines, painted pottery, and chipped stone forms (Tringham, 1971). Adjustments to climatic conditions encountered in Europe may account for such modifications as the use of **wattle and daub** and pitched roofs for building houses in the wetter and well-forested temperate regions.

The initial Neolithic phase in the Balkans is represented at sites such as Argissa-Maghula and Nea Nikomedeia, both of which date to around 8000 y.a.

Millet
Small-grained cereal grass native to Asia.

Horticulture
Farming method in which only hand tools are used.

Sorghum
Cereal grass with sweet juicy stalk.

Wattle and daub
A framework of woven sticks plastered with clay.

From there, farming cultures soon established themselves throughout southern and eastern Europe. Minor variations in settlements, pottery, and subsistence activities have permitted archeologists to distinguish among several
local subcultures; Karanovo I in southern Bulgaria and Starcevo in eastern
Yugoslavia are two important examples.

Over the next thousand years, a distinctively different farming culture
occupied several of the major river basins of central and western Europe,
especially the Danube. Its pottery, decorated with incised lines (and therefore
called *Linienbandkeramic* by European archeologists), is its most recognizable
hallmark. But sturdy timber longhouses, sometimes more than 120 feet in
length, used to shelter an extended family and its harvested grain, also set
this culture apart. The "linear pottery" (or Danubian) people may have been
shifting cultivators who preferred to farm on the well-drained loess plains
that had been neglected by earlier hunter-gatherers and farmers. As their
crops began to deplete the soil's nutrients, they would simply move on to
new locations. In this way, they spread rapidly through central Europe and
onto the northern plains. However, Dennell (1983) doubts that shifting cultivation was really practiced here, suggesting instead that a rapid acceptance

Figure 16-4 Stonehenge.

of Neolithic resources and techniques by Mesolithic Europeans accounts for the swift diffusion of farming throughout the area.

Descendants of these farmers may have been the first to convey Neolithic lifeways to the British Isles. We have no reason to suppose that there was anything particularly advantageous about the prospects for agriculture in this area, yet communities of these people found the wherewithal to erect the puzzling prehistoric structures known collectively as **megaliths**. (See Issue this chapter.) Megaliths include such famous and complex formations as Stonehenge and Avebury in England, and Carnac in France, as well as numerous unnamed single-stone sites throughout the British Isles and northwestern Europe. Burial chambers, or tombs, constructed of large stones and sometimes covered by earth, appeared during the earliest phases of the megalith-building era, which began some 6000 y.a. and continued through the next two millennia.

While the purpose of the tombs is fairly obvious, there is considerable debate about the significance of the individual standing stones, stone circles, and alignments. Some monuments, like Stonehenge, were built with great effort over the course of many centuries, some of the enormous stones having been moved substantial distances by land and sea. Some researchers have proposed that many of the megalithic constructions served as astronomical observatories, enabling ancient priests to predict solstices and eclipses with great accuracy. Many archeologists, however, remain skeptical of these explanations, while nevertheless agreeing that the monuments must have been inspired by some type of religious fervor (Daniel, 1980; Renfrew, 1983).

◇ Ancient Civilizations of the Old World

By about 5500 y.a. in the Old World, a number of Neolithic cultures were in the process of becoming **civilizations**. The changes they were undergoing were subtle, yet profound, and the societies that emerged represent the climax of Old World prehistory and the foundations of our modern world.

Considering Civilization

Conceptualizing "civilization" has proven to be a real challenge to archeologists and philosophers of history. The list of cultures in both hemispheres that might be included among the prehistoric civilizations is long and varied. Accounting for how and why such societies developed is a frustrating task. Archeologists realize that the material artifacts they have to work with are but imperfect reflections of complex social systems. And yet, because the objects were once part of those systems, they may serve as tangible evidence of the nature of early civilizations.

Some three decades ago, V. Gordon Childe enumerated the traits that he believed contributed greatly to the growth of early urban societies and civilizations. Writing, animal traction, wheeled carts, plows, metallurgy, standard units of weight and measure, sailing boats, surplus production, craft specialization, irrigation, and mathematics all had a stimulating effect, according to Childe (1951, 1957). Although these traits may have characterized many of

Loess
(luss)
Fine-grained soil composed of glacially pulverized rock.

Megalith
mega: large
lith: stone

Civilization
Large-scale, complexly organized society.

the Near Eastern civilizations with which Childe was familiar; his list was not universally applicable. For example, American Indian civilizations, such as those of the Maya and the Inca, lacked a number of the traits cited by Childe.

Prehistorians took a step toward a more dynamic perception of civilization in a symposium at the University of Chicago in 1958. Clyde Kluckhohn, a Harvard University anthropologist, proposed that civilizations were societies having (1) towns with at least 5,000 residents, (2) writing, and (3) monumental ceremonial architecture (Kraeling and Adams, 1960). Each of these criteria is outward evidence of the complex nature of the society. For instance, if a culture is able to maintain thousands of people in a permanent settlement, then it is clearly exercising some form of non-kin-based governance or administrative control, as well as redistribution of goods and services. Writing manifests an interest in keeping accurate records and accounts, ranging from economic reports and tax tallies to law codes, histories, and traditions. Large-scale construction activities that result in temples, pyramids, or other ceremonial architecture represent a society's surplus production, since such projects do not directly contribute to immediate and basic needs, such as food, in the same way that digging an irrigation canal might. A culture that can afford monumental ceremonial architecture shows it has attained a measure of success in supplying the needs of its population and in maintaining some control over it.

Definitions such as those of Kluckhohn and Childe are considered inadequate today because they do not really address the question of how or why civilizations emerged. It might be useful to consider civilization as an adaptive mechanism. For example, the rise of a large-scale and complexly oganized society may have been an accommodation to rapid population increases brought about by agricultural successes. Conversely, perhaps a concentrated and hungry population prompted the building of irrigation works necessary to increase crop yields. Did the need for controlling a water supply force entire societies to abide by the decisions of a dominant organizer and leader? Anthropologists have long argued among themselves about what stimulated the rise of civilizations in different areas. Did any come about as a result of warfare and a need for common defense? Perhaps religion or the rise of a theocratic state played a role in some cases. Or, possibly, the new order served mainly to legitimize and protect the differential access to resources and wealth initiated by increased production. These and other hypotheses have been tested against data from individual prehistoric societies, but with few conclusive results.

We should probably assume that there really is no single or prime factor that invariably impels a society along the path to civilization. Instead, anthropologists now rely on multidimensional explanations that recognize the complex nature of all societies. Any cultural system is comprised of a number of components, including its technology, subsistence economy, social organization, beliefs and symbolic expression, communication, and trade with other groups. Since each of these elements is interrelated with the others, the society as a whole may have to adapt whenever a change occurs in any one or more of these components or in their relationship with one another. If the culture has reached a critical threshold, it may achieve the degree of elaboration that we recognize as civilization.

As an illustration of how this systemic approach to culture change may be used to explain the development of a civilization, consider the following hypothetical example.

Intensive agricultural practices, often including irrigation, sometimes produced harvests that exceeded the requirements of the local population. Sustained surplus food production could, in turn, have stimulated a variety of further responses: population growth, trade or exchange with other societies, or possibly disproportionate accumulations of wealth leading to social stratification. Each of these consequences might prompt yet other transformations that would bring the society closer to what we consider civilization. Technological innovations, in part motivatd by these factors, would at the same time contribute to further new developments. Even an invention as simple as the potter's wheel, for example, could have revolutionized the craft of producing ceramic vessels by generating mass production techniques that would involve a number of specialists (mixers, potters, glazers, kiln masters, merchants, accountants, and so forth). As long as the society's food supplies were adequate, such specialists could be exempted from the obligation of producing food and would be enabled to practice their respective crafts on a full-time basis. Thus, pottery-making would contribute to a new order of social and economic relationships within the society. Civilizations thus may have emerged as a result of such interactions among various cultural components.

Like any other complex adaptive response, civilization involves adjustment to changing conditions. Robert J. Wenke aptly observes:

> We might suspect that the transition to social complexity was made in spite of its effect on the quality of life, and that its causes are not to be found in the choices of individuals or groups about how they want to live, but in the material factors of ecology, economics and technology (Wenke, 1984, p. 200).

Cities and Civilization   The most dramatic and dynamic invention associated with civilizations is the city. Civilizations are closely linked with the rise of city life, although not every civilization produced true cities. Archeologist Charles Redman has found that most early cities shared several major characteristics (Redman, 1978, p. 216). These include:

1. large and dense population
2. complexity and interdependence
3. formal and impersonal organization
4. many nonagricultural activities
5. a diversity of central services both for the inhabitants and for smaller communities in the surrounding area

No one is certain when city life really began, but a number of early citylike communities have been excavated in the Near East. Among the first of these settlements is the site known as Jericho, near the present city of the same name in the lower Jordan River valley. A large freshwater spring in an otherwise arid region seems to have been the principal attraction for Jericho's initial settlers, the Natufians, who arrived around 11,500 y.a. These people were not yet involved in many Neolithic activities. A thousand years later, the residents of Jericho were still lacking pottery and relying heavily on hunting and gathering. However, this society did have an interest in obtaining salt,

Tell
A mound of accumulated rubble on the site
of an ancient city.

Mesopotamia
meso: middle
potamos: river
Land between the Tigris-Euphrates rivers;
known as the Fertile Crescent.

sulphur, shells, obsidian, turquoise, and other stones, possibly for trade with other groups. The most surprising aspect of their residence at this site is their architecture. A massive stone wall one-half mile in circumference and 1.8 m (6 feet) thick, with towers 8 m (26 feet) in height enclosed the settlement of small dome-shaped mud and stone houses. An 8.5 m (28 feet) wide and 2.1 m (7 feet) deep trench cut into the bedrock beyond the wall afforded even greater security to Jericho's first citizens. From whom they were protecting themselves is not apparent (Kenyon, 1957).

In time, many of the early towns and cities of the Near East, like Jericho, became tells. Tells are mounds of archeological rubble, comprised of mud brick, stone, and other debris that accumulated from successive settlements. Some of these features reached the size of small hills and are prominent local landmarks. Others, such as Jerusalem, continue to be occupied to this day. As one might expect, the older components of the site are generally found closer to the base of the tell, nearer the original ground level. But neat layer-cake structures are the exception, since most tells accumulated in a sporadic way, as individual buildings or sections were erected or demolished.

Another early and notable site is Çatal Hüyük, represented by a 32-acre tell in south-central Turkey. Partially excavated by James Mellaart, this 8,000-year-old settlement may have been a religious and trade center of considerable importance (Mellaart, 1967). Its closely packed houses of timber and mud brick had rooftop entrances and painted plaster interiors. The several thousand inhabitants exploited nearby sources of obsidian, or volcanic glass. The beads, mirrors, and arrowheads they made from this stone were exported widely in exchange for various raw materials and finished goods. The wealth this trade generated apparently went in part to support religious activities in the more than forty elaborately decorated shrines found by Mellaart in the excavated portion of the city.

Jericho and Çatal Hüyük are probably somewhat extraordinary in that they grew as a result of specialized activities, such as trade or religious festivals, which took place there. They offer a contrast to contemporary settlements at Jarmo (Iraq), Çayönü (Turkey), and Hacilar (Turkey), which remained modest peasant villages. But even though the larger centers attained considerable size and local importance, they did not evolve into the kind of true city that characterized the first civilization.

Mesopotamia

During the centuries around 7000 y.a., pioneer farmers began to settle the vast alluvial plains bordering the Tigris and Euphrates rivers, an area known as **Mesopotamia**. These agriculturalists were undoubtedly relatives of the people who had long resided in such Neolithic communities as Jarmo in the Zagros foothills to the east and Cayonu on the edge of the Anatolian plateau. As they entered the lowlands, perhaps in search of vacant or more productive land, they encountered large flood-prone streams bordered by immense marshes and mud flats. But the deep stone-free silt that had accumulated along the great rivers held tremendous potential for the future.

These earliest farmers apparently did little to modify their new environment at first, choosing instead to plant their fields in naturally irrigated plots

Figure 16-5 Mesopotamia, showing extent of Sumerian civilization, and Upper and Lower Egypt.

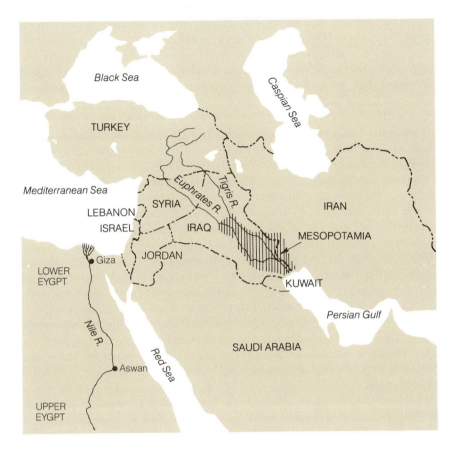

along the river. Barley was the primary grain, but wheat, millet, and emmer also grew well, along with the date palm and a variety of vegetable crops. Animals included pigs and many kinds of sheep. Donkeys and oxen performed many heavy tasks. Harvests were abundant, and the number and size of the floodplain communities increased dramatically.

The Ubaid villages as archeologists know them, flourished during the fifth and fourth millennia B.C. (7300–5000 y.a.). There was a degree of cultural uniformity shared by all the settlements along the Tigris and Euphrates. Each centered around a platform-based stepped temple. Ubaidians maintained contact among their own and more distant Neolithic peoples through trade in decorated pottery, obsidian, lapis (a valued blue stone), copper, and possibly grain. These exchanges have been traced as far to the west as the Semitic cultures of Syria through the analysis of distinctive trace elements found in some of the raw materials and artifacts.

Some major changes accompanied the latter part of the Ubaid period. The population of some communities, now protected behind massive walls, swelled to as many as 50,000 people as the outlying districts were abandoned. What do these events signify? Robert McC. Adams (1972) postulates that we are witnessing the birth of the true city, stimulated perhaps by developing economic and even military rivalry among the various population centers of the area. People fled to the protection of the city, leaving the hinterlands deserted

Extensive irrigation projects undertaken at this time outside many cities were perhaps expected to provide food for the concentrated populace. Altering the riverine environment by digging drainage and irrigation channels was a large-scale enterprise, one that could be accomplished only with organized communal effort, including a high degree of cooperation and direction. The activity no doubt transformed not only the landscape but the agricultural societies themselves. The cities and their expanded irrigation systems, along with plow agriculture, wheeled carts, draught animals, advanced copper metallurgy, massive architecture, and increasing social and religious complexity all contributed to a new order in southern Mesopotamia after 5000 y.a. Archeologists recognize this stage as the beginning of Sumerian civilization.

In many senses, the Sumerians were the world's first modern society (Kramer, 1963). Theirs was an urbanized and technological culture, economically dependent upon large-scale irrigation agriculture. Their many practical innovations included the use of wheeled carts, the plow, and probably sailing boats. They were among the first to refine metals such as gold, silver, and copper and to make bronze alloys. They had an advanced system of numeration and mathematics, including even the concept of the zero. Their sophisticated architecture incorporated the true arch and the dome. An accurate calendar reflected a knowledge of astronomy. Their system of law became a basis for later legal codes, and their contributions to literature included many of the traditions subsequently recorded in the Old Testament. Many skilled craftsworkers produced fine jewelry and textiles, while artists created music and sculpture.

Much like city dwellers everywhere, Sumerians experienced social problems and pollution in their urban environment. Sumer comprised about a dozen largely autonomous political units, called city-states, in the southern Tigris-Euphrates Valley. Each city-state included a major population center—Ur, Lagash, Kish, Nippur, and Uruk are examples—as well as some smaller satellite communities and, of course, a great deal of irrigated cropland. Perhaps governed at first by its citizens, the later city-state was controlled by hereditary kings, who contested for dominance over their counterparts in neighboring cities.

The focal point of the city-state was its central sacred district, called the *temenos*. Here rose the massive **ziggurat**, an impressive stepped temple built of millions of molded and baked mud bricks. Sumerians worshipped hundreds of major and minor deities who exhibited remarkably human characteristics. Chief among them was En-lil, the air god, who had a fatherly concern for mortals and their daily affairs, but who also meted out punishment and misfortune. Ringing the great civic center were the palaces of the priests and ruling elite. Beyond them, narrow unpaved alleyways twisted through crowded residential areas. The size and complexity of individual homes correlated with family wealth and position. The populace comprised three general classes: nobility, commoners, and slaves. Numbered among the latter were former free citizens who had fallen on hard times and sold themselves into bondage, as well as other Sumerians taken in conflicts with neighboring city-states. Many of the commoners engaged in craft or merchant activities, but most were farmers with fields and herds beyond the surrounding walls. The houses of all but the nobility were generally one-story, with several rooms opening onto a central courtyard. Wall and floor coverings brightened the interiors, which were furnished with wooden tables, chairs, and beds, and an assortment of household equipment for cooking and storage.

From our perspective, their writing system was perhaps the Sumerians' most significant invention, for it has enabled us to discover much more about them than their other artifacts and monuments could ever disclose. Using a wedge-shaped, or **cuneiform**, script formed by pressing a reed stylus into a damp clay tablet (later baked for preservation), specially trained scribes recorded everything from recipes and love poems to the great events and traditions of their times. Literacy was a hard-won accomplishment, limited to those willing to undergo years of formal study and practice. Over time, the original pictographic form of written Sumerian evolved into a phonetic system of some 2,000 symbols. Nine-tenths of their writing concerned economic, legal, and administrative matters, of course; like us, the Sumerians were part of a complex and bureaucratized society. But about 4500 y.a., scribes began recording more literary works, including several poetic accounts featuring the adventures of Gilgamesh, a culture hero who performed many brave deeds in the face of overwhelming odds.

Unfortunately, much of the energy of the society was expended in fruitless rivalries. Clustered together in an area about the size of Vermont, the city-states of Sumer were all too often vying with one another for supremacy in commerce, prestige, or religion. At the same time, their overreliance on irrigation was slowly poisoning the fields that supported the large populations. Soluble salts carried in the irrigation water accumulated in the soil, destroying its fertility, and the irrigation canals themselves continually filled with silt. The rise of a number of powerful Semitic city-states in the central Tigris-Euphrates Valley boded more ill for the Sumerians. Eventually, around 2370 B.C. (*circa* 4400 y.a.), Sargon, the king of Akkad, led armies from the north into

Ziggurat
Sumerian mud-brick temple-pyramid.

Cuneiform
cuneus: wedge
Wedge-shaped writing.

Figure 16-6 Ziggurat at Ur.

one after another of the Sumerian lands. The process was repeated several centuries later by the King Hammurabi of Babylon. After that episode, the ancient cities and culture of Sumer were absorbed into the powerful empire of the Babylonians.

Other early civilizations differed greatly in detail from the Sumerian example we have just considered. But pointing to this cultural diversity is not to deny that there were some basic similarities shared by most of the ancient societies at this level. We have already indicated that civilizations generally included focal points of production, trade, religion, and administration. Often these central places took form as cities, although some civilizations—Egypt and the New World's Inca, for example—did not develop true cities of large size. The economies of even the most advanced societies continued to be based primarily on domesticated plants and animals, of course. But increased social complexity, along with the development of technological innovations, stimulated the production of new kinds of products that contributed to the growth of a nonsubsistence economy. These new economic factors often fostered further societal changes. Thus, specialized production, utilizing trained craftspersons who were not obliged to grow their own food, created goods that could be consumed within the culture itself or, as was frequently the case, exchanged with other societies for comparable goods or desired raw materials. Access to these kinds of products usually varied according to some social or economic factor. Nowhere was this more true than in ancient Egypt.

Egypt

The pyramids of Egypt are without question the most imposing monuments of the ancient world. They have adorned the Nile's banks for so long that it is hard to imagine a time when they had not yet taken form. But, of course, the roots of Egyptian culture long predate the pyramids.

Geologists and paleoecologists believe that over the past 10,000 years or more the Nile remained essentially much like it was until the construction of the Aswan High Dam in the 1960s. During extended cycles of increased rainfall the river and its valley may have widened appreciably, while alternating drier periods saw a contraction of the river's life-giving influences. The river retained its seasonal rhythm, responding to the summer runoff by overtopping its banks in mid-July and flooding the lowlying basins for about three months annually. Dessication followed flood, but the fertile new silt grew lush with grasses through the dry season, long before farmers made the river's rhythm their own.

Remnants of the earliest Nile cultures are elusive and rarely encountered by archeologists digging in the much-disturbed river floodplain. But recent work has focused on tracing the beginnings of Egyptian civilization (Trigger, 1983). The Mesolithic foragers who occupied the Nile Valley by 8000 y.a. were equipped with bone-tipped harpoons for fishing. They also gathered wild produce, and probably ground starchy tubers on their milling stones. Their simple pottery and clay-daubed reed huts reveal their willingness to stay in one spot for at least a while. By some 1,500 years later, the descendants of these collecting and fishing people exhibited a Neolithic farming adaptation, one that already was familiar in southwest Asia. Although some local Nile species may have been domesticated initially, these were soon supplanted by crops and animals first brought under human control in the Fertile Crescent—barley and wheat, sheep and goats. Cattle, pigs, and donkeys were added later, and may represent locally domesticated varieties. Agricultural settlements scattered along the river's high banks consisted of reed-mat or skin-covered huts, with basket-lined storage pits or granaries. Pottery vessels of local clay, linen woven from flax fibers, flint work, and occasional hammered copper items were produced locally.

In the section of the Nile Valley just north of present-day Aswan (the "First Cataract" of ancient times), some of these Neolithic villages, collectively known to archeologists as the Gerzean culture, contrast with those of the delta region. Gerzean sites yield more evidence of Mesopotamian influence, introduced perhaps through direct contact or through Palestinian traders. Mineral resources, including gold, may have attracted the interest of the outsiders in the first place. By a little more than 5000 y.a., this part of the Nile Valley, called Upper Egypt, was using carved stone cylinder seals, vessel forms, artistic influences, and architectural techniques derived ultimately from the East. Other important innovations, apparently from the same source, changed the nature of this basic Nile culture profoundly (Hoffman, 1979).

Ancient Egyptians rather suddenly began using a complex pictographic script called **hieroglyphics**, a writing system that is Egyptian in form but probably Mesopotamian in inspiration. There are more advanced methods of copper working as well, including refining of ores and alloying, casting, and hammering techniques. An important by-product of copper metallurgy was **faience**, an Egyptian invention produced by fusing powdered quartz and copper ore. The blue-green glassy substance that resulted was molded into beads or statuettes. At the same time, archeologists find evidence for increasing political and social cohesion, as though the Gerzean settlements may be forming into small city-states under the leadership of a king. Again, these changes may have been stimulated by contact with the eastern Mediterranean. No evidence of comparable Egyptian influence in the other direction has been recognized.

According to historical tradition and contemporary Egyptian textual fragments, one of the early kings of Upper Egypt, named Narmer, dominated the other towns of this region and succeeded in extending control over the delta villages to the north as well. The unification of Upper and Lower Egypt under Narmer, the traditional beginning of the First Dynasty of Egyptian civilization, dates to around 3100–2900 B.C. (5100–4900 y.a.). The unification of these Nile Valley societies under one king marked another major step in the development of ancient Egypt. Old Kingdom times (4700–4400 y.a.) represent the fullest flowering of Nile Valley civilization. The ruler, or Pharaoh, was during this period the supreme power of the society, and under his direction Egypt became a wonder of the ancient world and a source of endless fascination for millennia to follow. The pharaoh was a godlike king who ruled with divine authority through a bureaucracy of priests and public officials. Memphis, about 15 miles southeast of present-day Cairo, was the royal center through most of this period. Local administrators, or nomarchs, governed about 40 individual districts, or nomes, each with a principal town. There were few

Hieroglyphic
hiero: sacred
glyphein: carving
The picture-writing of ancient Egypt.

Faience
(fay-ahnz′)
Glassy-surfaced pottery.

large cities or urban centers in the ancient Nile Valley. It is well to remember that Egypt remained basically a Neolithic culture, with the vast majority of its citizenry comprised of peasants and tradesmen carrying out their timeless routines (Aldred, 1961).

The great pyramids constructed during the Old Kingdom period best exemplify the pharaoh's absolute authority over the people and resources of his domain. In one sense, these monuments were immense public-works projects that undoubtedly served to solidify the power of the state while at the same time glorifying the memory of individual rulers. The familiar pyramids at Giza evolved out of a tradition of royal tomb-building that began by 5000 y.a. with a brick-lined burial pit and adjoining chambers stocked with offerings for the deceased king's afterlife, the whole of which was then capped by a low rectangular brick superstructure (Emery, 1957). The first stepped pyramids were raised a few centuries later, and after 4600 y.a., the massive tombs of Khufu and Khafra, Fourth Dynasty rulers, were built in true pyramid form. Khufu's Great Pyramid is 232 m (765 feet) square at the base and 147 m (485 feet) in height, with well over 2 million enormous stone blocks required in its construction (Mendelssohn, 1974). Khafra's tomb is about 20 percent smaller, but he compensated by having his likeness carved from a nearby outcrop that we now recognize as the Great Sphinx.

The stark structures that remain were once adjoined by extensive complexes of connecting causeways, shrines, altars, and storerooms filled with statuary and furnishings and ornamented with colorful friezes and carved stonework. These monumental tombs represent a remarkable engineering triumph and an enormous cultural achievement. We can also readily recognize that the mortuary cult of the pharaohs absorbed a great proportion of

Figure 16-7 Egyptian Old Kingdom pyramids at Giza.

◇ Box 16-2 Opening the Innermost Coffin of King Tutankhamen

"The lid was fastened to the shell by means of eight gold tenons (four on each side), which were held in their corresponding sockets by nails. Thus, if the nails could be extracted the lid could be raised. In the narrow space between the two coffins ordinary implements for extracting metal pins were useless, and others had to be devised. With long screwdrivers converted to meet the conditions, the nails or pins of solid gold, that unfortunately had to be sacrificed, were removed piecemeal. The lid was raised by its golden handles and the mummy of the king disclosed.

"At such moments the emotions evade verbal expression, complex and stirring as they are. Three thousand years and more had elapsed since men's eyes had gazed into that golden coffin. Time, measured by the brevity of human life, seemed to lose its common perspectives before a spectacle so vividly recalling the solemn religious rites of a vanished civilization. But it is useless to dwell on such sentiments, based as they are on feelings of awe and human pity. The emotional side is no part of archaeological research. Here at last lay all that was left of the youthful Pharaoh, hitherto little more to us than the shadow of a name.

"Before us, occupying the whole of the interior of the golden coffin, was an impressive, neat and carefully made mummy, over which had been poured anointing unguents as in the case of the outside of its coffin—again in great quantity—consolidated and blackened by age. In contradistinction to the general dark and sombre effect, due to these unguents, was a brilliant, one might say magnificent, burnished gold mask, or similitude of the king, covering his head and shoulders, which, like the feet, had been intentionally avoided when using the unguents. . . . The beaten gold mask, a beautiful and unique specimen of ancient portraiture, bears a sad but calm expression suggestive of youth overtaken prematurely by death. Upon its forehead, wrought in massive gold, were the royal insignia—the Nekhevet vulture and Buto serpent—emblems of the Two Kingdoms over which he had reigned."

SOURCE:
Carter, Howard, and A. C. Mace. *The Tomb of Tutankhamen*, London: Cassell and Co., Ltd., 1923, pp. 82–84.

the work and wealth of Egyptian society. But pyramid-building climaxed quickly; later rulers apparently channeled some of the energies that would have been used in erecting additional monuments into other kinds of projects. Subsequent kings contented themselves with burial in smaller but nonetheless lavishly furnished tombs. Discovered in the 1920s, the treasure-choked sepulcher of the young pharaoh **Tutankhamen**, who had died in 1346 B.C. (about 2450 y.a.) during New Kingdom times, is convincing evidence that dead royalty was not neglected after the era of pyramid-building had passed (Carter and Mace, 1923).

Much of what we know of ancient Egypt derives from the translation of countless hieroglyphic inscriptions. The 1799 discovery at Rosetta, a small Nile delta town, of a stone bearing an identical decree engraved in three different languages, including Greek and hieroglyphics, enabled the French linguist Jean-François Champollion to first decipher the mysterious writing. Egyptian hieroglyphics comprise a complex system that combines symbols representing ideas with those that indicate sounds. Because hieroglyphics were used primarily in formal contexts, in much the same way as Latin has been used in more recent times, their translation tells us much about pharaohs and their deeds, but reveals little of the commonplace events and people of the day. In fact, archeologists have been able to learn frustratingly little about daily life in Egypt's Old Kingdom period outside the major administrative and mortuary centers. Fortunately, somewhat more is known about the later periods of Egyptian civilization (Montet, 1981; Ruffle, 1977).

Egypt proved remarkably resilient through the centuries, surviving foreign invaders like the Hyksos and Hittites of southwest Asia, as well as occasional episodes of internal misrule. It enjoyed periods of resurgence and revival, although nothing equalled the original glory of the Old Kingdom period. Eventually, in a state of decline, and defeated by the Persians, Egypt was absorbed into the Greek sphere under Alexander the Great and eventually under the rule of Rome.

The Indus Valley

As the last great pyramids of the Nile Valley were being erected in the middle of the third millennium B.C., a less flamboyant civilization had begun to mature in another major valley far to the east, along the Indus River of India. People there had gained a tentative control over the flood-prone stream, repelling its silted waters with mud-brick walls and channeling part of its flow through irrigation sluices. They laid out fields for their vegetables and cotton and grain crops on its alluvial plains. They used the great river itself as a commercial highway.

These people were relative newcomers to the floodplains. Their ancestors had farmed the highland valleys to the west for thousands of years, harvesting cereals domesticated in the Near East, rice, and a variety of local wild grains. Why they began moving into the lowlands about 5000 y.a. is not understood. But for a time they prospered on the edge of the great river. The locations of nearly a thousand Indus Valley agricultural and pastoral villages have now been plotted by archeologists, but the two largest sites so far excavated are Mohenjo-Daro and Harappa, which flourished between about 4200 and 3700 y.a. (Wheeler, 1968; Fairservis, 1976). Built according to a precise plan, these major riverport cities were laid out in neatly gridded rectangles of approximately 400 by 200 meters. Windowless walls of standardized brick residence units bordered their broad streets. What was probably the world's first efficient sewage system conveyed waste away from thousands of densely packed dwellings. In other sections of the larger cities, roomier houses with interior courtyards probably sheltered members of a different social class. A "great bath," or pool, lies near what has been interpreted as Mohenjo-Daro's government center, a complex that also included elite residences and a large assembly hall. Close by was a capacious granary, serving perhaps as a state storehouse. Harappa, too, had such granaries, as well as rows of furnaces that probably were used for smelting ore.

Though its impressively large sites hint at some sort of central control and social complexity, the Indus Valley civilization remained a relatively simple **Bronze Age** culture. Nowhere, for example, is there evidence of a genuine palace or a monumental religious structure. Nor are there indications of international trade or warfare. In these regards, the culture stands in stark contrast to both Egypt and Sumer. Perhaps there was wider participation in economic and social aspects of Indus society than in others. The writing

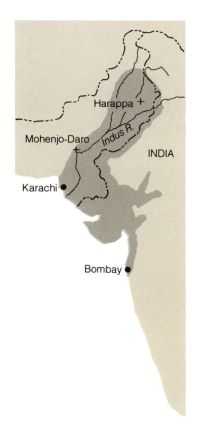

Figure 16-8   Location of the Indus Valley civilization.

system, consisting of brief pictographic notations on seal stones and pottery, is not yet fully translated, although there has been some recent headway on this front (Fairservis, 1983).

The river that spawned the principal urban centers may have played a role in their final chapter, gradually reclaiming the surrounding fields and eventually the cities themselves. But hundreds of other towns and villages outlasted them, some even persisting into the modern era as the peasant villages of western India.

Northern China

The final river valley civilization we will consider here is found in the Far East. The origins of Chinese civilization are rooted in the Neolithic villages of northern China. Farmers on the alluvial plains of the great Yellow or Huang Ho River valley were already cultivating millet, a small-grained cereal grass, by about 5500 y.a. Fertile deposits of deep loess soil helped ensure large yields and undoubtedly contributed to the growth of populous settlements during the Yangshao, or initial farming, period. Even at this stage, some characteristics of later Chinese culture were already apparent, including jade carving, painted ceramics, and possibly even silkworm cultivation. A shift to rice farming and the addition of domesticated horses, cattle, and water buffalo signalled the later Neolithic, or Lung-shan, period along China's central valleys, beginning around 4700 y.a. (Chang, 1977).

Perhaps as a consequence of successfully directing flood control efforts along the major rivers, local leaders who emerged in northern China over the next few centuries were able to command the allegiance of larger regions. These areas functioned almost like feudal states, giving rise to a noble ruling class that played a prominent role in the subsequent era of Chinese civilization, beginning with the Shang dynasty in the sixteenth century B.C. Material culture, architecture, art styles, and writing reflect a sophistication that emanated from a highly structured society.

The large population of peasant farmers labored and lived much as they always had, but an elite ruling class, supported by slaves, craftspersons, scribes, and other functionaries, had been added to the top of the social hierarchy. The power and actions of the rulers were apparently justified in many cases through the practice of **divination**, or prophecy. Divination was performed by first writing a question on certain specially prepared bones, such as turtle shells and ox or deer scapulae. Applying heat to the bone caused cracks to appear, whereupon the "answer" to the question could be "read." Divination was a vital activity in Shang society, and thousands of the marked bones still survive (Fitzgerald, 1978).

One of the early capitals of the Shang dynasty was located at the present-day city of Cheng-chou, along the Huang Ho River. Here, archeologists find remains of a large rectangular precinct comprising the residences of nobles and rulers as well as their temples and other ceremonial structures. A massive wall of packed earth nearly 10 meters in height separated the royal compound from surrounding huts and workshops. Among the latter were several bronze foundries. Shang artisans are most famous for their bronze work, which usually took the form of elaborate tripod cauldrons, cast in sectional molds.

Bronze Age
Period of early Old World civilizations, beginning with widespread use of metal tools after 5500 y.a.

Divination
A method of foretelling the future.

Figure 16-9 Centers of early Chinese civilization.

Figure 16-10   Bronze ritual vessel of
Shang dynasty.

Decorated with stylized animal motifs and dedicatory inscriptions, these
vessels were used by the nobility in making ritual offerings of wine and food
to ancestors and deities. Such vessels were also important funerary items
and are found in the royal tombs, including those in the vicinity of the later
Shang capital at Anyang. In addition to bronzes, the rulers were accompanied
in death by lavish offerings of carved jade, horse-drawn chariots, and scores
of human sacrificial victims (Chang, 1980).

Although limited in area, the Shang civilization influenced the future
course of Chinese culture. The social and cultural innovations introduced
by the Shang were adopted and expanded by succeeding rulers, until much
of China was apportioned among competitive Bronze Age warlords. Not until
the Han dynasty (206 B.C. to A.D. 220) was this huge region finally politically
unified into a cohesive Chinese empire.

Table 16-2   Chronological Chart Showing Major Cultural Events

Years Ago	Mesopotamia	Egypt	Indus Valley	China
5000		First dynasty	Earliest cities	Earliest cities
6000	Early Bronze Age	Fully agricul-tural villages		Incipient agriculture
7000	Irrigation			
8000				
9000				
10,000	Earliest cities			
11,000	Intensive agriculture			

The Mediterranean World

By comparison with the ancient cultures of Egypt and Mesopotamia and Asia, the Mediterranean societies of the second millennium B.C. were relatively late and unimpressive in scale and achievement. Their real significance for us is that they are the bridge between the old civilizations of the East and the formative societies of barbarian Europe. The Bronze Age Minoans had a sea orientation that kept them in contact with peoples of the Aegean. Their contemporaries and successors, the Mycenaeans, created the first civilization on the European mainland.

Minoans   Neolithic farmers were the first occupants of Crete, the large caterpillar-shaped island in the eastern Mediterranean. They brought with them domesticated sheep, olives, grapes, and lentils, all of which they found well adapted to the island's rough, semi-arid terrain. A desire to exchange their surplus products for those that were locally unavailable soon prompted the island's inhabitants to look seaward. First using oar-propelled galleys, then sailing vessels, the Minoans of Crete mastered the sea lanes of the eastern Mediterranean. They plied among neighboring islands and on to the mainland of Egypt, Anatolia, and the Levant, exchanging their foodstuffs, woolen cloth, pottery, and timber primarily for raw materials that they could convert into luxury goods. Attractively colored stones such as carnelian, agate, sard, and jasper became carved seals for impressing clay and other substances with an owner's personal mark. Copper and tin ores were smelted, alloyed, and cast into weapons, armor, tools, and ornaments. Minoans also gained fame as skilled artisans in gold and silver. Some of these finished goods reentered the exchange network, while others remained on Crete to supply the wants of the growing Minoan elite.

The rapid transformation of Minoan culture after 4500 y.a. reflects successful maritime trading (Hood, 1973). A number of urban centers formed around multistoried palaces and spacious homes that sheltered wealthy merchant-kings and others of privileged status. Crete's coastal towns dominated the Mediterranean trade for several centuries prior to about 3450 y.a. (1450 B.C.). Knossos, on the island's northern side, had been one of the earliest settlements on the island. Now it boasted a rambling palace of more than a thousand rooms. The local palaces were the focus of Minoan life, the centers of its economy, arts, crafts, and social hierarchy. The balconies of the Knossos palace overlooked tiled courtyards where religious celebrations took place. Within, the brightly frescoed walls revealed the Minoan love of art. Painted scenes of commerce and exotic ports were combined with views of lush gardens, dancers and daring athletes, mythological landscapes and imaginary creatures to capture the visitor's attention. Within palace workshops artisans created delicate jewelry and elegant drinking vessels. In some of the rooms, ranks of gaily decorated ceramic jars filled with olive oil awaited shipment. In others, scribes carefully impressed clay tablets with symbols that remain to this day an untranslatable script known as *Linear A*. Finally, one approached the colonnaded chamber that was the heart of the great palace—the royal court with its carved gypsum throne.

The civilization of Crete was highly distinctive. Despite long contact with the Nile valley and Near East, Minoans retained their cultural identity in every

Figure 16-11 Minoan and Mycenaean civilizations.

sphere, from art and architecture to statecraft and religion. Unlike many contemporary societies, the Minoans apparently remained content to worship at modest local shrines, sometimes tenanted by small figurines in the form of a buxom young woman holding a serpent on each arm. This so-called "snake goddess" may have been a fertility figure or mother goddess. Another prominent character in the Minoan pantheon was the bull, who may have signified virility. In one ritual, Minoan athletes performed somersaults over the back of a raging bull, and the familiar myth of the fierce half-man, half-bull Minotaur is closely associated with the Minoans of Crete.

This intriguing and colorful island civilization was relatively peaceful, yet it ended amid great devastation. Geologically recent, the island of Crete was earthquake prone. A number of Minoan cities had been damaged and reconstructed repeatedly. Then, some 3450 y.a. (1470 B.C.), one-third of the nearby island of Thera, a Minoan outpost 120 km (75 miles) off Crete's north coast, exploded into the sky. A surge of seawater instantly flooded the gaping crater formed by the volcano. Within minutes, severe tremors shook apart the great palaces and houses on Crete itself, and a huge tidal wave soon swept the island's north shore (Sparks and Sigurdsson, 1978). Damage was so extensive everywhere that, while rebuilding took place at a few sites, the Minoans were unable to retain control of the Mediterranean trade routes.

Mycenaeans   Even as Minoan civilization reached its zenith, other Mediterranean societies were responding to the stimuli of contact and trade. One of these emergent cultures was the Mycenaean. They had brought their proto-Greek language and simple Bronze Age culture into southeastern Europe about 4200 y.a. when they left their Anatolian homeland. Inspired by the Minoans, they soon secured a share of the lucrative sea trade by successfully establishing an exchange network that included Cyprus, Egypt, **Anatolia**, and the central Mediterranean. By 3600 y.a. they already could afford to richly stock the graves of their dead kings within their principal hilltop fortress-city of Mycenae. The massive stonework that protects this citadel reflects the militarism that pervaded Mycenaean society. Likewise, scenes engraved on finger rings, seal stones, and gold-inlaid weapons characteristically display a combat theme. Much Mycenaean bronze work (their primary commercial product) took the form of daggers, swords, helmets, and other armaments. Mycenaean militancy pervades the epics of Homer, whose *Iliad* and *Odyssey* recount the long struggle over the rival city of Troy, across the Aegean.

The degree to which Minoans and Mycenaeans competed or coexisted is not clear. But only when disaster weakened the culture of Crete could the Mycenaeans dominate. Over the two centuries following the decline of Knossos and other Minoan centers, Mycenaeans gained full control of the Mediterranean trade and of Crete itself. They incorporated the Minoan palace-based economic system, written recordkeeping, and artistic and technical achievements into their own culture (Warren, 1975). Now Mycenaean ships plowed the waves unchallenged. Wealthy merchant-kings enjoyed the highest positions in their society. Back home, their colonnaded palaces were virtual warehouses bulging with trade goods and imported luxuries. The elite, local administrators, landholders, craftsworkers, peasants, and slaves participated to varying degrees in the social and economic benefits of this stratified society.

Their insatiable need of raw materials for art objects and armaments drew

Anatolia
Asia Minor; present-day Turkey.

Figure 16-12   Throne room in the Minoan palace at Knossos.

the Mycenaeans to distant Mediterranean and Near Eastern ports. One crucial resource was metal. The key to bronze-making is the alloy added in small amounts to harden the copper. Arsenic can be used, but smiths who worked that substance rapidly experienced its lethal side-effects. Tin, the preferred alloy, was very scarce. Mycenaean demand for it stimulated mining activities as far away as western and central Europe and the Near East. Other northern European resources also attracted them. Amber, or fossil pine resin, a translucent yellow-brown substance that may have fascinated the ancients because of its static electrical properties, arrived from the far-off shores of the Baltic Sea. Mycenaean ships visited the Mediterranean seaports at the terminus of these overland supply and exchange routes, bringing articles of commerce to filter into the tribal societies of the European hinterlands (Harding, 1984; Bouzek, 1985). Their early exposure to Minoan trade and culture had transformed the Mycenaeans, and now the Mycenaeans themselves were having a similar, though indirect, impact on barbarian Europe. Mycenaean supply routes were cultural arteries, infusing the Europeans with new technologies and other far-reaching innovations (Piggott, 1965).

While we cannot yet precisely delineate the later relationship between western Europe and the Mediterranean world, we can observe that the Mycenaean sphere began to contract before collapsing altogether. Had these Europeans so quickly reached the point where they could seriously challenge Mycenaean trade and access to strategic resources? It seems doubtful. On the other hand, tribal peoples of the eastern Mediterranean, including some of Mycenae's near neighbors, appear to have become aggressive raiders. Early texts make cryptic references to "sea people" and "people of the north" who began to close in on the civilized world, armed with cutting-and-slashing swords. Thus began an unsettled era, a time of troubles for many of the ancient societies that bordered the Mediterranean. About 3200 y.a., the principal Mycenaean cities were destroyed, their populations dispersed, and their trade routes abandoned. From the Nile Delta to Anatolia, invaders swept through the old kingdoms, creating chaos. In the wake of this destruction came a dark age, a period that is but sketchily known to prehistorians. When the dust settled, centuries later, we find an Iron Age Europe peopled by Greeks, Etruscans, and Celts—the principals of a new era.

◇Summary

About 10,000 y.a., the world underwent significant climatic changes which in turn caused alterations in geography and in the configuration of animal and plant communities. These changes appear to have held some important consequences for humans, particularly in their subsistence economy. Post-Pleistocene human adaptations in the Old World were expressed in new technologies and in a more intensive utilization of local resources, a way of life that we call Mesolithic. Mesolithic cultures of northern Europe continued to develop specializations in their hunting-gathering-fishing economies for many centuries. Contemporary cultures of the Near East, such as the Natufian, were taking steps toward food production, and the success of such experimentation led ultimately toward a more self-sufficient and sedentary existence in the Neolithic period.

The rise of ancient civilization is another manifestation of post-Pleistocene adaptations following the technological achievement of agricultural food production. Appearing in scattered parts of the Old World, early civilizations flourished particularly on the alluvial plains of some of the major river systems: the Tigris-Euphrates, the Nile, the Indus, and the Huang Ho. Cities, monumental architecture, invention of writing, trade, social stratification, and development of art and science, all contributed to the formation of foundations on which much of our cultural heritage is based.

Amber
Fossil pine pitch or resin.

◇ Questions for Review

1. In what ways did the climatic changes at the end of the Pleistocene alter the natural environment of Europe?
2. Why and in what ways did the Mesolithic adaptations of northern Europe and southwest Asia differ?
3. What are several of the major theories that account for plant and animal domestication?
4. What kinds of archeological evidence are used to show plant and animal domestication?
5. Cite several of the important positive and negative consequences of food production.
6. What is the evidence for the spread of Neolithic lifeways from the Near East into Europe?
7. What was the nature of a typical Sumerian city-state?
8. Suggest why river valleys were the primary setting for early Old World civilizations.
9. Why was writing so closely associated with the rise of civilizations?
10. Explain why bronze technology stimulated cultural expansion and trade throughout the Mediterranean basin and Europe.

Prehistory of the Americas

CONTENTS

A surefire way to enliven any gathering of American archeologists is to ask for or express an opinion on the earliest evidence of people in the New World. There is a wide spectrum of positions on this issue. One extreme view even holds that modern humanity originated in the American Southwest and spread from there to the Old World! But most archeologists agree upon the Old World origin of American Indians, yet express varied opinions about the date of the first arrivals. The scanty evidence submitted as proof of the very early presence of people in the New World (in excess of 30,000 y.a.) is of questionable quality. In some cases, crude artifacts that have been recovered from erosion channels, blowouts, lake beds, or even plowed fields could be of considerable antiquity, but their disturbed contexts often prevent a realistic assessment of age. Other stone or bone fragments, some found within datable contexts, simply are not accepted by most archeologists as humanly produced artifacts.

Typical of these disputed claims is the Calico Hills site near Barstow, California. The late Louis Leakey, Ruth D. Simpson, and others contend that certain chert fragments recovered from geological deposits at depths of 6 m (20 feet) constitute artifacts dating to at least 50,000 y.a. and maybe 200,000 y.a. Most archeologists reject a human origin for these specimens, noting that their flaking angles could be the result of natural processes, such as soil movement. The geological dating of the site appears imprecise and highly questionable to many commentators.

At times, the preliminary results of experimental dating techniques have generated heated controversy and unwarranted assertions about the age of the earliest Americans. For example, the dating of bones by the amino acid racemization technique, which measures the postmortem changes in the body's protein components, produced estimates of 30,000 to 50,000 years for several human skeletons found between Los Angeles and San Diego, California. Most researchers, guided by the bones' relatively modern morphology, remained skeptical of these findings, while others reserved judgment on the dating technique itself. Similarly, some methods supported claims of extreme antiquity for other human remains: more than 40,000 years for the bones of an infant found at Taber in southern Alberta, Canada, and as much as 24,000 years for an adult skeleton found under a rock in the Yuha Desert of southern California. Fortunately, recent refinements in the radiocarbon dating technique now allow direct counting of the carbon-14 isotope in a specimen and produce much more reliable dates for even tiny samples of bone and other organics. Each of the controversial finds just cited has now been redated, using the improved procedure. The results in all cases are consistent with an age of between 4,000 and 6,000 years.

Currently, much of the debate about the New World's first inhabitants focuses on the span between 30,000 and 12,000 y.a. The former represents the period by which anatomically modern people were occupying the part of Asia that lies closest to North America. By the latter date, unquestionable sites associated with Paleo-Indians were already estab-lished in many parts of the Western Hemisphere.

Simple stone tools, in the form of crude choppers and large flakes or scrapers, have been found at various sites in the Americas. They are considered by some archeologists to be from a period that may have predated the use of bifacial projectile points (which were in use in North America by 12,000 y.a.). Unfortunately, many of these typologically "primitive" tools cannot be easily or securely dated. Some are merely surface finds, while others are from disturbed contexts. The lowest levels of Pikimachay (Flea Cave) in Peru's Ayacucho Valley contained bones of giant sloth and what the excavator, Richard S. MacNeish, interpreted as crude stone butchering tools of 15,000 to 20,000 y.a. But, here again, the nature and dating of the artifacts are disputed by many.

Purported bone artifacts have claimed considerable attention in recent years. Archeologist Robson Bonnichsen and others have shown that bone may have been of greater technological importance than archeologists previously recognized. Fresh bone could be worked into useful forms by controlled flaking and breaking techniques, which produce distinctive spiral fracture patterns not usually duplicated by natural processes. Thousands of Pleistocene animal bones lie scattered through the gravel bars and in the banks of the meandering Porcupine River and its tributaries in the Old Crow region of Alaska. (See Figure 1.) Among the bones found here are some that may show signs of human activity, including flakes, cuts, and even injuries induced by bone spearpoints. One

Figure 1   Flaked bone from the upper reaches of the Old Crow River, Alaska. The wavy lines are weathering caused by small roots.

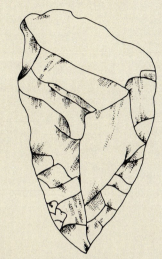

Figure 2   Knifelike implement from Stratum IIa at Meadowcroft Rockshelter, Pennsylvania.

notable implement is a caribou tibia fleshing tool, or scraper, with finely serrated teeth cut into its working edge. At first dated to more than 27,000 y.a. by conventional radiocarbon methods, this artifact has now been redated to only 1350 ± 150 y.a. However, mammoth bones showing green-bone fractures and flaking continue to indicate ages of 25,000 to 45,000 y.a. But few archeologists are willing to accept these specimens as tools.

In eastern North America, the Meadowcroft rock shelter near Pittsburgh, Pennsylvania, is a deeply stratified site containing cultural levels that have been dated to more than 19,000 y.a. by standard radiocarbon methods. Stratum IIa, from which this date derives, contained several prismatic blades, a retouched flake, a chipped biface, and a crude knifelike implement (Figure 2). Unfor-

tunately, none of the tools from this deep stratum are particularly distinctive, so it is difficult to assess their technological relationships to other assemblages. The unexpectedly early radiocarbon results for this site have not escaped challenge, either.

In short, there currently seem to be *no indisputable* sites, artifacts, or human remains in the New World older than about 12,000 years. The casualty rate for earlier claims has increased alarmingly in recent years, largely due to the new carbon-dating advances. Of course, we cannot rule out the possibility that older American sites exist, but the burden of proving claims of great antiquity is considerable.

SOURCES:

Bryan, Alan L. *New Evidence for the Pleistocene Peopling of the Americas*. Orono: University of Maine Center for Study of Early Man, 1986.

Dincauze, Dena F. "An Archaeological Evaluation of the Case for Pre-Clovis Occupations." In *Advances in World Archaeology*, Fred Wendorf and Andrea Close, eds., 3:275–323. New York: Academic Press, 1984.

Irving, William N. "Context and Chronology of Early Man in the Americas," *Annual Review of Anthropology*, 14:529–555, 1985.

Taylor, R. E., L. A. Payen, C. A. Prior, P. J. Slota, Jr., R. Gillespie, et al. "Major Revisions in the Pleistocene Age Assignments for North American Human Skeletons by C-14 Accelerator Mass Spectrometry: None Older than 11,000 C-14 Years B.P.," *American Antiquity*, 50(1):136–139, 1985.

◇ CHAPTER SEVENTEEN

◇ Introduction

The preceding chapter highlighted the major trends in Old World prehistory for the post-Pleistocene era. In this chapter, we will consider the somewhat parallel developments in the New World that occurred during approximately the same time span. The first problem we must deal with, however, is the matter of human arrival in the Western Hemisphere. Since evolution of advanced primates took place only in the Old World, the modern-type humans who occupied the Americas before the coming of the Europeans were clearly immigrants themselves. Archeologists are actively seeking to determine where and when the first people arrived in the New World.

As was the case in Europe, the inhabitants of the Americas made some major adaptations to rapidly changing environmental conditions in the period following the retreat of continental glaciers. Generally speaking, these cultural responses contributed to a way of life that was based upon a pattern of intensive and mobile foraging for a wide variety of plant and animal foods. In some cases a reliance upon selected wild resources led to experimentation that altered the natural species. Cultivated crops, and even a handful of animal domesticates, became locally significant in a few areas. Meanwhile, in Mesoamerica and the Andean region, these productive resources served as a primary economic base for several flourishing civilizations after about 5,000 y.a. These complex and highly sophisticated cultures in turn had an impact upon even wider areas of the New World through the diffusion of domesticates, trade, and even invasion.

While there seem to have been some basic regularities in the major features of Old and New World development, the distinctions cannot be overlooked. Transoceanic contact appears to have been minimal. The effect of this isolation was a divergence between the populations of the two hemispheres, particularly in the cultural dimension. With the recombination of Old and New World peoples that took place during the age of exploration, the long isolation came to an end; so, very nearly, did the New World societies themselves.

◇ Old World Origins of New World Peoples

Scientists generally agree that the original New World population was drawn from northeastern Asia. But questions of "How long ago?" and "What kind of people were they?" are still being debated. Was there more than one migration? What kinds of cultural equipment did the newcomers bring with them? Unfortunately, there is very little archeological debris or undisputed skeletal evidence that documents the earliest arrival of people in the New World.

The arrival of people in the Western Hemisphere represented a significant extension of the range of an Old World species. *Homo sapiens* had reached the farthest limits of Eurasia by the Late Pleistocene or Ice Age period. By some 30,000 y.a. Siberia and the east Asian mainland were occupied by *Homo sapiens* of a generalized, primitive "Caucasoid" type having long heads and short but slender body builds (Birdsell, 1981). Presumably, these people were the ancestral stock of the Amerinds. They apparently had not yet developed some of the physical traits prominently associated with modern Asian populations. Their cultural adaptation focused upon the hunting of large herbivores with stone- and bone-tipped weapons and probably also with the aid of domesticated dogs. Their use of fire, tailored skin clothing, and shelters made from the hides of butchered animals contributed to their survival in these bleak northern regions (Klein, 1969).

For long periods during the latest glaciation or **Wisconsin** stage (in New World terminology), northeastern Asia was linked to Alaska by a land connection or "bridge" that was fully 2,000 km (1,300 miles) wide from north to south (Hopkins, 1979). Exposure of this broad plain, known as **Beringia**, resulted from a lowering of worldwide sea levels by as much as 130 m (430 feet) due to the volume of water locked up on land in the massive ice sheets that blanketed much of the higher latitudes. Because of its cold, dry Arctic climate, Beringia itself remained an ice-free refuge, an area of low relief covered with vegetation of mosses, lichens, and sedges. Despite its treeless and barren appearance, Beringia's rich tundra supported large herds of grazing animals, as well as the hunters who preyed on them.

Beringia remained "open" for long periods. Geologists have determined that except for short spans, the passageway between the continents existed

Wisconsin
The period of the last major glacial advance in North America; analogous to Weichsel in the Old World.

Beringia
(Bare-in'-jya)
The dry-land connection between Asia and America that existed periodically during the Ice Age. Between 10,000 y.a. and 27,000 y.a., people could cross it into the New World.

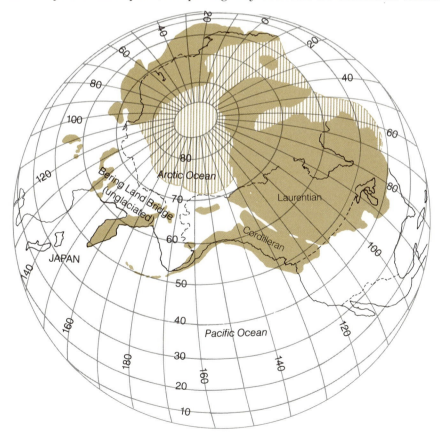

Figure 17-1 Cordilleran and Laurentide ice sheets during the height of the final glaciation. (Adapted from David M. Hopkins, "Landscape and Climate of Beringia during Late Pleistocene and Holocene Time," in *The First Americans: Origins, Affinities, and Adaptations*, William S. Laughlin and Albert B. Harper (eds.), figure 1.2. New York: Gustav Fischer. Copyright © The Wenner-Gren Foundation for Anthropological Research, Inc.)

Cordilleran
(cord-ee-yair'-an)

Paleo
"Ancient"; the early period of big-game hunting in the Americas, from about 12,000 y.a.–8000 y.a.

Fluting
Removal of large flakes in order to thin projectile point bases.

Lanceolate
Narrow and tapering form.

Clovis
Phase of North American prehistory, 12,000 y.a. to 11,000 y.a. in the West, during which short-fluted projectile points were used in hunting.

as dry land between 27,000 y.a. and 10,000 y.a., and for other extended periods even before that time. It probably was during one of these episodes that the New World received its first human inhabitants.

Precise dating of this entry is especially significant. If it took place earlier than some 40,000 y.a., one would have to conclude that a premodern physical type (most likely Neandertal) was the pioneering human species in the New World. To this point, however, no skeletal remains have been widely accepted in support of this possibility. Conceivably, the very first arrivals may have died out during the later stages of the Pleistocene. In that case, most archeological sites and all of the more recent Amerind peoples would derive from later, fully modern immigrants. In any event, with the exception of the late-arriving Eskimo and Aleuts, the American natives generally share a number of distinctive physical traits that could be the consequence of a small founding population.

The "founder effect" would explain the high incidence of shovel-shaped incisors, presence of rare blood types in relatively high frequencies, and absence of blood groups A^2, B, D, and r among Amerinds. On the other hand, the observable differences among these same native populations in body build, skin color, and the like may be credited to more recent genetic drift or microevolution due to natural selection pressures on isolated populations within local environments (Spuhler, 1979). Physical similarities shared by modern Asian and native American populations could be the result of either later infusions of Old World groups or the presence of developing "Mongoloid" genetic traits within the initial American population.

◇ Paleo-Indians

Access to the New World south of the Arctic entryway was limited because of the proximity of two great continental ice sheets (**Cordilleran** to the west, Laurentian to the east), which at times coalesced as one during stages of maximum glaciation. However, during milder periods, people and animals could gain entry to the south through an ice-free corridor along the eastern flank of the Canadian Rockies, when the edges of the ice sheets melted back from one another. Archeologists have found very few sites that they can confidently attribute to the earliest Americans. Many ancient camp locations undoubtedly were inundated when rising seas once more submerged Beringia at the end of the Pleistocene. In other areas, silt and gravels borne by glacial meltwaters must have deeply buried the sites.

Evidence of people in the New World prior to about 12,000 y.a. is very controversial (see this chapter's Issue). But archeologists generally acknowledge a great many sites formed after this time. The components are well dated and contain recognizable tools. The latter most often consist of bifacially chipped projectile points, scrapers, and knives, many of which apparently were used in securing and processing large game animals. The wide distribution of these sites throughout North America and into Central and South America within a short time after 12,000 y.a. suggests that early Americans made a rapid cultural adaptation to the varied environments of the New World during the late Pleistocene.

Figure 17-2 North American archeological sites mentioned in the text.

Specialists refer to this era of mobile hunters and gatherers with a big-game orientation as the **Paleo-Indian** period. Evidence of their way of life comes from widely scattered sites, including many in the western United States. The most spectacular of these sites have been the kill locations, where large herbivores, such as mammoth and giant bison, were killed and butchered. But the dramatic nature of such sites should not cause us to overemphasize the big-game hunting aspect of Paleo-Indian life and economy. It is very likely that the same people were exploiting a diverse range of both plant and animal foods within their environments. Still, their association with the preserved bones of the large herbivores is undeniable. At most of these places, butchered remains are accompanied by distinctive and finely flaked **fluted** projectile points of **lanceolate** shape. Each face typically displays a groove (or flute) that represents the removal of a channel flake to facilitate the special hafting technique.

On the basis of tool technology, chronology, and the primary prey species of each Paleo group, archeologists conclude that the period between about 12,000 and 11,000 y.a. was a time of hunters who employed **Clovis** type fluted

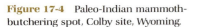

Figure 17-3   Clovis fluted point with reconstructed mounting. (Courtesy, Royal Ontario Museum, Toronto.)

points. At many sites in the West, these points are associated with mammoth remains. Although there has been less in the way of preserved animal bone found at sites in eastern North America, the same style of projectile point was in use in that area during approximately the same time span. At the Vail site in northern Maine, Clovis points were recovered in numbers from a caribou-hunting camp (Gramly, 1982), and in eastern Pennsylvania a mixed subsistence of smaller game and plant products supplied the Paleo-Indians at the Shawnee-Minisink site (McNett, 1985). Evidently, the Paleo-Indian's adaptation was flexible enough to accommodate the climatic and geographic diversity encountered throughout North America near the end of the Pleistocene.

The mammoth hunters who used Clovis points were succeeded in the West by people who concentrated their efforts on herds of giant long-horned bison. Around 10,000 y.a., some of these hunters in the Southwest were using another style of fluted point, called **Folsom**. These specialized weapons, however, were soon replaced by unfluted but finely parallel-flaked lanceolate projectile heads of the **Plano** type, which came into wide use throughout the West at about the time the ancient Pleistocene bison was being replaced by its smaller cousin, the modern-day *Bison bison occidentalis*.

A number of sites in the Great Plains demonstrate that the natives' favorite technique of hunting bison was to stampede them into arroyos, box canyons, or over cliffs, and then to quickly dispatch those that survived the trap (Wheat, 1972; Frison, 1978). Remember, the horse had not yet been reintroduced onto the Plains, so these early hunters were strictly pedestrians. In the East, the later Paleo-Indians employed different types of projectile points, such as the Dalton variety, but poor bone preservation again leaves us with little information about their hunting techniques or favored prey.

Circumstantial evidence like that found mainly in the West has led some researchers to ponder the question of human involvement in the extinction

Figure 17-4   Paleo-Indian mammoth-butchering spot, Colby site, Wyoming.

of major North American Pleistocene fauna, such as the mammoth, giant bison, horse, camel, ground sloth, and others. Paul S. Martin (1967) is fervent in his assertion that the overhunting of these animals by Paleo-Indians resulted in rapid extinctions throughout the New World. But the issue is complicated by the fact that some of the species may have been extinct by the time humans came to the New World. Others, like the gigantic ground sloth of the southwestern United States, seem not to have been hunted at all. Biologists point out that species extinction is an ongoing phenomenon that can result even today from a variety or even a combination of circumstances, ranging from climate change to human involvement. The matter of the human role in New World extinctions is still unresolved.

Distinctive Paleo-Indian artifacts may be found through Central America and all the way along western South America to Tierra del Fuego by 11,000 y.a. In South America, the hunters probably concentrated their efforts along the Pacific slopes of the Andes, where horse and ground sloth provided an important part of their diet, along with deer, camelids, and undoubtedly a wide variety of tuberous plants. An important part of the Paleo-Indian adaptation in this Andean region may have been the seasonal utilization of varied resource zones in their mountainous environment (Lynch, 1983). But just how advanced might these early societies have been? Recent excavations in southern Chile have revealed a unique and surprising site of apparent Paleo-Indian age (Dillehay, 1984). Remnants of the wooden foundations of a dozen rectangular huts are arranged back to back in a parallel row. The structures measured between 3 m and 4.5 m on a side; their sapling frameworks were once draped with hides. To the east of the main cluster was a separate "wishbone" shaped building containing distinctive stone tools and faunal remains. Numerous spheroids (possibly sling stones), a wooden lance, digging sticks, mortars, fire pits, mastodon and camelid bones, along with nuts, fruits, berries, wild tubers, and firewood testify to subsistence activities. Dillehay believes this site to have been a "planned settlement that was integrated both spatially and functionally," to a degree unknown for other contemporary sites in the Americas.

Folsom
Phase of southern Great Plains prehistory, 10,000 y.a.–8000 y.a., during which long-fluted projectile points were used for bison.

Plano
Great Plains bison-hunting culture of 8000 y.a.–7000 y.a., which used narrow unfluted points.

(a)   (b)   (c)   (d)

Figure 17-5 Varieties of Paleo-Indian projectile points. (a) Clovis point; (b) Plano point; (c) Dalton point; (d) Folsom point.

Archaic
Cultural stage of hunting and gathering after the end of the Wisconsin ice age; roughly equivalent to "Mesolithic" in the Old World.

Atlatl
A throwing board or spear-thrower.

Great Basin
Rugged, dry plateau between the mountains of California and Utah, comprising Nevada, western Utah, and southern Oregon and Idaho.

◇ New World Hunters and Gatherers

As in the Old World, in both North and South America, the end of the Pleistocene or Ice Age some 10,000 y.a. was accompanied by major changes in climate, landscape, flora, and fauna. The great continental ice sheets left behind them thick mantles of pulverized rock or till. This debris was subsequently sorted by wind and by streams that flowed in newly defined drainage systems. Midlatitude coastlines were drowned by rising sea levels, while the land in some northern areas rebounded once the earth's crust was no longer compressed by the tremendous weight of the glacial mass. As deglaciation proceeded, the major biotic zones expanded northward, so that areas once covered by ice were clothed successively in tundra, grassland, fir and spruce forests, pine and mixed deciduous forests—each with its distinctive complement of fauna (Bryson et al., 1970). The annual mean summer temperatures continued to climb until local climatic maxima were reached between 6000 y.a.–8000 y.a. in many areas. Pluvial lakes that had developed during the Ice Age from increased precipitation in nonglaciated areas of the American West evaporated under the modern arid conditions.

The changes associated with the end of the Pleistocene occurred slowly over many human generations, but their impact was cumulative. We see that human cultures made major adjustments in their ways of coping with the environment. For example, the disappearance of major Pleistocene herbivores required that new subsistence strategies be devised. In general, the period following the Pleistocene seems to be one characterized by the intensified hunting and gathering of a wide spectrum of natural resources. During this New World Mesolithic stage (or **Archaic** period, in North American terminology), people utilized a widening variety of plant species and both large and small animal species, including significant amounts of fish and shellfish where available. To make possible the effective exploitation of these food sources, hunters and gatherers developed a number of new technologies involving composite weapons (such as harpoons, the spear, and the throwing board, or **atlatl**), fishing gear, traps and snares, baskets and other containers, canoes, and many other items.

In most regions of the New World, hunter and gatherer bands adapted precisely to their local environments and resources. Most groups made seasonal movements through the often-diverse ecological zones of their own regions. They did so in order to take advantage of resources available at different locations during different times of the year. Culturally, and perhaps even biologically, these hunters and gatherers became more diversified as they adjusted to conditions within their own territories.

Figure 17-6 Use of the *atlatl*, or spear-thrower, with a stone weight for balance.

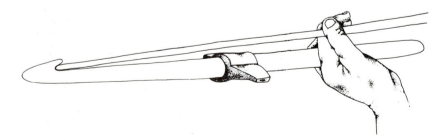

As we shall see shortly, this tradition of intensive foraging led in some cases to the domestication of selected plant species and the subsequent development of New World farming cultures. But for most of the native societies in the Americas, hunting and gathering remained the standard subsistence approach for thousands of years. In a few areas where they were not eventually replaced by horticulturalists (as in regions of too little water or too few frost-free days to promote crop development), hunters and gatherers persisted down to modern times.

The **Great Basin** of the American West, now a largely dry expanse between the Rockies and the Sierra Nevada mountains, was home to hunters and gatherers for at least 10,000 years. Evidence of their way of life has been preserved in dry caves and rock-shelters in the vicinity of the Great Salt Lake (Jennings, 1957; Heizer and Napton, 1970; Aikens, 1970). Excavations at Danger, Lovelock, and Hogup caves in Nevada and Utah have produced thousands of preserved weapons, milling stones, baskets, nets, fur-cloth blanket fragments, sandals and moccasins, bone tools, gaming items, animal bones, and even coprolites or dried human feces. The latter often contain seeds, insect exoskeletons, and often the bones of small rodents and amphibians, which provide direct dietary evidence (Bryant and Williams-Dean, 1975). Although large game animals were hunted whenever possible, it was the variety of seed-bearing plants and small animals such as jackrabbits and waterfowl that provided the greatest proportion of food for these hunters and gatherers.

Farther to the east, such major river valleys as the Mississippi, Tennessee, and Savannah provided ample resources to permit hunters and gatherers in those regions to establish fairly complex societies without relying upon the products of agriculture. Nuts of many kinds provided an important staple for the forest groups. Acorn, chestnut, black walnut, butternut, hickory, and beechnut represent high quality and palatable foods. Some were prepared by parching or roasting, others by crushing and boiling into soups; leaching neutralized the toxic acids in acorns. Intensive and efficient exploitation of these edible nuts, deer, shellfish, forest and riverine products (Caldwell, 1962), and the participation in regional exchange networks (Ford, 1974) enabled these southeastern societies to develop a degree of social organization, religious ceremonialism, and economic interdependence that is not usually observed among nonfarming peoples. Evidence of this sophistication is demonstrated by long-term residence at selected sites dating between 2000 and 6000 y.a. These include the Eva hunting, gathering, and fishing site on the Tennessee River (Lewis and Lewis, 1961); burials accompanied by significant grave goods at Indian Knoll, Kentucky (Webb, 1946); and even a great concentric mound complex at Poverty Point, Louisiana (Ford and Webb, 1956).

Figure 17-7 Yahgan hunter of Cape Horn, South America, late nineteenth century.

◇ Development of Agriculture in the New World

In both the Old and New Worlds, the initial steps toward a way of life that was based upon food production rather than hunting and gathering were taken by about 9000 y.a. There is little question today that these trends toward domestication occurred independently in the two hemispheres. Nevertheless, although different domesticates were involved, the process appears to have been broadly similar in both cases.

We considered the transition from food collecting to food production in the preceding chapter, emphasizing Old World examples. While that general consideration applies as well to the New World, there are some specific additional points worth noting. In contrast to the situation in the Old World, for example, the number of animal species brought under domestication in the Americas was minor, as was their economic importance outside a few areas. It is also apparent that domesticated plant resources in this hemisphere underwent longer periods of selection and evolutionary change, most likely as a result of human interference. Thus, it is more difficult to determine the precise ancestry of major New World domesticates. Nor did the products of agriculture so quickly replace wild produce as the primary components of the prehistoric American diet. The social consequences of farming, including the rise of complex urbanized societies, were not so quickly and dramatically obvious as in the Old World, either.

As in the Near East, the transition to food production in the New World began very early within some arid regions. There seems to be no agreement as to why plant domestication took place in these situations. Everyone acknowledges that in the semidesert areas of Central and South America, naturally occurring food resources were sparse, and were often widely scattered. To take optimal advantage of them, a hunter and gatherer band required a large territory. The members carefully scheduled their movements throughout the various biotic zones of this territory in order to exploit the most productive, nutritious, or reliable products at the most appropriate seasons. Thus, each band devised a well-defined set of subsistence strategies in order to cope with its environment.

From here, there is disagreement as to the exact route to domestication. The first view holds domestication to be the natural consequence of intensive foraging activities in a marginal environment (Flannery, 1968, 1973). Their exploitation of productive localities (or microenvironments) within their larger territories led hunders and gatherers to an increasing reliance upon selected plant resources, especially those preferred because of their concentrated growth pattern, ease of harvest, greater productivity, or food value. People sometimes sought to make more intensive and more efficient use of these resources through the development of new foraging strategies, new technological equipment, or even through experimentation with the plants themselves. Intensive human involvement with these plants readily could have favored significant genetic mutations in some species. Whenever more desirable traits might have resulted, people could be expected to respond to these "improvements" by quickly adapting their collecting behavior to take fullest advantage. As they intensified their focus on such species as maize or runner beans, the foragers eventually abandoned the rhythm of their traditional food-collecting schedule and committed themselves to further increasing the productivity of the chosen plant foods through horticulture.

An alternative explanation explored at length by Cohen (1977) is that plant domestication was an outgrowth of human overpopulation. Since population growth reached critical levels more quickly in marginal environments, it was here that domesticated plants first developed. In a conscious effort to encourage certain "weedy" plants that had been used customarily as secondary or even emergency food sources, people began to propagate maize, beans, and others. As Yudkin (1969) notes, given their choice people everywhere generally prefer fruit and meat, but will turn to root crops and grain when more desirable foods are in short supply. Yet, these low-priority foods share some important qualities as potential domesticates: (1) they grow in disturbed ground, (2) do well in dense concentrations, (3) respond to human manipulation and selection, and (4) are storable forms of protein or carbohydrate (Flannery, 1973). From this viewpoint, horticulture may be seen as an adaptation of a growing population to the natural poverty of its environment.

In either case, the role of wild plants eventually declined, while an increased interdependence, or symbiotic relationship, developed between the horticulturalists and their crops. In this partnership, humans obtained food, while the plant species were nurtured, genetically "improved," and often given an extended range by having their seeds traded, transported, or dispersed in feces.

Domestication of plants in the Americas did not take place within one restricted locale, nor did it occur at the same time in scattered locations. There were many regions in which local plant resources may have become essential to the foodways of native peoples through incipient or even full domestication. Some of these species retained only local significance: seed-bearing marshelder, **amaranths**, and **chenopods** in the eastern United States and the breadnut (*ramón*) in **Mesoamerica** are examples of locally important **cultivars**. But some of the most significant domesticates of the New World include maize (a grass), beans (legumes), and squashes (curcurbits), all of which were native to the dry highlands of Mesoamerica.

Research in several areas of Mexico has demonstrated that this portion of Mesoamerica was a stage for the development of food production in the millennia after 9000 y.a. Sites pertaining to the early history of maize, beans, and squash have been encountered in **Oaxaca**, **Tamaulipas**, and especially in the **Tehuacán Valley** southeast of Mexico City. Archeologist Richard MacNeish led an interdisciplinary research effort in this arid highland valley, where archeology, botany, and paleoecology have shed much light on the early stages of agriculture in the New World (MacNeish, 1964, 1978).

Initially, local microenvironments provided seasonally varied but scattered resources for small bands of foraging humans. Some of these food collectors in the Tehuacán Valley may have begun experimenting with certain of their plant resources, including wild maize, or the grass *teosinte*, in order to encourage a higher level of productivity. These methods could have involved eliminating competition by "weeding," transplanting young plants to more favorable locations, scattering seeds, or even altering the genetic makeup of the plant by cross-pollinating it with other varieties. In the case of maize, the result was a **cultigen** with much larger, more numerous, and more easily processed kernels. Today, maize or corn is one of the world's major crops.

Other plants which were probably under cultivation around the same time in highland Mexico include several varieties of beans and squash, gourds, chili peppers, and cactus fruit. Nevertheless, in the Tehuacán Valley, agricultural products were still providing less than one-third of the human dietary intake by as late as 4250 y.a. (MacNeish, 1964). It is possible that the shift in

Amaranth
(am'-ar-anth)

Chenopod
(keen'-o-pod)

Mesoamerica
("Meso" = middle); the region from southern Mexico through Panama.

Cultivar
A wild plant encouraged by humans.

Oaxaca
(wa-ha'-ka)

Tamaulipas
(tah-mah-leep'-ahs)

Tehuacán Valley
(tay-wah-kahn')
A dry highland region on the boundary of the states of Puebla and Oaxaca in southern Mexico.

Cultigen
A plant that is wholly dependent on humans; a domesticate.

Figure 17-8 Development and use of prehistoric maize in the Tehuacán Valley, Mexico.

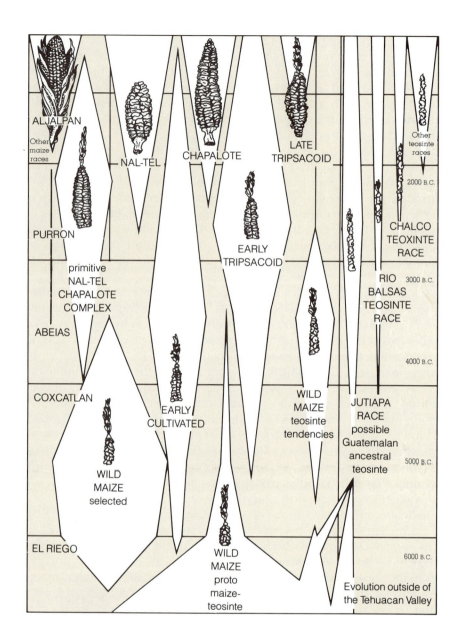

emphasis from collected foods to agricultural products took much longer in this dry highland region than it would have in more favorable environments.

As the residents of the Tehuacán Valley were experimenting with maize and slowly adding other domesticates to their subsistence economy, other peoples in the Andean region of South America were already making use of cultivated species such as beans and chilies by 10,500–9000 y.a. (Lynch, 1980, 1983). These foods added essential proteins and vitamins to a diet that apparently was high in starchy roots and tubers. Maize, which makes an appearance in South America after 6000 y.a. at Guitarrero Cave in Peru, contributed one more very significant component to the diet. Other major

South American cultigens include the white potato, peanuts, and **quinoa**. The probability of exchange of cultigens between the Americas is being pursued, but so far there is no substantial evidence bearing upon this question.

It is clear that domesticated plants from Mesoamerica were introduced into the southwestern United States. Maize and squash seeds as old as 3000 years are reported from Archaic sites in New Mexico (Simmons, 1986). The immediate impact of these early introductions on the subsistence economy of the region's hunters and gatherers appears to have been minimal. Probably the new species were simply encouraged by small-scale horticultural efforts and added to the wild food diet. But population growth and the development of settled village life were the long-run consequences in the following centuries as farming took precedence over hunting and gathering in this region. Between about 2300 y.a. and 1300 y.a., an increased reliance upon domesticated products, a growing population density, and a general cultural elaboration resulted in the emergence of several distinctive cultural traditions in the Southwest (Lipe, 1983). They included **Hohokam** (an archeological culture that may have been ancestral to modern **Pima** and **Papago** peoples); **Anasazi** (builders of the largest prehistoric pueblo villages and cliff dwellings and the forerunners of more recent Puebloan peoples); and **Mogollon** (a culture of pithouse dwellers that had dispersed before the arrival of Europeans in this area).

These regional traditions can be distinguished on the basis of their cultural traits, including pottery styles, architecture, religious ideas, and sociopolitical organization. These Southwestern societies may have been sustained in part by maintaining contact with Mesoamerica. Important Hohokam sites in the vicinity of Phoenix, Arizona, such as Las Colimas and Snaketown, date to around 1000 A.D. and include Mesoamerican-type ball courts and platform mounds, as well as shell jewelry, copper bells, mirrors, anthropomorphic figurines, and other artifacts in the Mesoamerican style (Haury, 1976). Charles DiPeso (1974) has suggested that the Casas Grandes district of northern Chihuahua, Mexico, may have served as a major exchange corridor between Mesoamerica and the Southwest.

Quinoa
(keen-oh'-ah)
Seed-bearing member of the genus *Chenopodium*, cultivated by early Peruvians.

Hohokam
(ho-ho-kahm')

Pima
(pee'-mah)

Papago
(pah'-pah-go)

Anasazi
(an-ah-saw'-zee)

Mogollon
(mo-go-yohn')

Figure 17-9 Anasazi "cliff palace" at Mesa Verde, Colorado, was built by early southwestern farmers.

Anasazi sites are among the most well known, due to their large scale and often excellent preservation. Some of their village ruins are protected as popular national parks today. The cliff dwellings of Mesa Verde, Colorado, and the structures of Chaco Canyon, New Mexico, represent the apex of this farming culture. Pueblo Bonito, the primary town in Chaco Canyon, was a D-shaped building of some 800 rooms that housed perhaps 5,000 people in 1250 A.D. It served as a marketplace and religious center connected to as many as 80 far-flung towns in an 800 km² (about 300 square miles) area.

Many people, such as the Indians of eastern North America and others who lived beyond the periphery of the nuclear zone of agricultural development, only gradually abandoned their hunter and gatherer lifeways. As we have seen, the productive river valleys of the Southeast and the rich forests covering much of the Northeast, as well as the broken prairies of the Midwest, provided adequate returns to support some degree of cultural elaboration even without maize agriculture. The widespread practice of moundbuilding and the rituals pertaining to death and burial persisted from Archaic times in this region and culminated about 2300 y.a. in the Hopewell Interaction Sphere (Struever, 1964). Well-organized groups throughout the southeast and midcontinent areas constructed earthen burial mounds of impressive size and participated in exchanges of ritual goods and ideological concepts that found expression in elaborate burials and their exotic furnishings. We have only recently recognized that, while these Indians were not yet growing maize, they may have adopted nonlocal species of squash and were already cultivating a number of indigenous domesticates (such as marshelder, *Iva annua*) by about 3000 y.a. (Conard et al., 1984). Only after 1500 y.a. in the Southeast and somewhat later in the Northeast, did new varieties of maize and the introduction of domesticated beans make agriculture more practical in these areas (Ford, 1974). Even then, wild nuts, seeds, fish, and game retained their primary place in the diet of most groups.

Among other New World societies, farming had not yet attained much importance even by the time the Europeans were arriving with their new way of life and their Old World domesticates. In fact, throughout much of the Far West, the Far North, and most of South America, hunting and gathering remained the principal way of making a living. Among a few of these non-agriculturalists—such as the coastal peoples of the northwestern United States and Canada—a combination of unusually rich and diverse resources

Figure 17-10 An early view of Monks Mound, part of the Cahokia group near East St. Louis, Illinois. Built in late prehistoric times, it is 300 m (1,000 feet) long and 30 m (100 feet) high.

and an elaborate redistribution system (known in historic times as the **potlatch**) enabled these Northwest Coast Indians to prosper without domesticated crops.

◇ New World Civilizations

The products of agriculture are not always superior in terms of nutritional value to the mixed diet that can be obtained by foraging. Yams, bitter **manioc**, and other starchy root crops domesticated by the peoples of the Amazon basin in South America before 1500 y.a. supplied bulk and carbohydrates, but relatively little protein. This deficiency required continued reliance upon hunting and gathering. But in other areas of the New World, the combination of maize, beans, and plants such as squash served as a suitable substitute for a diet containing animal protein. Nutritionists now recognize that maize and beans contain complementary amino acids, which, when consumed together, form a "complete" protein that can be synthesized by the human body. Squash and similar vegetables add other essentials to a reasonable diet. These major American domesticates formed the nutritional subsistence base for each of the New World's prehistoric civilizations.

It is intriguing that the earliest New World civilizations emerged and prospered exclusively in the low latitudes, within about 20° north or south of the equator. Although a humid lowland center along the southern Gulf of Mexico and the Yucatán Peninsula gave rise to the Olmec and Maya cultures, most advanced cultures of the New World appeared in arid or semiarid settings. Dry highland environments were homelands to a long succession of developed societies in central Mexico and western Peru, for example. Both these areas shared some general geophysical characteristics: steep and rugged terrain, stony soil supporting only sparse shrubs or grassland, little rainfall. In contrast, the advanced cultures of Egypt, Mesopotamia, the Indus Valley, and China all grew upon major river floodplains within arid regions between 25° and 40° north of the equator. Noting environmental associations is one matter; explaining their significance is another. Why did so many civilizations develop in arid regions? Perhaps the only significant connection is that it was in such areas that farming initially appeared, for reasons already considered in Chapter 16. We find that most highly advanced ancient societies were restricted to the same nuclear zones in which agriculture already had been flourishing for thousands of years. Neighboring regions, while not attaining the full elaboration of these primary centers, were sometimes profoundly influenced by them as we have seen in the example of the Hohokam, Anasazi, and Mogollon cultures in the Southwest.

Lowland Mesoamerica

A cultural complex that included ceramics, maize and bean agriculture, and residence in small hamlets characterized the **Purron** phase in the Tehuacán Valley of southern Mexico after 4250 y.a. (MacNeish, 1978). Within several centuries, the inhabitants of the tropical lowlands along the eastern portion

Hopewell
A culture centered in southern Ohio between 100 B.C. and 300 A.D., but influencing a much wider region through trade and the spread of a religious cult.

Potlatch
Ceremonial feasting and gift-giving among the Northwest Coast Indians.

Manioc
Cassava; a starchy edible root crop of the tropics.

Purron
(purr'-own)

Cuello
(quay′-yo)

Olmec
Culture in the Gulf Coast lowlands of Veracruz and Tabasco, Mexico, with a highly developed art style and high degree of sociopolitical complexity; flourished from 3500 y.a.–2500 y.a.

Anthropomorphic
anthro: man
morph: shape
Having or being given a humanlike appearance.

of the Yucatán Peninsula were sharing in a similar cultural development. At the **Cuello** site in the tropical forest zone of Belize, archeologists led by Norman Hammond have defined the 4,000-year-old Swasey Phase (Hammond et al., 1979). The people of this phase created sophisticated ceramics, public architecture in the form of a probable shrine or temple platform, and an economy that apparently was based upon a mixed diet of collected and cultivated seed crops. The remarkable aspect of the Swasey Phase is its clearly ancestral relationship to the Middle to Late Formative or Preclassic Maya culture of lowland Mesoamerica.

By the middle of the second millennium, sedentary farming villages existed throughout much of the lowlands region. Archeologists have long been especially interested in one of these formative cultures that was established along the southern and eastern Gulf Coast of Mexico. This culture is the **Olmec**, which dates from about 3450 to 2350 y.a.

It is likely that the Olmec derived from the same cultural base as other, less conspicuous cultures of Mesoamerica. But the Olmec is highly distinctive primarily because of its art and ceremonialism, which may have been promoted by the presence of an elite sociopolitical caste. The two best-known Olmec sites are the important ceremonial centers at San Lorenzo and La Venta (Adams, 1977). San Lorenzo, the earlier of the two, consists of a linear grouping of mounds on a modified salt dome in Veracruz. In addition to the mounds and their enclosed courtyards and plazas, there are other large-scale features involving the use of many tons of imported basalt rock. Inexplicably, San Lorenzo's demise, around 2850 y.a., is indicated by the startling destruction of most of its artwork and architecture. Following this tragic episode, Olmec culture persisted at La Venta, a remarkable ceremonial center located on a small island in a swamp near the Gulf Coast of Tabasco. An earthen

Figure 17-11 Mesoamerican archaeological sites mentioned in the text.

pyramid 120 m × 70 m (400 × 230 feet) at its base and several lesser mounds and platforms constitute the major features of the site, which probably served as a shrine and possibly also as an elite residence area. La Venta was occupied down to about 2550 y.a.

Both La Venta and San Lorenzo are notable for their art and sculpture, perhaps the most distinctive Olmec characteristics. **Anthropomorphic** forms are represented by sculpted figures and *bas-reliefs* of were-jaguars (half man, half feline) and by huge heads carved from blocks of basalt weighing many tons. The nearest source of the basalt was 100 km (60 miles) away. There are also buried pavements of serpentine blocks that had been set in a mosaic pattern to resemble stylized jaguar faces, and caches of valuable items such as beads, figurines, and implements of jade. Among the most impressive of these caches is a group of small jade carvings that includes sixteen anthropomorphized figurines and six upright posts representing some of the nearby basalt palisades in the La Venta ceremonial center itself. The entire group had been carefully arranged so that most of the figures were confronting another one, who was backed up against the posts. Then, still in position, the group had been intentionally buried.

The Olmec culture exerted its influence throughout a major portion of Mesoamerica. The primary agent of Olmec influence was probably trade. Their own culture required great amounts of raw materials, such as basalt, obsidian, and jade, which were available only in the adjacent foothills and highlands. In turn, Olmec artists and craftsworkers supplied quantities of hollow clay figurines, ceramic vessels, stone masks and sculptures, and many other items, especially those of a ritual nature, to neighboring peoples.

These contacts and exchanges of ceremonial and luxury goods continued even after Olmec times between the lowlands, the Valley of Mexico, and as far

Figure 17-12   Olmec head being excavated at San Lorenzo.

Figure 17-13   Cache of Olmec jade figurines, La Venta.

Maya
Prehistoric Mesoamerican culture that represented the climax of pre-European cultural development between 300 A.D. and 900 A.D.

Teotihuacán
(tay-oh-tee-wah-kahn')

Stela
(stee'-la)
(plural: stelae)
An upright post or stone, often bearing inscriptions.

Tikal
(tee-kal')

Uaxactún
(wash-akh-toon')

Milpa
Slash-and-burn or swidden agriculture.

west as the Pacific coast. The interchanges may have contributed to the further development of regional sociopolitical units that were already verging on civilization.

One of these emerging cultures was the **Maya**. We have already seen that some sophisticated ceramic and architectural traits of the Preclassic Maya have been traced back to the Swasey Phase at the Cuello site in Belize. Before 4000 y.a., then, elements of the later Maya culture already existed in lowland Mesoamerica. What may have stirred the small-village farming culture into a civilization has been long debated. It is possible that the stimulation came in part from the Olmecs and their descendants, or perhaps also through a commercial or even military influence from the flourishing empire of Teotihuacán in the distant Mexican highlands. But it is at least as likely that Maya civilization resulted from an internal reorganization of Maya society itself. Some areas occupied by Preclassic Maya, notably the scrub lands of Yucatán, were not capable of supporting an ever-increasing population that relied solely upon simple slash-and-burn farming. Moreover, some essential materials, among them suitable stone for making tools and milling slabs, were lacking altogether in this region. To increase their food supply and to obtain important products, the Maya resorted to more intensive farming techniques, including raised fields in lowlying areas, terracing, and irrigation. They opened trade with other Maya communities and more distant societies in order to exchange any surplus food and sea salt for useful stone. But establishing and maintaining the new agricultural system and commercial connections could be accomplished only under the authority and direction of a strong leadership. Thus, the transformation from small-scale villages to a more integrated and centralized society seems to have been an adaptive strategy to support a growing population in an area of scarce resources (Carneiro, 1970; Rathje, 1971; Adams, 1977).

Archeologists have made some progress in interpreting the complex hieroglyphic inscriptions on Maya **stelae**, temples, and other monuments. These efforts have rewarded researchers with a better understanding of Classic Maya sociopolitical organization, particularly in terms of the sometimes uneasy relationships among the various ceremonial centers and their hereditary aristocracies (Proskouriakoff, 1960; Graham, 1976). Detailed studies of calendrical notations on Maya sculptures have provided a precise chronology of major events in lowland Mesoamerica. When the Maya calendar system is correlated with our own, the beginning of the Classic period can be set at 292 A.D.

By then, the elements of Classic Maya civilization were in place. The most apparent of these traits was the formal, large-scale architecture of the ceremonial centers. The major features of these carefully designed districts were the large rubble-filled pyramids that served as substructures for temples. Secondary components were the "palaces," ritual ball courts, plazas, causeways, and often reservoirs for storing runoff from tropical rainfalls. Of smaller scale, but of great interest to archeologists, were the stelae or carved stone columns. Mayan ceremonial centers are one key to understanding this lowland civilization. The centers did not serve primarily as urban residence areas, although it is now apparent that some of the larger ones did house great numbers of people, including the ruling elite and their retainers, crafts-

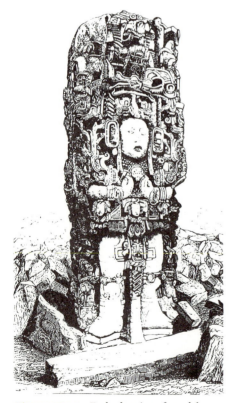

Figure 17-14   Early drawing of an elaborate Maya stela at Copán, Honduras.

◇ Box 17-1   How to Count Like the Maya

The Maya number system was closely linked to their elaborate calendar, which was comprised of 20-day months. The numbers from 1 to 19 were represented by a simple bar-and-dot notation, wherein a dot equalled 1 and a bar had a value of 5. Note the use of the 0, a device not recognized in Europe until the Middle Ages.

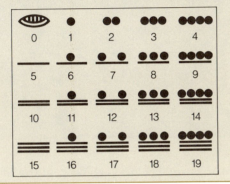

Numbers larger than 19 may be expressed as multiples of 20. The value of the number was determined by its position in a vertical column (much as the value of our numbers is indicated by their position relative to a decimal point). Thus, numbers in the first-place (lowest) position were multiplied by 1; those in the next higher position by 20; in the third, by 400 (20 × 20); in the fourth, by 8,000 (20 × 400), etc. The number for 1,987 may be written as follows:

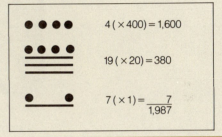

workers and other specialists, and at least some peasants. But much of the population lived in agricultural hamlets that were arranged over the landscape within a short radius from the ceremonial center. Despite their somewhat dispersed constituencies, the centers functioned essentially as cities in that they provided a focus for sociopolitical activity, religious ceremonies, and commerce. The size of the ceremonial centers ranged from those containing a couple of carved stelae or a small temple pyramid to such grand sites as **Tikal** in Guatemala, which, with its supporting area, covered 130 km² (50 square miles). It is now recognized that local centers, sustained directly by local hamlets, were subsidiary to regional centers, which were in turn under the domain of the major centers (such as Tikal) at the top of the hierarchy. Tikal may have achieved its status by controlling a primary river portage through the Maya heartland.

Archeologists historically have devoted much of their attention to the ceremonial centers of the Maya and to their obvious achievements in art and architecture. The more holistic approach of modern anthropological archeology demands a fuller understanding of Maya culture than could be obtained from their monumental constructions alone. Archeologists have now focused considerable effort on individual hamlets and local centers. One matter of basic concern to these researchers is the question of Maya subsistence. For example, the medium-sized center of **Uaxactún**, Guatemala, is estimated to have had as many as 15,000 people associated with it (Adams, 1977). Most of this population resided in small hamlets outside the central district itself. Their house mounds are encountered throughout the jungle wherever maize might have been grown by slash-and-burn or **milpa** techniques. According

Figure 17-15   Maya hieroglyphics on a stela at Copán, Honduras. (Courtesy, Mark A. Gutchen.)

Figure 17-16 View of ceremonial center complex, Tikal. (Courtesy, Mark A. Gutchen.)

to estimates compiled by Ursula Cowgill (1962), a shifting cultivation system in this region could provide for up to 200 people per square mile (2.6 km²).

We now recognize that the Maya continued to use the more intensive farming techniques mentioned earlier: raised and ridged fields, terracing, irrigation, and multiple-cropping. In addition, the Maya diet apparently included considerable quantities of the *ramón* or breadnut (*Brosimum alicastrum*), a reliably productive and high-quality nut that was stored in underground chambers called **chultúns** (Puleston, 1971). The produce of one area was

Figure 17-17 Maya Temple of the Inscriptions, at the site of Palenque, Chiapas, Mexico. (Courtesy, Mark A. Gutchen.)

redistributed to others in order to keep the entire region supplied. Altogether, then, the Maya population probably attained a large size but did so without a great degree of nucleation in urban settings.

For a time, Maya culture developed at an unabated pace, as ceremonial centers grew larger and more impressive. But between 534 A.D. and 593 A.D. there apparently was some disturbance (perhaps a breakdown in relations with Teotihuacán in highland Mexico) that resulted in a dramatic showdown of Maya construction and expansion. From the end of this period to about 790 A.D., Maya civilization at first seemed reinvigorated as it underwent un-paralleled population growth and monumental development, but then it fell into a rapid decline that was essentially complete by 909 A.D. After that date, only a modest and much-modified postclassic Maya culture persisted in northern Yucatán. The remarkable Maya collapse has intrigued scholars for years. Explanations have been offered ranging from theories of peasant revolt, widespread disease or famine, invasion by the militaristic Toltecs from the Valley of Mexico, to others which are marvelously imaginative (for review, see Willey and Shimkin, 1973; Culbert, 1973). The debate, however, continues (see Box 17-2).

Highland Mexico

The Valley of Mexico, in the central Mexican highlands, supported large urban populations beginning about 2150 y.a. with the rise of Teotihuacán. Several freshwater lakes and flowing springs at the southern end of the valley provided a favorable location for farmers, and excellent obsidian sources were worked nearby. Teotihuacán experienced especially rapid growth once the water was brought under better control through a system of irrigation canals. By about 1900 y.a. it had become the paramount urban center in the New World (G. Cowgill, 1974). While intensive agricultural activity took place outside the city, Teotihuacán itself was bustling with the activity of tens of thousands of residents, buyers and sellers at the markets, and visitors to its monumental shrines. At its height (around 1500 y.a.), Teotihuacán covered about 20 km² (8 square miles). Its population of 100,000 to 200,000 or more lived in some 2,000 large residence compounds. Many of these people were employed in one or another of the 500 workshops which specialized in the manufacture of ce-ramic vessels, obsidian blades and carvings, leather goods, and other practical and luxury items.

The city was well organized and carefully planned. Tradespeople and craftsworkers apparently lived in guild districts or **barrios** while the admin-istrative and religious leaders resided in luxurious complexes in the central area. The city itself was built on a grid pattern with a primary north-south axis and a secondary east-west orientation. Avenues, plazas, major monu-ments, and individual houses alike—and even the San Juan River—were aligned to the master plan. The main street (named by Europeans the "Avenue of the Dead") extended northward to a large pyramid ("Pyramid of the Moon"). An even greater structure ("Pyramid of the Sun"), as large at its base as the Egyptian Pyramid of Khufu, occupied a central position along the same avenue. At the very heart of the city were a great ceremonial center (the "Citadel"), which probably functioned as the major temple complex, and the "Great Compound," which may have been Teotihuacán's central marketplace.

Chultún
(shull-toon')
A storage pit used by the Maya for *ramón* or breadnuts.

Barrio
District or neighborhood.

◇ Box 17-2   The Classic Maya Collapse

The decline of Classic Maya culture rapidly encompassed all of southern lowland Mesoamerica during the course of the ninth century A.D. Everywhere in this region, archeologists have found that Maya artisans no longer turned out polychrome-decorated ceramics, nor did they carve and erect inscribed stelae. In fact, ceremonial center construction ceased altogether, and before long nearly all of them were abandoned. Maya culture never revived here.

There has been a great deal of speculation to account for the Maya collapse. Archeologists have sometimes invoked single-cause explanations, including soil erosion or exhaustion of soil nutrients, devastation by hurricanes or earthquakes, severe climatic fluctuations, insect infestations, epidemic diseases, malnutrition, overpopulation, an unbalanced male/female sex ratio, peasant revolts against the elite, competition and warfare between individual centers, and mass migrations. Other scholars have cited external factors, such as the breakdown of trade relations with the areas that supplied the resource-poor Maya, or invasion by people from highland Mexico.

Acknowledging that a collapse did occur, some archeologists argue that its effects have been overdramatized. Jeremy A. Sabloff and William L. Rathje view the collapse as part of a complex process. In the face of a degraded environment and reduced crop yields in the southern lowlands, the Maya elite demanded more temples to appease the gods, thus further burdening the farmers and precipitating an abandonment of the region's centers. Even so, sizable populations of peasants remained in the south. Moreover, some *northern* lowland sites actually expanded and continued to flourish for centuries. New cities, like Mayapán, emerged in late post-Classic times. The character of these sites was profoundly different, their architecture and achievements unspectacular. Recent research portrays these late-period Maya as merchants engaged in an active coastal trade throughout Central America until the Spanish arrived.

SOURCES:
Culbert, T. Patrick (ed.). *The Classic Maya Collapse*, Albuquerque: University of New Mexico Press, 1973.
Sabloff, Jeremy A., and William L. Rathje. "The Rise of a Maya Merchant Class," *Scientific American*, 233(4):72–82, 1975.

Teotihuacán clearly dominated the central highlands during the early centuries of the first millennium A.D. Ceramics, architectural and artistic styles, and other elements of Teotihuacán influence appear at secondary population centers throughout this region. But even well beyond central Mexico, Teotihuacán appears to have extended its hegemony through trade and possibly even military excursions. There are unmistakable signs of the Teotihuacán presence at the Maya site of Kaminaljuyú in the Guatemalan highlands, and at the lowland Maya sites of Tikal, Uaxactún, and Becán (Adams, 1977). Richard E. W. Adams has adopted the view that Teotihuacán may have had a hand in stimulating the transformation of Maya society from a "high chiefdom" level to that of an urban state or true civilization. It does appear that the fortunes of the Maya were somehow linked with those of Teotihuacán: The Maya Classic period was initiated at a time when Teotihuacán was just reaching its full bloom; the sixty-year period of stagnation that the Maya experienced after 534 A.D. may have resulted from a disruption of relations with Teotihuacán; and the period of greatest growth for the Maya corresponded with the fall of Teotihuacán and the dispersal of its population and craftworkers.

Teotihuacán's end apparently came in stages. Shortly after 600 A.D. the culture began to wane in terms of its influence on most other local societies beyond the Valley of Mexico. On the other hand, the population of the city itself remained fairly stable for another century or so before declining rapidly. The factors that brought about the dissolution of this first large urban center of the New World are not understood at present (Davies, 1983).

The demise of the great city-state of Teotihuacán left highland Mesoamerica devoid of its primary sociopolitical and religious center. Several smaller urban centers, located at the outer edges of the Valley of Mexico, contended for control of the region. The one which eventually emerged as the most powerful was **Tula**, located some 65 km (40 miles) northwest of Teotihuacán. Tula possibly had been established as a small colony of Teotihuacán, but after the fall of the capital city, Tula attracted many residents who had been living on the northern periphery of the area once dominated by the great center (Adams, 1977). During the tenth century A.D., a people known historically as the **Toltecs** set up their capital at Tula, and the city rapidly grew to cover an area about half that of Teotihuacán. Tula itself contained only a modest ceremonial center that could not rival those built during Classic times, but it did enjoy a brief period of success as the focus of a commercial and military enterprise that expanded through trade networks, colonization efforts, and possible conquest (Davies, 1983).

The Toltecs may well have been the agents by which copper objects and other exotic goods were introduced into the southwestern United States. Traditionally, they also have been viewed as intruders into the post-Classic Maya realm. The late Maya site of **Chichén Itzá** in northcentral Yucatán shares striking similarities with Tula itself, including details of art style and the form of its ball court, temple pyramids, and other major public buildings. Some archeologists who once interpreted the evidence as an indication of Toltec domination have now reassessed their opinions (Weaver, 1981). In the absence of archeological indications of a late Toltec invasion, and with a revised

Tula
(too'-la)

Toltecs
A central Mexican highlands people who created a pre-Aztec empire with its capital at Tula in the Valley of Mexico.

Chichén Itzá
(chee-chen' eet-zah')

Figure 17-18 Feathered-serpent figure on temple façade, Teotihuacán. (Courtesy, Mark A. Gutchen.)

Aztecs
A militaristic people who dominated the Valley of Mexico and the surrounding area at the time of the European conquest.

Chinampa
(cheen-ahm'-pah)
Aztec garden plots made by dredging muck from the lake bottom and canals.

Tenochtitlán
(tay-nosh-teet-lahn')

Figure 17-19 Toltec serpentine columns and votive figure, Temple of the Warriors, Chichén Itzá, Yucatán. (Courtesy, Mark A. Gutchen.)

chronology for architectural styles at Chichén Itzá, it now seems possible that the site had been begun during the Late Classic Maya era, when Mexican and Maya influences may have been shared more or less amiably during a period of extensive trade contact between Yucatán and the Valley of Mexico. This argument seems especially attractive since the Toltec city exhibits Maya influence in its carved stelae and polychrome pottery.

By the mid-twelfth century, Chichén Itzá had yielded its preeminence as a commercial center to Mayapán, an unspectacular city 125 km (80 miles) to the east. Meanwhile, in the highland, internal dissension, problems on the frontier, and perhaps even warfare resulted in the decline of Toltec power. Tula itself was finally abandoned around 1175 A.D., after an episode that saw the sacking of its temples and palaces. The result was that the Valley of Mexico was once again in turmoil, as people migrated into and out of the area, and as developing cities contended for superiority. One group that arrived on the scene around 1200 A.D. was the Mexica, later to be known as the **Aztecs**. These people seem to have been militarists eager to ally themselves with anyone who could further their own interests. In the mid-1300s they were able to establish their own city on an easily defended group of small islands near shallow Lake Texcoco's western shore, in the heart of the Valley of Mexico. With great industry they created causeways, canals, and **chinampas**, rich agricultural plots formed by dredging up muck from the lake bottom. They constructed a great central plaza that included palaces, administrative buildings, and huge twin pyramid-based temples for their gods. Until the arrival of the Spanish, **Tenochtitlán**, the Aztec capital, was a large and lively urban and religious center. Some of its impressive ruins recently have been discovered beneath the streets of modern Mexico City (Moctezuma, 1984).

The Aztecs shared and built on many of the accomplishments of earlier Mesoamerican cultures. Their calendar, for example, is a modification of that used by the Maya. Aztec religion, with its emphasis on the sun and on war and human sacrifice, seems to be derived from Toltec practices and, ultimately perhaps, from ancient Teotihuacán. Without doubt, the Aztecs also learned a great deal about social and political organization, warfare, and economic enterprise from their predecessors.

Through their well-trained military and an aggressive state-sponsored corps of professional merchants, the Aztecs dominated neighboring peoples and otherwise extended their influence well beyond the Valley of Mexico. As we shall see, however, their empire was brought to an end only a few decades after it began.

Peru

The great Inca Empire encountered by Europeans in the sixteenth century extended over most of highland and coastal South America from Colombia to Argentina and Chile. In many respects this Inca civilization was the culmination of much that had preceded it. Its foundations were rooted in the earlier prehistory of western South America, especially in Peru, where sociopolitical complexity developed together with an increasing proficiency in food production.

On first view, Peru seems an unlikely region for nurturing agricultural civilizations. Its Pacific shore forms a coastal desert averaging only a few miles in width, a dry fringe of land broken at intervals by dozens of deeply entrenched valleys that cross it laterally from the Andes to the ocean. Mountains rise abruptly and dramatically behind this narrow coastal plain to create a rugged and snow-capped continenal spine that extends along the whole Pacific flank of South America. These geographical contrasts figured prominently in Peru's prehistory.

The zone lying between the sea and the mountains probably served as the major thoroughfare and attraction for the continent's earliest humans, as well as for their late Pleistocene prey animals and edible plant foods. A generalized hunter and gatherer adaptation to this resource belt resulted in a pattern of

Figure 17-20 Peruvian archeological sites mentioned in the text.

Transhumance
Seasonal migration from one resource zone to another.

Chavín de Huántar
(cha-veen' day wahn'-tar)

Raptor
A hunting bird with talons and hooked beak, such as an eagle.

Oracle
A person believed to be in touch with the deities.

Huaca del Sol
(wah'-ka dell soul)

Polychrome
Many-colored.

Huari
(wah'-ri)

Tiahuanaco
(tee-eh-wahn-ah'-co)

Chimu
A powerful culture that dominated the northern Peruvian coast between about 1000 A.D. and 1476 A.D.

transhumance, or carefully scheduled movements between coastal and upland locations, where various plants, animals, or seafoods would be available at different times of the year. By about 6000 y.a., this exploitation pattern was modified by groups who began to rely on coastal resources year-round. At Chilca, a site on the coast a short distance south of Lima, people lived in permanent villages as they consumed sea mammals, fish, shellfish, turtles, and sea birds. Sometime around 4500 y.a., some of the central coast fishing villagers had begun growing cotton for weaving fabric. Their small-scale agriculture also furnished chilies, squash, and beans as supplements to the primarily seafood diet.

For reasons not yet fully understood, a new subsistence emphasis on agricultural products after about 3750 y.a. correlates with a population shift from coastal fishing villages to the upper valleys of rivers, such as the Chillón and Ancón. Here, organized communities excavated irrigation canals reaching into the adjacent desert to water important new staples, particularly maize and peanuts. The success of these early farming practices is evident at the site of Las Haldas, on the plateau between the Casma and Culebra valleys of northern Peru. Some 2,000 residents lived in a town that boasted a large terraced mud-brick pyramid and plazas for ceremonial use. Finely crafted artifacts were made by specialists and included loom-woven fabric of cotton and llama or alpaca wool, molded ceramic vessels, and small objects formed from precious metals. Similar settlements are found on other river valley sites during the period from 3750 y.a.–2850 y.a. (Moseley, 1975b).

In the highlands, meanwhile, there appear to have been parallel developments. Maize farming and the domestication of the potato and other crops may have occurred initially in the uplands. The ruins of Kotosh at an elevation of 1,800 m (6,000 feet) in the central Andes, reveal a large and surprisingly sophisticated farming settlement (Willey, 1971). An even more remarkable highland site is located north of Kotosh. **Chavín de Huántar** is an impressive ceremonial center with elaborate stone temples and platforms that contain underground chambers and labyrinthine passageways. Much of the associated artwork is highly distinctive, featuring sinister anthropomorphic figures that combine human characteristics with the features of snakes, jaguars, **raptorial** birds, and mythological beings. While Chavín de Huántar itself may have served as a religious retreat or perhaps as the seat of an **oracle**, the Chavín art style was disseminated widely throughout Peru. Chavín, much like the Olmec art of Mesoamerica, constituted an agent of cultural unification, at least on a stylistic and ideological level. It represents the first episode of expansionism in the highlands.

By about 2100 y.a., the appeal of Chavín had faded, and there was once again a trend toward more isolated developments in Peru. The next few centuries saw the establishment and growth of influential urban centers in the Moche Valley of the north coast and Nazca in the south. Associated constructions in these two areas indicate that the cities also served as major ceremonial centers. One massive mud-brick pyramid, **Huaca del Sol**, at Moche measured 228 × 136 m and rose 41 m above its base (750 × 450 × 135 feet). Monumental architecture is also found in the Nazca Valley. Both areas seem to have had a high degree of social organization and control. Not only the large-scale construction of pyramids, canals, and major buildings, but also the specialization of crafts would indicate a complex society under effective management.

Artists in both areas produced fabulous objects that adhered to formally defined local styles. Beautifully modelled **polychrome** ceramic vessels, often taking the form of portrait heads, buildings, three-dimensional scenes, or imaginative fantasies, were a Moche speciality. Nazca pottery had an appeal of its own with its brightly painted surfaces. Metalsmiths in both regions produced superb gold, silver, and copper work as status objects for the elite. Many of the luxury items were produced especially as grave furniture. Nazca dead were customarily wrapped in richly embroidered, multicolored textiles that display highly stylized animal and human figures. The most intriguing feature of Nazca culture may be the mystifying lines, geometric designs, and animal figures that are "drawn" in gigantic scale on the flat desert tableland of the southern coast. Many of these motifs seem to be shared with the burial wrappings and decorated ceramic vessels (Kosok and Reiche, 1949; Isbell, 1978).

Moche and Nazca influences were localized largely within their respective coastal valleys. But the southern highlands witnessed its second period of expansionism around 1400 y.a. **Huari** and **Tiahuanaco** were well-organized polities that used religion, trade, control of food and labor, and military conquest to further their interests in the central Andes. Neither of these kingdoms endured for long, but the impetus toward unification of ever larger regions did not end with them. In fact, Peru's north coast was involved in a parallel development about 1000 y.a.

The **Chimu** Empire had its roots in the earlier Moche Valley culture. Its capital was Chan Chan, a city whose mud-brick architecture still blankets

Figure 17-21   Nazca ceramic vessel, southern Peru. (Courtesy, Katherine Pomonis.)

Figure 17-22   Detail of Paracas textile, Nazca culture, Peru.

15 km² (6 square miles) of the coastal desert (Moseley, 1975a). Its major features are nine spacious compounds that had been enclosed by walls standing as high as 10 m (35 feet). These enclosures perhaps served as grand but secluded residence units for each of the successive monarchs of the ruling dynasty. The crowded adobe quarters of the urban peasants were spread under the shadow of the massive walls. The Chimu state seems to have maintained its control over the north coast through the establishment of local administrative centers that watched over local populations and directed large-scale projects of canal construction and agricultural terracing (Kus, 1984).

Some archeologists have pointed out that the prehistory of western South America reflects a theme of increasing sociopolitical integration (Moseley, 1983). To this point, we have seen that the process varied between northern coastal areas and the southern highlands. The highland people tended to push "downward," toward the lowlands; those along the coast spread laterally, incorporating adjacent coastal valleys. In either case, the object was to gain access to additional resource zones (Murra, 1972). Overpopulation, resource depletion, or environmental degradation could have stimulated the aggressive expansionism observed periodically in Peru's prehistory.

The Chimu state set the stage for the final episode of native empire-building. Lessons learned and taught by the Chimu were not lost on their rivals and successors, the **Inca**. Beginning as a minor highland culture centered around present-day **Cuzco**, the Inca gained rapid ascendancy over the southern highlands after some bold military enterprises in the mid-fifteenth century. The aging Chimu Empire offered relatively little resistance in the north, and by 1476 the Inca had consolidated their imperial domain over all

Figure 17-23 Aerial view of one of the royal enclosures at Chan Chan, the Chimu capital.

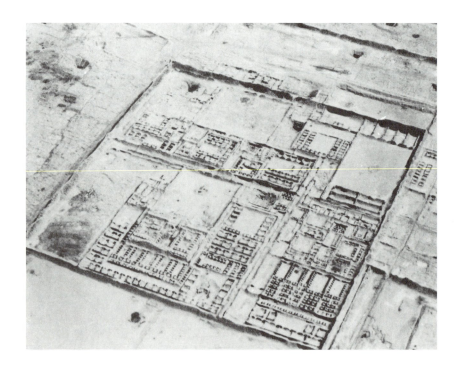

of modern Peru and several adjacent regions. The Inca army had had a major role in this success, but equally important in maintaining it was an efficient administration that established communication and supply systems to hold the empire together. The absolute rule of the divine emperor, or *Inca*, was effectively carried out by subordinates who oversaw the collection of taxes, allotment of communal lands, dispersal of malcontents, and selection of the "Chosen Women" who were destined for marriage to the nobles or sacrifice to the gods.

Cuzco became the capital of an empire whose population is estimated to have been six million (Lanning, 1967). In contrast to the principal cities of other prehistoric American civilizations, the highland town of Cuzco was surprisingly small and rural in character. Its central area comprised a simple ceremonial district with several villages in close proximity. On a hill overlooking Cuzco was the **Sacsahuamán** fortress. Its mortarless walls were formed by huge stone blocks that had been expertly dressed and fitted together. This distinctive architectural style is seen throughout the territory of the Inca.

Well-maintained roads led out of Cuzco to the four quarters of the Inca Empire, crossing mountains, valleys, and deserts to tie the far-flung domains together. Beyond Cuzco, the only other large settlements were Pachacamac, the seat of a respected oracle on Peru's central coast, and Quito, in Equador, established as a second capital by Inca Huayna Capac. The population of the Inca Empire consisted almost exclusively of rural peasants. Most grew maize, potatoes, quinoa, or other crops on terraced hillsides or in irrigated alluvial valleys. Herders in the highlands drove flocks of domesticated llama and

Inca
The people whose sophisticated culture dominated Peru at the time of the Europeans' arrival; also, the term for that people's divine ruler.

Cuzco
(coos'-co)

Sacsahuamán
(sack-sa-wah-mahn')

Figure 17-24   Inca stone walls at Sacsahuamán, near Cuzco, Peru. (Courtesy, Katherine Pomonis.)

alpaca, which supplied transport, wool, dung for fuel, religious sacrifices, and food, although the only meat consumed by most people was the domesticated guinea pig, a small tailless rodent.

The Inca had deliberately resisted the development of major urban centers because they feared the possibility that large numbers of city dwellers might be a potential source of unrest. Careful resettlement programs broke up established population clusters in newly conquered areas. Yet, despite the precautions, the Inca Empire lasted for only about sixty years.

◇ European Conquest of the New World

By the first quarter of the sixteenth century, many Europeans were well aware that what Columbus had come upon was truly a new world, rather than the new route to the East Indies that he and his sponsors had hoped for. It is not too much to say that disappointment was the main feeling expressed by most who had any interest at all in the episode. After disappointment came a determination to make the best of the situation. Spanish, Portuguese, English, Dutch, and French parties were sent off, each to see what could be wrung from this "new found land" that lay across the path to the exotic wealth of the Orient. In the meantime, all would be searching for any possible way over, around, or past America.

Perhaps it is unfortunate that there were no anthropologists in the 1500s to alert their fellow citizens to the unique circumstances that were coming to a climax not only in America but in Africa and Asia as well. Never before and never again would there be such a large-scale confrontation between peoples and cultures that had evolved in isolation over hundreds of generations. On the other hand, it is doubtful that the painful course of events that was to follow could have been altogether avoided even if the situation had been fully appreciated.

The Western Hemisphere was populated by perhaps 100 million people (Dobyns, 1966) who shared a remarkable range and richness of genetic, cultural, and linguistic variation. Small bands of hunters and fishers peopled the northernmost and southernmost extremes of the continents. Foragers and tribes of horticulturalists occupied most of the middle latitudes. A few large agricultural chiefdoms maintained sway in the southeast United States, the Caribbean Islands, and northern South America. But more than a third of all the New World's peoples were subjects of one or the other of the great societies that still prevailed in highland Mexico and Peru in the early 1500s.

Aztec and Inca were the nuclear civilizations of America. Both represented the culmination of many centuries of cultural tradition and development in their respective areas. Each had reached an apex of achievement in every dimension—art, social organization, commerce, technology, learning, government, and religion. The Aztec and Inca states commanded the resources, talents, and vigor of vast territories. At the same time, their influence radiated into even larger regions of the two continents. These centers of wealth and power attracted the armored Europeans like a magnet.

Their end came with shocking swiftness. The two decades following 1520 saw both the Aztec and the Inca and their domains thoroughly enslaved by Spanish conquerors (Prescott, 1906). Leaving Cuba in 1519, Hernán Cortés and his fellow adventurers pressed through the swampy lowlands of Veracruz and onto the central highlands of Mexico, where, in 1521, they were received with some justifiable suspicion by the Aztec emperor Moctezuma II. As Cortés and his 400 soldiers entered Tenochtitlán, they were reminded of the principal cities of their native Spain, which hardly surpassed the Aztec capital in size or grandeur. Their admiration notwithstanding, the newcomers resolved to seize Tenochtitlán. Almost immediately Moctezuma found himself imprisoned and the Spanish in control. An uprising against the European invaders was quelled with the willing assistance of thousands of the Aztecs' disenchanted former subjects. By 1524, the Spanish were the uncontested successors to the great empire in the heartland of Mesoamerica.

The conquest of Peru shared some similarities. An expeditionary force of 180 men led by Francisco Pizarro entered the Inca domain in 1527, just as **Atahuallpa** claimed victory in a bitter five-year struggle for succession to the throne of his father, **Huayna Capac**. Pizarro found many disappointed followers of Huascar, Atahuallpa's half-brother and rival for the throne, eager to assist in deposing the new Inca. Through treachery, the Spanish were able to eliminate both of the contenders, but not until they had first amassed a fabulous ransom in gold and silver from the unfortunate Atahuallpa, who was then put to death. Despite some resistance that followed these episodes, the Spanish had firm control of Peru by 1538.

In one brief and tragic, yet remarkable moment of history, the crowning achievements of half a world had been undone. Successive decades would witness the wholesale devastation of peoples and cultures that had represented tens of thousands of years of development and adaptation. The Spanish conquest proceeded outward from the Mexican and Peruvian centers while other Europeans began the process anew in the more peripheral areas occupied by tribal peoples and bands. The cost of the confrontation, in human and cultural terms, was enormous; the foregone potential will be forever incalculable. The loss, if not the shame, is borne by all humankind.

Atahuallpa
(at-a-wall'-pah)

Huayna Capac
(why'-na kah'-pak)

◇ Summary

In this chapter, we have considered the long prehistory of the New World's inhabitants. We began by tracing the original American cultural and genetic stock back to northeastern Asia. While the date of human entry into the New World via a now-submerged Bering land bridge cannot presently be dated with precision, it undoubtedly occurred at least by 12,000 y.a., when sites of big game hunters appear in many parts of the Americas.

After the end of the Pleistocene, groups in most regions were engaged in the intensive hunting and gathering of a wide variety of plant and animal resources. In a few areas, such as highland Mexico and Peru, some of these foragers gradually increased their reliance on a few favored species, then eventually began to produce a significant portion of their food from fully domesticated crops. The impact of agriculture spread well beyond these initial zones and in some cases stimulated further cultural elaboration.

The development of highly complex societies in Mesoamerica and the western coast and Andean areas of South America after about 4000 y.a. set the trends for the later stages of prehistory. The alternate flourishing and waning of successive civilizations affected the larger regions that were linked to these centers through military, political, religious, and/or economic ties. The final dissolution of America's native cultures was a tragic consequence of the Old World's rediscovery of the New.

◇ Questions for Review

1. What kinds of biological and cultural clues support the idea that the Amerinds originated in Asia?
2. Why is it so difficult to address the question of whether people were living in the New World before the last glaciation?
3. How does the nature of the archeological evidence for Paleo-Indians bias our view of them as big-game hunters?
4. What explanation can be offered to account for the early development of food production in such marginal environments as the Tehuacán Valley, rather than more favored regions such as the woodlands of the eastern United States?
5. What are some of the qualities of maize that contribute to its great importance as a New World domesticate?
6. What functions did ceremonial centers serve in the cultures of Meso-america?
7. In what ways does it appear that Olmec and Chavín had a similar impact on their respective culture areas?
8. What was the nature of the relationship between the lowland Maya and the early civilizations of the Valley of Mexico?
9. What are some of the historical parallels between the Aztec and Inca cultures?
10. What are some of the ways in which the early civilizations of the New World contrasted with those of the Old World?

Human Evolution: A Biocultural Process

What does it mean to be human? Certainly, part of the answer is understandable in terms of organic evolution—as it applies to any animal. Indeed, we are animals, and the evolutionary process acts similarly on humans through the combined action of the evolutionary forces: mutation, genetic drift, migration, and natural selection. Human populations have evolved and continue to do so as gene frequencies shift in response to these forces.

Thus, our origins are ultimately traceable to the roots of life on this planet, close to 3.5 billion years ago (Gurin, 1980). The last 500 million years of evolution, as told by the fossil vertebrate record, informs us more directly of our immediate precursors. Even more specifically, we can trace our roots to the placental mammal radiation and from here to the beginnings of the primate order more than 60 m.y.a.

Through comparative studies of modern primates, prosimians, monkeys, apes, and ourselves, we are able to flesh out the bits and pieces of bones and teeth that comprise the fossil record of our primate ancestors. From such comparisons we know that early anthropoids began diverging in the Old World by probably 40 m.y.a. and the first hominoid was already on the scene by 20 m.y.a. (perhaps close to 30 m.y.a.).

When, however, did the unique evolutionary radiation occur that produced the first hominid? The exact timing of this evolutionary event is still disputed, but evidence suggests a date somewhere between 10–5 m.y.a. for the appearance of the first member of the human family.

The first half of hominid evolutionary history is still clouded in mystery, but ongoing research by Richard Leakey, Donald Johanson, David Pilbeam, and others is aimed at filling in this gap. We now know considerably more about the last 5 million years. Abundant evidence from the Plio-Pleistocene of South and East Africa tells of a variety of early hominid forms. The earliest definite hominid—*Australopithecus afarensis*—is an extremely small-brained, but completely bipedal, hominid. It remains to be seen if this primitive hominid consistently made tools, but to date no stone artifacts have been found in association with this fossil form. Despite its relative primitiveness, *A. afarensis* may indeed be our ancestor.

A more definitive biocultural interaction among our ancestors is indicated by 2 m.y.a. At this time, early members of our genus (*Homo*) are emerging in Africa (also possibly Asia), and they are associated with stone tool remains at several localities. Not surprisingly, then, early members of the genus *Homo* show significantly larger brains than their australopithecine cousins—whom they eventually outcompeted.

The fossil record of our ancestors continues its saga with *Homo erectus*, transitional forms, a variety of *sapiens* forms (among them, Neandertal), and finally the appearance of fully modern humans (*Homo sapiens sapiens*) around 40,000 years ago (and perhaps as early as 100,000 years ago).

This then, briefly, is the human evolutionary journey. But it is told to us in more than just morphological details of tooth and bone, for we *and* our ancestors are more than just physical organisms blindly following the dictates of organic evolution. Several million years ago our early hominid ancestors began culturally to modify their environments, thus drastically altering their ecological niche and henceforth setting a new direction for human evolution.

What we are and how we came to be that way can only be answered in terms of biocultural processes. Whether we are talking about the first crude attempts to knock a flake off a lava cobble or the landing of human beings on the moon, the process is a unified one. It may well be true that "man makyth tools" but it is equally true that "tools makyth man."

The results of our unique evolutionary history are recounted in the size and the structure of our brain, our dental apparatus, and our bipedal gait (with its manifold physical requirements). We, however, can also see the imprint of our special hominid origins in our behavior: our cultural abilities to make and use tools, our symbolic language, our passion to be social.

Indeed, as we have emphasized repeatedly, the physical structure of our body has been molded by evolutionary factors relating to concomitant development of *all* these behavioral characteristics. Does our evolution, then, *explain* our behavior? Today, there are those in biology and anthropology who believe that it does.

A new emphasis in behavioral biology developed over the last decade has been given the name "sociobiology" (Wilson, 1975; Barash, 1982). In its more restrained pragmatic applications, this approach attempts to understand social behavior among insects and birds in terms of natural selection models. In other words, sociobiology assumes that social behavior among these animals can be best understood by relating such behavior to reproductive success of individuals. In some cases, such as sterile "altruistic" worker castes among social insects, such a perspective is most helpful (Hamilton, 1964).

What, however, can we say about human behavior? Many popular writers have argued that humankind's current behavior involving territorial nation-states, organized warfare, etc. is merely an extension of hominid behavioral propensities developed during the last several million years. Often emphasized as a primary determinant in shaping human behavior is the role of hunting (Ardrey, 1976), creating a "killer-ape" (Morris, 1967).

We have seen that systematic hunting of big game did become an important factor in *erectus* times around 1 m.y.a. The behavioral demands of such social hunting *may* have selected for more cohesive social organization, more effective means of communication, and more specialized tools. These demands in turn *may* have placed a higher selection benefit on larger brains. It makes a neat model, but even at this level it is highly speculative. Neither the fossil record nor archeological traces inform us directly concerning the exact circumstances that caused increases in hominid brain size.

Even more speculative are the postulations concerning the determining influence of hunting on human aggression, territoriality, male/female differences, and so on. Given the nature of the evidence, such wanton speculation—no matter how intellectually appealing—is to be avoided.

What then can we say about the evolution of human behavior? The development of culture most assuredly has shaped our behavioral *capacities*. The fact, that *Homo sapiens* characteristically has such a complex neurological foundation and that we are all capable of symbolic language reveal our biocultural evolutionary heritage. However, the development of culture also created an entirely new realm of behavioral possibilities. Our hominid ancestors, like us, were symbol-making, cognitively complex animals. Their behavior, and ours, thus has a large element of choice built in. The capacity for language and culture is inherited, but the form it will take is *learned*. As such, our behavior is subject to considerable modification even during one individual's lifetime.

Humans are not blind gene-machines simply pursuing the ultimate end of greater individual reproductive success. *Unlike any other animal on earth* we have the possibility of almost infinite behavioral creativity; what is more, we have the self-awareness that such flexibility exists. By means of cognitive devices that Richard Dawkins calls "memes," humans have forever departed from the course of gene-determined biological evolution into the sphere of a culturally and symbolically mediated development (Dawkins, 1976).

While cultural norms (as applied to the group) and biological success (as applied to the individuals within the group) may occasionally come into conflict, over the long run they should harmonize to some degree (Cavalli-Sforza and Feldman, 1981). Without a viable interaction of biocultural elements, neither human beings—nor the human groups upon which we depend for survival—could be expected to long endure.

Hominid evolutionary development has created *Homo sapiens*, an animal with behavioral flexibility. In a sense, we are products of our evolution. But unlike any other organism on this planet we can infinitely mold our own behavior through exercise of our own uniquely human creativity.

Homo sapiens groups increased the pace of cultural modification around 10,000 years ago. We have seen how the physical geography as well as plant and animal communities changed as the glaciers receded. So, too, with human groups. Our species is not immune to evolutionary forces. As environments change, evolution does not stop; it changes direction. With the development of agriculture and dense permanent settlements came new selection pressures, especially infectious disease. For example, the spread of the sickle-cell trait in response to malarial pressures demonstrates how such a natural selection process acts on human populations within their cultural environments.

The rate of cultural changes has continued to accelerate over the last ten millennia. We have traced how—in the span of just a few thousand years—agriculture developed in several areas in the Old World. At about the same time, human groups began to experiment with plant domestication in the New World. We have likewise noted the emergence of advanced and complex societies—civilizations—in both hemispheres. What is most intriguing (barring unlikely transoceanic contacts) is that these developments occurred *independently* in both areas of the globe.

Many cultural anthropologists/archeologists have used such evidence to argue for regular patterns—even laws—governing the direction of cultural change. Some have gone so far as to postulate models explaining how culture *evolves*. We must bear in mind, however, that the processes underlying cultural evolution are fundamentally different from those of biological evolution:

There are no discrete units of cultural transmission (analogous to genes) nor does cultural selection (measured by success of groups) parallel natural selection (measured by success of individuals).

Given these considerations, it still cannot be denied that cultures do change, that these changes have direction, and that some cultures survive and grow while others perish. In fact, if we are meaningfully to understand anything of the last few thousand years of human history, it is only through studying these *cultural* factors.

Does this mean we have at last left the realm of biological evolution completely? By no means. Mutation still occurs, and the potential mutagenic effects of artificial radiation and chemicals pose the danger of still further increasing the frequency of genetic "mistakes." Natural selection is also still operating in a very powerful way; perhaps as many as 85% of all the zygotes conceived never reproduce. Moreover, results of the accelerated pace of migration in the last five centuries are visible all around us.

What we are saying is that our profound ability to modify our environments has outdistanced our biological capacity to respond. As slowly maturing mammals, our generation span is considerably longer than that of most other animals. Unlike the mosquitoes that have biologically (adaptively) responded to massive environmental changes such as DDT, we cannot adapt so quickly. If mosquitoes had sprayed us continually with equal amounts of insecticides (which they might call "humanicides"), we almost certainly would have been completely wiped out.

How then can we be expected to cope with the new biological pressures of the modern technological world? Clearly, the biggest dangers are the cultural ones we have created for ourselves: overcrowding, pollution, radiation, and so forth. Equally clearly, the only viable answers are also cultural ones. As human beings we possess the capability to remake our world—for better or worse. The choices are ours.

Atlas of Primate Skeletal Anatomy

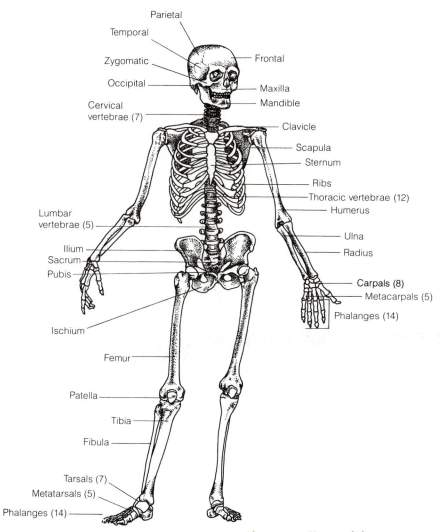

Parietal
Temporal
Zygomatic
Occipital
Frontal
Maxilla
Mandible
Cervical vertebrae (7)
Clavicle
Scapula
Sternum
Ribs
Thoracic vertebrae (12)
Humerus
Lumbar vertebrae (5)
Ulna
Ilium
Radius
Sacrum
Pubis
Carpals (8)
Metacarpals (5)
Phalanges (14)
Ischium
Femur
Patella
Tibia
Fibula
Tarsals (7)
Metatarsals (5)
Phalanges (14)

Figure A-1 Human skeleton (*Homo sapiens*)—bipedal hominid.

527

Figure A-2   Chimpanzee skeleton (*Pan troglodytes*) A knuckle-walking pongid.

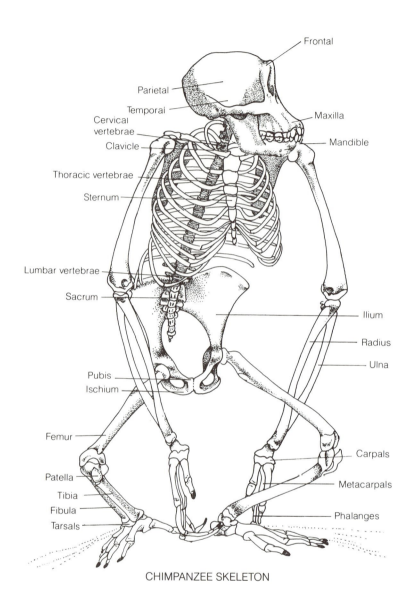

CHIMPANZEE SKELETON

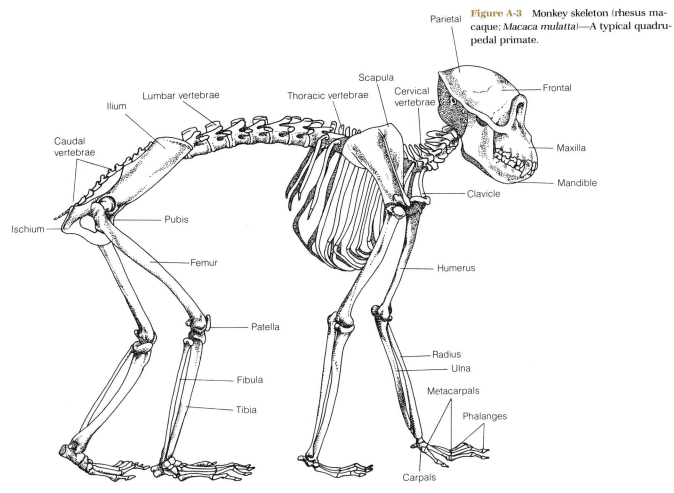

Parietal

Scapula

Cervical vertebrae

Frontal

Lumbar vertebrae

Thoracic vertebrae

Ilium

Maxilla

Caudal vertebrae

Mandible

Clavicle

Ischium

Pubis

Humerus

Femur

Patella

Radius

Ulna

Fibula

Metacarpals

Tibia

Phalanges

Carpals

MONKEY SKELETON

Figure A-4 Human cranium.

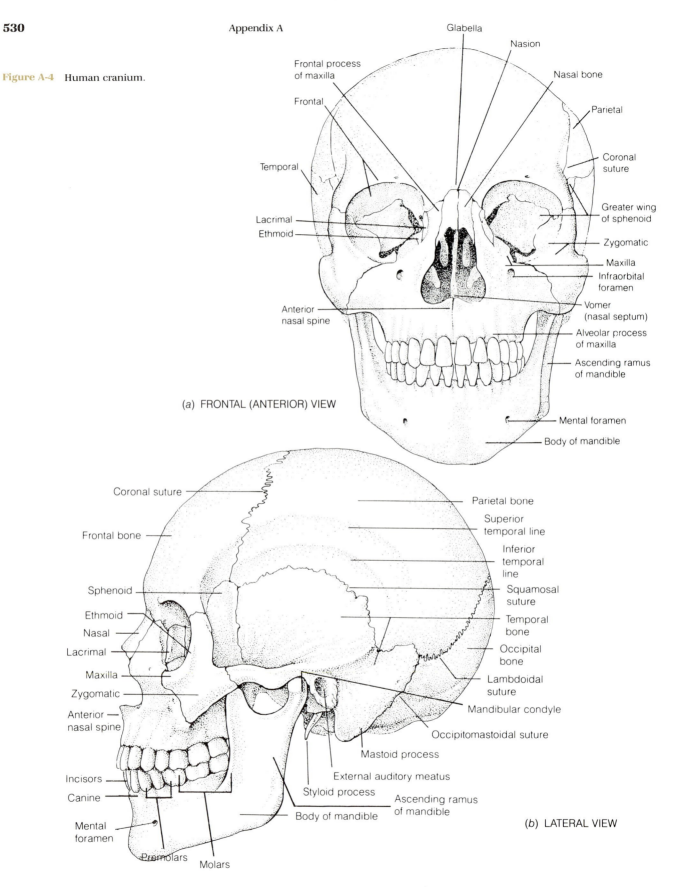

(a) FRONTAL (ANTERIOR) VIEW

Frontal process of maxilla

Frontal

Temporal

Lacrimal

Ethmoid

Anterior nasal spine

Glabella

Nasion

Nasal bone

Parietal

Coronal suture

Greater wing of sphenoid

Zygomatic

Maxilla

Infraorbital foramen

Vomer (nasal septum)

Alveolar process of maxilla

Ascending ramus of mandible

Mental foramen

Body of mandible

(b) LATERAL VIEW

Coronal suture

Frontal bone

Sphenoid

Ethmoid

Nasal

Lacrimal

Maxilla

Zygomatic

Anterior nasal spine

Incisors

Canine

Mental foramen

Premolars

Molars

Parietal bone

Superior temporal line

Inferior temporal line

Squamosal suture

Temporal bone

Occipital bone

Lambdoidal suture

Mandibular condyle

Occipitomastoidal suture

Mastoid process

External auditory meatus

Styloid process

Ascending ramus of mandible

Body of mandible

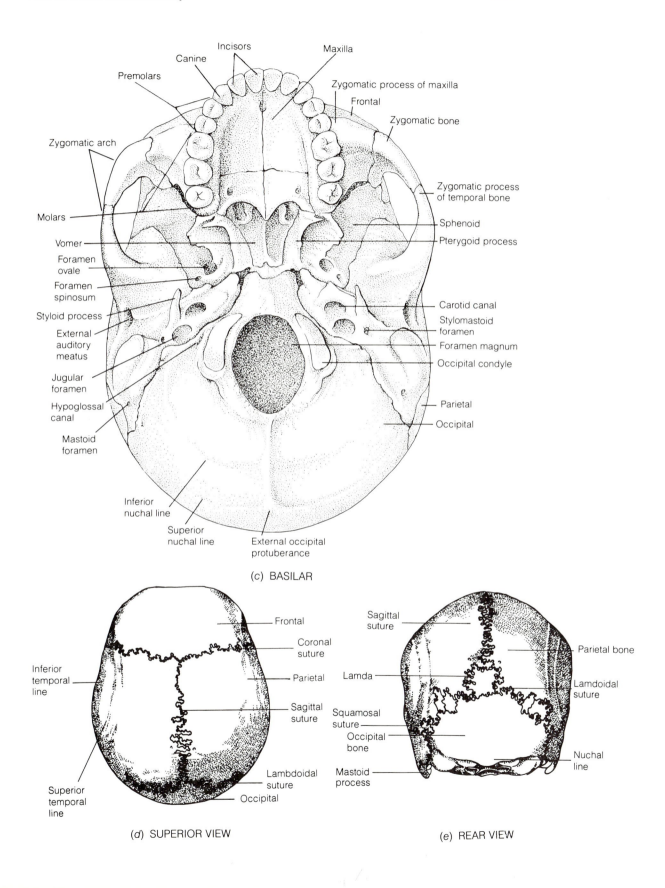

Incisors

Canine

Premolars

Maxilla

Zygomatic process of maxilla

Frontal

Zygomatic bone

Zygomatic arch

Zygomatic process
of temporal bone

Molars

Sphenoid

Vomer

Pterygoid process

Foramen
ovale

Foramen
spinosum

Styloid process

Carotid canal

External
auditory
meatus

Stylomastoid
foramen

Foramen magnum

Jugular
foramen

Occipital condyle

Hypoglossal
canal

Parietal

Mastoid
foramen

Occipital

Inferior
nuchal line

Superior
nuchal line

External occipital
protuberance

(c) BASILAR

Frontal

Coronal
suture

Inferior
temporal
line

Parietal

Sagittal
suture

Superior
temporal
line

Lambdoidal
suture

Occipital

(d) SUPERIOR VIEW

Sagittal
suture

Parietal bone

Lamda

Lamdoidal
suture

Squamosal
suture

Occipital
bone

Nuchal
line

Mastoid
process

(e) REAR VIEW

Figure A-5 Gorilla crania.

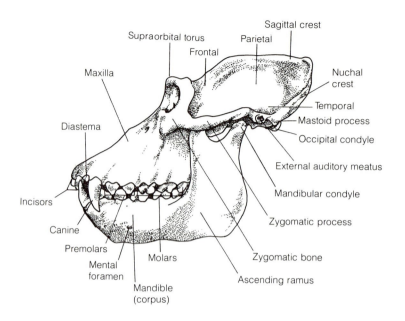

(a) MALE

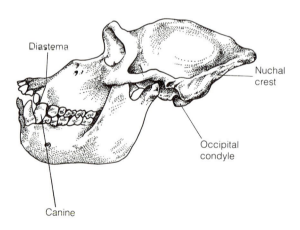

(b) FEMALE

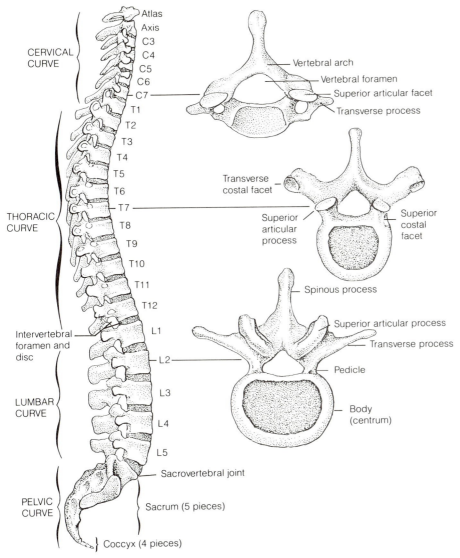

CERVICAL CURVE

Atlas
Axis
C3
C4
C5
C6
C7

T1
T2
T3
T4
T5
T6
THORACIC CURVE
T7
T8
T9
T10
T11
T12

Intervertebral foramen and disc

LUMBAR CURVE

L1
L2
L3
L4
L5

Sacrovertebral joint

PELVIC CURVE

Sacrum (5 pieces)

Coccyx (4 pieces)

Vertebral arch
Vertebral foramen
Superior articular facet
Transverse process

Transverse costal facet
Superior articular process
Superior costal facet

Spinous process
Superior articular process
Transverse process
Pedicle
Body (centrum)

Human vertebral column (lateral view) and representative views of selected cervical, thoracic, and lumbar vertebrae (superior views).

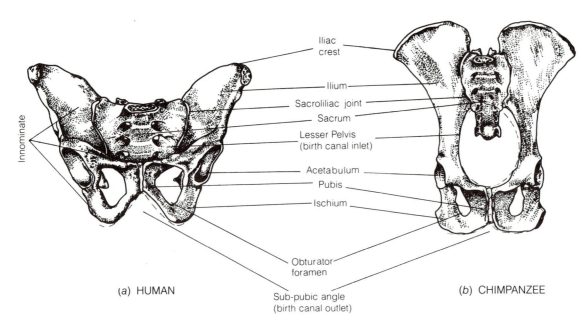

Figure A-7 Pelvic girdles.

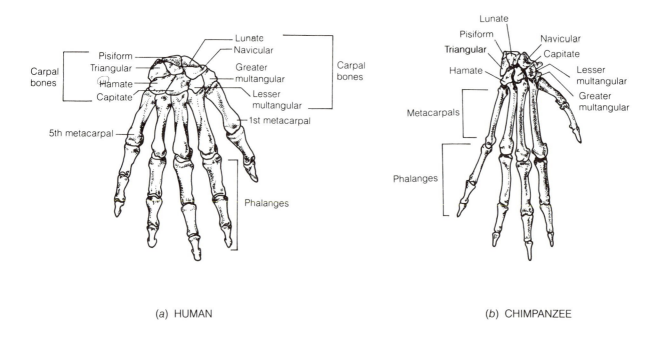

Figure A-8 Hand anatomy.

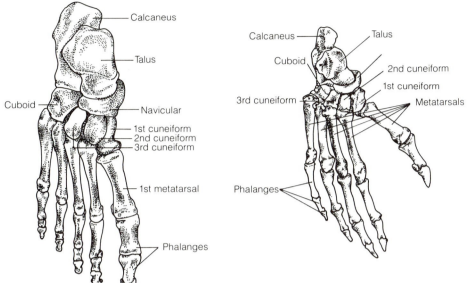

(a) HUMAN (DORSAL VIEW)

(c) CHIMPANZEE

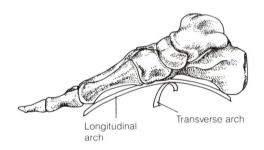

(b) HUMAN (MEDIAL VIEW)

Forensic Anthropology

Upon death, our so-called "soft" tissues, such as skin, hair, and muscle, deteriorate, leaving behind the "hard" tissues—bones and teeth—as human skeletal remains. The analysis of this material involves a knowledge of *skeletal biology*, a specialty practiced by some physical anthropologists.

It is a fascinating and startling fact that there are hundreds of millions of humans buried around this planet, and often their bones come to light for one reason or another. Indeed, thousands of skeletons have been excavated and are now curated in various natural history and anthropology museums. Skeletal biologists (also called *human osteologists*) are often asked to assist in unearthing these human remains and to perform various specialized analyses on them when prehistoric or, occasionally, historic burial sites are excavated. In some places (as recent controversies in Australia and Israel demonstrate), the excavation of human remains has become a highly emotional issue. Obviously, any disturbance of human burials can have profound religious implications for those people who, for cultural reasons, feel closely linked to the deceased individuals.

In the United States, ethical concerns in recent years have limited the circumstances under which Native American burials may be unearthed and studied. Quite often, such burials now are removed *only* when they are imminently threatened—for example, by construction work. Consequently, skeletal biologists are often requested to assist in the excavation of these threatened burials, to study them for a short time, and finally to supervise their reinterment in a more secure resting place.

In addition, human burials are occasionally excavated from sites that have a quite recent historical context. For example, one of the authors (R. J.) directed the removal and osteological study of the partial skeletons of four sailors who were drowned in a shipwreck in 1865 along the California coast. When the beach site where the sailors were buried began to erode and expose their graves, it was decided to remove the skeletons and to provide opportunity for their study.

Another situation that often calls for the expertise of a skeletal biologist comes about when skeletonized or partially skeletonized remains are found in what are clearly *very* recent contexts. For example, when a body with most of the soft tissue decomposed is found in a garbage bag in a wooded area outside a large city,* the coroner asks immediate questions: What is the identity of the person (actual identity, but failing that, age and sex)? What was the manner of death?

The key individuals who try to provide answers to these questions include a forensic dentist (who examines the teeth and tries to match them with

*The example cited here is based on an actual case, one that is not out of the ordinary. In fact, all the examples discussed in this appendix are drawn from real cases.

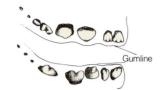

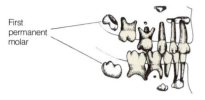

Gumline

(a) Birth: The crowns for all the deciduous (milk) teeth (shown in color) are present; no roots, however, have yet formed.

First permanent molar

(b) 2 years: All deciduous teeth (shown in color) are erupted; the first permanent molar and permanent incisors have crowns (unerupted) formed, but no roots.

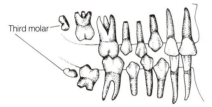

Third molar

(c) 12 years: All permanent teeth are erupted except the third molar (wisdom tooth).

Figure B-1   Skeletal age: dental development.

dental records) and a skeletal biologist who, from the bones, attempts to ascertain the age, sex, stature, and race of the victim, along with other information, such as the presence of any unusual injuries.

This appendix, then, serves as an introductory visual guide to the techniques used by skeletal biologists in their analysis of human skeletal remains. It is not intended as a complete summary of osteological methods, but as an illustration of some of the specialized techniques used by osteologists—especially as they pertain to forensic applications.

◇ Skeletal Age Determination

During its growth and development, the skeleton exhibits regular stages of change that allow osteologists to establish quite accurately the age of an individual at death. For example, the ages of infants and children can be determined by inspecting the degree of dental development or the regular fusion of the separate ends of long bones (called *epiphyses*) to the bone shafts.

However, once maturity is attained (by the early twenties), determining age by skeletal analysis becomes considerably more difficult. The most commonly used method for discovering the age of adults involves rating progressive

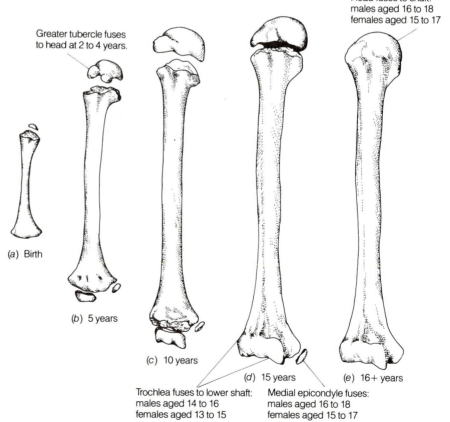

Head fuses to shaft: males aged 16 to 18 females aged 15 to 17

Greater tubercle fuses to head at 2 to 4 years.

(a) Birth

(b) 5 years

(c) 10 years

(d) 15 years

(e) 16+ years

Trochlea fuses to lower shaft: males aged 14 to 16 females aged 13 to 15

Medial epicondyle fuses: males aged 16 to 18 females aged 15 to 17

Figure B-2   Skeletal age: epiphyseal union in the humerus. Some regions of the humerus exhibit some of the earliest fusion centers in the body, while others are among the latest to complete fusion (not until late adolescence).

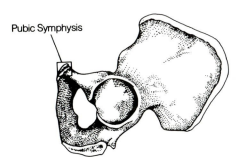

Pubic Symphysis

(a) Position of the pubic symphysis. This area of the pelvis shows systematic changes progressively throughout adult life. Two of these stages are shown in (b) and (c).

(b) Age: 21. The face of the symphysis shows the typical "billowed" appearance of a young joint; no rim present.

(c) Age: mid-50s. The face is mostly flat, with a distinct rim formed around most of the periphery.

Figure B-3   Skeletal age: Remodeling of the pubic symphysis.

changes in the area where the two halves of the pelvis join (called the *pubic symphysis*). Other areas—for example, the ends of ribs—are also sometimes used. In addition, some microscopic techniques, in which progressive cellular changes are observed, have also proven useful.

AGING A SKELETON: AN EXAMPLE

A forensic case requiring knowledge of age at death came about when three skeletons were discovered months after a small plane crashed in a remote region of northern California.

The identities of the three passengers, all male, were known, and the teeth of the individuals did conform to these personal identifications. However, the bones of all three were mixed together when they were received by the coroner (having been scattered at the crash site by predators, perhaps, as well as being mixed by authorities who collected the bones).

Since the crash victims were of different ages (one in his teens, one in his 30s, and one in his 40s), it was helpful to use aging criteria to separate the bones. The teenager was the easiest, since many of his epiphyses were just about to complete fusion or had just done so (leaving a telltale line). The bones of the two adults were much more difficult to distinguish, emphasizing the complexity of accurately specifying the age of mature individuals. In this case, the best that could be done was to attempt to match the bones mainly on the basis of size.

◇ Sexing the Skeleton

Ascertaining the sex of a person from skeletal remains presents a set of problems opposite to those posed by aging methodologies. While, for aging, young individuals are easiest, determining sex is achieved most accurately for mature skeletons. Like other secondary sexual characteristics, skeletal sexual dimorphism is most clearly manifested after puberty. As a result, it is relatively straightforward to find the sexual identity of teenage or older skeletons. On the other hand, for skeletons of infants and children, it is often impossible to determine their sex.

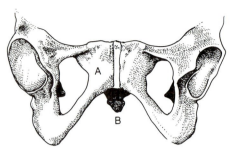

(a) FEMALE PELVIS

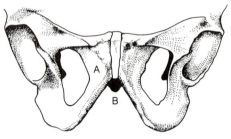

(b) MALE PELVIS

Figure B-4   Sexing the skeleton: the pelvis. The most diagnostic area of the body displaying skeletal sexual dimorphism is the pelvis, especially the anterior (front) aspect. The width of the pubis (A) is relatively greater in females, and the subpubic angle (B) is also more open. Both these features reflect the proportionately wider pelvic outlet in females that forms the bony birth canal.

The most consistent skeletal sexual indicators are found in the pelvis, reflecting, of course, the modifications in the female pelvis associated with childbearing.

While not as reliable, the cranium is also used (and sometimes is *all* that the osteologist has to work with). Here, differences are seen in size and especially in proportions: Males have relatively bigger and more prominent faces, larger browridges, and heavier (more robust) muscle insertions.

SEXING THE SKELETON: AN EXAMPLE

The almost completely skeletonized remains of a young individual were found rather haphazardly buried in a streambed outside a large city. To confirm more accurately the sex of this individual, the pelvis was cleaned of all remaining tissue. The osteologist was then able to see the proportions of the pelvis (wide pubis and subpubic angle, etc.) to ascertain confidently that this was a female. Interestingly, while cleaning the pelvis, the assistant coroner found a bullet lodged in the hip (smashed against the femur head).

◇ Assessing Stature

Another aspect of the skeleton that relates directly to a condition of a *living* individual is stature. Since the skeleton (especially the long bones of the lower limb) contributes directly to a person's body height, it is possible to estimate height even when only some bones remain.

The methods for stature estimation were developed from skeletal collections in which the stature of the individuals was known (for example, cadavers were measured before they were dissected in medical school anatomy labs). From such studies, standard formulae have been developed to allow stature estimates from long-bone measurements. The femur provides the most accurate estimates, but the tibia, fibula, and long bones of the upper limb can also be used. It must be noted, however, that these formulae apply most directly to *the samples from which they were drawn*. They can be reasonably extended to the *populations* these samples represent (White females, Black males, and so forth). Since the formulae differ for the two sexes and for different racial groups, it is crucial to know sex and race *beforehand* in order to select the appropriate stature estimation formula.

DETERMINING STATURE: AN EXAMPLE

Over the last few years, several skeletons have been returned to the United States by the North Vietnamese. It has been assumed that these individuals were missing American servicemen (mostly pilots whose planes were shot down).

An immediate concern, of course, was to ascertain that a returned skeleton was not simply that of a North Vietnamese. A very quick check could be done by estimating stature, since the range of variation among Vietnamese males overlaps very little with that of American servicemen.

In the case of the returned remains, stature was checked immediately by forensic anthropologists, and it was found that the skeletons almost certainly were *not* those of Vietnamese.

Confirming positive identification (exactly *which* person a particular skeleton represented) turned out, of course, to be more difficult. Dogtags were returned with given skeletons, so there were apparently clear identifications, but these had to be checked. Unfortunately, in some cases, however, no dental records existed. Consequently, less reliable indicators had to be employed. In one instance, the estimated stature from the long bones matched to within one-half inch of the missing serviceman's actual stature. Moreover, other indicators, such as a healed ankle fracture, also matched, making it extremely likely that the skeleton was, in fact, the individual identified on the dogtags.

The total length of the femur is obtained on an osteometric board. In this case, this eighteenth-century sailor's femur measured as 461 mm.

From standardized formulae (see text), tables can be constructed to obtain stature estimates from femur length. A portion of such a table is shown below:

Femur length (mm)*	Stature	
	cm	inches
452	169	66
456	170	66
461	171	67
465	172	67
469	173	68

From these comparisons, the sailor's stature is thus estimated as 171 cm (67 inches).

*Note: Data drawn from White males with known statures at time of death.

Figure B-5   Estimating stature: measuring the length of the femur.

◇ Attribution of Race

Another aspect of osteological analysis, especially relating to forensic work, is the attribution of race. For example, is a particular skeleton that of an individual who was Caucasian or Black?

Here, however, the skeletal differences are far from clearcut. Accordingly, the best that can be done is to make scientific "best guesses" on the basis of statistical inference. Techniques employed for race attribution primarily involve the use of special formulae which, like those for stature estimation, are abstracted from dissecting-room skeletal samples. Measurements taken from the cranium are the most reliable, but the pelvis, femur, and other bones can also be used.

ATTRIBUTION OF RACE: AN EXAMPLE

In mass disasters (for example, the crash of a commercial jetliner), it is obviously important to establish accurately the identity of each victim. Initially, age and sex are ascertained. Beyond this, another way to sort the remains is by race. Therefore, measurements can be taken on the cranium of each adult, applied to a formula, and a "best guess" can be made. It must be pointed out that, first, sex needs to be established (the formulae vary for males and females) and, secondly, the formula is devised to answer only a limited question. For example, Is a particular cranium from a Caucasian or from a Black individual? The mathematical statement discriminates between these two choices. If we asked the same question of an unknown individual who turned out to be Asian, the answer (telling us only whether the person was Black or White) would be meaningless.

The question of race attribution was also addressed in the preceding section concerning stature estimation. In the example concerning identification of the skeleton of an American serviceman from that of a Vietnamese, the problem was really one of race identification. In this example, stature was useful, since the ranges of variations are known to overlap very little between the two respective populations (American White—or Black, for that matter— compared to Southeast Asians).

◇ Facial Reconstruction in Human Identification*

Facial reconstruction (also termed *facial reproduction*) is a process used when other identification procedures (including fingerprints and dental matches) have been unsuccessful. Two different methods of producing a face on the skull are employed: a portrait of the individual using clues from the bones of

*Contributed by Diane L. France, Ph.D., Colorado State University, and Sandra C. Mays, Supervisor, Crime Laboratory Section, Wyoming State Crime Laboratory. Stages of reconstruction are from both authors; finished reconstruction by Sandra Mays.

the face; and a more direct, three-dimensional method of applying clay to the skull (or to a plaster cast of the skull). These techniques employ both science and art: The physical anthropologist discovers the age, sex, and race of the skull, but there is no direct evidence from bone that indicates the eye color, hair color and style, lip form, or degree of wrinkling or fleshiness in the individual. Therefore, there is a great deal of subjectivity in the rendering of the finished product; an exact reproduction is not expected only a general likeness.

The following photographs show a facial reproduction taking shape. Erasers or blocks of clay marking tissue depths (arrived at experimentally from cadavers) are commonly glued to the skull. Clay strips, graduated to the various tissue depths, then "fill in the dots" between erasers, and the face is "fleshed out." The eyes, nose, lips, and sometimes ears are then fashioned according to various guidelines, and a wig is usually added.

Figures i and j show the reproduction of a Caucasoid female, over 60 years old. The first figure shows a nearly complete reproduction, but without the effects of aging, while Figure 5j is the finished product, including the features characteristic of a woman of that age.

Figure B-6   Facial reconstruction from a skull.

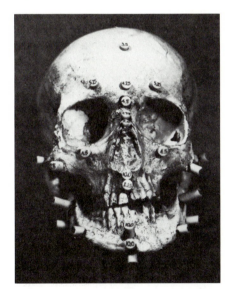

Figure a   Erasers precut to experimentally determined tissue depths are glued to skull.

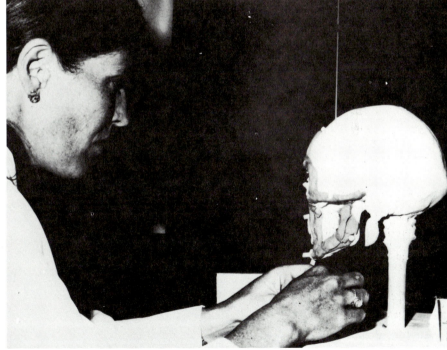

Figure b   Sandra Mays applies strips of clay between erasers, graduated to eraser depths.

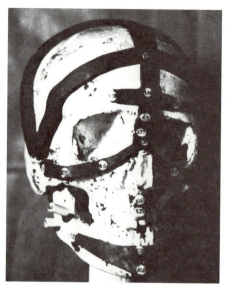

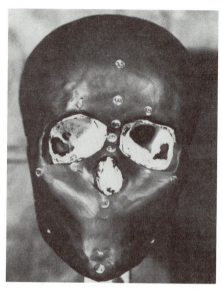

Figure c   Strips of clay connect erasers.

Figure d   Clay is added to "flesh out" the face.

Figure e and f   A nose and lips are added and refined.

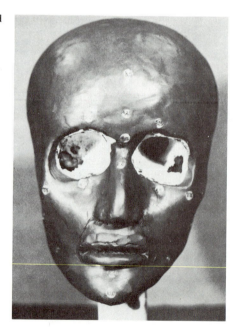

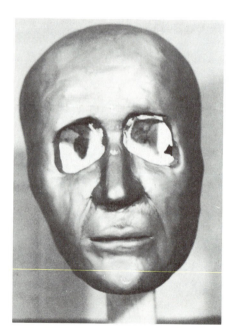

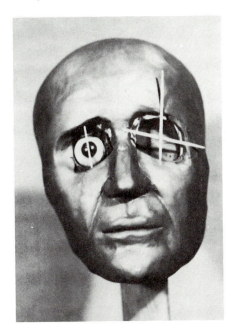
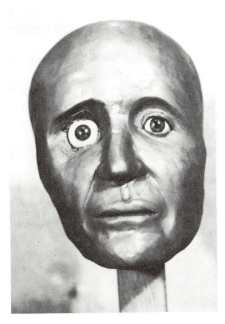

Figure g and h Glass (or plastic) eyes are placed into orbits and eyelids are fashioned.

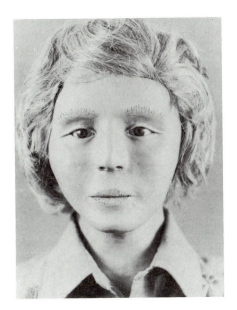
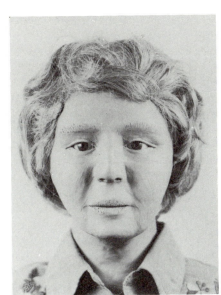

Figure i and j Completed reproduction. (i) Before adding aging features. (j) After "aging" the face to correspond with aging indicators ascertained from other parts of the skeleton.

The Archeological Research Project

To the uninitiated, archeology sometimes seems like a technique for discovering interesting or valuable objects that once were associated with ancient and exotic cultures. At times, archeology may have been little more than a glorified treasure hunt. But modern archeology is a method of scientific investigation with the goal of learning something about humans and their behavior. Archeologists may focus on one people or time period or site, but ideally each individual project should contribute to a broader understanding of what it means to be human.

◇ 1. Formulating a Research Program

Modern research archeology is problem-oriented, meaning that today's archeologists are seeking answers to specific questions. Depending on the extent of previous work in an area, it usually should be possible to go beyond basic matters of *where* or *when*: "Where did people settle in this valley?" "When was this site occupied?" Archeologists are most interested in seeking explanations about the past: "*Why* did farming develop in the Tehuacán Valley at such an early date?" "*How* did the impact of European exploration affect the balance of power among West African societies in the sixteenth century?"

To address topics such as these, archeologists have adopted the general scientific method of hypothesis-testing. Considerable background research is necessary even before the archeologist steps onto a site. Familiarity with all previous archeological study of the problem or the region, examination of ethnographic accounts covering the more recent cultures that could provide clues to ancient lifeways, and a consideration of nonanthropological topics that may have a bearing on the issue at hand—all may assist the archeologist in framing a reasonable hypothesis that can be examined archeologically: "Overexploitation of their environment forced the people of Mesa Verde to abandon their sites in the thirteenth century A.D."

Once the problem has been defined and a hypothesis proposed, the archeologist must devise a research design, a specific strategy to test the hypothesis by collecting new data. Where might appropriate sites be sought? How can the essential resources—money, labor, equipment—be obtained? What permissions are needed? What specialists from other disciplines must be contacted for their assistance?

◇ 2. Gathering Data

A site is a location of past human activity. The archeologist seeks to find the right site—or portion of a site—that will yield some pertinent information about the research question or hypothesis. To delimit the area of investigation, archeologists use various survey and sampling techniques:

(a) Walkover Survey—team members walk across the surface of potential sites, usually in a series of parallel transects, marking locations of all finds; any concentration of appropriate artifacts or features may merit further investigation

Figure C-1 Survey and sampling techniques of the archeologist.

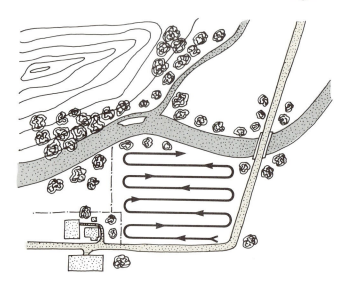
(a) Walkover Survey

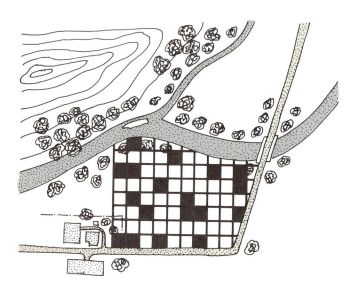
(b) Simple Random Sampling

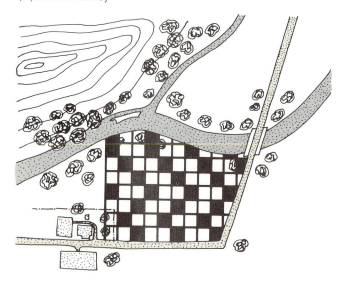
(c) Systematic Sampling

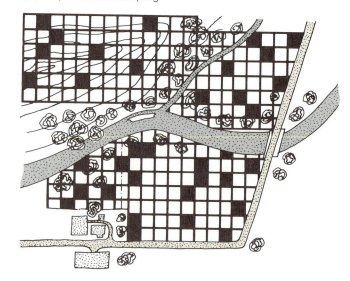
(d) Stratified Random Sampling

(b) Simple Random Sampling—a map of the study area is gridded into sampling units of standard size ($10 m^2$, $100 m^2$), and a predetermined percentage of these units (perhaps 10% or 20%) are selected randomly for collection or testing

(c) Systematic Sampling—the grid of the proposed study area is again used to guide the on-the-ground surveyors. This time, units are selected for examination in some systematic way—every tenth unit (for a 10% sample), every fifth unit (for a 20% sample), etc.

(d) Stratified Random Sampling—if the archeologist has some basis for differentiating the study area into distinct zones, he or she may then wish to randomly sample each zone separately, to assure that all are represented and examined for sites

The use of standardized survey and sampling techniques makes it possible to use statistics and apply probability predictions with confidence. Nonprobabilistic techniques, such as intuition, informants, or incantations often have been used successfully to locate sites, but they do not enable the researcher to make any statistically valid statements about the representativeness of the site.

Excavation is, of course, the activity most closely associated with archeology by the general public. At one time, archeologists routinely excavated entire sites, sometimes employing enormous numbers of untrained diggers. Excavation is a labor-intensive activity, and as techniques have become more refined and costs have risen, large-scale excavation is less common. Fortunately, probabilistic sampling and the use of innovative analytical techniques and interdisciplinary research efforts have largely eliminated the need for total site excavation. In fact, archeologists prefer to preserve untouched portions of their sites for the benefit of future scientists, who may develop even better ways of extracting archeological information. Thus, much excavation today is a sampling procedure.

Sites may be classified on the basis of their culture histories. Was the site occupied for a long time, or only briefly? The answer to this question often determines the techniques required to excavate the site. Single-component sites were occupied by only one culture and usually for a relatively short period. Therefore they generally produce only one cultural "layer" or stratum in the otherwise natural stratigraphy of the site. On the other hand, multicomponent sites are those that preserve evidence of several cultures, or perhaps a long-term occupation by one culture, and so produce successive layers or strata of cultural debris or overlapping features.

On multicomponent sites it is especially important that each stratum be recognized and individually excavated in order to keep the cultural materials from each component separate. At times, such a site may be comprised of a vertical stack of stratigraphic layers, all easily distinguishable from the others. More often, though, the strata may be undulating, or may disappear intermittently, or may have been thoroughly mixed by later activities, such as laying foundations or digging ditches. Archeologists use any and all characteristics to distinguish between strata: color, texture, artifact contents, degree of disturbance by earthworms or rodents, or even the variable sound of a trowel scraping across them!

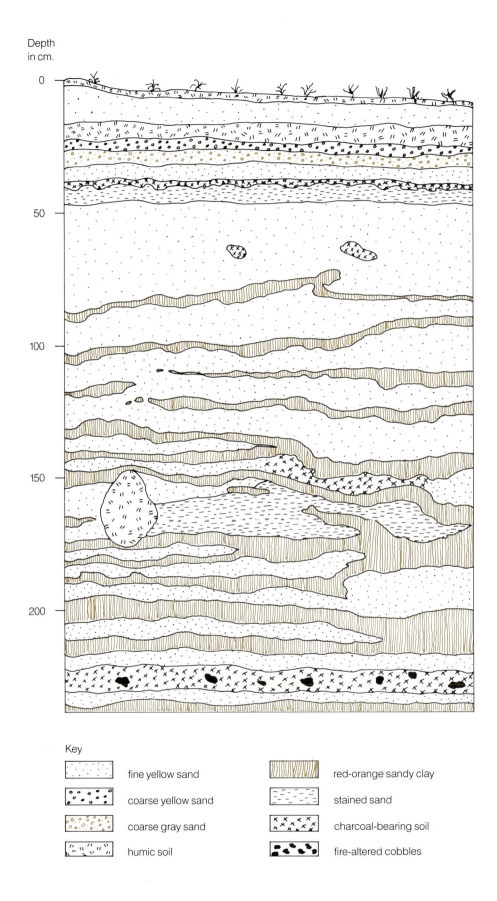

Depth
in cm.

0

50

100

150

200

Key

fine yellow sand

coarse yellow sand

coarse gray sand

humic soil

red-orange sandy clay

stained sand

charcoal-bearing soil

fire-altered cobbles

Figure C-2 Stratigraphy.

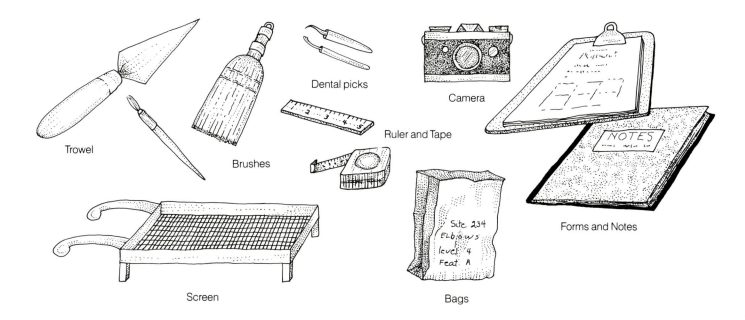

Trowel

Brushes

Dental picks

Ruler and Tape

Camera

Screen

Bags

Forms and Notes

Excavation is a meticulous process, and the most useful hand tools of the archeologist reflect the delicacy of the operation: trowel, brushes, dental picks. Keeping records is as important (and equally as time-consuming) as digging itself. The archeologist carefully notes the nature of each stratum, photographs artifacts and features as they are uncovered, and records the exact provenience or location of each find. Archeologists lay out their sites in a gridwork of squares, or excavation units, usually 1 or 2 meters on a side. These units are keyed to a central datum point, or permanent marker. In this way, excavators can precisely locate the horizontal position of anything they find. By carefully noting the depth of the find as well, they can pinpoint its location in three dimensions. This information is faithfully recorded and mapped and will enable the archeologist to reconstruct the context of the artifact after the fieldwork has ended.

Naturally, the kinds of data recovered from a site will depend upon several factors: past and recent site environment, earlier disturbance by people or

Figure C-3   Tools of the archeologist.

Figure C-4   The excavation unit.

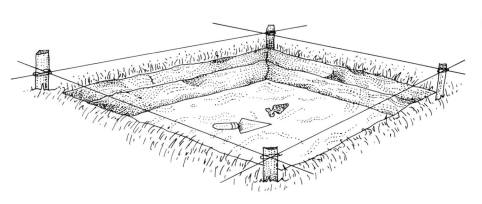

animals, original nature of the site and its contents. During its period of occupation, a site represents an interplay between additive and subtractive processes: building vs. destruction, growth vs. decay. When a site is finally abandoned, the subtractive processes are seldom interrupted. Organic matter decays, structures and other features become disarranged, weathering and breakdown proceed unchecked. Depending upon when the archeologist breaks into this process, and what recovery and conservation techniques are used, the site may yield much or little pertaining to the research topic.

It is the goal of the archeologist to maximize the recovery of data, of course, since a site can be excavated only once. To this end, a barrage of special equipment and techniques are routinely employed. For example, flecks of animal bone and microflakes from stone tools are caught in fine-mesh screens, while minute fragments of charcoal, seeds, and nut hulls are retrieved from flotation, or wet-sieving, devices.

Materials recovered from a site undergo immediate processing. Artifacts are recorded and photographed even while they are in the ground. Everything is quickly bagged and tagged with provenience data and forwarded to the field lab or on to specialists who will begin their detailed analyses.

◇ 3. Analyzing Data

Archeology today makes use of the expertise of numerous specialists from many disciplines. As a result, field archeologists must recognize and collect many previously ignored kinds of data from their sites. Artifacts, the products of human behavior, remain a primary focus of archeologists. In addition, a site may yield identifiable faunal remains ranging from large prey species to tiny snails. Plants may be represented by carbonized wood, preserved seeds, pollen, or even leaf impressions on a clay floor. Soil samples yield evidence of past environments and human activity through analysis of composition and chemistry. And, of course, some materials may be collected for dating purposes. Few archeologists can be competent in working with more than one or two of these categories of material, which is why interdisciplinary research is so important in the study of the past.

Artifacts themselves are cleaned, numbered, and sorted into major categories: ceramics, lithics, organics. The archeologist may then turn some materials over to a colleague who specializes in ceramic studies or lithic technology, for example. These people will now begin to classify and study the artifacts in order to extract cultural information.

Artifacts may be classified in several ways. Archeologists create "types," categories of artifacts that share selected characteristics:

(a) Morphological Types—recognize common attributes of size, shape, color, etc.; this classification is descriptive and does not presume a specific purpose for the objects (example: "bifacially flaked lanceolate object")

(b) Functional Types—artifacts sometimes preserve evidence of use: food residue in cooking vessels, edge wear on lithic blades; if function can be determined by objective means, it is proper to assign the artifact to a specific functional category (example: "arrowhead," "hide scraper")

(c) Temporal Types—many categories of cultural artifacts undergo stylistic changes through time, making it possible to assign an example of a given type to a specific position in the stylistic sequence (a modern example would be the yearly models turned out by automobile manufacturers); in the same way, a prehistoric artifact may be placed in its proper position in a series from one site, and perhaps even dated by comparison with artifacts of the same style from another site of known age

Archeologists use these classificatory techniques to enable them to deal with a few groupings of related artifacts rather than countless individual specimens. Typology enables one to note significant trends and associations that might otherwise be obscured by minor stylistic details and individual variations.

With the advent of radiocarbon and other physico-chemical dating methods, the age of archeological materials often can be established with some precision. Carbon 14, potassium-argon, and dendrochronology produce chronometric (or "absolute") dates, expressed in terms of years. Other dating techniques provide only "relative" ages, indicating merely that an object or site is older/younger than another. Relative dating techniques include stratigraphy and fluorine analysis. Most dating techniques (and all of those mentioned here, except stratigraphy) require the use of specialized laboratory equipment and procedures. Each method also has its own limitations and shortcomings, including the kinds of materials that can be dated, upper and lower age limits, sources of error, and precision.

Much of the remaining data collected in the field can be examined for clues about past environments. Some residual categories are considered ecofacts (as opposed to artifacts, which are cultural products). Plant and animal remains can help archeologists identify probable foods and reconstruct the native ecology of the site and its vicinity. There may also be clues about how humans interacted with their environments: What kinds of wood they collected for fires, where they planted their fields, how they processed acorns, and when they hunted deer.

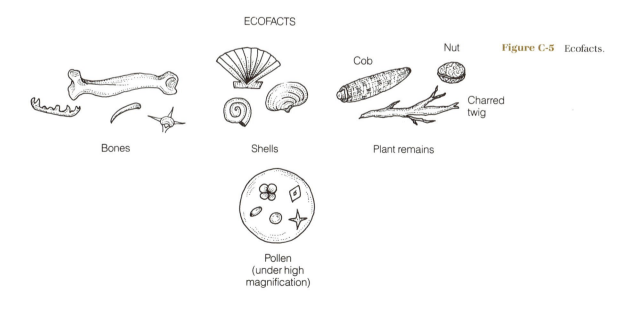

ECOFACTS

Figure C-5 Ecofacts.

Bones   Shells   Plant remains

Cob   Nut   Charred twig

Pollen
(under high
magnification)

TYPOLOGY OF MODERN ARTIFACTS

Morphological types

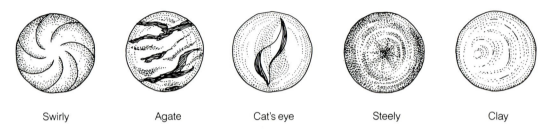

| Swirly | Agate | Cat's eye | Steely | Clay |

CHILD'S MARBLES

Functional Types

CONTAINERS

Temporal Types

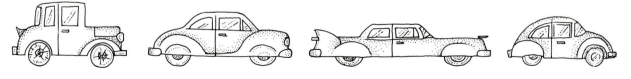

| Model T Ford | 1940s Chevrolet | Late 1950s Cadillac | 1960s Volkswagon |

AUTOMOBILES

Figure C-6   Typology of artifacts.

TYPOLOGY OF PREHISTORIC ARTIFACTS

Morphological types

| Side-notched | Corner-notched | Straight-stemmed | Contracting-stemmed | Expanding-stemmed | Triangular | Lanceolate |

FLAKED BIFACES

Functional Types

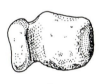

| Axe | Drill | Spearhead | Knife | Pipe |

IMPLEMENTS

Temporal Types

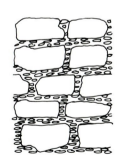

Type 1
Tenth century A.D.

Type 2
Eleventh century A.D.

Type 3
Late eleventh century A.D.

Type 4
Late eleventh century A.D.

McElmo
Early twelfth century A.D.

STONE MASONRY TYPES AT CHACO CANYON, NEW MEXICO

◇ 4. Interpreting the Data

Many seasons of fieldwork are sometimes necessary to produce enough data to address the investigator's research questions. Each hour a person spends digging on a site may later require at least several more hours away from the site spent in processing artifacts or records or in analyzing nonartifactual samples. The increasingly sophisticated laboratory techniques employed by archeologists often are available from only a small number of specialists or labs, so the time needed to process these samples may run into many months. When, at last, everything has been examined, considered, re-examined, and argued about, the time has arrived to synthesize the data into a comprehensive final report. To do so obviously demands that the archeologist be thoroughly conversant with the results of any specialist studies commissioned for the project.

Documenting a project and making its results available to colleagues, funding agencies, and the interested public is an important obligation. Although a "final report" may eventually be published for a project or a site, it probably will contain very few final answers. A fruitful archeological project is one that has tested a hypothesis or two and shown it to be reasonable or not. Very likely, new questions will have arisen out of the work, which may in turn lead to new or more refined hypotheses to be tested on yet another site.

◇ GLOSSARY

Acheulian   The culture period, or stone tool industry, of the Middle and part of the Lower Pleistocene; characterized by the handaxe.

Acquired characteristics   The notion developed by Lamarck that traits acquired during the lifetime of an organism could be passed on to offspring. Known as the theory of acquired characteristics.

Acrocentric chromosome   A chromosome with its centromere towards one end.

Adaptation   Genetic changes within populations in response to selection (environmental) pressure; usually takes many generations.

Adaptive niche   The whole way of life of an organism: where it lives, what it eats, how it gets food, and so forth.

Adaptive radiation   The rapid increase and spread of an evolving group of organisms which diversify and adapt to new niches.

Adenine   One of the chemical bases (purines) found in both DNA and RNA.

Advanced   In evolutionary terms, an organism further removed from an evolutionary divergence than a more primitive one; usually now termed "derived." *See* Primitive.

Aegyptopithecus   An early hominoid form from the Oligocene; Fayum, Egypt.

Agonistic behavior   Behavior actively related to fighting—aggression, conciliation, or retreat.

Allele   Alternative form of a gene that may be present at the same locus. In the ABO blood-group system, for example, any one of these three alleles (A, B, or O) may be present at the ABO locus.

Allo   Combining form indicating different or other.

Allometric growth   Differential patterns of growth whereby some parts of the body are disproportionately related to other parts.

Altruism   Helping others without direct benefit to oneself. In natural selection terms: sacrificing your own reproductive success to help another.

Alveolar   Tooth-bearing portion of the upper jaw.

Alveolar prognathism   Forward projection of the maxilla (much reduced in anatomically modern humans).

Amber   Fossil resin or pine pitch, often prized by ancient cultures because of static electrical properties.

Ameslan   American sign language. AMESLAN (ASL) is used among deaf humans and also to teach language to some apes.

Amino acids   Small molecules that are the building blocks of protein.

Amniote egg   The developing reptilian embryo is surrounded by three sacs: one for food, one for waste matter, and one filled with liquid—amniotic fluid—for protection. This egg evolved with reptiles.

Analogous structures   Similarities in parts of the anatomy not based on descent from a common ancestor (the bird wing and butterfly wing, for example), but based on common function.

Analogy   Similarities between organisms based on common function, not due to evolutionary relationship. *See* Homology.

Anatolia   Asia Minor; present-day Turkey.

Anatomically modern *H. sapiens* (or human beings)   Populations of the Upper Paleolithic who physically resemble populations of today.

Anomaly   Different, irregular deviation.

Anthropoidea   The suborder (of Primates) of anthropoids, including New World monkeys, Old World monkeys, and hominoids (apes and hominids).

Anthropology   The study (or science) of humankind.

Anthropometry   Measurement of the human body.

Anthropomorphic   Having or being given a humanlike appearance; usually applied to art.

Anticodon   A triplet of bases in tRNA which complements the triplet of bases in mRNA. The anticodon corresponds to a particular amino acid.

Arboreal   Tree-living. Many prosimians and monkeys, as well as the gibbon and the orangutan, are arboreal.

Archaic   New World cultural stage of hunting and gathering; equivalent to the term "Mesolithic" in the Old World.

Archeology   The study of prehistoric culture through remains left by ancient humans.

Artifacts (archeological traces)   Traces of hominid behavior. Very old artifacts are usually made of stone.

Artiodactyl   Even-toed hoof (e.g., cows, pigs, camels).

Ascending ramus   Rear upright portion of the mandible.

Association   What an archeological trace is found with (other archeological traces, bone refuse, etc.).

Atlatl   A throwing board or spearthrower, used in both the Old and New Worlds.

Aurignacian   A culture period (*circa* 30,000 y.a.) of the Upper Paleolithic; probable beginning of Upper Paleolithic art.

Aurochs   European wild ox, ancestral to the modern cattle.

Australopithecine   The common term for members of the genus, *Australopithecus.*

Australopithecus   The extinct genus of Plio-Pleistocene hominids found in South and East Africa; usually divided into: *A. africanus* and *A. robustus* (S. Africa), and *A. boisei* and an early primitive representative, *A. afarensis* (E. Africa).

Autosome   Any chromosome except a sex chromosome.

Autosome   Any chromosome except a sex chromosome.

Aztecs   A militaristic people who dominated the Valley of

Mexico and surrounding area at the time of the European conquest.

Barrio   A district or neighborhood in a Mesoamerican or South American town site.

Base   One of the four chemicals attached to a sugar molecule and a phosphate to make up a nucleotide. In DNA, a base is always paired with another base.

Behavior, social   The behavior of animals that live together as a group; gregariousness, sociability.

Beringia   The dry-land connection between Asia and America that existed periodically during the Ice Age. Between 27,000 y.a. and 10,000 y.a. people could have crossed it into the New World.

Binomial   The binomial (two-term) system of classification developed by Linnaeus. Every organism is identified by two Latin names: the first word is the generic term; the second, the specific.

Biocultural   An approach to the study of human beings, their evolution and behavior. The biocultural approach considers both human biology and culture.

Biological adaptation   Genetic changes within populations in response to selection (environmental) pressure; usually takes many generations.

Biosphere   The entire area inhabited by organisms.

Biostratigraphy   Dating method based on evolutionary changes within an evolving lineage.

Bipedalism   Walking on two legs as the natural means of locomotion.

Blade   A parallel-sided flake at least twice as long as it is wide.

Brachiation   Arm-over-arm suspensory locomotion beneath branches.

Brachycephalic   Broad-headed. A skull in which the width of the skull is 80% or more of the length.

Breccia   Cemented conglomerate containing limestone, sand, and bone.

Breeding isolate   A population geographically and/or socially separate and, therefore, relatively easy to define.

Bronze Age   Period of early Old World civilizations, beginning with the widespread use of metal tools and weapons after 5500 y.a.

Burin   A chisellike stone tool used for engraving on horn, wood, and ivory; characteristic of the Upper Paleolithic.

Calva (or callote)   Uppermost portion of the braincase.

Calvaria   The skull minus the face and mandible.

Calvarium   The skull minus the mandible.

Cambrian   The first period of the Paleozoic.

Canine   Usually a long and pointed (conical) tooth in front of the mouth, lateral to incisors; used for piercing and grasping.

Carbon 14 (^{14}C) dating   A method of determining the age in years of an organic specimen by measuring the loss of the radioactive isotope, ^{14}C.

Carboniferous   Fifth period of the Paleozoic. The first reptiles appear during this period.

Carnivore   A meat-eating animal. Also the common name for a member of the mammalian order, Carnivora (for example, dogs, cats, bears).

Catastrophism   The idea that there were a series of violent and sudden catastrophes which destroyed most living things. This would explain the extinction of many species. Also part of catastrophism was the belief that after each catastrophe, a new set of creations established new species. Associated with Cuvier.

Catarrhine   The group (infraorder) comprising all Old World anthropoids, living and extinct.

Ceboidea   The anthropoid superfamily of New World monkeys, including marmosets and cebids.

Cenozoic Era (65 m.y.a.–present)   The present era; the era following the Mesozoic.

Centromere   A circular body that attaches the two arms of a chromatid.

Cercopithecoidea   The anthropoid superfamily of Old World monkeys including colobines and cercopithecines.

Cerebellum   Hind portion of brain. The cerebellum is the center of unconscious control of skeletal muscles.

Cerebrum   The front portion of the brain; the largest portion of the brain in placental mammals.

Cervical   Pertaining to the neck, as in cervical vertebrae.

Chatelperronian   An early culture period (*circa* 32,000 y.a.) of the Upper Paleolithic; perhaps transitional between Mousterian and later Upper Paleolithic culture.

Cheek teeth   Premolars and molars.

Chimu   A powerful culture that dominated the northern Peruvian coast between about 1000 A.D. and 1476 A.D. Chan Chan was its capital city.

Chinampa   Aztec garden plots built up and fertilized by dredging organic muck from adjacent canals and lake beds.

Chromatid   Each of the two subunits of a duplicated chromosome.

Chromosomal mutation   A rearrangement of large sections of DNA (whole pieces of chromosomes) such as deletions, translocations, inversions, and duplications.

Chromosome   A rod-shaped structure, composed of nucleic acid and protein, found in the nucleus of the cell. Chromosomes occur in pairs and contain the DNA responsible for inheritance.

Chronometric dating   Determining the age of a specimen in number of years. Potassium-argon, ^{14}C, ^{238}U, dendrochronology (and others) are used to obtain chronometric dates.

Chultún   A stone-lined pit used by the Maya for storing ramón or breadnuts.

Civilization   Large-scale, complexly organized society.

Cladistics   The school of evolutionary biology that seeks to make ancestral-descendant hypotheses through interpreting patterns of primitive/derived characteristics.

Cladogram   A diagrammatic representation of population relationships using several genetic traits simultaneously.

Class   A category of classification in the Animal (or Plant) Kingdom; a subdivision of subphylum. A class includes those animals (or plants) that have adapted to a similar way of life. Vertebrate classes are Pisces, Amphibia, Reptilia, Aves, and Mammalia.

Classic Neandertals   Western Europe and Near Eastern Neandertals who lived during the early Würm.

Clavicle   Collar bone.

Cline   A gradual distribution of gene frequencies over space.

Clovis   Phase of North American prehistory, 12,000 y.a. to 11,000 y.a. in the West, during which fluted projectile points were used in hunting.

Codon   A triplet of bases in mRNA that codes for a specific amino acid. The triplet is matched by another triplet of bases in tRNA, known as anticodon.

Composite   Made of several parts; a harpoon or a bow and arrow are examples of composite implements made in prehistoric times.

Condyle   A rounded protuberance of bone which articulates with another bone (that is, forms a joint with or moves against another bone).

Context   The environmental setting where an archeological trace is found.

Convergence (convergent evolution)   Evolution of similar adaptive traits in unrelated forms; for example, the wings of birds and wings of butterflies. *See* Parallelism.

Coprolite   Preserved dung or fecal matter which may be examined for ancient dietary evidence.

Core   Stone reduced by flake removal.

Core area   Area, within the home range, of greatest regular use.

Coronal suture   The suture running transversely across the skull joining the frontal and parietal bones.

Cosmology   The study of the creation of the universe and the laws that govern it.

Cranium   The complete skull; bone of the head, face, and mandible.

Crepuscular   Active at twilight or dawn.

Cretaceous   Final (third) period of Mesozoic. Dinosaurs become extinct. Probable appearance of first primates.

Crossing-over   The exchange of genetic material between homologous chromosomes during meiosis.

Crossopterygians   Lobe-finned fish; probably gave rise to amphibians.

Cultigen   A plant that is wholly dependent on humans; a domesticate.

Cultivar   A wild plant encouraged by humans.

Culture   The ways humans discover, invent, and develop in order to survive. Culture is the human strategy of adaptation.

Cuneiform   Wedge-shaped writing, usually associated with Mesopotamia.

Cytoplasm   That portion of the cell lying outside the nucleus.

Cytosine   One of the chemical bases (pyrimidines) found in both DNA and RNA.

Dental arcade   The shape of the tooth row: posteriorly divergent, parallel, parabolic, etc.

Dental formula   The number of each kind of tooth present. Shown usually for one-quarter of the mouth as: Incisors; Canine; Premolars; Molars.

Devonian   Fourth period of the Paleozoic. Age of Fish. Appearance of amphibians.

Diastema   Gap, space, especially between the upper lateral incisor and canine (also seen in the lower jaw between the canine and first premolar); found in many monkeys and pongids.

Diploid number (2n)   The full complement of chromosomes—46 in humans—in a somatic cell or in a sex cell before meiosis.

Display   Stereotyped behavior that serves to communicate emotional states between individuals. Display is most often associated with reproductive or agonistic behavior.

Diurnal   Active during daylight hours.

Divination   A method of foretelling the future.

Division of Labor   Activities performed only by members of a particular status, such as age or sex.

Dizygotic   Twins derived from two zygotes, genetically related the same as any full sibs; differences between them are caused both by the environment and genetic variation.

DNA (deoxyribonucleic acid)   A large molecule composed of adenine, guanine, cytosine, and thymine plus phosphate and sugar; DNA carries the genetic code.

Dolichocephalic   Narrow or long-headed. A skull in which the width is less than 75% of the length.

Dominance (dominance hierarchy)   The physical domination of some members of a group by other members. A hierarchy of ranked statuses sustained by hostile, or threat of hostile, behavior which results in greater access to resources such as food, sleeping sites, and mates.

Dominant   A trait determined by a dominant allele. A trait that is visible or measurable and that prevents the appearance of the recessive.

Dorsal   Pertaining to the back (toward the backbone) of an animal.

Double helix   The structure of DNA composed of a pair of matching helixes.

Dryopith   The common term for *Dryopithecus* and *Proconsul*; distributed mostly in Africa, but with some representatives in Europe.

Dryopithecus   The genus name referring to a diverse group of extinct hominoids from the Miocene.

East Lake Turkana A Plio-Pleistocene locality in northern Kenya which has yielded dozens of fossil hominids. Hominid-bearing levels date 1.8–1.0 m.y.a.

Ecological niche (econiche) The life-style of a particular organism (species) in a particular habitat.

Eemian "Third" interglacial; between the Riss and Würm glaciations.

Effective breeding population Those individuals in a population actually producing offspring; usually about one-third total population size.

Empirical Derived from or depending on experience or experiment.

Endocast An impression of the inside of the skull showing the size, shape, and some details of the surface of the brain.

Endogamy Mating within the social unit (that is, the population). *See* Exogamy.

Endoskeleton An internal bony skeleton, characteristic of vertebrates. *See* Exoskeleton.

Eocene Second epoch of Tertiary. Radiation of prosimians. Possible appearance of anthropoids.

Estrous cycle An hormonally initiated cycle in female mammals correlated with ovulation. Estrus may involve observable physical and behavioral changes.

Ethnography The study of surviving, nonliterate societies.

Eutheria The most numerous subclass of Mammalia. Embryo and fetus of these (placental) mammals are nourished by a placenta.

Evolution A change in gene frequency in a population from one generation to the next.

Evolutionary reversal The reacquisition of a structure previously lost in the evolution of a life form—an extremely unlikely event.

Evolutionary trend A set of anatomical and/or behavior traits which tend to characterize a group of evolutionarily related organisms. For example: pentadactyly, retention of complete clavicle, and stereoscopic vision among the primates.

Exogamy Mating outside the social unit (that is, the population).

Exoskeleton A hard, supporting external covering, characteristic of many invertebrates such as ants and lobsters. *See* Endoskeleton.

F₁ First filial generation; offspring resulting from a cross of homozygous dominants and homozygous recessives. All individuals resulting from such a cross are heterozygous.

F₂ Second filial generation; offspring of a cross of F₁ individuals—a mating of two heterozygous individuals (or selfing in a species where this is possible, as in the case of Mendel's peas).

Faience Pottery with a glassy glazed surface, developed by Egyptians.

Family Members of a family usually inhabit a similar environment; a category that includes genera and species.

Fayum An Oligocene fossil primate site in Egypt yielding several early anthropoid forms.

Femur Thigh bone.

Fibula The narrow long bone of the lower leg. *See* Tibia.

Fixity of species The belief that species, once created, never changed but remained fixed. This belief was firmly held by most scholars in the eighteenth century.

Fluorine dating A method of relative dating by measuring the amount of fluorine in a specimen. More fluorine indicates a greater age.

Fluting Technique of removing large flakes in order to prepare projectile points for hafting; popular during the Paleo-Indian period in the New World.

Folsom Phase of southern Great Plains prehistory, 10,000 y.a. to 8000 y.a., during which long-fluted projectile points were used for killing bison.

Foramen magnum Opening in the base of the skull through which the spinal cord passes.

Forensic Pertaining to courts of law. In anthropology, the use of anthropology in questions of law.

Founder effect (Sewall Wright Effect) A type of genetic drift resulting from the isolation of a small non-random population drawn from a larger gene pool.

Frontal bone The front bone of the skull including the forehead and the brow region over the eyes.

Gamete A mature sex cell. A sex cell following two meiotic divisions—sperm for male; ovum for female.

Gene That section of DNA responsible for the ultimate synthesis of a specific polypeptide chain of amino acids; that portion of DNA with a detectable function.

Gene frequency (allele frequency) A numerical indicator of the proportion of genes (alleles) in a population. *See* Hardy-Weinberg Equilibrium.

Gene pool The total complement of genes in a population.

Generalized Pertains to a trait capable of several functions. The human hand is generalized because it is used for a number of functions; the human foot is specialized and is used in a very limited way. *See* Specialized.

Genetic drift (random genetic drift) The evolutionary factor which accounts for evolutionary changes (shifts in gene frequency) due to random events. A function of population size.

Genetic screening Testing programs to ascertain individuals with genetic diseases or carriers of potentially deleterious genes.

Genotype The genetic makeup of a particular organism; an individual's "genetic formula"; the genes at one or more loci.

Genotypic proportion The relative frequency of the genotypes in a population. For a two-allele system (such as A, a), there will be three genotypes (AA, Aa, aa). Hardy-Weinberg equilibrium makes idealized predictions of these genotypes according to the formula: $p^2 + 2pq + q^2 = 1$. *See* Hardy-Weinberg Equilibrium.

Genus (pl. genera) A category of classification in the Animal (or Plant) Kingdom. Genus groups together closely related species usually inhabiting similar ecological niches; for example, *Homo, Pan, Felis, Canis*.

Geochemistry The study of the chemical composition of the earth's crust.

Geology The study of the history and structure of the earth as recorded in rocks.

Gracile Small, lightly built; used to refer to smaller australopithecines. *See* Robust.

Gravettian A culture period (*circa* 25,000 y.a.) of the Upper Paleolithic; associated with Lascaux Cave art.

Great Basin Rugged, dry plateau between the mountains of California and Colorado, and southern Oregon and Idaho.

Grooming Cleaning the body of another by picking through the hair and fur with the fingers or teeth. Grooming is common among primates.

Guanine One of the chemical bases (purines) found both in DNA and RNA.

Günz First glacial of the Pleistocene.

Habilis A species of genus *Homo*, first applied by Louis Leakey to Plio-Pleistocene hominids from East Africa.

Hadar A Plio-Pleistocene hominid locality in northeastern Ethiopia. Hominid-bearing levels dated ?3.7–2.6 m.y.a.

Haploid number (n) The number of chromosomes in the gamete after meiosis (23 in humans).

Haplorhini The classificatory term used to group tarsiers with monkeys, apes, and humans (either suborder or semiorder).

Hardy-Weinberg Equilibrium The mathematical relationship expressing—under ideal conditions—the predicted distribution of genes in populations; the central theorem of population genetics.

Helix A spiral or anything with a spiral form.

Helix, double The structure of DNA resembles a double helix (spiral).

Herbivore A plant-eating animal.

Heritability The relative amount of variation in a trait due to genetic causes as part of total phenotypic variation.

Heterodontism Having different teeth. Characteristic of mammals whose teeth consist of incisors, canines, premolars, and molars.

Heterozygote A cell or individual that is heterozygous. (A hybrid is heterozygous for a particular trait.)

Heterozygous Having different alleles at a given locus on a pair of homologous chromosomes.

Hieroglyphics Sacred "picture-writing" used in ancient Egypt and elsewhere.

Holistic Viewing the whole as an integrated and interdependent system. Anthropology includes as its concern all aspects of human beings—physical and behavioral.

Holocene Second (present) epoch of Quaternary; begins with end of Pleistocene glaciation.

Holstein Second interglacial between the Mindel and Riss glaciations.

Home range The area utilized by an animal; the area the group is most familiar with and which provides the group with food.

Hominid Popular form of Hominidae, the family to which humans belong. Hominids include bipedal primates such as *Australopithecus* and *Homo*.

Hominidae The family, of the order Primates, to which humans belong.

Hominization Process of becoming more human.

Hominoid Abbreviated or popular form of Hominoidea, the superfamily to which hominids, pongids, and gibbons belong.

Homo The genus to which humans belong, including *erectus* and *sapiens*.

Homodontism Having the same teeth. Refers to the situation wherein all teeth of the mouth are similar, as in fish and reptiles.

Homoiothermy Pertains to an organism that maintains the same temperature (mammals and birds, for example). Warm-blooded.

Homologous chromosomes Paired chromosomes. Chromosomes that are paired during meiosis and participate in cross-over. Homologous chromosomes contain the same loci.

Homologous structures Similarities in parts of the anatomy based upon common descent.

Homologue Occurs in meiosis when a chromosome duplicates itself. The double-stranded chromosome is a homologue.

Homology Similarities of organisms based on common evolutionary descent.

Homo sapiens The species which appeared 200,000 to 300,000 years ago; includes Neandertals and anatomically modern humans.

Homo sapiens sapiens The subspecies to which modern humans belong; beginning with the Upper Paleolithic; anatomically modern human beings.

Homozygote A cell or individual that is homozygous. (A purebred is homozygous for a particular trait.)

Homozygous Having the same allele at a given locus on a pair of homologous chromosomes.

Hopewell A culture centered in southern Ohio between 100 B.C. and 300 A.D., but influencing a much wider region through trade and the spread of a religious cult.

Horticulture Farming method in which only human energy and hand tools are used for cultivation.

Human A term now generally applied to *H. erectus* and *H. sapiens*.

Human evolution Biological changes over time leading to anatomically modern human beings.

Human variation Physical differences among humans.

Humerus Upper arm bone.

Hybrid Offspring of parents of mixed ancestry. A heterozygote.

Hypothesis   Unproved theory. A theory is a statement with some confirmation.

Inca   The people whose sophisticated culture dominated Peru at the time of the Europeans' arrival; also, the term for that people's divine ruler.

Incisors   Front teeth, usually spatulate in primates; used for cutting and nipping.

Independent assortment   Where gene pairs on one set of homologous chromosomes do not influence the distribution of gene pairs on other chromosomes—they separate independently from one another during meiosis and are randomly assorted in the gametes. Known as Mendel's second law.

Innominate   The fused half-portion of a pelvis; contains three bones—the ilium, ischium, and pubis.

In situ   In its original or natural position.

Interspecific variation   Variation between two separate species.

Interstadial   A temperate period during the phases of a glacial period.

Intraspecific variation   Variation within a species due to age, sexual dimorphism, individual genetic differences, or geographic separation.

Intron   Within a genetic locus, a section of DNA that is not translated.

Ischial callosities   Hardened sitting pads found on the rear ends of Old World monkeys. Also seen to some degree in chimpanzees.

Jurassic   Second period of Mesozoic. Great age of dinosaurs. First appearance of birds.

Kabuh   Middle Pleistocene geologic formation.

Kanapoi   A Plio-Pleistocene hominid site in northern Kenya. Estimated age approximately 4 m.y.a.

Karyotype   The chromosome complement contained in a cell, especially the diagram of chromosomes arranged according to size and banding patterns of each chromosome.

KNM-ER   Kenya National Museum—East Rudolf (the former name for Lake Turkana). The prefix preceding paleontological discoveries from East Lake Turkana.

Kromdraai   A Plio-Pleistocene hominid site in South Africa yielding remains of robust australopithecines.

Laetoli   A Plio-Pleistocene hominid site in northern Tanzania. Dated 3.77–3.59 m.y.a.

Lamarckism   Lamarck's ideas about evolution. *See* Acquired characteristics.

Lambdoid suture   The horizontal or transverse suture at the back of the top of the skull joining the parietal and occipital bones.

Lanceolate   Narrow and tapering form.

Lemuroidea   The prosimian superfamily of lemurs, today confined to Madagascar.

Levant   Countries bordering the eastern Mediterranean.

Lineage   An evolutionary line of related forms distinct from other such lines.

Living floor   A narrow horizon of archeological remains. Corresponds to brief period of hominid occupation.

Locus (pl. loci)   The place a gene occupies on a chromosome.

Loess   Fine-grained soil composed of glacially pulverized rock dust.

Lorisoidea   The prosimian superfamily of lorises. Today all are nocturnal forms, found in Africa and southern Asia.

Lothagam   A Plio-Pleistocene hominid site in northern Kenya. Estimated age, approximately 5.5 m.y.a.

Macroevolution   Large evolutionary changes (result of long-term major shifts in gene frequencies) produced only after many generations. *See* Microevolution.

Magdalenean   Final period of the Upper Paleolithic (*circa* 15,000 y.a.) (in Europe) and a time of spectacular technological growth; associated with art from Altamira Cave in Spain.

Makapansgat   A Plio-Pleistocene hominid site in South Africa yielding remains of gracile australopithecines.

Mammals   The class of animals that nurse their young from mammary glands. Primates belong to this class.

Mandible   Lower jaw.

Manioc   Cassava; a starchy edible root crop of the tropics.

Marsupials   A subclass of mammals—metatheria—that bear live young; infants are nursed in the mother's pouch, Marsupium pouch.

Masseter   Chewing; refers to muscles used in the operation of the jaw—originating on the zygomatic (cheek) bones and inserting on the mandible.

Mastoid process   A triangular bone behind the ear hole on a human skull; usually more pronounced in males than females.

Maxilla   Upper jaw.

Maya   Prehistoric Mesoamerican culture that represented the climax of pre-European cultural development between 300 A.D. and 900 A.D.

Megalith   "Large stone" construction associated especially with the Neolithic farmers of western Europe. Stonehenge is the best-known example.

Meiosis   Cell division, consisting of two divisions, in which the total complement (diploid number) of chromosomes is reduced by half (haploid number) in the gametes (sperm in males; ova in females). Also known as reduction division.

Melanin   The biochemical compound produced by specialized cells in the basal layers of the epidermis. Melanin is very important in influencing skin pigmentation.

Mendelian trait (simple trait)   An inherited trait with a straightforward pattern, controlled by one genetic locus.

Mesoamerica   The region from southern Mexico through Panama.

Mesolithic   A cultural phase dominated by a foraging and fishing economy in the Old World, where it is also referred to as the Middle Stone Age; equivalent to Archaic in the New World.

Mesopotamia   Land between the Tigris and Euphrates rivers; known also as the Fertile Crescent.

Mesozoic Era (225–65 m.y.a.)   The era following the Paleozoic. Known as the Age of Reptiles.

Metacentric chromosome   A chromosome with its centromere near the center.

Metatheria   A subclass of mammals (marsupials); infants are nursed in the mother's pouch.

Metazoa   Multicellular animals. A major division of the Animal Kingdom.

Microevolution   The small-scale evolutionary changes occurring over just a few generations and involving relatively small changes in gene frequencies. What the Hardy-Weinberg formula measures. *See* Macroevolution.

Midden   A refuse heap marking a Mesolithic campsite.

Migration   Movement of individuals (and, necessarily, genes) between populations. An evolutionary factor that may cause changes in gene frequencies.

Millet   Small-grained cereal grass native to Asia and domesticated there by early farmers.

Milpa   Slash-and-burn or swidden farming; usually applied to Mesoamerica.

Mindel   Second glacial of the Pleistocene (correlated with the Elster).

Miocene   Fourth epoch of Tertiary. Radiation of hominoids. Possible appearance of hominids.

Mitosis   Cell division into two daughter cells in which the chromosome complement is identical to the mother cell and to each other.

Molars   Cheek teeth, following the premolars. In anthropoids these are the last three teeth of the tooth row; used for grinding and chewing.

Molecule   Smallest portion of a substance that acts like that substance and is capable of existing independently. Several to many atoms constitute a molecule.

Mongrelization   Racial mixture.

Monogenists   Term applied to those who believe that all races derived from a single pair (Adam and Eve).

Monotreme   A subclass of mammals—prototheria—that lay eggs.

Monozygotic   Twins derived from one zygote, genetically identical. Differences between the twins are caused solely by the environment.

Mosaic evolution   Term applied when the rate of evolution in one functional system varies from other systems.

Mousterian   A culture period, or stone tool industry, of the Middle Paleolithic; usually associated with Neandertals. Characterized mainly by stone flakes.

Multivariate   Pattern for several variables assessed simultaneously.

Mutation   An alteration in the genetic material (DNA). The

true "creative" factor in evolution. Mutation is the only way to produce new variation and the starting point of all evolutionary change.

Natural selection   The evolutionary factor, first articulated by Charles Darwin, that causes changes in gene frequencies in populations due to differential net reproductive success of individuals. *See* Net reproductive success.

Neandertal, classic   Neandertals of the early fourth (Weichsel or Würm) glaciation, especially those of Western Europe.

Neandertals   *H. sapiens* form that preceded anatomically modern human beings (*H. sapiens sapiens*); usually associated with Mousterian culture and the Middle Paleolithic.

Neolithic   Literally, "New Stone" Age; associated with the development of domesticated resources and farming practices.

Neopallium or Neocortex   A covering of the cerebral hemispheres begun in reptiles, expanded in mammals, and reaching its greatest expansion in humans. Higher mental activity is concentrated in this area.

Net reproductive success   The number of offspring successfully raised; the bottom line of natural selection.

Nocturnal   Active during nighttime. *See* Diurnal and Crepuscular.

Nomadism   Lifeway of wandering in search of food.

Nuchal   Pertaining to the neck.

Nucleotide   A purine or pyrimidine base attached to a sugar and a phosphate group: a subunit of DNA and RNA.

Nulliparous   Never having given birth.

Nucleus   A body, present in most types of cells, containing chromosomes.

Occiput (occipital bone)   The rear bone of the skull. The occiput also forms most of the base, including the occipital condyles and foramen magnum.

OH   Olduvai Hominid. The prefix preceding hominid discoveries (numbered sequentially) from Olduvai Gorge.

Olduvai Gorge   A paleoanthropological site in northern Tanzania yielding remains of Plio-Pleistocene hominids and a wealth of biocultural data.

Olfactory   Smell.

Oligocene   Third epoch of Tertiary. Radiation of anthropoids.

Olmec   Culture in the Gulf Coast Lowlands of Veracruz and Tabasco, Mexico, with a highly developed art style and high degree of sociopolitical complexity; flourished from 3500 y.a. to 2500 y.a.

Omnivore   An animal that will eat both plants and meat.

Omo   A Plio-Pleistocene hominid locality in southern Ethiopia. Hominid-bearing levels dated 2.9–1.0 m.y.a.

Order   A category of classification in the Animal (or Plant) Kingdom. A subdivision of Class. Members of an order usually inhabit a similar environment; for example, Carnivora, Rodentia, Primates.

Ordovician The second period of the Paleozoic. First fishes appear.

Orthograde Upright walking.

Oracle A person believed capable of communicating with the deities on behalf of others.

Osteology The study of bones.

Ostracoderm Shell-skin or armored.

Oviparity Egg birth, characteristic of most animals..

P₁ The parental generation in which homozygous dominants and recessives are crossed. Parents homozygous (pure) for round seeds and parents homozygous for wrinkled represent such a parental cross.

Paleo "Ancient"; in the Americas, refers to the early period of big-game hunting cultures, from about 12,000 y.a. to 8000 y.a.

Paleoanthropology The multidisciplinary approach to the study of human biocultural evolution. Includes physical anthropology, archeology, geology, ecology, and many other disciplines.

Paleocene First epoch of Tertiary. Prosimians present.

Paleolithic Old Stone Age. The culture period that includes the beginning of culture up to approximately the end of the Pleistocene glaciation. Usually divided into Lower, Middle, and Upper.

Paleolithic, Lower The earliest period of the Paleolithic, characterized by Oldowan (pebble tools) and Acheulian (hand-axe) industries.

Paleolithic, Middle A stone flake industry associated with the Mousterian culture period and Neandertals.

Paleolithic, Upper The final stage of the Paleolithic, associated with more sophisticated culture such as cave painting, sculpting, engraving, and stone tools made from blades. Appearance of anatomically modern humans.

Paleomagnetism Dating method based on the shifting nature of the earth's geomagnetic field.

Paleontology The study of the fossils of ancient animals.

Paleopathology The study of ancient diseases.

Paleospecies A group of organisms found in paleontological contexts and usually separated by large amounts of time, thus adding to the amount of variation seen in extant groups.

Paleozoic Era (570–225 m.y.a.) The era following the Proterozoic, beginning 570 million years ago. The first era in which fossils are relatively abundant.

Palynology The analysis of pollen found in the soil of archeological excavations to determine the kinds of plants present at the ancient site.

Parallelism (parallel evolution) Evolution of similar adaptive traits in forms that were once related but then diverged, developing along similar lines. *See* Convergence.

Paranthropus The genus name sometimes used to refer to robust australopithecines and, therefore, making a generic distinction between them and gracile australopithecines (*Australopithecus*).

Parietal The right and left side bones on top of the skull, joined by the sagittal suture.

Pentadactyly Having five digits. A generalized trait of mammals and primates.

Penultimate Last but one; next to last.

Peptide A compound of two or more amino acids joined by peptide bonds. Linked peptides form polypeptides which, in turn, join to form proteins.

Periodontal Gum and jaw disease.

Perissodactyl Odd-toed hoof (e.g., horse).

Permian Final period of the Paleozoic. Appearance of mammallike reptiles.

Phenotype The observable or measurable characteristic of an organism. Roundness in a seed is an observable phenotype. In blood groups, A, B, and O are measurable phenotypes.

Phenotypic ratio The ratio of phenotypes, especially from a hybrid cross. Mendel's famous F₁ hybrid cross of peas produced a 3:1 phenotypic ratio.

Phylogeny The study of evolutionary lines of descent. A "family tree."

Phylum (pl. phyla) A primary division of the Animal (or Plant) Kingdom; for example, Arthropoda, Chordata.

Piltdown A forged "fossil" hominid from England, "discovered" in 1911. Combining a fully *sapiens* cranium with a modern pongid jaw, it served to confuse anthropologists for four decades.

Pithecanthropus Name originally given to *H. erectus* by Eugene Dubois.

Placenta Tissue connected to the uterus that nourishes the fetus and absorbs its waste. This structure is characteristic of most mammals and has given its name to that form—placental mammals.

Placental mammals (eutheria) Mammals whose embryonic development is associated with a placenta.

Plano Great Plains bison-hunting culture of 8000 y.a. to 7000 y.a., which used narrow unfluted lanceolate points.

Platycephaly Flatheadedness, as opposed to the dome shape of the skull of anatomically modern humans.

Pleistocene First epoch of the Quaternary. *H. sapiens* becomes widespread throughout Old World. *H. sapiens sapiens* evolves toward end of Pleistocene. Ice Age.

Pliocene Final (fifth) epoch of Tertiary. Hominids definitely present.

Point mutation Change in just one base in the DNA sequence. Probably the most common kind of mutation with evolutionary impact.

Polychrome Many-colored.

Polygenic Traits controlled by two or more loci; usually such traits (for example, stature, weight, IQ) are also influenced considerably by the environment.

Polygenists Term applied to those who believe in a multiple origin of races.

Polygyny One male and two or more females in a mating relationship.

Polypeptide   A group of peptides linked together. One or more polypeptide chains make a protein.

Population   Within a species, a community of individuals where mates are usually found.

Population genetics   Studies in contemporary populations through measurement of gene frequencies. *See* Hardy-Weinberg Equilibrium.

Postcranial   The skeleton behind (below) the skull.

Postorbital bar   The bony element that closes in the outside of the eye orbit—a characteristic of primates.

Potassium-argon (K/Ar) dating   Determining absolute age (in years) by measuring the amounts of potassium-40 (^{40}K) and argon-40 (^{40}Ar). The greater the amount of argon that has built up, the older the specimen. Used only on rocks once heated to a very high temperature, such as that generated by volcanic activity.

Potlatch   Ceremonial feast and gift-exchange among the Northwest Coast Indians.

Prehensility   Adaptation for grasping.

Premolars   Cheek teeth similar in form to the molars; situated between canines and molars. Old World anthropoids possess two premolars and New World forms normally three in each quadrant. Human premolars have two cusps, compared to four or more in molars, and are known as bicuspids.

Presenting   A behavior, often indicating subordination or appeasement, in which an animal places itself on all fours and elevates its rear end toward another. During estrus a female may present for purposes of copulation.

Primates   The order of mammals to which humans, apes, monkeys, and prosimians belong.

Primitive   In evolutionary terms, an organism that is closer to an evolutionary divergence than a later (more derived) one. *See* Advanced.

Principle of independent assortment   The distribution of one pair of genes does not influence the distribution of other pairs of genes.

Principle of segregation   Chromosomes occur in pairs. In the production of a gamete, the pair is separated so that each gamete contains only one of the pair.

Prosimian   Common form for Prosimii; the suborder of primates, including lemurs, lorises, and tarsiers.

Protein   A macromolecule, composed of one or more polypeptide chains of amino acids. Proteins are responsible for carrying out most of the cell's metabolic activities, and are thus the basic structural and functional compounds of the cell.

Protein synthesis   The manufacture of a protein from the DNA to the final product. The process by which amino acids are linked (by a peptide bond) to form a polypeptide chain. The completed chain or chains form a protein.

Proterozoic   A geologic era immediately preceding the Paleozoic. Not much evidence of life.

Prototheria   A subclass of mammals (monotremes) that lay eggs and nurse their young.

Punctuated equilibrium   The view that evolutionary rates are not constant, but proceed slowly (equilibria) until "punctuated" by rather sudden spurts.

Purines   A class of chemical bases—adenine and guanine—found in DNA and RNA.

Pyrimidines   A class of chemical bases—cytosine, thymine, uracil—found in nucleic acids.

Quadrumanual   Using all four limbs for grasping during locomotion, as in the orang.

Quadrupedal (quadrupedalism)   Using all four limbs as weight supports while moving. Trunk typically horizontal. The basic mammalian, and primate, form of locomotion.

Quaternary   Second (present) period of Cenozoic. Period of *Homo erectus* and *Homo sapiens*.

Quinoa   Seed-bearing member of the genus Chenopodium, cultivated by early Peruvians.

Race   Currently defined by anthropologists as a breeding population; formerly applied to a group of people who resembled each other in physical appearance. Many anthropologists do not believe the term to be a useful one when applied to humans.

Rachis   On a plant, a short stem by which individual seeds are attached to the main stalk.

Ramapithecus   An extinct hominoid from the Miocene (13–9 m.y.a.) thought by some to be an early hominid. Now usually included within *Sivapithecus*. *See Sivapithecus*.

Raptor   A hunting bird with talons and hooked beak, such as an eagle or owl.

Recessive   A trait that is not phenotypically expressed in heterozygotes. A trait that is phenotypically expressed only in the homozygous state.

Recombination   The reshuffling of genetic material every generation as the result of sexual reproduction. Recombination occurs during meiosis (through crossing-over and random assortment) and provides variation for natural selection to act upon.

Ribosomes   Small, spherical particles, composed of rRNA and proteins, found in the cytoplasm. The ribosome is the site of protein synthesis.

Rift Valley (Great Rift Valley)   A massive (1,200 mile long) geological feature in East Africa associated with mountain building, volcanoes, faulting, etc. The results of "rifting" have provided preservation and access to several superb Plio-Pleistocene sites (Olduvai, East Lake Turkana, Hadar, etc.).

RNA (ribonucleic acid)   A nucleic acid found both in the nucleus and the cytoplasm. RNA differs from DNA in that its sugar component is ribose.

   mRNA   Messenger RNA. This RNA carries genetic information from DNA in the nucleus to the ribosomes in the cytoplasm.

   rRNA   Ribosomal RNA; a major constituent of ribosomes.

   tRNA   Transfer RNA. This RNA brings amino acids together to form a polypeptide chain.

Riss The third major glaciation of the Alpine system; equivalent to the Salle of the Scandinavian system.

Robust Larger, more heavily built; used to refer to the larger australopithecines. *See* Gracile.

Saale The third major glaciation of the Scandinavian system; occurred during the Pleistocene; equivalent to Riss, of the Alpine system.

Sagittal crest Raised ridge along the midline of the skull where the temporal muscle (used to move the jaw) attaches.

Sagittal suture The suture joining the left and right parietals; extending the length of the skull from the coronal suture in front to lambdoidal suture behind.

Savanna A grassland with a scattering of trees, usually in the tropics or subtropics.

Scapula Shoulder blade.

Sectorial Compressed single-cusped tooth (1st lower premolar) seen in pongids (and many extinct hominoids); compared to the bicuspid form found in most hominids.

Segregation Genes exist on paired chromosomes. At meiosis, the pairs are segregated so that a gamete has only one of the pair. Mendel's first law.

Sex cells Cells that divide by meiosis and become gametes.

Sexual dimorphism Marked physical differences between adult males and females of a species. Examples: greater size of gorilla and baboon males; sagittal and occipital crest of male gorilla.

Shovel-shaped incisors (shoveling) Incisors with raised ridges of enamel on both sides of the teeth.

Silurian Third period of the Paleozoic. Jawed fishes appear. First air-breathing animals.

Sinanthropus The name originally given by Davidson Black to hominid specimens from Zhoukoudian; now known as *H. erectus pekinensis*.

Sivapithecus An extinct hominoid from the Miocene (*circa* 13–7 m.y.a.) found mostly in Eurasia. Some species are probably closely related to orangs.

Sociobiology An evolutionary approach to the explanation of behavior—largely in terms of natural selection (individual reproductive success).

Solutrean A culture period (*circa* 20,000 y.a.) of Europe; known for its magnificent flintwork.

Somatic cells Cells that do not divide by meiosis and do not become gametes. Body cells.

Sorghum A cereal grass native to Africa, with a sweet juicy stalk.

Specialized A trait that evolved for a specific function is said to be specialized. The human foot is specialized, the hand generalized. *See* Generalized.

Speciation The evolutionary process that produces new species from previous ones.

Species A category of classification of the Animal (or Plant) Kingdom. A population or group of populations living in the same econiche that can, or actually do, interbreed and produce fertile offspring.

Stela An upright stone or post, often bearing inscriptions.

Sterkfontein A Plio-Pleistocene hominid site in South Africa yielding remains of gracile australopithecines and, perhaps, early *Homo*.

Stratigraphy Sequential layering of deposits. The sequence of layers is used as a means of dating, relatively, the layers as well as the materials in the layers.

Strepsirhini The classificatory term used to group lemurs and lorises (either suborder or semiorder).

Subphylum A major division of a phylum—such as Vertebrata.

Substrate The physical surface on which an animal moves or rests.

Superfamily A group of closely related families.

Supraorbital torus Ridge above the orbits on a skull. The supraorbital torus is very pronounced in *erectus*, Neandertals, and some australopithecines.

Swartkrans A Plio-Pleistocene hominid site in South Africa yielding remains of robust australopithecines and, perhaps, early *Homo*.

Symbiosis Mutually advantageous association of two different organisms.

Taphonomy Study of how bones come to be buried in the earth and preserved as fossils.

Tarsiioidea The prosimian superfamily of tarsiers, a nocturnal form found in southern Asia.

Taung A South African Plio-Pleistocene australopithecine site. The location of the first australopithecine discovery (1924).

Taurodontism Enlarged molar pulp cavities found in cattle and some early humans.

Taxon A population (or group of populations) judged to be sufficiently distinct to be assigned to a separate category (such as genus or species).

Taxonomy The science of the classification of organisms, including the principles, procedures, and rules of classification.

Tectonic movement Movements of the earth (along fault lines, during mountain building, and so forth).

Tehuacán Valley A dry highland region on the boundary of the states of Puebla and Oaxaca in southern Mexico; location of early New World domestication and farming activities.

Tektite A round, glassy body of unknown origin.

Tell A mound of accumulated rubble on the site of an ancient city.

Terrestrial Living on the ground. Humans, gorillas, and some monkeys are terrestrial.

Territoriality Behavior in defense of the territory of a group; establishment of exclusive right to the use of a territory. Some primates are much more territorial than others.

Territory   That part of the home range used exclusively by one group. The area defended by one group against other groups of the same species.

Tertiary   First period of the Cenozoic. Period of primate radiation. (Includes: Paleocene, Eocene, Oligocene, Miocene, and Pliocene.)

Thymine   One of the chemical bases (pyrimidines) found in DNA, but not in RNA.

Tibia   The large long bone of the lower leg; the shin. *See* Fibula.

Toltecs   A central Mexican highlands people who created a pre-Aztec empire with its capital at Tula in the Valley of Mexico.

Traissic   First period of Mesozoic. First dinosaurs.

Transhumance   Seasonal population movement from one resource zone to another.

Trinil fauna   Animal remains associated with the Middle Pleistocene Trinil period in Java.

Triplet   A sequence of three bases; found in mRNA and tRNA. Codes for a specific amino acid. A codon or anticodon.

Tuff   A solidified sediment of volcanic ash.

Typology, racial   Dividing humans into discrete racial types.

Uniformitarianism   A concept maintaining that the ancient changes in the earth's surface were caused by the same physical principles acting today. The earth's crust was formed slowly and gradually. Mountains, rivers, valleys, etc., were the result of purely natural forces such as erosion by wind, water, frost, ice, and rain. Although not originated by Charles Lyell, uniformitarianism is associated with him because he popularized it.

Upper Paleolithic   A culture period noted for technological, artistic, and behavioral innovations. Also known for the appearance of anatomically modern human beings.

Uracil   One of the chemical bases (pyrimidines) found in RNA, but not in DNA.

Variation (genetic)   Inherited differences between individuals. The basis of all evolutionary change.

Ventral   Toward the belly; the front of an organism (as in man) or the undersurface of an animal that does not stand erect (as a dog).

Vertebra (pl. vertebrae)   A single bone of the spinal or vertebral column (backbone).

Viviparity   Live birth; characteristic mainly of mammals.

Wattle and daub   A building technique, using a framework of woven sticks plastered with clay.

Weichsel   The fourth glacial advance in the Old World.

Weir   A brush or stone obstruction placed across a stream or inlet for the purpose of trapping fish.

Wisconsin   The period of the last major glacial advance in North America; correlates with Würm in the Old World.

World view   A literal translation from the German, *Weltanschauung*. A personal or group philosophy explaining history; a way of looking at the world.

Würm   The fourth glacial in the Old World.

Y-5 pattern (Dryopithecine Y-5)   A pattern of cusps on the molar teeth characteristic of hominoids.

Ziggurat   Sumerian mud-brick temple-pyramid.

Zygomatic (or zygomatic bone)   Malar or cheek bone.

Zygomatic arch   The bone along the side of the skull below the orbit providing attachment for jaw muscles.

Zygote   A fertilized ovum; formed by the union of a sperm and ovum.

◇ BIBLIOGRAPHY

Adams, Richard E. W.
1977   *Prehistoric Mesoamerica.* Boston: Little, Brown.

Adams, Robert McC.
1972   "Patterns of Urbanization in Early Southern Mesopotamia." *In: Man, Settlement, and Urbanism,* Peter J. Ucko, Ruth Tringham, and G. W. Dimbleby (eds.), London: Duckworth, pp. 735–749.

———
1981   *Heartland of Cities.* Chicago: University of Chicago Press.

Aigner, Jean S. and Wm. S. Laughlin
1973   "The Dating of Lantian Man and His Significance for Analyzing Trends in Human Evolution." *American Journal of Physical Anthropology,* 39:97–110.

Aikens, C. Melvin
1970   *Hogup Cave.* University of Utah Anthropological Papers, 93.

Aldred, Cyril
1961   *The Egyptians.* New York: Frederick A. Praeger.

Alland Jr., Alexander
1971   *Human Diversity.* New York: Anchor Press/Doubleday.

Altman, I.
1978   "Crowding: Historical and Contemporary Trends in Crowding Research." *In: Human Response to Crowding,* A. Baum and Y. M. Epstein (eds.), New York: John Wiley and Sons.

Altmann, Jeanne
1981   *Baboon Mothers and Infants.* Cambridge: Harvard University Press.

Altmann, Stuart A. and Jeanne Altmann
1970   *Baboon Ecology.* Chicago: University of Chicago Press.

Amos, D. Bernard and D. D. Kostyu
1980   "HLA—A Central Immunological Agency of Man." *In: Advances in Human Genetics* (Vol. 10), H. Harris and K. Hirschhorn (eds.), New York: Plenum Press, pp. 137–208.

Andersson, J. Gunnar
1934   *Children of the Yellow Earth.* New York: Macmillan.

Andrews, P. J.
1983   "The Natural History of *Sivapithecus.*" *In:* R. Ciochon and R. Corruccini (eds.), q.v., pp. 441–463.

Andrews, Peter and Elizabeth Evans
1979   "The Environment of *Ramapithecus* in Africa." *Paleobiology* 5(1):22–30.

Ardrey, Robert
1976   *The Hunting Hypothesis.* New York: Atheneum.

Aronson, J. L., R. C. Walter, and M. Taieb
1983   "Correlation of Tulu Boi Tuff at Koobi Fora with the Sidi Hakoma Tuff at Hadar." *Nature,* 306:209–210.

Baba, M. L., L. L. Darga and M. Goodman
1981   "Maximum Parsimony Test of the Clock Model of the Molecular Change Using Amino Acid Sequence Data." Paper presented at the Annual Meetings, American Association of Physical Anthropologists, April 1981.

Bailey, G.
1975   "The Role of Molluscs in Coastal Economies." *Journal of Archaeological Science,* 2: 45–62.

Baker, Paul T.
1966   "Human Biological Variation as an Adaptive Response to the Environment." *Eugenics Quarterly,* 13:81–91.

Baker, Paul T. and Michael A. Little
1976   "Environmental Adaptations and Perspectives." *In: Man in the Andes,* P. T. Baker and M. A. Little (eds.), Stroudsburg, Penn.: Dowden, Hutchinson, and Ross, Inc., pp. 405–428.

Barash, David
1982   *Sociobiology and Behavior.* 2nd Ed. New York: Elsevier.

Barzun, Jacques
1965   *Race: A Study in Superstition.* New York: Harper and Row.

Bayanov, Dmitri and Igor Bourtsev
1974   "Reply (to comments on Proshner's article)." *Current Anthropology,* 15(4):452–456.

———
1976   "On Neanderthal vs. Paranthropus." *Current Anthropology,* 17(2):312–318.

Beck, Benjamin B.
1980   *Animal Tool Behavior.* New York: Garland Publishing, Inc.

Behrensmeyer, Anna K. and Andrew P. Hill
1980   *Fossils in the Making: Vertebrate Taphonomy and Paleoecology.* Chicago: The University of Chicago Press.

Bennett, Kenneth A.
1979   *Fundamentals of Biological Anthropology.* Dubuque: Wm. C. Brown Co. Publishers.

Biddiss, Michael D.
1970   *Father of Racist Ideology: The Social and Political Thought of Count Gobineau.* New York: Weybright and Talley.

Binford, Lewis R.
1968   "Post-Pleistocene Adaptations." *In:* Sally R. Binford and Lewis R. Binford (eds.), q.v., pp. 421–449.

———
1981   *Bones. Ancient Men and Modern Myths.* New York: Academic Press.

———
1982   Comment on White's article, "Rethinking the Middle/Upper Paleolithic Transition." (*See* White, 1982)

———
1983   *In Pursuit of the Past.* New York: Thames and Hudson.

Binford, Sally R., and Lewis R. Binford (eds.)
1968   *New Perspectives in Archaeology.* Chicago: Aldine.

Birdsell, Joseph B.
1981   *Human Evolution.* (3d Ed.), Boston: Houghton Mifflin Co.

Black, Francis L.
1975   "Infectious Diseases in Primitive Societies." *Science,* 187:515–518.

Boas, Franz
1940   "Changes in the Bodily Form of Descendants of Immigrants." *Reprinted In:* F. Boas (ed.), *Race, Language and Culture.* New York: The Free Press, pp. 60–75.

———
1940   "New Evidence in Regard to the Instability of Human Types." *Reprinted In:* F. Boas (ed.), *Race, Language and Culture.* New York: The Free Press, pp. 76–81.

569

Boaz, N. T.
1977   "Paleoecology of Early Hominidae in Africa." *Kroeber Anthropological Society Papers*, 50:37–62.

Boaz, N. T., F. C. Howell, and M. L. McCrossin
1982   "Faunal Age of the Usno, Shungura B and Hadar Formation, Ethiopia." *Nature*, 300:633–635.

Bodmer, Walter F.
1972   "Race and IQ: The Genetic Background." *In: Race and Intelligence*, Ken Richardson and David Speers (eds.), Baltimore: Penguin Books, Inc., pp. 83–113.

Bodmer, W. F. and L. L. Cavalli-Sforza
1976   *Genetics, Evolution, and Man.* San Francisco: W. H. Freeman and Company.

Bökönyi, S.
1969   "Archaeological Problems and Methods of Recognizing Animal Domestication." *In:* Peter J. Ucko and G. W. Dimbleby (eds.), q.v., pp. 207–218.

Bonner, T. I., R. Heinemann and G. J. Todardo
1980   "Evolution of DNA Sequences Has Been Retarded in Malagasy Primates." *Nature*, 286:420–423.

Bordes, François
1968   *The Old Stone Age.* New York: McGraw-Hill Book Co.

Boserup, Ester
1965   *The Conditions of Agricultural Growth.* Chicago: Aldine.

Bouzek, Jan
1985   "Relations between Barbarian Europe and the Aegean Civilizations." *Advances in World Archaeology*, 4:71–114.

Bowler, J. M. and A. G. Thorne (eds.)
1976   "Human Remains from Lake Mungo: Discovery and Excavation of Lake Mungo III." *In: The Origin of the Australians*, R. L. Kirk and A. G. Thorne (eds.), Canberra: Australian Institute of Aboriginal Studies (Humanities Press Inc., New Jersey), pp. 127 138.

Boyd, Wm. C.
1950   *Genetics and the Races of Man.* Boston: Little, Brown.

Brace, C. Loring
1964   "The Fate of the 'Classic' Neanderthals: A Consideration of Hominid Catastrophism." *Current Anthropology*, 5:3–43.

——— 1967   *The Stages of Human Evolution.* Englewood Cliffs, N.J.: Prentice-Hall, Inc.

——— 1973   "Sexual Dimorphism in Human Evolution." *In: Man in Evolutionary Perspective*, C. L. Brace and J. Metress (eds.), New York: Wiley Publishing Co., pp. 238–254.

——— 1979   "Biological Parameters and Pleistocene Hominid Lifeways." *In: Primate Ecology and Human Origins*, Irwin S. Bernstein and E. O. Smith (eds.), New York: Garland Publishing Co., pp. 263–289.

Brace, C. Loring and Frank B. Livingstone
1971   "On Creeping Jensenism," *In: Race and Intelligence*, C. L. Brace, G. R. Gamble and J. T. Bond (eds.), Anthropological Studies, No. 8, American Anthropological Association, Washington, D.C.

Brace, C. L. and Ashley Montagu
1977   *Human Evolution* (2nd Ed.). New York: Macmillan.

Brace, C. Loring, Harry Nelson and Noel Korn

1971   *Atlas of Human Evolution.* New York: Holt, Rinehart and Winston. (2nd Ed. 1979)

Braidwood, Robert J.
1975   *Prehistoric Men* (8th Ed.). Glenview, Ill.: Scott, Foresman and Co.

Brain, C. K.
1970   "New Finds at the Swartkrans Australopithecine Site." *Nature*, 225:1112–1119.

——— 1975   "The Bone Assemblage from the Kromdraai Australopithecine Site." *In: Paleoanthropology: Morphology and Paleoecology*, R. Tuttle (ed.), World Anthropology Series, Chicago: Aldine, pp. 225–243.

——— 1981   *The Hunters or the Hunted? An Introduction to African Cave Taphonomy.* Chicago: University of Chicago Press.

Bramblett, Claud A.
1976   *Patterns of Primate Behavior.* Palo Alto, Ca.: Mayfield Publishing Co.

Brock, A., P. L. McFadden and T. C. Partridge
1977   "Preliminary Paleomagnetic Results from Makapansgat and Swartkrans." *Nature*, 266:249–250.

Brose, David and Milford H. Wolpoff
1971   "Early Upper Paleolithic Man and Late Middle Paleolithic Tools." *American Anthropologist*, 73:1156–1194.

Bryan, Alan L.
1986   *New Evidence for the Pleistocene Peopling of the Americas.* Orono: University of Maine Center for Study of Early Man.

Bryant, Vaughan M., Jr. and Glenna Williams-Dean
1975   "The Coprolites of Man." *Scientific American*, 232: 100–109.

Bryson, Reid A., David A. Baerreis, and Wayne M. Wendland
1970   "The Character of Late Glacial and Post-Glacial Climatic Changes." *In: Pleistocene and Recent Environments of the Central Great Plains*, Wakefield Dort, Jr., and J. Knox Jones, Jr. (eds.), pp. 53–74. Lawrence: Department of Geology, University of Kansas.

Buettner-Janusch, John
1973   *Physical Anthropology: A Perspective.* New York: John Wiley and Sons.

Buffon, George Louis Leclerc, Compte de
1860   "Histoire Naturelle Generale et Particuliere." Translated by Wm. Smellie, London. *In:* Louis L. Snyder, q.v., pp. 102–103.

Bugliarello, G., A. Alexander, J. Barnes and C. Wakstein
1976   *The Impact of Noise Pollution: A Sociotechnical Introduction.* New York: Pergamon Press.

Bunn, Henry T.
1981   "Archaeological Evidence for Meat-eating by Plio-Pleistocene Hominids from Koobi Fora and Olduvai Gorge." *Nature*, 291:574–577.

Busse, Curt D.
1978   "Do Chimpanzees Hunt Cooperatively?" *American Naturalist*, 112:767–770.

Butynski, Thomas M.
1982   "Vertebrate Predation by Primates: A Review of Hunting Patterns." *Journal of Human Evolution*, 11:421–430.

Butzer, Karl W.
1974   "Paleoecology of South African Australopithecines: Taung Revisited." *Current Anthropology*, 15:367–382.

Butzer, Karl W. and Glynn L. Isaac, (eds.)
  1975 *After the Australopithecines.* The Hague: Mouton Publishers and Chicago: Aldine Publishing Co.

Bygott, J. David
  1979 "Agonistic Behavior, Dominance, and Social Structure in Wild Chimpanzees of the Gombe National Park." *In*: Hamburg and McCown (eds.), q.v., pp. 405–427.

Caldwell, Joseph R.
  1962 "Eastern North America." *In*: *Courses Toward Urban Life*, Robert J. Braidwood and Gordon R. Willey (eds.), Wenner-Gren Foundation for Anthropological Research, Publications in Anthropology, 32:288–308.

Campbell, Bernard
  1974 *Human Evolution.* Chicago: Aldine Publishing Co.

———
  1976 *Humankind Emerging.* Boston: Little, Brown and Co.

Carneiro, R.
  1970 "A Theory of the Origin of the State." *Science*, 169:733–738.

Carpenter, C. R.
  1965 "The Howlers of Barro Colorado Island." *In*: I. DeVore, (ed.), q.v., pp. 250–291.

Carter, Howard and A. C. Mace
  1923 *The Tomb of Tutankhamen.* London: Cassell and Co., Ltd.

Cartmill, Matt
  1972 "Arboreal Adaptations and the Origin of the Order Primates." *In*: *The Functional and Evolutionary Biology of Primates*, R. H. Tuttle (ed.), Chicago: Aldine-Atherton, pp. 97–122.

———
  1974 "Rethinking Primate Origins." *Science*, 184:436–443.

Cavalieri, Liebe F.
  1976 "New Strains of Life—or Death." *New York Times Magazine*, 22:8, August.

Cavalli-Sforza, L. L. and M. W. Feldman
  1981 *Cultural Transmission and Evolution: A Quantitative Approach.* Princeton, N.J.: Princeton University Press.

Chang, Kwang-chih
  1977 *The Archaeology of Ancient China* (3rd Ed.). New Haven: Yale University Press.

———
  1980 *Shang Civilization.* New Haven: Yale University Press.

Chard, Chester S.
  1975 *Man in Prehistory.* New York: McGraw-Hill Book Co.

Chargaff, Ervin
  1976 "On the Dangers of Genetic Meddling." *Science*, June 4.

Charteris, J., J. C. Wali, and J. W. Nottrodt
  1981 "Functional Reconstruction of Gait from Pliocene Hominid Footprints at Laetoli, Northern Tanzania." *Nature*, 290:496–498.

Chia, Lan-Po
  1975 *The Cave Home of Peking Man.* Peking: Foreign Language Press.

China Pictorial
  1981 "A Complete Ape-Man's Skull Unearthed at Longtan Cave." *China Pictorial*, 3:20–21, Beijing, China, March 1981 (no author).

Chippindale, Christopher
  1986 "Stonehenge Astronomy: Anatomy of a Modern Myth." *Archaeology*, 39(1):48–52.

Chopra, S.R.K.
  1983 "Significance of Recent Hominoid Discoveries from the Siwalik Hills of India." *In*: R. Ciochon and R. Corruccini (eds.), q.v., pp. 539–557.

Ciochon, Russel L.
  1983 "Hominoid Cladistics and the Ancestry of Modern Apes and Humans. A Summary." *In*: R. Ciochon and R. Corruccini (eds.), q.v., pp. 783–843.

Ciochon, R. L. and A. B. Chiarelli (eds.)
  1980 *Evolutionary Biology of the New World Monkeys and Continental Drift.* New York: Plenum Publishing Co.

Ciochon, Russel L. and Robert S. Corruccini
  1983 *New Interpretations of Ape and Human Ancestry.* New York: Plenum.

Clark, W. E. LeGros
  1967 *Man-apes or Ape-men?* New York: Holt, Rinehart and Winston.

———
  1959, *The Antecedents of Man.* New York:Quadrangle/
  1971 The New York Times Books (3rd Ed.).

Clarke, R. J.
  1976 "New Cranium of *Homo erectus* from Lake Ndutu, Tanzania." *Nature*, 262:485–487.

Clarke, R. J. and F. Clark Howell
  1972 "Affinities of the Swartkrans 847 Hominid Cranium." *American Journal of Physical Anthropology*, 37:319–336.

Clodd, Edward
  1897 *Pioneers of Evolution from Thales to Huxley.* New York: Freeport (Reprinted 1972).

Clutton-Brock, T. H., F. E. Guiness, and S. D. Albon
  1982 *Red Deer Behavior and Ecology of Two Sexes.* Chicago: University of Chicago Press.

Cohen, Mark N.
  1977 *The Food Crisis in Prehistory.* New Haven: Yale University Press.

Conard, Nicholas, David L. Asch, Nancy B. Asch, David Elmore, Harry Gove, Meyer Rubin, James A. Brown, Michael D. Wiant, Kenneth B. Farnsworth, Thomas G. Cook
  1984 "Acceleration Radioactive Dating of Evidence for Prehistoric Horticulture in Illinois." *Nature*, 308:443–446.

Conroy, G., C. J. Jolly, D. Cramer and J. E. Kalb
  1978 "Newly Discovered Fossil Hominid Skull from the Afar Depression." *Nature*, 276:67–70, November 2.

Constable, George
  1973 *The Neanderthals* (Emergence of Man Series, Time-Life Books). Waltham, Mass.: Little, Brown and Co.

Cook, J., C. B. Stringer, A. P. Currant, H. P. Schwarcz and A. G. Wintle
  1982 "A Review of the Chronology of the European Middle Pleistocene Hominid Record." *Yearbook of Physical Anthropology*, 25:19–64.

Cooke, H.B.S.
  1978 "Faunal Evidence for the Biotic Setting of the Early African Hominids." *In*: *Early Hominids of Africa*, C. Jolly (ed.), New York: St. Martin's Press.

Coon, C. S., S. M. Garn and J. B. Birdsell

1950   *Races—A Study of the Problems of Race Formation in Man.*
        Springfield, Ill.: Charles C. Thomas.

Corruccini, R. S.

1975a   "Multivariate Analysis of *Gigantopithecus* Mandibles." *American Journal of Physical Anthropology*, 42:167–170.

1975b   "The Interaction Between Neurocranial and Facial Shape in Hominid Evolution." *Homo*, 26:136–139.

Corruccini, R. S. and H. M. McHenry

1980   "Cladometric Analysis of Pliocene Hominids." *Journal of Human Evolution*, 9:209–221.

Corruccini, R. S., M. Baba, M. Goodman, R. L. Ciochon and J. E. Cronin

1980   "Non-Linear Macromolecular Evolution and the Molecular Clock." *Evolution*, 34:1216–1219.

Count, Earl W. (ed.)

1950   *This Is Race.* New York: Henry Schuman.

Cowgill, George L.

1974   "Quantitative Studies of Urbanization at Teotihuacán." *In: Mesoamerican Archaeology: New Approaches*, Norman Hammond (ed.), Austin: University of Texas Press, pp. 363–396.

Cowgill, Ursula M.

1962   "An Agricultural Study of the Southern Maya Lowlands." *American Anthropologist*, 64:273–286.

Cronin, J. E.

1983   "Apes, Humans, and Molecular Clocks. A Reappraisal." *In: R. Ciochon and R. Corruccini (eds.), q.v., pp. 115–150.

Cronin, J. E. and V. M. Sarich

1980   "Tupaiid and Archonta Phylogeny: The Macromolecular Evidence." *In*: W. P. Luckett (ed.), q.v., pp. 293–312.

Crook, J. H.

1970   "Social Organization and Environment: Aspects of Contemporary Social Ethology." *Animal Behavior*, 18:197–209

Culbert, T. Patrick (ed.)

1973   *The Classic Maya Collapse.* Albuquerque: University of New Mexico Press.

Curtis, Garniss

1981   "A Matter of Time: Dating Techniques and Geology of Hominid Sites." Paper delivered at the symposium, "Our Ancestors, Ourselves," Davis, Ca., May 10, 1981.

Curtis, G. H., T. Drake, R. Cerling and A. Hampel

1975   "Age of KBS Tuff in Koobi Fora Formation, East Rudolf, Kenya." *Nature*, 258:395.

Dalrymple, G. B.

1972   "Geomagnetic Reversals and North American Glaciations." *In*: Calibration of Hominoid Evolution, W. W. Bishop and J. A. Miller (eds.), Edinburgh: Scottish Academic Press, pp. 303–329.

Damon, Albert

1977   *Human Biology and Ecology.* New York: W. W. Norton and Co.

Daniel, Glyn

1980   "Megalithic Monuments." *Scientific American*, 243(7):15, 78–81.

Dart, Raymond

1959   *Adventures with the Missing Link.* New York: Harper and Brothers.

Darwin, Charles

1859   *On the Origin of Species.* A Facsimile of the First Edition, Cambridge, Mass.: Harvard University Press (1964).

Darwin, Francis (ed.)

1950   *The Life and Letters of Charles Darwin.* New York: Henry Schuman.

Davies, Nigel

1983   *The Ancient Kingdoms of Mexico.* New York: Penguin.

Dawkins, Richard

1976   *The Selfish Gene.* New York: Oxford University Press.

Day, Michael

1965   *Guide to Fossil Man.* Cleveland: The World Publishing Co.

Day, M. H., M. D. Leakey and C. Magori

1980   "A New Fossil Hominid Skull from Nu Ngaloba Beds, Laetoli, Northern Tanzania." *Nature*, 289:55–56.

Day, M. H. and E. H. Wickens

1980   "Laetoli Pliocene Hominid Footprints and Bipedalism." *Nature*, 286:385–387.

DeBonis, L.

1983   "Phyletic Relationships of Miocene Hominoids and Higher Primate Classification." *In*: R. Ciochon and R. Corruccini (eds.), q.v., pp. 625–649.

De Luce, Judith and Hugh T. Wilder

1983   *Language in Primates.* New York: Springer-Verlag New York Inc.

De Lumley, Henry

1969   "A Paleolithic Camp at Nice." *Scientific American*, May, 220:42–50.

De Lumley, Henry and Marie-Antoinette

1973   "Pre-Neanderthal Human Remains from Arago Cave in Southeastern France." *In: Yearbook of Physical Anthropology* 1973, 16:162–168.

De Lumley, Marie-Antoinette

1975   "Ante-Neanderthals of Western Europe." *In: Paleoanthropology: Morphology and Paleoecology*, Russel H. Tuttle (ed.), The Hague: Mouton Publishers, pp. 381–387.

Dene, H. T., M. Goodman and W. Prychodko

1976   "Immunodiffusion Evidence on the Phylogeny of the Primates." *In: Molecular Anthropology*, M. Goodman, R. E. Tashian and J. H. Tashian (eds.), New York: Plenum Press, pp. 171–195.

Dene, H., M. Goodman, W. Prychodko and G. Matsuda

1980   "Molecular Evidence for the Affinities of Tupaiidae." *In*: W. P. Luckett (ed.), q.v., pp. 269–291.

Dennell, Robin

1983   *European Economic Prehistory: A New Approach.* New York: Academic Press.

Dillehay, Tom D.

1984   "A Late Ice-Age Settlement in Southern Chile." *Scientific American*, 251(4):106–117.

Dincauze, Dena

1984   "An Archaeological Evaluation of the Case for Pre-Clovis Occupations." *Advances in World Archaeology*, 3:275–323.

Dingle, Herbert

1959   "Copernicus and the Planets." *In: A Short History of Science*, Jean Lindsay (ed.), New York: Doubleday & Co., pp. 18–26.

DiPeso, Charles C.

1974 *Casas Grandes, A Fallen Trading Center of the Gran Chichimeca, I, II, III.* Flagstaff: Northland Press.

Dobyns, Henry F.
1966 "Estimating Aboriginal American Population: An Appraisal of Techniques with a New Hemisphere Estimate." *Current Anthropology*, 7:395–449.

Dobzhansky, Theodosius
1970 *Genetics of the Evolutionary Process.* New York: Columbia University Press.

——— 1971 "Race Equality." *In: The Biological and Social Meaning of Race*, Richard H. Osborne (ed.), San Francisco: W. H. Freeman Co., pp. 13–24.

Drake, R. E., et al.
1980 "KBS Tuff Dating and Geochronology of Tuffaceous Sediments in the Koobi Fora and Shungura Formations, East Africa." *Nature*, 283:368–372.

Draper, Patricia
1973 "Crowding Among Hunter-Gatherers: The !Kung Bushmen." *Science*, 182:301–303.

Dunn, Frederick L.
1968 "Epidemiological Factors: Health and Disease in Hunter-Gatherers." *In: Man the Hunter*, R. B. Lee and I. DeVore (eds.), Chicago: Aldine, pp. 221–228.

Dunn, L. C.
1951 *Race and Biology. The Race Question in Modern Science.* UNESCO.

——— 1965 "Mendel, His Work, and His Place in History." *In: Proceedings of the American Philosophical Society*, Vol. 109, No. 4 (Commemoration of the publication of Gregor Mendel's pioneer experiments in genetics), August 18, Philadelphia: American Philosophical Society.

Durham, William
1981 Paper presented to the Annual Meeting of the American Anthropological Association, Washington, D.C., Dec. 1980. Reported in *Science*, 211:40.

Eiseley, Loren
1961 *Darwin's Century.* New York: Anchor Books.

Ekberg, Douglas R.
1979 *Intelligence and Race.* New York: Praeger.

Eldredge, Niles and Joel Cracraft
1980 *Phylogenetic Patterns and the Evolutionary Process.* New York: Columbia University Press.

Emery, Walter B.
1957 "The Tombs of the First Pharaohs." *Scientific American*, 197(7):36, 106–112.

Fairservis Jr., Walter A.
1976 *The Roots of Ancient India* (2nd Ed.). New York: MacMillan.

——— 1983 "The Script of the Indus Valley Civilization." *Scientific American*, 248(3):58–66.

Falk, Dean
1980 "A Reanalysis of the South African Australopithecine Natural Endocasts." *American Journal of Physical Anthropology*, 53:525–539.

——— 1983 "The Taung Endocast: A Reply to Holloway." *American Journal of Physical Anthropology*, 60:479–489.

Fedigan, Linda Marie
1983 "Dominance and Reproductive Success in Primates." *Yearbook of Physical Anthropology*, 26:91–129.

Fisher, R. A.
1930 *The Genetical Theory of Natural Selection.* Oxford: Clarendon.

Flannery, Kent V.
1968 "Archaeological Systems Theory and Early Mesoamerica." *In: Anthropological Archaeology in the Americas*, Betty J. Meggers (ed.), Washington, D.C.: Anthropological Society of Washington, pp. 67–87.

——— 1969 "Origins and Ecological Effects of Early Domestication in Iran and the Near East." *In: The Domestication and Exploitation of Plants and Animals*, Peter J. Ucko and G. W. Dimbleby (eds.), Chicago: Aldine, pp. 73–100.

——— 1973 "The Origins of Agriculture." *Annual Review of Anthropology*, 2:217–310.

Fleagle, J. G.
1983 "Locomotor Adaptations of Oligocene and Miocene Hominoids and their Phyletic Implications." *In*: R. Ciochon and R. Corruccini (eds.), q.v., pp. 301–324.

Fleagle, J. G. and R. F. Kay
1983 "New Interpretations of the Phyletic Position of Oligocene Hominoids." *In*: R. Ciochon and R. Corruccini (eds.), q.v., pp. 181–210.

Fleischer, R. C. and H. R. Hart, Jr.
1972 "Fission Track Dating, Techniques and Problems." *In: Calibration of Hominoid Evolution*, W. W. Bishop and J. A. Miller (eds.), Edinburgh: Scottish Academic Press, pp. 135–170.

Flynn, L. J. and G. Qi
1982 "Age of the Lufeng, China Hominoid Locality." *Nature*, 298:746–747.

Fobes, James L. and James E. King (eds.)
1982 *Primate Behavior.* New York: Academic Press.

Ford, James A. and Clarence H. Webb
1956 *Poverty Point: A Late Archaic Site in Louisiana.* Anthropology Papers of the American Museum of Natural History, 46.

Ford, Richard I.
1974 "Northeastern Archaeology: Past and Future Directions." *Annual Review of Anthropology*, 3:385–413.

Fossey, Dian
1981 "The Imperiled Mountain Gorilla." *National Geographic*, 159(4):501–523.

——— 1983 *Gorillas in the Mist.* Boston: Houghton-Mifflin.

Fouts, Roger S.
1983 (See Friends of Washoe, 1981).

Fouts, Roger S. and Richard L. Budd
1979 "Artificial and Human Language Acquisition in the Chimpanzees." *In*: D. Hamburg and E. McCown (eds.), q.v., pp. 375–392.

Fox, Michael W.
1978   "Man, Wolf, and Dog." *In: Wolf and Man*, R. L. Halland and H. S. Sharp (eds.), New York: Academic Press, pp. 19–30.

Fox, Robin (ed.)
1975   *Biosocial Anthropology.* New York: John Wiley & Sons.

———
1971   "The Cultural Animal." *In: Man and Beast*, John F. Eisenberg and Wm. S. Dillon (eds.), The Smithsonian Institution Press (reprinted in Yehudi A. Cohen, *Man in Adaptation, The Biosocial Background*, 2d Ed., Chicago: Aldine Publishing Co., 1974).

Francoeuer, Robert T.
1965   *Perspectives in Evolution.* Baltimore: Helicon.

Frayer, David
1973   "*Gigantopithecus* and Its Relationship to *Australopithecus*." *American Journal of Physical Anthropology*, 39:413–426.

———
1980   "Sexual Dimorphism and Cultural Evolution in the Late Pleistocene and Holocene of Europe." *Journal of Human Evolution*, 9:399–415.

Freeman, L. G.
1975   "Acheulian Sites and Stratigraphy in Iberia and the Maghreb." *In:* K. W. Butzer and G. L. Isaac (eds.), q.v., pp. 661–743.

Friends of Washoe
1981   Central Washington University, Ellensburg, Wa.

Frison, George C.
1978   *Prehistoric Hunters of the High Plains.* New York: Academic Press.

Galdikas, Biruté M.
1979   "Orangutan Adaptation at Tanjung Puting Reserve: Mating and Ecology." *In: The Great Apes*, D. A. Hamburg and E. R. McCown (eds.), Menlo Park, Ca.: The Benjamin/Cummings Publishing Co., pp. 195–233.

———
1981   Public Lecture at the California Institute of Technology, May 2, 1981.

Galdikas, B.M.F. and G. Telecki
1981   "Variation in Subsistence Activities of Male and Female Pongids: New Perspectives on the Origins of Hominid Labor Division." *Current Anthropology*, 22:241–256.

Gantt, D. G.
1983   "The Enamel of Neogene Hominoids. Structural and Phyletic Implications." *In:* R. Ciochon and R. Corruccini (eds.), q.v., pp. 249–298.

Gardner, Beatrice T. and R. Allen Gardner
1975   "Evidence for Sentence Constituents in the Early Utterances of Child and Chimpanzee." *Journal of Experimental Psychology: General*, 104:244–267.

Gardner, Eldon
1965   *History of Biology.* Minneapolis: Burgess Publishing Co.

Garn, Stanley M.
1969   *Human Races.* Springfield, Ill.: Charles C. Thomas.

Gavan, James
1977   *Paleoanthropology and Primate Evolution.* Dubuque, Iowa: Wm. C. Brown Co.

Gelvin, Bruce R.

1980   "Morphometric Affinities of *Gigantopithecus*." *American Journal of Physical Anthropology*, 53:541–568.

Gerson, Donald
1977   "Radiation in the Environment." *In: Human Biology and Ecology*, A. Damon (ed.), New York: W. W. Norton and Co., pp. 246–265.

Gingerich, P. D. and A. Sahni
1979   "*Indraloris* and *Sivaladapis*. Miocene Adapid Primates from the Siwaliks of India and Pakistan." *Nature*, 279:415–416.

Ginger, Ray
1958   *Six Days or Forever?* Boston: Beacon Press.

Glass, Bently (ed.)
1959   *Forerunners of Darwin, 1745–1859.* Baltimore: Johns Hopkins Press.

Goodall, Jane
1965   "Chimpanzees of the Gombe Stream Reserve." *In: Primate Behavior*, I. DeVore (ed.), New York: Holt, Rinehart and Winston, Inc., pp. 425–473.

———
1968a   "A Preliminary Report on Expressions, Movements and Communications in the Gombe Stream Chimpanzees." *In: Primates*, P. C. Jay (ed.), New York: Holt, Rinehart and Winston, pp. 313–374.

———
1968b   "The Behavior of Free Living Chimpanzees in the Gombe Stream Reserve." *Animal Behavior Monographs*, 1:(3).

———
1971   *In the Shadow of Man.* Boston: Houghton Mifflin Co.

———
1978   Public Lecture at San Jose State University. April 26.

———
1979   "Life and Death at Gombe." *National Geographic*, 155(5):597–620.

Goodall, Jane, A. Bandora, E. Bergmann, C. Busse, H. Matama, E. Mpongo, A. Pierce and D. Riss
1979   "Intercommunity Interactions in the Chimpanzee Population of the Gombe National Park." *In:* D. A. Hamburg and E. R. McCown (eds.), q.v., pp. 11–53.

Goodman, M., M. L. Baba and L. L. Darga
1983   "The Bearing of Molecular Data on the Cladogenesis and Times of Divergence of Hominoid Lineages." *In:* R. Ciochon and R. Corruccini (eds.), q.v., pp. 67–86.

Goodman, Morris and Gabriel W. Lasker
1975   "Molecular Evidence as to Man's Place in Nature." *In: Primate Functional Morphology and Evolution*, R. H. Tuttle (ed.), The Hague: Mouton Publishers, pp. 71–101.

Gorcyca, Diane A., Patrick Garner and Roger Fouts
1975   "Deaf Children and Chimpanzees." Paper presented at the Speech Communication Association Convention, Houston, Texas, December.

Gossett, Thomas F.
1963   *Race, the History of an Idea in America.* Dallas: Southern Methodist University Press.

Gould, Stephen Jay
1976   "Darwin and the Captain." *Natural History*, January, 85:32–34.

Gould, S. J. and N. Eldredge
1977   "Punctuated Equilibria: the Tempo and Mode of Evolution Reconsidered." *Paleobiology*, 3:115–151.

Graham, Ian

1976   *Corpus of Maya Hieroglyphic Inscriptions* (Vol. I, Introduction). Cambridge, Mass.: Peabody Museum of Archaeology and Ethnology.

Gramly, Richard Michael

1982   "The Vail Site: A Palaeo-Indian Encampment in Maine." Bulletin of the Buffalo Society of Natural Sciences, **30**.

Greenberg, Joel

1977   "Who Loves You?" *Science News*, 112:139–141, August 27.

Greenfield, L. O.

1979   "On the Adaptive Pattern of *Ramapithecus*." *American Journal of Physical Anthropology*, 50:527–548.

——   1980   "A Late Divergence Hypothesis." *American Journal of Physical Anthropology*, 52:351–365.

——   1983   "Toward the Resolution of Discrepancies between Phenetic and Paleontological Data Bearing on the Question of Human Origins." *In*: R. Ciochon and R. Corruccini (eds.), q.v., pp. 695–703.

Grobstein, Clifford

1977   "The Recombinant DNA Debate." *Scientific American*, 237:22–31, July.

Grootes, P. M.

1978   "Carbon-14 Time Scale Extended: Comparison of Chronologies." *Science*, 200:11–15.

Gurin, Joel

1980   "In the Beginning." *Science 80*, 1(5):44–51.

Hadingham, Evan

1979   *Secrets of the Ice Age.* New York: Walker & Co.

Haldane, J.B.S.

1932   *The Causes of Evolution.* London: Longmans, Green (reprinted as paperback, Cornell University Press, 1966).

Hamburg, David A. and E. R. McCown

1979   *The Great Apes.* Menlo Park, Ca.: The Benjamin/Cummings Publishing Co.

Hamilton, W. D.

1964   "The Genetical Theory of Social Behavior: I and II." *Journal of Theoretical Biology*, 7:1–52.

Hammond, Norman, *et al.*

1979   "The Earliest Lowland Maya: Definition of the Swasey Phase." *American Antiquity*, 44:92–109.

Harding, A. F.

1984   *The Mycenaeans and Europe.* New York: Academic Press.

Harding, Robert and Shirley C. Strum

1976   "The Predatory Baboons of Kekopey." *Natural History Magazine*, 85(3):46–53.

Harlow, Harry F.

1959   "Love in Infant Monkeys." *Scientific American*, 200:68–74.

Harlow, Harry F. and Margaret K. Harlow

1961   "A Study of Animal Affection." *Natural History*, 70:48–55.

Harrison, Richard J.

1985   "The 'Policultivo Ganadero,' or Secondary Products Revolution in Spanish Agriculture, 5000–1000 B.C." *Proceedings of the Prehistoric Society*, 51:75–102.

Hatley, T. and J. Kappelman

1981   "Bears, Pigs, and Pliopleistocene Hominids: A Case for the Exploitation of Belowground Food Resources." *Human Ecology*, 8:371–387.

Haury, Emil W.

1976   *The Hohokam. Desert Farmers and Craftsmen: Excavations at Snaketown, 1964–1965.* Tucson: University of Arizona Press.

Hausfater, Glenn

1976   "Predatory Behavior of Yellow Baboons." *Behaviour*, 56:44–68.

Heizer, Robert F. and L. K. Napton

1970   *Archaeology and the Prehistoric Great Basin Subsistence Regime as Seen from Lovelock Cave, Nevada.* University of California Archaeological Research Facility Contribution, 10.

Herre, Wolf

1969   "The Science and History of Domestic Animals." *In*: Don Brothwell and Eric Higgs (eds.), q.v., pp.257–272.

Hoffman, Michael A.

1979   *Egypt Before the Pharaohs.* New York: Alfred A. Knopf.

Hoffstetter, R.

1972   "Relationships, Origins, and History of the Ceboid Monkeys and the Caviomorph Rodents: A Modern Reinterpretation." *In*: *Evolutionary Biology*, Th. Dobzhansky, T.M.K. Hecht and W. C. Steere (eds.), Vol. 6, New York: Appleton-Century-Crofts, pp. 323–347.

Holloway, Ralph L.

1969   "Culture: A Human Domain." *Current Anthropology*, 10:395–407.

——   1981   "Revisiting the South African Taung Australopithecine Endocast: The Position of the Lunate Sulcus as Determined by the Stereoplotting Technique." *American Journal of Physical Anthropology*, 56:43–58.

——   1983   "Cerebral Brain Endocast Pattern of Australopithecus Afarensis Hominid." *Nature*, 303:420–422.

Hood, Sinclair

1973   *The Minoans.* London: Thames and Hudson.

Hooton, E. A.

1926   "Methods of Racial Analysis." *Science*, 63:75–81.

Hopkins, David M.

1979   "Landscape and Climate of Beringia During Late Pleistocene and Holocene Time." *In*: *The First Americans: Origins, Affinities, and Adaptations*, William S. Laughlin and Albert B. Harper (eds.), New York: Gustav Fischer; pp. 15–41.

Howell, F. Clark

1966   "Observations on the Earlier Phases of the European Lower Paleolithic." *American Anthropologist*, 68(2):88–201.

——   1978   "Hominidae." *In*: *Evolution of African Mammals*, V. J. Maglio and H.B.S. Cooke (eds.), Cambridge: Harvard University Press, pp. 154–248.

——   1982   "Ambrona." *Leakey Foundation News*, Spring.

Howells, W. W.

1971   "The Meaning of Race." *In*: *The Biological and Social Meaning of Race*, Richard H. Osborne (ed.), San Francisco: W. H. Freeman and Co., pp. 3–10.

——   1973   *Evolution of the Genus* Homo. Reading, Mass.: Addison-Wesley.

——— 1974   "Neanderthals: Names, Hypotheses, and Scientific Method." *American Anthropologist*, 76:24–38.

——— 1975   "Neanderthal Man: Facts and Figures." *In: Paleoanthropology: Morphology and Paleoecology*, R. H. Tuttle (ed.), The Hague: Mouton Publishers, pp. 389–407.

——— 1980   "*Homo erectus*—Who, When, Where: A Survey." *Yearbook of Physical Anthropology* 1980, 23:1–23.

Hrdy, Sarah Blaffer
1977   *The Langurs of Abu*. Cambridge, Mass.: Harvard University Press.

——— 1981   *The Woman That Never Evolved*. Cambridge: Harvard University Press.

Hudson, Liam
1972   "The Context of the Debate." *In: Race and Intelligence*, K. Richardson and D. Spears, Baltimore: Penguin Books, Inc., pp. 10–16.

Iltis, Hugo
1966   *Life of Mendel*. New York: Hafner Publishing Co. (first published in Germany, 1924).

Irving, William N.
1985   "Context and Chronology of Early Man in the Americas." *Annual Review of Anthropology*, 14:529–555.

Isaac, G.
1971   "The Diet of Early Man." *World Archaeology*, 2:278–299.

——— 1975   "Stratigraphy and Cultural Patterns in East Africa During the Middle Ranges of Pleistocene Time." *In*: K. W. Butzer and G. L. Isaac (eds.), q.v., pp. 495–542.

——— 1976   "Early Hominids in Action: A Commentary on the Contribution of Archeology to Understanding the Fossil Record in East Africa." *Yearbook of Physical Anthropology* 1975, 19:19–35.

Isbell, William H.
1978   "The Prehistoric Ground Drawings of Peru." *Scientific American*, 239(10):20, 140–142.

Jacob, François
1975   "Morphology and Paleoecology of Early Man in Java." *In: Paleoanthropology: Morphology and Paleoecology*, R. H. Tuttle (ed.), Chicago: Aldine Publishing Co., pp. 312–325.

Jacobs, Louis L. and David Pilbeam
1980   "Of Mice and Men: Fossil-Based Divergence Dates and Molecular 'Clocks.' " *Journal of Human Evolution*, 9:551–555.

Jarvis, J.V.M.
1981   "Eusociality in a Mammal: Cooperative Breeding in Naked Mole-Rat Colonies." *Science*, 212:571–573.

Jaeger, Jean-Jacques
1975   "The Mammalian Faunas and Hominid Fossils of the Middle Pleistocene of the Maghreb." *In*: K. W. Butzer and G. L. Isaac (eds.), q.v., pp. 399–418.

Jelinek, Arthur J.
1982   "The Tabun Cave and Paleolithic Man in the Levant." *Science*, 216:1369–1375.

Jennings, Jesse D.
1957   *Danger Cave*. Society for American Archaeology Memoir, 14.
Jennings, Jesse D. (ed.)
1983a   *Ancient North Americans*. San Francisco: W. H. Freeman.

——— 1983b   *Ancient South Americans*. San Francisco: W. H. Freeman.
Jensen, Arthur
1969   *Environment, Heredity, and Intelligence*. Cambridge, Mass.: Harvard Educational Review.

——— 1974   "Kinship Correlations Reported by Sir Cyril Burt." *Behavior Genetics*, 4:1–28.

——— 1980   *Bias in Mental Testing*. New York: The Free Press.
Jerison, H. J.
1973   *Evolution of the Brain and Behavior*. New York: Academic Press.
Johanson, Donald and Maitland Edey
1981   *Lucy: The Beginnings of Humankind*. New York: Simon and Schuster.
Johanson, Donald C. and Maurice Taieb
1976   "Plio-Pleistocene Hominid Discoveries in Hadar, Ethiopia." *Nature*, 260:293–297.

——— 1980   "New Discoveries of Pliocene Hominids and Artifacts in Hadar." International Afar Research Expedition to Ethiopia (Fourth and Fifth Field Seasons, 1975–77). *Journal of Human Evolution*, 9:582.
Johanson, D. C. and T. D. White
1979   "A Systematic Assessment of Early African Hominids." *Science*, 203:321–330.
Johanson, D. C., T. D. White and Yves Coppens
1978   "A New Species of the Genus *Australopithecus* (Primates: Hominidae) from the Pliocene of Eastern Africa. *Kirtlandia*," No. 28, pp. 1–14.
Johnson, A. E., Jr.
1979   "Skeletal Estimates of *Gigantopithecus* Based on a Gorilla Analogy." *Journal of Human Evolution*, 8:585–587.
Jolly, Alison
1985   *The Evolution of Primate Behavior* (2nd Ed.). New York: Macmillan.
Jolly, C. J.
1970   "The Seed Eaters: A New Model of Hominid Differentiation Based on a Baboon Analogy." *Man*, 5:5–26.
Jungers, W. L.
1982   "Lucy's Limbs: Skeletal Allometry and Locomotion in *Australopithecus afarensis*." *Nature*, 297:676–678.

Kamin, Leon
1974   *The Science and Politics of IQ*. New York: John Wiley & Sons.
Kan, Yuet Wai and Andrée M. Dozy
1980   "Evolution of the Hemoglobin S and C Genes in World Populations." *Science*, 209:388–391.
Kawamura, Syunzo
1959   "The Process of Sub-culture Propagation among Japanese Macaques." *In: Primate Social Behavior*, C. H. Southwick (ed.), Princeton: D. Van Nostrand Co. Inc., pp. 82–90 (originally published in the *Journal of Primatology*, 2(1):43–60).
Kawanaka, Kanji

1982   "A Case of Inter-Unit-Group Encounter in Chimpanzees of the Mahale Mts." *Primates*, 23(4):558–562.

Kay, John P., et al.
1981   "Normalization of Low-Density Lipoproteins Levels in Heterozygous Familial Hypercholesterolemia with a Combined Drug Regimen." *New England Journal of Medicine*, 304:251–258.

Kay, Richard F.
1981   "The Nut-Crackers—A New Theory of the Adaptations of the Ramapithecinae." *American Journal of Physical Anthropology*, 55:151–156.

Kay, R. F., J. G. Fleagle and E. L. Simons
1981   "A Revision of the Oligocene Apes of the Fayum Province, Egypt." *American Journal of Physical Anthropology*, 55:293–322.

Kay, R. F. and E. L. Simons
1983   "A Reassessment of the Relationship Between Late Miocene and Subsequent Hominoidea." *In*: R. Ciochon and R. Corruccini (eds.), q.v., pp. 577–624.

Keeley, Lawrence H.
1980   *Experimental Determination of Stone Tool Uses: A Microwear Analysis*. Chicago: University of Chicago Press.

Keeley, Lawrence H. and N. Toth
1981   "Microwear Polishes on Early Stone Tools from Koobi Fora, Kenya." *Nature*, 293:464–465.

Kelso, A. J.
1974   *Physical Anthropology* (2nd Ed.). New York: J. B. Lippincott Co.

Kennedy, G. E.
1980a   *Paleoanthropology*. New York: McGraw-Hill Book Co.

_____

1980b   "The Emergence of Modern Man." *Nature*, 284:11–12.

_____

1984   "The Emergence of *Homo sapiens*: The Post Cranial Evidence." *Man* (N.S.), 19:94–110.

Kenyon, Kathleen M.
1957   *Digging Up Jericho*. New York: Frederick A. Praeger.

King, J. L. and T. H. Jukes
1969   "Non-Darwinian Evolution." *Science*, 164:788–798.

Klein, R. G.
1969   *Man and Culture in the Late Pleistocene*. San Francisco: Chandler.

_____

1974   "Ice Age Hunters of the Ukraine." *Scientific American*, June.

_____

1977   "The Ecology of Early Man in Southern Africa." *Science*, 197:115–126.

Kortlandt, Adriaan
1965   "A comment on 'On the Essential Morphological Basis for Human Culture.'" *Current Anthropology*, 6:320–326.

Kosok, Paul and Maria Reiche
1949   "Ancient Drawings on the Desert of Peru." *Archaeology*, 2:206–215.

Kramer, Samuel N.
1963   *The Sumerians*. Chicago: University of Chicago Press.

Kraeling, Carl H. and Robert M. Adams (eds.)
1960   *City Invincible*. Chicago: University of Chicago Press.

Kummer, Hans
1971   *Primate Societies*. Chicago: Aldine-Atherton, Inc.

Kus, James S.
1984   "The Chicama-Moche Canal: Failure or Success? An Alternative Explanation for an Incomplete Canal. *American Antiquity*, 49(2):408–415.

Lack, David
1966   *Population Studies of Birds*. Oxford: Clarendon.

Lancaster, Jane B.
1975   *Primate Behavior and the Emergence of Human Culture*. New York: Holt, Rinehart and Winston, Inc.

Lasker, Gabriel W.
1969   "Human Biological Adaptability: the Ecological Approach in Physical Anthropology." *Science*, 166:1480–1486.

Latimer, Bruce
1984   "The Pedal Skeleton of *Australopithecus afarensis*." *American Journal of Physical Anthropology*, 63:182.

van Lawick-Goodall, Hugo and Jane
1970   *In the Shadow of Man*. London: Wm. Collins Sons and Co., Ltd.

Leakey, L.S.B.
1966   "*Homo habilis*, *Homo erectus*, and the Australopithecinae." *Nature*, 209:1279–1281.

Leakey, L.S.B., J. F. Everden and G. H. Curtis
1961   "Age of Bed I, Olduvai Gorge, Tanganyika." *Nature*, 191:478–479.

Leakey, L.S.B., P. V. Tobias and J. R. Napier
1964   "A New Species of the Genus *Homo* from Olduvai Gorge." *Nature*, 202:7–10.

Leakey, Mary D.
1971   "Remains of *Homo erectus* and Associated Artifacts in Bed IV at Olduvai Gorge, Tanzania." *Nature*, 232:380–383.

Leakey, M. D. and R. L. Hay
1979   "Pliocene Footprints in Laetolil Beds at Laetoli, Northern Tanzania." *Nature*, 278:317–323.

Leakey, R.E.F.
1974   "Further Evidence of Lower Pleistocene Hominids from East Rudolf, Kenya, 1973." *Nature*, 248:653–656.

_____

1976   "New Hominid Fossils from the Koobi Fora Formation in Northern Kenya." *Nature*, 261:572–574.

Leakey, R.E.F. and Alan C. Walker
1976   "*Australopithecus*, *Homo erectus* and the Single Species Hypothesis." *Nature*, 261:572–574.

Lee, Richard B.
1979   *The !Kung San*. Cambridge: Cambridge University Press.

_____

1984   *The Dobe !Kung*. New York: Holt, Rinehart and Winston.

Lerner, I. M. and W. J. Libby
1976   *Heredity, Evolution, and Society*. San Francisco: W. H. Freeman and Company.

Lewellen, Ted C.
1981   "Aggression and Hypoglycemia in the Andes: Another Look at the Evidence." *Current Anthropology*, 22:347–361.

Lewin, Roger
1981   "Biggest Challenge Since the Double Helix." Research News, *Science*, 212:28–32.

_____

1983   "Is the Orangutan A Living Fossil?" *Science*, 222:1222–1223.

Lewis, Thomas M. N. and Madeline Kneberg Lewis

1961   *Eva, an Archaic Site.* Knoxville: University of Tennessee Press.

Lewontin, R. C.
1972   "The Apportionment of Human Diversity." *In: Evolutionary Biology* (Vol. 6), Th. Dobzhansky et al. (eds.), New York: Plenum, pp. 381–398.

Lieberman, P. and E. S. Crelin
1971   "On the Speech of Neanderthal." *Linguistic Inquiry,* 2:203–222.

Lindsay, Jean
1959   *A Short History of Science.* New York: Doubleday & Co.

Lipe, William D.
1983   "The Southwest." *In:* Jesse D. Jennings (ed.), q.v., pp. 421–493.

Little, M. A., R. Brooke Thomas, Richard B. Mazess and Paul T. Baker
1971   "Populational Differences and Developmental Changes in Extremity Temperature Responses to Cold Among Andean Indians." *Human Biology,* 43:70–91.

Livingstone, Frank B.
1964   "On the Nonexistence of Human Races." *In: Concept of Race,* A. Montagu (ed.), New York: The Free Press, pp. 46–60.

———
1969   "Polygenic Models for the Evolution of Human Skin Color Differences." *Human Biology,* 41:480–493.

———
1980   "Natural Selection and the Origin and Maintenance of Standard Genetic Marker Systems." *Yearbook of Physical Anthropology,* 1980, 23:25–42.

Lovejoy, Arthur L.
1959   "Buffon and the Problem of Species." *In: Forerunners of Darwin, 1745–1859,* Bentley Glass (ed.), Baltimore: Johns Hopkins Press, pp. 84–113.

Lovejoy, C. Owen
1981   "The Origin of Man." *Science,* 211:341–350.

———
1983   Paper presented at the Institute of Human Origins Conference on the Evolution of Human Locomotion (Berkeley).

Lovejoy, C. O., G. Kingsbury, G. Heiple and A. H. Burstein
1973   "The Gait of *Australopithecus.*" *American Journal of Physical Anthropology,* 38:757–780.

Löwenberg, Bert James
1959   *Darwin, Wallace, and the Theory of Natural Selection.* Cambridge, Mass.: Arlington Books.

Luckett, W. Patrick
1980   "The Suggested Evolutionary Relationships and Classification of Tree Shrews." *In: Comparative Biology and Evolutionary Relationships of Tree Shrews,* W. P. Luckett (ed.), New York: Plenum Press, pp. 3–31.

Lynch, Thomas F.
1983   "The Paleo-Indians." *In:* Jesse D. Jennings (ed.), San Francisco: W. H. Freeman, q.v., pp. 87–137.

Lynch, Thomas F. (ed.)
1980   *Guitarrero Cave.* New York: Academic Press.

MacNeish, Richard S.
1964   "Ancient Mesoamerican Civilization." *Science,* 143:531–537.

———
1978   *The Science of Archaeology?* North Scituate, Mass.: Duxbury Press.

Mai, L. L.
1983   "A Model of Chromosome Evolution and Its Bearing on Cladogenesis in the Hominoidea." *In:* R. Ciochon and R. Corruccini (eds.), q.v., pp. 87–114.

Maier, W.
1977   "Chronology and Biology of the South African Australopithecines." *Journal of Human Evolution* 8:89–93.

Mann, Alan
1975   "Some Paleodemographic Aspects of the South African Australopithecines." *University of Pennsylvania Publications in Anthropology* (No. 1), Philadelphia.

Marschak, A.
1972   *The Roots of Civilization.* New York: McGraw-Hill Publishing Co.

Martin, Paul S.
1967   "Prehistoric Overkill." *In: Pleistocene Extinctions: The Search for a Cause,* Paul S. Martin and Herbert E. Wright, Jr. (eds.), New Haven: Yale University Press, pp. 75–120.

Maw, B., R. L. Ciochon, and D. E. Savage
1979   "Late Eocene of Burma Yields Earliest Anthropoid Primate, *Pondaungia cotteri.*" *Nature,* 282:65–67.

Mayr, Ernst
1962   "Taxonomic Categories in Fossil Hominids." *In: Ideas on Human Evolution,* W. W. Howells (ed.), New York: Atheneum, pp. 242–256.

———
1970   *Population, Species, and Evolution.* Cambridge: Harvard University Press.

———
1982   *The Growth of Biological Thought.* Cambridge: Belknap Press.

McGrew, Wm. C.
1979   "Evolutionary Implications of Sex Differences in Chimpanzee Predation and Tool Use." *In:* Hamburg and McCown (eds.), q.v., pp. 441–463.

McHenry, Henry
1975   "Fossils and the Mosaic Nature of Human Evolution." *Science,* 190:425–431.

———
1982   "The Pattern of Human Evolution: Studies on Behavior, Mastication, and Encephalization." *Annual Reviews of Anthropology,* 11:151–173.

———
1983   "The Capitate of *Australopithecus afarensis* and *A. africanus.*" *American Journal of Physical Anthropology,* 62:187–198.

McKenna, James J.
1982   "The Evolution of Primate Societies, Reproduction, and Parenting." *In:* J. Fobes and J. King (eds.), q.v., pp. 87–133.

McKusick, Victor
1980   "Anatomy of the Human Genome." *Journal of Heredity,* 71:370–391.

———
1983   *Mendelian Inheritance in Man* (6th Ed.). Baltimore: Johns Hopkins Press.

McNett, Jr., Charles W. (ed.)
1985   *Shawnee-Minisink: A Stratified Paleoindian-Archaic Site in the Upper Delaware Valley.* Orlando: Academic Press.

Mech, L. David

1966   *The Wolves of Isle Royale.* Washington, D.C.: U.S. Government Printing Office.

Mellaart, James
1967   *Çatal Hüyük: A Neolithic Town in Anatolia.* New York: Mc-Graw-Hill.

Mendel, Gregor
1965   "Experiments in Plant Hybridisation" (A paper read before the Natural History Society of Brünn in 1865). Cambridge: Harvard University Press.

Mendelssohn, Kurt
1974   *The Riddle of the Pyramids.* New York: Frederick A. Praeger.

Menosky, Joseph A.
1981   "The Gene Machine." *Science 81* (July-Aug.):38–41.

Merrick, H. V. and J. P. S. Merrick
1976   "Archeological Occurrences of Earlier Pleistocene Age from the Shungura Formation." *In: Earliest Man and Environments in the Lake Rudolf Basin,* Y. Coppens et al. (eds.), Chicago: University of Chicago Press, pp. 574–584.

Moctezuma, Eduardo Matos
1984   "The Great Temple of Tenochtitlan." *Scientific American,* 251(2):80–89.

Montagu, Ashley (ed.)
1980   *Sociobiology Examined.* New York: Oxford University Press.

Montet, Pierre
1981   *Everyday Life in Egypt in the Days of Ramesses the Great.* Philadelphia: University of Pennsylvania Press.

Moore, Lorna G. and Judith G. Regensteiner
1983   "Adaptation to High Altitude." *Annual Reviews of Anthropology,* 12:285–304.

Moore, Ruth
1961   *Man, Time and Fossils.* New York: Alfred A. Knopf.

Morbeck, M. E.
1975   "*Dryopithecus africanus* Forelimb." *Journal of Human Evolution,* 4:39–46.

———
1983   "Miocene Hominoid Discoveries from Rudabánya. Implications from the Postcranial Skeleton." *In:* R. Ciochon and R. Corruccini (eds.), q.v., pp. 369–404.

Morris, Desmond
1967   *The Naked Ape.* New York: McGraw-Hill.

Moseley, Michael E.
1975a   "Chan Chan: Andean Alternative to the Preindustrial City." *Science,* 187:219–225.

———
1975b   *The Maritime Foundations of Andean Civilization.* Menlo Park, Calif.: Cummings Publishing Company.

———
1983   "Central Andean Civilization." *In:* Jesse D. Jennings (ed.), q.v., pp. 179–239.

Mturi, A. A.
1976   "New Hominid from Lake Ndutu, Tanzania." *Nature,* 262:484–485.

Mueller, William H. et al.
1979   "A Multinational Andean Genetic and Health Program. VIII. Lung Function Changes with Migration between Altitudes." *American Journal of Physical Anthropology,* 51:183–196.

Murra, John V.
1972   "El 'control vertical' de una maximo de pisos ecologicos en la economia de los sociedades andines. *In: Vista de la Prov-*

incia de Leon de Huanaco (1562), John V. Murra (ed.), Huanaco, Peru, Universidad Nacional Hermilio Valdizen, vol. 2, pp. 427–476.

Murray, R. D.
1980   "The Evolution and Functional Significance of Incest Avoidance." *Journal of Human Evolution,* 9:173–178.

Napier, John
1967   "The Antiquity of Human Walking." *Scientific American,* 216:56–66.

———
1973   *Bigfoot.* New York: E. P. Dutton & Co., Inc.

Napier, J. R. and P. H. Napier
1967   *A Handbook of Living Primates.* New York: Academic Press.

Napier, Prue
1977   *Chimpanzees.* New York: McGraw-Hill Book Co.

Newman, Marshall T.
1975   "Nutritional Adaptation in Man." *In: Physiological Anthropology,* Albert Damon (ed.), New York: Oxford University Press, pp. 210–259.

Ninkovich, D. and L. H. Burcle
1978   "Absolute Age of the Base of the Hominid Bearing Beds in Eastern Java." *Nature,* 275:306–308.

Nishida, Toshisada
1979   "The Social Structure of Chimpanzees of the Mahale Mountains." *In: The Great Apes,* David A. Hamburg and E. R. Mc-Cown (eds.), q.v., pp. 73–121.

———
1983   "Alloparental Behavior in Wild Chimpanzees of the Mahale Mts., Tanzania." *Folia Primatologica,* 41:1–33.

Nishida, Toshisada, S. Uehara, and R. Nyundo
1979   "Predatory Behavior among Wild Chimpanzees of the Mahale Mts." *Primates,* 20(1):1–20.

Norikashi, Kohshi
1982   "One Observed Case of Cannibalism Among Wild Chimpanzees of the Mahale Mountains." *Primates,* 23(1):66–74.

Oakley, Kenneth
1963   "Analytical Methods of Dating Bones." *In: Science in Archaeology,* D. Brothwell and E. Higgs (eds.), New York: Basic Books, Inc.

Olby, Robert O.
1966   *Origins of Mendelism.* New York: Schocken Books.

Oldroyd, D. R.
1980   *Darwinian Impacts: An Introduction to the Darwinian Revolution.* Atlantic Highlands: Humanities Press.

Olson, Everett C.
1980   "Taphonomy: Its History and Role in Community Evolution." *In: Fossils in the Making,* K. Behrensmeyer and A. Hill (eds.), Chicago: University of Chicago Press, pp. 5–19.

Osborne, Richard (ed.)
1971   *The Biological and Social Meaning of Race.* San Francisco: W. H. Freeman Co.

Ovey, C. D. (ed.)
1964   "The Swanscombe Skull." Royal Anthropological Institute, Occasional Paper 20.

Oxnard, C. E.
1975   "The Place of the Australopithecines in Human Evolution: Grounds for Doubt?" *Nature,* 258:389–395.

Parker, Seymour
1976   "The Precultural Basis of the Incest Taboo: Toward a Biosocial Theory." *American Anthropologist*, 78:285–305.

Parks, Michael
1981   "Skulls Found in China Important in the Puzzle of Man's Evolution." *San Jose Mercury News*, Sunday, May 17, 1981.

Pauling, Linus
1974   "The Molecular Basis of Biological Specificity." *Nature*, 248:769–771.

Petit, Charles
1981   "Ancient Skull Raises New Storm." *San Francisco Chronicle*, September 26, 1981.

Pfeiffer, John E.
1978,   *The Emergence of Man* (3d Ed.). New York: Harper and Row,
1985   Publishers.

Pickford, M.
1983   "Sequence and Environments of the Lower and Middle Miocene Hominoids of Western Kenya." *In*: R. Ciochon and R. Corruccini (eds.), q.v., pp. 421–439.

Pilbeam, David
1972   *The Ascent of Man*. New York: Macmillan.

_____
1975   "Middle Pleistocene Hominids." *In*: K. W. Butzer and G. L. Isaac (eds.), q.v., pp. 809–856.

_____
1977   "Beyond the Apes: Pre-*Homo* Hominids: The Ramapithecines of Africa, Asia, and Europe." Symposium Lecture, March 5, Davis, Calif.

_____
1979   "Recent Finds and Interpretations of Miocene Hominoids." *Annual Reviews of Anthropology*, 8:333–352.

_____
1981   "New Fossil Hominoid from Pakistan." Paper presented at the Annual Meeting, American Association of Physical Anthropologists, April, 1981.

_____
1982   "New Hominoid Skull Material From the Miocene of Pakistan." *Nature*, 295:232–234.

Pilbeam, David, G. E. Meyer, C. Badgley, et al.
1977   "New Hominoid Primates from the Siwaliks of Pakistan and Their Bearing on Hominoid Evolution." *Nature*, 270:689–695.

Popp, Joseph L. and Irven DeVore
1979   "Aggressive Competition and Social Dominance Theory." *In*: *The Great Apes*, David A. Hamburg and E. R. McCown (eds.), q.v., pp. 317–318.

Potts, Richard and Pat Shipman
1981   "Cutmarks Made by Stone Tools from Olduvai Gorge, Tanzania." *Nature*, 291:577–580.

Poulianos, Aris N.
1981   "Pre-*sapiens* Man in Greece." *Current Anthropology*, 22(3):287–288.

Prescott, William H.
1906   *History of the Conquest of Peru*. New York: Everyman's Library.

Proshnev, B. F.
1974   "The Troglodytidae and the Hominidae in the Taxonomy and Evolution of Higher Primates." *Current Anthropology*, 15(4):449–450.

Proskouriakoff, Tatiana

1960   "Historical Implications of a Pattern of Dates at Piedras Negras, Guatemala." *American Antiquity*, 25:454–475.

Puleston, David E.
1971   "An Experimental Approach to the Function of Maya Chultuns." *American Antiquity*, 36:322–335.

Radinsky, Leonard
1973   "*Aegyptopithecus* Endocasts: Oldest Record of a Pongid Brain." *American Journal of Physical Anthropology* 39:239–248.

Ransom, Timothy W.
1981   *Beach Troop of the Gombe*. Lewisburg: Bucknell University Press.

Rathje, William
1979   "Modern Material Culture Studies." *Advances in Archaeological Method and Theory*, 2, pp. 1–37.

Rathje, William L. and Michael McCarthy
1977   "Regularity and Variability in Contemporary Garbage. *In*: *Research Strategies in Historic Archaeology*, Stanley South (ed.), New York: Academic Press, pp. 261–286.

Raza, S. Mahmoud, et al.
1983   "New Hominoid Primates from the Middle Miocene Chinji Formation, Potwar Plateau, Pakistan." *Nature*, 306:52–54.

Redman, Charles L.
1978   *The Rise of Civilization*. San Francisco: W. H. Freeman and Co.

Reed, Charles A. (ed.)
1977   *Origins of Agriculture*. The Hague: Mouton Publishers.

Renfrew, Colin
1983   "The Social Archaeology of Megalithic Monuments." *Scientific American*, 249(5):152–163.

Repenning, Charles A. and Oldrich Fejfar
1982   "Evidence for Earlier Date of 'Ubeidya, Israel, Hominid Site." *Nature*, 299:344–347.

Rightmire, G. P.
1976   "Relationships of Middle and Upper Pleistocene Hominids from Sub-Saharan Africa." *Nature*, 269:238–240.

_____
1978   "Florisbad and Human Population Succession in Southern Africa." *American Journal of Physical Anthropology*, 48:475–486.

_____
1979a   "Cranial Remains of *Homo erectus* from Beds II and IV, Olduvai Gorge, Tanzania." *American Journal of Physical Anthropology*, 51:99–116.

_____
1979b   "Implications of the Border Cave Skeletal Remains for Later Pleistocene Human Evolution." *Current Anthropology*, 20:23–35.

_____
1983   "Lake Ndutu Cranium and Early Homo sapiens in Africa." *American Journal of Physical Anthropology*, 61:245–254.

Rindos, David
1984   *The Origins of Agriculture: An Evolutionary Perspective*. Orlando: Academic Press.

Roberts, D. F.
1973   *Climate and Human Variability*. An Addison-Wesley Module in Anthropology, No. 34, Reading, Mass.: Addison-Wesley.

Robinson, J. T.

1953   "Telanthropus and Its Phylogenetic Significance." *American Journal of Physical Anthropology*, 11:445–501.

——   1972   *Early Hominid Posture and Locomotion*. Chicago: University of Chicago Press.

Romer, Alfred S.
1959   *The Vertebrate Story*. Chicago: University of Chicago Press.

Rose, M. D.
1983   "Miocene Hominoid Postcranial Morphology. Monkey-like, Ape-like, Neither, or Both?" *In*: R. Ciochon and R. Corruccini (eds.), q.v., pp. 405–417.

Rose, Noel R.
1981   "Autoimmune Diseases." *Scientific American*, 244(2):80–103.

Rose, Steven
1972   "Environmental Effects on Brain and Behavior." *In*: *Race and Intelligence*, Ken Richardson and David Speers (eds.), Baltimore: Penguin Books, Inc., pp. 128–144.

Rovner, Irwin
1983   "Plant Opal Phytolith Analysis." *Advances in Archaeological Method and Theory*, 6:225–266.

Rowell, Thelma E.
1972   *The Social Behaviour of Monkeys*. Baltimore: Penguin Books.

Rudnai, Judith
1973   *The Social Life of Lions*. Wallingford, Pa.: Washington Square East.

Ruffle, John
1977   *The Egyptians*. Ithaca: Cornell University Press.

Rumbaugh, D. M.
1977   *Language Learning by a Chimpanzee: The Lana Project*. New York: Academic Press.

Rumbaugh, Duane M., E. Sue Savage-Rumbaugh and John L. Scanlon
1982   "The Relationship Between Language in Apes and Human Beings." *In*: James E. King and James L. Fobes (eds.), q.v., pp. 361–385.

Sabloff, Jeremy A., and William L. Rathje
1975   "The Rise of a Maya Merchant Class." *Scientific American*, 233(4):72–82.

Sanderson, Ivan T.
1969   "The Missing Link." *Argosy*, May, pp. 23–31.

Sarich, Vincent
1971   "A Molecular Approach to the Question of Human Origins." *In*: *Background for Man*, P. Dolhinow and V. Sarich (eds.), Boston: Little, Brown & Co., pp. 60–81.

Sarich, V. M. and A. C. Wilson
1967   "Rates of Albumen Evolution in Primates." *Proceedings, National Academy of Sciences*, 58:142–148.

Sartono, S.
1975   "Implications Arising from *Pithecanthropus* VIII." *In*: *Paleoanthropology: Morphology and Paleoecology*, R. H. Tuttle (ed.), Chicago: Aldine Publishing Co., pp. 327–360.

Savage-Rumbaugh, E. Sue, D. M. Rumbaugh and Sally Boysen
1978   "Symbolic Communication between Two Chimpanzees (*Pan Troglodytes*)." *Science*, 201:43–56.

Scarr, Sandra
1981   "The Effects of Family Background: A Study of Cognitive Differences among Black and White Twins." *In*: *Race, Social Class, and Individual Differences in I.Q.*, S. Scarr (ed.), Hillsdale, N.J.: Lawrence Erlbaum Associates, Inc., pp. **261–315**.

Scarr, Sandra and R. A. Weinberg
1976   "IQ Test Performances of Black Children Adopted by White Families." *In*: S. Scarr (ed.), q.v., pp. 109–159.

Schaller, George B.
1963   *The Mountain Gorilla*. Chicago: University of Chicago Press.

——   1972   *The Serengeti Lion*. Chicago: University of Chicago Press.

Scheidt, Walter
1924   "The Concept of Race in Anthropology and the Divisions into Human Races from Linnaeus to Deniker." *In*: *This Is Race*, E. W. Count (ed.), New York: Henry Schuman, pp. 354–391.

Scheller, Richard H. and Richard Axel
1984   "How Genes Control Innate Behavior." *Scientific American*, 250:54–63.

Schiffer, Michael B., Theodore E. Downing, and Michael McCarthy
1981   "Waste Not, Want Not: An Ethnoarchaeological Study of Reuse in Tucson, Arizona." *In*: *Modern Material Culture: The Archaeology of Us*, Richard A. Gould and Michael B. Schiffer (eds.), New York: Academic Press, pp. 67–86.

Scopes, John T. and James Presley
1967   *Center of the Storm*. New York: Holt, Rinehart and Winston.

Schull, William J., M. Otuke and J. V. Neel.
1981   "Genetic Effects of the Atomic Bombs: A Reappraisal." *Science*, 213:1220–1227.

Sebeok, Thomas A.
1980   *Speaking of Apes*. New York: Plenum Press.

Senut, Brigett
1981   "Humeral Outlines in Some Hominoid Primates and in Plio-pleistocene Hominids." *American Journal of Physical Anthropology*, 56:275–283.

Sergi, Sergio
1967   "Morphological Position of the Prophaneranthropi (Swanscombe and Fontechevade)." *In*: *Ideas on Human Evolution*, Wm. Howells (ed.), Garden City, N.Y.: Doubleday and Co., pp. 507–520. (First published by Harvard University Press, 1962.)

Service, Elman R.
1966   *The Hunters*. Englewood Cliffs, N.J.: Prentice-Hall, Inc.

Shapiro, Harry
1936   *The Heritage of the Bounty*. New York: Simon and Schuster.

Shipman, P. L.
1983   "Early Hominid Lifestyle. Hunting and Gathering or Foraging and Scavenging?" Paper presented at 52nd Annual Meeting, American Association of Physical Anthropologists, Indianapolis, April, 1983.

Simmons, Alan H.
1986   "New Evidence for the Use of Cultigens in the American Southwest." *American Antiquity*, 51(1):73–89.

Simons, E. L.
1969   "The Origin and Radiation of the Primates." *Annals of the New York Academy of Sciences*, 167:319–331.

——   1972   *Primate Evolution*. New York: Macmillan.

Simons, E. L. and P. C. Ettel
1970   "*Gigantopithecus*." *Scientific American*, 222:76–85.

Simpson, G. G.
1945   "The Principles of Classification and a Classification of Mammals." *Bulletin of the American Museum of Natural History*, 85:1–350.

1961   *Principles of Animal Taxonomy.* New York: Columbia University Press.

Simpson, G. G., C. S. Pittendright and L. H. Tiffany
1957   *Life.* New York: Harcourt, Brace and Co., Inc.

Singer, Charles
1959   *A Short History of Scientific Ideas to 1900.* London: Oxford University Press.

Smith, Fred H.
1982   "Upper Pleistocene Hominid Evolution in South-Central Europe." *Current Anthropology,* 23:667–703.

Snyder, Louis L.
1962   *The Idea of Racialism.* New York: Van Nostrand Reinhold Co.

Solecki, Ralph
1971   *Shanidar, The First Flower People.* New York: Alfred A. Knopf.

Solheim II, Wilhelm G.
1972   "An Earlier Agricultural Revolution." *Scientific American,* 226(4):10, 34–41.

Sparks, Stephen and Haraldur Sigurdsson
1978   "The Big Blast at Santorini." *Natural History,* 87(4):70–78.

Speth, J. D. and D. D. Davis
1976   "Seasonal Variability in Early Hominid Predation." *Science,* 192:441–445.

Stanyon, Roscoe and Brunetto Chiarelli
1982   "Phylogeny of the Hominoidea: The Chromosome Evidence." *Journal of Human Evolution,* 11:493–504.

Stern, Curt
1973   *Principles of Human Genetics* (3rd Ed.). San Francisco: W. H. Freeman and Company.

Stern, Jack T. and Randall L. Susman
1983   "The Locomotor Anatomy of *Australopithecus afarensis.*" *American Journal of Physical Anthropology,* 60:279–317.

Stocking, George W. Jr.
1968   *Race, Culture, and Evolution.* New York: The Free Press.

Stringer, C. B. (ed.)
1981   *Aspects of Human Evolution.* London: Taylor & Francis Ltd. (Symposia of the Society for the Study of Human Biology, Vol. XXI).

———
1982   "Towards a Solution to the Neanderthal Problem." *Journal of Human Evolution,* 11(5):431–438.

Stringer, Christopher B., F. Clark Howell and John K. Melentis
1979   "The Significance of the Fossil Hominid Skull from Petralona, Greece." *Journal of Archaeological Science,* 6:235–253.

Stringer, C. B. and E. Trinkaus
1981   "The Shanidar Neanderthal Crania." *In: Aspects of Human Evolution,* C. B. Stringer (ed.), London: Taylor & Francis Ltd., pp. 129–165.

Struhsaker, Thomas T. and John F. Oates
1975   "Comparison of the Behavior and Ecology of Red Colobus and Black-and-White Colobus Monkeys in Uganda: A Summary." *In: Socioecology and Psychology of Primates,* R. H. Tuttle (ed.), Chicago: Aldine Publishing Co.

Strum, Shirley C.
1981   "Processes and Products of Change at Gilgil, Kenya." *In: Omnivorous Primates,* R.S.O. Harding and Geza Teleki (eds.), New York: Columbia University Press.

1983   "Baboon Cues for Eating Meat." *Journal of Human Evolution,* 12:327–336.

Sugiyama, Yukimaru and Jeremy Koman
1979   "Tool-Using and -Making Behavior in Wild Chimpanzees at Bossou, Guinea." *Primates,* 20:513–524.

Suomi, Stephen J., Susan Mineka and Roberta D. DeLizio
1983   "Short- and Long-Term Effects of Repetitive Mother-Infant Separation on Social Development in Rhesus Monkeys." *Developmental Psychology,* 19(5):710–786.

Suzman, I. M.
1982   "A Comparative Study of the Hadar and Sterkfontein Australopithecine Innominates." *American Journal of Physical Anthropology,* 57:235.

Szalay, Frederick S.
1968   "The Beginnings of Primates." *Evolution,* 22:19–36.

Szalay, Frederick S. and Eric Delson
1979   *Evolutionary History of the Primates.* New York: Academic Press.

Tanner, J. M.
1977   "Human Growth and Constitution." *In: Human Biology,* G. A. Harrison, et al. (eds.), New York: Oxford University Press, pp. 299–385.

Tattersall, Ian and Niles Eldredge
1977   "Fact, Theory and Fantasy in Human Paleontology." *American Scientist,* 65:204–211.

Tauxe, Lisa
1979   "A New Date for *Ramapithecus.*" *Nature,* 282:399–401.

Taylor, R. E., L. A. Payen, C. A. Prior, P. J. Slota, Jr., R. Gillespie, *et al.*
1985   "Major Revisions in the Pleistocene Age Assignments for North American Human Skeletons by C-14 Accelerator Mass Spectrometry: None Older than 11,000 C-14 Years B.P." *American Antiquity,* 50(1):136–139.

Teleki, G.
1973   *The Predatory Behavior of Wild Chimpanzees.* Cranbrook, N.J.: Bucknell University Press.

Terrace, Herbert S.
1979   *Nim.* New York: Alfred A. Knopf.

———
1982   "Why Koko Can't Talk." *The Sciences,* 22(9):8–10, Columbia University.

———
1983   "Apes Who 'Talk': Language or Projection of Language by Their Teachers?" *In: Language in Primates,* J. de Luce and N. T. Wilder (eds.), New York: Springer-Verlag, Inc., pp. 19–42.

Thomsen, Dietrick E.
1978   "Radioisotope Dating with Accelerators." *Science News,* 113:29–30, January 14.

Thorne, A. and P. Macumber
1971   "Discoveries of Late Pleistocene Man at Kow Swamp, Australia." *Nature,* 238:316–319.

Thouveny, N. and E. Bonifay
1984   "New Chronological Data on European Plio-Pleistocene Faunas and Hominid Occupation Sites." *Nature,* 308:355–358.

Tobias, Phillip
1967 *Olduvai Gorge* (Vol. 2). *The Cranial and Maxillary Dentition of* Australopithecus (Zinjanthropus) boisei. Cambridge: Cambridge University Press.

_____ 1971 *The Brain in Hominid Evolution*. New York: Columbia University Press.

_____ 1972 "Early Man in Sub-Saharan Africa." *In: The Functional and Evolutionary Biology of the Primates*, R. Tuttle (ed.), Chicago: Aldine-Atherton, pp. 63–93.

_____ 1976 "African Hominids: Dating and Phylogeny." *In:* G. L. Isaac and E. R. McCown (eds.), q.v., pp. 377–422.

_____ 1980 "*Australopithecus afarensis* and *A. africanus*. Critique and an Alternative Hypothesis." *Palaeontologica Africana*, 23:1–17.

_____ 1983a "Hominid Evolution in Africa." *Canadian Journal of Anthropology*, 3:163–185.

_____ 1983b "Recent Advances in the Evolution of the Hominids with Especial Reference to Brain and Speech." Potifical Academy of Sciences, *Scrita Varia*, 50:85–140.

Tobias, P. V. and G.H.R. von Koenigswald
1964 "A Comparison between the Olduvai Hominines and Those of Java and Some Implications for Hominid Phylogeny." *Nature*, 204:515–518.

Tomkins, Jerry R. (ed.)
1965 *D-Days at Dayton*. Baton Rouge: Louisiana State University Press.

Trigg, Roger
1982 *The Shaping of Man. Philosophical Aspects of Sociobiology*. New York: Shocken Books.

Trigger, Bruce G., Barry J. Kemp, David O'Connor, and Alan B. Lloyd
1983 *Ancient Egypt: A Social History*. Cambridge: Cambridge University Press.

Tringham, Ruth
1971 *Hunters, Fishers, and Farmers of Eastern Europe, 6000–3000* B.C. London: Hutchinson University Library.

Trinkaus, Eric
1982 "The Shanidar 3 Neandertal." *American Journal of Physical Anthropology*, 57:37–60.

_____ 1983 *The Shanidar Neandertals*. New York: Academic Press.

Trinkaus, E. and W. W. Howells
1900 "The Neandertals." *Scientific American*, 241(6):118–133.

Trinkaus, Eric and Marjorie LeMay
1982 "Occipital Bunning Among Later Pleistocene Hominids." *American Journal of Physical Anthropology*, 57:27–35.

Trinkaus, Eric and M. R. Zimmerman
1982 "Trauma Among the Shanidar Neandertals." *Ibid*, pp. 61–76.

Trivers, R. L.
1971 "The Evolution of Reciprocal Altruism." *Quarterly Review of Biology*, 46:35–57.

_____ 1972 "Parental Investment and Sexual Selection." *In: Sexual Selection and the Descent of Man*, B. Campbell (ed.), Chicago: Aldine, pp. 136–179.

Turner, C.
1975 "The Correlation and Duration of Middle Pleistocene Interglacial Periods in Northwest Europe." *In:* K. W. Butzer and G. L. Isaac (eds.), q.v., pp. 259–308.

Ucko, Peter J. and G. W. Dimbleby (eds.)
1969 *The Domestication and Exploitation of Plants and Animals*. Chicago: Aldine.

Ucko, Peter J., Ruth Tringham, and G. W. Dimbleby (eds.)
1972 *Man, Settlement, and Urbanism*. London: Duckworth.

Van Couvering, A. H. and J. A. Van Covering
1976 "Early Miocene Mammal Fossils From East Africa." *In: Human Origins*, G. Isaac and E. R. McCown (eds.), Menlo Park, Ca.: W. A. Benjamin, pp. 155–207.

Vandermeersch, B.
1981 "A Neandertal Skeleton from a Chatelperronian Level at St. Cesaire (France)." *American Journal of Physical Anthropology*, 54:286.

van Lawick-Goodall, Jane
1971 *In the Shadow of Man*. Boston: Houghton Mifflin Co.

Van Valen, L. and R. E. Sloan
1965 "The Earliest Primates." *Science*, 150:743–745.

Vaughan, Patrick C.
1985 *Use-Wear Analysis of Flaked Stone Tools*. Tucson: University of Arizona Press.

Vleck, F.
1978 "New Discovery of *Homo erectus* in Central Europe." *Journal of Human Evolution*, 7:239–252.

Vogel, F., M. Kopun and R. Rathenberg
1976 "Mutation and Molecular Evolution." *In: Molecular Anthropology*, M. Goodman, et al. (eds.), New York: Plenum Press, pp. 13–33.

Von Koenigswald, G.H.R.
1956 *Meeting Prehistoric Man*. New York: Harper & Brothers.

Walker, A.
1976 "Remains Attributable to *Australopithecus* from East Rudolf." *In: Earliest Man and Environments in the Lake Rudolf Basin*, Y. Coppens, et al. (eds.), Chicago: University of Chicago Press, pp. 484–489.

_____ 1981 Presentation of New Miocene Hominoid Material from East Africa. Annual Meetings, American Association of Physical Anthropologists, April, 1981.

Walker, Alan, Dean Falk, Richard Smith and M. Pickford
1983 "The Skull of *Proconsul africanus*: Reconstruction and Cranial Capacity." *Nature*, 305:525–527.

Walker, Alan and Richard E. F. Leakey
1978 "The Hominids of East Turkana." *Scientific American*, 239:54–66.

Walker, A. C. and M. Pickford
1983 "New Postcranial Fossils of *Proconsul africanus* and *Proconsul nyanzae*." *In:* R. Ciochon and R. Corruccini (eds.), q.v., pp. 325–351.

Walker, A., D. Pilbeam, and M. Cartmill
1981   "Changing Views and Interpretations of Primate Evolution."
       Paper presented to the Annual Meetings, American Associa-
       tion of Physical Anthropologists, April, 1981.

Ward, Steven and William H. Kimbel
1983   "Subnasal Alveolar Morphology and the Systematic Position
       of *Sivapithecus*." *American Journal of Physical Anthropology*,
       61:157–171.

Ward, S. C. and D. R. Pilbeam
1983   "Maxillofacial Morphology of Miocene Hominoids From Af-
       rica and Indo-Pakistan." *In*: R. Ciochon and R. Corruccini
       (eds.), q.v., pp. 211–238.

Warren, Peter
1975   *The Aegean Civilizations*. Oxford: Elsevier/Phaidon.

Washburn, S. L.
1963   "The Study of Race." *American Anthropologist*, 65:521–531.

Watson, J. B.
1924   *Behaviorism*. New York: W. W. Norton.

Watson, James D.
1968   *The Double Helix*. New York: Atheneum.

Wendorf, Fred and Romuald Schild, *et al.*
1984   "New Radiocarbon Dates on the Cereals from Wadi Kubba-
       niya." *Science*, 225:645–646.

Weidenreich, Franz
1946   *Apes, Giants, and Man*. Chicago: University of Chicago Press.

_____
1951   "Morphology of Solo Man." *Anthropological Papers of the
       American Museum of Natural History*, Vol. 43, No. 3.

Weiner, J. S.
1954   "Nose Shape and Climate." *American Journal of Physical An-
       thropology*, 12:615–618.

_____
1955   *The Piltdown Forgery*. London: Oxford University Press

_____
1977   "Human Ecology." *In*: *Human Biology*, G. A. Harrison et al.
       (eds.), New York: Oxford University Press, pp. 387–483.

Weiner, J. S. and B. G. Campbell
1964   "The Taxonomic Status of the Swanscombe Skull." *In*: *Royal
       Anthropological Institute of Great Britain and Ireland*, Occ.
       Paper 20, D. Ovey (ed.), pp. 175–215.

Weiss, Mark L. and Alan E. Mann
1981   *Human Biology and Behavior* (3rd Ed.). Boston: Little, Brown,
       and Co.

Wendt, Herbert
1963   *In Search of Adam*. New York: Collier Books.

Wenke, Robert J.
1984   *Patterns in Prehistory* (2nd Ed.). New York: Oxford University
       Press.

Wheat, Joe Ben
1972   "The Olsen-Chubbuck Site: A Paleo-Indian Bison Kill." Mem-
       oirs of the Society for American Archaeology, **26**.

Wheeler, Mortimer
1968   *The Indus Civilization* (3rd ed.). Cambridge: Cambridge Uni-
       versity Press.

White, Randall
1982   "Rethinking the Middle/Upper Paleolithic Transition." *Cur-
       rent Anthropology*, 23:169–192.

_____
1982   "On the Middle/Upper Paleolithic Transition: A Response to
       Mellars." *Current Anthropology*, 23:358–359.

White, T. D.
1980   "Evolutionary Implications of Pliocene Hominid Footprints."
       Science, 208:175–176.

_____
1983   Comment Made at Institute of Human Origins Conference
       on the Evolution of Human Locomotion (Berkeley, Ca.).

White, T. D. and J. M. Harris
1977   "Suid Evolution and Correlation of African Hominid Locali-
       ties." *Science*, 198:13–21.

White, T. D., D. C. Johanson and W. H. Kimbel
1981   "*Australopithecus Africanus*: Its Phyletic Position Reconsi-
       dered." *South African Journal of Science*, 77:445–470.

Willey, Gordon R.
1971   *An Introduction to American Archaeology, Vol. 2: South Amer-
       ica*. Englewood Cliffs, N.J.: Prentice-Hall.

Willey, Gordon R. and D. B. Shimkin
1973   "The Maya Collapse: A Summary View." *In*: T. Patrick Culbert
       (ed.), q.v., pp. 457–501.

Williams, G. C.
1966   *Adaptation and Natural Selection: A Critique of Some Current
       Evolutionary Thought*. Princeton: Princeton University Press.

Wilson, E. O.
1975   *Sociobiology, The New Synthesis*. Cambridge: Harvard Univer-
       sity Press.

Wolbarsht, M. L.
1975   "Letter to the editor." *Science*, 187:600.

Wolpoff, Milford H.
1980a *Paleoanthropology*. New York: Alfred A. Knopf.

_____
1980b "Cranial Remains of Middle Pleistocene European Homin-
       ids." *Journal of Human Evolution*, 9:339–358.

_____
1983a "*Ramapithecus* and Human Origins An Anthropologist's
       Perspective of Changing Interpretations." *In*: R. Ciochon and
       R. Corruccini (eds.), q.v., pp. 651–676.

_____
1983b "Lucy's Little Legs." *Journal of Human Evolution*, 12:443–453.

Wolpoff, Milford H. et al.
1981   "Upper Pleistocene Human Remains from Vindija Cave,
       Croatia, Yugoslavia." *American Journal of Physical Anthropol-
       ogy*, 54:499–545.

Wood, B.
1976   "Remains Attributable to *Homo* in the East Rudolf Succes-
       sion." *In*: *Earliest Man and Environments in the Lake Rudolf
       Basin*, Y. Coppens et al. (eds.), Chicago: University of Chicago
       Press, pp. 490–506.

Wood, C. S., G. A. Harrison, C. Dove and J. S. Weiner
1972   "Selective Feeding of *Anopheles gambiae* According to ABO
       Blood Group Status." *Nature*, 239:165.

Wu, Rukang
1981   "Where Did Humankind Originate?" *China Pictoral*, No. 7,
       pp. 16–18.

_____
1982   "Paleoanthropology in China, 1949–79." *Current Anthropol-
       ogy*, 23:473–477.

Wu, Rukang and S. Lin
1983   "Peking Man." *Scientific American*, 248(6):86–94.

Wu, Rukang and C. E. Oxnard
1983   "Ramapithecines from China: Evidence from Tooth Dimen-
       sions." *Nature*, 306:258–260.

Wymer, John
    1981   *The Paleolithic Age*. New York: St. Martin's Press.

Yellen, John E.
    1977   *Archaeological Approaches to the Present*. New York: Academic Press.

Yudkin, J.
    1969   "Archaeology and the Nutritionist." *In: The Domestication and Exploitation of Plants and Animals*, Peter J. Ucko and G. W. Dimbleby (eds.), Chicago: Aldine, pp. 547–554.

Yunis, Jorge J. and Om Prakesh
    1982   "The Origin of Man: A Chromosomal Pictorial Legacy." *Science*, 215:1525–1530.

◇ INDEX

587